Declinations

Joseph Silveira deMello

Copyright 2002 by Joseph Silveira deMello
All rights reserved.

No part of this book may be reproduced or transmitted in any form or by any means, electronic or mechanical, including photocopying or recording, or by any information storage and retrieval system, without written permission from the author and publisher. Requests and inquiries may be mailed to: American Federation of Astrologers, Inc., 6535 S. Rural Road, Tempe, AZ 85283.

ISBN: 0-86690-540-5

First Printing: 2003

Published by:
American Federation of Astrologers, Inc.
PO Box 22040
6535 S. Rural Road
Tempe, AZ 85285-2040

Printed in the United States of America

Dedication

To the memory of my mother,
who refused to tell me my hour of birth lest I become interested in astrology.
To all astrologers of the past who taught me
and to future students of astrology who will write, publish, teach
and keep the great science and art of astrology alive.

Acknowledgements

I wish to thank the many astrologers mentioned throughout this book
for the many charts they submitted for my study and for their constant support
throughout the writing of this book. Needless to say, this book
could not have been written if I had not read many other previously published
astrology books and countless astrology articles in astrological journals and magazines.
Most of what is written in this book is hardly the sole product of the creative self.
Kt Boehrer
Macelle Brown
Don Borkowski and his late wife Georgie Borkowski
the late Nan Burket
Karen Christino
the late Henrietta "Mike" Cramton
The late Edith Custer
The late T. Patrick Davis
Edward L. Dearborn
The late Shirley Decker
Guy de Penguern
Defiance Gregg
Eleonora Kimmel
Diane Lawson
J. Lee Lehman
Margaret Meister
Rev. Joy Morris
Rev. H. Lee Poteet
The late Lois Rodden
Mollie Sommer
Helena Stansfield
Norma Storey
Jan Van Schuyler

Contents

Preface	vii	Barman	75
Introduction	xi	Student of Hindu Guru	78
George Washington	3	Cabby/Attorney	78
William Henry Chaney	5	No-Show Male Client	78
Ivy Goldstein-Jacobson	8	Oil Field Worker	82
Female Astrologer	10	Maritha Pottenger	84
Astrologer's Grandmother	12	Troubled Young Wife	86
Joseph McCarthy	12	The Big Heist	88
Lew Ayres	15	Advertising Woman	90
Barry Goldwater	17	Male Bartender	90
Victor Borge	19	Male Nurse	90
Male Student	21	Daughter of Gender Identify	94
Jan Van Schuyler	21	Male Porn Star	94
Jacqueline Stallone	24	Oscar Gutierrez, Jr.	97
Lady Astrologer	24	Computer Engineer	97
Ophthalmologist	24	Grand-nephew	97
Astrologer's Father	28	Jackpot	101
Jeannie Miller	30	Jackpot #2	103
Retired Travel Agent	30	Eileen Garrett	105
John B. Anderson	33	20th Century Lady	105
X-ray Technologist	35	Nelson Aldrich Rockefeller	105
Fidel Castro	37	Lyndon B. Johnson	109
John McCormick	39	Entrepreneur	111
Travel Agent	39	Retired WAAC	113
Cargo Handler	39	Ex-Nun and Teacher	113
Barman	43	Mark O. Hatfield	116
Cellist	43	Saddam Hussein	116
Barman	43	Wealthy Heir	119
Roger Elliot	47	Retired Waiter	121
Artist	47	Café Pianist	121
Computer Analyst	50	Richard Ideman	121
Lady with Back Problem	52	Medical Technologist	121
Churchman	52	Service Garage Employee	121
Neti Leo	56	John Valle	127
Fabricator	56	Publisher's Representative	127
Entrepreneur	56	Jerry Brown	127
Male Astrologer	61	Architect/Restaurateur	131
Sculptor and Bar Owner	61	Groupie	131
Restaurateur	64	Artist and Chef	131
Kitchen Designer	66	Tennis Pro	131
Astrologer and Pilot	66	Waiter	131
Chef	69	Robert Schmidt	137
Barman	69	Mother with Problems	137
Male Author	69	Divorcee	137
Remittance Man	73	Barman	141
Accountant	75	Rush Limbaugh	141

Female Bank Clerk	141	Hawaiian Male	199		
One-Time Female Client	141	Hip Replacement	201		
Male Office Manager	146	Lesbian Lady	201		
Band Vocalist	146	Businesswoman	201		
Canadian Female Astrologer	149	Unknown Lady	205		
Female Astrologer	149	Lee Harvey Oswald	205		
Policewoman	149	The Mathematician	207		
Maitre'd	153	Psychic Healer	209		
Psychologist	153	Barman	209		
Dorian Bagwell	153	Quiet Young Man	209		
Archaeologist	157	Man with Alias	213		
Princess	157	The High Roller	213		
John Sutter	160	Cemetery Dweller	216		
Sir Richard Burton	162	Female Attorney	216		
Woodrow Wilson	162	Carpenter	216		
Gertrude Stein	165	Astrologer and Author	220		
Herbert Hoover	165	Lady Psychiatric Patient	220		
Josef Goebbels	168	Neighbor Lady	220		
Golda Meir	168	Chef	224		
Robert W. Cooper	171	Male Referral	224		
Lady Doctor	173	Female Student	227		
Architect	173	Scorpio Lady	227		
Man with Broken Elbow	176	Lady Librarian	227		
Prison Guard	176	Cystic Fibrosis Victim	231		
Marrying Man	176	The Girlfriend	233		
Psychic's First Husband	180	Man About Town	233		
Man with Brittle Bones	182	Career Woman	236		
The Bon Vivant	182	Male Client	236		
General's Aide	182	Upscale Man	236		
The Irishman	185	Career Concerns	240		
Union Administrator	185	Female Client	240		
Male Nurse	185	Troubled Brother	243		
Male Astrologer	188	Spiritual Lady	243		
Robert Nicholas Denham	188	Blond Young Man	246		
Career Manager	191	Pretty Girl	246		
Singer-Dancer	193	Thomas, Earl of Craven	246		
Porn Star	193	Jennifer Collegio	250		
Legal Lady	196	Kidney Patient	253		
Potential Suicide	196				

Preface

The author feels it is important from the outset that the reader understand his point of view, and to that point the chart of the author is given. Ascendant and Moon in Gemini balance the Scorpio Sun. Despite having air and fixed in major proportions, the author will insist, first of all, that he is a practical astrologer who has learned that clients are seeking answers which they can easily accept. Since there is little earth in this chart, the author has had to teach himself to be practical. Air gives multiple interests and general distraction. Fixity is the enemy of intellectual research; if one's mind is already made up, one is stuck with it and not very open to intellectual inquiry. The author has tried to make air blend with fixity in his own life and discover how to develop what is in short supply in the chart.

The important message is that we should teach our clients how best they may live with the charts they have and discover the options which will open their world. It is hoped that astrologers can find alternate approaches to aid clients to live life smoothly.

The author's interest in astrology came of a need to discover what the future had in store for him and in order to better understand himself and his past. Neither pop psychology or analysis seemed to be of much help. Astrology was a huge help from the very beginning of its study. It has done so with such strength of meaning that the author is sure the study will aid any serious student. In the course of study the author became acquainted with mythology, reincarnation, mysticism and spiritual approaches. Practical help proved far more productive. Most astrologers profess some form of religious belief. The author feels his religious beliefs should be his alone and remain private to himself and not to be imposed on other people.

Astrology has endured for more than four thousand years. Anything which has lasted that long certainly deserves the attention of any thinking person. Astrology is both an art and a science. The science lies in the cosmic and mathematical cycles of the heavens and our methods for setting up charts. As does a doctor, the astrologer examines the person and his chart and has an experience of how what he sees should work. The doctor uses the art of diagnosis to aid his patient. The astrologer examines all the information for the well-being and ease of his clients' lives. Astronomy as understood today has lost much by refusing to see the role of astrology in the concerns of men. The astrologer is often asked if he "believes" in astrology. There is no need for blind faith when astrology proves its worth every day.

The author immediately informed his physician of being an astrologer. As a Gemini rising there might be lung problems. As a Scorpio Sun there might be problems with lower body plumbing, but with Libra ruling the sixth house there might also be kidney problems. The doctor had just performed a thorough physical, smiled and hastened to assure me that all was well. I then mentioned that my mother, one of her sisters and three of her brothers all died of various kidney problems, and that these problems have come down to her children and grandchildren. One grand-nephew has twice rejected kidney transplants. The doctor made serious and appropriate notes into my history or medical record. At every annual physical, extensive blood work and kidney function exams are done routinely. Fifteen years later when the author discovered he had gout, a rather basic kidney malfunction, the doctor had a gleeful expression as though he had predicted it himself. Then he behaved very doctorly. Gout is where the patient can no longer process certain foods. He raced for a huge diet list, was not willing to prescribe pain medication and suggested that the malfunction be controlled by me eating a proper diet.

But you see the author's chart. Libra with a Scorpio interception is not the whole story, for in that sixth house there is Mars in Libra, Sun, Saturn and Mercury all in Scorpio. Between them, those planets can produce falls, heart attack or stroke, skin and bone problems and still bow to all sorts of Gemini problems. Moreover, over the years, planets have progressed and transited through the sixth house, and most recently Pluto has spent some time there without bringing any specific health problems. Sun and Saturn are trine to Pluto. Yet when Pluto progressed over the fourth house there was an obvious change of lifestyle. But when Pluto went into the seventh, there was no particular event. Of course no astrologer should ever predict on seventh house events. It is

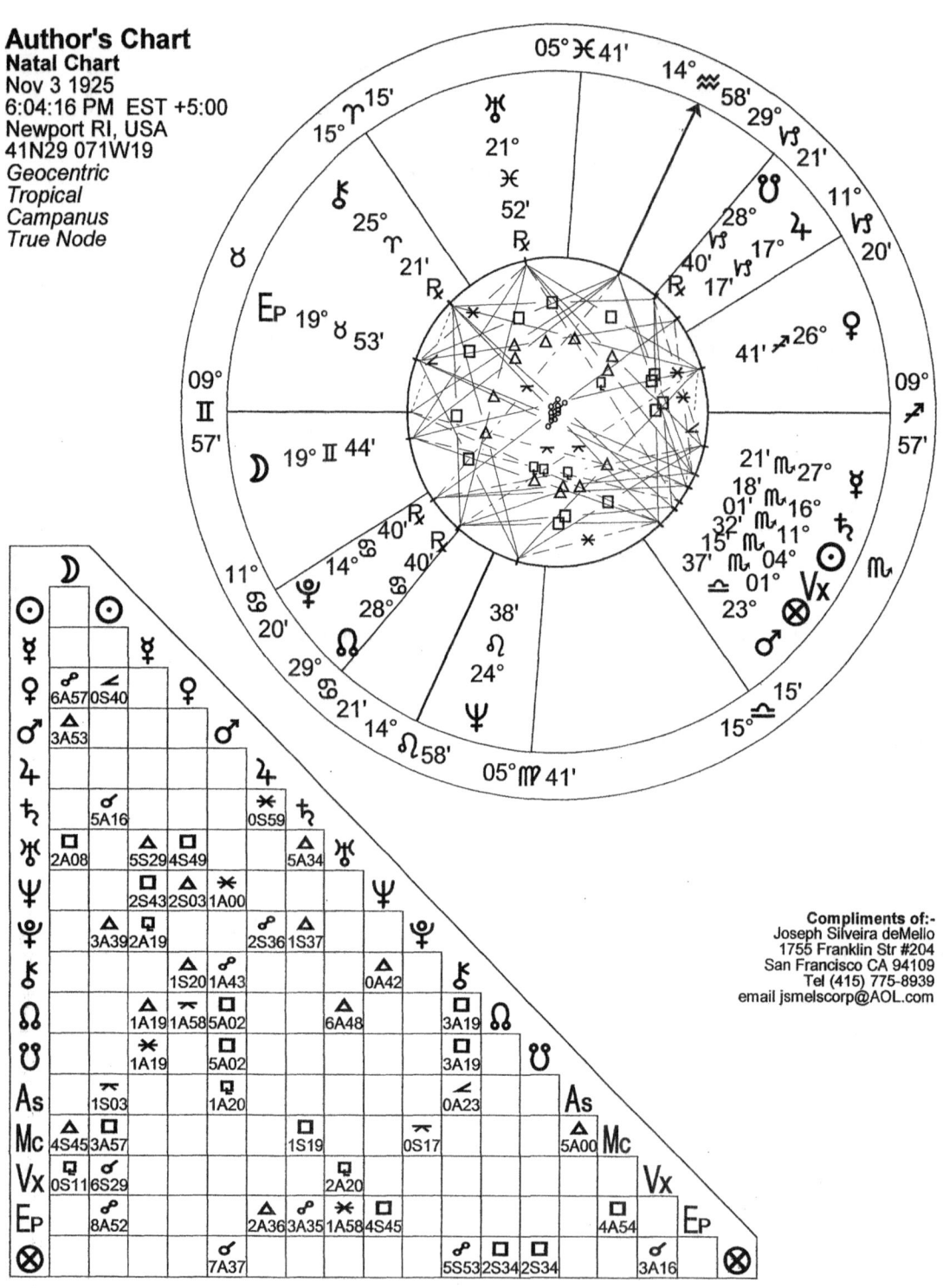

nigh impossible to predict what other people are doing to or for a person. Successful predictions in that area are rare. Any astrologer who furnishes such reports to clients cannot have the needs of the client at heart.

If astrology can explain the life and history of men, and if it is men who make history (and women), then astrology is also a determiner of history. In our world of intense cause and effect, all things depend on and contribute to each other. It has too often been said that those who do not learn from history are condemned to repeat its mistakes. In round discussions of fate and free will, we have the freedom of choice but we also have the indicators allowing us to make the choices which entirely fulfill our own astrological indicators.

The author's chart is fairly obvious. The heavy preponderance of planets in the sixth house, energetic Mars weak in Libra, the ego Sun in Scorpio, karmic Saturn and chart ruler Mercury all tell unmistakably that the person of the chart is destined for a life of work and service. The chart then goes on to have all manner of aspects, those easy to see and some not. Sun, Jupiter and Uranus are not in aspect of each other, but Jupiter is at the midpoint of the other two (See #0259 in Ebertin's *Combination of Stellar Influences*). But then, in all fairness, see Neptune at the midpoint of Sun-Ascendant or Sun at the midpoint of Mercury-Mars. The Moon is quincunx both Jupiter and Saturn. The same for Uranus with Neptune and Mars. Some of these aspects do not make a computer printout because they are separating aspects. A recognizable problem is Jupiter opposite Pluto, which has taught some lessons about money, but there is also the saving grace with Pluto trine Sun and Saturn so that transiting Pluto went through my sixth house with no attributable problems. The fourth house Neptune in Leo gives a sensitivity toward prescription drugs and the overuse of tobacco, but no recreational drug use or excessive alcohol.

x

Introduction

Until the last few years the entire subject of declinations was hardly discussed or taught. Forty years ago, we looked at declinations for merely one thing, were they conjunct each other by one degree orb, both North or both South, or one north and the other south. The explanation was that if both were north or both were south, this was as strong as if the planets were in conjunction in the chart. But if one was north and the other south, then they were in the nature of oppositions. This is very plain, quite simple, and it left it up to the astrology students to think in terms of those specific planets either conjunct or opposed.

That was all so simplistic that there had to be something wrong with it, nothing in astrology is ever that simple or insignificant. Several astrologers, led by Edward L. Dearborn of Norwood, Pennsylvania, undertook to start a Special Interest Group (SIG) under the NCGR banner to study declinations. Various members of the group undertook to study the cyclical loops of the declination of the Moon in progressed charts, to study what happened to planets when they went "out of bounds" or beyond the declination of the Tropics of Capricorn and Cancer. Here the author has chosen to study Saturn and Jupiter at zero degrees of declination for the karmic planet and for the planet which indicates our ability to accept our circumstances. As a control group, he also checked charts of those with Saturn beyond the one degree orb. The effort was taken in an effort to find if zero declination showed any particular special significance in the natal charts and lives of those people examined. What resulted is this workbook of charts with brief commentaries to allow other astrologers to look at for similarities.

All example charts shown, unless otherwise noted, use the Campanus house system, but full data is furnished for those wishing to see charts in any other style.

Study of Declinations

At some time in our study of astrology we were made aware of declinations as another element in the study of astrology. Declinations were either north or south of the equator and pretty much stayed in a belt determined by the seasonal tilt of the earth toward the Sun. Not much emphasis was put on how they got that way, nor was there any discussion of the astronomy involved. We needed deeper knowledge, we were to check out the geography and astronomy for ourselves.

The ephemeris listed the declinations and we students were to note what declinations we had for the planets in our natal charts. The important element was that it gave us parallels (like conjunctions) or contraparallels (acting like oppositions). We were told not to allow more than one degree of orb in looking at these parallels. The important thing was that such parallels might exist between planetary positions which were not in any other aspects to each other. The beginning student is always eager to acquire yet another possibly favorable indicator. It took some time for us to become suspicious of something so glibly explained. This subject of parallels, having been mentioned, was then dropped. Absolutely no attention was given to the fact that declinations have a manner of movement which is as important and cyclically repetitive. In fact, so little further mention was thereafter made of declinations that some astrologers stopped looking at them. If we had the luck to talk to seasoned astrologers, we would be surprised to be told that if we did not pay attention to declinations we were missing more than half of what each astrological chart had to say to us. The best example of declination in action is to check the declinations of the two great NASA space accidents.

Another thing very suspicious about declinations was that we gave declinations to the Ascendant, the Midheaven and the Part of Fortune. It seemed to me these were quite artificially derived, for we gave these positions the declination which the Sun would have had were it in that degree and sign. Later on, when we proceeded to the study of horary astrology, suddenly we found that declinations were important factors. Moreover, all those other columns in the ephemerides, latitudes, also had special significance.

Kt. Boehrer had studied out of bounds planets with Minnie McNutt and had written an early article on out of bounds planets in a long ago *Today's Astrologer*, the AFA bulletin. Los Angeles sidereal astrologer Jim Haynes remembered exactly when, April 12, 1975, and I was able to find it on my own shelves and add to my knowledge of declinations. Finally Kt. Boehrer wrote a book on the subject. Friends of Edward Dearborn got together to start a special interest group in the NCGR format to study declinations. That these made patterns, moved North a certain distance, and they may or might not go out of bounds before they turned South to zero and proceeded until they reached as far south as they were going and turned northward again. I felt this approach to zero, the change from north to south or south to north should have special significance. Special meanings were developed for planets that were natally out of bounds, and now we were going to be extending and charting declinational movement. North was not better than South or vice versa. Once the special interest group was established, we had a landmark article in their newsletter written by astrologer Karen Christino in which she traced graphically the progressed movement of lunar declinations in her progressed lifetime and correlated it with earning swings. I dare say other astrologers immediately graphed their own progressed Moons and thought deeply about their own charts. Even at that moment I was already collecting information for this book.

This was quickly followed by an article which cautioned us to give special thought to planets in northern signs but in a southern declination, or vice versa. Perhaps the next thing would be to check when the planets with which we were born in parallel journeyed to be in contra-parallel in our progressed charts or, looking at our transits, created a pictograph of the loops made in our lifetimes. Would the return to natal parallel have special meanings for us? It should have. These advanced studies were a far road from our limited elementary introduction to declinations.

The boundaries of normal declinations are set by those to which the Sun reaches on the solstices due to the tilt of the earth, summer and winter, for in summer the declination of the Sun is as far north as it ever is going to be, while in winter, it is as far south as it will ever go. If you remember what you learned in geography, the Earth tilts so that the Sun reaches as far north or south of the equator in the torrid zone. The Sun reaches at the Summer solstice to 23N27 or the Tropic of Cancer, loops down across zero at Libra and at the start of Capricorn will reach to 23S27 which is the Tropic of Capricorn. Eventually the Sun comes back to zero when we come back in the spring to Aries. Bear in mind always that it is the earth which tilts to capture the rays of the Sun, and it is the earth which rotates and tilts to give us our seasonal effects.

The Sun never goes outside its geographic boundary. However, the other planets may go further out than this solar boundary. When the declinations of other planets go beyond this degree and minute, such a planet has gone Out of Bounds or "beyond the awareness of human comprehension." (Great heaven, another astrological loophole and alibi.) But planets nearing the boundaries of the Sun's declination were said to become more powerful, more potently involved with action and life. Alas for those who have planetary declinations beyond the boundary of the Sun's path for they shall have less control over the manifestations of whatever planet is involved.

In that *Today's Astrologer* of April 12, 1975, Katherine Boehrer wrote that "the closer they approach the 23N27 or 23S27 limitation, the more extreme, eccentric, unusual, far-reaching and enduring their influence will be." This is better than "beyond control." She then followed this remark by reminding us that on December 7, 1941, Pearl Harbor Day, Pluto's declination was at 23N22, a mere five minutes from being out of bounds.

Later in her article, she also wrote: "It would not be reasonable to expect to find Uranus out of bounds in the natal chart of every murderer. Nor is it reasonable to expect that every natal Uranus out of bounds will prove to be the chart of potential murderer. With declination as with all else in astrology, it is necessary to relate the out of bounds planet to the entire chart. Look for natal parallels and parallels by progression and transit." Whether this is in any way some kind of indicator, we do have to concede that Uranus is quite important in the chart of O.J. Simpson. He had at birth Venus at 23N16, Uranus at 23N24, and Pluto actually out of bounds at 23N29. Why does Uranus have the responsibility of murder when Pluto is available? Astrologers, however, must be prepared to find people with Uranus out of bounds who are not murderers. And we did not have far to go to find just such a person in Mark Spitz, Olympic swimmer, who has Pluto at 23N40, Uranus at 23N43 and the Moon at 26S10. Simpson is two and a half years older than Mark Spitz.

One final observation by Katherine Boehrer piqued my curiosity. Charts of the early astronauts had Moon out of bounds "with surprising frequency." As space exploration became more common, fewer astronauts had out of bounds Moons natally. "I have found," she wrote, "that the natal Moon out of bounds is not uncommon in the charts of the victims of drowning." In my own research, there was a time when I was ready to assign Moon out of bounds as responsible for homosexuality after a run of several charts of homosexuals with far out Moons. Fortunately I found charts of two men who are absolutely heterosexual before I carved an idiot conclusion in stone. After all, since early astronauts, our best and brightest, had out of bounds Moons and are thoroughly investigated, it is hardly likely that any of them was homosexual. We will have to examine the emotionality of people with the Moon out of bounds, or the lengths to which they might go to manifest the sign in which they have their Moons, a thing which many feminist astrologers seem to think is impossible for any man or visible in any male chart.

Kt. Boehrer has written the definitive work on planetary declinations out of bounds. People with Venus out of bounds love "too strongly but seldom very wisely." Those with Mercury out of bounds are especially skilled at communications, particularly in writing. They seem to write with a felicity and have the facility for finding just the right turn of phrase. How I envy this, for when I write, there is hardly a sentence that could not be written more clearly or thoroughly rewritten. Mars out of bounds could be indicative of the compulsive military man.

Articles published in periodicals tend to get lost and remembered by only a few of us. Now, fortunately, Kt. Boehrer has written and published her own book *Declination, the Other Dimension*, 1994, Fortunate Press, Box 12476, El Paso, Texas, 79913. One would hope this book were a collection of various articles she has written, but it is not exactly that. She is primarily concerned with planets which go out of bounds. She has researched these and found them very significant. One may be born with planets beyond the boundaries to which the Sun reaches, and one may by progression live to a time when a planet goes out of bounds by progression (not to mention times in our lives when planets do so by transit), and then, the things of that planet and where it rules will be of great prominence in our lives. Even as I write, I note that Mercury is now out of bounds in my progressed chart. Unfortunately, it does not seem to have the same meaning in my current life that it has in the charts of those who natally have out of bounds Mercury, and I have done much editing and rewriting.

So if we can be affected by planets going out of bounds in the course of secondary progressions, there has to be special meaning when planets do so by transit. It was recently reported that Saturn was at zero declination all during the Munich Olympics in 1996, and that at the same time when Mars was out of bounds there were many news reports of Mars research.

In the course of this work I discovered in my own chart that I was born with Venus out of bounds, and I checked other charts of others born with Venus out of bounds, just as Kit. Boehrer had researched. The meaning I read was "one who loves too well but not too wisely." and it brought from me a mighty harumph. Talent and expertise without judgment! Another big harumph, for if you use judgment in love, it isn't exactly love. I still don't feel I chose to love people unworthy of me. Isn't the general thing that you fall in love with people of whom you are unworthy? Our sense of values eludes us. I was working on charts of children born in 1996 and noticed them all having Saturn at zero declination. I felt that this should have some special meaning, and I went looking for charts in my files of other people who were born with Saturn at zero.

Pulling these charts, I thought it would be a good idea to pull charts of persons born with Saturn at zero declination and allow a degree and a half of orb, but other astrologers convinced me to stick with a one degree orb. Then I saw that there were periods where Jupiter was at zero. Someone told me that at the same time Saturn was at zero so was Jupiter, but that, unfortunately was arrived at by mixing up the ephemeris declinations columns with the latitude column for Jupiter. Still, at that time, I also began by making a list of people born when Jupiter was at zero declination as a contrast to zero Saturn types.

As I examined the charts I pulled, I found a great variety of people in the Saturn group engaged in politics. When I decreased my orb to one degree, these politicians divided and some went into the further away list. However, I have kept the two sets separated in this study in hopes of showing a contrast of types. I decided to go no further than a one degree orb for the Jupiter group, the third section of declination study.

In all research one tries to be objective and keep an open mind. Nevertheless, one has a background of opinion on what one can expect of a basic Saturn or a basic Jupiter. All who have studied astrology are going to have similar ideas what these planets rule or influence, and are not likely to get mixed up by the meanings of Venus or Moon or Mars. Certain things are expected of Saturn, thinking along the lines of lessons, cautions, delays, the conservative and the conventional. As the work progressed, I expected I would find differences and tried to start with an open mind. There was much to think about.

In my own chart, and you will want to start out by checking out your own charts, I have to note that Venus was out of bounds at 26S19 and stayed out there my first thirty years, and Jupiter was within a degree of the boundary but never went out. If I live to age ninety, Mars will go out of bounds. At birth Mercury was 21S20, and I follow it by progression to where at age seven, it went out of bounds and stayed out there until I was thirty-two. Four years before that, Mercury went retrograde by progression, and it stayed that way until I was forty-nine. By declination, Mercury came in as far as 19S13 when I was age forty-seven and began going further out to where, at age seventy-one, it went again out of bounds and will return inside in the year 2004. There is no correlation between declination and retrograde periods. Mercury should have reference to Mercury things, rule Mercury houses (first and fifth in my case), and it should have been relevant to getting a formal and systematic education, which I did not. I studied what interested me rather than what would be cohesive and more well-rounding. I could very glibly make myself understood in several languages. I got about, I was very social, and being social is a Venus activity. I had a lot of fun, never a dull moment. I feel no different now than what I remember of life from age seven to age thirty-two. With Venus out of bounds, I must report that at age seven, I was not loving unwisely; I was a late-bloomer sexually and emotionally. And what of the time between age thirty-two and age seventy-one? Many changes took place in that span. I am faced with a pattern that was surely set by the time I got to my thirties and did not change simply because Venus came back within bounds by age thirty. Or, more importantly, what about life from now on? Not having the answer now, I will worry about that tomorrow.

Jupiter was at 22S42, and I checked to see that it was going outward until I was seven years old, at which time it then started coming toward the equator, which it will never reach by progression in my lifetime. Planets farther out—Saturn, Uranus, Neptune and Pluto (and Chiron)—pretty much stay at the declination where they were at birth throughout a reasonable progression. If they move little by progression in longitude, they do not move much by declination. Indeed, it is rare to find the three outer planets out of bounds. Remember to limit progressed movement to no more than three months after birth, a day for a year. Later you will want to explore declination movement by transits.

The charts in this sample are those of historical and notable persons, astrologers, and clients. Except for charts of notables and astrologers who have given special permission or who have previously published their own charts, attempts have been made to keep client identities confidential by use of identifying tags. This is followed by a "code" of three numbers, the first of which is the Ascendant, the second being the Sun sign, and the third being the Moon sign. So that our first chart below is a Taurus rising, Pisces Sun with Moon in Capricorn or 2-12-10, the chart of George Washington. Those given an identifying tag, an effort is made to tell the gender of the person. All of these charts have birth data furnished by the subjects or, in the case of public figures, previously published birth data from various official source records.

1. George Washington, 2-12-10
Saturn: 0S57
Data: February 22, 1732, 10:00 a.m. LMT,
Pope's Creek, Virginia, 38N12, 76W56

This chart was discovered after all others, and I could not resist inserting it chronologically at the start. The data comes from the family Bible, and the place is somewhat vague. It is east of Wakefield, Virginia, where Pope's Creek empties into the Potomac River. It may never have been more than the name for the private landing place on the river that served the Washington farm. Today it is Washington's Birthplace National Monument.

Everybody knows who Washington was, the honest child who chopped down the cherry tree and could not tell a lie, a man whose early career as a surveyor made

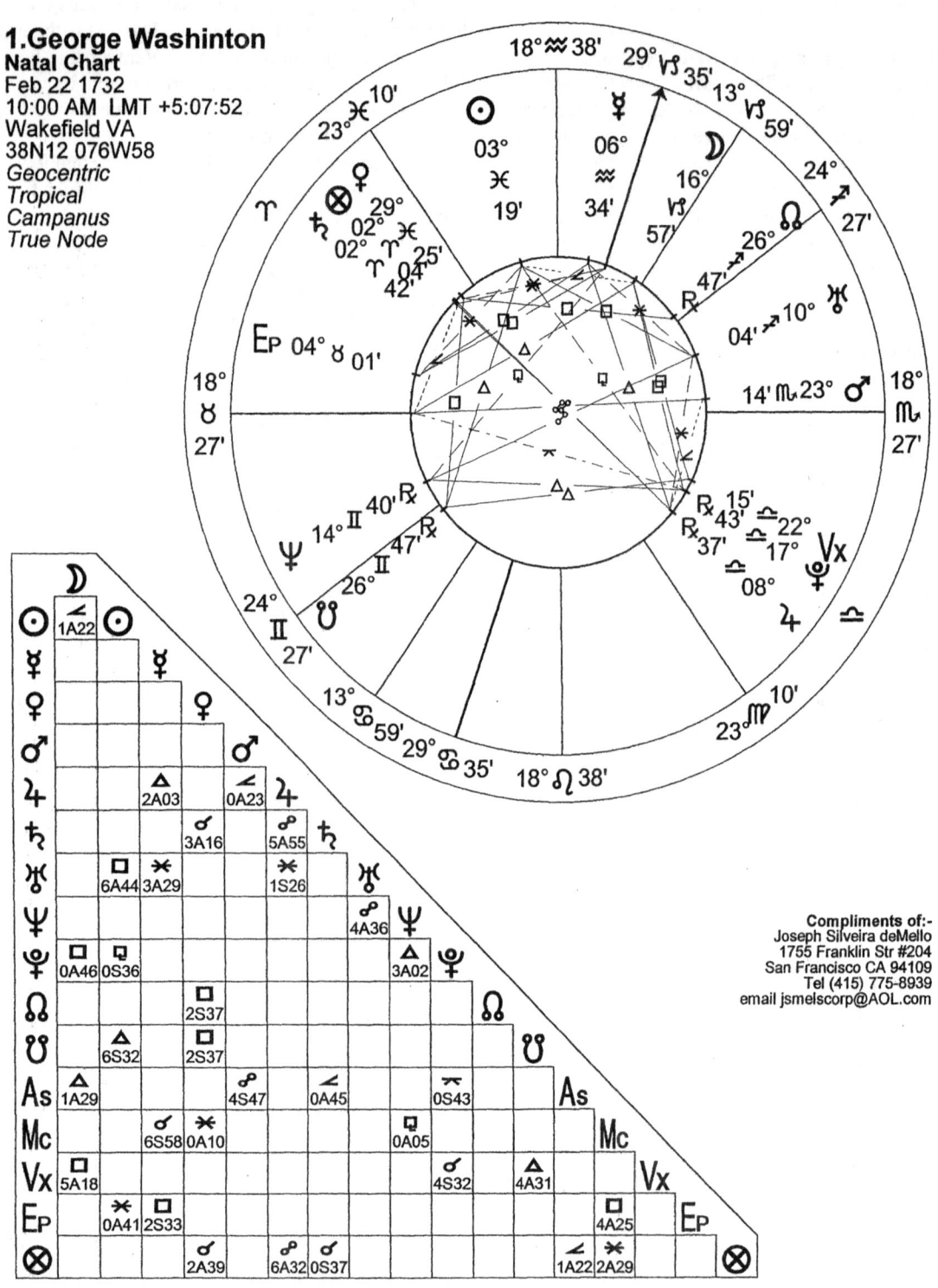

him a reliable leader in the French and Indian War, and finally he was chosen to head the Continental Army in our Revolutionary War, and is known as Father of his Country. Gilbert Stuart painted him, getting slight jaw differences due to the ill-fitting wooden false teeth of his time. More advanced academics tell us that the father of our country was also the father of the expense account. Given the choice of salary or expense account, he chose the latter and kept meticulous records. Never spent a penny if he could avoid it, and was a welcomed guest everywhere he went, often using his diamond ring to sign a window pane of the room he occupied. Even so, he wanted nothing better than to retire from public life to his own Potomac River farm at Mt Vernon. Now political correctness prefers to criticize him for having had slaves because people today do not realize there was no way to work a plantation without slaves, there being no white workers lowly enough to do any menial work. Virginia settlers were all well born second sons seeking to make their fortunes more easily done here than to have stayed in England.

Here we have Taurus rising with a Pisces Sun and the Moon in Capricorn. These three major points of any chart start us doing a methodical reading. The Ascendant is the way others see you and your personality; the Sun is your individuality and ego, while the Moon is how you think you appear to others as if you yourself were on stage. Although our plan is to look at charts where Saturn was at zero declination, we start with a chart where one of the three primaries already has a strong Capricorn presence in the Moon. The Capricorn Moon alerts us to see Washington as a man who suffered a great deal of opposition. But these do not loom large in his life. After all he was the one leader who was acceptable to both northern and southern colonies. The Moon of course indicates the subject's mother, a lady who seems never have been pleased by anything her son did or accomplished. We are told she refused to attend his inaugurations when we should realize that any such a journey at her age and in her times presented unimaginable difficulties. If Washington wanted nothing more than to get back to his home farm, his mother sternly refused to leave her home.

Venus, his chart significator is in the twelfth house, a location which tells us that matters of the affections are hidden behind the scenes. This is doubly indicated by Venus underlined by being conjunct Saturn which traditionally gets the person thought of as a cold fish. We all know that Venus in the first house gives us an attractive person, but I have found Venus in the twelfth often gives us a person with some facial mark or visible beauty flaw. Remember those false teeth. Along Venus lines, we know he had an eye for the ladies, and the refinement and courtliness to go with it, but he never did marry his first light of love. And what is intercepted in the twelfth is the sign Aries of military persons. He certainly accepted no criticism of the way he handled his position as leader of the Continental Army.

What is important in the study of his sixth is that it is ruled by Mercury, highest planet in his chart. His earliest career was as a surveyor mapping the boundaries of uncharted territories. Boundaries of property are of great interest to a proper Taurus rising. We have to notice other things about this chart. Mercury in the tenth rules the second and sixth making property and work and service focused to status. We note that Saturn rules Midheaven carrying that into the twelfth where we find Saturn in Aires. The things of where Saturn is and where Saturn rules come to every person later rather than earlier in life. Saturn in the twelfth frequently questions whether the subject will survive his early years, but then Saturn transits into his first house, and he proceeds to know himself (first), like himself (second), learn to communicate (third) and proceeding in orderly twenty-eight year round to complete the entire cycle. We are also looking at a man born at a time when length of life was shorter than it is today and people matured earlier, worked earlier, married sooner, and died sooner except that many important Revolutionary men did manage to live a longer life than did most of their peers. We must also note that the Midheaven signifies the end career of man, decidedly an executive, and a man who refused to be a king of the new republic, which was a popular sentiment of the time. He was entirely against such a title. It is well to remember that Neptune and Pluto did not exist in his lifetime. Note Virgo ruling the sixth; the details never escaped him.

There is one more consideration in personality evaluation and that is Mars here in his Scorpio seventh. Where we find Mars is where we put our energies, and the seventh concerns close associates, mates, and open enemies. We are so accustomed to seeing Mars in the seventh of our leaders who have been involved in the country's wars. We can see Uranus in generational opposition to Neptune. John Adams, the next President, three years younger than Washington, had the same aspect.

Washington was propelled into a position of leadership. He was neither fiery orator nor lawyer. As a Taurus landowner and farmer, and he thought of himself always as the latter, it would be natural for him to be a conservative and a Tory. Did Saturn in a northern sign and southern declination have any responsibility for that? The owners of plantations, contrary to modern opinion, were very involved in the welfare of his slave dependents and would never have treated any of them harshly. Indeed, he emancipated his slaves in his final will and testament at his death.

2. William Henry Chaney, 7-10-3
Saturn: 0N55
Data: January 13, 1821, 11:31 p.m. EST,
Chesterville, Maine, 44N38, 70W06

W.H. Chaney has the distinction of being the first American born astrologer. He was one of many children born to early farmers in rural Maine. His mother died in his infancy, and his father died when he was nine years old. Returning to their farm, he had an accident, was thrown from his carriage and his head fatally struck a large rock. The orphaned Chaney children were parceled out in the community, and young Chaney was by turn apprenticed to six men in various trades, none of

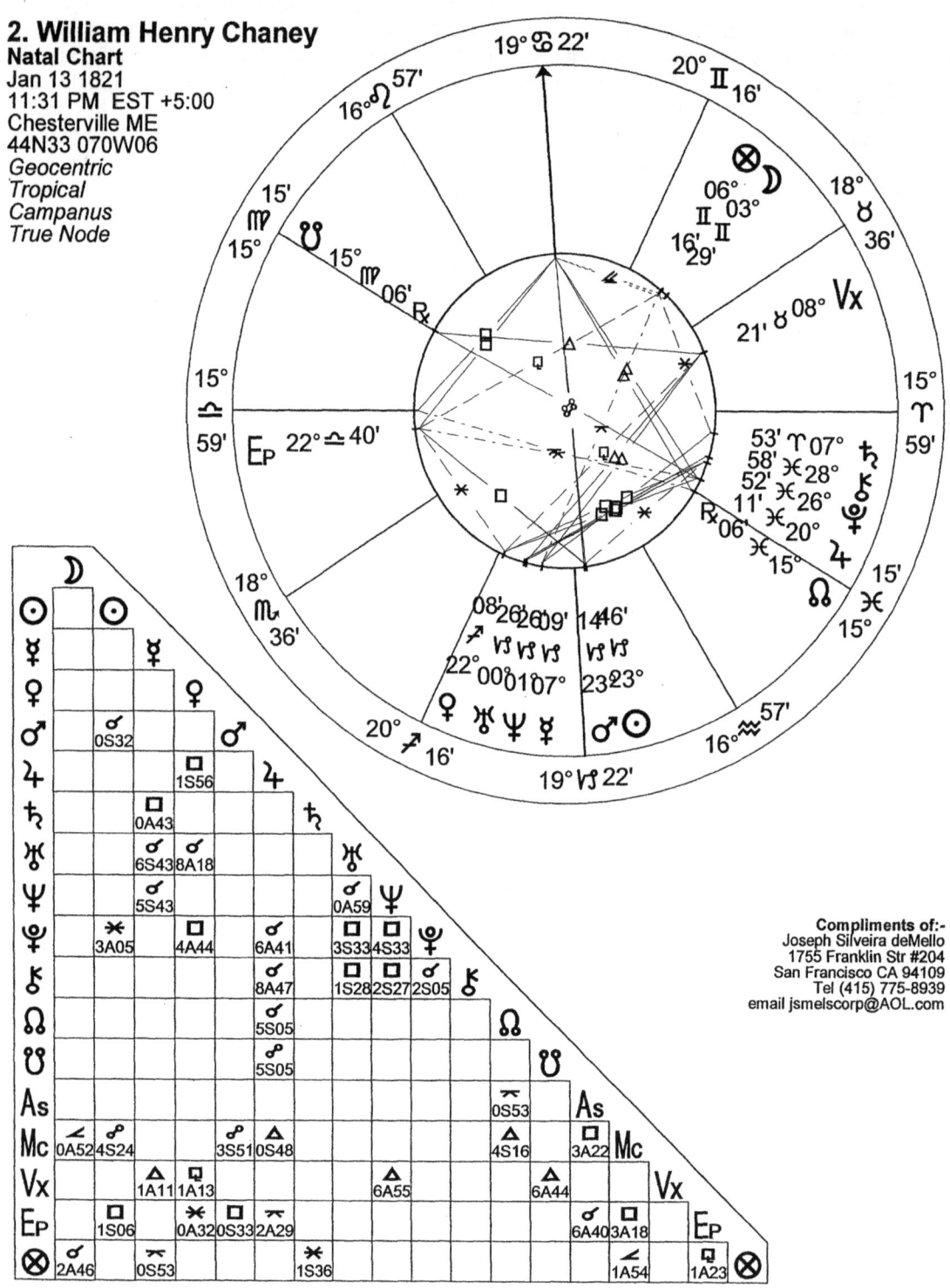

which quite suited his dreams of adventure and glory. In his teens, he found himself in Boston, an enlistee in the Navy, a dead-end position. He deserted before his enlistment was up.

His months of Navy service, swapping tales with his mates, got Chaney to dream of going down the Ohio and Mississippi, working his way to New Orleans where he would sign on a ship and eventually take it over to set himself up as a highly successful pirate. Upon reaching the river, his plans were thwarted by an untimely illness. Sick, ragged, impoverished, he was rescued by a local gentleman who took Chaney home to his family and saw promise in the youth, outfitted him and set him up as a rural schoolmaster in a nearby community. Chaney was soon contributing writings and poetry to the local weekly newspaper and even schooled himself to the point of becoming a country lawyer. Chaney did not lack in enterprise. He remained in Ohio and West Virginia for twenty years. During the Civil War, he was probably beyond military age.

Around 1867, he chanced on some writings by Dr. Luke Broughton, and immediately he set off for New York City to apprentice himself to this learned English third generation astrologer-doctor. Broughton took Chaney in and taught him astrology. Both men were arrested for practicing astrology and taken to Ludlow Street Jail. Broughton, being a learned professional man and head of the New York Medical Society, was soon released. But Chaney, being contentious, the typical jail house lawyer, was kept there for eight months without charges ever being brought against him.

Further travels took him to San Francisco, where he set up astrology classes and giving public lectures on every subject of current public interest. He traveled up to Salem, Oregon, gave his first lecture there in 1871. He had clients in Portland and in Seattle. The then mayor of Seattle had come from Ohio, and had taken into his home a young woman who had run away from her prominent Ohio family.

Chaney moved to a boarding house and discovered that the young woman he had met in Seattle was also living there supporting herself as a psychic and tarot reader. With Ohio in common, she put herself at his disposal to run his errands, take care of the door receipts when he lectured or taught astrology, played the musical intervals at his lectures, even delivered his written horoscopes to clients. He had a flourishing astrology practice, but learned that, when she delivered his charts, she tried to make his clients her own.

There is some question what Chaney's relationship was with this lady. She seems to have given up on emancipation. She was then determined to marry as well as she could. When she announced that she was pregnant and told Chaney he was the father, he told her it was impossible as early illness and much brain work had made him sterile. He suggested she have an abortion. When this idea failed, he moved away. She made a hash of trying to kill herself, attempted to blame Chaney, but Chaney got himself officially exonerated and went up to Oregon to work in Salem.

This story followed him and was picked up by the famous pioneer feminist newspaper publisher and editor of *New West*, Abigail Scott Dunniway. The fact that he had been officially cleared of any responsibility in the San Francisco scandal was disregarded. She refused to publish a retraction or cease her continual attacks against him.

In the meantime, in San Francisco, the Ohio lady gave birth to a son, on the day before Chaney's fifty-fifth birthday. She gave herself up to child care and worked for a seamstress to support herself and her son. Thus she came to meet an Iowa widower with children who was looking for a mother for them, and he married her and adopted her son John, giving the boy his own name. This son was to become Jack London, noted American writer-adventurer, but Chaney always denied his paternity, though every placement in London's chart bears close testament otherwise. You can check this yourself with the data for London, January 12, 1876, 2:10 p.m. PST, San Francisco, California. Jack London was to write Chaney on this subject and was continually rebuffed, and by the time Jack London passed through Chicago, Chaney had already died, so the two never met.

Chaney moved back to St. Louis where he taught astrology and issued his astrological pamphlets which became the *Primer of Astrology*. He later moved on to Chicago (1897) where he operated astrology schools at two locations, one of them the Chicago College of Astrology at 509 Ogden Avenue, and he died January 6, 1903. In his latter years he was gray, lost a goodly portion of his teeth grew increasingly deaf; he went blind toward the end of his life. He described himself an a cantankerous old curmudgeon, and indeed he was.

An easy person he never was. He could always justify any stance he took, being a Libra rising. Capricorns are happiest being their own master, and there seldom were times he was not. Three times in his life, and perhaps more, he was rescued from the depths of ill luck, rescues he attributed to Jupiter although Jupiter was not in his twelfth house. His third house planets, Venus, Uranus, Neptune and Mercury, are square to his Jupiter, Pluto, Chiron and Saturn in the sixth (he would not have known of Pluto or Chiron). His eighth house Moon in Gemini is conjunct his Part of Fortune but aspected to nothing else in his chart. This is interesting since he has both Moon and Mercury in declinations out of bounds. His chart is predominately cardinal and earth. His cantankerousness may be seen by Sun separating from a conjunction to Mars, only thirty-one minutes apart. This is too far apart for cazimi (seventeen minutes or less). so the ego overtakes his Mars. It is significant his Moon's only aspect is a semisquare to the Midheaven.

Here was a man who did exactly what he wanted to do and was not lax to strike back at those he perceived as his enemies. And we hear more of his enemies than we do of his friends. Of astrologers he had good words only for Pearce, a writer whose books may be found in the libraries of older astrologers. Reading the astrology pamphlets of W. H. Chaney is both instructive and amusing. I was introduced to them by astrologer Don Borkowski who found a bound collection of those pamphlets. Chaney knew himself and his chart, had no hesitation to use events in his life to illustrate astrological principles. But he still leaves one feeling he withheld or did not tell all. This was somewhat the same when he practiced law. He would not stick to classical precedents and judges criticized him.

There are things of which we should be careful in his chart. As a Libra rising, those who furnished him mail order charts commented on his fine appearance and slender weight. He was stocky, weighed between 200 and 220, and rued his lack of beauty. He constantly abjured his students against relying entirely on aspects in chart delineation. The Moon is just two degrees beyond being quincunx Uranus. A planet which makes no aspects, the Moon, is usually a very strong planet. Chaney was indeed a man of many parts. There was no subject on which he could not get up and speak. His considerable Ohio literary output is totally lost. His chart delineation is published in *A to Z Horoscope Maker and Delineator*. Some of his lecture topics are just what one could expect of a flower child of the 1960s full of environmental concerns. In a lecture of 1874 he was awaited the imminent Age of Aquarius as people did again almost a hundred years later. His published chart had in it neither Neptune nor Pluto, let alone Chiron, and the East Point and Vertex were not calculated. None of his natal planets is retrograde. His Mercury has only a square to Saturn. If we use the same dictum as in the previous chart, the Sun in the fourth makes security the heart of the matter, yet he was seldom secure. His Mars and Saturn are in mutual reception, so if we give him courtesy placements of Mars, we get a seventh house Mars at 23 Aries, and a third house Saturn conjunct his Mercury. He worked hard and was entirely sincere, but he was also not above tilting at as many windmills as he could find.

3. Ivy Goldstein-Jacobson, 4-1-12
Saturn: 0S50
Data: April 13, 1893, 12:12 p.m. LMT,
Brisbane, Queensland, Australia, 27S28, 153E02

I have always wanted to write about this wonderful lady who was a great influence on my study of astrology. I like to credit this lady for her insistence that astrologers use their heads for thinking. I have all but one of her astrology books and do not have her volume of poetry. From her *Foundations of the Astrological Chart* I learned to erect horoscopes in a simple and reliable process.

The data for this chart is the data she used for herself and was probably rectified by her. Note that she was born just below the Tropic of Capricorn. The chart has Cancer rising, Moon therefore being chart significator is in Pisces in the eighth house. The Sun, highest planet in her chart is in Aries just short of her Midheaven in the ninth house of philosophical ideas and higher teachings. The chart is further enhanced by Jupiter in Taurus in the tenth house, and few placements are more glorified in astrology than Sun or Jupiter in the tenth house. While the chart divides the planets equally to east and west sides, most of the planets are above the horizon. Mars which is a strong component in any chart is almost in the twelfth house in Gemini and conjunct Neptune and Pluto, also in Gemini. Mars is almost close to out of bounds, a thing Mars does once a year. Mercury-Mars are in mutual reception.

Although we exchanged notes three or four times, I hardly knew Ivy Jacobson. Her responses to any question were always brief and to the point, and there was never any chit chat of any kind. Unlike Chaney, her books contain no personal references. She practiced astrology and taught it at the First Temple of Astrology in Pasadena. I found all of her books wonderful and grumbled that they were not indexed. One could never find again some half-remembered gem. One can only gain by reading her books over and over again. When I taught horary astrology, her book on horary was the text I used.

The main thing about reading and teaching from these books is the author's style of writing. Her punctuation has to be heeded. She says you have to have this and this and a third other, the two with the third have a specific meaning. Students had to learn that if they did not have all three things, they could not have that specific meaning in their charts. So if the student had two of those three things, and in the place of the third thing she gave, they had something else, students had to find their own meaning. It was not easily on the next page. She was pointing the path to astrological perfection, stressing the usual astrological need of a presence of three indicators to prove any specific astrological judgment. She insisted that astrology remain astrological. She saw no need to set out meanings for every astrological combination to be found. That sort of thing was left to be done by Reinhold Ebertin in *The Combination of Stellar Influences*, a must in any library of astrology books. It was not the aim of Ivy Jacobson to give us a nice cookbook of astrology for such defeat learning to think. Every once in a while I look at my book shelves and vow to go back to her books the next time I lack something to read.

And thereby hang several tales. The publisher Don Weiser proposed that he take over the publishing of Ivy's books and got her to agree. Accordingly, he set the wheels in motion and got his editors to do all those things editors do, like making decisions on fonts typesetting and design and bindings and jackets, and eventually a set of proofs was sent to the author for corrections, changes or additions. And the roof fell in. Ivy felt her great work had been ruined, that the books she lovingly crafted had been defiled. She did not want her books to look like any other astrology books. It was her typing that made her books unique, and she refused to allow them to be published in any other way. Here we see the fine hand of Mercury opposite Saturn. The project had to be scrubbed. And then she died.

There is one interesting set of aspects about this chart. Count around the circle how many planets seem to be fifteen degrees apart, or then thirty degrees apart, and note where the midpoints fall. For example Saturn and Uranus are thirty degrees apart and make 165 degree aspects to the Sun (at their converse midpoint). You might see that Mercury and Jupiter almost have Venus at their midpoint. This is not exact in the natal chart but it

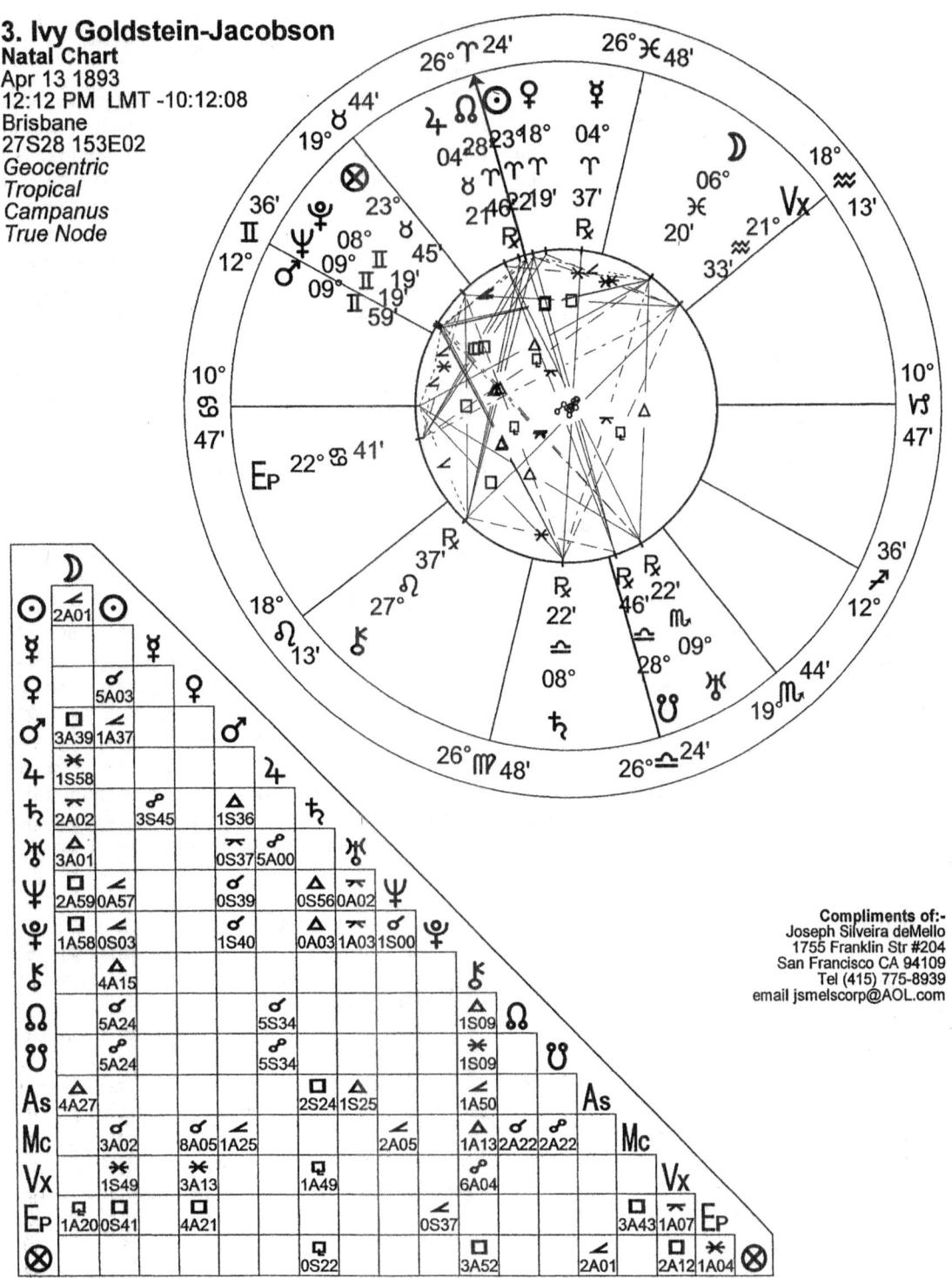

3. Ivy Goldstein-Jacobson
Natal Chart
Apr 13 1893
12:12 PM LMT -10:12:08
Brisbane
27S28 153E02
Geocentric
Tropical
Campanus
True Node

will at some time be touched by progressions or most certainly by transits.

This chart is interesting as the chart of a writer. Her third house has Saturn in Libra so that communication is a karmic issue, but the house is ruled by Virgo (it could not be any other sign) which is, in turn, ruled by her Aries Mercury in the ninth house. Mercury and Mars are in mutual reception. No one who reads these astrology books can doubt her seriousness. I have never heard any astrologer argue with her interpretations. But even the best of astrologers can make chart errors as she did in rectifying the chart of the Duchess of Windsor, assuming a birthplace of Baltimore, Maryland, rather than at Blue Ridge Summit, Pennsylvania. She did note the very real suspicion that some family effort was made to alter the birth record so that it not show that the Duchess was born out of wedlock.

Ivy had Cancer rising, the sign of nurture, then an intense Aries Sun softened by the Moon in Pisces. What one sees most easily is the Ascendant, but the ego is the Sun, not easily concealed in Aries, while the Moon is how the person wishes to come across to the public. She certainly was successful in expressing much of the good side of Pisces. The final personality indicator is Mars in Gemini (mutual reception to Mercury) and you see graphically how this worked. But we cannot avoid seeing Mars tightly with Neptune and Pluto almost on the edge of her twelfth house. (See my interest as these three planets fall on my own Ascendant!) This trio of planets is quincunx her Uranus (close to my natal Sun). It is almost routine that astrologers compare any chart they see to their own charts.

Analyzing Saturn at zero declination, we noted it is opposite Mercury. Both of them are retrograde. Mercury retrograde is the abstract mind. Saturn retrograde gives us people who have a mission that all people around them relate to each other and the world. This is not a debility for it keeps such people avidly interested in all that goes on around them. Note the aspects of this opposition. Saturn is square the Ascendant and Saturn trines Pluto-Neptune-Mars, which then sextile Mercury. But think of the mutual reception and do not fail to see the grand trine of Moon, Ascendant and Uranus.

4. Female Astrologer, 4-2-12
Saturn: 0S07
Data: April 26, 1908, 9:00 a.m. CST,
Chicago Illinois, 41N49, 87W37

This lady is a student astrologer I have known for many years. We were originally both students together, and later on she attended classes I taught. I could always gauge whether other students understood the lesson by watching her reactions. She was never too shy to ask the questions other students were too timid to ask. She only did horoscopes for people she met and in whom she became interested. These charts were always puzzles she had to solve. She was a shrewd observer of people. She studied them and their charts, and never would she think of herself as a professional astrologer. She was a marvel. She would put a chart on a side table and go about her daily tasks, now and then coming back to the chart for another look at it. She was never satisfied until she could point to several reasons revealed in any chart which pointed to the correctness of her observations. If there was a serious problem to be solved for one of her friends, a problem she felt inadequate to tackle, she would then telephone me to ask what I thought about it. Moon in the ninth house is often given to the study of ancient arts such as astrology. The Moon in Pisces can be sensitive and perceptive but tends to lack confidence, no matter how often you praise their consistent successes.

I welcomed her calls for help. It was a good exercise for me, and I enjoyed her thorough approach. She would tell me something of the person, and we would look at the chart together. Then she would tell me a bit more about the person and add something further, until she got around to telling me what the current problem was, by which time, we were halfway to our conclusions. Bit by bit, piece by piece, we would find order in the chart and a routine system of looking at any chart and considering only those factors involved in whatever the problem. Then we would check current transits to the chart. All of it was interesting and full of native humor and understanding.

Note that she is fifteen years younger than the previous chart, the same Ascendant and Moon, but now the Sun is in Taurus. She had been married seven times, and married yet another time after I got to know her. These marriages ended equally in divorced or widowhood. Many years ago, she had worked in restaurants and even owned one of her own, but she hit on a way that she could work and live well with a minimum of hard labor, and she and her various husbands eked out fine incomes by managing large apartment buildings in the San Francisco area. She and her husbands were both salaried and rent free. She was a larger than life personality with a boisterous and earthy sense of humor. She had an avid zest for life and was open and forthright to one and all.

If we pause to examine the individuality of this chart, there it is, everything on top, as in the saying "what you see is what you get," but for Jupiter in the first house. She was sturdy but petite. She might have been larger had Jupiter been in her rising sign, but it is in Leo, so, even if in the first house, Jupiter in the first house is effective only to give her a larger than life and a sanguine personality. The Moon in Pisces as her chart significator in the tenth, tied to karmic Saturn square to the Ascendant and Neptune. She had no thoughts of suicide as Neptune in the twelfth so often gives. I can only say that I have seldom seen an ascending Neptune working as favorably as it did for her. See the mutual reception of Moon and Neptune and recognize it as a key to this charming lady. The validity of putting mutual reception planets as extras in their own signs would give her a first house Moon, and she was very outspoken. Another mutual reception in this chart involves Mercury and Mars. Astrologers glibly say of mutual receptions that the trouble one of the placements gets you into, the other gets you out of it. To this I can only add that mutual receptions are found in the charts of those who need them.

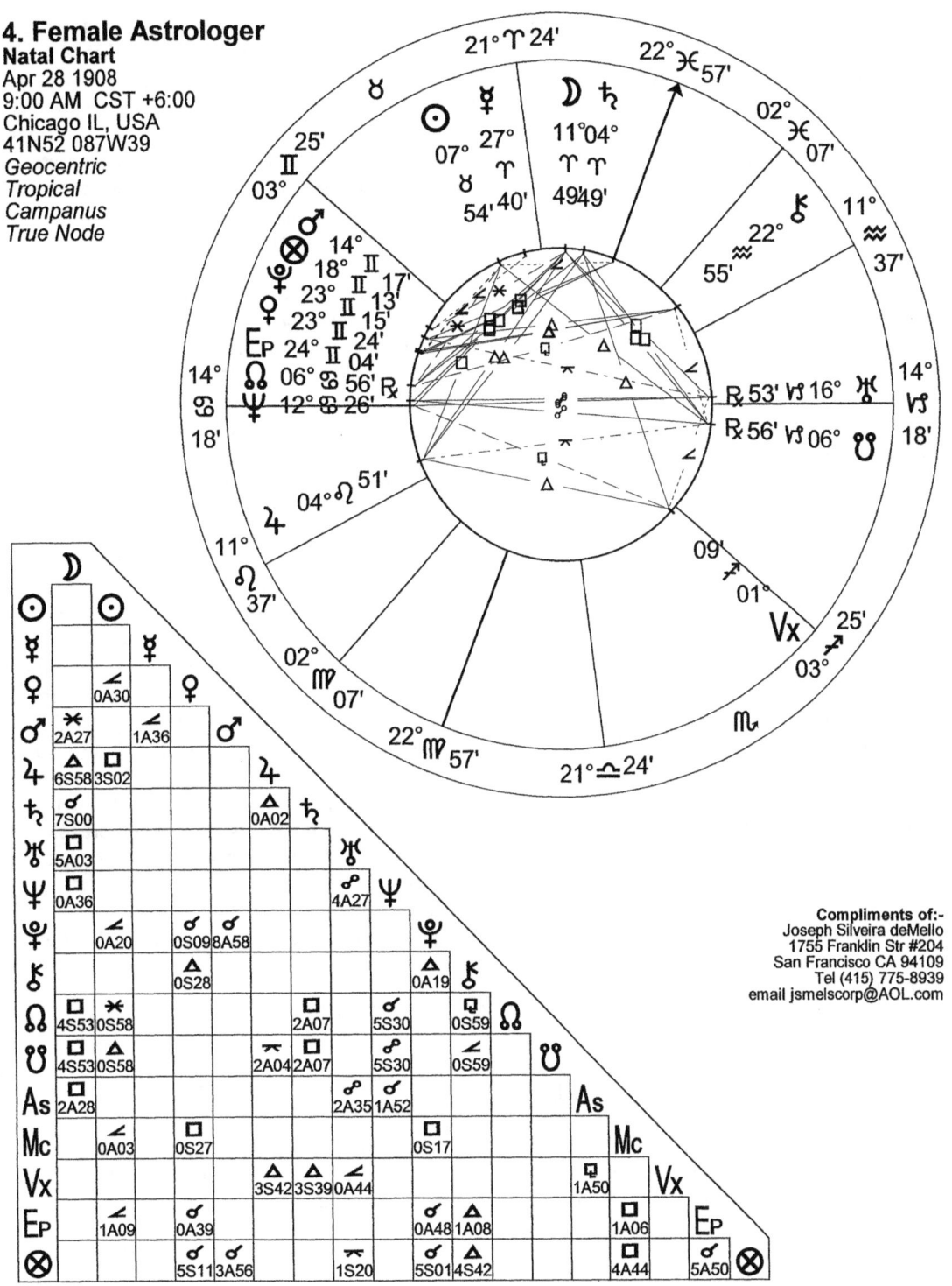

4. Female Astrologer
Natal Chart
Apr 28 1908
9:00 AM CST +6:00
Chicago IL, USA
41N52 087W39
Geocentric
Tropical
Campanus
True Node

Though open and forthright, woe unto anyone who every tried to pull any sort of scam on her. She pulled no punches with such people. They were out of her life even before they heard her slam the door.

She had much experience of life. My notes in her file say that from the age of five until sixteen she had been raised a Catholic in an orphanage. She had been married twice to alcoholics, once to a Mafioso. She joined the Mormon church when she was 41 or 42 years of age. At that same time, she gave cesarean birth to two children who did not live. The husband she had when I first met her was a retired motorcycle policeman whom she married when she owned and operated a restaurant. They were a great couple, well suited to each other.

I used to do a little drawings of aspect patterns for all the charts I did. I had a feeling that when the aspects produced a picture pattern, you would be looking at a special person. The diagram of all her aspects turned out to form a rakishly folded turban, just as the pattern for Eleanor Roosevelt chart is a tilted garrison cap. I would simplify by drawing only those aspects which made double aspects and obvious pattern midpoints.

5. Astrologer's Grandmother, 7-7-5
Saturn: 0S19
Data: October 18, 1908, 6:30 a.m. PST,
Middletown, Idaho, 43N42, 116W37

This chart was contributed by a fellow astrologer whom, like most astrologers, finds it important to find astrological continuums between family charts. This lady was his maternal grandmother. The main point here is that she was born with Saturn at zero declination, and now we are back to finding Saturn in a northern sign but a southern declination. He also sent me the chart of his paternal grandmother, but she had Mercury at zero declination. We have to bear in mind that Mercury is a quickly moving planet and is at zero but briefly, but will be there frequently in a lifetime of transits.

The lady of this chart was born in 1908, in a small town far from major city centers. We must also consider her times. She was a housewife who added to the family income by working as a waitress. Beginning life at the beginning of a century which was going to bring people face to face with more innovations and inventions per year than any previous century, she was ten at the end of World War One, in her twenties during the depression, almost forty at the end of World War Two.

The chart has the late degree of Libra rising, with a Libra Sun. Quite early in life, both progressed into Scorpio. The natal Moon is in Leo, and highest planet in her chart, so she is not taking a back seat to anyone, not with this combination. The Sun is in fall and behind the scenes in the twelfth house, where we also find Mars not in its best sign. But the Moon indicates that she wishes drama though her status is not entirely satisfactory. A Leo Moon makes up for the absence of other things in her life. Venus her chart significator is in the eleventh with Jupiter and both in Virgo. I believe signs usually go well with adjacent signs. It was not only economics which brought her into the work area and the public area. This is not the chart of someone who would have been happy to stay home. She needs people contact. And then Saturn in the sixth tells us of a karma of works and services, with Pisces ruling the sixth house, she was a fine waitress and probably ran the place with greater control of what happened there than such a servile position indicates. One can be sure she touched the lives of all her clientele. Yet with her twelfth house, there was a large interest in background and subconscious. You see that Mercury, the interest in the life is fenced off in her first house and retrograde.

The chart is dominated by two oppositions, Uranus and Neptune, and Mars and Saturn, but they are far enough out of orb that they do not make a cardinal square. Both of these oppositions are a problem but one which she probably learned to work out. The opposition is not the worst of aspects since one gets to select sides with every event. Uranus gives us unconventional or modern communications, while Neptune brings its element of imagination and delusion. Difficult aspects between Mars and Saturn are always evocative of frustration. But the opposition is more manageable than the square. It has the choice of whether for forge ahead or to hold back. A third opposition between Moon and Fortune to Chiron might tell us some personal security or home measure went by the board where her public life was given more attention. I tend to dislike mythological symbolism but note that Chiron's son is Uranus, and Uranus is father of Saturn. Here we have good fortune playing counterpoint to overlooking the obvious.

When faced with the charts of waiters and waitresses, I always check the condition of the sixth house, here in Pisces, ruled by Neptune in the area for state actresses, in the ninth house. But being a waitress is a sensible occupation if one has to go out to work as it does not require an extensive wardrobe, perhaps a uniform, sometimes merely an apron, so every cent you make is not spent dressing to impress. It is made more tolerable if, as in this chart, the job allowed for some role playing. Plus, with Saturn retrograde, the person who tries to make everyone and everything relate to each other, she took a serious and lively interest in the problems of others.

6. Joseph McCarthy, 1-8-5
Saturn: 0S52
Data: November 14, 1908, 3:00 p.m. CST,
Grand Chute, Wisconsin, 44N17, 88W18

In February 1950, the Republican senator from Wisconsin alleged a fantastic number of State Department employees were known active Communist sympathizers.

The fantastic number was halved in his next speech. But this was the impetus for chairing the House Un-American Activities Committee. The war was won, and the media had covered the Nazi war crimes trials. The US was ready to go back into its former isolationism. But the stage has been set in the thirties, when all ef-

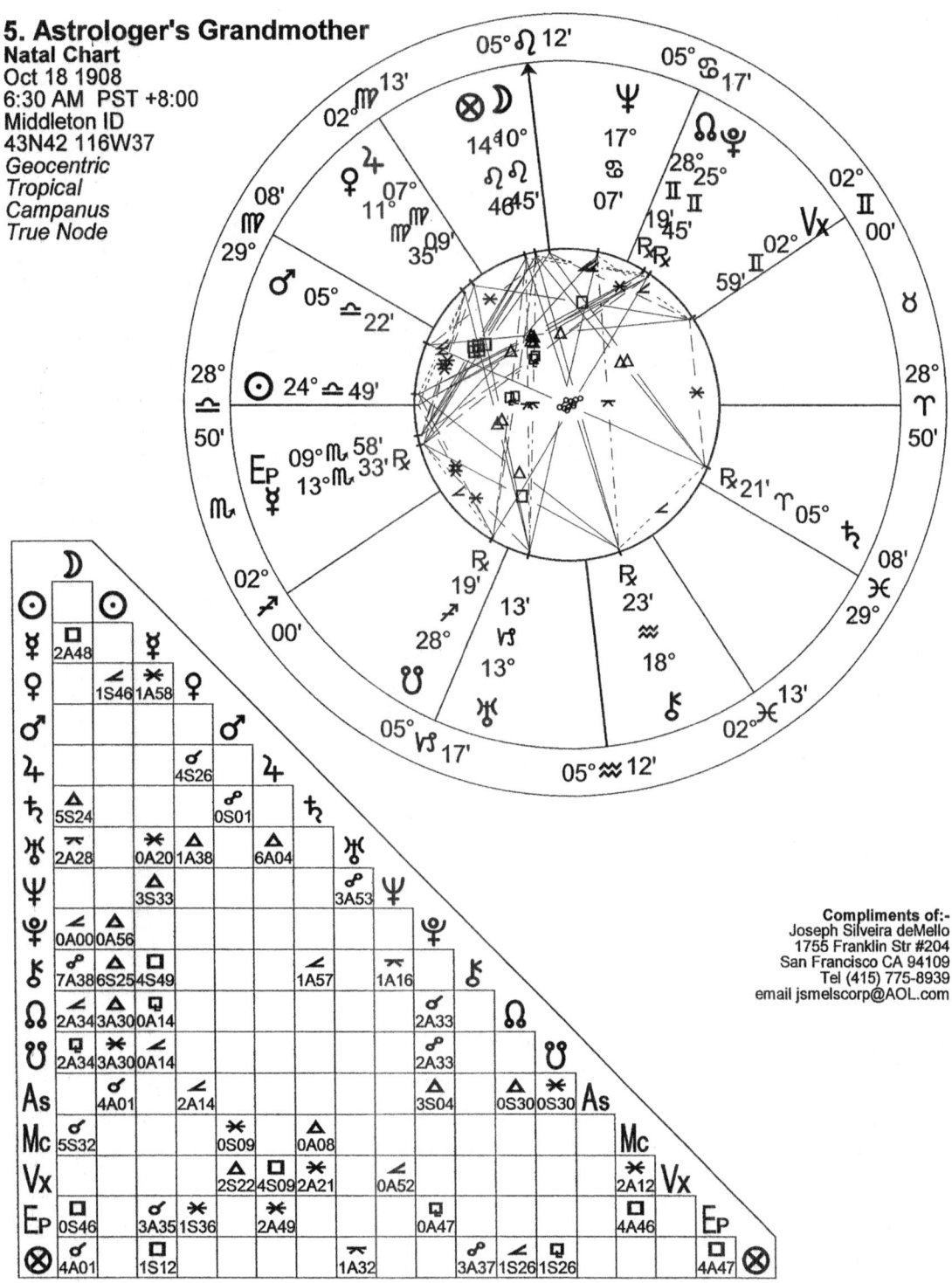

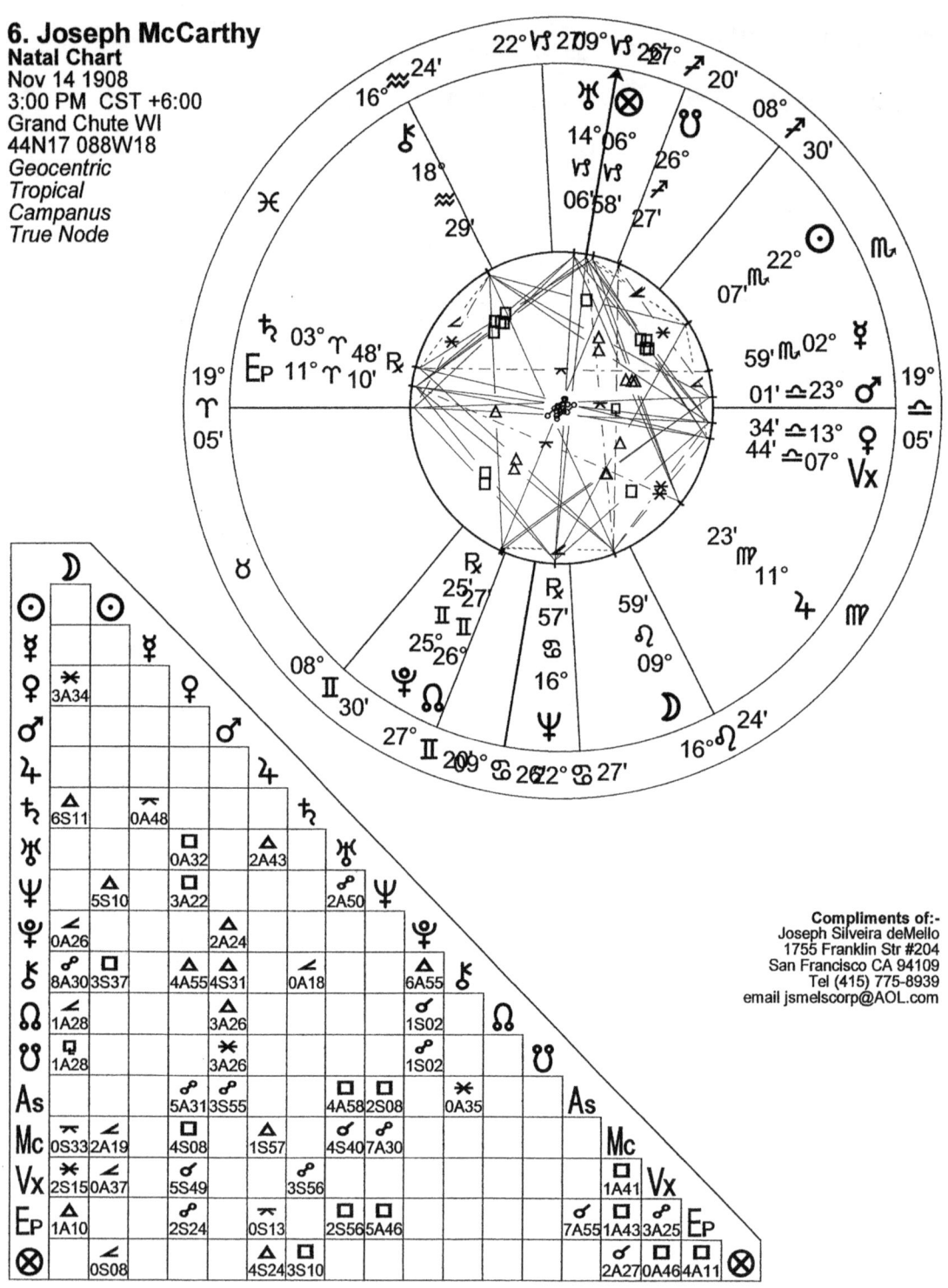

forts to unionize labor in one American industry were labeled as communistic, principally by the Hearst press. When the war made Russia an ally, Roosevelt quietly asked media and movies to treat Russia more favorably. This was forgotten, and warming to his thesis, McCarthy found an apt source of publicity by routing communists in the movie industry, since movies were recognized to influence public opinion and mores. Purging homosexuals from the State Dept. and the Army was an alternate issue. It never dawned on him that several members and advisors of his committee themselves were homosexuals.

McCarthy's style was complete bombast. He would wave a fistful of papers and say they were documents naming State Dept. communists, but not one was ever read into the record. Allegations were never factually supported. Once accused, however, there was no way anyone was permitted to deny association as a communist or a homosexual. Someone even wondered if it was possible to be both those things at the same time. In typical Aries fashion, if his tactics came under question, he changed the subject. Nor did it occur to him what image of America he was broadcasting to the world. It was the first investigation carried on television. The public got full bonus watching these antics.

I have often said Scorpios naturally like other Scorpios, but Joseph McCarthy was a person I thoroughly disliked. As a Republican, it was McCarthy and later Richard Nixon which were the straws which raising personal doubts and embarrassment. And way back before I had astrology to assist me. McCarthy was quintessentially his Aries rising, and I might say his Scorpio was not too evident. The Scorpio Sun is intercepted in his seventh house, fenced off from the criticism of other people, while the Leo Moon, a talent for self-dramatization, is very front and center. Anything an Aries says is automatically correct simply because he has said it. His Libra Mars in the warlike seventh house, and his Sun, Moon and Venus are in critical degrees. Critical degrees have been found to be quite powerful. His Mars, like my own, is conjunct Spica.

The chart has a cardinal grand cross under which no man stands still. With that he would go out to find opportunity if it did not come to him. He has the generational Uranus opposed to Neptune, here from tenth to fourth, an unconventional status to a home situation somewhat nebulous. We know how the most debilitated people have no temerity about criticizing others when they are themselves are not paragons. Uranus, the highest planet in this chart, is going well toward an out of bounds status. The Saturn retrograde is here in the twelfth house which says he learns from his own mistakes, often at great cost, must, in that house be reliving some sort of past life karma. One wonders at Saturn in zero declination. He seemed to pull out all the stops to do the thing he wanted to do. I do not believe he was as conservative as his political pose.

Possibly the worst thing that could happen to an Aries rising is to have his chart significator in the house of other people, and in a chart with the majority of the planets on the other people side of the chart, hence his life is pulled by the whims and machinations of other people, which an Aries would instantly deny. It would have been the last straw had McCarthy himself been accused of homosexuality. He was a bachelor who close to the end of his life married his secretary. He started life as a middle-weight boxer in college, he later went into Wisconsin politics and was elected to the US Senate 5 Nov 46. It was his speech of the February 9, 1950 at Wheeling, West Virginia, which ignited the anti-Communist paranoia. In December 1954, Congress condemned his beliefs but did not condemn his conduct. In the course of his life he became alcohol dependent, eventually dying of liver failure at 5:02 p.m. EDT, May 2, 1957, at Bethesda, Maryland.

7. Lew Ayres, 7-10-12
Saturn: 0S43
Data: December 28, 1908, 12:15 a.m. CST,
Minneapolis, Minnesota, 44N58, 93W15

Discovered for films at the age of twenty while playing in a night club band in Hollywood, this former University of Arizona medical student found the banjo, guitar and piano more fun. Do the fates laugh that he soon graduated into playing opposite to Greta Garbo in "The Kiss," and in 1930, he played the lead in Lewis Milestone's acclaimed war film "All Quiet on the Western Front" based on the great novel by Erich Maria Remarque. His role as the disillusioned German soldier was to have great impact on him. The book and film were regarded as the greatest indictment against war. So strongly did this part influence him that he became a conscientious objector to active duty in the Second World War. L.B. Mayer told him he was finished in pictures when at age thirty-four he was drafted and declined to serve in combat. Motion picture houses refused to run any of the very popular *Dr. Kildare* series when theaters which booked them were picketed.

He then served three and a half years as a medic and chaplain's aide, earned three battle stars, and this restored him to favor in Hollywood. He was booked to play opposite Olivia deHavilland in *The Dark Mirror*. In 1948, his work opposite Jane Wyman (need I say she was the first wife of Ronald Reagan) in *Johnny Belinda* earned him a nomination for an Oscar and won her an Oscar for her role as a raped deaf woman being treated by a sympathetic doctor. An active Christian who had studied world religions, he wrote *Altars of the East*, which he later made into a five-part documentary which won a Golden Globe Award for Best Documentary in 1976, and this was the lifetime achievement of which he was the most proud.

Lew Ayres was married to actress Lola Lane, 1931 to 1933, and to Ginger Rogers 1934 to 1941. Then with the war and twenty-five years of almost ascetic living during which he painted, studied and traveled, he married in 1964 to a British airline flight attendant Diana Hall by whom he had a surviving son. He died in his sleep on Monday, December 30, 1996, after being in a coma for several days, and just past his eighty-eighth birthday.

In movies, image is the thing. Lew Ayres was a thin, sincere-looking young man befitting Libra rising even

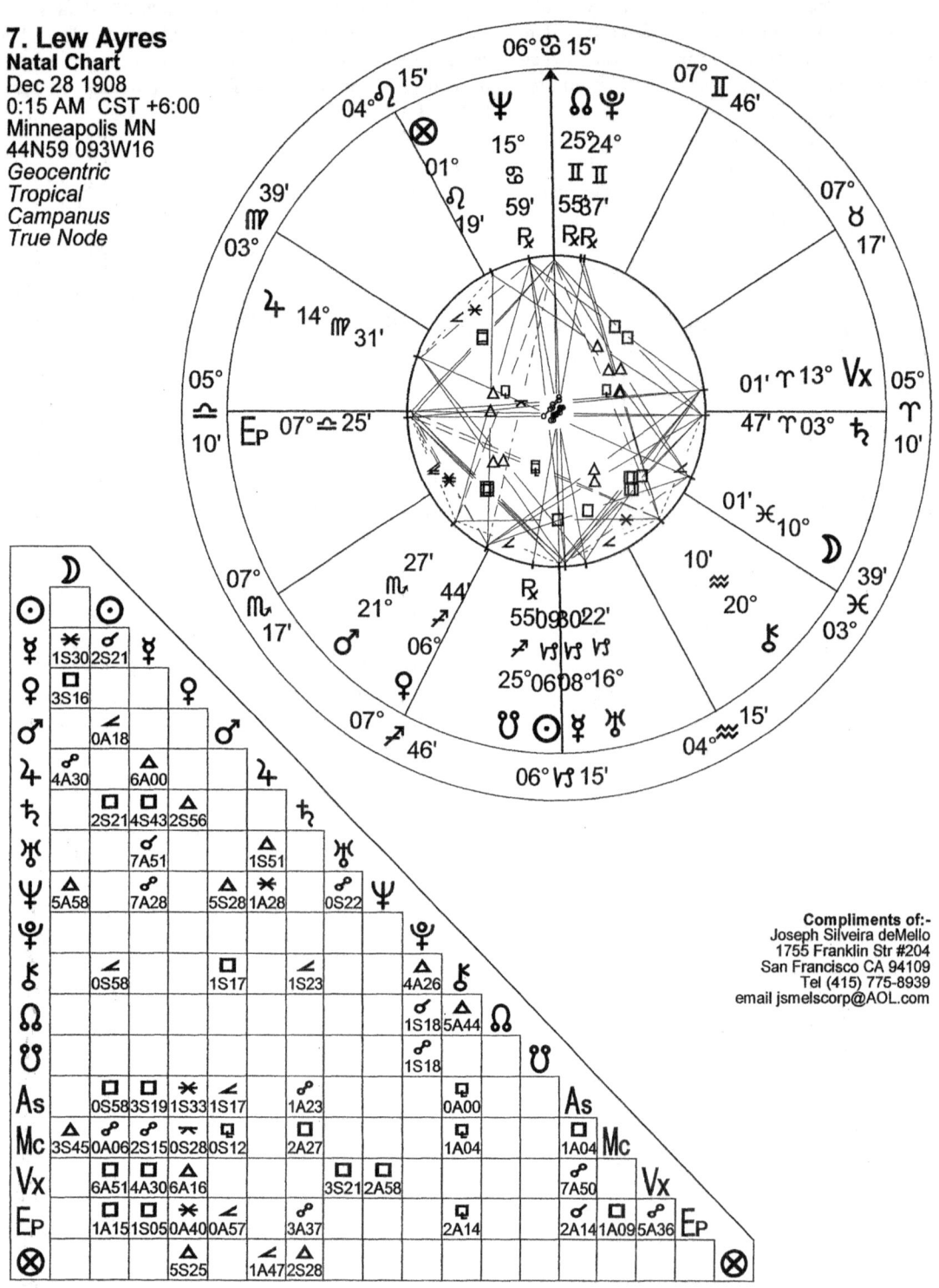

with Venus in Sagittarius. You could see the idealism leaking out of him, fit for Moon in Pisces. He easily projected disillusionment when the realities of the world impinged on the characters he played. He was easily type-cast from his very first role. And then he modestly led the life of a Hollywood star.

Here is a chart a mere six weeks later than that of the previous example, but what a difference. Now, we have Libra rising with the Venus significator in Sagittarius with Fortune on his third house of communications, music, writings. The Sun is exactly on the bottom of his chart, rather too close to Mercury, and Uranus close by so that we inevitably furrow our brows over what must have happened when he was ten years old, when the Sun progressed to Uranus. The Pisces Moon in his sixth house, separating from a sextile to Sun and a quincunx to the Ascendant. Repeated work with the quincunx has proven a five degree orb is not too wide an orb for this serious nervous aspect.

Consistency in astrological reading is the best path. This is a nocturnal birth chart, and we give to its planets chief support of the nocturnal rulers. Discussing his sixth house and the Moon, we think more of Jupiter than of Neptune. As a motion pictures actor, a career which astrology usually points to having Neptune in the fifth house, some times the ninth, and often Pisces on the Midheaven. But, because Neptune is the highest planet in his chart, we are brought up short and have to think of him as a Neptunian. But with here the difference that he made the Moon a very viable and positive force in his life. Astrologers tend to shrink from significators that are retrograde. Jupiter may rule, but Neptune is still a presence not to be denied. It is good to see the Guardian Angel twelfth house placement of Jupiter which must have aided his life to work for his benefit.

The fourth personality determinant is Mars, here in its own sign Scorpio and in his second house of his immediate future. Mars is doubly important here as final dispositor of this chart. It is the nocturnal ruler of Scorpio. Mars in Scorpio gives depth to his energies but not what made him a pacifist. In the second house, Mars wants nothing so much as to make money and have a good self image. We check that Mars makes a semisquare (friction) aspect to the Ascendant, a sesquiquad (agitation) aspect to the Midheaven, and a square to Chiron (at odds with something overlooked). Mars is Square Sun, and, more importantly, trine to Saturn.

Saturn at zero declination is almost on the cusp of his seventh house and most would interpret it there. But we have to decide whether his karma is work and service or of relationships to those close around him. The Moon in sixth ties in with rulership of his Midheaven, and then we have to check Saturn and see it as part of the cardinal square to Sun, Ascendant and Midheaven. What we do have here is a man who did exactly what he wanted to do, and a man who managed to turn what he did entirely to his benefit.

This is a chart where it behooves us to see all of the problems of the chart and then to discover all the mitigations present. We have Uranus in his fourth house and the generational Uranus opposite Neptune. Ponder also Pluto in the ninth house of higher mind and philosophy. This Pluto is on his North Node. It makes only a trine to Chiron. In this chart, Mercury is well out of bounds, while due to his birth close to the solstice, the Sun is close to its boundary of declination.

8. Barry Goldwater, 7-10-2
Saturn: 0S38
Data: January 1, 1909, 1:00 a.m. MST,
Phoenix Arizona, 33N27, 112W04

On the first day of 1909, and four days after our previous example, we have the birth of this one time contender for Presidential office. But the even stranger thing is its similarity to the chart of Joe McCarthy, both of them Republicans. It is always a puzzle for us to see similarities for they usually prove they are not really alike. And then we see another chart to compare, that of Nelson Rockefeller. But Goldwater was no liberal Republican, much more a McCarthy foot-in-mouth conservative. Yet, he did have a disdain of the religious right, "hypocrites all of them." And still we have the generational Uranus-Neptune aspect seen in the same house locations as McCarthy, but reversed to fourth to tenth in the Ayres chart.

Barry Goldwater was the scion of a Phoenix department store family. But he had to be more, so he entered politics and become Governor of the State of Arizona and served five terms as Senator from Arizona, a favorite son who acquired two lifetime titles and sought a third. ``Governor'' and ``Senator'' were his, titles retained after leaving office and to this he felt he could perform the greatest service by being President. He was regarded as highly conservative in his views, but when moderation was seen as the order of the times, he found a centrist stance with which his party was never entirely comfortable. A man of high personal integrity, he realized that some of the hard right-wing lines were absurd, but he created more unease in the eyes of voters and made them feel unsure about his specific nature and beliefs.

His chart offers us Libra rising, Sun in Capricorn, Moon in Taurus, and Mars is in Scorpio in the second house. Mars is strong for being in its own sign and as final dispositor. Mars in second should tell us he has a fine opinion of himself. There is never a time, no matter how well off one is, that one could not use more money. The Sun is in his third house and certainly communications and business were his thing. He went everywhere, knew everybody. Capricorn is a lawyerly, executive, serious, controlling sort of person. Capricorn manipulates people as well as motivating them. The Moon toward the end of his seventh house, though exalted in Taurus, put dissatisfaction in the area of gains from other people. Yet, no on-the-road politician was more in demand as a guest speaker. As Governor, he was criticized for traveling too widely, not being home minding the store.

As befits Libra rising, he was a handsome looking man, had charisma, seemed able to charm people in a party becoming increasingly conservative. But no evaluation is proper unless we look at the liabilities of his

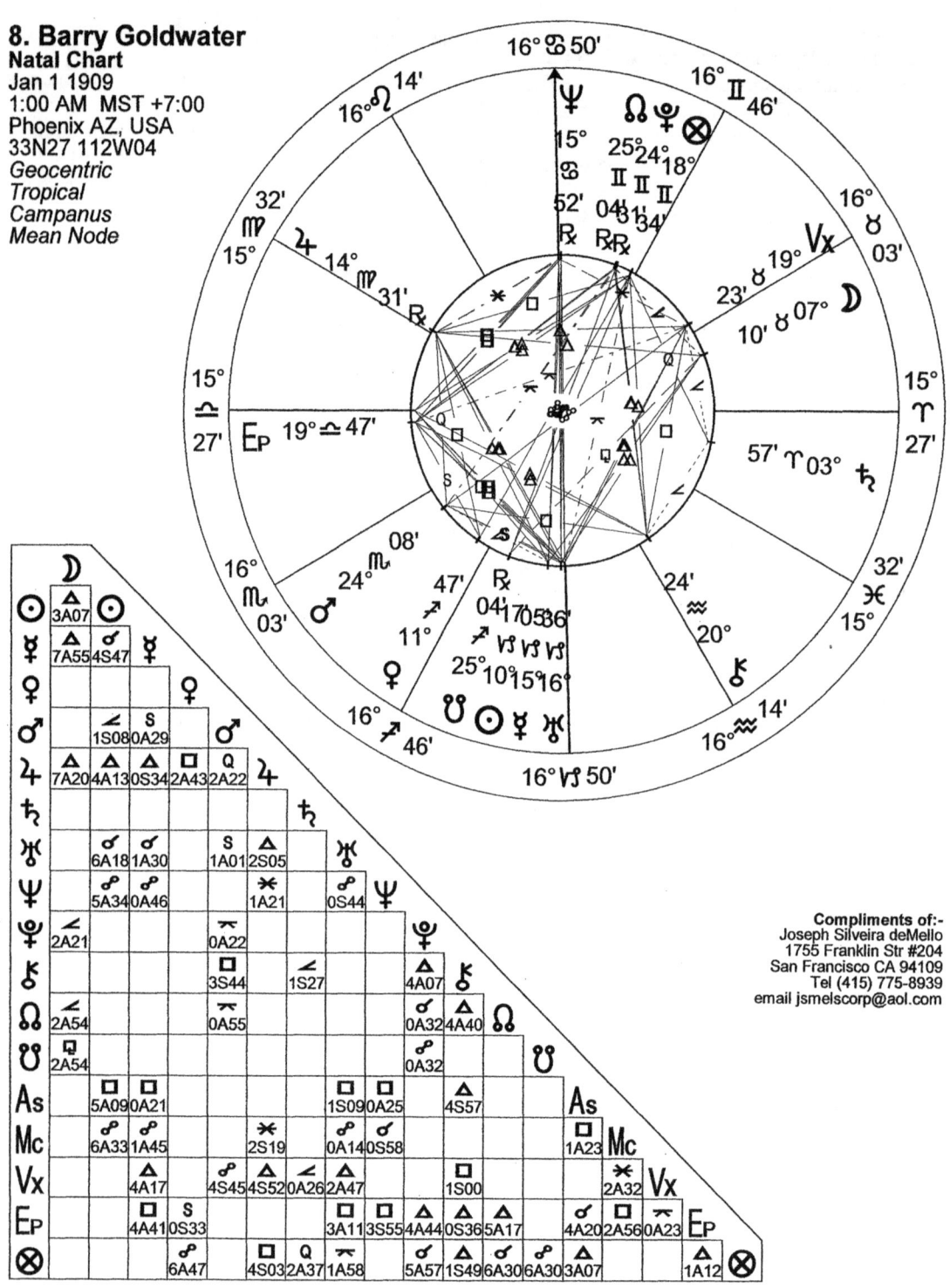

chart which will reveal his down side.

Capricorn can be seen as a "user" of other people. Taurus can be seen to indicate an overwhelming self-interest in personal promotion. Jupiter is retrograde and has just backed out of the Guardian Angel position of Jupiter in the twelfth. Jupiter went stationary retrograde the day before he was born. Neptune is at the top of the chart, indicator of a person who processes information and draws from it conclusions no one else would get. We have to have Pluto somewhere in a chart, and it is retrograde in his ninth of higher ideals. Saturn of karma is in the sixth house, and he went into government to perform a national service.

Goldwater was gregarious and outgoing. He thrust himself into national prominence. Eisenhower did his political bit by endorsing Goldwater over other potential Republican nominees. Unfortunately the men who wrote his speeches seemed oblivious of the type of man Goldwater was. A month prior to the convention, California voters had gone to a primary where they had endorsed Rockefeller as their potential nominee. The Republican Convention occurred at the San Francisco Cow Palace in July 1964, and the quick astrologer will see that Saturn was transiting retrograde in Pisces, cyclically on its way from a lower square to a Saturn return. During this period people are usually advised to get rid of the superfluous lumber in their life before the Saturn return acts to do the job for them. I felt that the Saturn return might deal him a low blow. But his own words in his acceptance speech are what damned him. He made two statements: "Extremism in the defense of liberty is no vice" and "Moderation in the pursuit of justice is no virtue." Do we blame Mars, Pluto or Neptune for these two gems? He would never understand why these two statements struck a chord of chills and dread in the electorate and laid the quietus to his eventual election. He got the Republican endorsement, was expected to pick up the votes of Republicans in the southern states, but Johnson owned the majority of the Southern vote. Goldwater received only thirty-nine percent of the vote, the smallest percentage ever got historically by any presidential candidate. He carried only his home state. When I was first writing on this chart, Goldwater was coming to the end of his life. He died May 28, 1998, at age eighty-nine. Through 1996, he suffered a bad series of strokes. Obituary writers were universally kind to his memory, spoke of how his ideas were picked up by the later Reagan administration. All called him an "American original" and spoke of him as a man ahead of his times.

9. Victor Borge, 11-10-3
Saturn: 0S35
Data: January 3, 1909, 10:30 a.m. MET,
Copenhagen, Denmark, 55N40, 12E35

This man is well known for his one-man comedy turns at the piano. He was born Borge Rosenbaum in Copenhagen, two days after the previous example. The given data is birth certificate documented. Although trained in the classic piano repertory, he turned to using the piano as a background to spoof classic fairy tales which he narrated with explosions of special sound effects for all punctuation marks. His delightful sense of humor had him consistently playing to full-house audiences.

The chart we see for him is now as remarkably skewered as are all charts of persons born at the great northern latitudes. Ninety degree first and seventh houses and over average length sixth and twelfth houses in this Campanus house chart, deemphasize all other houses which are extremely shortened. Note that it takes the fast Moon a whole week to go through each of his two longest houses, which leaves two weeks of every month to rush through all his other houses. Therefore the slower planets take longer to go through the long houses, emphasizing matters of those houses for longer periods of time.

We are faced here with a challenging chart. It will be noticed that Mercury and Gemini rule the third, fourth and fifth houses, while Jupiter rules the ninth, tenth and eleventh houses. We remember the corollary that when two houses are ruled by the same sign and planet, the second of the two is the more important house. With that in mind, we well might ponder which house is the more important when a third of same shows up.

Early teachers gave us a picture of Aquarius which was all political tact and humanistic empathy. But when astrologers and psychiatrists/psychologists came into the picture, definitions had to be revised. The keyword most used for Aquarius is "I know." And do they ever. Tact in Aquarius lasts only so long as you do not ask Aquarius for a personal opinion. Then all tact is lost, and Aquarians will give it to you with both barrels of the shotgun to say something like: I've been watching your situation for quite a while now wondering how long it would take you to see what the only solution to your problem could be. And then they propose a solution which is absolutely untenable for the person involved. An Aquarian will suggest you get a cat even when he knows you have a dandruff allergy.

As an entertainer, his muse is his chart significator, Uranus. The Sun, Uranus and Mercury are in a Capricorn stellium. I insist five degrees orb to the Sun as detrimental, and then consider the transference of light. Uranus close to the Sun retains the Uranus power and buffers Mercury. The presence of Mercury-Uranus is volatile and creative. Moreover, Mercury is out of bounds. This Mercury must describe the genius used in fashioning his lively and entertaining skits.

The Sun in the twelfth house, I usually describe as a placement for a diffident or mistrustful ego expression, perhaps somewhat concealing rampant ego expression. Then we see that wonderful aspect Sun trine Jupiter. His comedy style makes constant use of "throw-away" lines. He gets his greatest laughs by alternating between emphasis and clever asides. I emphasize this since we seldom expect humor from a Capricorn Sun usually too serious; but Aquarius humor can be quite witty and sardonic. Ah, then, you will see that the Moon, projecting as though on stage, is all the livelier by being in Gemini. But he has complete control and management of his ma-

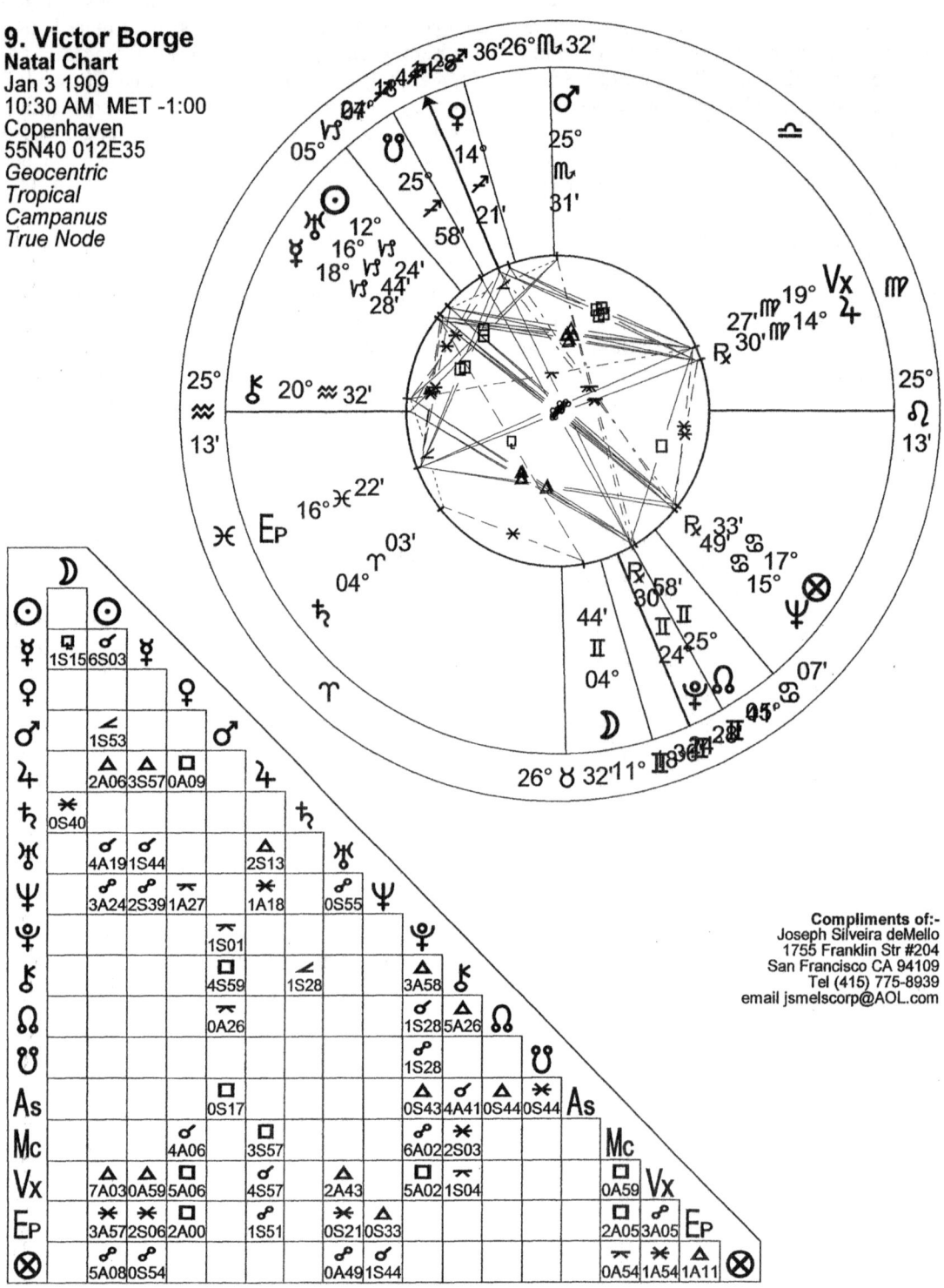

terial. And then he plays it as if he were Jack Benny, appears so serious and as if he did not know he was being hilarious. Like most Capricorns he seldom smiled so that the audience was always surprised when he did smile and changed his whole facial expression. His change of career came about due to a dissatisfaction with a stalled concert career. Then consider Mars in Scorpio on the edge of his ninth house and the fact he has no mitigating kite aspects for his oppositions.

10. Male Student, 6-8-9
Saturn: 0N42
Data: November 3, 1921, 1:30 a.m. CST,
Pine Bluff, Arkansas, 34N14, 92W01

This is the chart of an astrology student I had in 1978, data from birth certificate. He was Black, well-educated, and I was surprised to find I had been born on his fourth birthday. My natals were his transits. It was with great interest that I compared it to my own. Not only do we look at every chart to discover our affinities with students and clients but the revelations are often startling.

Where I am a Gemini rising, he had Virgo rising, so we see the two faces of Mercury at work, and we both have Mercury in Scorpio. I could see the problems of a Gemini teacher trying to reach the structured Virgo student. His Mercury is the more important for ruling both the Midheaven and the Ascendant. There is but a slight difference that his Mercury is before the Sun, while mine comes after. And then his Mercury was retrograde, blending logic and the abstract. And those describe exactly his style of operation. The fact my Sun fell in his in his third house speaks of a brotherly feeling I was ready to have for him, while his Sun falling in my sixth house told me I would only be around as long as he needed me. Then, too, his Mercury is in mutual reception to his Mars in Virgo. The extra courtesy placements put Mercury into his twelfth house above the Ascendant, and the extra Mars falls on my Mercury and after his Sun. Add to that his Sagittarius Moon was opposite my Moon in Gemini. Like myself, he was born with Mars before Saturn, so as it happened in my life, it must have been quite frustrating for him when Mars progressed over his natal and progressed Saturns.

This is one of the earliest charts I saw of Mars in the first and in the rising sign. He was never ready to take a back seat. His energy was thoroughly Aries, and he was quick with it. Yet he tended to deny the power of his Mars even while showing it at every turn. A student with this amount of mettle in any class enlivens every session. It was hard to keep him from leaping ahead of the rest of the class, and to keep him from trying to convert every session in to an analysis of his chart. But Scorpio also shone through, and he shared very little of his own life with either teacher or fellow students.

11. Jan Van Schuyler, 9-8-2
Saturn: 0N17, Mars: 0S44
Data: November 14, 1921, 9:25 a.m. CST,
Chicago, Illinois, 41N49, 87W37

Jan Van Schuyler is an astrologer I met through correspondence in Mercury Hour and responded directly to me to offer chats for this study. In her study of astrology her teachers were Zip Dobyns, Mark Robinson and Richard Ideman. When she first began to study, she called home to ask her father to read the time from her birth certificate, and he read it as 9:45 a.m. which gave her a later Sagittarius rising, but later when she checked the birth certificate herself, she found that the flowery script of the recorder was actually 9:25 a.m. She describes herself as optimistic, enthusiastic and outgoing, with an ability to learn from any situation in which she has found herself.

In this chart, eleven days after the previous chart, the Mercury-Mars mutual reception turns into a Venus-Mars reception which become chart dispositors. Sagittarius rising points our attention to Jupiter in the ninth house, for we see there the separating close conjunction of Mars and Saturn and the presence of the North Node of the Moon. The ninth house is Virgo, the detailed mentality, ruled by Mercury in Scorpio which deepens the mentality, close to Venus in Scorpio, not much help to Venus, but Mercury in the tenth is favorably placed in the house after that which it rules.

When she was ten, the country was about to go into the depression. She reports that her father lost his job, and they lost their home and had to move to another location. She also reports that when Saturn crossed her IC, age sixteen going on seventeen, life opened up for her. She became attractive and easily made friends in a new town, and as Saturn transited through her fourth house, she fell in love and went away to college. All her life, she has been at acute observation points. Her second transit of Saturn over the IC was also preceded by times of difficulty, but she went to work managing the office of a surgeon.

The ninth house to third house balance of the Nodes of the Moon is very indicative of the student and the teacher. Here, the North Node of the Moon in the ninth intakes from an understanding of why things are as they are, to a third house South Node of release to an understanding of the status quo, how things in fact are. This is a reversal of what is generally considered the best and proper order for the nodal axis, so we are going to get an entirely new slant in learning from her. The subject herself sees Mars and Saturn as exemplifying the men in her life and as indicators of a past life karma which must in the present life be expiated. Basically Mars and Saturn, in any aspect of togetherness, are responsible for frustration. Mars asks for immediate action (even in Libra detriment) and Saturn, exalted in Libra, demands caution to temper any tendencies toward rash action. Although Mars is separating, progressions will bring Saturn over Mars, and in her sixties, Saturn turned retrograde. Jupiter will someday go over the top of her chart. This is a strong chart with fine mental capabilities, and the normal reticence of Sagittarius is underlined by Scorpio, so I consider it a nice surprise that she wished to help with this work. Perhaps I am the beneficiary of her very active ninth house. Then too, Jupiter as chart significator is well placed in the ninth, called being accidentally mun-

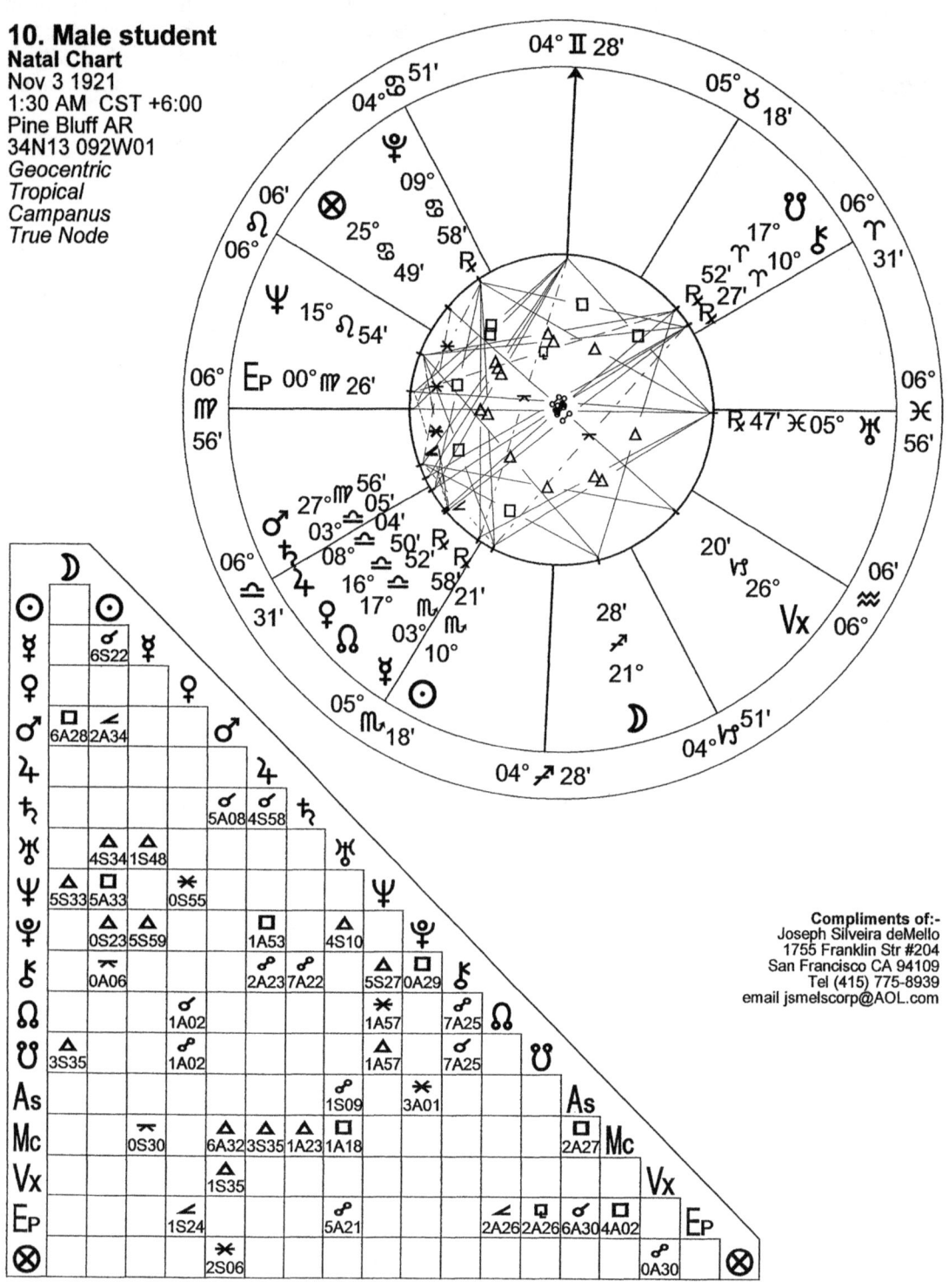

10. Male student
Natal Chart
Nov 3 1921
1:30 AM CST +6:00
Pine Bluff AR
34N13 092W01
Geocentric
Tropical
Campanus
True Node

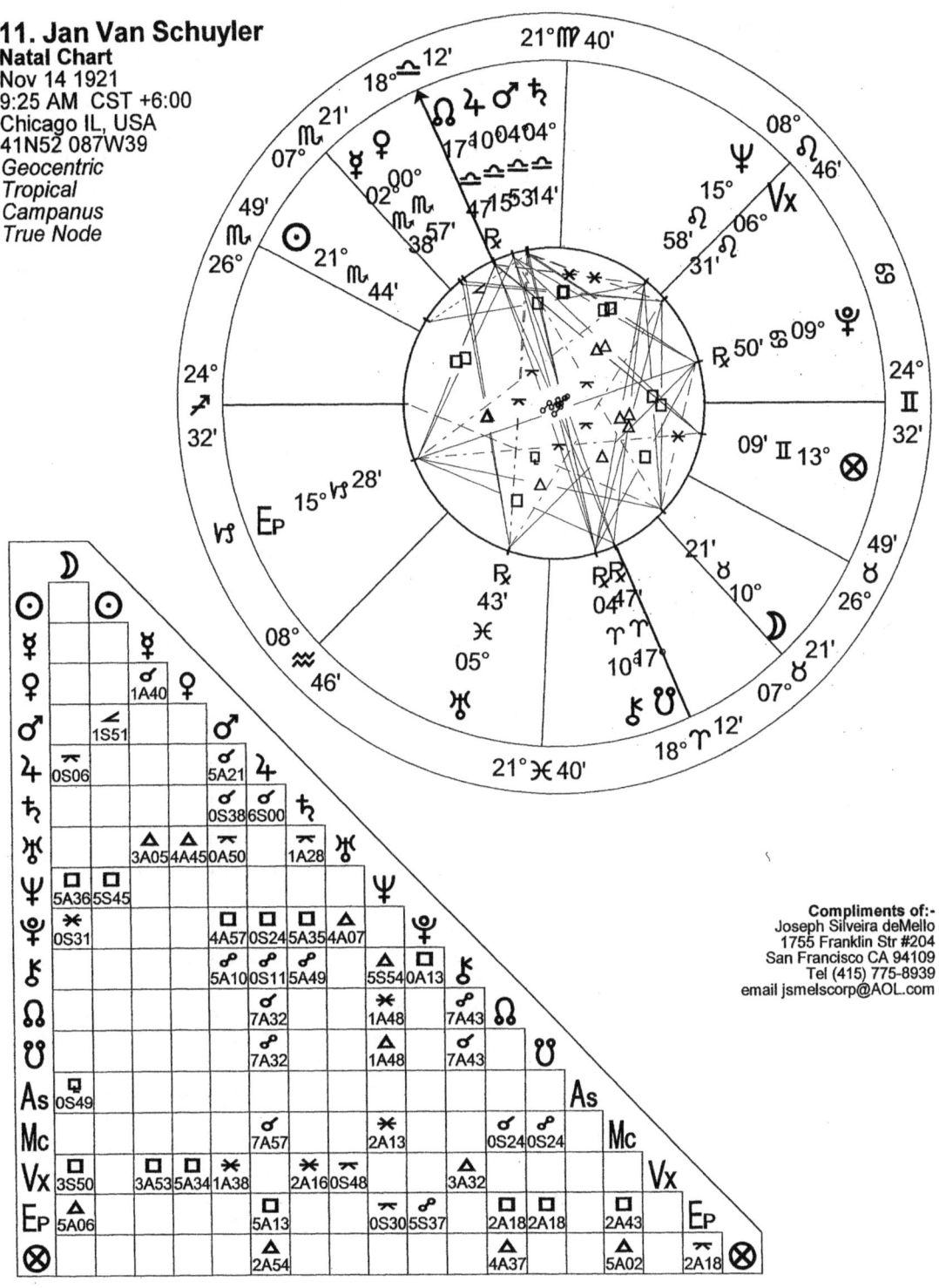

danely dignified. I do believe anyone could count on her to do the right thing with the right attitude and can suppose a studied lack of astrological bias in her own interpretation of her chart. The ninth is a house which can be given great elasticity of interpretation. It means distant travel, or perhaps living in a place far from her birthplace, and, as a cadent house, is a planning area for tenth house considerations, career, personal status. But because of its tenants and their quality, the ninth is active at all times in her life, not just when transits go through it.

Since she made her own statement about karma, I would say it is as much signified by the ninth as it is by the twelfth—intellect and subconscious. In a chart with a ninth house Saturn, she was deciding on her status and friends, and then analyzing puberty years before Saturn transited her first house of learning about the self, and then the second house of how well she liked herself and her things around her. Always study the Saturn orientation because not everyone can begin life with Saturn in the first house. Where Saturn starts in any chart emphasizes how we all go through different phases. This interesting chart gives us the peculiarity owned by most Scorpios. Scorpios may be in public situations yet manage to retain personal privacy as the special essence of being.

Concerning ourselves with the zero declination Saturn, we have the presence of Mars also at zero declination and contra-parallel. Saturn in North declination is in a southern sign, while Mars is South and in a southern sign. Add to that, Mars in detriment and Saturn exalted, and our delineation is up for grabs. We are forced to weigh which of these is the more powerful or the least afflicted. Both are conjunct and both are square Pluto. We have a conjunction mitigated by contraparallel to act as an opposition. She herself says she has taken her option, as we do working with oppositions, of choosing whether to go with Mars or to go with Saturn and acts accordingly. The action of Mars and Saturn have always been highly visible to her. We should follow her example with ultimate profit in all our chart work.

12. Jacqueline Stallone, 7-9-9
Saturn: 0S13
Data: November 30, 1921, 2:52 a.m. EST,
Washington, DC, 38N53, 77W01

Sixteen days after our previous example, we have the chart of the mother of a big box office movie star, who is also a prominent east coast astrologer, seen and heard on many talk shows. She is identified here because her birth data has been made public, and she is a very public person. No shrinking violet she, not by any means, and talk show hosts delight in having such a vitally responsive personality for which Mars in Libra on the Ascendant is most likely responsible. She takes a back seat to no one and sees no reason for doing so. She has to believe that she who toots her own horn toots best.

As we begin to look at this chart, note that it is a nocturnal birth so that we resort to using all the old rulers. Note, too, the Venus-Mars mutual reception. We also see that Mars and Jupiter are further from Saturn, that here Venus is the chart significator, but the mutual reception is chart dispositor. Saturn in the twelfth learns from her own experience, often fails in early career endeavors before finally settling on a career, perhaps has a difficult infancy until Saturn transits out of the twelfth, and Jupiter is in the Guardian Angel position, usually said to rescue from any brink of misfortune.

Here we have the eternal quandary of Libra rising, wanting everything balanced and harmonious, but you never know which way she will leap, demanding all the facts, starting small wars to become the peacemaker. She has obviously decided what her chart means and has exploited it to the utmost. She makes no bones that her son has had misfortune when he failed to heed her advice. And it is well known that she has never much cared for her son's wives and girl friends. Every mother does that, going from doting mother to dragon mother-in-law, the liberated woman with all the most modern in attitudes exuding off-hand sophistication.

We see here that she was born just after a New Moon, that the second and twelfth houses demand our interest, as well as being a double Sagittarius with Libra prominent. Should we interpret her Pluto in the tenth and her Neptune in the eleventh or both Sun and Moon in the third. Those who use Placidus houses might do so, but my use of Campanus (as I have done in most of these charts) would only push ahead Neptune and Moon. Giving the mutual reception courtesy placements of Venus in Libra (so in the first house) and Mars would then be on the edge of her second house, she is nowadays less Libra pretty and much more the sort of woman described best as handsome. This reminds me that a favorite astrologer I know once said that persons with Venus close to Mars are people you either like or dislike, or they like or dislike you with no quarter given either way.

13. Lady Astrologer, 7- 9-12
Saturn: 0S22
Data: December 6, 1921, 3:19 a.m. EST,
Worcester, Massachusetts, 42N18, 71W48

Six days after our previous example, here is the chart of a Texas astrologer, also a Libra rising with Sun in Sagittarius and Moon in Pisces, and a very private person, who studies astrology to apply it to family and friends. She is not the least interested in being a professional astrologer or having clients. Although there are great similarities to the previous chart, we have here Leo instead of Cancer Midheaven. This, too is a nocturnal chart. And it still has Venus-Mars in mutual reception. The Moon in Pisces is a big difference. But notice now that Mars further away from the Moon.

14. Ophthalmologist, 12-9-1
Saturn: 0S27
Data: December 9, 1921, 12:00 p.m. EST,
New York City, New York, 40N40, 83W58

And then three days later, we now see a Pisces Ascendant with Sagittarius Sun and Moon in Aries and a

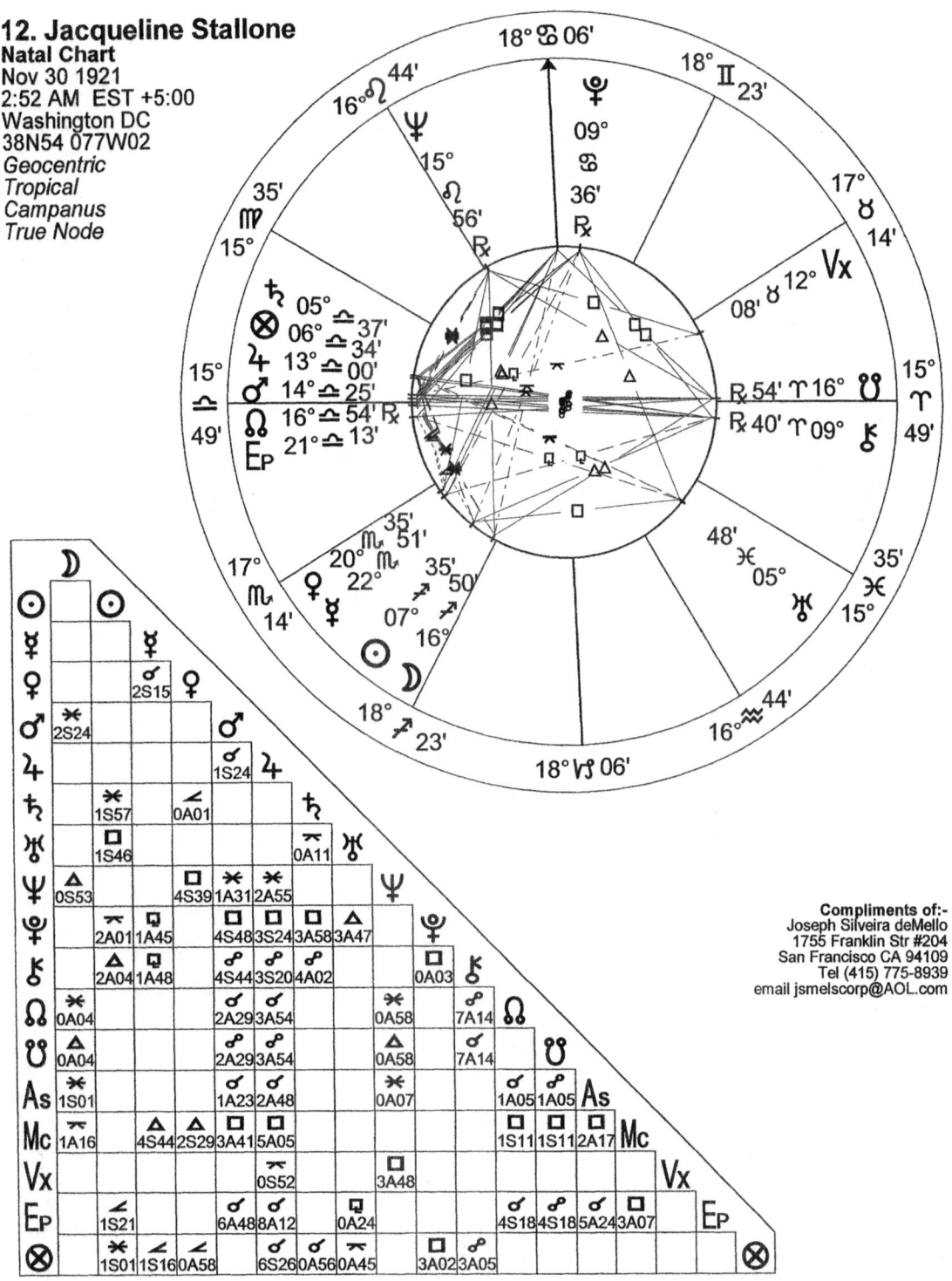

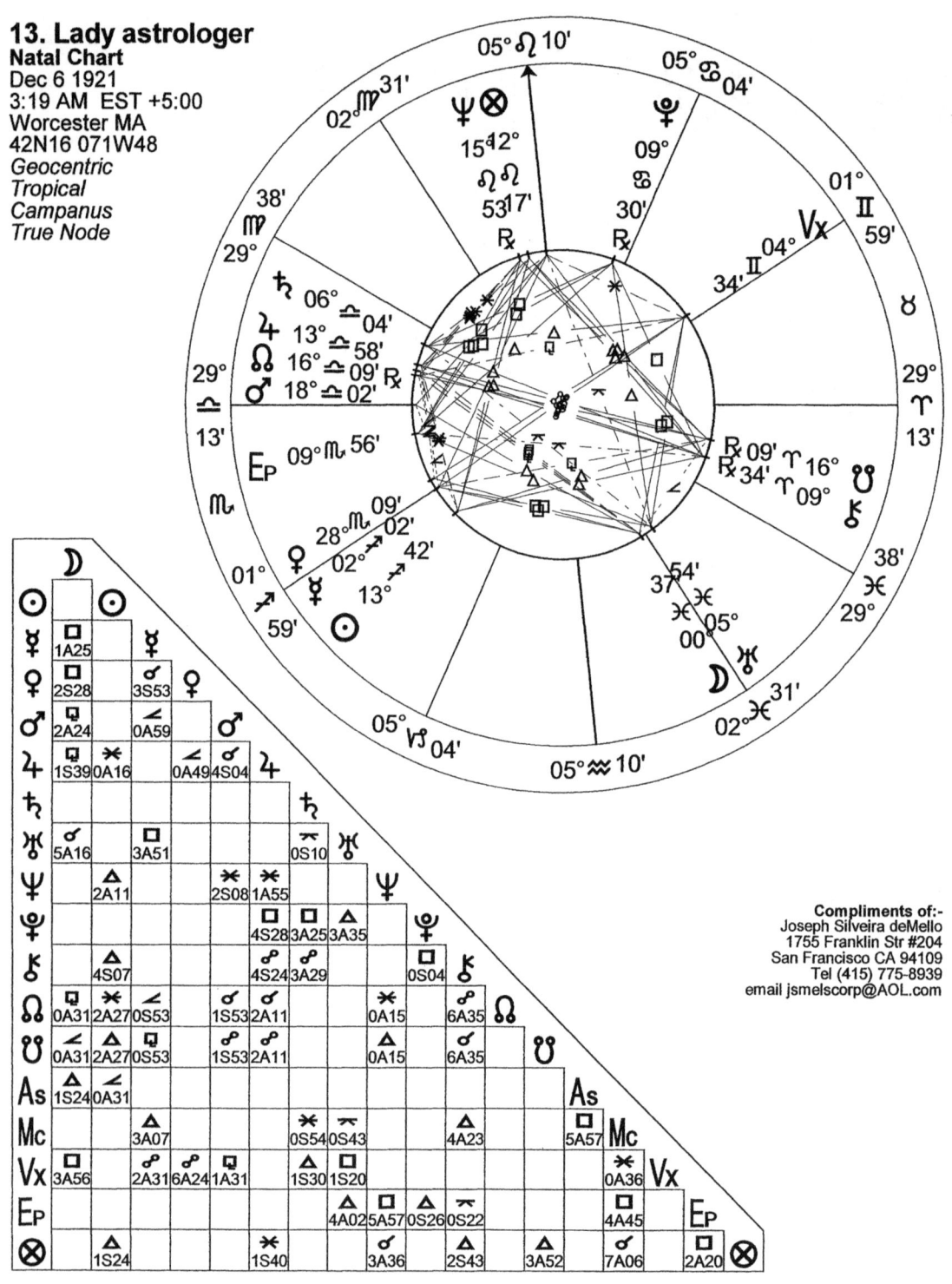

13. Lady astrologer
Natal Chart
Dec 6 1921
3:19 AM EST +5:00
Worcester MA
42N16 071W48
Geocentric
Tropical
Campanus
True Node

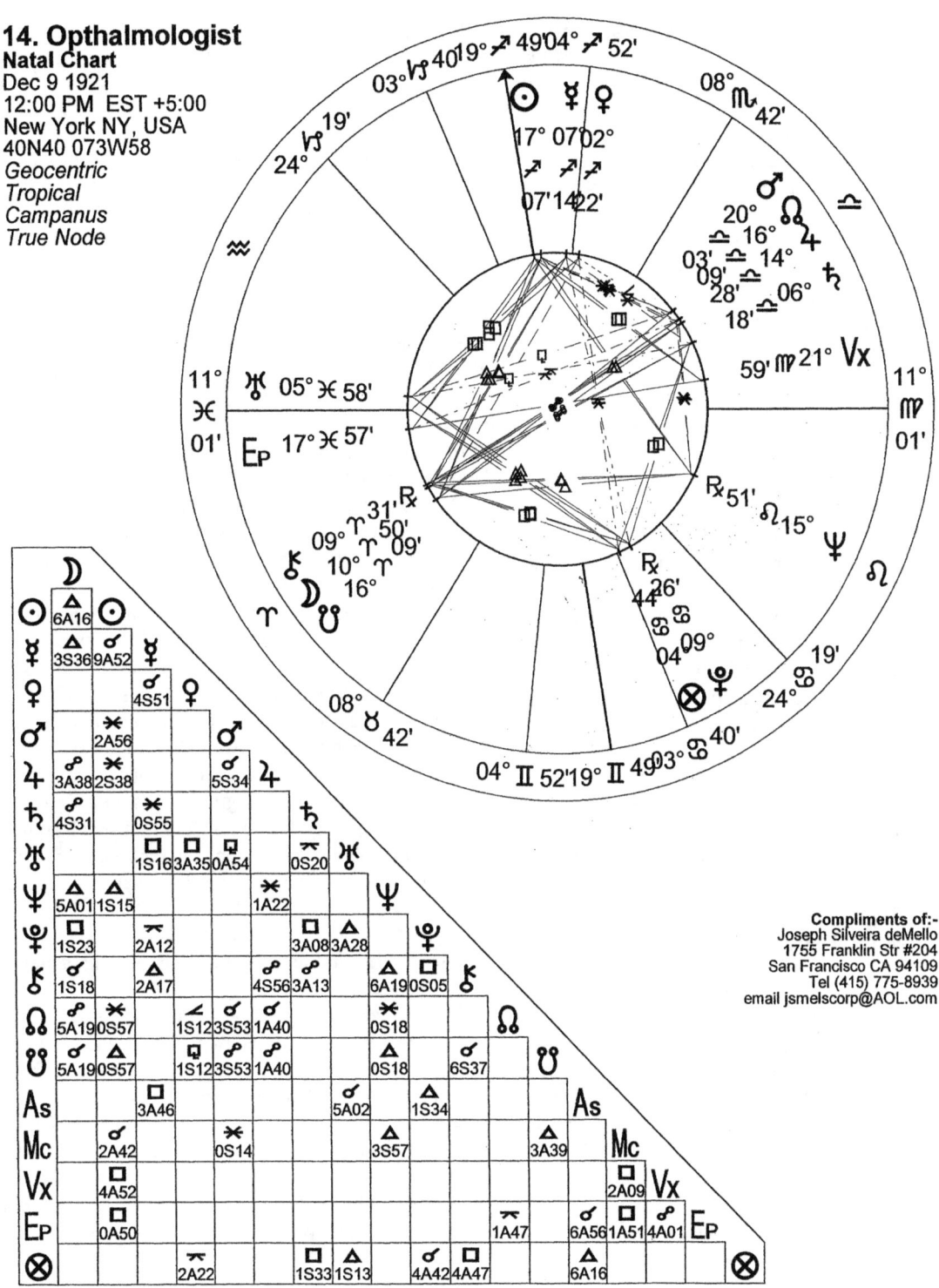

14. Opthalmologist
Natal Chart
Dec 9 1921
12:00 PM EST +5:00
New York NY, USA
40N40 073W58
Geocentric
Tropical
Campanus
True Node

chart for high noon. Astrologers love the Sun at the top of the chart. An astrologer I have known for twenty-five years contributed this chart of a man who has been both old friend and client. He is a retired ophthalmologist, and during 1999, he with no apparent reason ceased all communication with his long-time friendly astrologer.

My astrologer friend and I talk frequently on the telephone. In 1997, two years earlier, she was boiling hot when I called. Once a year she has an informal gathering of friends. This year he asked her who would attend. She wondered why he did not suppose it would the same people who always attended, but perhaps because she is a Scorpio with Gemini rising, same as I, she felt there was more to his question. There was, he wanted to know if anyone very interesting would be there as he was "disinclined to waste his time on people who were no-bodies." I'd have boiled over, too. She told him that before he could expect others to be interesting that he should be an interesting person himself. She determined not invite him that year, he made her so furious. I was rather curious why he allowed the intercepted Aries Moon to surface on this occasion.

The chart significator here is Neptune in Leo retrograde and intercepted in the sixth house. People who have such a Neptune usually make fine waiters. But an eye doctor? Bills says that is mainly Moon, Mercury and sometimes Pluto. Moon is trine Mercury and square Pluto, and Mercury is quincunx Pluto. And now we have Venus and Jupiter in no aspect but in mutual reception. Courtesy positions due to mutual reception give us a Venus close to Saturn in the seventh house, and a Jupiter rather too close to the Sun (where we originally had Sun sextile Jupiter).

Now there is nothing whatsoever wrong with being a Pisces rising except for the burden such people put on everybody else. In astrology, you never can tell them enough good things about themselves, and so you have failed them. But no amount of careful questioning will ever reveal specifically what was omitted. Pisces rising can be as intent as neighboring Aries on getting his own way, does what he wants to do, usually forgets being specifically told it is not what you want to do. If Pisces is sensitive, it is mainly toward himself. If you go out with any water sign, you go where they want to go, and they will tell you where you want to go is too pretentious for them.

A not so endearing habit of this man is that he tells stories at such length and in such gross detail that the point of the story is lost before the story ends. Fire signs use conversation as a way of holding people in their control. Aries controls the flow of talk, and people talk about what Aries wants to talk. Leos hold by dramatic and often fictional twists to stories which hardly need embellishment. Sagittarians, on the other hand, specifically fits the bill for the way this man tells stories. On and on and on.

Of the many things that Pisces rising can be, good as well as bad, there is usually an internal problem about them knowing what is real. The more especially if Neptune is in the first or tenth house, which it is not here. If Pisces does something for you, you must in turn do something much greater for them. Most of the time what you do for Pisces will not measure up to what Pisces does for you. It is a constant in their minds that they always do more for others than others do for them. They can remember the exact date on which they have done these things and are very pleased if you thank them again on any anniversary date. Once a Pisces refuses to tell you something, that refusal will never get changed over the passage of time.

15. Astrologer's Father, 8-10-12
Saturn: 0S48
Data: January 4, 1922, 2:10 a.m. PST,
Seattle Washington, 47N37, 122W20

When I wrote to astrologer Diane Lawson about her mother's chart, she also gave me the chart of her father who was born earlier the same month. The father's chart is Scorpio rising, Sun in Capricorn, with the Moon in Pisces. And here again Neptune at the top of the chart, another Neptunian, processing the same truths anybody knows but getting strange conclusions. When Mars is in any rising sign and in the first house, it gives the person of the chart an Aries personality. It does not, as in this case make the person more of a Scorpio. Aries is the keyword for this Mars which is also chart significator, and it is in a tight grand trine to Uranus and Pluto.

Although we are now a year later than the preceding charts, we still find Saturn and Jupiter in Libra, and in this chart in the twelfth house where things are not so bad for either planet. Of course it might be that his health in infancy was dubious until Saturn should transit over his Ascendant, and any other time in his life when Saturn transited through the twelfth house area. With Saturn he will rebound well from failure; with Jupiter a Guardian Angel will always be looking of over his shoulder to save him. Diane works with a house system which puts his Saturn in the eleventh house. Diane says his Saturn accounts for his great ideals and big plans which never quite worked out. I would say that Neptune in Leo must share some responsible for this, subjecting him to ideas to which he gives inflated value. Note that both this and his wife's chart below both have Neptune as highest planets in the charts. This would almost amount to the blind leading the blind, but I have never noted such people as unhappy.

He has been married three times and remained on friendly terms with his three ex-wives. Diane accounts for much of his basic temperament and liberality from his education and long stay in Berkeley, California where liberal ways often border on the fantastic. One of his many plans which went awry involves a gold mine he inherited from his father. He made money from the mine, sometimes receiving as much as $4,000 a month for its lease to operators, but when gold was taken out of the mine, it turned out that it cost more to mine than the gold itself was actually worth. Diane does not consider that in any way her father sought perfection, nor does she describe him in Stamina terms. It is almost as if the Neptune were more prominent. Venus-Saturn are in mutual reception.

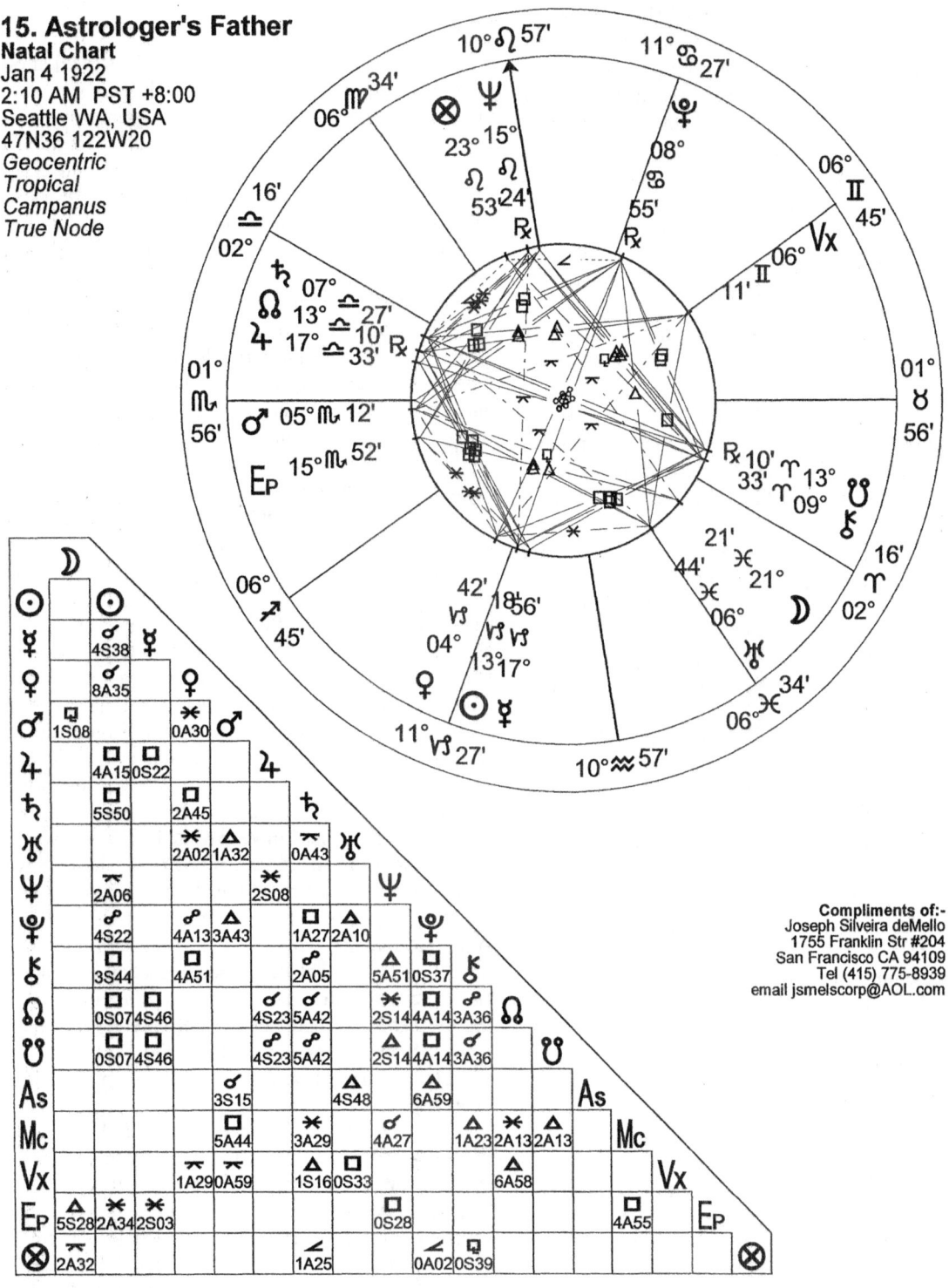

16. Jeannie Miller, 10-10-3
Saturn: 0S49
Data: January 11, 1922, 6:25 a.m. CST,
Cincinnati, Ohio, 39N06, 84W31

This lady is the mother of Kansas astrologer Diane Lawson and ex-wife of the man of the previous example. They were born just seven days apart. Diane published this data in Mercury Hour puzzled that the chart she had done for her mother did not fit or match. Diane was asking fellow readers if they could see in the chart the lung problems her mother was having. Don Borkowski wrote to inform her that in 1922 Cincinnati used CST rather than EST (EST was adopted there in 1927), whereupon the subsequently corrected chart fit. Note that the Vertex, always a health indicator, is in Gemini.

From the time she was six years old, she had chronic lung problems which caused her family to move to Arizona. Note that the Moon at birth was in 18 Gemini, the degree of asthma. We should remember that prescriptions of a change of climate were quite routine in the Twenties and Thirties, perhaps even later. Only recently that we have had alternative treatments for asthma. Yet she was aided by the climatic change, went to school in Arizona, married there and had her first daughter there. She subsequently married and divorced a second time, but also remained on good terms with her former husband.

Dianne attributes her mother's love of art to Neptune. Her mother spent a lot of time painting and some time making pottery. She always saw the best of people and seldom said a harsh word of anyone. Note that the first house Mars is not in the rising sign not altering the Libra personality. But we are to make no mistakes about this lady who did as much of what she wanted to do as she could do. Although her mother got a degree in education and qualified to do social work, she retired from teaching when she was forty-five as her health prevented her from a regular work schedule. Yet she traveled extensively, her medical problems and frequent lack of energy may have intruded greatly from time to time, but these hardly held her back. Dianne says her mother is not conservative; although brought up a Republican, she voted Democrat. She was married (the second time) to a successful doctor and had a servant to help with housekeeping. Dianne says she never let anyone know of her lack of energy and always, Libra like, appeared impeccably and charmingly turned out. She died September 4, 1990 of chronic obstructive pulmonary disease.

Diane Lawson feels that Saturn meant that her mother's life was severely restricted. I don't think she was "restricted" at all. She seems to have done things when she wanted to do them. Neptune retrogrades tend to have great pride. This shows when they think someone is going to say something difficult about them, so they compensate by bringing up the very things she feels is coming as it will hurt her less to admit to it than have someone else bring it up. And then they find that the person was not thinking along those lines at all. Despite the artistic interests which lasted through her life, she was not a seeker of perfection. Many people with Saturn at zero declination do have a reticence about discussing their personal problems, but I am beginning to think the clue lies in them doing what they want to do. But she would have been as Neptunian as her ex-husband.

17. Retired Travel Agent, 1-11-9
Saturn: 0S45
Data: January 24, 1922, 10:30 a.m. EST,
Montpelier, Vermont, 44N16, 72W35

The death of this man was a severe loss to all at our local watering hole. Every day after his favorite news program, he would arrive just after 7:00 p.m., have a few drinks and go on to dinner. Our local bar is a lot like the bar in *Cheers*, almost everyone is a regular, and everyone knows something about everyone else. For a long time this man would say "good evening" to the bartender, drink his drinks, say "good night" and go to dinner without talking to any of his neighbors at the bar. He did not have to order his drink, the bartender prepared it as he came through the door. He was a mystery to all, but a quiet one. One day, the bartender saw him trying not to laugh at a nearby conversation. The bartender smiled and quietly said, "You're eavesdropping," and that broke the ice. From then on he began talking to the bartender and a few other people. He could talk or sit as happily in companionable silence.

He was at first skeptical about my involvement with astrology, but did not demure about giving me his birth data. The man was dignified, enigmatic and politely reticent so I was surprised when the chart came up Aries rising. He was more Scorpio than Aries. His chart significator Mars was in Scorpio and intercepted in his seventh house. Privacy was a serious factor. I would have thought Taurus rising, which would have needed an hour later birth time, but experimentation did not work. Venus is too close to the Sun in the eleventh house, and once he made a friend, it was after serious consideration. He was tall and a bit heavy. His head was crowned by a full head of very white hair. There was no sign of the usual Aries pattern baldness. His face was square rather than pointy chinned, and his features were evenly matched to both sides of his face in the classic Aquarian manner. There was nothing bellicose about him. What he thought was reasoned, factual and logical. If his facts were disputed, he would go home, research the problem and report next night whether he or you were right or in error. He did this without crowing, if he was right, and not exactly eating humble pie if he had been in error.

Little was known of his personal life. In his career of mapping and routing trips for AAA members, he retained a fantastic memory for routes and places. At work he had often been offered promotions which he turned down to stay with an activity he enjoyed. He had a daily routine almost rigidly and neatly followed. For years he had lived in a fine apartment on one of the best hills in San Francisco. His apartment had a fantastic 270 degree view of the bay from the Bay Bridge, past Alcatraz, to the Golden Gate Bridge, the sort of view which is the

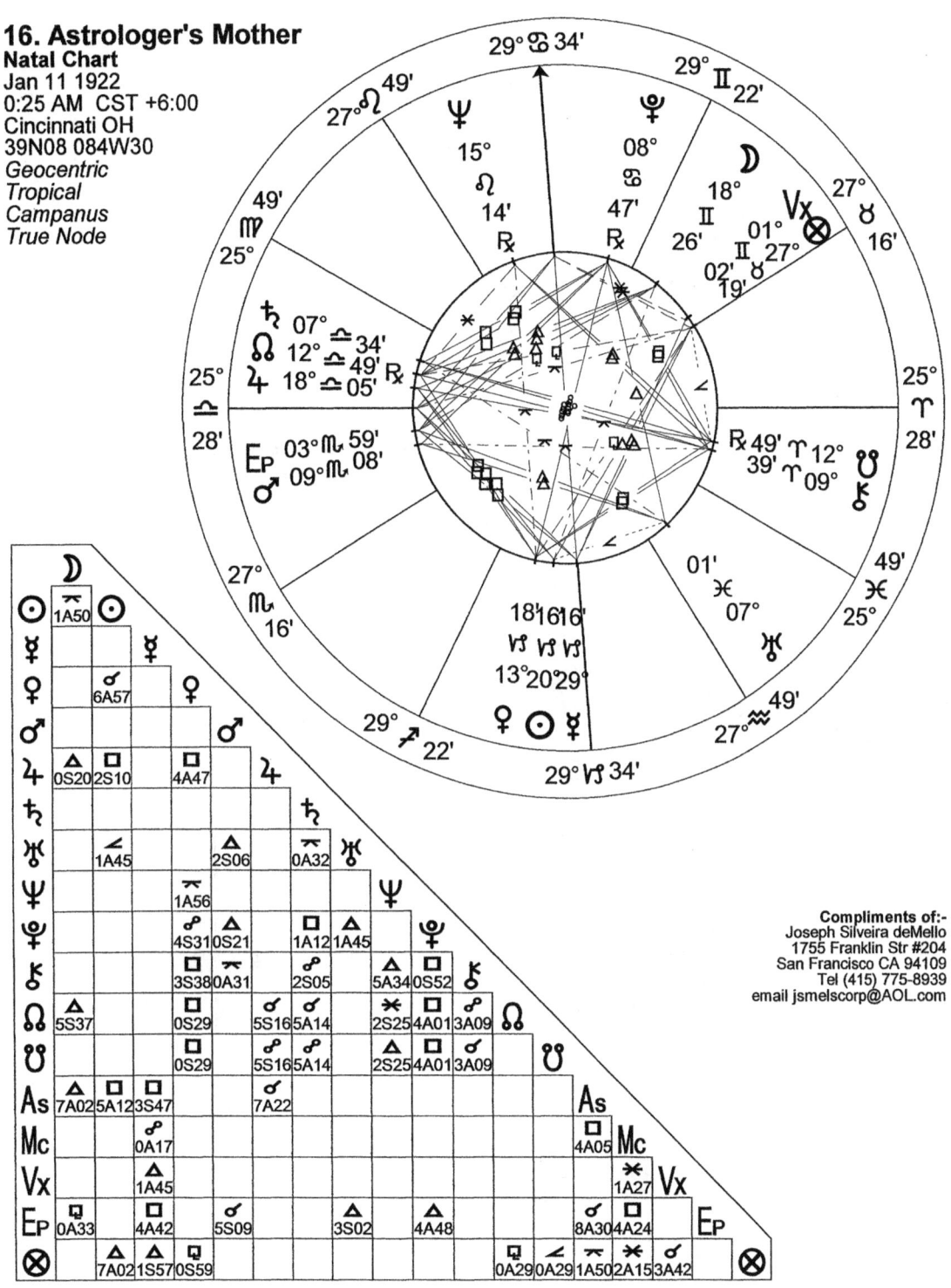

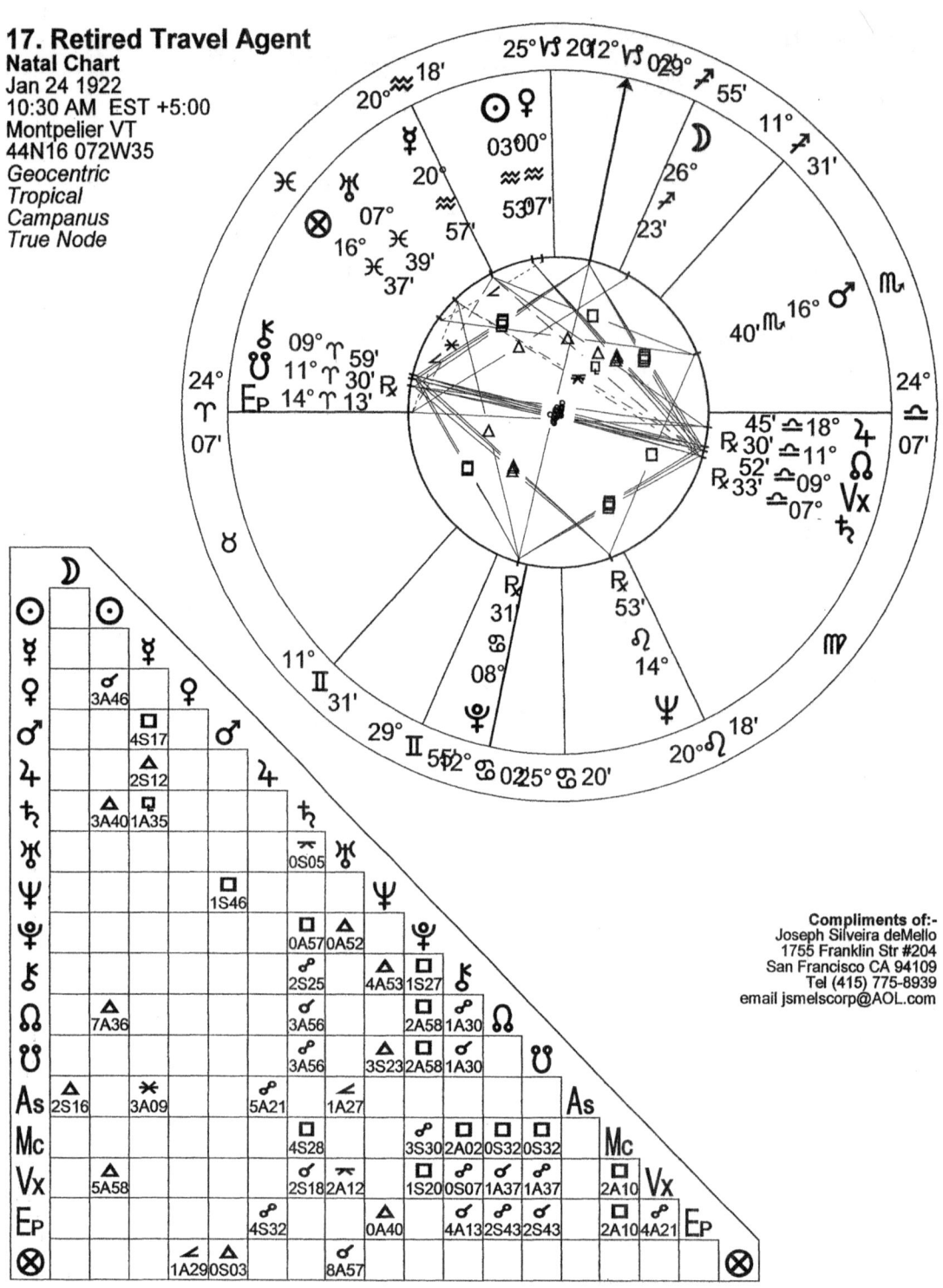

premium local desire of everybody. He long held onto an old Gremlin almost exclusively used only for shopping and going to a monthly luncheon of a group of retired co-workers. After a discussion of the cost of auto insurance, he decided he would live and get around without that car and sold it.

One of his main interests was theater. Monday evenings at the bar were quiet and less well attended. It was the night when the half dozen or ten people present would talk and bring up unusual conversational topics and really oddball facts. On such a night, I took by a visiting astrologer to the bar and introduced her. She happened to mention a long past theater experience, and to our surprise, this man was immediately able to recall it in detail. There was instant accord and a very successful gathering. He was always current on news, read the papers, watched television sparsely. His memory was excellent. He never closed off conversations, never joined any talk about sexual matters, but he inevitably made the final remark which was so germinal to any topic it left nothing better anyone else could add. He did this with a sardonic humor which upset no one.

Saturn here is at zero declination. He was quite conservative but also had liberal attitudes in his general outlook on life. He was a born and bred New Englander with a fine Yankee humor. His only relives with whom he kept in touch were cousins back east. Toward the last year he had quiet medical concerns. Medications forced him to change from martinis to a ginger ale thinned down by soda water, and when he arose from his bar stool to leave, he began to have to work out stiffness from sitting too long. He mentioned bone cancer, and this was never brought up again. From time to time I would join him for dinner, last doing so on July 14, 1998, the evening before I left to attend the AFA Orlando convention. When I returned home, I was informed he had been found dead in his apartment on Friday, July 17, probably dying some time earlier of a cerebral aneurysm. His death was a shock to us all.

At our bar, if a regular fails to appear for two days, one of the bartender-owners would get on the phone. They knew where everyone worked, lived, banked. Thus we learned a neighbor had called the police to check his apartment and find his body. No one knew if his retirement group had been notified, so I called AAA to make sure they knew and was routed to man who had his "file" that moment on his desk. As we talked, this man revealed that the executor of our friend's will was his wife who had also been notified. He had never mentioned having been married. A bit of Yankee humor ends the story. The bar has a treacherously steep staircase to the office-storeroom. Many have fallen on those stairs to the point that this man brought in luminous duct tape to be put on every stair tread. The accidents ceased. Weeks after his death, there came a note in the deceased's own handwriting that the enclosed check for twenty-five dollars from his estate was to endow the purchase of future luminous duct tape as needed. Typically this came in an envelope without any hint of source or other explanatory note. As he might have guessed, this check was spent immediately on a bottle of the best whiskey.

18. John B. Anderson, 7-11-7
Saturn: OS22
Data: February 15, 1922, 8:55 p.m. CST,
Rockford, Illinois, 42N16, 89W06

How soon we forget and how lax some of our record keeping. When I pulled these zero Saturn declination charts, I found this as a study chart which originally appeared in Mercury Hour. I failed to reference the issue date or make any notes that would in any way identify the person of the chart. Such a common name, I was not even aided by having progressed the chart to the year when it was acquired, so I found myself in a quandary to identify the person of the chart. Luckily, his place of birth is the same as that of the town where astrologer Norma Story lives. I have known her for more than twenty-five years. I applied to her for help. Norma informed me that there were at present thirteen John Andersons in the local telephone book, but she rather thought this would be John Bayard Anderson who was, in 1976, a third party presidential candidate.

And of course that was why I had the chart, briefly at that time studied it. Third party candidates held greater interest for younger generation voters. Such candidates usually lose, and siphon off the votes of major party candidates. But now I needed to know more, and Norma reported that he graduated from Rockford Central High School in 1939, and from Harvard Law in 1949. For a while he had been States Attorney for Winnebego County and in 1960 was elected to the House of Representatives where he served for sixteen years. He began as very conservative and was that way until Barry Goldwater was defeated (1964). Then he decided that he would have to become more liberal and not depend for re-election on the fact that he was a native son of Swedish stock. Local legend had it that no one whose name ended in a vowel would ever be elected to any office in that voting district. He decided to run for the presidency as an independent when it appeared that Republicans were either going to nominate Ronald Reagan or Phil Gramm.

This chart is reminiscent of that of Richard Nixon who will remain immortal as prime example of Pluto as the highest planet in the chart, so this was the first thing that hit my eye in this chart. I wondered how Anderson had sabotaged himself. Untouched by any career faux pas or scandal, he could have run and won any office in his constituency. He remains a popular figure in his home town. His presidential campaign may also have left him seriously in debt. Then I was startled to see Saturn on his Libra Ascendant and retrograde. I rushed to my ephemeris to see in 1976 that transiting Saturn was at 16 Leo (in orb of natal Neptune) still some distance from his next Saturn return, but not yet transiting his twelfth house (universally unfavorable for election), going from the lower square to his natal Saturn, headed for the difficult twelfth house transit before hitting his Ascendant and next Saturn return. Had he won election, his term of office might be very difficult. In such times of

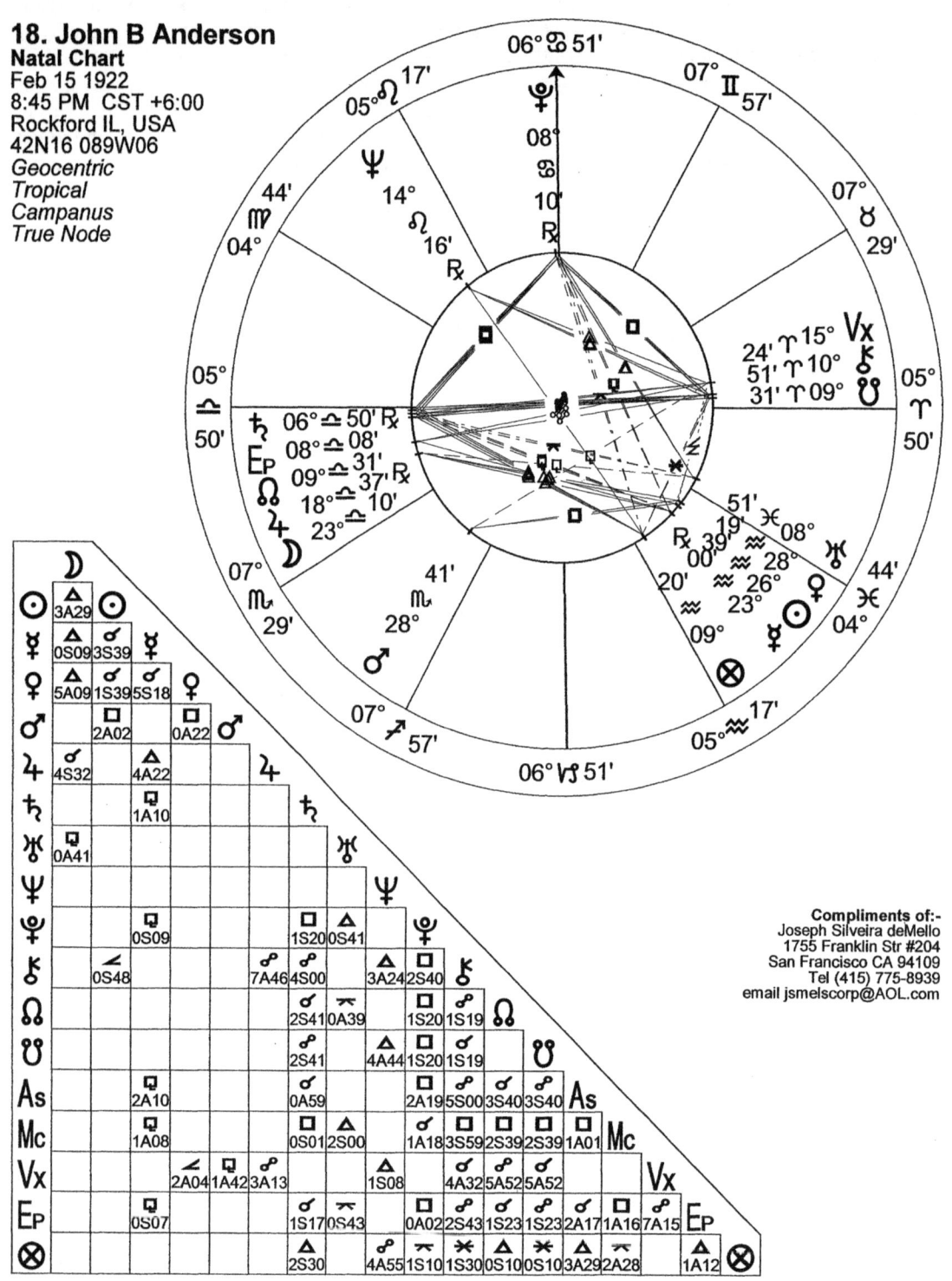

serious affliction it is best not to add lumber to one's regular load of problems.

Libra is such a politician's sign. But we cannot obviate the season in which he lived. From the loftiness of history, Anderson can be assumed to have appealed in a climate where the voters had little liking for the nominees of both major parties. At each election, astrologers get interested in the charts of all candidates. In such a study we always find that the bias of astrologers surfaces to read favorably the chart of whichever candidate is the personal preference of each astrologer.

Looking at Anderson's chart, we have to wonder how a politician with the majority of his planetary placements below the horizon could have summoned popular appeal. This testifies to a man of hidden depths. With Chiron, Pluto and Neptune as the only planets in the upper half, one has to honestly wonder about his local fame and wonder if that could be translated to the national scene.

Additionally we worry about five planets in retrograde—abstract Mercury, Jupiter, which makes out well with ideas and things abandoned by others, the Saturn of relatedness, then prideful Neptune and the champion of the underdog, Pluto. My first teacher, Macelle Brown, said that retrogrades were like driving a car. You might operate a car easily with three retrogrades, but if you have to do more than three things at the same time, expert driving gets too complicated. My teacher also said that retrogrades do not bother those who have them but give us a person off from the norm with which others find difficult to cope.

A person with Moon in the first house, in the same sign as his rising sign, will at some time in life stand up and tell it as it is. Libra, which wants to balance life, often procrastinates in wait for further facts which will help them made a final decision. Howard Hammitt, Jr., another great teacher, used to call them the mugwumps of political life, sitting on fences, their mugs to one side, their wumps on the other, and no one knows which way or when they will jump. We have also come to regard the Aquarian Sun as a political certainty (since the advent of FDR) though one astrologer, Carl Tobey, told us all that's wrong with the world is due to Capricorns and Aquarians.

Aquarians are argued to have social consciousness and the good of the people uppermost in their minds. Anderson is one of a remarkable group of turncoats, basically conservative, but ready to turn to the needs of his constituency. In that heyday of "liberal Republicans" some of whom felt that, if they were going to be liberal, they might as well be Democrats. John B. Anderson survived even though he did not win election. He today teaches political science.

Anderson had great appeal, but it was the movie-star charisma of his chief opponent that won the day. Reagan could smile and make everyone feel easier about any situation. A serious man like Anderson, who might bring some thought and real philosophy to political office, was more of an enigma than the public was ready to understand. But Anderson held on to his own integrity and retired emeritus to his own native place.

19. X-ray Technologist, 9-1-1
Saturn: 0N50
Data: March 28, 1922, 11:58 p.m. MST,
Dickinson, North Dakota, 46N53, 102W48

When I managed and revamped the x-ray film library of the County Hospital, there was a petite redhead who was the hardest working x-ray technician in the department. The chest x-ray is the most frequently used routine diagnostic tool of any radiology department. There was always a line of people outside her room, and she processed a new patient every five or six minutes. Her films never had to be repeated. And she had taken the unheard of initiative to learn how to instruct her patients in their own languages which included all sorts of Oriental dialects. She never had to wait on finding a translator. The chest x-ray machine was therefore the most used piece of equipment. From time to time it broke down from overuse or required to be fed new film, both of which took time away from waiting patients. The radiologists, medical men who are doctors who read x-rays, knew they had a paragon worker and were determined that she be let alone to do her job.

Not so a new civilian administrator or even her co-workers. Doing more work than others, none of whom wanted her job, does not get approbation of others who would never work so hard. And the administrator with the whip was of the sort who refused to give anyone favorable job evaluations, in fact always wrote out less than average assessments and tended to blame this worker whenever her x-ray machine went down or she had to pause to load fresh film. There was also a nasty meanness about clocking the worker's luncheon time or any mandated breaks. Good deeds never go unpunished.

The birth data here is from the subject's mother, two minutes before midnight. The chart is Sagittarius rising, Sun exactly on the IC and South Node in Aries, and the Moon is also in the Aries fourth house. Jupiter the chart significator is in the tenth, a most favorable placement. But the real point is that Mars is in the first house and in the rising sign, and everything about her was very much Aries. It is no wonder that this lady created her own fiefdom from what others did not want. The fourth to first house trine is part of the grand trine to Neptune retrograde in Leo in the eighth house.

This whippet of a lady, a whiz at her job, never late, hardly ever out sick, was not going to accept a poor evaluation report meted by our administrator. She neither became angry nor broke down in tears, she sat firmly in the office of the administrator and challenged every point of the poor review and refused to budge until each rating was upgraded to what it should have been. Every one of her coworkers knew exactly what was going on and contrived to walk past the office to catch odd bits of what was going on behind the door. Outwardly, she was very upbeat and friendly, but she wasted no time on jollification with her fellow workers who envied her tenacity and felt either jealous or threatened by her success.

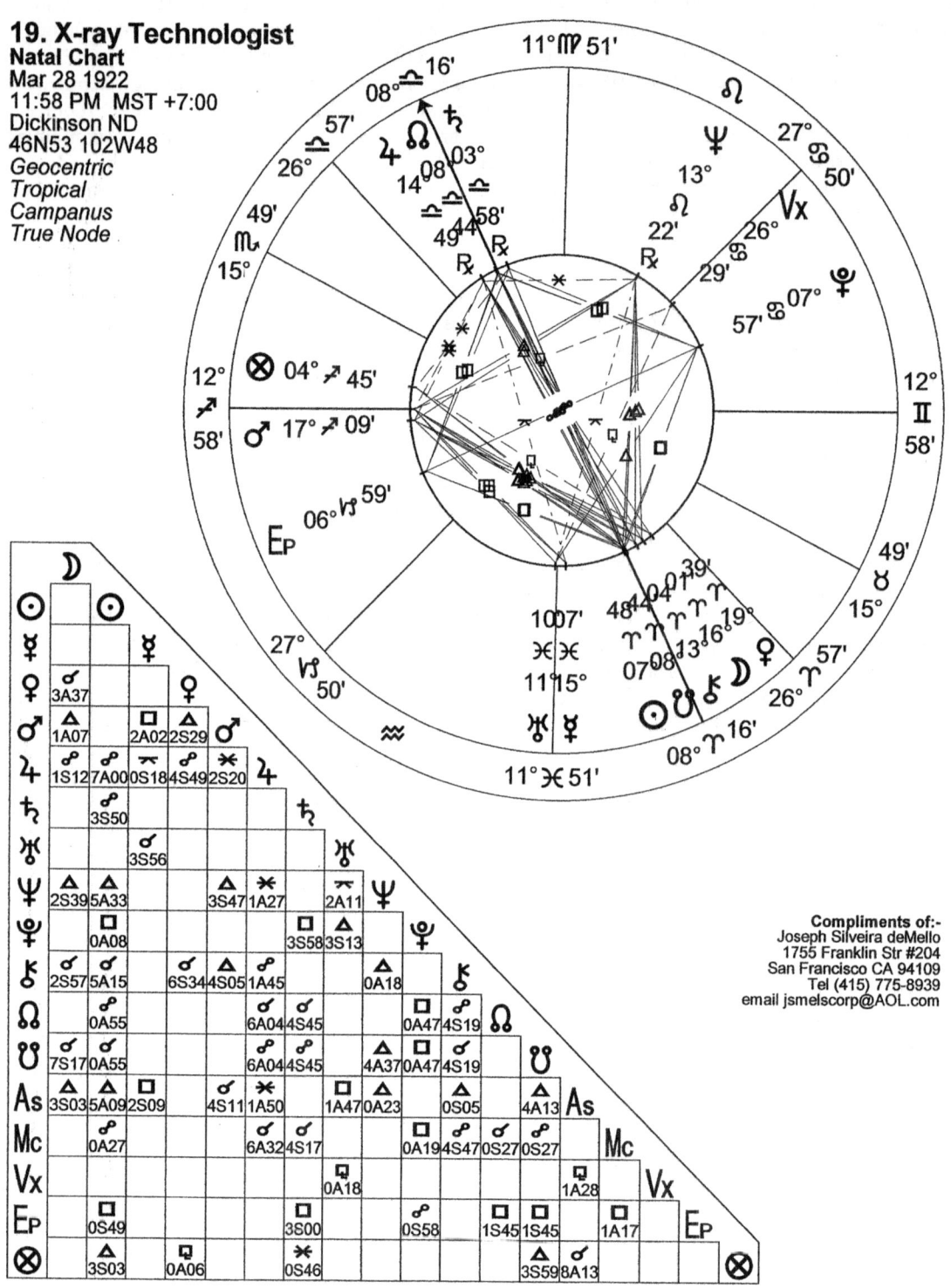

20. Fidel Castro, 8-6-8

Saturn: 0S24
Data: August 27, 1922, 11:00 a.m. EST,
Mayari, Cuba, 20N40, 75W41

There has been a great deal of controversy about the birth data for this world leader. He was born in a mountain village, Mayari, in Oriente Province, Cuba. Today Oriente province has been incorporated with its neighboring province which has the same name as its major city, Santiago de Cuba. It is difficult to understand why this place of birth has been so confusing to American astrologers.

Castro began life as the son of a well-to-do sugar planter and his servant whom the planter later took as his second wife. Castro was educated by Jesuits and Christian Brothers and received advanced education at the Colegio Belen in Havana where he got his first interest in political science. He associated with a number of diverse political student groups and joined protest rallies in Columbia and the Dominican Republic. In 1948, he married Mirtha Diaz Balart, member of a conservative family. His political leftist leanings led him to work in the Orthodox Party which opposed the corrupt administration of Fulgencio Batista. For a time, he was in the Assembly, but after the Batista coup in 1952, Castro turned more toward armed opposition. In 1956, he led a small band of exiled students and professionals from Mexico to the Sierra Maestra mountains in his native province, and he engaged in guerrilla warfare from then until 1959.

Castro, for a time, lived in the United States (New York) where his love of baseball began. He originally had help from the United States, which abetted his revolutionary takeover, so badly did the United States want to end Batista corruption. In the days of Batista, Havana was a flashy Latin capital where gambling and night life were major tourist attractions. However, as soon as he was successful in taking over his country, Castro refused to allow the United States to oversee or advise him on the running of his country. Those ideas he liked from the United States, he accepted, but he objected to a great deal more. Cuba had gained independence from Spain only to find itself shackled to the paternalism of the United States which held long term leases on strategic naval bases there. But his social reforms were seen as leaning toward communism, and the USA was not going to have a potentially dangerous communist presence ninety miles from Florida's shores. The United States led the Organization of American States in voting political and economic sanctions against Cuba. The United States then passed the Helms-Burton Act, named after two Republican Senators from N. Carolina and Indiana, which raised an economic embargo on trade with stopping all Cuban goods and exports and effectively shut of American trade with Cuba as well as American tourism.

This of course predictably turned Castro and Cuba directly into the arms of Russia for aid and trade, and European and African nations still trade with Cuba. The fragmentation of the USSR has been a blow to the Cuban economy. Unfortunately Cuban goods have not improved with the quality of its "superior" ideology and even the quality of its once famous cigars has deteriorated. Castro retains his charisma. No matter how his people may complain about the red tape and the bureaucracy, no blame accrues to him. Over six feet tall, he is a renown speechmaker who can talk for eight hours at a time and without pause. He has grown heavier and older, but his philosophy is unchanged.

In this chart, Scorpio rising, chart significator Pluto in the eighth house might direct us to think that he sabotages himself in what he expects to gain from others or perhaps on ninth house philosophies. The Moon in Scorpio is in the twelfth house, but if the birth time were a bit earlier where the Moon in the first house would account for his speechmaking. However, it is Neptune which has prominence of place at the top of the chart that is of real significance. If we rectified for the Moon position, we would also change the placement of Neptune which is more viable as it is with the given birth data. We are drawn to think of him as reality-challenged with such a Neptune position. It is not so much that he makes mistakes in judgment as it is more likely that he habitually processes information in ways which produce conclusions that are easily seen as excessive or bordering on conspiracy theories. There is a bonus in this chart, no retrogrades at birth. That only means retrogrades by progression will have to be checked.

The Sun in the tenth house is always favorable (as is Jupiter there), but in Virgo and paying attention to details, no wonder his regime is tied up in red tape. Virgo fragments to each tree in the forest rather than to a large overview of the forest. Note that Sun, Mercury, Venus, and Uranus are all very favorably placed by being in the houses which they rule. Sun in Leo in a Leo house is far better than the Sun in the sign beyond the cusp sign. Meaning that I would give full values to Sun tenth in Leo, but take off marks for Sun in tenth in Virgo. He is further permitted to make strange judgments with the Neptune in a grand trine to Mars and Chiron. Chiron is on the cusp of the sixth house ruled by Mars, and is of questionable value to his workers and labor force. But since this devolves to Mars in the second house, his energies are compelled to issues of money, self esteem, his immediate future (or the national economy). Bear in mind that we are dealing with the needs of people of a different culture than our own. Cubans are a volatile, potentially explosive, religion of Rome people who behave with frivolity as a masque against their real troubles. They have enthusiasms as an escape. They have not gone the way of most Latin American states where nepotism and oligarchy rule. But public service still means to them, quite logically, that services obtained should come with nice quid pro quo bribes, so if bribery was rampant in the Batista regime. it is still as natural in the Castro years. Human nature and its tendencies survive.

See the grand trines in fire and water and reflect that trines are permissive. They allow things to happen. They are not simplistically lucky, only more easy going. Castro is a public man with most of his planets above the horizon. The chart is fixed and water. Its dispositors are Mercury and Venus. The Moon and Pluto are in mutual

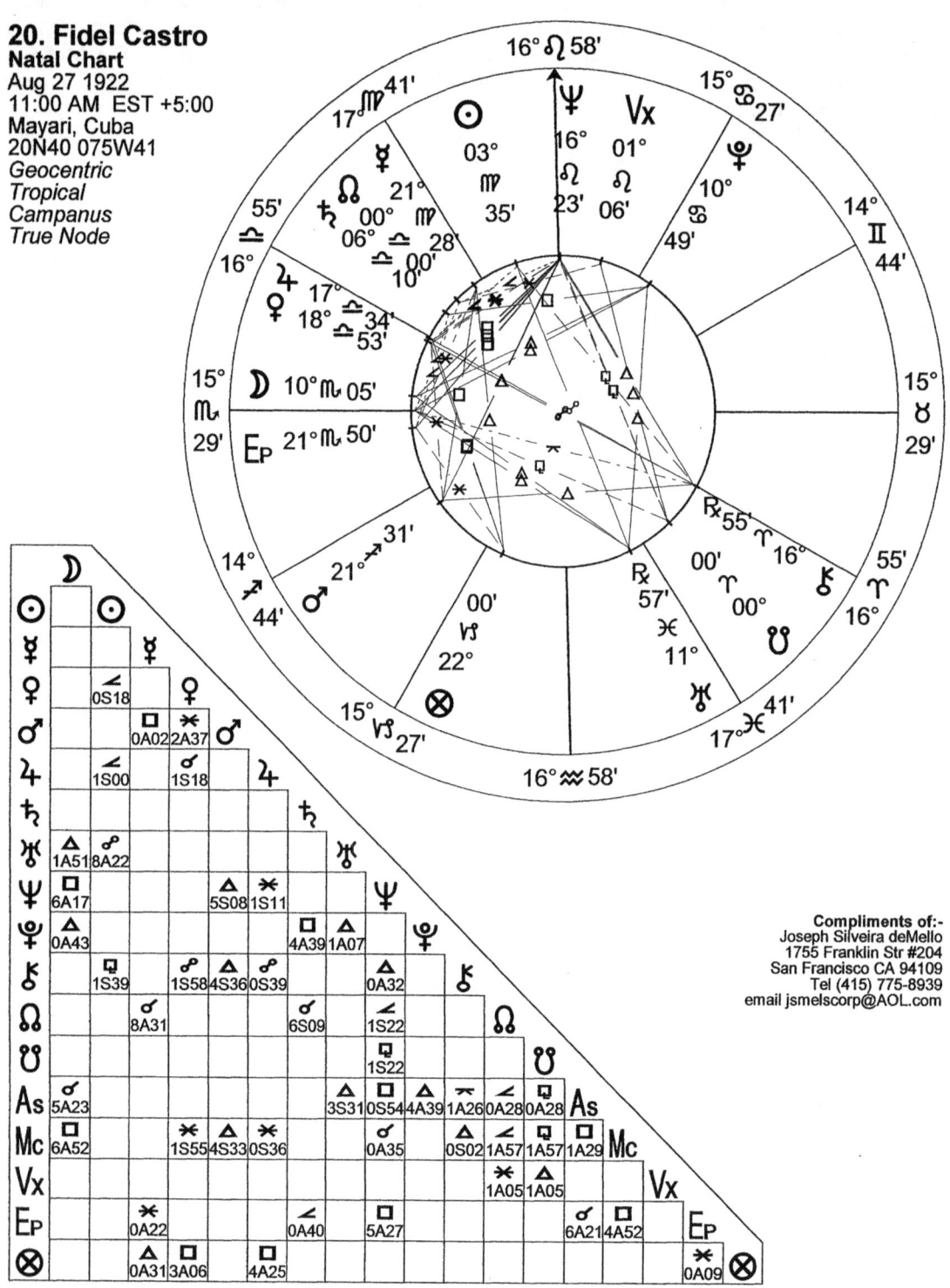

reception and turn their trine aspect into a couple of conjunct aspects. Watching the transits of Saturn in any chart is the foremost indicator in the timing of events in both the life of the leader and the general events of the country. This is a classic chart for the study of Scorpio rising. But, wait a minute to note that his Moon falls on my Sun, his rising sign on my Saturn. With this latter, I should probably not strive to be his astrologer as critical as I might be of him.

It rankles many that Castro and Cuba can manage to live without the USA. Forty years later Castro and Cuba are still there and still not a territory of the USA. It is moot that the fortunes of Castro and Cuba would profit from an open relationship. If it was an innate right for us to become a sovereign nation, it has to be equally correct for Castro to believe in Cuba as a self-governing nation true to its own standards. Remember it was Hearst journalism which launched the Spanish-American War and that we got Puerto Rico instead of getting Cuba, a move as poorly conceived as the Bay of Pigs invasion.

21. John McCormick, 9-6-9
Saturn: 0S30
Data: August 29, 1922, 1:30 p.m. EST,
Newark, New Jersey, 40N44, 74W10

Astrologer John McCormick was well known and is well remembered by many astrologers. He went to conventions, sat in hotel lobbies surrounded by a crowd of ten deep and talked astrology. He left his lobby seat only when he had to deliver a lecture. He knew his astrology, and he loved its manifestations. He wanted other people to have as great an understanding of it as he did. He was also extremely outspoken and was able to resort to satire and humor as his tools for combating the more woolly-minded, pompous and self-important. He did not suffer fools gladly and stuffed-shirts got no tolerance from him. As one of the original five of the Mercury Hour group, he left behind much evidence of his quick wit and wisdom. Although two days younger than Fidel Castro there is little similar between them except a lot of the same aspects.

The man was his chart, and once he called it the chart of a drunken Irishman. Sagittarius rising people are ultimate consultants, as are those with a Sagittarius Midheaven. Note immediately that his Sagittarius Moon just above the Ascendant and as good as being in his first house and with as much propensity as Fidel or I to tell people exactly how things really are. With the addition that Mars is in the rising sign he never got really Aries with anyone unless it was that other Aries Al H. Morrison. Anything Morrison said, John could easily disagree with, and Morrison could never best him. Well, Morrison was not too swift on reading his own chart, and John saw his own very clearly. The whole Mars thing is interesting since he and Fidel have Mars out of bounds. To say that John was a retired civil servant (so am I) just does not quite tell us anything. Edith Custer says he taught piano, had to do with helping indigent immigrants, was an efficiency expert, was involved in social services and put together her first computer.

His Virgo Sun and Mercury are well separated in the ninth house, and this is ambitious locale, paying attention to the details of course, but with Mars for swiftness This is John McCormick's own given birth data as he used it, despite the fact that EDT was officially in use in 1922. It was his habit to convert all chart times to standard time, perhaps as a side-swipe at those who insist on conversion to UT. I heavily favor using clock time and making the proper zone notations and subsequent arithmetic.

Other things to note in this chart, as in the chart of the x-ray technician, are to be found in the tenth house with the nodal axis on the chart's vertical axis. Saturn tenth is exalted in Libra, and Jupiter is in tenth for leadership, and Venus there is in its dignity. His eight year participation in Mercury Hour has been collected and published, and "John From Beginning to End" perpetuates his memory and may enliven new astrologers who did not personally know this erudite astrologer. Edith Custer supplied his death data as May 7, 1981, 2:45 p.m. EDT, Newark, New Jersey.

22. Travel Agent, 1-6-12
Saturn: 0S50
Data: September 5, 1922, 8:30 p.m. CST,
Hartshorne, Oklahoma, 34N51, 95W33

This is the chart of a casual acquaintance, of interest due to his place of birth, who was not very much the Aries type. He was medium height, conservatively dressed, very low key, did not have red hair and was socially affable. His Virgo Sun with three other Libra planets in the sixth house, definitely tuned in to the details. He was homosexual. but not overtly so if you note Sun opposite Moon conjunct Uranus which has no sextile-trine formation to mitigate this opposition.

23. Cargo Handler, 9-3-10
Saturn: 0S42
Data: May 28, 1937, 8:26 p.m. MST,
Ogden, Utah, 41N13, 111W58

Note that we have an interval of fourteen years since the previous example. This is the chart of a man who was an airport cargo loader whom I first met in 1976. He was very interested in astrology, had several friends who had looked into it, and informed me he was a Gemini, and he told me his time of birth. I immediately told him (without knowing his occupation) he should watch how he lifted things in order to avoid back injury. Whenever you see Sagittarius rising or on the cusp of the sixth house, any astrologer can always very confidently make that observation. He laughed wryly and told me he had just managed to break the tip off his coccyx. In early 1976, transiting Saturn was in Leo but had been in Cancer on natal Pluto and would return retrograde to Cancer.

Of course his disability was contested. Is there ever a time when insurance companies do not vacillate in accepting that injuries are real. The course of his future was very iffy for better than two years. But once his dis-

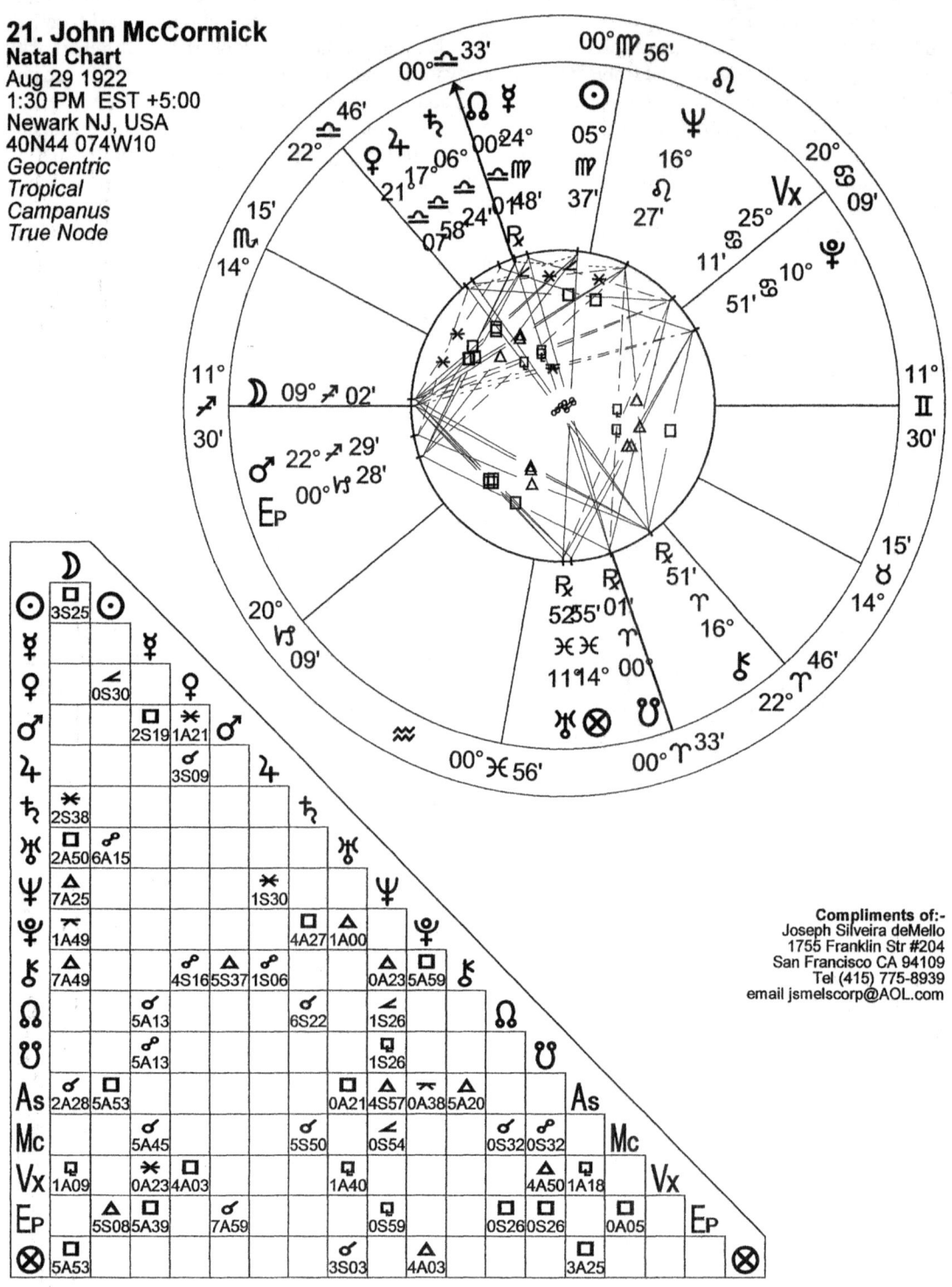

21. John McCormick
Natal Chart
Aug 29 1922
1:30 PM EST +5:00
Newark NJ, USA
40N44 074W10
Geocentric
Tropical
Campanus
True Node

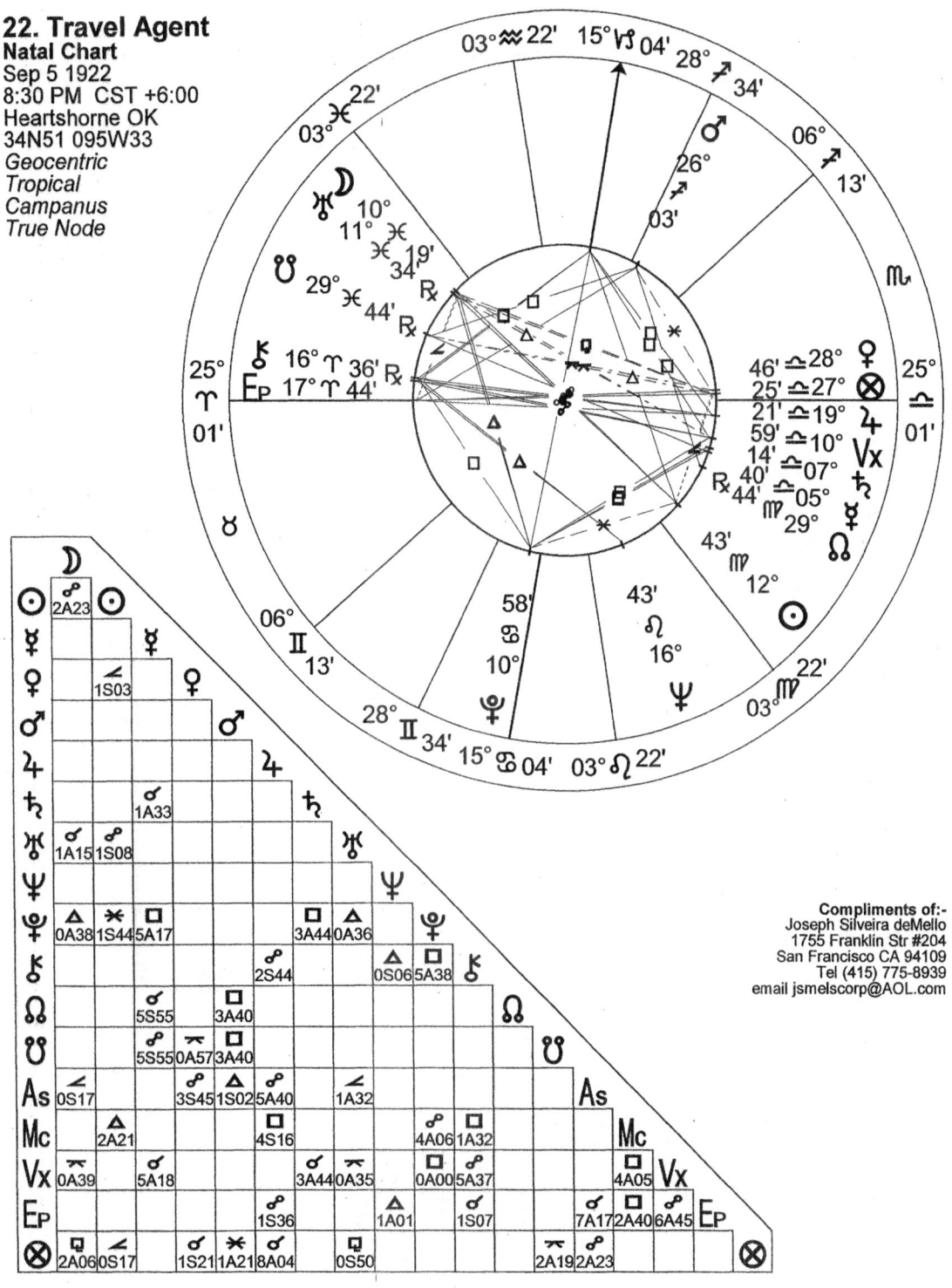

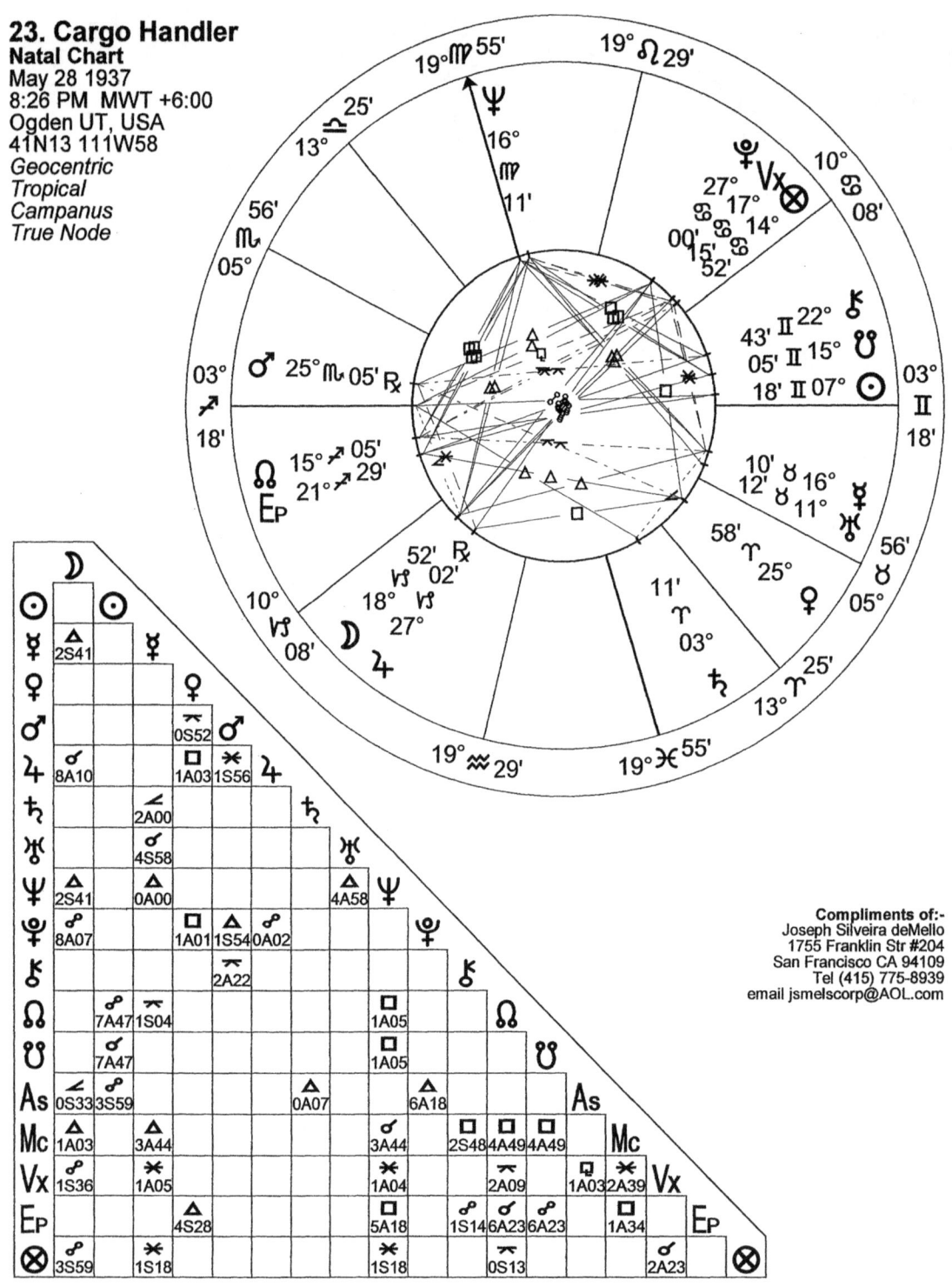

ability status was accepted, he has since then been in retirement. This was indeed a difficult case since treatment and therapy did little for him; therapy too often holds unfulfilled promises. Lack of exercise has allowed him over the years to gain quite a great deal of weight. Much of his time is spent traveling in Utah, Wyoming and Arizona visiting with a long list of family and old friends, driving a Volkswagen van he has owned for years. Typically Sagittarian, he loves the outdoors and non-competitive sports activity. He is not too eager to form any people attachments and habitually distances himself from all but a select group of old friends.

Many an astrologer might well be cautious with this chart. Jupiter as chart significator in the second house might well state that he is financially well fixed but for that Jupiter being in retrograde; while he may receive a regular stipend, he counts his pennies and lives from month to month. Jupiter is sextile and parallel to Mars, also retrograde, and the latter in the twelfth is the final dispositor of this chart. Saturn at the nadir of the chart shows a lack of father figure in his life, and that is factual. Note that Jupiter is also opposite to Pluto and Fortune in the eighth house (mitigated by a trine or kite to Mars), and Venus is at the focus of a T-square to the Jupiter opposite Pluto. We also have to make up our minds about the benefits of Moon conjunct to Jupiter, and Moon applying to a separating sextile to Mars. Note how the Sun stands alone and makes a sextile to Saturn. With the random trines in this chart, we have to think about allowing that there is a grand trine involving the ninth house Neptune, the Moon, and the Uranus-Mercury in the sixth house. He has accepted his situation with resignation. He could pick up the telephone, or I could, to communicate, but, instead, he knows exactly where I will be every day at cocktail hours and comes along two or three times a year. There seems to be a karmic bond that permits us to quickly pick up from where we last parted. His Sun falls in my twelfth, and mine in his twelfth, so I daresay we've known each other previously. Note his ninth house Neptune, highest planet in his chart. I would of course question is Neptunian side only to find he has a fair grasp of the realities but has over the years indulged in occult studies and philosophies, has high ideals more than spirituality, and was one of the first to tell me of the wonders of Sedona, Arizona.

24. Barman, 12-3-12
Saturn: 0S36
Data: June 2, 1937, 1:38 a.m. CST,
Ft. Worth Texas, 32N45, 97W20

My neighborhood supermarket, no matter how I get to it or leave it, involves the climbing and descending one of the formidable San Francisco hills. It was such a chore to go there once a week that I always treated myself to a drink at an old Irish bar across the street before beginning the trip homeward. The bar was staffed by bartenders I have known for years (and some are now dead) and, indeed, the place has changed hands. But I had the charts of every bartender and half the customers. Indeed, one customer had studied astrology in a class I had attended years ago. At the illness of one of the regular bartenders, this man was hired to fill in. He was a newcomer to the area, but he fit in nicely, not the only Pisces or Gemini among regulars, and was easily accepted, stayed a while and finally disappeared moving to southern California. He even has Neptune in the sixth although Jupiter is chart significator in the nocturnal chart.

Jupiter ruled Pisceans are very different than those ruled by Neptune, Also note the sixth is ruled by Leo. I have noticed Pisceans with a Leo ruled sixth gives us dynamos in full control while they work. But once they come out from behind, they suffer a total reversal of charisma. I assure you Saturn in the first house has nothing to do with the case. When he left, he maintained no contacts, simply moved away, and he is singularly not remembered by former co-workers or customers. I wish I had known him better and asked all the questions the reader may well be asking.

25. Cellist, 9-4-9
Saturn: 0S14
Data: June 22, June 1937, 6:00 p.m. PST,
San Francisco, California, 37N45, 122W26

Scandinavian by family heritage and education, he was quiet and pleasant, but was not silent about things musical. He was a musician who performed in ensemble and solo occasions, was very involved in helping the education of promising musical students, and he was very involved in the local Scandinavian community. Years before the trendy coffeehouses we find in every shopping area, he also worked in a bakery-café, very clean, very Scandinavian in decor and very Scandinavian goodies on the menu. And there with Saturn in the fourth, he was ten when his father died.

Two things I do not like are Mars retrograde at the difficult 19 Scorpio, and his Neptune in orb of a cesquin or quindecile from his IC which French astrologer Guy de Penguern has found predispositional to weakness of the immune system. Guy's research has found many charts with this aspect singly, as here, our doubly to both sides of the Midheaven. This man was homosexual and did die of AIDS. I clipped his obituary to send to a mutual acquaintance but forgot to make a note in his file.

26. Barman, 4-4-10
Saturn: 0S13
Data: June 24, 1937, 5:00 a.m. BST,
Liverpool, England, 53N25, 0W58

By total accident, a client suggested a drink at a bar in a commercial hotel where I ordinarily would never have gone. Turns out my client had been there previously, and he introduced me to the bartender as his astrologer. The bartender immediately gave me his data as if I could give me an instant reading. I politely made note of it, seeing double Cancer and smiling that my client was a Cancer Sun. Only later did my client tell me that this was one of the hideaways where, while still married to his first wife, he had for years been meeting the lady who would become his next wife.

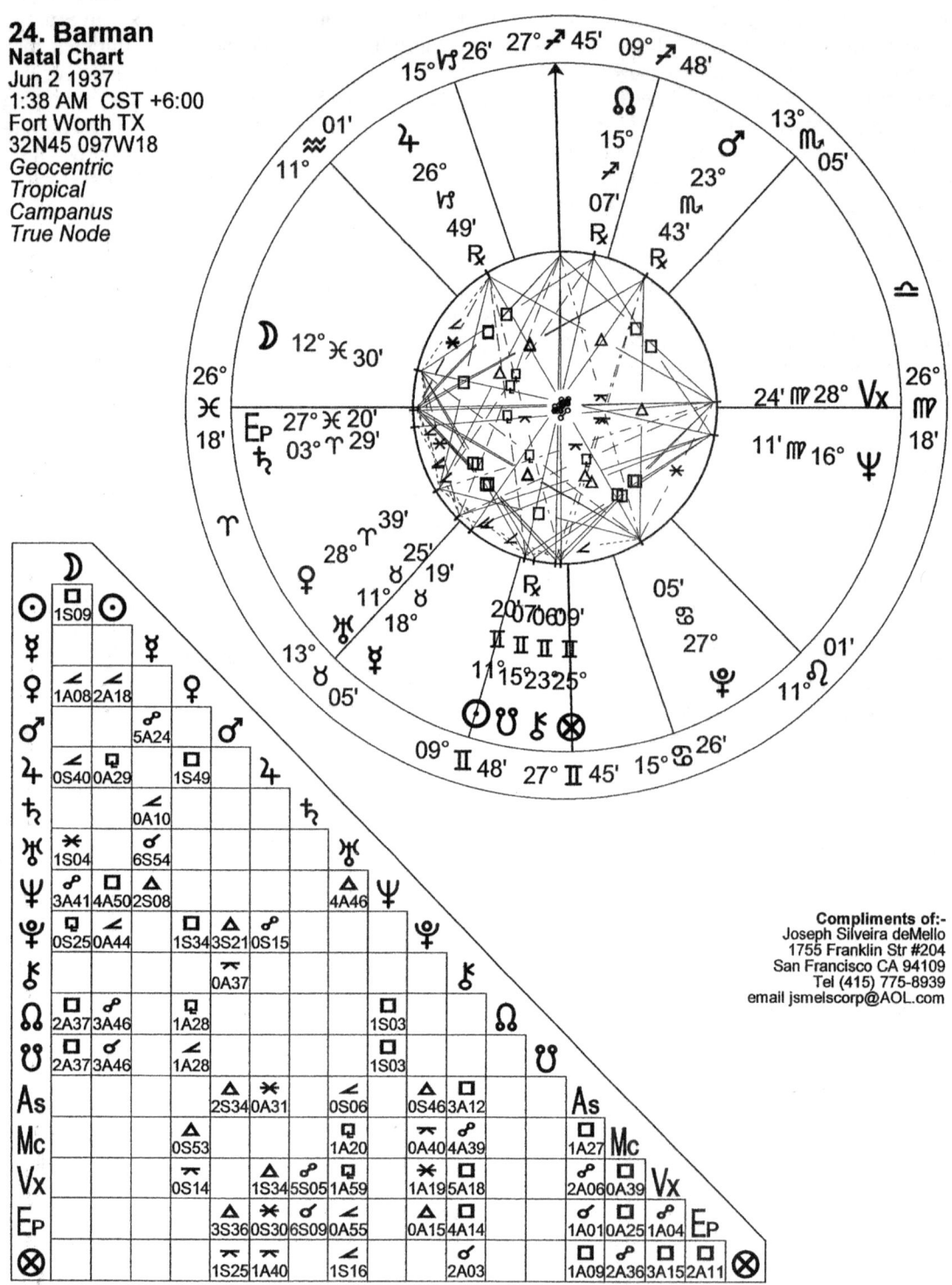

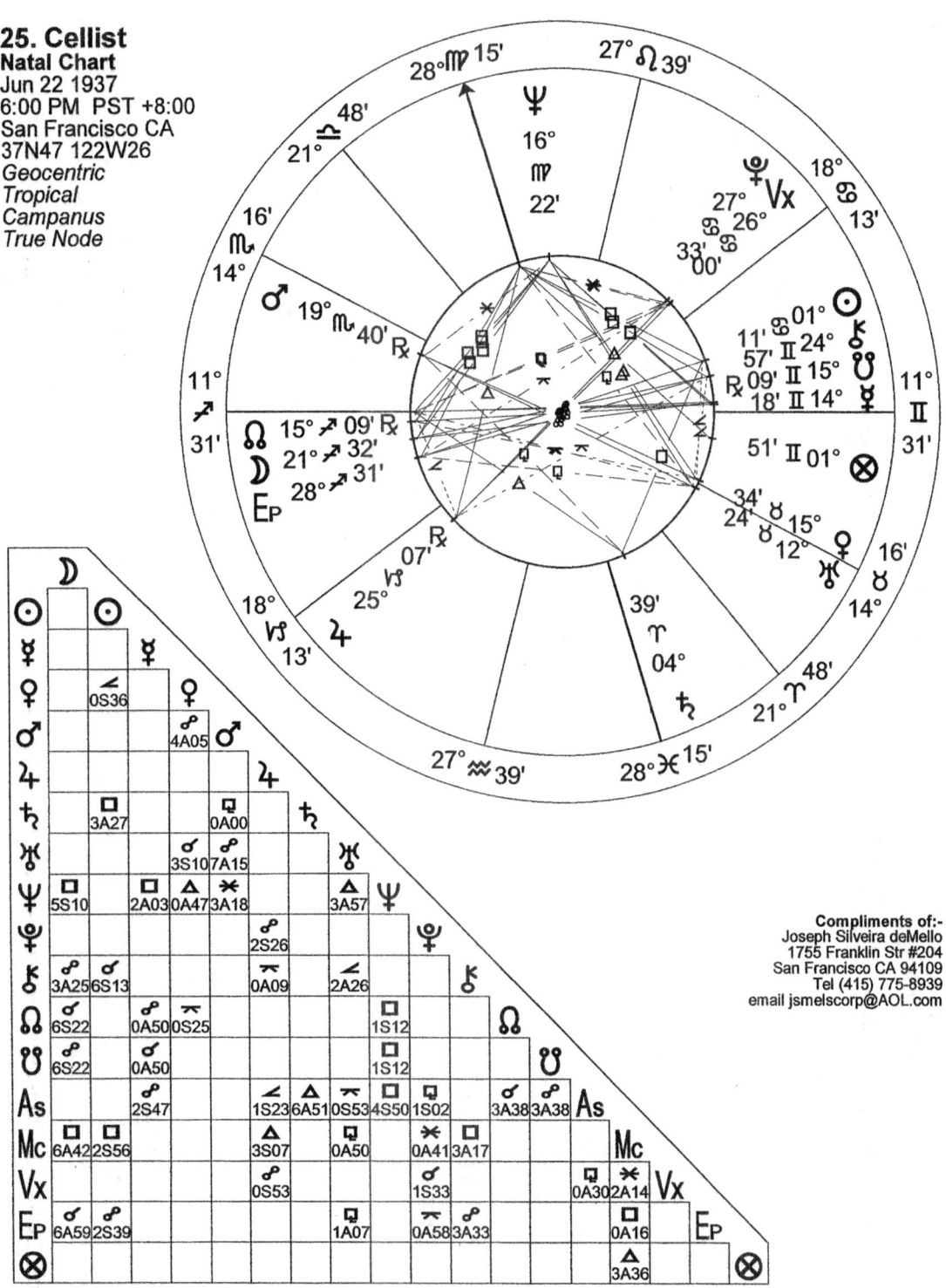

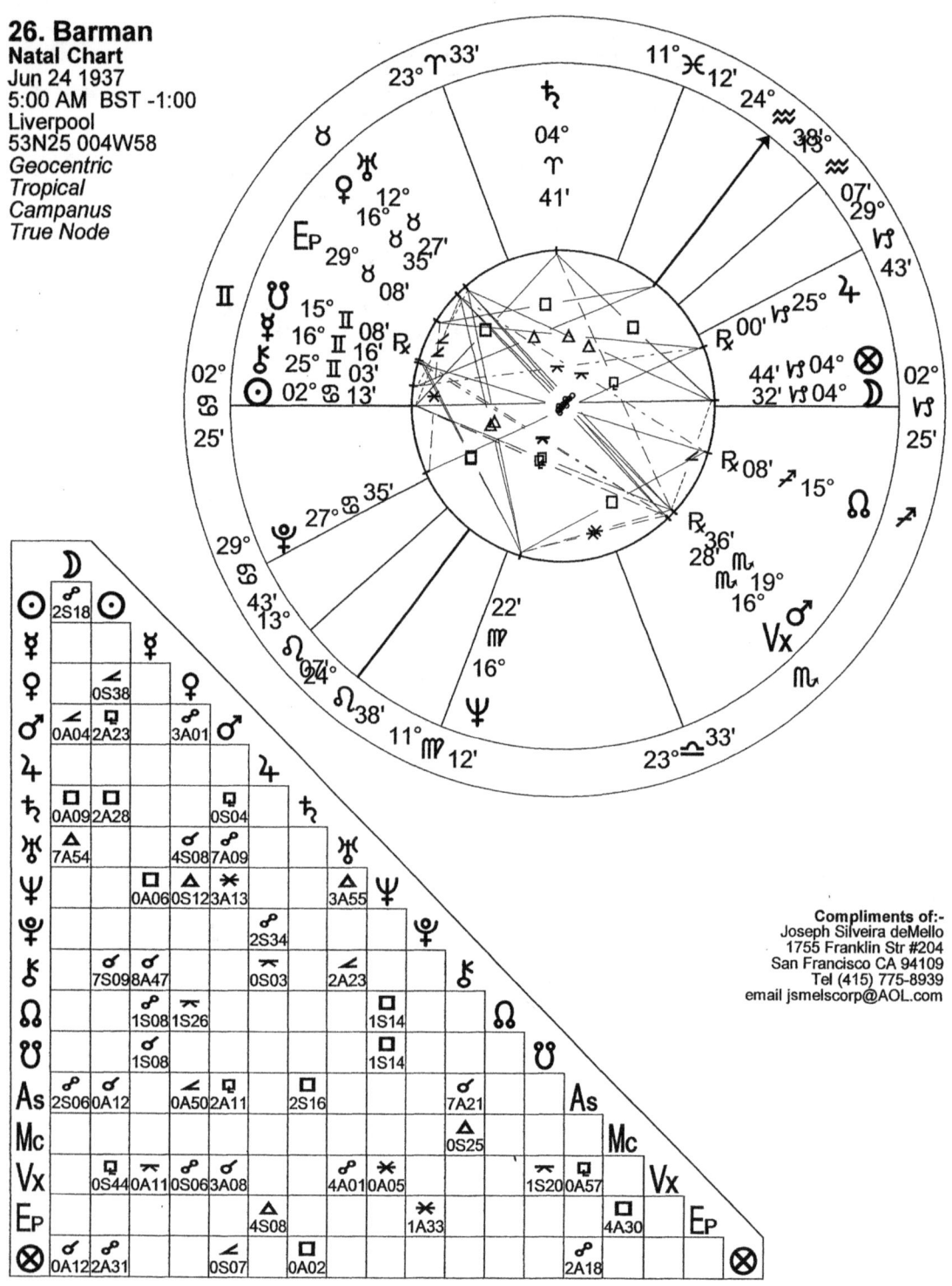

But myself as Scorpio watched this British born bartender who would wander in our direction and join our conversation. He volunteered he had been twice married and twice divorced. He was enjoying the single life and free lancing among the many birds available to him. He was of better than medium height, thin and blond and of average good looks. He informed us, out of the clear, that, when it came to sexual experiences, he had and would try anything, and enjoyed it all. Something clever he had read somewhere, I did not react. This was, after all, San Francisco, where your barber is straight and your plumber is gay, and any bartender is an amateur psychologist. This was just the sort of venue where the lovely waitresses might be available for a price, and the bartender a social facilitator. My client was also checking out the waitresses, but when the bartender came near, his interest switched as if he was trying to cement a rapport with the bartender. I saw the bartender was entirely professional and mechanical toward the waitresses, and that they seemed coldly businesslike toward him. There was no warmth or friendliness.

When I got home after several cocktails and a good luncheon, the afternoon was useless for anything but doodling, and I set up his chart, to see he was born just a bit after a Full Moon. He was indeed a double Cancer with the Moon in Capricorn, in detriment and in the seventh. I remembered the early warning of a teacher, when Capricorn is on the Descendent astrologers should check their calculations for errors. I was at odds with a Capricorn seventh that had been twice married and divorced until I saw Jupiter retrograde there and the Moon. The Moon is where you keep changing your mind about things, and obviously he was a person in quandary about what he wanted from those close to him. Pluto is in his first house, suitable for sabotaging his own image. Even though he had paused to talk to us, his eyes were always attentive to the rest of the bar. The chart had Neptune in the fifth perhaps not favorable for his speculations or love affairs. And the fifth is ruled by Virgo which should prohibit gambling as such people always feel there is a system to winning if only they can only find it. Mars in the sixth, is retrograde, opposite Venus, and made a kite to Neptune. Venus was with Uranus in the twelfth, and also in the twelfth were widely spaced Mercury, Chiron and Sun. There was one more thing, Mars at the focal point of sesquiquads to Sun-Ascendant and to Saturn square each other. He had said he did not date coworkers, and boasted that, if the timing was right, half the people in any room were available to him. I concluded he played roles to make his shift pass more quickly. Later I learned he had changed jobs to work in a more trendy yuppie location.

27. Roger Elliot, 3-4-10
Saturn: 0S12
Data: June 25, 1937, 3:15 a.m. GET,
Torque, England, 50N28, 3W30

Hardly 24 hours later, we have the chart of this cheerful, urbane, and very bright British astrologer who has provided happy moments by his writings and lectures. He easily drew large audiences who experienced levity in astrology while still getting the reliable word. He fell more to the side of the Theosophists than to the "scientific" astrologers. Unfortunately, he died 8:28 p.m. GDT, September 29, 1993, in Bristol, England, during heart by-pass surgery, according to data furnished in Data News (#41).

I have one lasting memory of this bright star. We were both in the audience of a convention presentation by an astrologer whose psychological interpretations were neither in line with astrology nor with any psychology I would have cared to see practiced. And it is not surprising that these wrong-headed psychological practices and interpretations are routinely accepted in our, otherwise, enlightened times. My blood was boiling with protest. The speaker advocated giving astrological readings that aroused and caused pain to his clients. I cannot agree with that sort of thing, and I was ready to give the speaker a twelve-gun broadside as we got to the question and answer portion of his lecture. But Roger Elliot got up, and I gave way. In a few good humored words, he laid the speaker by the wayside so satisfactorily that my anger was quelled by joining the majority of those present who spontaneously applauded Elliot. And since Elliot was doing a presentation in the next session, I was among those who eagerly went along to hear him. Surprise benefits such as this are why more people ought to attend conventions.

Devon's northwest coast is still quite high in northern latitudes. Here our chart has a huge sixth and twelfth houses, four signs intercepted, as did the previous example. There is Saturn in the twelfth, and there is Venus conjunct Uranus in the twelfth (all privately intercepted). We have just backed up the Ascendant of the previous chart. Here it was nice to see the chart significator in the first house getting away from the South Node. Mars is powerful in Scorpio, and in the sixth house, contributing to a high work ethic, but this Mars is also retrograde, sign of he who tries to drive with the brakes on, and in the degree of snakebite (Serpentis). This is like shooting yourself in the foot. I was about to say that this was like having an aspect to Chiron, and sure enough, Mars is quincunx Chiron, like a speaker who lost his notes or brought the wrong set of notes and has to wing it.

Roger Elliot was the author of an astrology column in a British tabloid which was said to be read by twenty percent of all England. It was a column noted for his sense of humor. I easily saw why so many other astrologers admired his expertise. He had a depth of knowledge, and admired his facility for remember every chart he ever studied.

28. Artist, 12-4-7
Saturn: 0S08
Data: July 14, 1937, 10:30 p.m. MET,
Venice, Italy, 45N25, 12E18

This chart belongs to the son of an astrologer. She had told me he was a Pisces rising, and it was a good thing she told me that. The first chart I did was not Pis-

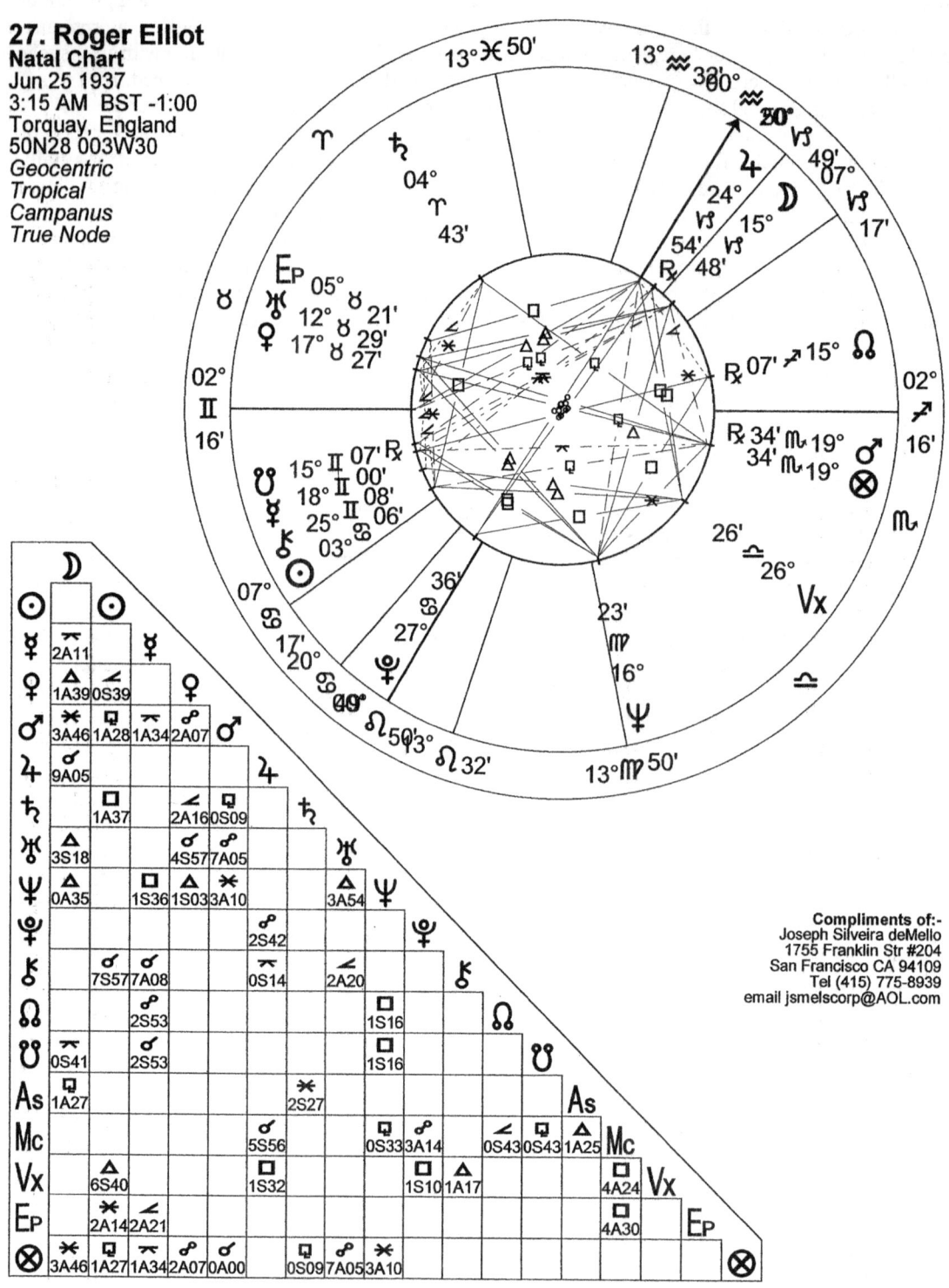

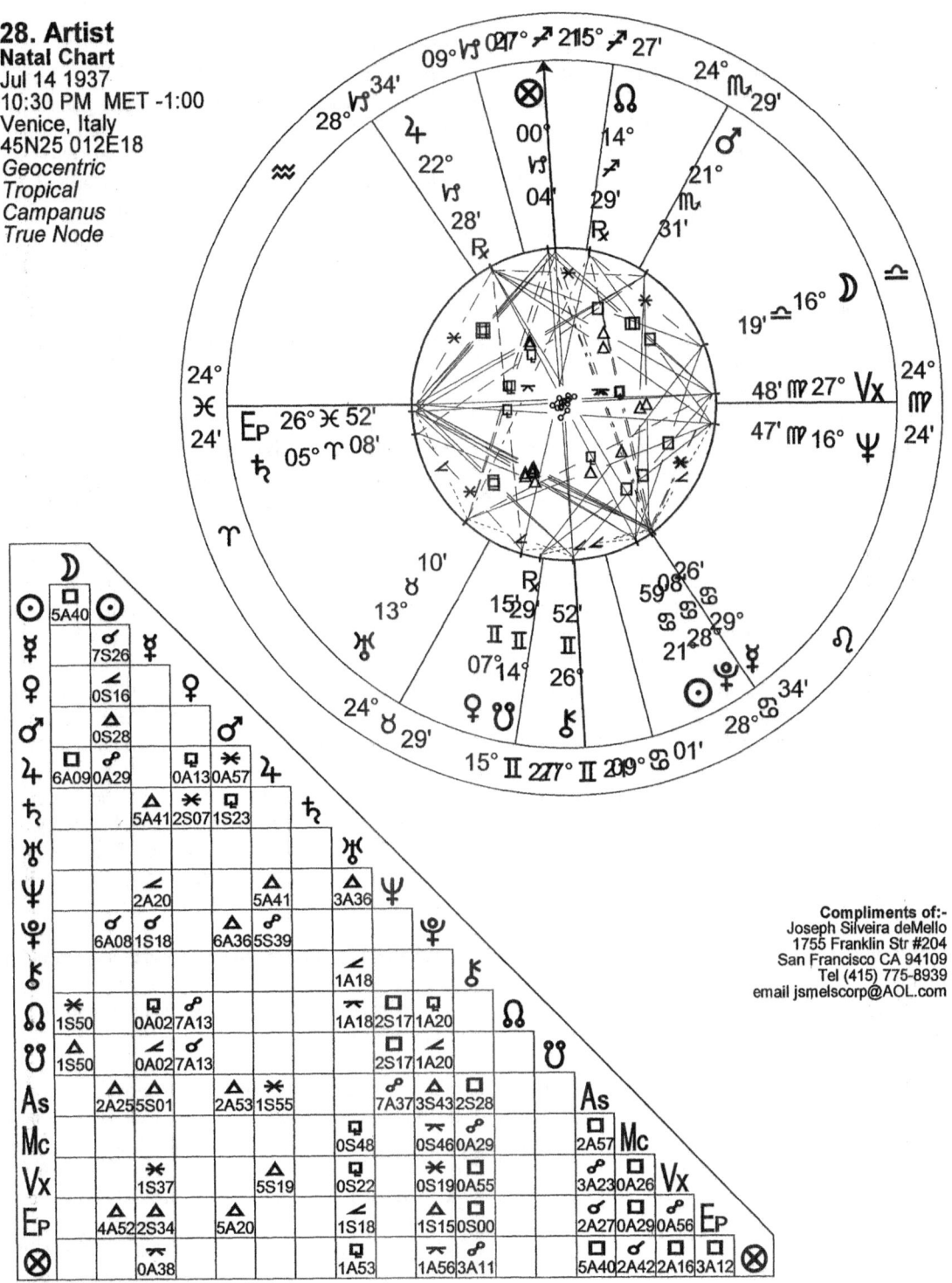

ces, and it was frustrating to find how my slippery fingers had erred on the computer keyboard. My program calculates Fortune to suit diurnal or nocturnal charts, so I was glad to see both Fortune and Sagittarius on the Midheaven. Such people tend to become consultants in their careers.

Born in Venice prior to World War Two, he and his British-born mother were interned in a concentration camp in southernmost Italy during the war. One day, camp officials were gone and the gates were open and unguarded. All the internees had to do was sit and await liberation by the approaching American forces. Mother and son followed the American army northward, often hitchhiking with the army, until they reached Rome and eventually returned to Venice. He grew up in Venice without any fatherly presence. At times they lived frugally, and much thought went to the real basics, so he early learned to cook. He started painting as a child and, before his teens, he had his first gallery showing which was very well received. He emigrated to the USA in 1956 as a representative of European color printing houses which specialize in art reproductions for coffee table gift books brought out by various American publishers. He has been very successful in his work, has a fine home and is happily married to his second wife.

The curious thing about this chart has four signs intercepted, but the only planets involved are the first house Saturn and the seventh house Moon in Libra. Where Saturn indicates the father and Moon the mother, we see these are out of orb of opposition.

The Moon rules the fifth and sixth, while Saturn rules the eleventh and twelfth. This is another case of Pisces rising ruled by Jupiter, the only retrograde in his chart, and in the eleventh house. Mars is on the eighth house cusp of gains from others is fairly well aspected. It must be significant that this chart has Ascendant, east point and Vertex all practically on the same horizon. To the sensitive Ascendant we find an agreeable trine to the Sun and grand trine to Mars. But then we still have to note that Sun is square Moon. I am always involved in a search of aspect patters, so it is interesting to see the overlap of semi-squares along the bottom of the chart starting with Uranus to Chiron, then Venus to Sun, South Node to Mercury, and Mercury to Neptune. Of these, only Neptune square South Node shows a Mercury midpoint.

The subject is involved in a quest for perfection. He competes against himself, not against others. Whether it is a new picture he is painting, a business coup he is pursuing, each must always manifest as an improvement over any previous endeavor. He is also something of a gourmet chef, very proper, for Cancerians solve their problems over a cookstove. He is very directed on any problem until it is solved and bested. But, as becomes more prominent as we go through this study, he does what pleases him.

29. Computer Analyst, 3-4-10
Saturn: 0S10
Data: July 22, 1937, 3:00 a.m. EDT,
Boston Massachusetts, 42N20, 71W00

This man was a computer analyst who was working for an American company in Bonn, Germany, when I first met him in San Francisco. I met him through #34 Entrepreneur later in this group of charts. He had an adventurous childhood, with serious whooping cough at age six months, being severely burned by hot water at age three years, and the first home burned down while he was still in preschool. By the time he was eight years old, his family was moving into their third home. He had a background of personal insecurities and yet a great sense of personal dignity.

There is a great deal to see in this Gemini rising chart, and it would be a big mistake to dismiss this person as a frivolously spread out Gemini, however serious thought must be given to Chiron on the Ascendant, and we struggle to find what we think of this modern placement. For me, Chiron is indicative of our easy ability to overlook the obvious, give ourselves a kick in the pants for obliviously sliding down the easiest path and later wryly laugh at our ineptness. If laughter be healing, that is the only way I see Chiron acting as a healer. He and his friend, both with strong charts, backed each other in joining AA and staying with that program, but healing and stabilizing are two things these partners did excellently for each other.

Here the Cancer Sun is overshadowed by a very close Pluto exerting great power. A frequent large problem facing any Cancerian is a natural propensity to harbor resentments and difficulty seeing how non-productive these persistent memories can be to successful daily living. The Moon is not well regarded in Capricorn, being in detriment, a propensity to encountering opposition from others. And here we have the Moon making a double quincunx to Mercury and Venus in sextile each other. The worst thing a quincunx can do is to create an element of nervousness between these planets and what they rule. Perhaps it of some benefit that he was born going into a Full Moon.

Mercury as chart significator in Leo lending more creative drama to the mental processes is blessedly distant from the Sun's rays. To interpret it in the third house, so close it is, we see the creativity in communication and business. We also note Mars in the sixth, the area of people who are born with a work ethic, made more powerful for being in Scorpio and being dispositor of the chart. So, though we begin with a versatile Gemini rising who has to watch his money, he does want to project as a stable person.

By way of sideline understanding, we see Jupiter retrograde seventh drawing to himself those rejected by others and attesting that such relationships are going to succeed due to his own efforts. And we also see Saturn retrograde which brings an interest in having all people relate to themselves and the world around them. Give a quick glance to the principal things in the chart of his companion, Capricorn rising, Sun in Aquarius, Moon in Leo. If the study of chart comparison in close relationships appeals to you, you may well indulge yourself studying these charts as a pair. People with Saturn retrograde will have a Saturn return in infancy, so that most recently he has already had his third Saturn return. I was

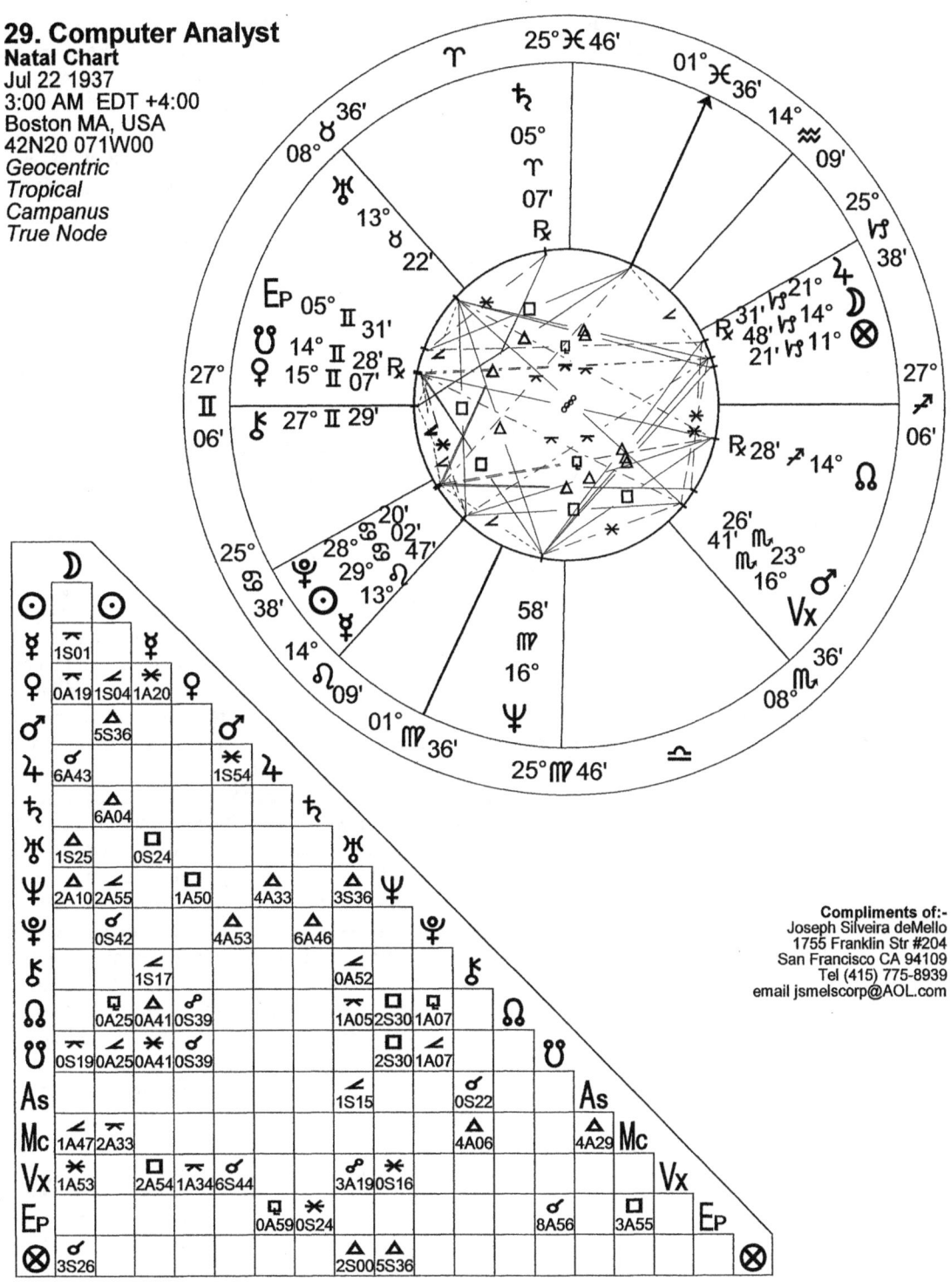

nearby when they met in 1976, but did not make a note of the date when #34 Entrepreneur asked me to do a comparison chart for them. On the February 3, 1976, I did a horary question when they were coming to terms about which would abandon his career in favor of the other if they joined forces. Where we have a same-sex partnership, we have to meld career needs of both and decide which partner leads. Their relationship has succeeded, both are happy and different persons, seen only at AA meetings, retaining no friends from "the old days."

30. Lady with Back Problem, 11-5-2
Saturn: 0S16
Data: July 30, 1937, 7:32 p.m. MST,
Salt Lake City Utah, 40N45, 111W53.

This unlucky woman fell down a flight of stairs and became paralyzed three years before I came to know her, by which time she was no longer visibly afflicted by her injury. We immediately spot Mars on the Scorpio Midheaven, and we are struck by two placements to either side of the Midheaven, fifteen degrees in both directions, right and left, which sets up the infamous 165 degree aspect, the quindecile, to the IC. This is a strange minor aspect which, although considered by astrologers of the past, has had a resurgence to our attention only since the early Nineties. It was the basis for studies on AIDS by Guy de Penguern in his book *Cosmos and AIDS* and the subject of an article by Noel Tyl in the Mountain Astrologer, Dec 97-Jan 98 issue, but which is much featured in Noel Tyl's book *Astrological Timing of Critical Illness*. In his book, de Penguern noted that persons born with planets in this aspect to the IC had a great deal to do with immune systems, and that progressions and transits forming such an aspect were germinal in charts of persons who developed positive HIV factors or full-blown AIDS afflictions. So far as I know, this affliction has not manifest itself. But self-care suggestions would not go awry.

Of course when I first did this chart I was unaware of the quindecile in delineating this chart. I saw Aquarius rising with Sun in Leo, and I saw the Moon and Uranus in Taurus, which I today see as quindecile Mars on the Midheaven in Scorpio. We go looking for it and find that the chart significator Uranus is with the Moon opposite to Fortune, so Moon and Uranus are 165 degrees from Mars and Midheaven. From Mars, looking the other way, we see Mars and Midheaven 165 degrees from the South Node. Minor aspects in close orb and forming double patterns are a circumstance which should not be overlooked. Danger is ever present in this chart.

31. Churchman, 3-5-2
Saturn: 0S16
Data: July 31, 1937, 1:52 a.m. MST,
Eunice New Mexico, 32N26, 103W09

I have followed this chart more than thirty years, have charts for his parents, his siblings, both his wives, his five children, and their extended families, and now of several grandchildren. As a child, his family moved about a great deal because his father was an oil prospector, but his formative years were spent in Oklahoma. He was the U.S. Air Force recruiting poster boy in his youth, a tribute to Venus on the Ascendant. He worked in advertising on Madison Avenue, an obvious Gemini occupation, and then he married a woman with two children whom he adopted, and they had three children of their own. They moved west to settle in the San Francisco area. Out here, his first marriage eventually dissolved, and he married a lady with three children by two previous marriages, and of whom he is now a widower.

He and his first wife became civil servants in San Francisco, and they worked first in the Welfare Department, but his wife eventually surpassed his grade and became a personnel officer. He transferred to a community college, where he was in charge of finances, and then to the Commission on Aging, where he held a similar job overseeing the letting of $3 million in city contracts, in many cases himself writing those contracts. The then city attorney praised him for writing tighter contracts than his own staff could produce. He then moved into the Tax Department, where he was promised a large staff that never materialized. He never had more than one assistant, and oversaw on- and off-street parking fees, as well as assisting in real estate taxation when that division needed more help. He was the only person in his department who was capable of conducting auctions on tax delinquent properties, and after his departure no adequate replacement was found for that activity. He went into this assignment at the Tax Department in the midst of a major scandal involving parking meter collections that were so loosely handled that employees were taking home the not-so-random bag of change. The culprits were not charged but were given mandatory early retirement. In the course of his tenure, he raised parking fee collections from $5 to $11 million per annum. Again, on the promise of job importance, he moved to the newly created Department of Parking and Traffic, where he was again third man down from the top. In all of his civil service jobs he was kept from the top job slots by affirmative action that discriminated against him racially and sexually. He is male and white, and saw promotions go to minority or female employees who were in all cases inferior to him in ability and job performance. In fairness, he must shoulder some of the blame for being a very outspoken conservative Republican in a city where every major departmental job is headed by Democrats, most of whom have actively worked on political campaigns and become political appointees, which he has not done.

In every public stance he has always been very conservative, and in private life has gone from deacon to priest to bishop in the Continuing Church. His church affiliation is more right wing than the Roman church for which he has always been very conservative, and in private life has gone from deacon to priest to bishop in the Continuing Church. His church affiliation is more right wing than the Roman church for which he has only disdain and contempt. His church is against

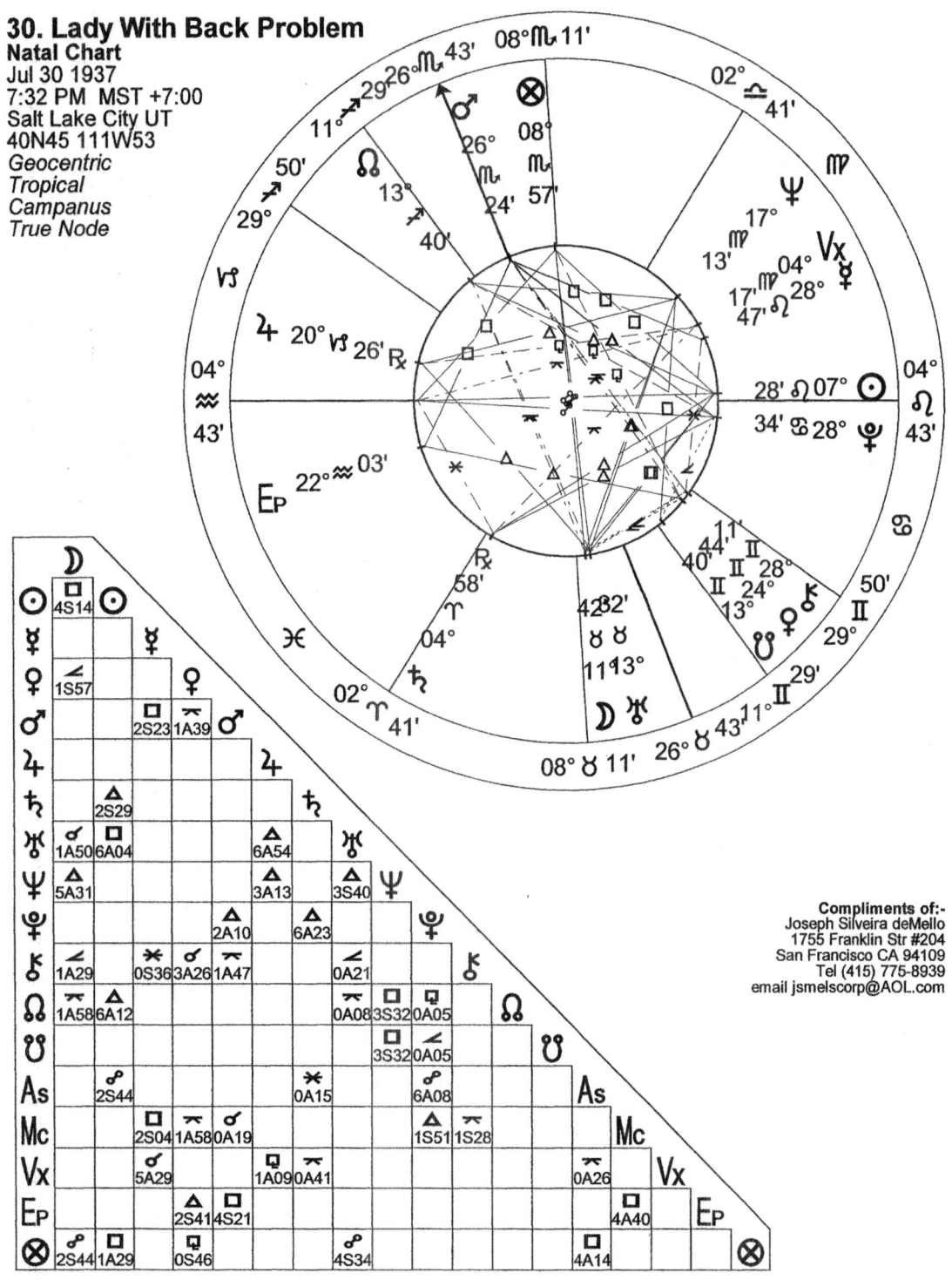

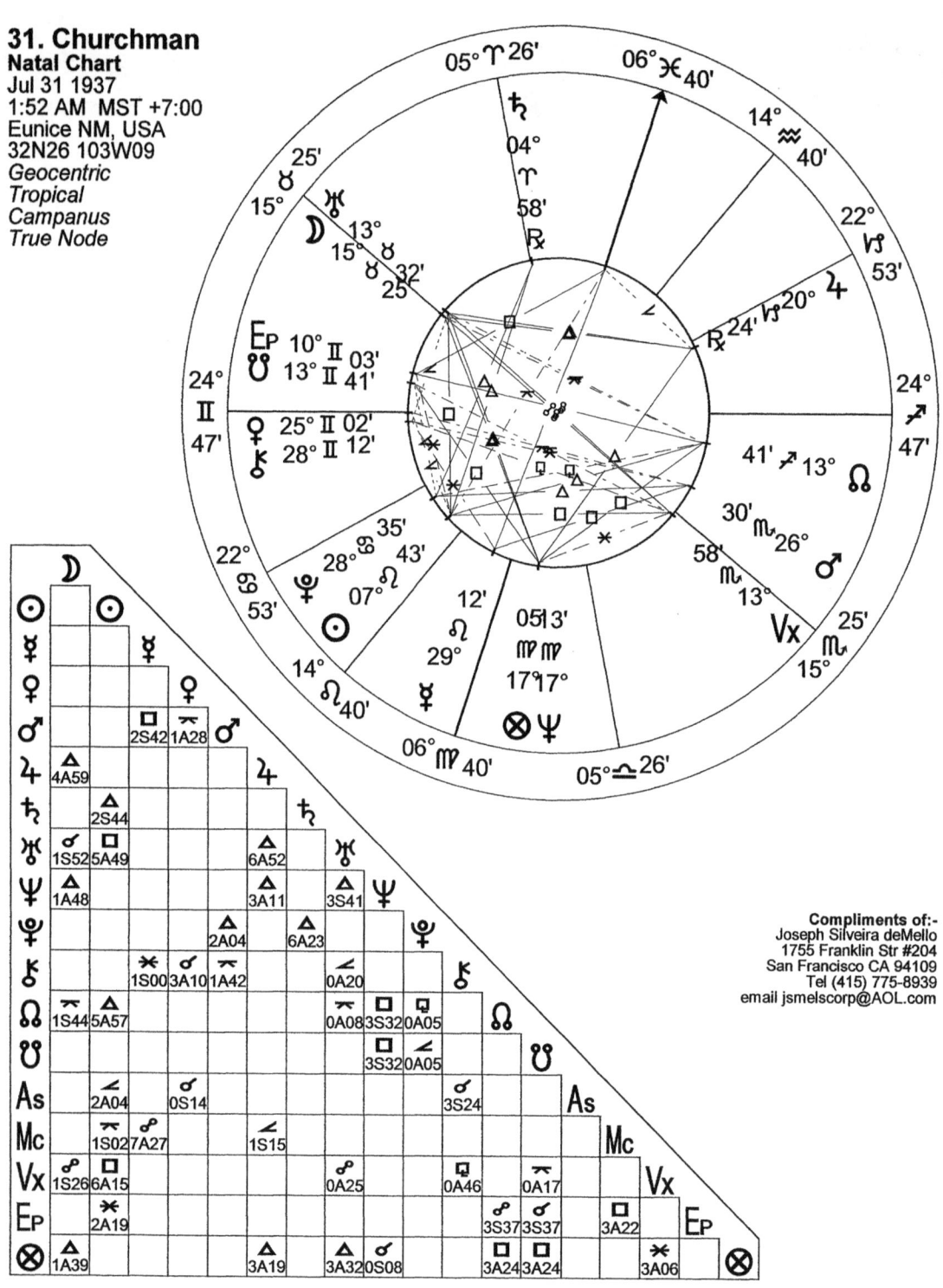

31. Churchman
Natal Chart
Jul 31 1937
1:52 AM MST +7:00
Eunice NM, USA
32N26 103W09
Geocentric
Tropical
Campanus
True Node

divorce, and a fellow bishop who originally sponsored him, held up his promotion to Bishop on the basis that "there were too many women in his past." He is a widower of his second wife, but his first wife is still very much alive. Ironically he would like to marry again, but he cannot do so and retain his position in his church.

His second wife, a wonderful person and able business manager of a city department, was his mistress long before he was divorced and able to marry her. She was of his similar religious persuasion, and urged his churchly aspirations. She died of cancer just as he was to be ordained a priest. She worked to within two weeks of her death, dying the same morning when, hours later, a hearing was held to contest her disability status.

He is a Gemini rising, Leo Sun and Taurus Moon. Those who know him closely see large manifestations of both Gemini and Leo, and quite a few astrologers who have seen his chart have said it is a wonder he can find his way home. One the one hand, known as an able administrator, well regarded for bringing in every project ahead of schedule and under budget, never being late for work or business appointments, he cannot be relied upon to know the time of day when keeping social engagements. Until he married his second wife, he never wore a watch, and wearing one has not improved his chronic lack of a sense of time. On any simple errand to the grocery or drug store, he can get lost for two hours if he pops into any book store.

He has always had many interests and plans. At one time, and I helped him do so, he dug up his front lawn into beds in which to plant a great variety of roses, intending to go into the rose business. This of course never materialized, partly from the well known Gemini tendency to get projects going and then regard them as accomplished and giving them no further thought. Furthermore, the roots of his rose plants were discovered by a hoard of local gophers who found them delectable. His children would not let him poison the noxious beasties, and he was at a loss of how to cope with the problem. He kept Arab horses (hay burners, I called them) but only had a shelter for them half built when he finally disposed of them. He planted an orchard of various types of apple trees in the lowland beside the creek at the bottom of his property, and then had to fence them off when his horses found apple tree bark desirable. He is allergic to every conceivable sort of pollen, cannot bear to mow grass, indeed, cannot keep a mower repaired and in fuel, but his self-image is that of the proper suburban family man. Playboys live in cities; proper family men live in the suburbs or in the country. And while his opinions, religious and political, are conservative, and he says he's never met a Democrat who was not a liar and thief, he leads a thoroughly liberal lifestyle.

Fed up with dead end jobs and no prospects, he retired from civil service at an early age, to devote himself to church observance and business. Unfortunately he receives no stipend for his church activities, his travel expenses being paid only when he travels on assignment. His mother died, and his father wanted no more than to die and join her. His brother was finding it difficult to cope, so he brought his brother and father to live with him. The situation provided him with a sense of *deja vu* since he sees the likeness between his father and himself and a probable shadow of his own future. He could not commit his father to a nursing home. As 1998 came to an end, his father fell and broke his hip, was hospitalized, and his father's doctor mandated nursing home care, absolving our subject of guilt feelings. He easily combines his conservative stance with his liberal life style. The Moon is separating from Uranus on the twelfth house cusp, and in a separating square to his Leo Sun. An earth grand trine to Fortune and Neptune to Jupiter. This really justifies my stance that grand trines are very permissive. He has several overt Leo traits that would make any astrologer smile. He tends to believe that he is the only friend his friends have. He has a fund of stories he has been retelling for years, striving to tell them each new time with embellishments the stories actually do not need for greater drama. But then, with all the facts at hand, if he is thrown a question he has not foreseen, he is at a loss as to where to begin a rebuttal. Mars in Scorpio is trine Pluto which is trine Saturn but a bit out of line to make the grand trine back to Mars.

His Ascendant and Sun are at semi-square neither aiding nor assisting in getting it together. In this nocturnal chart and using the old rulers, the rise of his churchly ambitions are easily seen as Jupiter transited his Midheaven. Even with Jupiter retrograde (also see Saturn retrograde), he does well with previously rejected people and ideas. While he does have a sense of humor and personal drama, he has had more than his share of cares and woes. Nonetheless, he is a serious, sincere, caring and generous person.

Notice that Mars and Jupiter are in the houses they rule, Venus is in the house ahead of the one it rules, but Sun and Mercury are in the houses behind those they rule (which makes for a twelfth house effect). When criticized he dismisses critics as having insufficient sense or status to judge him. I have noticed that it must be the Leo Sun which attracts and draws to himself many young men in search of a temporary father figure, and at his request I have done charts on those young men to help him advise them. Of course he has studied astrology, is quite capable of erecting any charts he wishes to see, but he always consults me astrologically. I am more than repaid by what I have thereby learned of astrology, and by his open generosity. Over the years, I have been treated to many luncheons and dinners in some of our finest restaurants. Recently when I had an accidental fall, he drove in from the country to get me to a hospital as he did fifteen years ago after I had a knee operation and insisting I recuperate at his country place. In those serious times he was quick to help and to run errands for me.

Finally note, if we calculated Fortune for a daytime chart, Fortune would have come conjunct Saturn. Doing it for a nocturnal chart, we see it with Neptune. Because we have written Neptune out as ruler of his Midheaven, giving it to Jupiter, we still have to think of Neptune, deal with its presence in his fourth house where I myself have Neptune. From personal experience, this does not make either of us great housekeepers. Our office desks were always well ordered, but at home there is chaos. He is a gourmet chef, and very ambitious and dramatic with it, but he uses every pot, pan, and utensil in these creations and never cleans up as he goes along. His youngest son, and spitting image, is chart #55 in this study.

32. Neti Leo, 5-5-6
Saturn: 0S25
Data: August 9, 1937, 5:24 a.m. CST,
Chicago, Illinois, 41N52, 87W39

Publicized data from the files of Don Borkowski. This lady is a well known astrologer, writer, lecturer. I was surprised to find Saturn at zero declination. Her Sun falls in my fourth house, while mine falls in her third house. I hesitate to comment of her chart as she has often disagreed with me astrologically. She is an astrological mentor to many astrologers. With Leo rising, she has the Sun in the twelfth house where she also has Pluto about to leave Cancer. She comes off as always right but not as a big ego. There is no denying the Leo prominence in her chart. Mercury, Neptune and Moon form a stellium in Virgo, in the first house but for Moon in the second house. Uranus of astrology is prominent the very top of the chart. Because Mars and Jupiter seem ready to go out of bounds, a check was made of the ephemeris, and only Mars really swings widely out of bounds by progression from age 6 to age seventy-four (at of this writing, not yet reached). Jupiter stays at where it is by declination. But Jupiter turned direct when she was thirty-seven, while Saturn stays retrograde all of her life (by progression). This is another case of Saturn retrograde giving a Saturn return in infancy and one Saturn return ahead of those born with Saturn direct. Although Mercury is a chart dispositor, Mars, Jupiter and Saturn form a constant ring to dispose of each other without Mercury or the Sun. Sun is quincunx Jupiter and Mercury is trine Midheaven and Uranus. She lives and thinks astrology.

33. Fabricator, 6-6-1
Saturn: 0S45
Data: August 24, 1937, 6:00 a.m. PST,
San Francisco, California, 37N47, 122W26

This man is the former son-in-law of an astrologer who has given me the data of five generations of family members all with birth certificate data. He has had an unusual career as fabricator of miniature machine and computer parts so minuscule that he often designs and carves them under a microscope. Many of the things he does are for NASA, intricate experimental parts which go up into outer space. Yet he always shows up to help his former mother-in-law to help with house maintenance chores.

With such devotion to detail in everything he does, it is hardly a surprise that he is a double Virgo involved in scientific engineering perfection. He is another twelfth house Sun in the rising sign. This man is an expert in his field, but no great ego. He recently (spring 1998) lost his job just as he was about to retire. I believe he would do well in bringing a group together to form any computer start-up venture. The Moon in Aries with Saturn and Fortuna on the cusp of his eighth house, are certainly germane. Such a Moon should increase the ego, except Moon is conjunct retrograde Saturn. Mars is in Sagittarius in his fourth house indicating his energies go into home or security. He has an independent nature, but Mercury in first and ruling first and tenth and with Neptune in his first and ruling his seventh, these have to be considered in any personality assessment. He has never remarried.

Be as surprised as I was that the conjunction of Moon and Saturn on the edge of his eighth house, is a repeat element inherited from the chart of his father. One of the problems of his life has been expectations that he live up to an ideal father. Notice that Saturn retrograde rules his fifth house. Either the tension of his work or the looseness of the times in which he lived, he went through a serious three year period of substance abuse that ended his marriage. He may be rather mistrustful of ego expression and his ego Sun does not impinge on his Mercury which stands alone. Angular Neptune has to be an important personality influence. He has Jupiter in his fifth retrograde, creative with things others would discard, Saturn retrograde in his eighth of what he gets from others, and Uranus retrograde in his ninth which certainly pertains to a creative sense of why things are as they are. Born here, and with Uranus in the ninth, some might expect that he would live far from his place of birth, but he continues to live in the San Francisco area while his creations have done all the stratospheric wandering.

34. Entrepreneur, 10-11-5
Saturn: 0S56
Data: February 13, 1938, 5:15 a.m. EST,
Wellsburg, West Virginia, 40N16, 80W37

This is the chart and data for a man with great flair for entrepreneurial business management. He is a Capricorn rising with Aquarius Sun and Moon in Leo. Capricorn is the ultimate executive manager, Aquarius has flair and knowing, and the Leo Moon tends to project dramatically and in a thoroughly controlling manner. He is also the life partner of #29 Computer Analyst.

I first regularly encountered this man in the close knit social group of an excellent and very clubby saloon. An impressively tall businessman, he sloughed his cares of the day by indulgence in a great deal more alcoholic intake than most of the people in the same group. It was a classic case of he who, having worked hard, played fervently. In the club atmosphere, we all knew a little something about each other. He was running a candy business and was obviously very successful and lived on nearby Nob Hill. And if we knew about each other, we also kept a casual eye open to the changes in the group. So I saw him develop several personal relationships, none of which lasted very long. On the other hand, he must have known I was an astrologer, as I had several clients in that club. We had never spoken except in greeting, so it came as a surprise to me when he came and sat next to me and launched into a serious discussion

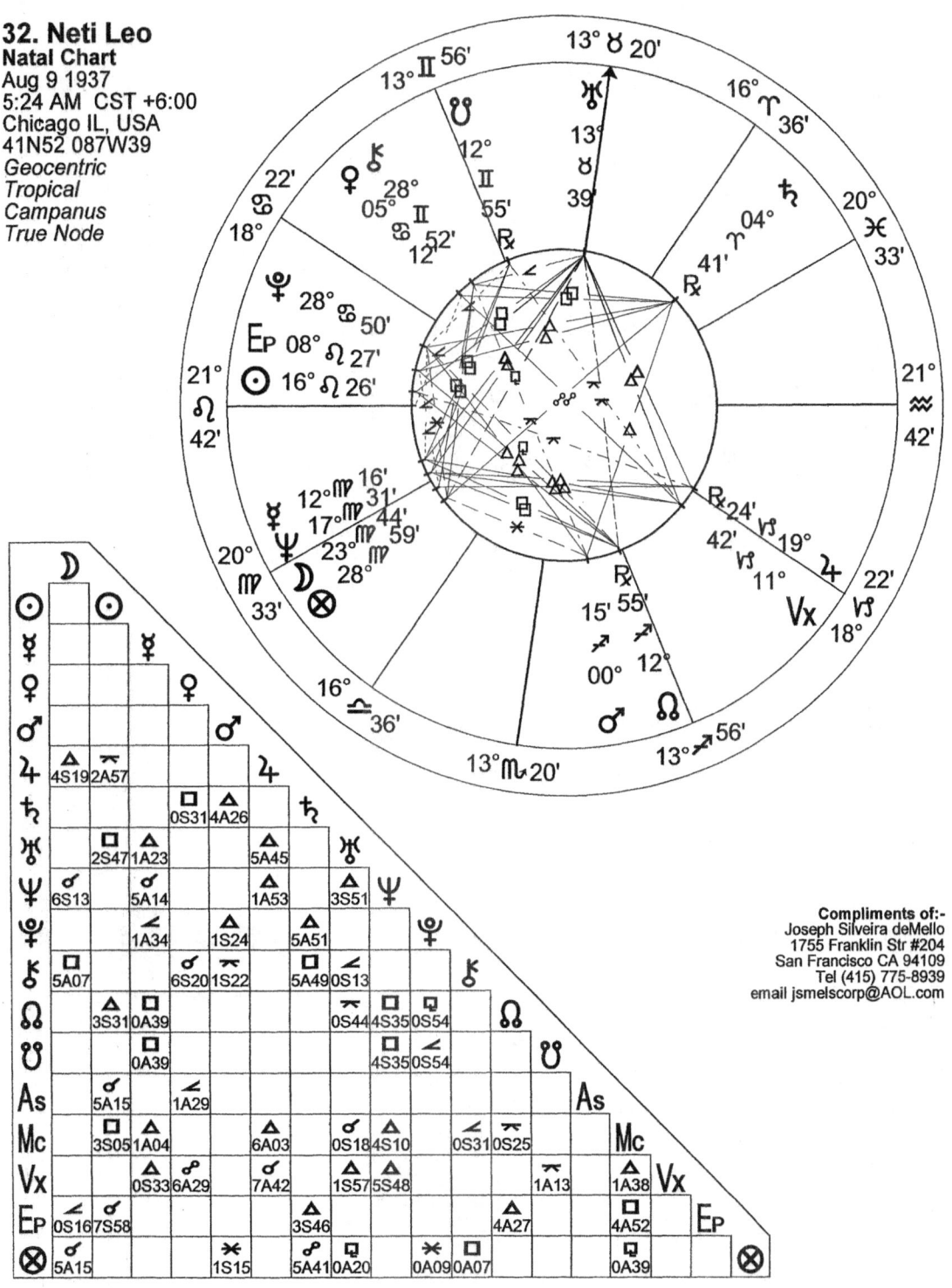

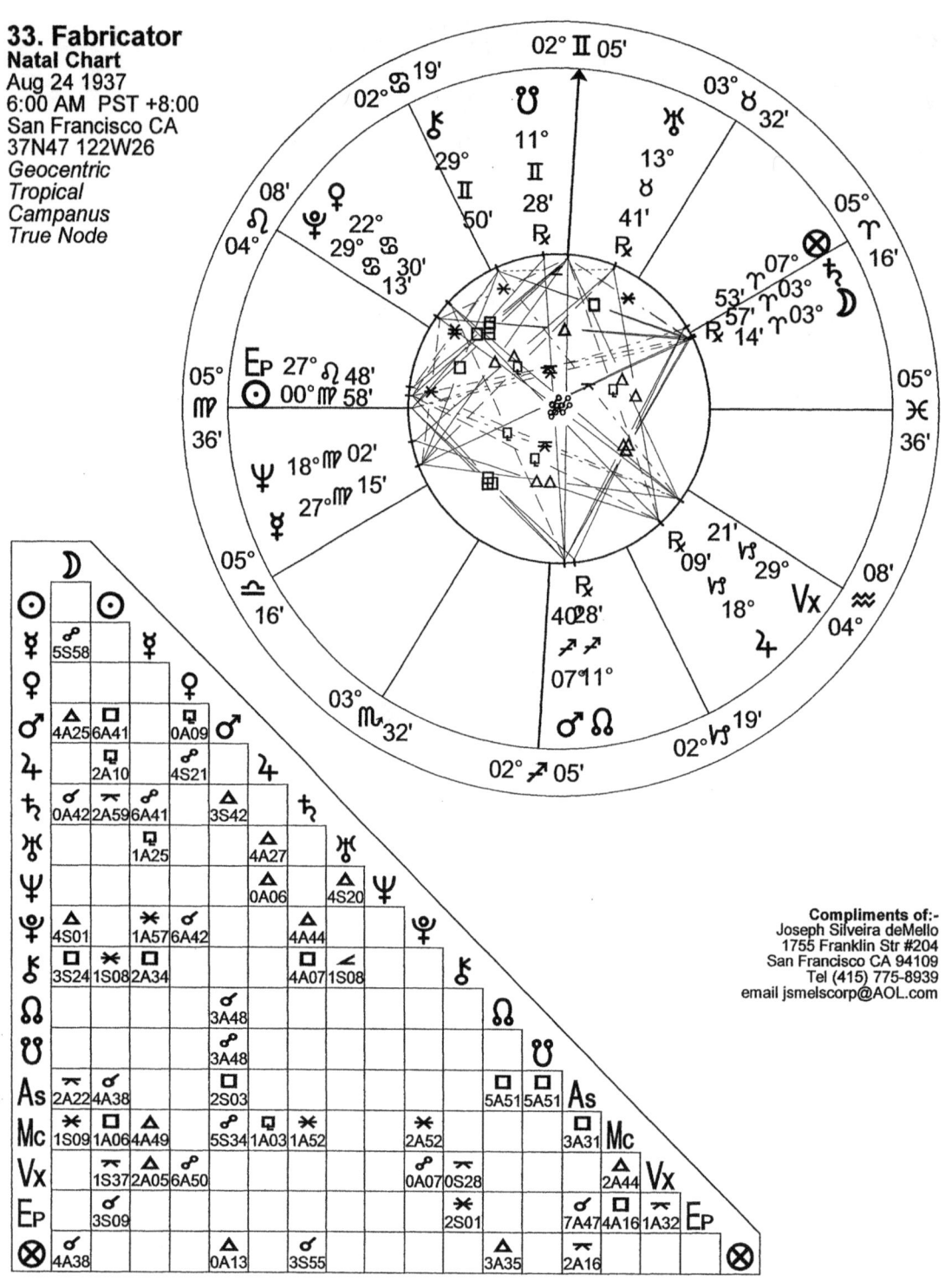

33. Fabricator
Natal Chart
Aug 24 1937
6:00 AM PST +8:00
San Francisco CA
37N47 122W26
Geocentric
Tropical
Campanus
True Node

Compliments of:-
Joseph Silveira deMello
1755 Franklin Str #204
San Francisco CA 94109
Tel (415) 775-8939
email jsmelscorp@AOL.com

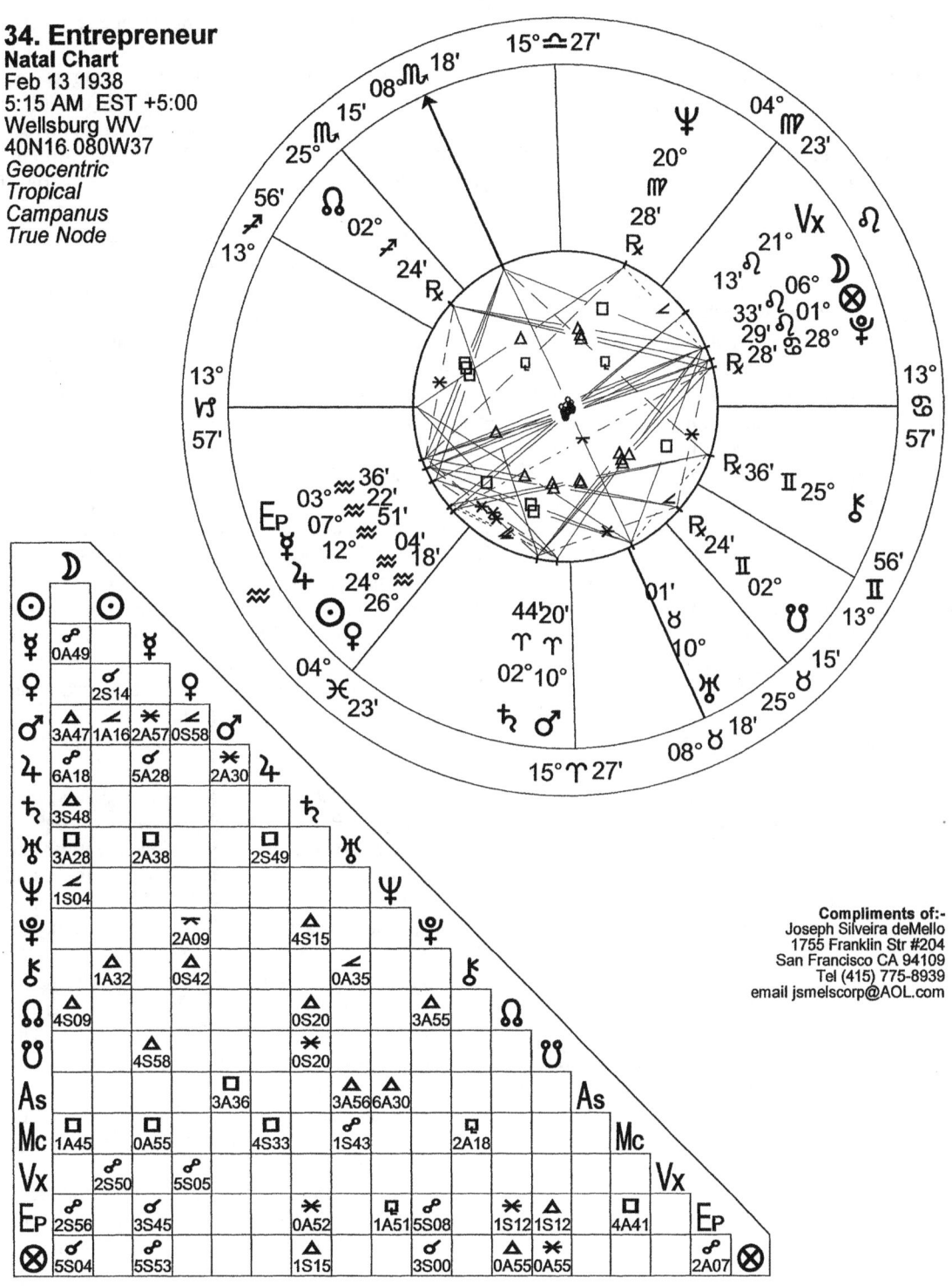

of his business activities and wanted to know whether or not astrology would show him what was really going on.

He had gone to work in the candy business and expanded it, and then discovered the company President was doing some shady bookkeeping practices. When he brought these to the attention of the owners, the executive was fired, and this man succeeded his predecessor. Taking over, he first added ice cream to the candy business, and then he proceeded to franchise the business to other locations throughout the city. At this point a national conglomerate was seeking to buy out the business. While this would be a landmark that established his success, it also left him wide open to a search for something new to do. And he had a very good idea of what that was going to be.

Thus he became a client. I did his chart noting Capricorn rising which indicated to me, first, that I may have bit off more than I could chew. Up to then, my experience of Capricorns was that any consultation with them always ran into overtime while they repeatedly asked the same questions either to clarify, to get better answers, or to get their money's worth. I felt I was going to do a great deal of work for this client. On the other hand, Capricorn is the executive, very happy when working for himself or running everything. My first reading on the business side was limited to showing him how to go with the flow of his chart, the times which told him when to go ahead and the times when things were more routine. Like most people, he expected to live life as if every day brought a crest of accomplishment and success. The first reading must have impressed him because I was soon doing charts of the various young men with whom he was seeking to form meaningful and lasting partnerships. To my surprise, the expected problems of dealing with a Capricorn did not occur. He never wasted his time or that of anyone else.

He could have stayed on with the new owners, but he decided he would rather work where he had the pulse of the business rather than take impersonal direction from afar which the conglomerate would demand of him. An idea for an entirely new business was developing in his head, and he was more than ready to explore new frontiers.

It is interesting how his new idea developed. One of the club owners was an Oscar winning set designer. Several fellow club members were in various aspects of interior design. My client's basic business philosophy was to take something quite common and make it important. Wallpaper was just the right sort of thing. For the very rich there were expensive wallpaper companies which sold to interior designers, sales to the trade rather than at retail, but when the less affluent wanted wallpaper, they were limited to the line carried by the local hardware store or mail order houses. He decided to open a store devoted exclusively to wallpapers at retail. It took him no time at all to find a location on a well-traveled street, on a main bus line, and which also had off-street parking. His special concept would feature innovative and fashionable designs which had up until then been unavailable to the general public.

This was in the mid-1970s. Naturally every phase of the development of this idea was fully checked and timed astrologically. So much time allowed for decorating the shop and getting in stock toward a favorable opening date. Look at this chart and see that he was very creative in merchandising, displays, and every facet of business from ordering to shipping and bookkeeping. He had learned the lesson that nothing would more quickly kill a business than loose bookkeeping.

As hard as he worked and played, he kept both entirely separate. Anyone else might have developed an ulcer, but he had an incredible tolerance for alcohol. The late evening always found him at the club. Nor did he discuss business or astrology at the club. Evenings were play time. He would make an appointment to consult on astrology and these appointments never had to be reaffirmed next day. Strangely, our client relationship began at a time when I was researching the charts of alcoholics.

The trouble with this chart is not Capricorn rising, for people of that sign have no problems if they have leeway to range about and act on their own. Capricorns are very self-motivated. They can pick and surround themselves with willing workers whom they can easily manage. And they know how high or low on the backs of those people, and how soft or hard to pat or prod them to doing exactly their wishes. Born just before a Full Moon, he has the Sun in Aquarius (absolute assurance that his way is the only answer) and the dramatic Moon in Leo which is often an even larger control and power factor. Note also that he has three other planets in the first house and that they and the Moon are in intercepted signs. Those intercepted planets took care of seven houses of his chart, the affairs of which were channeled through his first or seventh houses. I smiled to myself when I realized that my Sun fit on his natal Midheaven and that his also fell in my tenth house. I also noted the fixed square of his chart, and the fire grand trine.

The romantic search of his life is made difficult by a seventh house Moon which is changeable about what people he really wanted close to himself and the seventh house presence of Pluto which too often attempts to change other people to his ideal vision. We must have gone through doing half a dozen totally unsuitable comparison charts. A person with Pluto retrograde in the seventh house can easily chose unsuitable underdogs as close companions. Matters are not helped by Venus so close to the Sun that his need for affection is burned by his ego needs. One of the biggest lessons for a Capricorn to learn is how to give and receive compliments. They know a well placed bit of flattery will be motivational, and they are realists enough to realize others may use those same tactics. Capricorns seldom smile, but when they do, they amaze everyone by the dazzling light which can light up the whole room.

The chart significator is Saturn in Aries in the second house where we also see a widely separating conjunction from Mars which might just be wide enough that it does not manifest in frustration. I checked the ephemeris to see if Saturn would ever progress close to natal Mars and noted that it would do so in the 1980s, years ahead of when we were working with his chart. Of course I mentioned this to him at the time. Saturn is in

Fall in Aries, which might afflict his money. At the same time, I had to notice progressed Jupiter to the natal Sun and Venus. Saturn was trine the Moon and made a grand trine to the Moon's North Node. This grand trine made double trine-sextile aspects to somewhat mitigate the oppositions and T-squares of the chart. In a search for positives in this chart, it could be seen that my client had all the energy he needed and a bit of self-made luck which might allow him an escape hatch. And, finally, I saw that every placement in the chart is disposed of by the mutual reception of Venus-Uranus except Mars.

There is one more thing to notice about Saturn in zero declination. Saturn is in a northern sign but here is in south declination. Kt. Boehrer talked about this in an article published in *The Other Dimension*, the newsletter of Declination SIG (Vol. 1 #4, December 1996, p. 14) where she concluded that a lot of research needs doing before we can put a cogent delineation to that sort of crossover. In that article she discussed the Clinton Inauguration Chart of Jan 20, 1997, 12:04:42 p.m. EST, Washington DC. That chart had this same Saturn crossover and also a Mars in a south sign but actually in north declination. There is always a great deal more to study and seek from astrology.

In the present chart we do not have Mars involved in that way, but a check of progressions shows that Mars continues northward until, when this man reaches age seventy-three, Mars will go out of bounds. When we began to work together, Mars had progressed to within two degrees of his natal Uranus. In his future, the client would also come upon transiting Uranus square his natal Uranus which might bring about mid-life crisis or another need for a career change. Back then his progressed Ascendant was on his second house cusp showing major changes. He suddenly met the man who became his life partner. The progressed Moon was just past his natal Ascendant and going through his first house.

But now a large question was to be solved. If these two men became partners, who's career would give way to the other. His new friend was working in Germany, here only on vacation. My client was ready to entertain the idea of a personal move to Germany. I would have put my money on both of them staying right here, which is exactly what happened. Suddenly it was also time to dry up the alcoholic intake. They found an apartment, joined AA, disappeared from saloon society. For a while the client and his friend lived five blocks from me, but neither man was ever seen in any of the neighborhood shops, only seen at one of the two neighborhood church AA meeting places.

35. Male Astrologer, 9-11-6
Saturn: 0S51
Data: February 15, 1938, 2:37 a.m. EST,
Greenville, South Carolina, 34N51, 82W24

This is the chart of an astrologer and writer who was born just two days after the previous example. Since I thought I could see him as a military man in his immediate past life experience but not so obviously in his present chart, I tried to contact him in order to gain his input on his chart. He did not reply. Astrologer and writer show up easily, Sun in the third house, mutual reception of Venus which rules the sixth and Uranus which rules the third, even if entering complimentary extra position of Venus and Uranus in their own signs give us the extra Venus in the sixth and the extra Uranus in the second close to his Mercury.

The chart has mutable angles for versatility and adaptability. Sagittarius is rising here, and while there well many be Sagittarians with military careers, this is not the sign of a team player or a competitive spirit. Sagittarius manifestations seems less a fire sign than Aries and Leo. Virgo on the career tenth is more a project engineer and would be more applicable to the military Engineering Corps or the Navy Seebees. I wanted to know more about the responsibilities of his military career. Taurus on the sixth cusp with Venus in the fourth did indicate an army career, and Mars in the twelfth seemed no more indicative. It may well be that circumstances connived to his finding himself in the army during the Korean War, deciding he could do the job as well as any other job, perhaps being sucked into the Vietnam War, and, surviving that horror, it could only be downhill to retirement. Having simply culled this chart due to Saturn in zero declination, and lacking any elucidation from the subject, the chart stays here as a conundrum. Jupiter as his chart significator is on his second house is in mutual reception to Saturn.

36. Sculptor and Bar Owner, 7-11-7
Saturn: 0S46
Data: February 16, 1938, 10:45 p.m. PST,
Crescent City, California, 42N00, 124W13

And now, born the next day after the previous example, this is the chart of a sculptor who found great success as a tavern keeper. Half Greek by heredity, this puts us in mind of the Mediterranean notion that at least you will always eat if you own a restaurant. He had previously worked for others, but suddenly the time was right to have his own place. In 1968, he found a modest hole in a wall close to the financial district, a long bar, with a not too wide passage between bar stools and a row of booths. And he found a partner who would work with him as bartender. They hired a cook and a waitress. Although the bar immediately drew the three martini luncheon group, it also served a hearty menu of excellent quality. There were always lines of people waiting to actually eat, and the place was always crowded at cocktail time. It opened just before lunch time and closed at nine in the evening, thus staying open for a long cocktail hour.

The success of this place was phenomenal. Where there was a mixed crowd for luncheon, in the late afternoon the clientele was almost exclusively male only. The latter circumstance caused him to cringe, he found himself in no position to argue with success. All he had wanted was a business he could handle single-handedly. What he did not want was a gay bar. Yet, in two years, it was evident a larger place was needed, and a location around the corner and a block away was found. The new

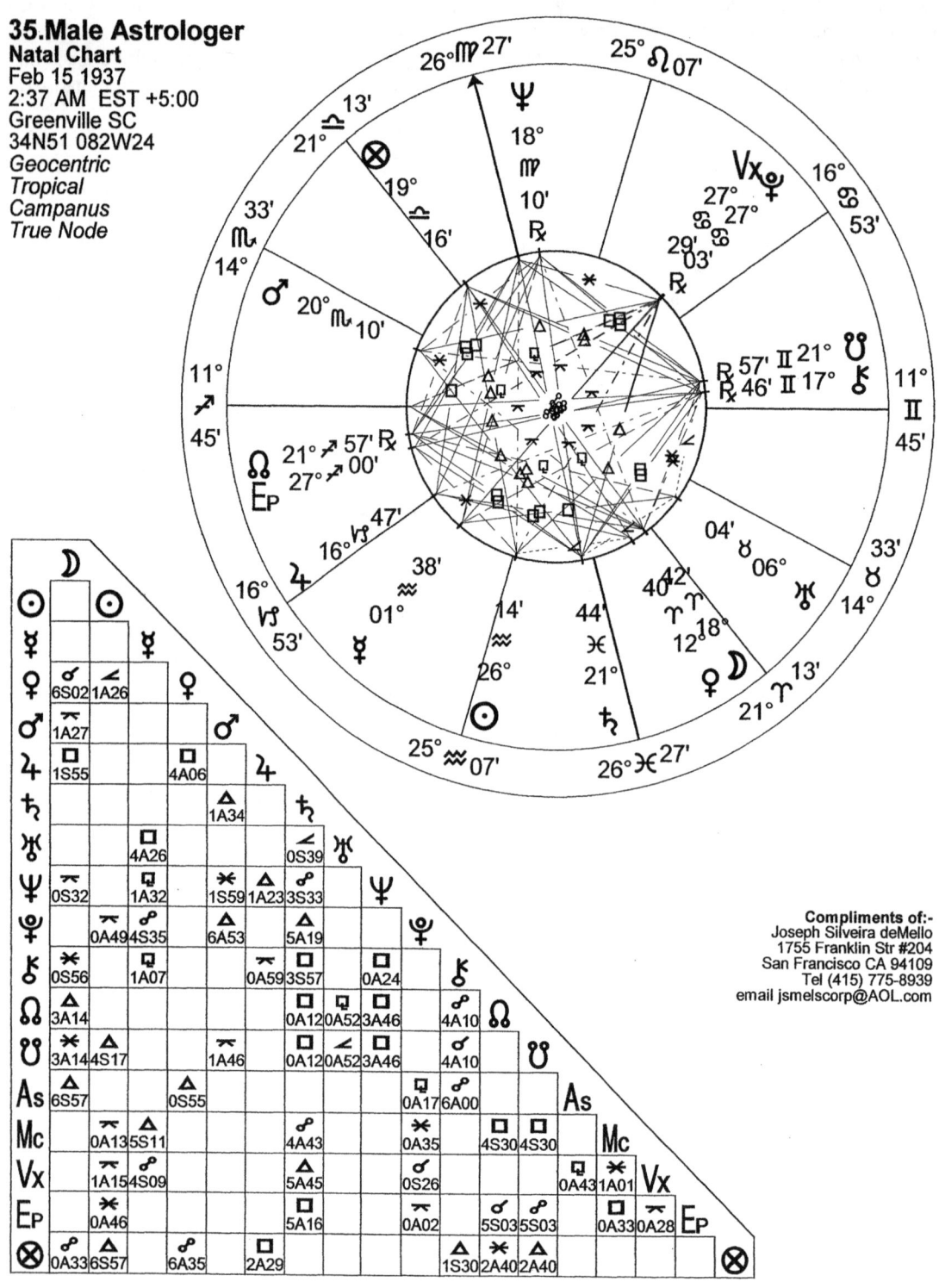

35. Male Astrologer
Natal Chart
Feb 15 1937
2:37 AM EST +5:00
Greenville SC
34N51 082W24
Geocentric
Tropical
Campanus
True Node

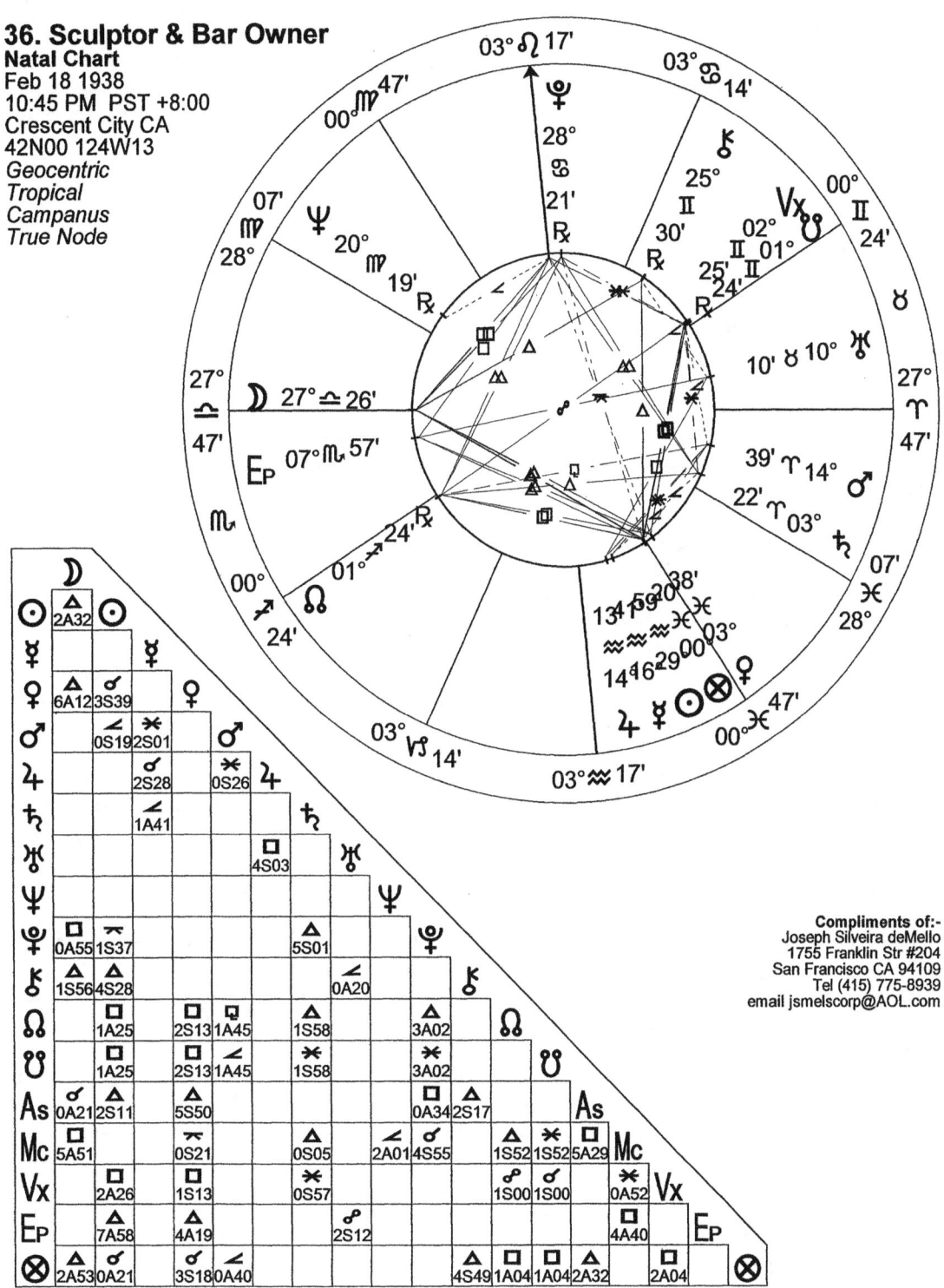

place had two huge rooms, the front one with three rows of booths, a good sized kitchen behind it, and, to the right of the kitchen, another big room with tables and its own bar. The original two partners took on two more partners to man the bar in the back room. Of course, pretty soon, more waiters were hired, and a larger kitchen staff. Over one weekend the move was accomplished and the customers followed to the new premises and quadrupled in numbers. The business expanded to occupy the increased space and was soon as overcrowded as the original. A favored few learned how to enter and exit by kitchen door.

Suddenly it was all wrong. From a small manageable business it had grown to where all the partners not only had to work one daily long shift but all had management chores, schedules, ordering, bookkeeping, banking. What had started as a simple idea in 1968, was now too much. Our subject had wanted something to tide him over a series of sculpture projects, and now he had little time for his studio. Our subject was the first to put up his partnership for sale and was out of there.

I was an early luncheon regular, and as an astrology student, eager to do charts on anyone who crossed my path, I soon had the charts of all the partners and key personnel and expanded my files to the new place of business. Soon after the move to the new premises, this subject approached me to do a chart for one of the luncheon regulars who was a longtime friend but whom I knew only by sight. It was to be a birthday gift. I did the chart and one of the things I said was that, if this man was not a doctor, he had missed his vocation. This line got me instant success when the mystery guest turned out to be a doctor. More clients flowed to me. One Christmas our sculptor made and passed out to special customers small wooden trolls, and I still have mine. Just over age forty, after he sold out, he never returning to the place. Years later, he bought another saloon in the middle of the commuter path but away from the financial district, and he still operates that place. He was a well built man of only middle height, a youthful unlined appearance but with advanced early hair loss.

This is a nocturnal chart calling for primary use of old rulers. Libra rising gives us chart significator Venus in Pisces. Mars disposes of all. Venus is too close to the Sun (which I do not regard as favorable, for ego dominates affections). Of course this Sun and Venus as well as Fortune on his fifth cusp speak for a prime interest in creativity, and then Pisces rules both the fifth and sixth houses ruled by Jupiter. This also speaks for his restaurant success. The Sun is in the final degrees of Aquarius, brings Pisces very much into the picture as a dominant force in this chart. The Moon is in Libra in the twelfth house, and very little was known of his private or emotional life, and he never spoke of his sculpture projects. Mars in the sixth house and strong in Aries is well ahead of Saturn. While Mars is dignified in Aries, Saturn is in fall there. Saturn is in a Northern sign but in a Southern declination. Mars establishes a strong work ethic, and Saturn speaks for more measured a pace. Bear in mind that Saturn rules the Aquarian planets of which Mars disposes. Note that the grand trine is in fire to the Midheaven but that Pluto must be considered part of this trine though it is out of element by being in Cancer. He conveyed the easy image of the affable tavern keeper who was friend and philosopher to all his clientele.

An interesting thing about this chart is the number of semi-square aspects which lend friction to the chart. While it has trines and squares and sextiles, the only real opposition is between Uranus and the East Point (intercepted), and there are no T-squares. It is also interesting to see which of his aspects are separating and which are applying. Pluto is highest planet in the chart with a mixed bag of aspects including a quincunx the Sun. Another interesting things is the North Node in the second house ruled by Jupiter with the South node in the eighth house. Bear in mind that a full time sculptor has long periods between cash flow, the tavern keeper or restaurateur has a day to day cash flow. With this nodal axis, it was his idea and direction which made the money which greatly benefited others.

The quirky thing about this man and his Libra rising chart is that Libras want and need people around them. While he enjoyed the presence of clientele, he was also a bit reticent though not quite formal or distant. Uranus is in the seventh house which says that his people must be different, unusual or non-conventional, perhaps even gay.

37. Restaurateur, 9-12-10
Saturn: 0S34
Data: February 21, 1938, 3:36 a.m. MST,
Great Falls Montana, 47N30, 111W17

Now, five days later than the previous example, we have another restaurateur born into an Italian restaurant family, and there are many such families in San Francisco. From early youth, this man was involved in all phases of running a family style Italian eating place. Italian families are often so large that inheritance of any family business can hardly provide for all sons in the family, and some sons have to go further afield. By the time I met this man in the spring if 1974, he was working in restaurant management, relegated to a job done behind the scenes, and, even though he had just been promoted, he was not exactly happy with his career position. Also at the same time, he was having problems with growths which proved not to be malignant cancers but were, nevertheless, the products of virus. This brush with thoughts of his own mortality had a significant impact on him, forced him to think of how much lifetime remained for him to attain significant career goals, the chief of which was to own and operate his own place. It is every man's dream.

It was in February 1976 that he asked me about making changes. His progressions for 1974 showed Saturn and Sun were then in 8 and 9 degrees of Aries, while his progressed Moon was in the final degree of Pisces headed to conjunctions with natal Saturn and Mars. With all this action in his natal third house, it was the right time for him to be thinking of those things, but not the right time to make a move or change. Saturn then

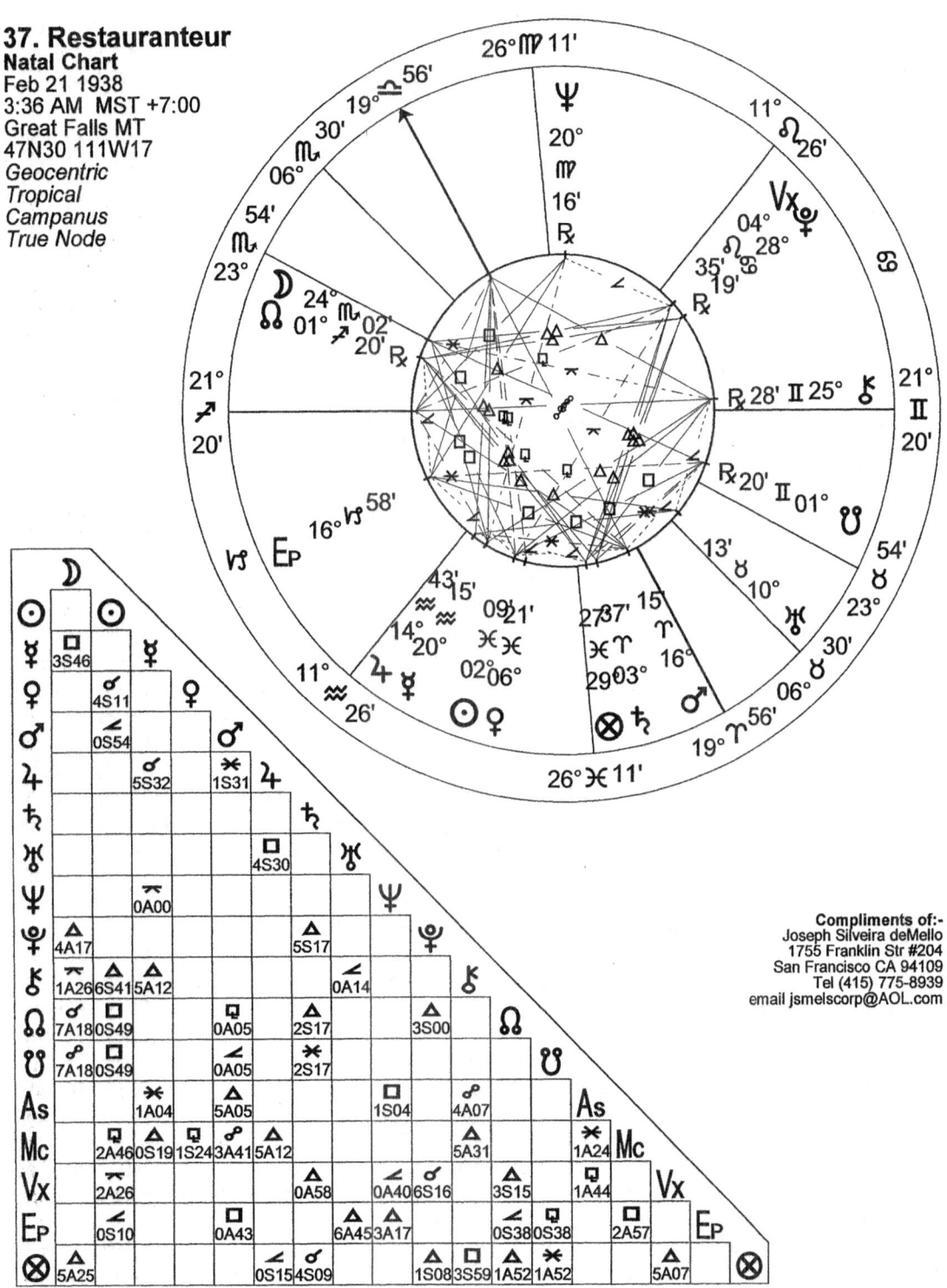

37. Restauranteur
Natal Chart
Feb 21 1938
3:36 AM MST +7:00
Great Falls MT
47N30 111W17
Geocentric
Tropical
Campanus
True Node

was transiting retrograde over his natal Pluto in his seventh house, and I made it a point to discuss this and subsequent Saturn movement in my reading for him. Obviously when a client asks if the present is the right time and you tell him it is not, it is incumbent that you point out when times will be more favorable as well as discussing thoroughly ways in which the intervening time should best be spent. But that day in February, the question had been posed as a horary question, and that horary chart was much less favorable than his natal chart. I wanted him to wait until after his progressed Moon was with his progressed Sun, and I wanted transiting Saturn to get from the conjunction to his natal Pluto.

38. Kitchen Designer, 2-12-9
Saturn: 0S31
Data: February 22, 1938, 10:30 a.m. EST,
Havana, Cuba, 23N08, 82W24

In 1982, a neighbor down the hall moved around the corner, and a visit to his new place brought about the meeting of two of his new neighbors, both Cuban refugees, very interested in astrology, who became clients. Both had interesting charts, but this is the chart of the only one of them with Saturn at zero declination, a kitchen designer who had done wonders with the 1920s kitchens common to most San Francisco apartments. When I studied architecture, I took a long interest in kitchen design and have two other clients in the same field. None of those other men were homosexual, but this man and his Cuban neighbor both informed me that they had tested HIV positive and were potential AIDS patients. In 1982, the AIDS epidemic was just being noticed. At the hospital I had seen x-rays of AIDS patients. I was eager to study their charts even though I then had no idea of where to begin except that it should be with Pluto or Mars or Scorpio. Uranus and Neptune were then transiting in early and late Sagittarius (with Uranus retrograding over his North Node), and Mars and Saturn were in Libra. I was rather taken by Mars in the twelfth exactly opposite his Vertex and felt this might have some significance, not to mention Pluto on the IC of the chart and out of bounds. It was to be fifteen years before I learned about the role of the quindecile to the IC, and this chart has Jupiter and Fortune in that position. But in 1982, when doctors were treading gingerly and quite unsure, so was I. The progressions from 1982 through the following fifteen months did not bode well, the Moon progression from Cancer into Leo. There simply was not much reassurance with which to placate a client. He was interested in knowing how long he could pursue his career unimpaired by temporary indispositions. He did not ask how long he would live but wanted to so order his projects around potential bad spells. Hispanics have a different view of death which is also a bit casual. I can report that the kitchen designer was to live fourteen years after his condition was discovered, while his countryman and neighbor, a choirmaster, lived for only eleven years after our initial meeting.

So, sharing an interest in his career, I got a first hand look into how he worked. Jobs in various stages occupied side tables in his studio, collections of photographs, drawings, plans of electrical and plumbing layouts, as well as renderings of how jobs would look when completed. The detail amazed me as I examined his work, and when I did his chart, I was still surprised to find Virgo ruling his sixth house, and with Capricorn on the tenth, a self-employed career was indicated. With Mars in the twelfth, working behind the scenes. With Moon in Sagittarius, coming off as a consultant, all part of his stock in trade, his approach to clients. Saturn in the twelfth usually makes a success no matter how many obstacles. The Sun and Venus in the eleventh house revealed itself I learned that he was extensively involved in the local community of Cuban immigrants. This man had a quite sensibility, great artistry and an entirely professional approach.

39. Astrologer and Pilot, 8-12-11
Saturn: 0S12
Data: February 28, 1938, 11:45 p.m. EST,
12 miles west of Uhrichsville, Ohio, 40N24, 81W34

This is the chart of a male astrologer and writer in *Mercury Hour*, from data he uses for himself, via the files of Don Borkowski. He is also a commercial airline pilot. The question here might be how well a Pisces Sun would fit with Scorpio rising and Moon in Aquarius. Scorpio rising could only help, and again a nocturnal chart going with the old rulers end right up against Saturn and Mars in Aries. There is that dread fifth house Saturn whose parents demand more and yet more from him, and he will do the same toward any of his offspring. How should we worry about an airline pilot who has Pluto in his ninth house? We should also carry the nocturnal rulerships through all the chart houses. Mars in Aries in the sixth, shows a solid work ethic. Uranus, planet of astrology, in the sixth would say astrology is a service he performs. However, his primary concerns probably involve fourth house things. See the measured distances from Jupiter through Venus. Expect this man to be more a basic Scorpio rising, who is a big believer and would like to be seen as knowing everything. Privacy is no issue since most placements are at the bottom of the chart. He could use astrology to get to know other people really well.

Where some might curl their lips over Scorpio rising, being myself a Scorpio Sun, I would probably like this man if I knew him, since Scorpios always like other Scorpios, Additionally we would sure be friends with his Sun falling in my eleventh, and he is a person from a past life with me since my Sun falls in his twelfth. On the other hand, my Saturn falls on his Ascendant, so I should not give him astrological advice. We might be sure to argue and point. You've read what a fuss I make over planets too close to the Sun. I don't think I have mentioned that my boundary for this is usually five degrees, and in this chart neither Mercury nor Venus are that close to the Sun. And we should still consider that Mercury is in mutual reception with Neptune. The courtesy Neptune put in Pisces lands at the midpoint of natal Mercury-Saturn. A quick look at Ebertin's *The Combination of Stellar Influences* gives us a definition which, in part

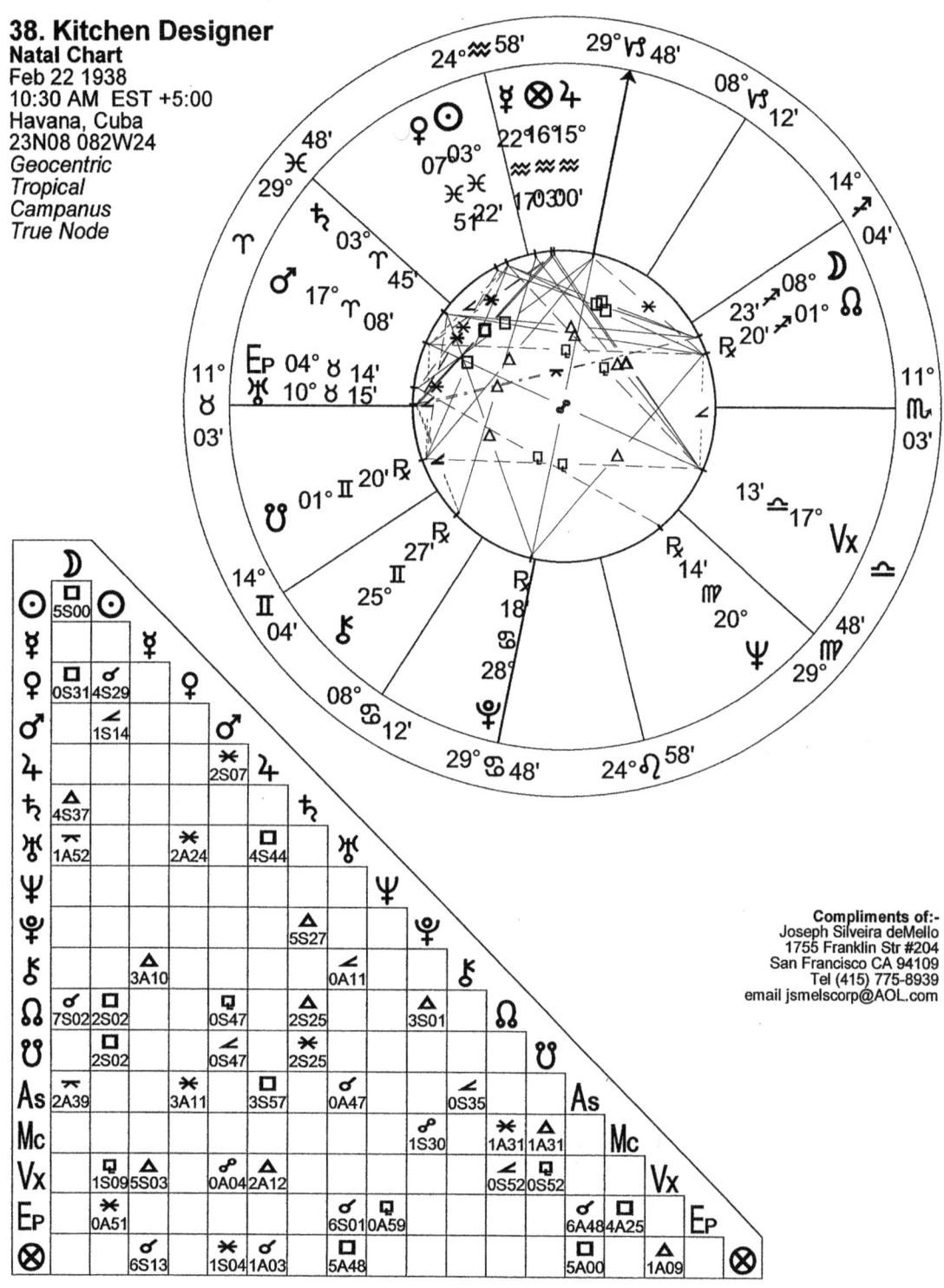

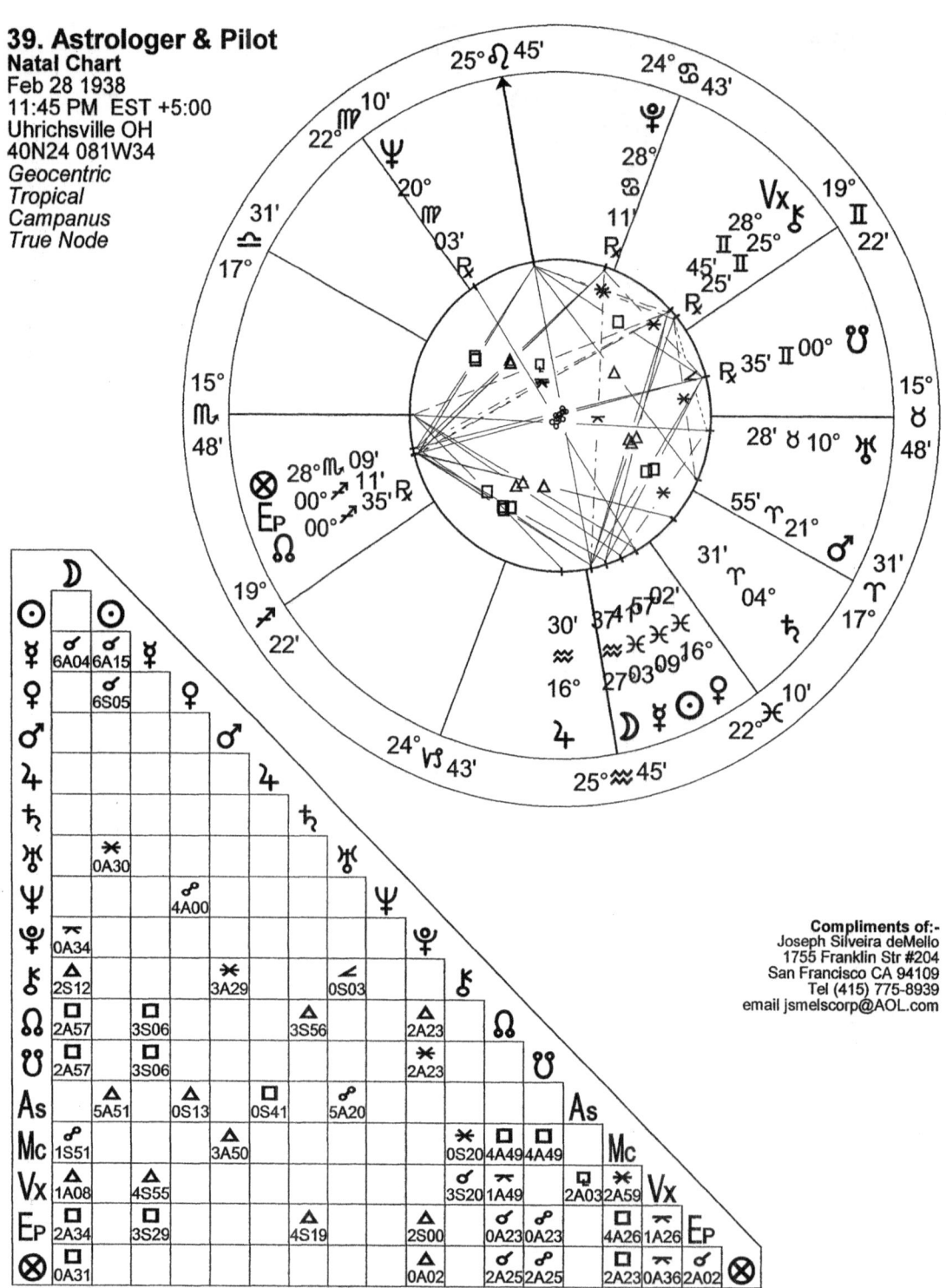

39. Astrologer & Pilot
Natal Chart
Feb 28 1938
11:45 PM EST +5:00
Uhrichsville OH
40N24 081W34
Geocentric
Tropical
Campanus
True Node

Compliments of:-
Joseph Silveira deMello
1755 Franklin Str #204
San Francisco CA 94109
Tel (415) 775-8939
email jsmelscorp@AOL.com

reads "a journey by air or sea, the longing for far-distant places" which certainly bends to the occupation of airline pilot. I have to smile in wonder how I ever came to look that up.

The next two charts are of two men born seven hours apart in the same city, Chicago. Of course neither of them knew the other. It does, however, give us the opportunity to look at the sameness and difference of two close charts.

40. Chef, 11-12-2
Saturn: 0N03
Data: March 6, 1938, 4:50 a.m. CST,
Chicago, Illinois, 41N52, 87W39

The first of these belongs to a chef who briefly worked in a favorite French restaurant I frequented. The chart has Aquarius rising, the sign of the person who always knows exactly what is best for everyone else but not for himself. His Sun may be sensitive in Pisces, but the Aquarian Ascendant is going to win out in every exigency. I dislike describing Pisces as sensitive. The Pisces sensitivity is selective, parceled out differently by each Pisces, always sensitive to himself, much less sensitive to the desires or needs of others. He fairly dripped sensitivity every chance he got. This is always a judgment call, and this Pisces is aided by being ruled by Jupiter in the first house, does not make him big or large, but underlines Aquarius rising. He was fussy and busy and careless and self-involved and loved to hear himself talk. Bear in mind that the three Pisces planets are fenced off in interception, unreachable by mere mortals (all the rest of us).

The restaurant where he worked was one of the first neighborhood French country cuisine gems, and of a fine reputation. While there was a hidden large kitchen, all finishing was done in a raised open kitchen visible from every table. If he was busy chatting, the food in his oven could be burning, smelled by the patrons but not by him. And Pisces has the world's own devil of a sense of smell. Whatever this man was doing was far more important than the job he was supposed to be doing. Going with Aquarius rising, he was a star, totally self-absorbed, striving to be original, and the world should only bow with respect. During the course of his tenure he managed to pervert the classic recipes of the French country cuisine to the Slavic flavors of his mother's kitchen. That this was inappropriate cut no ice with him. Criticism never quite got through.

The son of Czech immigrants, he originally studied for the ballet. So much time had been devoted to ballet that he was a blank on many things others would have learned in early schooling. It was never told why he abandoned the ballet, but he was tall and ungainly and probably could not keep to the basic steps of classical ballet, interposing his own notions of how he would dance. But his mother had seen to it that he learned to cook, and he liked cooking. But you do see Pluto in his sixth. He was obviously homosexual in attitudes and demeanor but that is not a problem in San Francisco. It was important to him that he make a lot of money, and he knew no reason why he could not make money at an occupation at which he claimed he felt so at home. He was quite irate and heavily put upon when he was dismissed, unable to understand why his services were no longer required.

41. Barman, 4-12-2
Saturn: 0N04
Data: March 6, 1938, 11:47 a.m. CST,
Chicago, Illinois, 41N52, 87W39

The second of these charts is of a man born seven hours later in the same city. These men as different as the night the day. While they were both homosexual, this man was handsome, well formed, understated and unpretentious and had good manners. I would never have brought them together. They would have disliked each other at first sight. The latter was briefly a bartender at a Nob Hill social club and bar. He fit well into the philosophy of the club operation. Yet, in the preparation of these remarks, I checked around to see if anybody knew what had become of him, and he is not remembered by either former coworkers or clientele. When the club was sold, not wishing to work for the new owners, he left San Francisco for Los Angeles.

I am sure you will see this as the better of the two charts. We still have the Sun too close to Mercury, but here it is in the tenth house. The Mercury and Neptune are in mutual reception. Mars in Aries is now in the eleventh house and he was community oriented and made good money working as a bartender, an occupation fitting both Midheaven and his Scorpio sixth house. His Moon is in Taurus on Uranus in the eleventh house. I remember that the moment he stepped behind the bar and began to be introduced to the clientele, he was an instant success. He had worked in other San Francisco bars before being hired in this club, and his North Node in the sixth house gives him a service-work intake that made it easy for him to be an employee. To find him unremembered rather underlines the fact that people are often callous of those who serve them.

Give some thought about these two examples of men who moved west from their natal place and form your own notions of whether this was or was not a good idea for them. Would they have done better to live in a location that would take their Neptunes out of angular houses? Astrologers have to learn that changing locations may for a few months of settling in go with a relocation chart, but, once acclimated, it is still the natal chart for natal place to which we always return.

42. Male Author, 10-1-10
Saturn: 0N56
Data: March 24, 1938, 2:06 a.m. PST,
Los Angeles, California, 34N03, 118W04

Having had one pair of same day charts, here is another pair, two men also unknown to each other. The first is the chart of a former neighbor and author who has never published under his own name. This man rises daily, goes to his desk, and works at his craft in a businesslike manner with which no other activity is allowed to interfere. There is no waiting around for inspiration to show up. His output consists of erotic male pornography. There was little in his deportment that was homo-

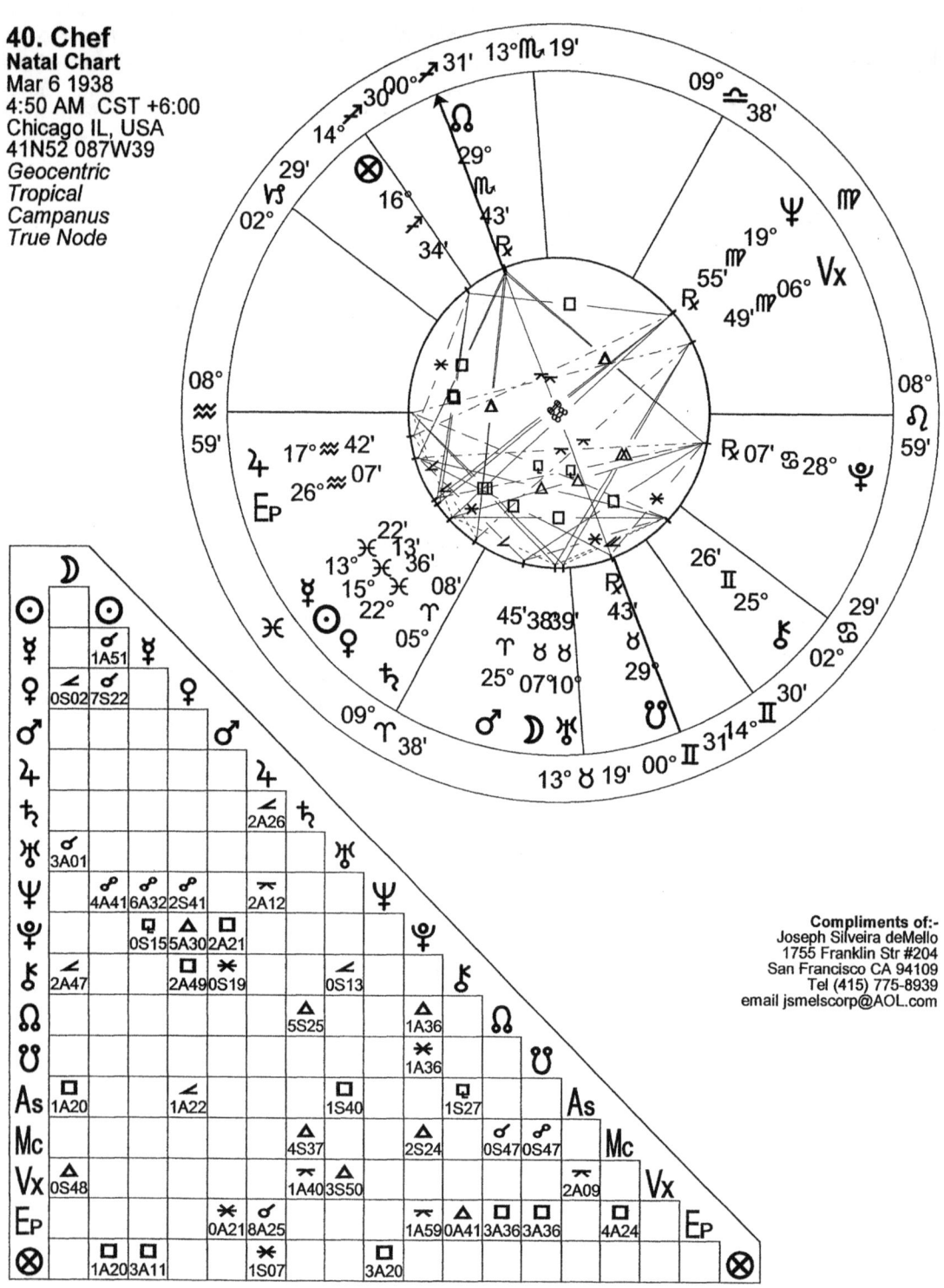

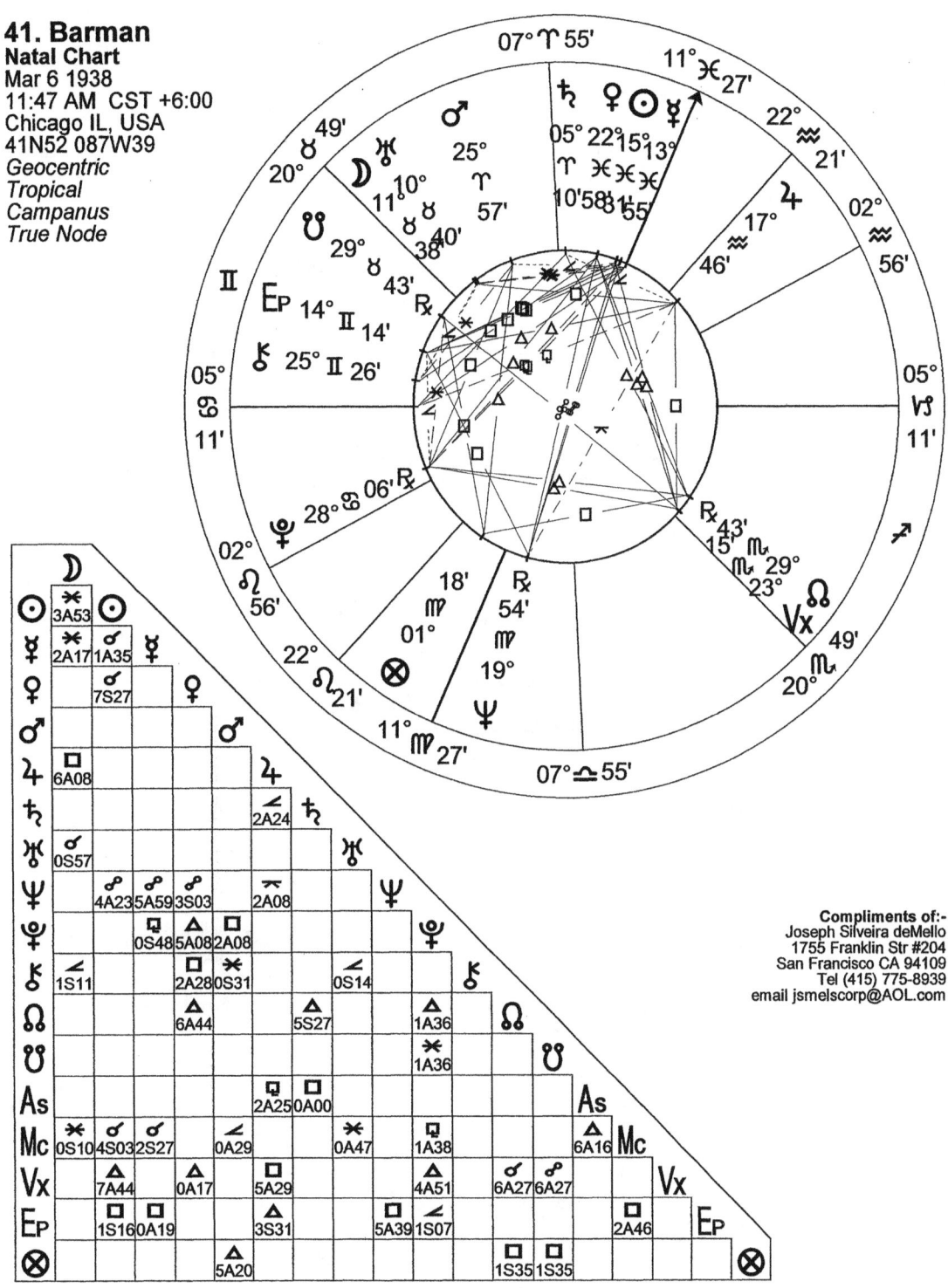

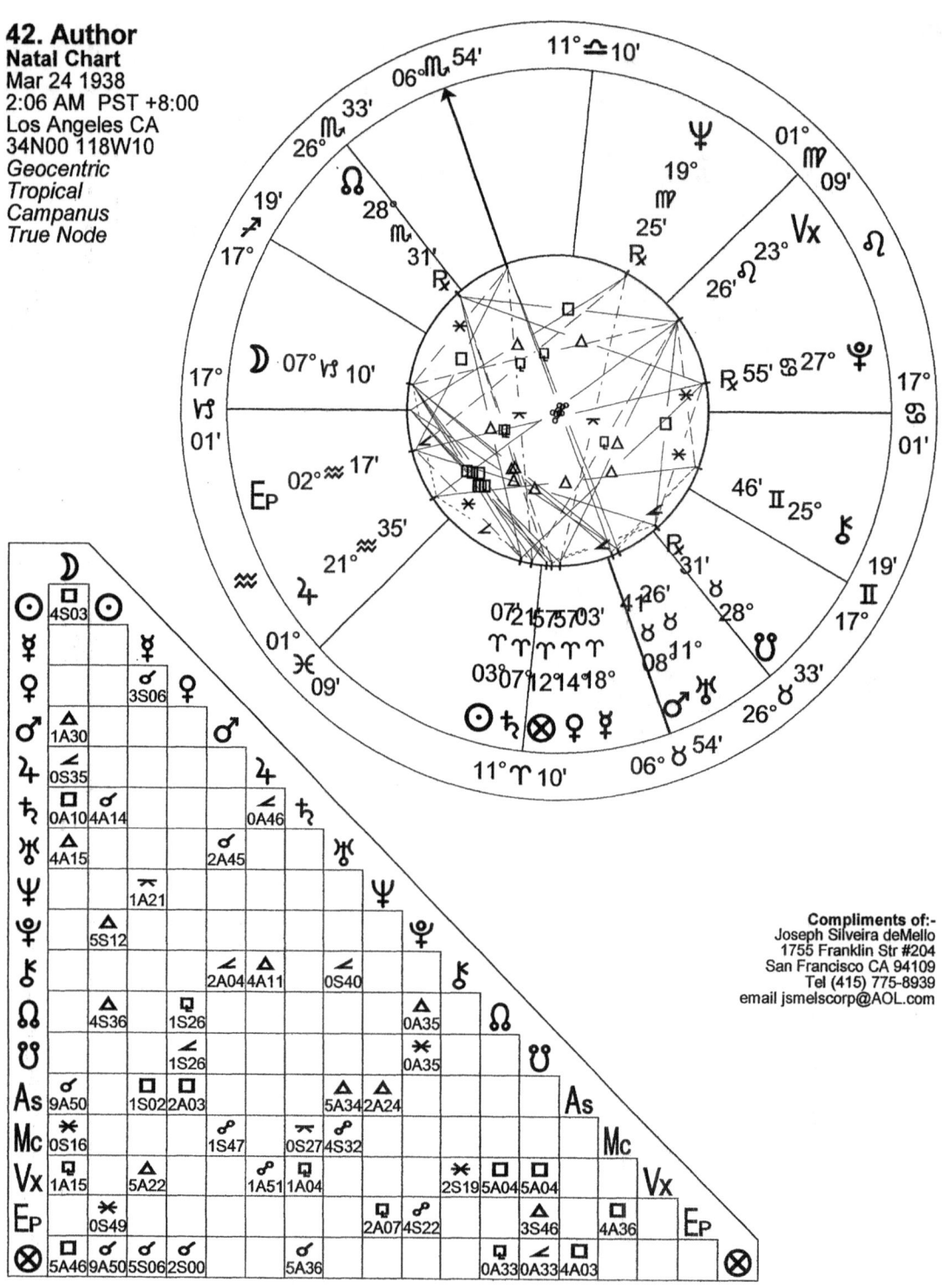

42. Author
Natal Chart
Mar 24 1938
2:06 AM PST +8:00
Los Angeles CA
34N00 118W10
Geocentric
Tropical
Campanus
True Node

sexual. He had a neutral grave dignity as might be expected of Capricorn rising. He is successful as a writer in that he supports himself entirely by his craft. Of course, a Capricorn rising is going to be most happy when self-employed, and anyone with Sun in second is going to be interested in making money. Saturn is chart significator, rather too close to his Sun (usually indicative of a problem father) is too close to his Sun in an Aries stellium, and Venus and Mars are in mutual reception. In this nocturnal chart, Jupiter is behind one of the houses it rules, while Venus is similarly set, a condition that gives these planets a twelfth house flavor. Writing is indicated by a fully packed third house and Gemini on the fifth, while the subject matter is indicated by tenth and eleventh houses as well as by some planetary aspects. The Capricorn Moon which usually provides for a life of many obstacles, here only compliments the rising sign. He very much knows who he is, is in touch with himself as he is. Mars teamed with Uranus in the fourth of home is a natural for churning out erotica at home.

Although to all intents and purposes this man's image was staid and quiet, he was not as conservative as he appeared. But with Saturn scorched by proximity to the Sun and Saturn in fall in Aries, there was little that could stop him. The Aries Sun is exalted and powerful, probably more powerful than his Mars. He does not lack in ego, but he did go from a ribald humor to a total lack of it more often than expected. You might not wish to have this man as a friend, but as an astrologer, you can see he has a very interesting chart. The combination of Capricorn and Aries, square each other, and therefore energizing each other is just a start in analyzing this chart. Parse now the four planet stellium. Like so many of these examples, nothing interferes with what he wants to do.

If you get the sense that this man is in some sort of rebellion against his past, you would not be in error. The well known Mars conjunct Uranus of extreme high energy and tenseness, somewhat close to breaking point all the time, and not very tolerant of others, particularly seeing others as a danger to himself. Although opposite his Midheaven, Mars and Uranus are trine the Moon and semi-square Chiron. Sexuality is not absent from this chart, nor is it absent in himself. He is rather better looking that the usual Capricorn and Aries. The Capricorn sobriety and the Capricorn inability to give or receive compliments, meld with the Capricorn and Aries capability for self-absorption. But on the rare occasions when he chooses to smile, his smile does light up the room. For him there are things more important than the having of a sense of humor.

43. Remittance Man, 2-1-10
Saturn: 0N56
Data: March 24, 1938, 8:47 a.m. CST,
Tulsa Oklahoma, 36N10, 95W55

Shortly after moving from living next door neighbor to the previous example, I took a break and went to check the mail. Out of the building next door rushed a young man who immediately started talking to me as if we had been having a conversation which had been briefly interrupted. Yet we had never met. He found I was an astrologer, gave me his data, and I found I had sort of swapped neighbors and now had a manic-compulsive for a neighbor. Son of an Oklahoma oilman, he was paid to live anywhere as long as it was not in his city or state of birth. His father was still alive, and his mother, usually said to be dead, was nevertheless a long time patient at a psychiatric hospital in the East. This man had never worked in his life. He was well educated at Princeton and the University of California-Berkeley. I was not surprised that he was under regular psychiatric therapy. Added to all this was his flagrant homosexuality, very defiantly out of the closet. He had all the earmarks of a burnt out case, although he had no history of drug use, and his alcoholism was confined to beer drinking. Because he could not cope, his affairs were all handled by a conservator who paid all his bills, saw to his health care, kept him in pocket money. He could not cope with handling his own banking and checking account.

In the fall of 1977, he made a trip home to visit his father but returned in two days, hardly enough time to get there, have the predictable argument with his father, and fly back. On his return, he went directly into the psychiatric ward of a nearby hospital where his liver and kidneys seemed to be afflicted and there was some throat problem. Today, the throat problem, thrush, is an early symptomatic occurrence toward an active AIDS condition. In those days AIDS was not yet recognized. For the next four months I saw him between stays in the nearby hospital and convalescence at home. He snacked at home, but generally he ate all his meals out. His social life revolved around visits to his medical doctors, his psychiatrist, his AA meetings. In the Spring of 1978, not having seen him for two weeks, I asked his apartment manager of him and learned that he had died at 4:35 p.m. PST, March 17, 1978, San Francisco. This was on his death certificate. An autopsy gave his official cause of death as arteriosclerotic cardiovascular disease. It is very possible he was one of the earliest AIDS victims. But now just count the quindeciles in this chart, IC to Jupiter, Sun to Neptune, Moon to Chiron and Pluto being the most obvious. These aspects exist in his "twin" chart, but that man is not even HIV positive.

This young man was short and tubby, soft, a bit bloated, his features regular but unexceptional, his complexion somewhat sallow. He fit most classic descriptions of Taurus rising. Venus his chart significator and the Aries stellium of the previous chart (#42) are here in the long twelfth house with Mars and Uranus, and there is the Venus-Mars mutual reception. With his Sun in the twelfth house, he was definitely short on ego. His father was rich enough to support him but had no need to like him. His father's own life had fallen apart, a wife who was institutionalized most of her life, a son who, in the father's eyes, inherited his mother's deficient genes, or worse, and who would never amount to other than an embarrassment, borne out by the chart closeness of Sun-Saturn. On the other hand, surely the affairs of ten houses of this chart are channeled into the area of the subconscious, into twelfth house needs.

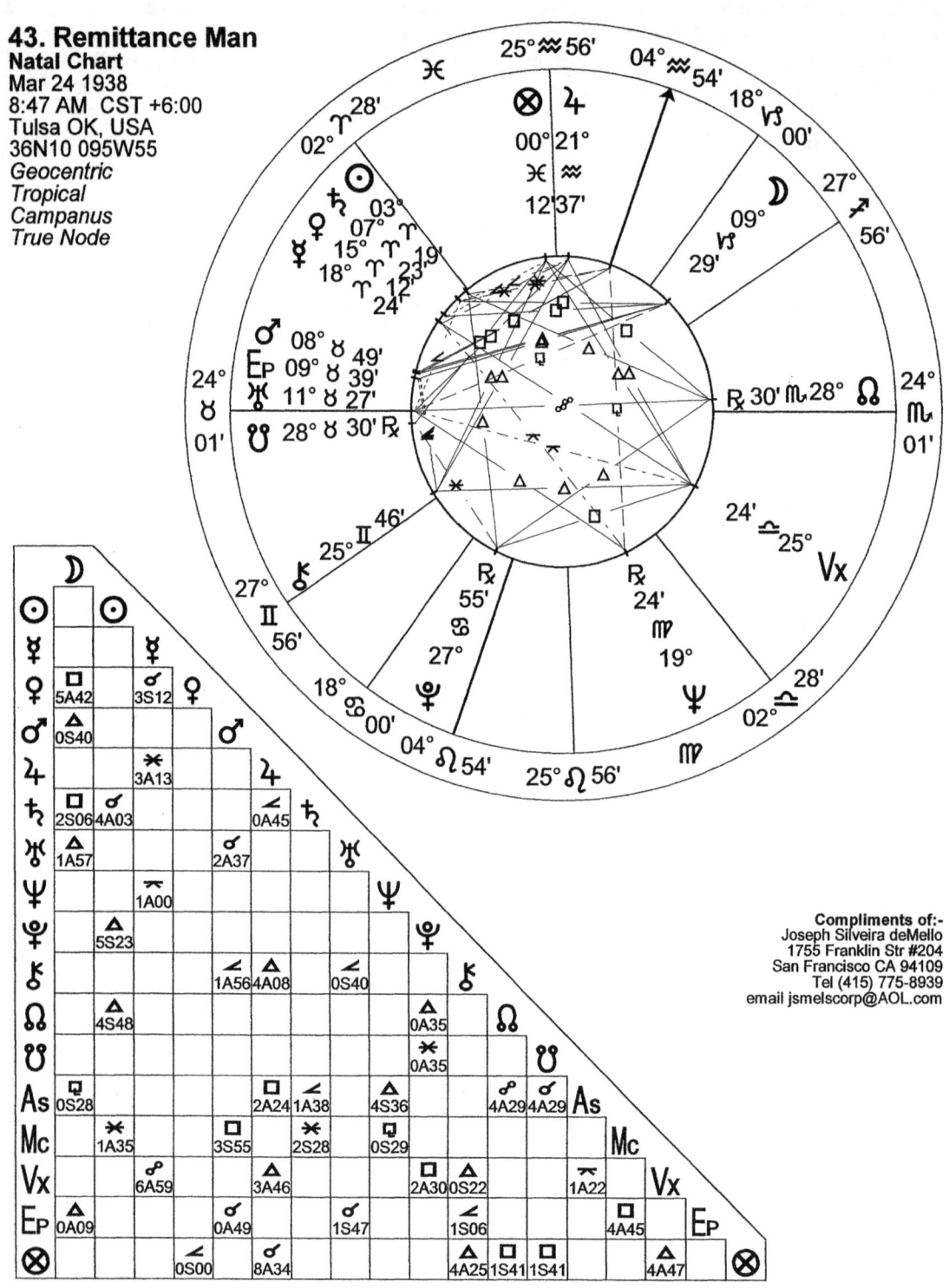

Surprisingly there is a loaded fourth quadrant which usually points to a need of objective self-knowledge. He did not tell me that his therapy was court ordered, but that it provided support he needed, being alone. I momentarily worried he might see me as a father figure, but I quickly realized he was so focused on his own father to mistake either me or his therapist with his real father. He had a great need of that man's affection. He loved his father, but it was a love that required sexual relations with his father, which his father told him was sick, sicker than his mother had been. I found it strange that his therapist could not accept this as a serious need or as a desire fantasy. In dealings with sexuality, psychiatrists tend of assume the adult figure as guilty and refuse to see predatory behavior in the children. This man could not realize that his father could not and would not cope with him. His father lived quite alone and modestly (perhaps due to the drain on his finances). From what I saw, this young man was being well provided with bromide alibis to make him more accept his condition rather than beneficially alter his thinking. Any astrology done for him would become another alibi system. Acquaintance with this man was like going from zero to sixty and back again in no time flat. My contact with the previous man was casual, and with this man I was a sounding board sympathizer. My former neighbor was reticent. This young man knew no reticence, was naively wide open and totally vulnerable.

44. Accountant, 10-6-9
Saturn: 0N48, Venus: 0N55
Data: September 8, 1951, 4:08 p.m. EDT,
Albany, New York, 42N39, 73W45

Two and a half years after I moved into my present residence, this man moved into the same building, and today he is the second most senior tenant in the building. A quiet young man of medium height and wearing rather thick eye glasses, for years we never more than greeted each other as we entered or left the building. I was aware that he took both the Wall Street Journal and the local morning paper. Much of his life seemed to involve commuting to faraway jobs rather than working as an accountant in any downtown financial office. From twenty years of coming and going, and gradually two or three minutes of conversation, we have seldom been in each other's apartments. He is a bachelor and lives alone in a Spartan and uncluttered quarters. He reads a great deal, despite which, his apartment seems to contain no books. Stores them in a closet. He is a Virgo, and, I guessed, a Capricorn rising, for he seldom smiles, but it is a smile which takes twenty years off his age. Two years ago he found some astrological references in a Greek translation of Dorotheus he was reading, and he Xeroxed those pages for me, and then gave me his birth data which confirmed the Capricorn rising.

The big surprise with this chart that has zero declination Saturn is that he also has zero declination Venus and both planets, not in aspect, are parallel. On the other hand, he has Moon way out of bounds in Sagittarius. Since he has Capricorn rising and an exalted Saturn in Libra to soften things, he has a natural talent for management but, rather than be in a large organization, he would rather work for firms where he works alone and carries responsibility for his area of expertise. He would like to know other people without being especially or intimately drawn to them. This negates the normal interpretation we would give to a crowded third quadrant. Yet his seventh house has Uranus there and Mars and Pluto are intercepted or private to him while Mercury, Venus and Sun are in a Virgo stellium in the eighth. He admits to being an alcoholic, a thought that never crossed my mind. He regularly attends a couple of AA groups. His forays into social life take place in coffee shops where people sit alone at their own tables, reading books or writing.

I was not surprised his Spartan lifestyle echoed by Virgo Sun, Capricorn rising and Sagittarian Moon, a bit surprised at a Gemini sixth house. He has the Moon in the twelfth house, and the general attitude of Sagittarius, not readily making close friends. I have long found that Sagittarius often blends well in combination with Capricorn rising. He seems to have no close or intimate friends. Where we might see Uranus in the seventh house as indicative of the presence of unconventional and quite modern people in his life, perhaps even of homosexuals as partners, simply is not brought out by his daily life. He is plain, unassuming, and private. For at least five years, he has occasionally dated a woman neighbor who lives in an apartment close to his own.

45. Barman, 9-6-2
Saturn: 0N13
Data: September 20, 1951, 1:00 p.m. EDT,
Niagara Falls, New York, 43N06, 79W03

In the late 1960s and early 1970s, I achieved some notoriety as a saloon astrologer and the writer of a Sun sign column. In the Seventies, we saw the first of the multiplex entertainment centers which franchised nationwide. It was no longer sufficient to own a bar or to own a restaurant and bar. These early multiplexes had three bars, a formal dining room, a billiards area, and a huge cabaret, all of which required a huge staff of waiters, bartenders, bar backs, swappers, bus boys, kitchen staff, entertainers, publicity people, musicians and disk jockeys, accountants and administrative staff. And all of this myriad staff was repeated in all of their branches cross country. I became involved when a former student invited me to visit the place, was quickly introduced around and found myself house astrologer of their San Francisco and Los Angeles venues.

This young man was a bartender, slender and attractive as the young usually are. He was, as were many of his co-workers, homosexual, and he was the intimate friend of one of the entertainers who was a female impersonator and singer. In 1974, less than six months after I got to know this crowd, his friend was sensationally murdered in the early morning hours in Golden Gate Park, quite far from where he worked. His friend's sister, a great favorite, wanting to talk to him seriously, had come in from the suburbs and picked him up after his last show. She was suspected but released to her

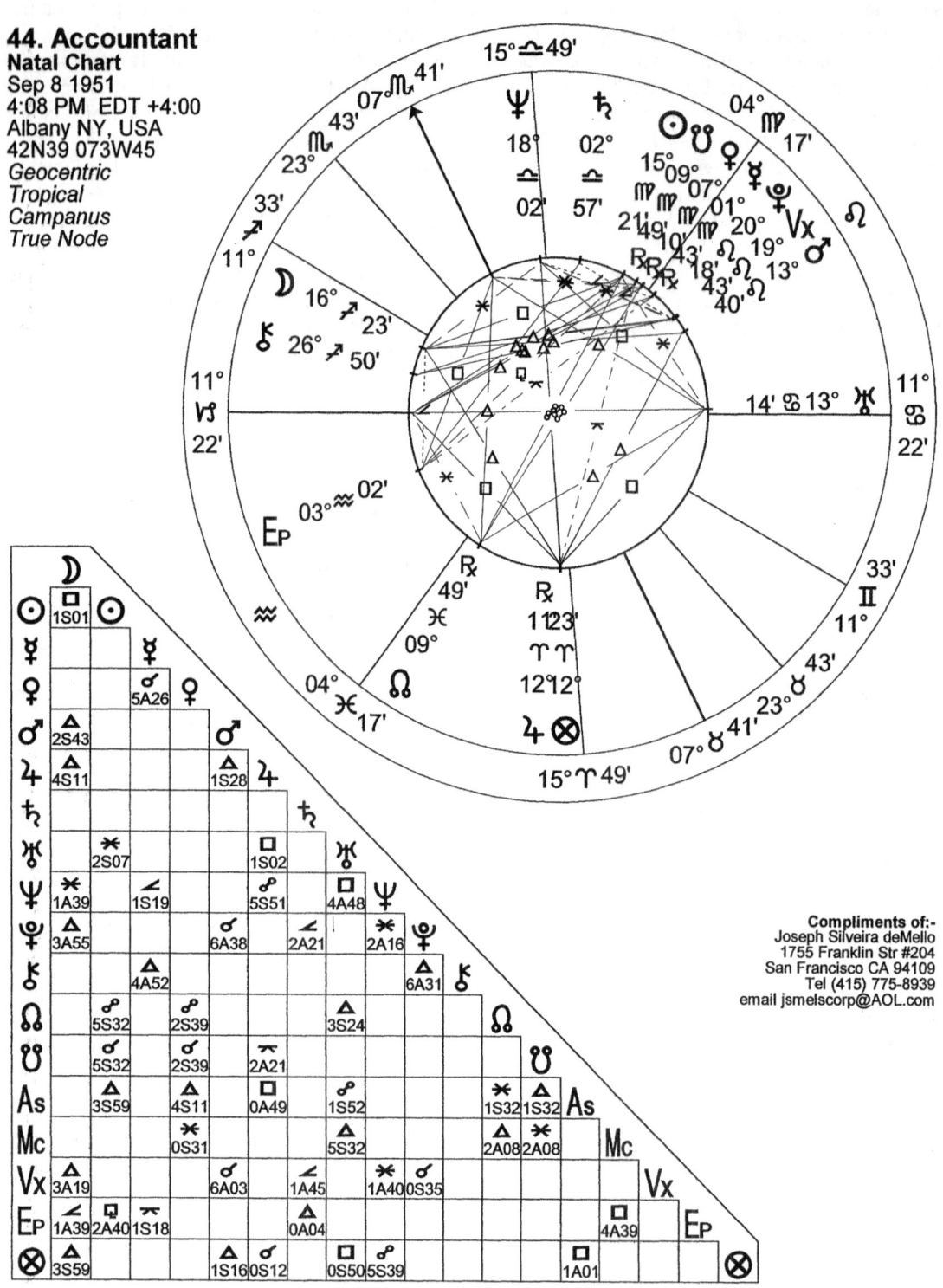

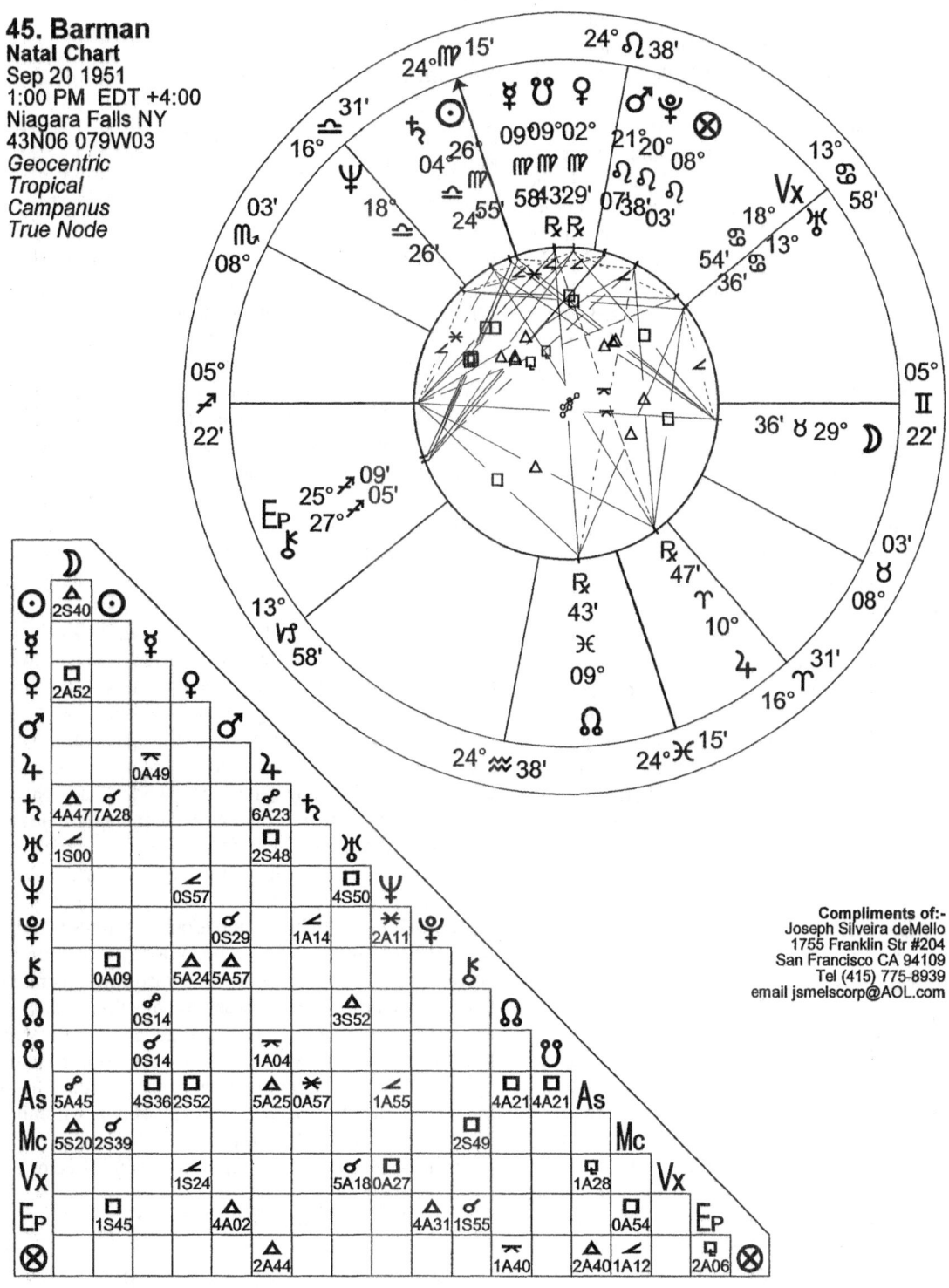

45. Barman
Natal Chart
Sep 20 1951
1:00 PM EDT +4:00
Niagara Falls NY
43N06 079W03
Geocentric
Tropical
Campanus
True Node

mother's custody. A few days later, she attacked another sister who came to visit their mother, and police and firemen responding to a fire in the home, found the hacked up and partially burned body parts of the mother. Now this favorite sister was finally adjudged to be criminally insane and hospitalized, never to be tried for either murder.

The young man of this chart received much sympathy and his employers quickly gave him a transfer to their complex in Los Angeles. He had undergone police investigation, but was found to have been working through to the morning setting up for next day.

At the time I met this young man, then just over 21, he was entirely serious and capable. The interesting thing about this chart is that he has the Moon very far out of bounds is in the final degree of Taurus, the Pleiades, which would prompt many astrologers to deduce that there would be many tears in his emotional life. The Sun is rising before Saturn, both in the tenth house. He worked nights and went to school by day. At the time of the murder of his friend, his progressed Venus was within one minute of his progressed South Node, and his progressed Moon had just gone into Aries. At the same time, his progressed Sun and Mercury were on his natal and progressed Neptune.

This is a chart with a number of problems. This Sun as highest planet in the tenth, is far from favorable, makes a square to Chiron and a trine to his late Taurus Moon. Venus is at the midpoint of the Ascendant and Moon. The Moon is in the sixth house and rules the eighth. I cannot remember what he was studying, but he was very set on obtaining a solid education. If we are looking at AIDS potentials, knowing today what we then could not have known, notice how Mercury is 15 degrees from the midheaven, how the IC has the North Node and Jupiter 15 degrees either side of it, quindecile the midheaven and Sun and then Mercury and South Node quindecile the IC and think of how progressed and transiting placements could easily fill in his tenth house. Since he disappeared from this area six years before the discovery of AIDS, I can only pause to wonder what possibly became of him.

46. Student of Hindu Guru, 8-6-3
Saturn: 0N07, Sun: 0N28
Data: September 22, 1951, 11:45 a.m. EDT,
Milford, Connecticut, 41N14, 73W04

I met this lady and her husband at a big party given by old friends interested in Hindu music. She and her husband were interested in astrology and gave me their birth data. Besides being into Hindu music, she was also a pupil of a celebrated guru. They were a very attractive young couple, she being quite beautiful. Our hostess asked me to do their horoscopes.

I was not surprised to find Scorpio rising, and a thoroughly occupied ninth house ruled by Leo. It contained Pluto, Fortune, Mars and Venus, while Mercury in Virgo was exactly on her Midheaven, and the Virgo Sun was in the tenth not far from Saturn in Libra.

When choosing charts for these samples, I noticed her Moon was far out of bounds, Saturn at zero declination, and because of the date on which she was born, her Sun was also at zero declination, parallel her Saturn. Mercury is dispositor of the chart. Another bit about this chart is that Venus is retrograde, finding sadness in what others find humorous, and humor in where most find sadness. Jupiter is also retrograde, but that is in the fifth house and rules the intercepted portion of the first house. Moon opposite Chiron forms a T-square to the Sun. I knew this young couple all too briefly.

47. Cabby/Attorney, 5-7-4
Saturn: 0S00
Data: September 25, 1951, 2:31 a.m. EST,
Hertford, North Carolina, 36N11, 76W28

I met this man through a fellow astrologer. He and this man were both taxi drivers, and I was told this man was also waiting to take and pass his bar exams. Very ambitious, not one to sit around and wait for things to happen, he was out there happening to things and gaining a special education from every situation he encountered. He was also earning a living in the easiest possible way for him. My friend insisted I take this man's birth data, saying I would find it an interesting chart. I was curious about how he would do with his bar exams, seeing from his data that he was possibly a Leo rising. Many people have to take their bar exams several times before it dawns on them that they have to stick to classical precedents. Products of liberal schools where students are encouraged to do their own thinking do not usually fair well in bar exams.

Indeed, he did turn out to be a Leo rising, but one with Pluto and Mars, which ruled his fourth house, here placed quite close to the Ascendant. Mars in the first house and in the rising sign always produces an Aries personality. His Libra Sun was too close to Saturn in the second house, ruled by and with Mercury on its cusp. Besides the fact that he cannot have had an easy childhood, I saw that the three planets in the first house tie the matters of five houses of his chart to his immediate needs. This, added to other things in this chart, usually produces a very self-centered person. The Moon is in Cancer in his twelfth house and is out of bounds by declination. But I wondered how he viewed the downtrodden and how he saw himself. Mars also rules his ninth house, which increases aggressive projection with high ambitions. Pluto on the Ascendant generally sabotages one's own personality image. His disposition seemed optimistic, but he was not laid-back, not relaxed. Due to the path of transiting Saturn, I felt success was a number of years in the future. If he is practicing law in San Francisco, he is not listed in the current telephone directory.

48. No-Show Male Client, 6-7-6
Saturn: 0S13
Data: September 29, 1951, 5:52 a.m. PDT,
San Francisco, California, 37N47, 122W26

We all have these, I suppose. I usually ask half my fee when charts are commissioned, the second half fee to be

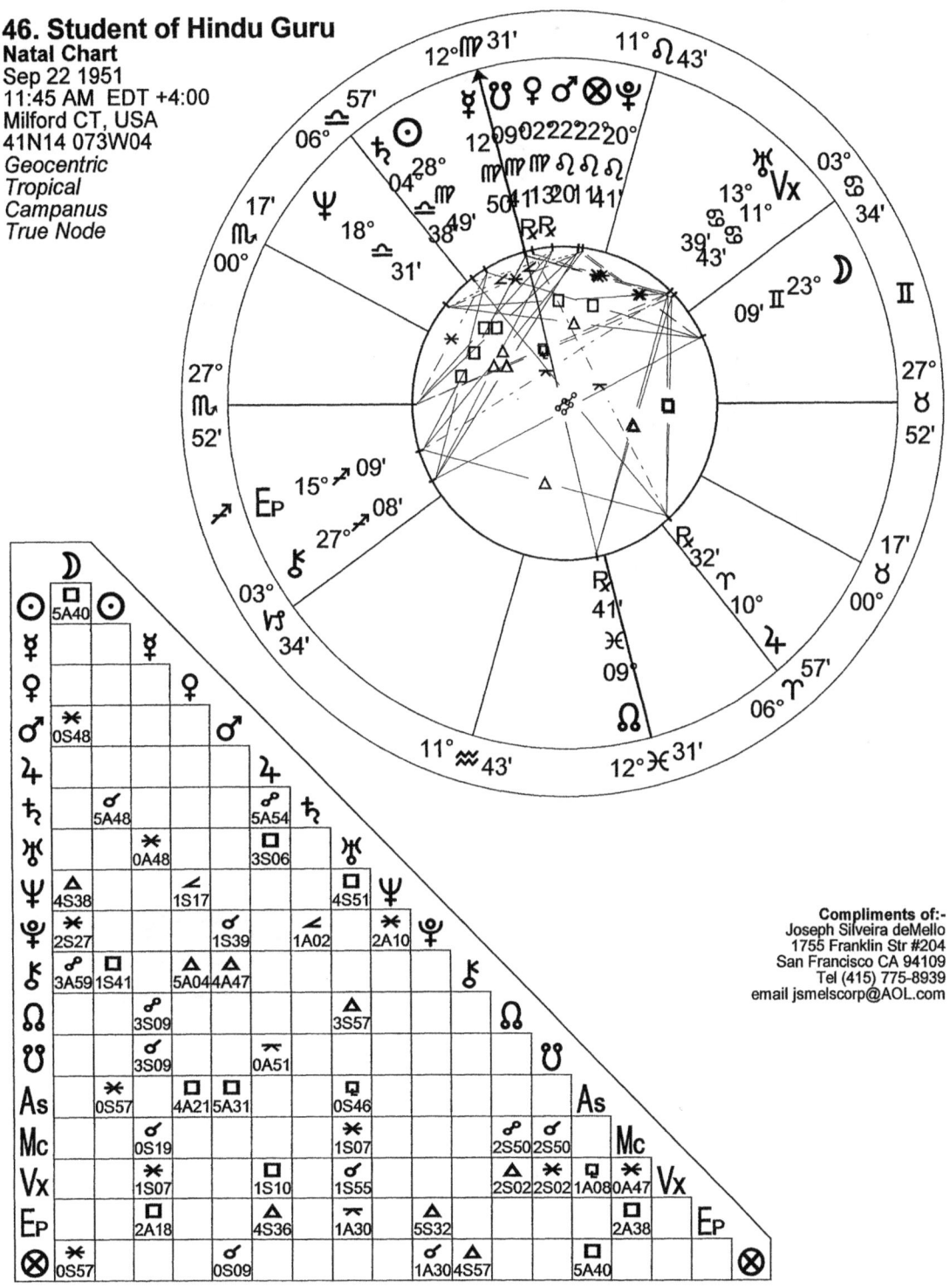

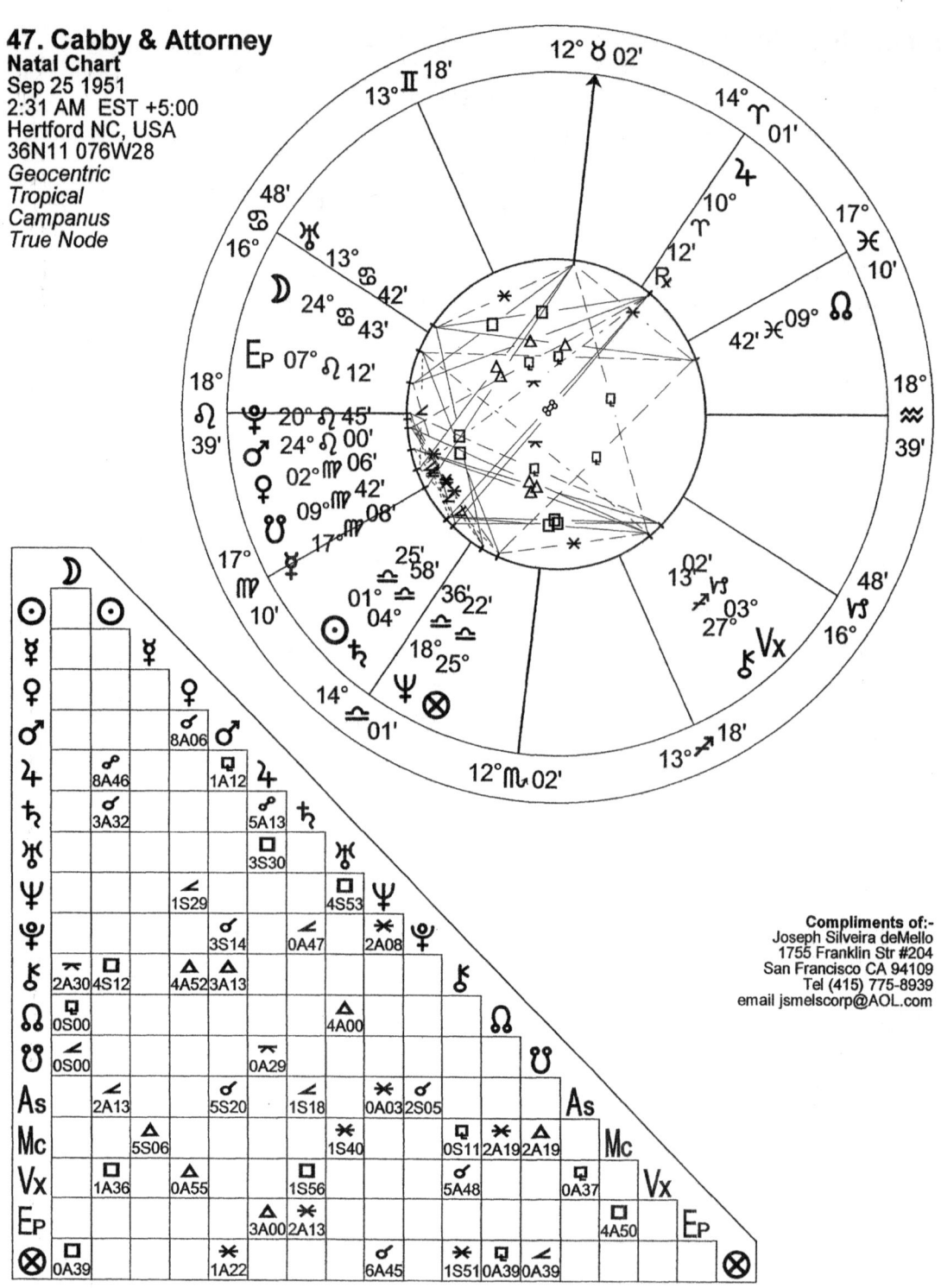

47. Cabby & Attorney
Natal Chart
Sep 25 1951
2:31 AM EST +5:00
Hertford NC, USA
36N11 076W28
Geocentric
Tropical
Campanus
True Node

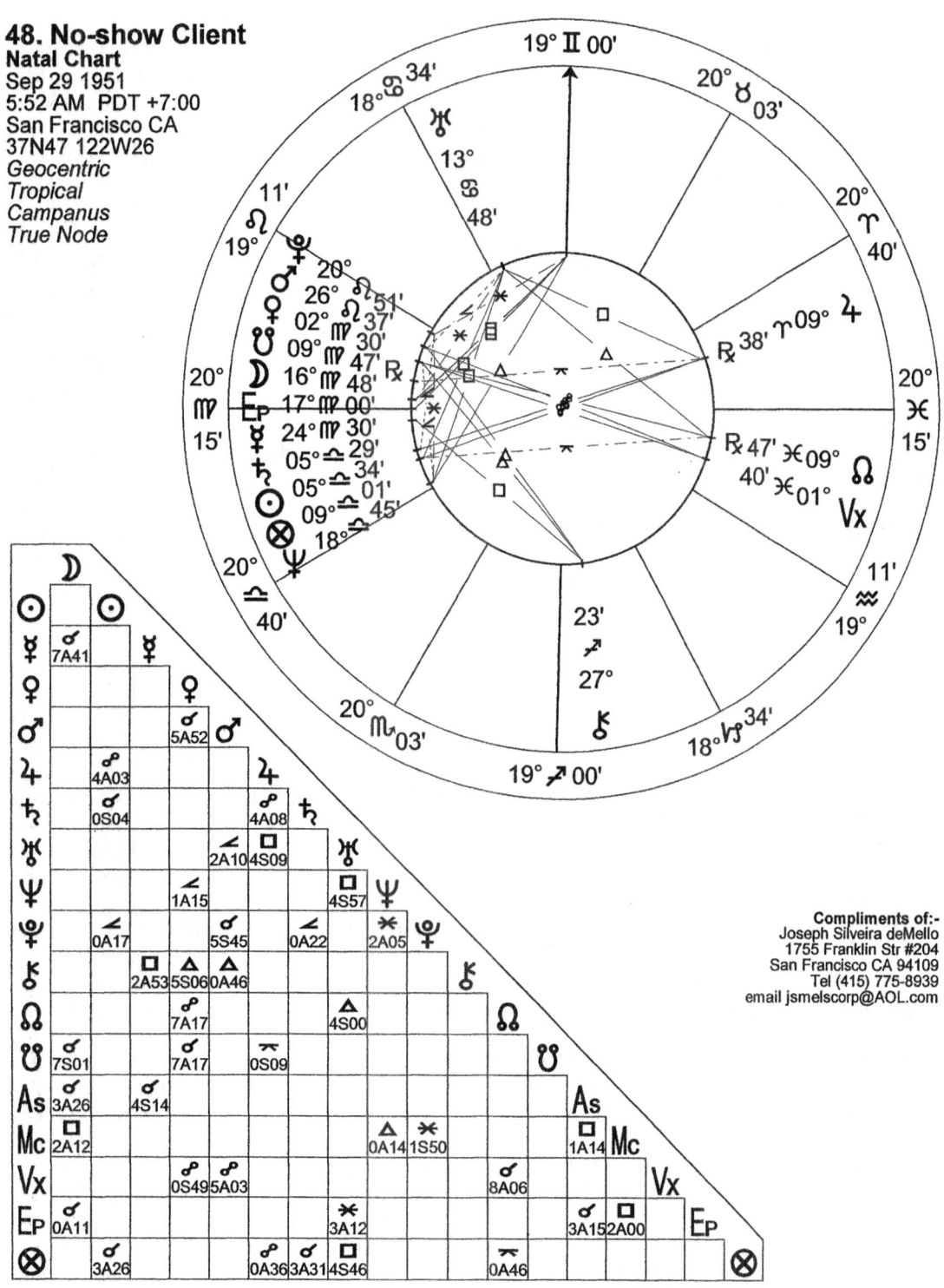

paid at the time of consultation. I this case I did not do so, and, having done the work, found myself lacking in eagerness to have this couple as clients. Although I saw him more in need than she of astrological counseling, I also felt that she was more interested in getting her own chart done, no matter how much she acted as if her fiancé was the client. She did ask about their relationship and duration. I checked the relationship and was not eager to tell them that there was not much between them that was favorable. Although I did see them after the broken appointment, I did not press to reschedule and have to deal with a negative reading and give a poor prognosis.

This is now the fourth chart at about the same time, showing a quick progression to having all those close placements in the twelfth and first houses. She initiated the contact with me, and he had sat back and listened to us. She was much in command of the situation. They had decided to marry and were shooting the works on the honeymoon. Perhaps they had tight money considerations. I saw that if she led, he would follow. His chart has Virgo rising, Sun in Libra and a Virgo Moon in the twelfth. The Sun and Saturn are exactly conjunct (cazimi) in the first house, so Saturn is the more powerful. Mars and Venus are equally close in the twelfth house and both in Virgo, Venus in fall and of no special help to Mars, but one might say, inclined to secret affairs. Mercury is dispositor of the chart, and the four planets in the first house take care of the activities of six houses of the chart processed through the subject's personal needs. But the four planets in the twelfth house take care of the activities of five houses of the chart.

49. Oil Field Worker, 11-7-10
Saturn: 0S37
Data: October 7, 1951, 3:55 p.m. CST,
Corpus Christi, Texas, 27N47, 97W24

An old friend of mine told me her son-in-law was so weird that he must have a strange chart which I might like to study. Mind you, she is not unhappy with him as husband to her daughter. He treats his wife like a princess and is totally devoted to her. He worked in the Texas oil fields and knew of no work for a he-man unless the man gets thoroughly dirty doing it. He worked four days at a time hundreds of miles from home, working days one week, nights alternating weeks. He and his wife are a happy couple though they come of different backgrounds and value systems.

His life is perfect the way it is. He has found a job that suits him just fine, and has found the ideal wife. Everything in his life is ordered, even his most ordinary routines, and he insists upon the status quo. He has a strong dislike of anything he has not previously experienced. He had a very stringent Texas upbringing on plain fare and fundamentalism. He will not eat anything that his mother did not fix for him when he was growing up. This is rather wild since he is married to a woman who is a gourmet chef, who at one time owned a restaurant in California which critics rated a four-star establishment. Many of her recipes have been published in big home and cooking magazines. From the world of cuisine, she has become very active and highly successful in Texas real estate and works only because she cannot sit idly around her spacious home. Returned from the oil fields, he now manages all her financial affairs.

His Capricorn Moon, far from the easiest of Moon signs, is out of bounds. He knows no opposition. Having found charts of several men with out of bounds Moons who were homosexuals, I am happy to note that this man is decidedly heterosexual. Mars and Venus are intercepted in his seventh house, and Venus is in mutual reception with Mercury which brings a courtesy Mercury into the interception. A courtesy position of Venus puts it next to his Saturn, but he is far from being a cold person emotionally. Sun is seven degrees beyond Saturn, which may be sufficiently out of orb to not afflict him, though I do not expect a strong father presence in his formative years. I find it interesting to have astrological myths blasted to kingdom come or finding exceptions that prove the rules, and I welcome that this example disallows the further proliferation of general conclusions.

His attitudes exactly mirror Aquarius rising, fixated on what he knows and the notion that his way is the only right way for him and everyone around him. A long time ago, an astrologer invented a phrase for this sort of thing, describing fixation as tantamount to a lack of intellectual curiosity. But this man has neither great intellect nor curiosity. He is just dead set in his ways and thoroughly dislikes change. With late degree of Aquarius rising, he may take on the worst characteristics of the next sign, in this case Pisces. Two of the chief detriments of the Pisces personality are procrastination and dislike of change. In examining the personality, we must combine rising sign with Sun and Moon and the chart significator, Uranus in Cancer in the fifth house, any planets in the first house, here only Jupiter in Aries which is perhaps best interpreted in his second house, and the location of Mars, here in Virgo and not auspiciously placed in his seventh house. The seventh house explains his attitude toward others, and Mars in seventh meets those around him with, at least, initial combat in mind. Note that he has Neptune in the eighth house, Sun on the cusp of eighth, with Mercury, Saturn, and the extra Venus close behind. Neptune as the last planet in this stellium might have much more bearing on an interpretation of what he expects of other people, probably disbelief. The closeness of Mars and Venus is amusing in hygienic Virgo, and Venus gains robustness from Mars, while Venus blunts the full energy expression of Mars. He gets along well with other people, but he is not open to any criticism from others. There is always an initial trial period for all people he meets.

At the time I first did this chart, I had a spate of charts of people with the Moon in Capricorn and correspondence with other astrologers about this. This man's Capricorn Moon is opposite Uranus and forming a T-square to the Sun-Mercury. In cardinal signs, this T-square should give enterprise. Yet what he does is solidly routine. Moon opposite Uranus can connote versatility. But he has a fixed horizontal axis, and what gives versatility

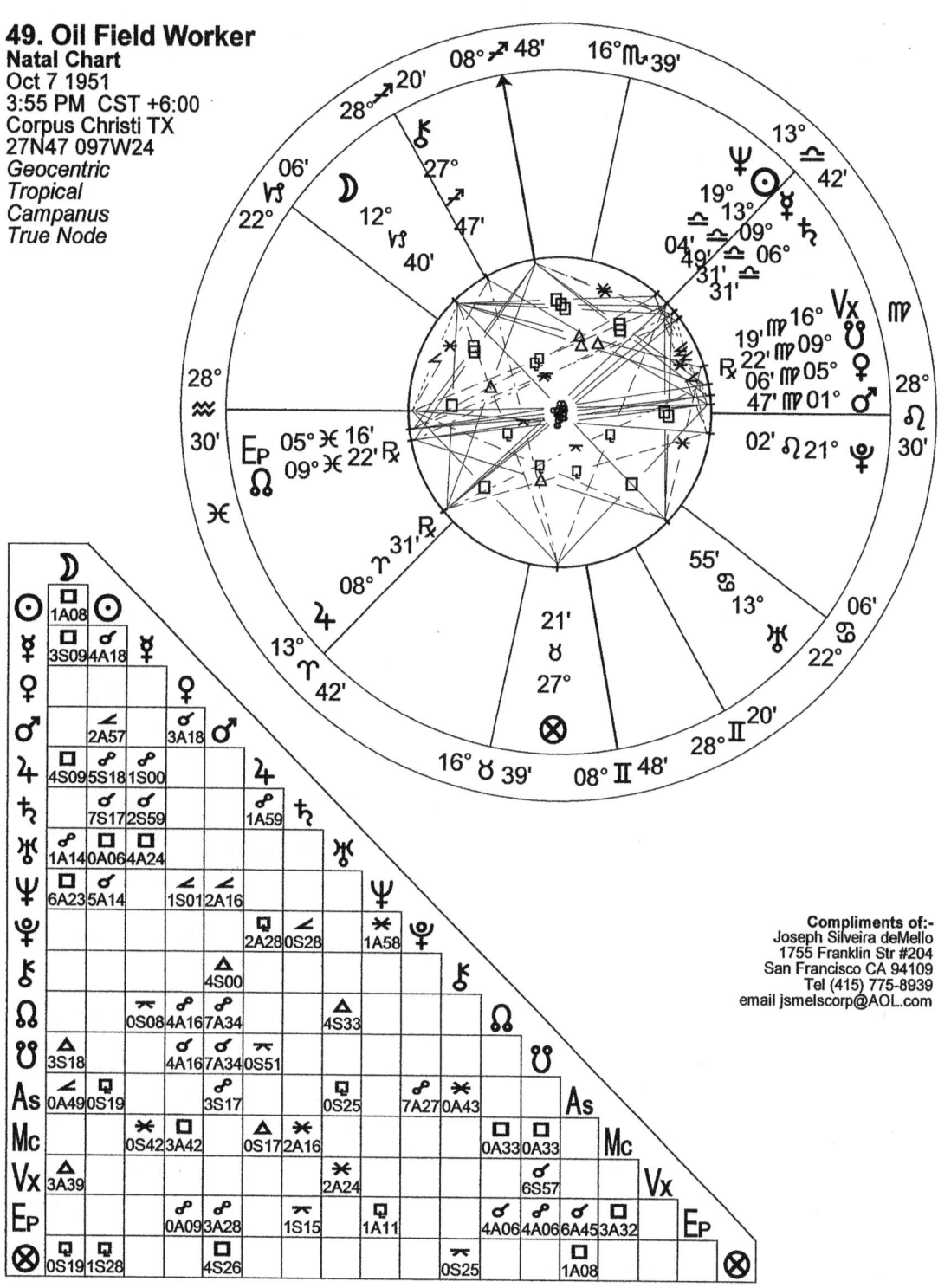

49. Oil Field Worker
Natal Chart
Oct 7 1951
3:55 PM CST +6:00
Corpus Christi TX
27N47 097W24
Geocentric
Tropical
Campanus
True Node

is his vertical axis. He will mellow with the years. He knows his job and is called upon to make independent decisions in the course of his work. I should think this would promote independent thought and assist him in making solutions. But he only takes these as matter of course and does not talk about his work because he deems it beyond the understanding of his women-folks. Uranus in the fifth house should give him creativity, even make him some sort of gambler (which he is not). The problem may lie with our perceptions of the opposition, and we should bear in mind that the opposition gives us the choice to go with one side of it or with the other, by turn, not a blending aspect but one of seesaw choice.

Examining this chart for career and vocation or work and status, we begin with an examination of the personality, a modern rising sign, a balancing Sun sign, a restraining Moon sign, a discriminating Mars. The Moon rules his sixth house of which we can only say that he works with fluids and nurtures the work he does. The career and status sign is Sagittarius on his Midheaven which I always take to indicate a potential for becoming a consultant in any chosen field. This chart puts any astrologer to the test about how consultantship might come about and when. Transiting Saturn has been going through his first quadrant, and things will open up for him when it reaches his IC. Give a second thought to the oil field worker's Neptune in the eighth house and check Pluto in the sixth, his only Neptune aspect. Moon in the eleventh indicates his ambivalent attitudes toward friends and community, and note Chiron on the cusp of the eleventh. Pluto rules the ninth of higher thought, but matters of the ninth are sorted through what he needs in his sixth where Pluto is located. He is free of tensions, happy with life as it is. And he is not the least bit bothered that his wife is highly successful in her field.

50. Maritha Pottenger, 4-3-2
Saturn: 0S58
Data: May 21, May 1952, 7:38 a.m. MST,
Tucson Arizona, 32N13, 110W58

Maritha Pottenger is a very well known astrological author, editor and lecturer and the daughter of Zip Dobyns. She studied with her mother, and her subsequent books go toward an effort to systematize the interpreting of any horoscope. In particular, her *Complete Horoscope Interpretation* involved a great deal of thought and single-minded dedication. Any astrologer could learn a great deal from adopting her and her mother's methods of reading astrological charts.

When I discovered that she had Saturn at zero declination, I wrote for permission to use her chart as one of these samples. I wanted to find what she thought of having Saturn at zero declination. Did she have a need to find perfection? She replied that, because of how she had seen what harm the pursuit of perfection did to people around her, she was not trying for perfection. She and her significant other forwarded a list of her strengths and a list of what challenges her, all of which show a combination of Gemini and Cancer. Her Moon is in Taurus, and her Mars is in Scorpio (fifth house), are also in line with her comments about herself.

As an astrology book editor she does not always draw good reviews. It would seem she has stepped on the tootsies of many of our colleagues. Some see her as arrogant, sanctimonious, elitist, feminist and thin-skinned. She and those around her regard her as non-confrontational, though she confesses to be enraged by injustices. She certainly holds back from making snap judgments, perhaps because her Mars, though in Scorpio, is also retrograde. I have found her thoughtful, serious and careful of speech, not exactly fitting a Gemini Sun, unless we see the Sun in the twelfth house as prone to hold back from ego displays. I always put rising signs as first in importance. Cancer is no less talkative than Gemini. Exchanges and reciprocity are descriptive of Cancer, and constancy, as will be realized by anyone who has ever tried to shake off a Cancerian connection. It is the Cancer risings who keep their families together. They give 100 percent of what they want to give (which is not usually or specifically what others want to receive). The only real detriment of Cancerians is that they build and harbor resentments easily and have to make a real effort to learn to shake them off.

If we consider Saturn, exalted in Libra and retrograde, this is a strong indication of a need to relate and an equal need to make sure that everyone around them also relates. I have found that retrograde Saturn is not a debility. Those who have this are avidly interested in all that goes on around them. She had her first Saturn return in infancy, and is one Saturn return ahead of most of her contemporaries. This Saturn is the focal point of a T-square to the opposition of Chiron-Uranus (mix a bit of mythology here, Saturn the father, but Uranus is his father, and Chiron is grandfather), Saturn is also trine to Fortune and a trine from the Sun which happened by progression when she was eight years old. Watch it when you start moving things. Fortune is going to move into exact trine to Saturn a lot sooner because Fortune moves as the Moon moves.

We see also Mars retrograde (those who try to drive with the brakes on), Neptune retrograde (for those with personal pride and some insecurity about that). Mars is the next to final piece in personality judgment. Mars in Scorpio makes the detective and the policeman, the researcher and delver into greater depths, and here placed in the fifth house of everything speculative, it is finely placed for her. To this Mars she may owe more bracing assistance. But, wait, there is more. Venus in her own sign disposes of all other chart positions. And, what every astrologer probably saw first, Uranus in the first house, and the aspects Uranus makes, have to be also part of the personality.

The very first thing I learned about Uranus in the first house was that such people could be exceptionally attractive or unpredictably homely. So much for first learnings.

Uranus is modern, contemporary, signifying things not around fifty years ago, and of course it is the unexpected, the less conservative. The second thing I have found about Uranus in the first house is that it often happens in children born with a clef palate. Well that must

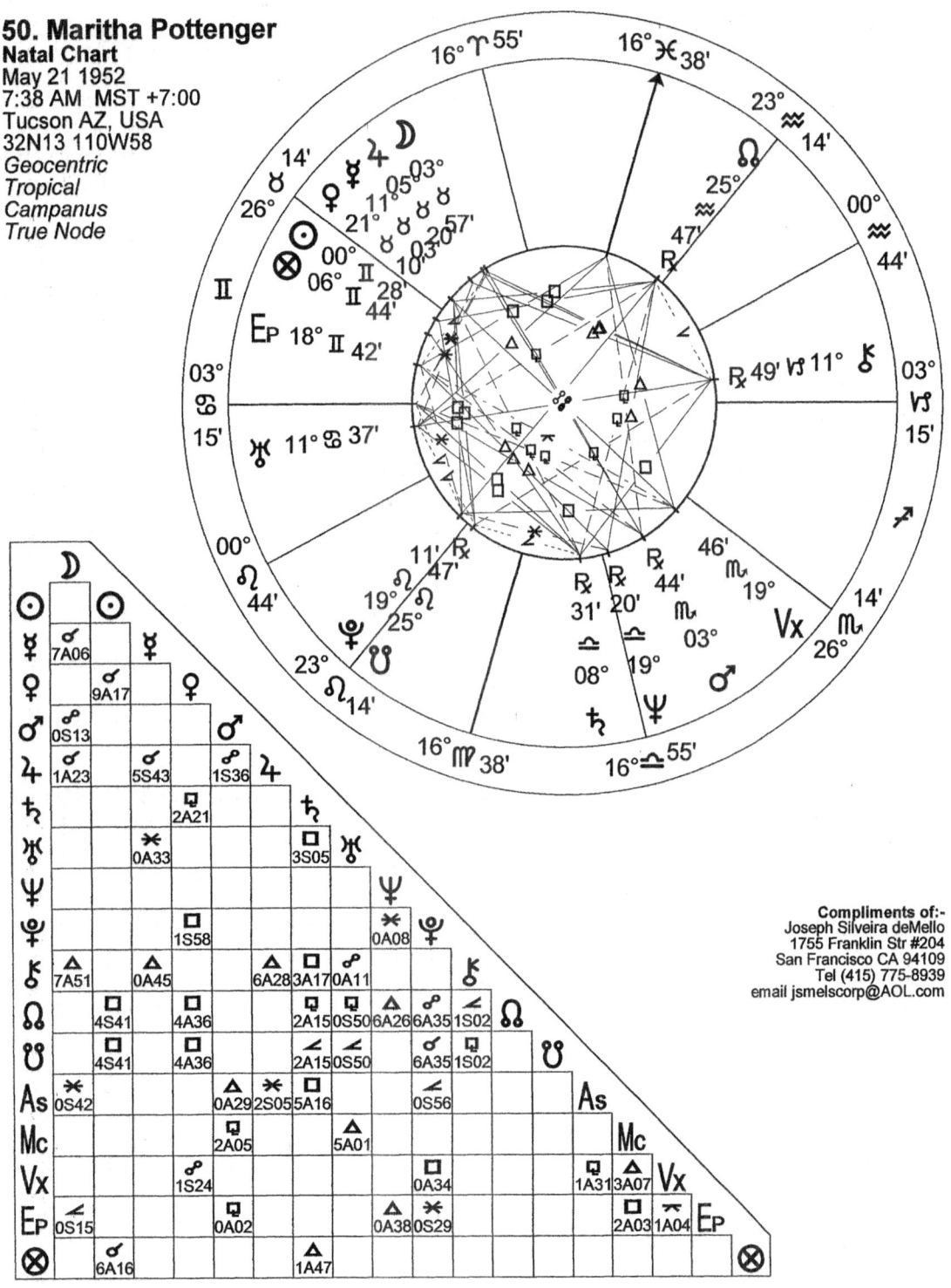

also have Uranus aspected to other significators, does not stand alone. This is the chart of a woman, and to all women styles and cosmetics exist as disguises. With her, the unexpected manifests in that she hardly bothers with cosmetics, but you cannot look at her and not see her as contemporary and liberated and her own person.

It amazes me she does not see herself as detailed (she made no Virgo comments and denied perfection), yet she has written a book which manifests painstaking care and rigid attention to organized logical thought and writing. An astrologer once said that the world's final summation of anyone is seen in their Midheaven, while their own summations of themselves is seen as the sign on the IC, in this case Virgo. Astrologers have to be careful of what they accept for the exception is inevitably the next chart you look at.

She admits to being an impatient and fast driver. She feels she needs to put more energy into all relationships (Saturn's need that all relate to everything). She is interested in only the things that interest her and has not time for those which at the moment do not. She finds it easy to learn what interests her and is reluctant to work on what does not. She says she is quite happy to have much of what she does be "good enough." Except for the first of these, she is loading her bases in favor of her Sun sign Gemini. She did not emphasize Cancer rising, did not say much of Moon in Taurus. We can see the togetherness of Moon and Jupiter which should lay testament to having higher standards and a flair for obtaining these. She admits that she is lazy about her body, does not exercise, eats heartily what foods she wants. And then she says her "thinking can be too literal" to the extent that she will miss the point of jokes.

51. Troubled Young Wife, 7-3-8
Saturn: 0S53
Data: June 4, 1952, 2:50 p.m. PDT,
Vancouver, BC, 49N14, 123W07

In the sixties and seventies, the Metaphysical Center in San Francisco, now long gone, was a very active place. There was a regular schedule of all sorts of classes, and it was where I began to study and teach astrology. Starting in the Seventies, a friend and I took turns keeping it open in the evenings and closing up at night. We can remember people who then gave and attended classes for five dollars a session, and considered this fee as really exorbitant, who now would not consider holding the same classes for less than ten times that amount. On the other hand, great stars, some now dead, but others still living, came to lecture at Metaphysical, and tickets were quite reasonable. Working as we did, we knew every teacher and student, were at the very hub of all movements, and got first look at any new book or product that came into the shop.

My friend first noticed and talked to the lovely blond lady of this chart, but I did not meet her until I took part in a psychic fair held on February 15, 1976. My friend brought her up to me and asked me to help her. It seems that three days earlier her husband had disappeared under rather incredible circumstances. He worked for an armored car company and had walked off the job with the day's collections, a half million, in a champagne crate on his shoulder. She was a young mother with an infant daughter, and she had been attending various types of occult and metaphysical lectures over the previous two or three months, including a Silva Mind Control series.

Otherwise she lived a very routine suburban lifestyle. She was as attractive a Libra rising as could be, with the Sun in Gemini and the Moon together with Mars just into Scorpio in the first house. About three weeks before I met her, her progressed Moon was squaring her natal Sun and was sextile her progressed Uranus. So, although her data is birth certificate time, it could stand to be corrected. Her progressed Sun and Venus were at her Midheaven, the Sun at 7 Cancer 11, Venus at 8 Cancer 19, and these were square her natal and progressed Saturn. It did not seem to me that she was headed for a marital breakup or divorce due to her tenth house Uranus at least for a few years yet. Very much in love with her husband, she wanted everything in her life to be perfect and tended very much to blame herself for what she saw as her inability or failure to attain perfection. Note what our previous example said of the difficult lives of those who try for perfection.

After years of reading that people who have Saturn in the first house close to the Ascendant are usually reticent and shy, finally I had found such a person. A western Canadian by birth, she was certainly not the usual rowdy cowboy playgirl type. Although she had been married at least a year, everyone referred to her as a newlywed. Many of the men who took courses at the Center did so strictly in order to meet women, and many of them, including some teachers, were attracted to her, even as she held her baby daughter but they had to back off when her very tall, very attractive husband came to pick her up.

When her husband disappeared, many were solicitous. The few times we had seen him, he had been very much the new father delighting in how quickly his daughter was growing in so few months. He was attentive to mother and child, but was not very interested in the Metaphysical scene. We knew little of him other than he had been a Marine. She came to the psychic fair to see what she could learn from the various readers of what had happened, and a fellow student and myself both carefully took down the data for father, mother and child. Also data of when all of this happened.

For months after this happened, her Silva Mind Control teacher took an interest and began to be somewhat serious about her. Especially when, as time went by, it became obvious that her husband had no intention of contacting her or returning. She really had little hope of that since, after his first marriage was over, he had told her that he never thought of or saw any reason to contact his first wife.

Twenty years have passed, but I know two people with whom she stayed in contact over the years after she left this area. I called them before I sat down to write this. No one had heard from her in four years. No sooner did I collate my notes than one of these old friends called

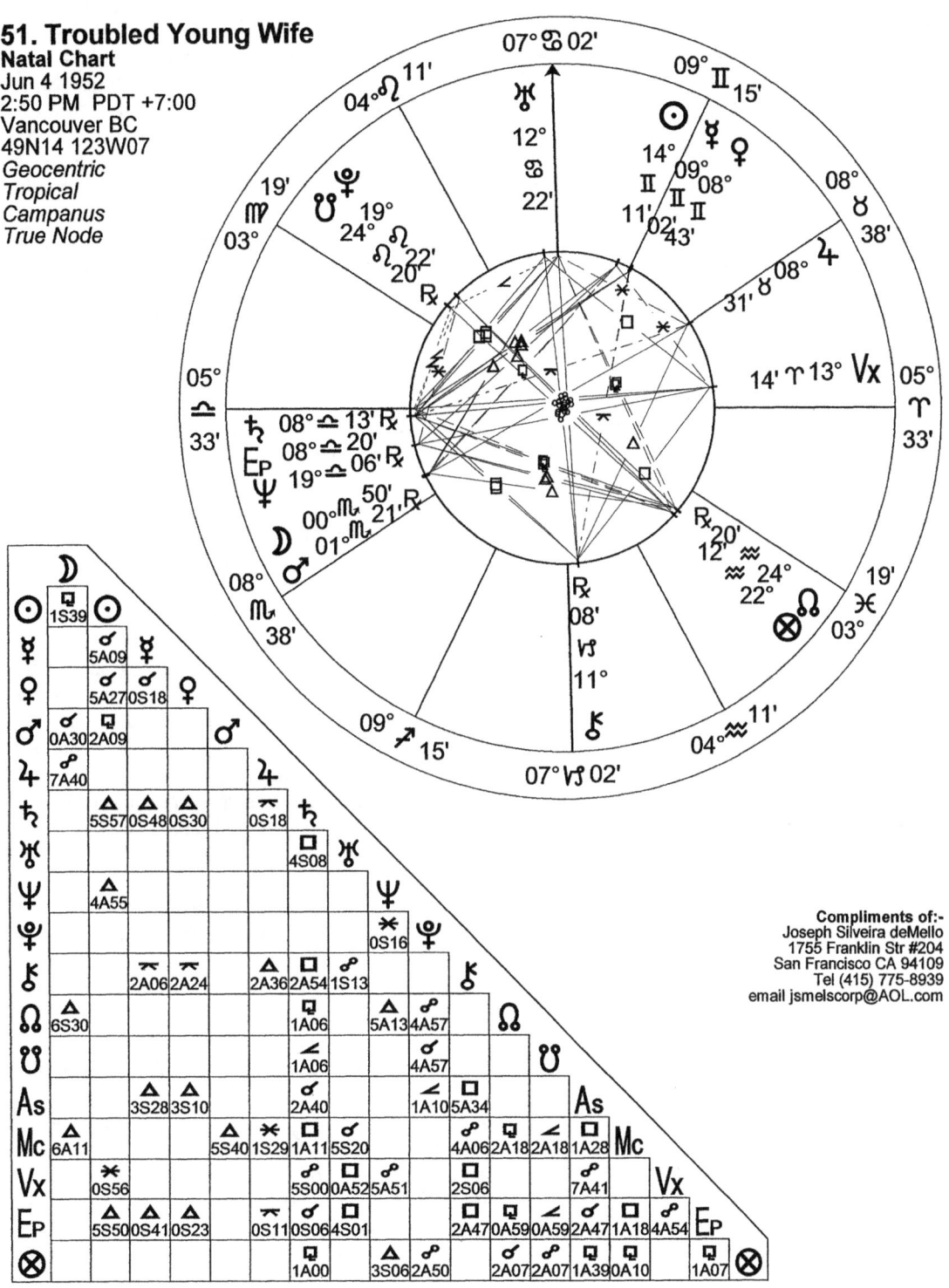

51. Troubled Young Wife
Natal Chart
Jun 4 1952
2:50 PM PDT +7:00
Vancouver BC
49N14 123W07
Geocentric
Tropical
Campanus
True Node

back to say that she had just had a telephone call from the subject. Her husband has still never tried to call her, she has never remarried, but their daughter, now out of school, married, and has had two children.

This chart, Libra rising, Sun in Gemini and Moon in Scorpio, has Venus as chart significator in Gemini in the eighth house. The first house of the chart is crowded by Saturn, Neptune and Mars, all retrograde, and the Moon in Scorpio (as well as Mars) are not in the rising sign. The retrograde Saturn is avid to achieve relativity with people and the world around her, while Neptune retrograde testifies to pride in self, and Mars in retrograde to trying to drive with the brakes on. Note that Mars is not well placed behind one of the houses it rules, the second, but it also rules her seventh. Neptune rules the sixth, and Saturn rules the fourth, and Moon rules the tenth, so that the matters of five houses are channeled to her first house of what she wants of those matters. This heavy first house testifies to a complex personality. But perhaps due to her Sun in Gemini, her Venus chart significator also in Gemini, and Libra rising, she was not very self-centered. Uranus is opposite Chiron making a T-square to Saturn and rising degree, and Moon and Mars oppose Jupiter. In this chart the zero declination Saturn is also trine to Mercury-Venus which are too close to her Sun. The Sun is trine Neptune but sesquiquad Moon and Mars. No planets out of bounds although Uranus and Pluto are nearly so.

52. The Big Heist, 4-3-4
Saturn: not applicable
Data: May 30, 1949, 8:05 a.m. EDT,
Wellsboro, Pennsylvania, 41N45, 77W18

Having looked at her chart, I should not deprive you of her husband's chart to fill out the rest of the story, even if he has no zero declination planets. He does have the Moon quite far out of bounds, and Venus, Uranus and Pluto also out of bounds. This might offer germane clues to out-of-bounds placements. His chart is most occupied in the fourth quadrant, especially in the twelfth house, where he has Sun in Gemini with Mercury and Venus and Uranus, and Moon in Cancer just above the Cancer Ascendant.

The newspapers instantly dubbed him the Brink's Guard with Class. He had worked all morning with a buddy, and going onto lunch time he had told his co-worker he would be gone for a few minutes to deliver a case of champagne to a friend working in that mall where they had been collecting. And off he shambled. But as the minutes ticked away, he never came back. With him disappeared an estimated five hundred thousand dollars, and it could only have gone in the champagne crate. In early 1976, he was a clean-cut, clean-shaven, 180 pound, twenty-seven-year-old ex-Marine who had served in Vietnam. He had been working for Brink's for two years, had an excellent record and was well thought of when this incident occurred. He and his bride (his second wife) had just had a baby daughter and had been living ordinary lives in a suburb. His crime surprised and dismayed everyone who knew him.

My own notes say he was more than six foot tall in stocking feet, but he habitually wore western boots which made him six-four. His wife told me his trousers had a 36" inseam, and the size of his wedding ring was eight or eight and a half, big wide hands. He was light brown haired and brown eyed. In Vietnam he sustained many shrapnel wounds, (while under capture, he had sustained many additional blows to his head). His list of injuries from his service record show both feet were broken, back was broken, there was shrapnel in his private parts and a "hole" in one of his buttocks. He had been awarded three Purple Hearts. He routinely wore a back brace, and his back was stiff after vertebrae were fused. He therefore walked with a sort of duck walk or waddle. No matter how he disguised himself, it is amazing that he came close to FBI men in the ten months he was on the lam and was never recognized and detained.

In those ten months, he blew it all on wine, women and song. Not to mention good booze, and luxurious nose candy. Finally broke, and with the FBI and a hit man hired by a former female companion, seemingly about to close in on him, he turned himself in by writing a seventeen page letter to San Francisco newspaper columnist Herb Caen in which he gave enough clues of his whereabouts and the direction in which he was moving. Now the FBI was able to catch up with him in a motel in New Mexico, and they brought him back to face California justice. He pled guilty, was quickly sentenced in 1977 to ten years, served but a fraction of it with a cut for good behavior.

His twelfth house planets were well spaced from each other. Although we can still look upon this as a stellium, it is nice to see the Sun not exactly burning up its surrounding planets. At the time of his capture, the newspapers treated us to a long story. One day he found himself in conversation with an FBI man who never cottoned to who he was. He had let his hair grow to his shoulders and acquiring a great beard, all of which he dyed black. But even he thought he should easily have been spotted, apprehended any time.

When he walked away with the cash, the progressed Moon had been conjunct his natal Uranus and his progressed Uranus, and the Moon was sextile his natal Saturn. That was January 1976. In April 1976 the progressed Moon was conjunct progressed Sun. And in August and September 1976, the progressed Moon was semi-sextile natal Sun and then conjunct natal Moon. When apprehended he was watching television on the evening of January 12, 1977, sixty miles south of Santa Fe, New Mexico. The arrest was described as routine and uneventful. He spent his time in jail carving wood toys, a model of his Brink's truck which he sent to his former employers who then legally forestalled him from duplicating such models commercially. Obviously he would have been out of jail in the early 1980s. He is now a successful wood sculptor.

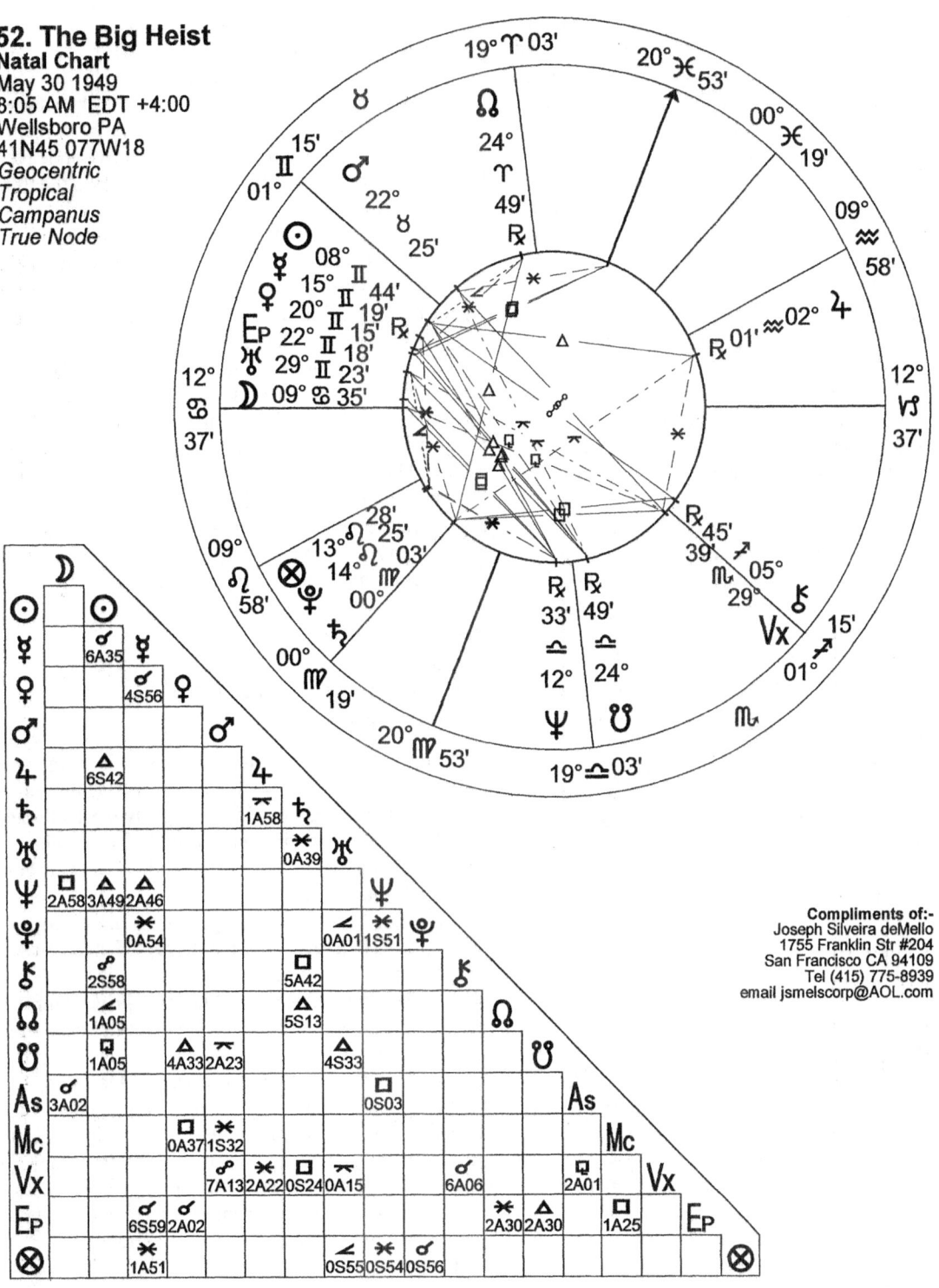

53. Advertising Woman, 11-3-8
Saturn: 0S53
Data: June 6, 1952, 12:20 a.m. EDT,
Toronto, Ontario, 43N39, 79W22

This young woman and her girl friend, two lesbians, had the good heart to take in as a roommate an editor and graphics artist friend of mine who worked with her during a brief rough period in his life. I met her only briefly. She had Aquarius rising, Gemini Sun and Scorpio Moon. She was not very interested in astrology, and I did this chart at the behest of my friend. She was very attractive and artistically talented. The Sun, which creates the declination boundary (at that time of year) was at its full extent of declination, and Moon, Mercury and Uranus are almost out of bounds, and Pluto just outside. These planets are on the verge of going beyond her personal control (though it is a difficult concept that anyone is ever really in charge of his or her Pluto). She was confident in what she knew.

The chart provides a number of surprises. The chart is disposed mainly by Mercury in its own sign and Mars in Scorpio and retrograde. Saturn is chart significator on the edge of the eighth, and the focus T-square of the Uranus-Chiron opposition. The many aspects are a mixed bag of energies and permissiveness. I dare say that what is not aspected is perhaps as important as what is. She had wide interests, and the Sun on the cusp of her fifth house was indeed a creative force, and she was clever in graphic arts design. Here we see another chart with Sagittarius on the Midheaven—optimistic confidence in her continued success. The earth grand trine which brings together Jupiter and Chiron with the Vertex is not one which can be looked up in the cookbooks. First we make up our minds whether to read Jupiter in the second or third house, see Chiron as the thing easily and obviously overlooked, the Vertex as health, and Fortune as protection. We could make a case for that. The Sun, as heart of the matter, nicely in the creative fifth, but Venus and Mercury, the latter showing security as interest, are both too close to Sun. Pay attention to what is not intercepted in the seventh house.

54. Male Bartender, 11-3-11
Saturn: 0S55
Data: June 12, 1952, 10:30 p.m. EST,
Augusta, Georgia, 33N28, 81W58

Personable and pleasant, this bartender has been on the local scene for some years now, serving for short periods at a time as a relief bartender, available to fill in for any colleague taking a sick day. With all that much air in his chart, this man is a prime example of the triumph of education. He would like to attend law school full-time but has to support himself in the meantime. Any discussion with him gives evidence that he has a well grounded education and remembers it all. He is also very open to looking at what he has learned from other viewpoints than the criteria of his professors. When he thinks, you can see his wheels spinning. Versus the previous example, his Aquarius rising has Scorpio on the Midheaven. As a Gemini Sun person, one might expect him to be more of a talker, but this man does a great deal of listening. Of course Aquarius rising people do have the ability to keep quiet, the ability to keep confidentiality and to respond only when asked point blank what he thinks someone ought to do in a given case. When that happens, such a person pulls out all stops and tells them exactly what he thinks and forgets all tact. Add to this that he has the Moon first house and in the rising sign and unequivocally speaks his own mind. Although Aquarius is an air sign, it is fixed and weighs more than Gemini.

He is remarkably ambitious, as attested by his Scorpio Mars on the cusp of his ninth house. His chart shows several problem spots for the interpreter. Sun, Venus and Mercury are in the fifth house of creative endeavor, but he is also creative with a partner. Jupiter in the third should insist on involvement in communications and business. However with Pluto in the seventh I doubt I would push that notion very far. He is strong enough to succeed in changing any would be partner thereby losing the person he found attractive, so that is not very productive. He firmly believed few people are living up to their personal potentials. Combine Venus-Sun-Mercury in the fifth with Uranus in the sixth being a bartender is insufficient and probably temporary, especially with Mars at the ninth cusp and in Scorpio. Do you think he will ever be a lawyer? I think not criminal law. If only Saturn were not intercepted, but it is, so we can't change that. We have what we have in our charts for a purpose and our duty is to find the purpose. Scorpio on the tenth will be a telling factor in his total career..

55. Male Nurse, 4-3-12
Saturn: 0S55
Data: June 14, 1952, 6:21 a.m. PDT,
Burbank, California, 34N11, 118W19

This man is primarily a male nurse specializing in geriatric care and working in the homosexual community. Never a client, I know him through two friends and found him as interesting as you will find his chart. I should tell you that he has a twin brother who was born six minutes later than he.

His chart has Cancer rising, notably nurturing, but his Gemini Sun and Venus are intercepted in the twelfth house, yet he cannot be said to act entirely behind the scene. He is very conscious of his own privacy, probably due to his Mars in Scorpio. His twelfth house Mercury is in early Cancer. And Uranus in his first makes him unusual and less than conservative. Moon, as chart significator is in his tenth house in Pisces, sensitive to something lacking in his status, yet it is the push that puts him into public life. Uranus in the first does not make him either physically attractive or homely, as it usually does, but here concentrates on an emanation of personality that is electrical and contagious.

In the area of declinations, his date of birth gives Sun at its boundary, Mercury out of bounds gives him facility in communication, Venus is out of bounds, usually saying he loves well but not too wisely. Uranus and Pluto are close to being out of bounds. Such planets on

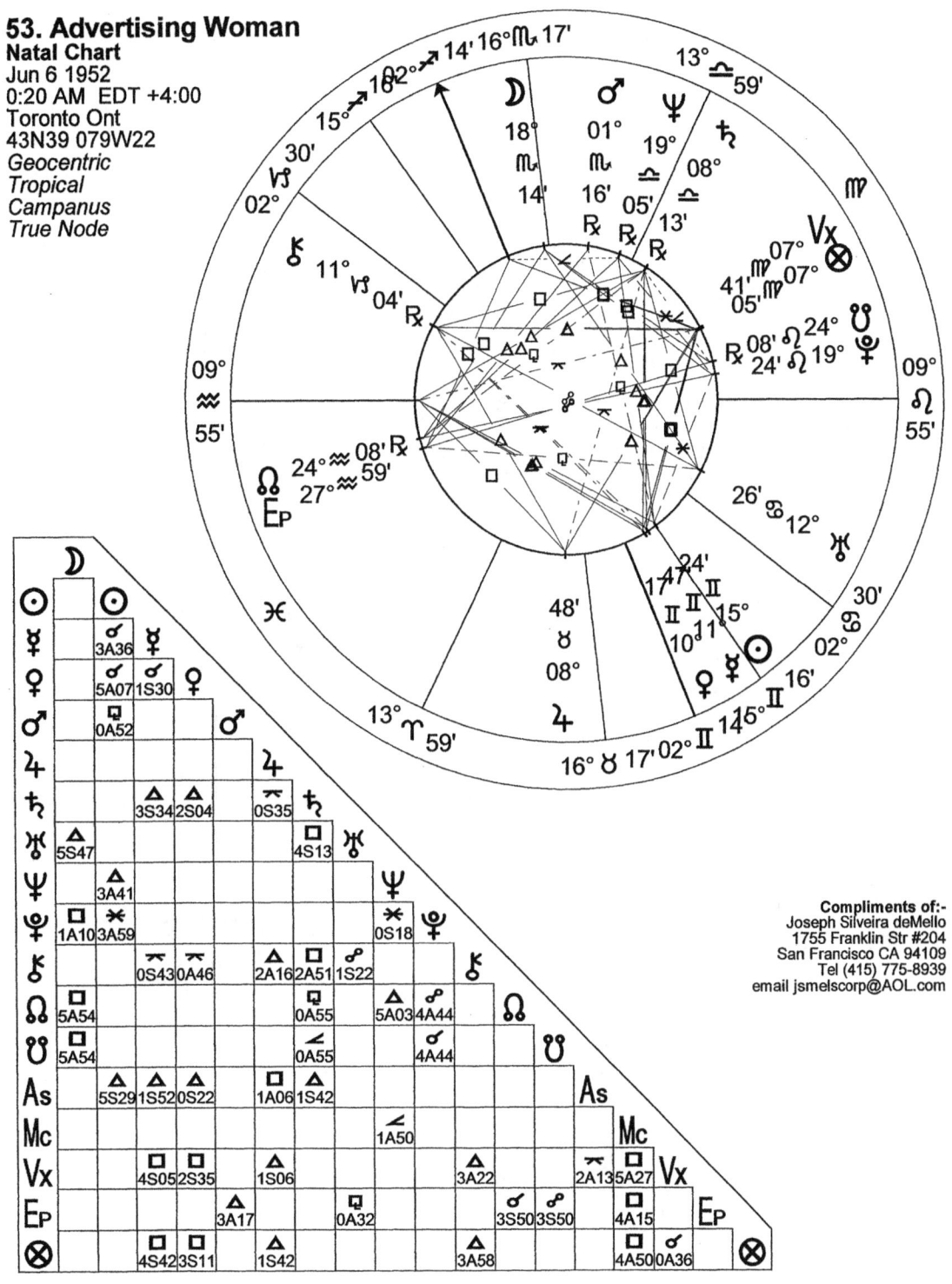

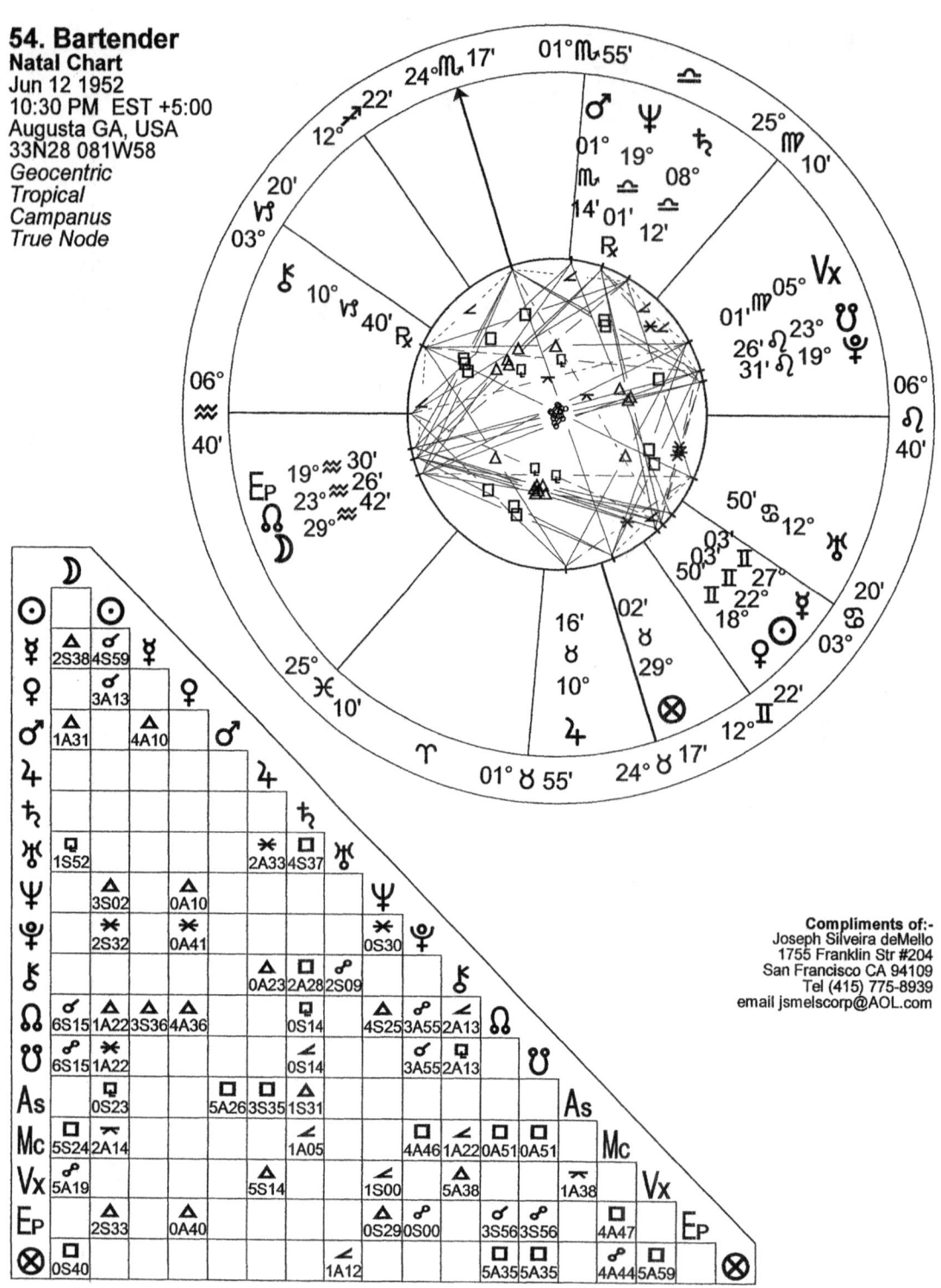

55. Male Nurse
Natal Chart
Jun 14 1952
6:21 AM PDT +7:00
Burbank CA, USA
34N11 118W19
Geocentric
Tropical
Campanus
True Node

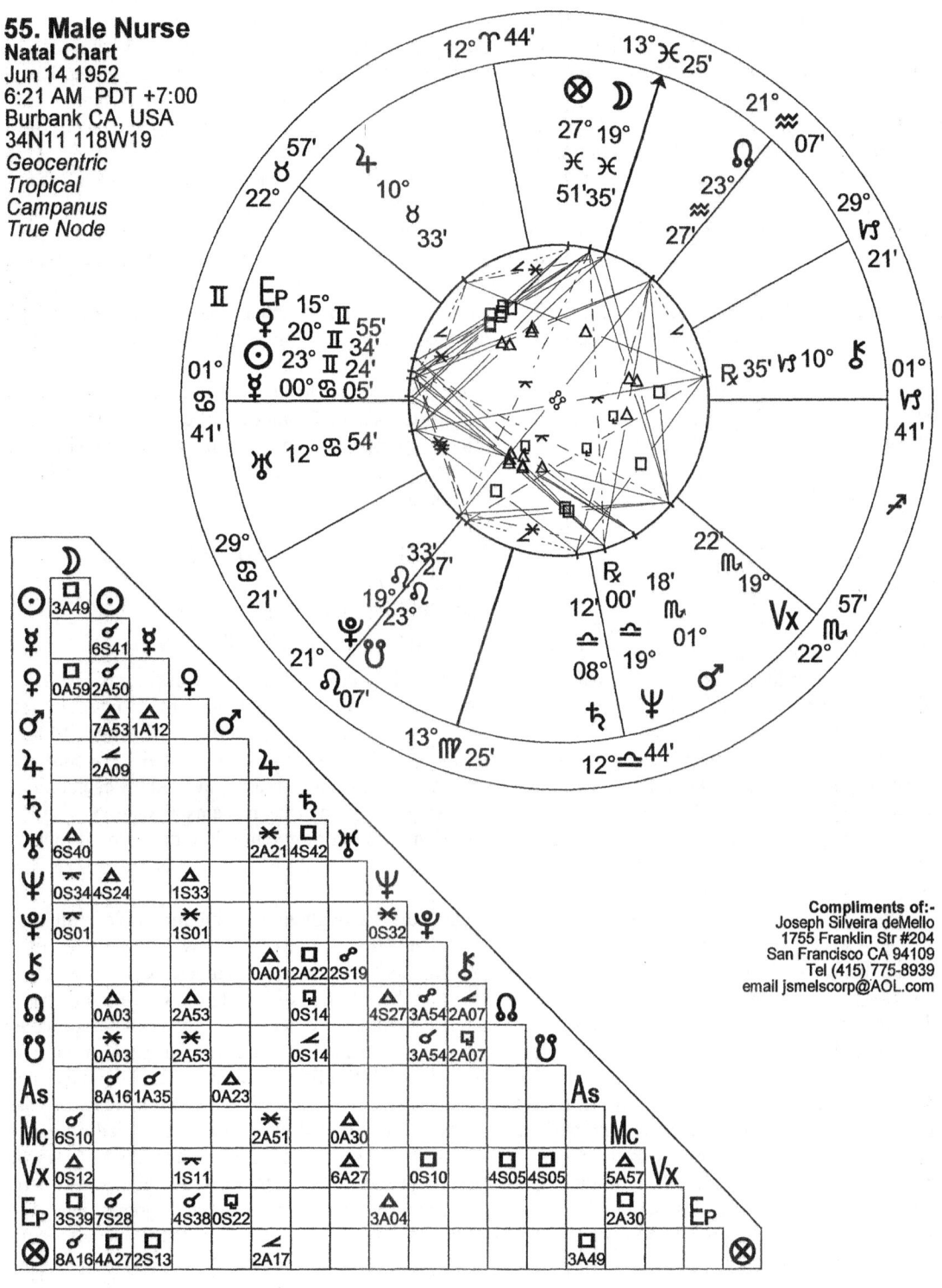

Compliments of:-
Joseph Silveira deMello
1755 Franklin Str #204
San Francisco CA 94109
Tel (415) 775-8939
email jsmelscorp@AOL.com

the edge, not quite out of bounds, still tickle the edges of personal control. What he does control are Sun and Venus because these are fenced off in interception, private to himself, not open to the criticism of others. In this matter of interception, many astrologers refuse to allow special significance and believe such geographical anomalies to be artificial. I find them both factual and special, as the reader may already have guessed. They are no problem for those who have them. The problem is that they create circumstances into which others cannot intrude, hence a problem for those who would and find they are locked out.

This chart has many trines, but only one grand trine, and that in air. Look upon the squares in this chart as energizers, aware that the person of the chart must control these to make them work well for himself. With half his planets in the fourth quadrant, this man is more interested in objective knowledge of himself. And note that the Moon is the focal point of a double quincunx to Neptune-Pluto. Finally, note the nodal axis from ninth to third, intaking from philosophy with release through the knowledge of the status quo.

Whether this nodal axis exists from the third to ninth or, as we see here, those persons are students and teachers. Another interesting aspect is Uranus opposite Chiron which has Jupiter trine Chiron and Jupiter sextile Uranus.

56. Daughter of Gender Identity, 4-1-1
Saturn: 0S10, Moon: 0S24
Data: April 8, 1967. 9:51 a.m. PST,
Oakland, California, 37N48, 122W16

Twenty years ago, many of us participated in a psychic fair to open a new occult and astrology bookshop. I met the couple and two pre-school children, and the parents of the father as well as his brother and brother's wife. Except for the children's mother, who was an astrologer, all the others were of markedly Hispanic ancestry. At a lull in the general activities, I got the birth data for all of them. I normally dislike doing charts for very young children on the grounds that they are too young to understand a reading and such charts are usually done for the parents and grandparents. The father's relatives seemed apprehensive about astrology, and I thought they looked upon me with great apprehension and suspicion. I only gave the charts a light reading, and got sighs of relief. But I had the family data, took it home and eventually did all the charts.

It was at least ten years before I was to learn that the dark and heavy-set father had actually started life as the biological mother of the two children, and that, soon after the children were born, she deciding that she should take a male gender identity for the rest of her life. She had undergone various medical treatments so that the final result was to take on a masculine appearance, corpulence, and a lot of facial hair. He Anglicized the family name, and, as a man, he had married the attractive blond young woman who took on the role of his children's mother. There never has been any word about the biological father of the children. I like to take Saturn as the father and Moon as the mother, and see here how they are conjunct.

This obviously was the secret which the Catholic family had been forced to accept. It bothered me that his wife, herself an astrologer, had not told the family members that no astrologer can tell gender variants in the horoscope. When events finally revealed the true story, it is very unhappy, for the father finally succeeded in killing himself on his third attempt. Since that psychic fair, I have had no contact with any of the people involved.

I doubt the children were ever told then of their mixed up parentage. Everyone could have relaxed that I would be brilliant enough to guess their secret. I have seen many other charts were it was obvious there was no father on the scene, and this chart is unlike any of those others. The father/mother person was Pisces rising, by the way, but the woman who was acting mother was neither Pisces nor Virgo in any way. I made nothing special of Neptune ruling the tenth house. There is a grand trine from Saturn to Jupiter to Vertex-Neptune, and Venus is opposite the latter pair, and Mercury is opposite Uranus- Pluto. These oppositions all have trine-septile mitigators. Now looking at this chart many years later I notice that this child not only has Saturn at zero declination but also has the Moon parallel although the Moon is in a Northern sign. Moon rules the rising sign, and Saturn rules the seventh, making an interesting dichotomy, rulers of Ascendant and Descendant together in the tenth house.

57. Male Porn Star, 10-2-6
Saturn: 0N27
Data: April 21, 1967, 11:50 p.m. EST,
New Haven Connecticut, 41N20, 72W55

I met the man of this chart working as a relief or fill-in cocktail waiter at my neighborhood bar. It was at a time when regular people were vacationing, and there was a run of new people which lasted for a couple of months. This man and another even knew each other in Los Angeles. At any rate, it seems when they wished to vacation between movie making, they would pick the town and scout for jobs which would finance their vacations.

Oh dear, I thought on meeting him, he's in the movies, and I hardly ever go to movies. I am also the sort of person incapable of recognizing celebrities if I pass them on the street. As I wondered what I would say, it got even worse. Everyone else there knew this young man and his friend as stars in male porn movies. He found it hard to believe I never see such films and nonplused when I revealed I did not own a VCR. But then we were all diverted when it was revealed both were gymnasts and proceeded to do smooth handstands without any fuss at all. When they discovered I was an astrologer, the two gymnasts immediately jotted down their birth data for me. This is the chart of the one with Saturn at zero declination. To compound the issue, this man also has Venus out of bounds.

While there are many homosexuals of both sexes in mainstream Hollywood, there is no crossover between those who act in porn and those who do not. Neither of

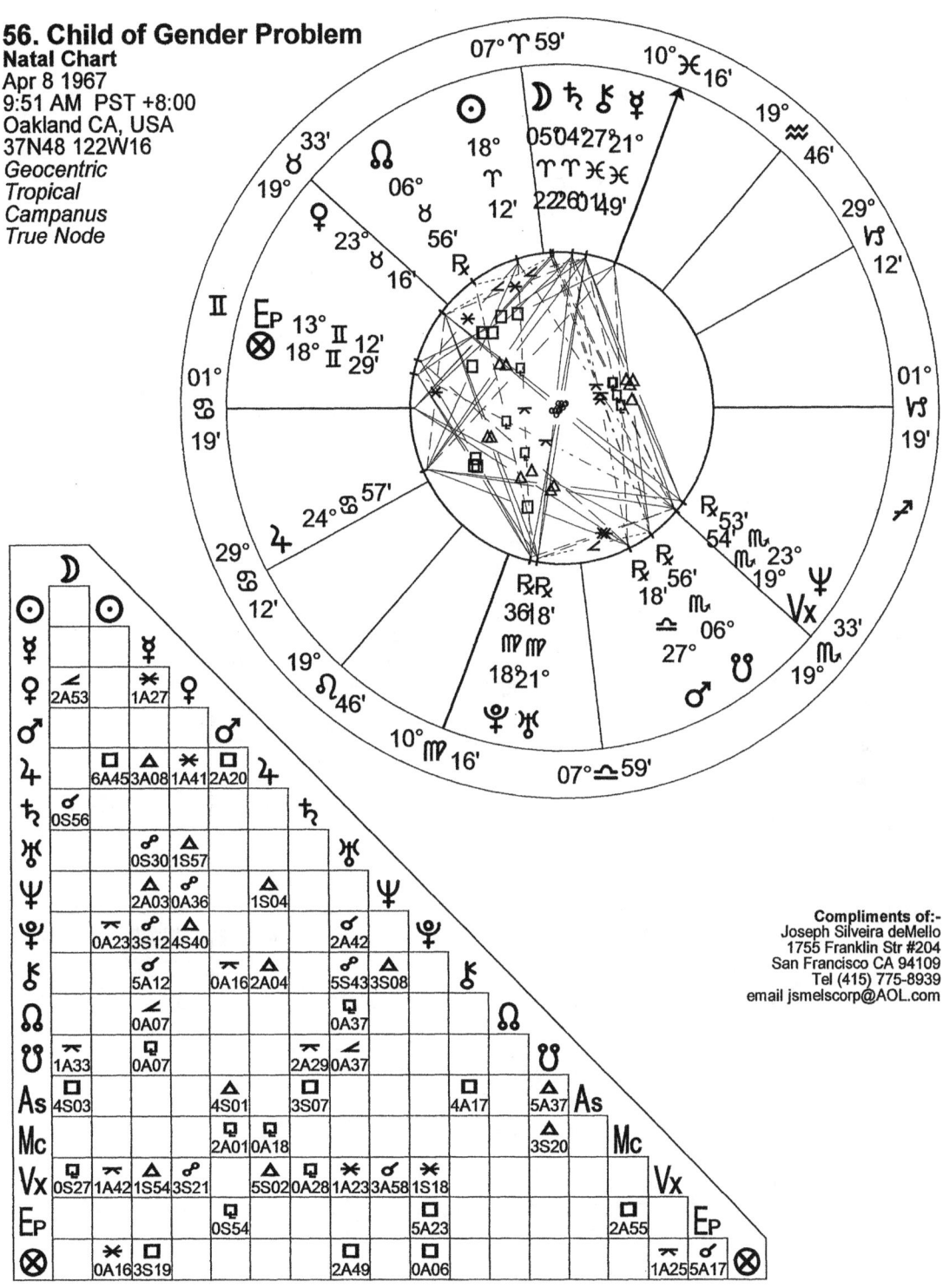

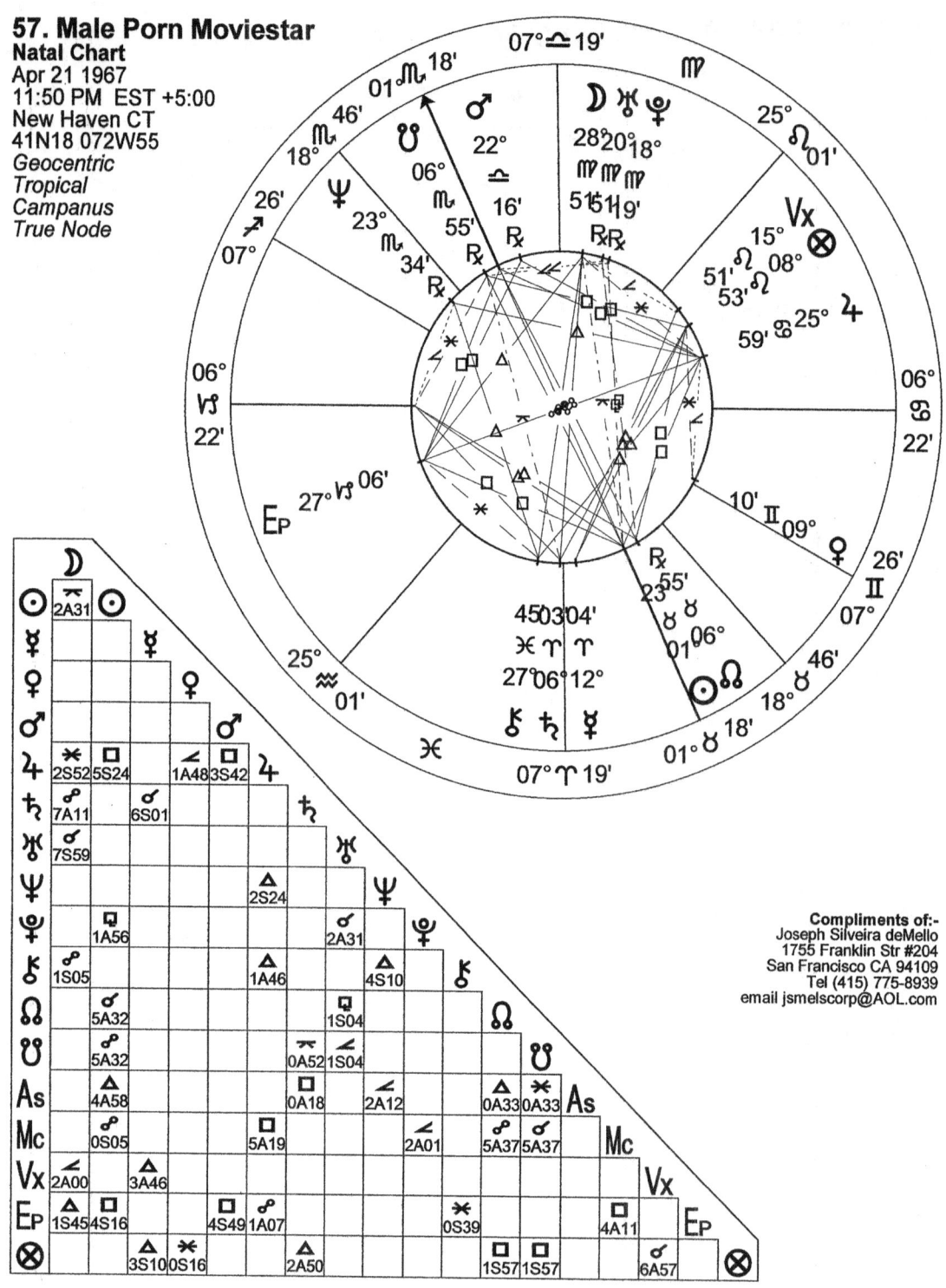

these young men had any ambition to be part of mainstream Hollywood. Porn was a lark which gave them some notoriety among their friends. Their schedules did not tie them up for months at a time. But they had egos as large as any movie star. I was very surprised to find a Capricorn rising engaged in an occupation he goes into as a lark. Then, with the Sun in Taurus, he had a long thin neck, and a gymnast's body. The Moon is in Virgo. The sixth house is Gemini and the career tenth is Scorpio. Certainly as a cocktail waiter, he maneuvered easily through the crowd and was entirely professional and capable. Mars in Libra in the ninth house is both ambitious and here is indicative of living far from his natal place.

58. Oscar Gutierrez, Jr., 7-2-8
Saturn: 0N38
Data: April 25, 1967, 4:45 p.m. AST,
Santiago, Chile, 33S27, 70W40

This chart comes from the files of Don Borkowski who tells me he knows nothing about this person. A fellow student when Don was studying astrology got the charts of the whole Gutierrez family of Chile. The class teacher, astrologer and author Press Roberts, decided to use this chart as a drill to teach the class how to do Southern hemisphere charts. I noticed the data was sent me with the time zone notation of PST, which, if you look at a map, you will see this is rather impossible. Chile is so far east that they are on Atlantic Standard Time, and that is the zone for which I have set up this chart.

In the classroom there was no endeavor to interpret the chart, that of a ten year old of an entirely different culture. At the same time, we have no idea of the social status. He might as well be a fictional person of infinite potential. But we have Libra rising and Mars Libra in the first house and note that it is retrograde, so we, I at least, will see him as predominantly Aries with a Taurus Sun and Scorpio Moon. The Moon is with Neptune in the second house would indicate some unease in material things as well as self-esteem. Additionally, the Moon-Neptune conjunction is part of a grand trine with Jupiter and Chiron, and I regard trines as a thoroughly permissive influence. All the more so as the Midheaven is a focal point to the Ascendant-Saturn opposition.

59. Computer Engineer, 6-10-3
Saturn: 0N27
Data: January 11, 1968, 9:14 p.m. PST,
San Francisco, California, 37N45, 122W26

I have known this young man since infancy. His father is the Churchman (chart #31 of this study). There is no mistaking them on sight as father and son as this young man looks exactly as his father did in his youth. Through the divorce of his parents, he remained in the custody of his mother but was always in contact with his father. He has gone through periods where he might have studied architecture, and he supported himself through school by working in banking jobs where he was so well regarded that he could have stayed in that as a career. But he was studying engineering all the while.

In mid-October of 1996, his father telephoned to ask me when this, his youngest son, would get the job he had interviewed for at Hewlett-Packard where his eldest sister was also an engineer. Although I took the time of the question as if I might do a horary, I did a diurnal instead and saw that on the following Wednesday he would have favorable contacts to the diurnal angles, so I predicted that he would get an engineering job with Hewlett-Packard either that coming Wednesday or that he would have to wait until April of 1997 to get it, because he was in the middle of a retrograde Saturn period around his first Saturn return which would not be over until March. From his progressed chart I saw that he would have excellent aspects for the following April (1997). But not to worry. His Wednesday, October 17, 1996 was so good he landed the job right then.

Where his father is Gemini rising, this young man has Virgo rising and is taller than his father. The resemblance between them is entirely physical. He gives much more attention to details, and has the Sun in Capricorn. Unfortunately his Gemini Moon is on his Midheaven, and he will have diverse interests. But with the Ascendant as one type of Mercury, and his Midheaven the other type of Mercury, we have an interesting combination to study. His Mercury is in Aquarius. His Mother is an Aquarius rising with Pisces Sun and Gemini Moon, as liberal as his father is conservative. His Moon was quite far out of bounds at birth, and it will periodically repeatedly do so throughout life. He was born with Jupiter, Uranus and Pluto retrograde. Toward late in life he will have progressed Uranus at zero declination.

60. Grand-nephew, 8-12-3
Saturn: 0S35
Data: March 11, 1981, 10:21 p.m. EST,
Norfolk, Virginia, 36N51, 78W18

This is the chart of a grand-nephew I have never met. Another chart where my Saturn sits close to his Ascendant. But since my Sun falls in his twelfth, he is out of my karmic past. His Sun falls in my eleventh house of friends and is on my natal Uranus. His Moon falls on my Ascendant. His Pluto is on my Mars, and his Neptune is trine mine and on my Venus. Since we both have Moon in Gemini, an astrological myth is that we should understand each other's emotional needs. I have never found this to be true. People with same sign Moon can just as easily disregard or be oblivious to each other's emotional needs. His parents are divorced, and he lives most of the year with his mother and visits his father in Florida usually in summer. Our visits to Florida have never coincided. All I have seen are very shadowed pictures of a very quiet, thin young boy who I am told is very polite and quite proper as indeed is his father.

His story has unusual beginnings. His father was a Navy career man on sea duty when there was a fire at the second story apartment where they lived in Virginia. Only his mother, a half-sister (daughter of mother's first

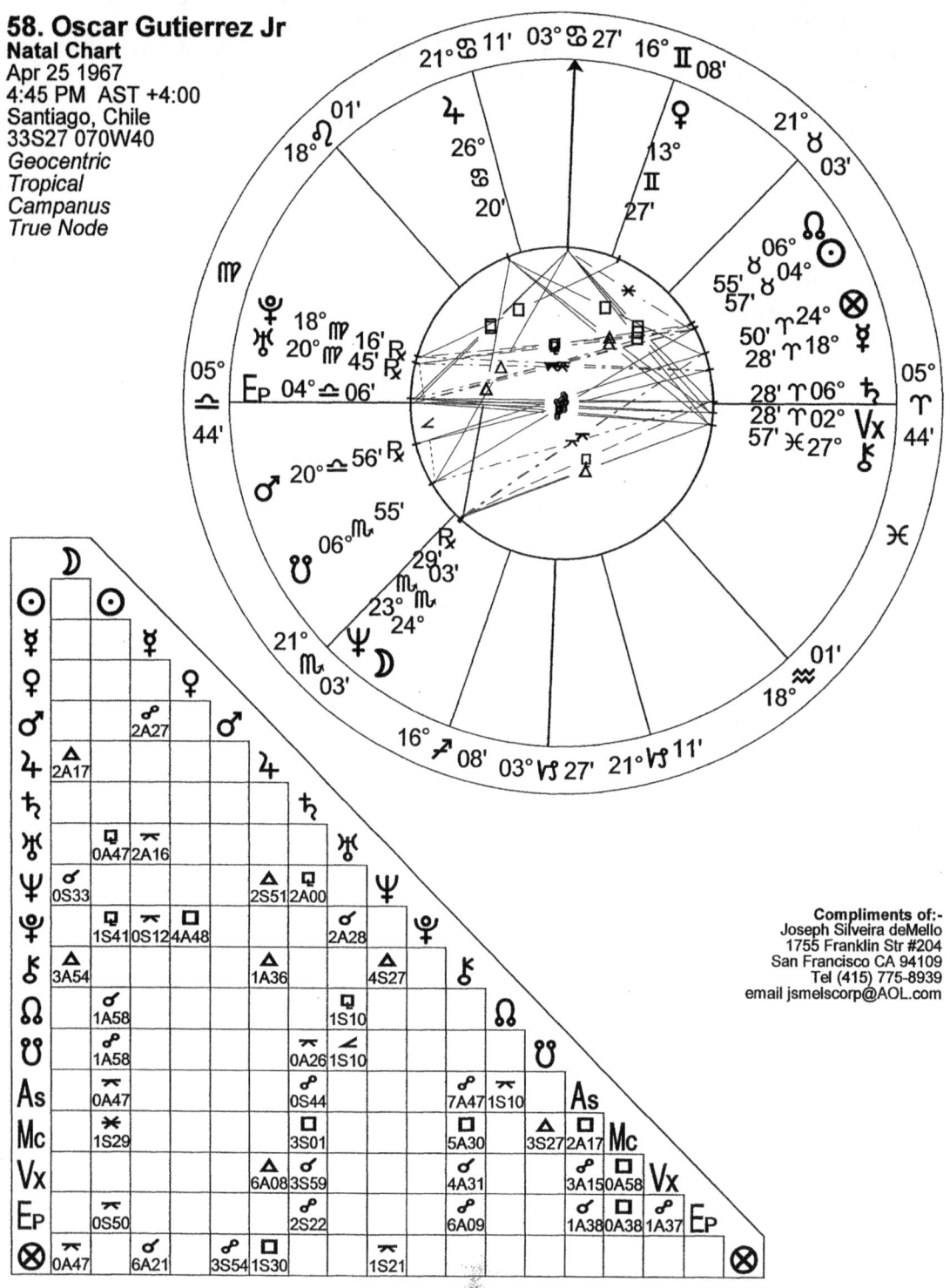

59. Computer Engineer
Natal Chart
Jan 11 1968
9:14 PM PST +8:00
San Francisco CA
37N47 122W26
Geocentric
Tropical
Campanus
True Node

Compliments of:-
Joseph Silveira deMello
1755 Franklin Str #204
San Francisco CA 94109
Tel (415) 775-8939
email jsmelscorp@AOL.com

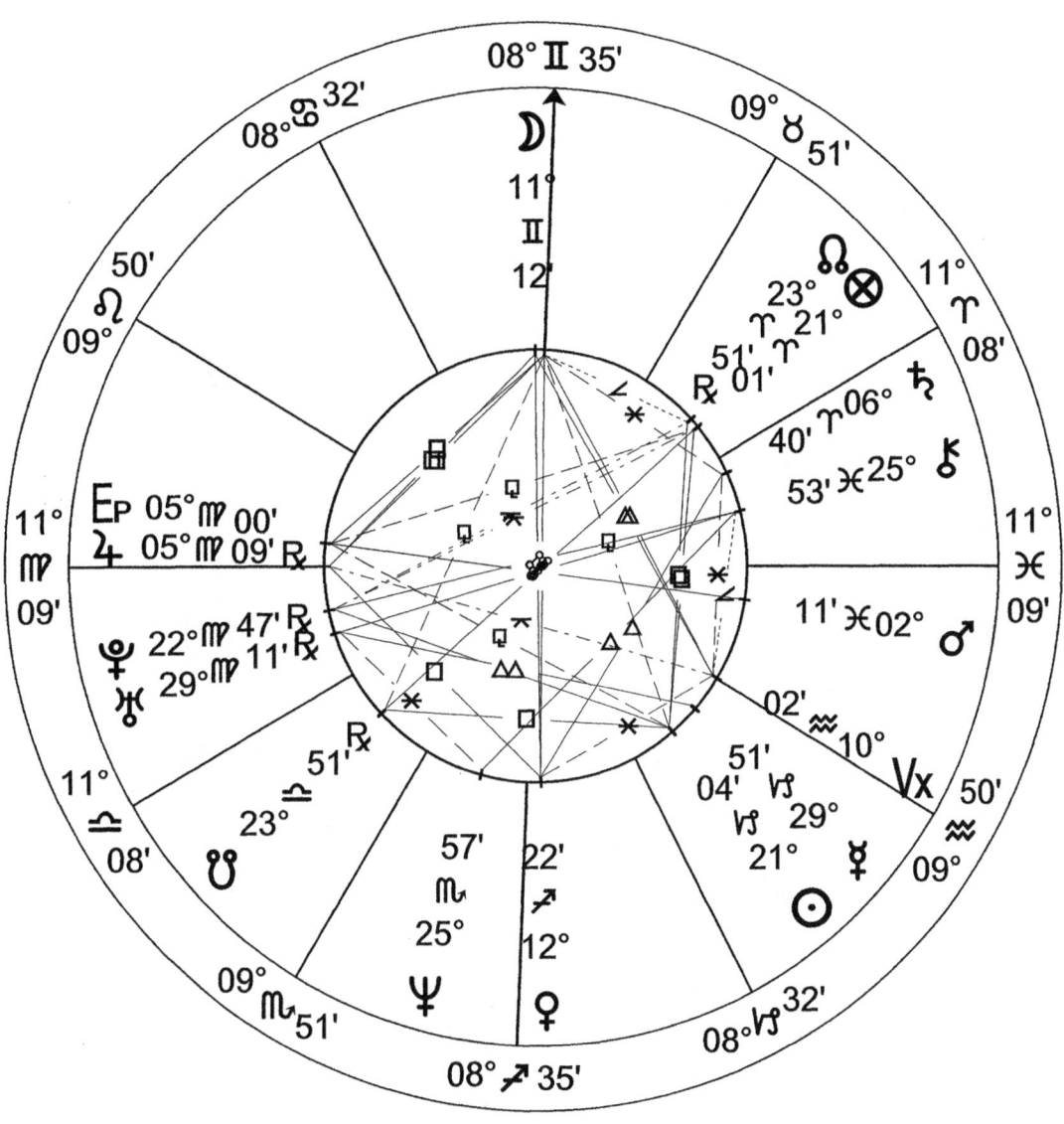

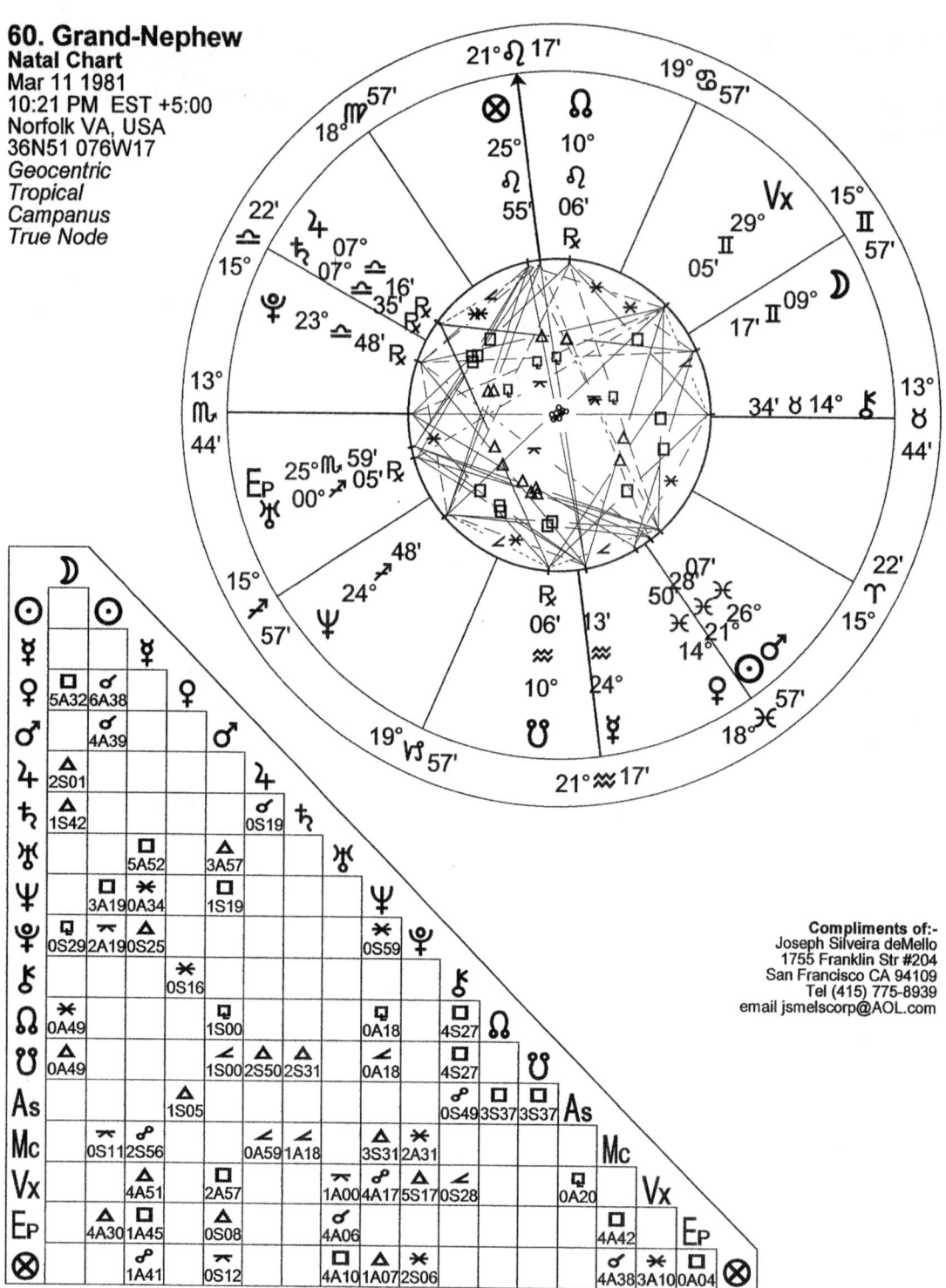

marriage), and he were at home. His mother dropped him out the window to a passersby. When his older half sister saw this, she ran and hid, and in the smoke filled room, her mother could not find her. The mother was rescued, but the little girl perished. When her husband would not leave the Navy, the wife divorced him and returned to her place of birth taking the surviving child with her. And shortly after, his father gave up on his naval career.

He is a Scorpio rising (and on that basis we should get along as Scorpios always like Scorpios). The chart is nocturnal. Scorpio is therefore ruled by Mars in Pisces, and Pisces is ruled by Jupiter in Libra which leads us to see a mutual reception between Venus and Jupiter, Jupiter is conjunct Saturn and both are retrograde. Quite a few of our family members have Jupiter in various ways aspected to Saturn. Also the threads of Gemini and Pisces abound in our family charts. At the time of the home fire Saturn was transiting his twelfth house.

The Sun is between Venus and Mars both not too close. He graduated from high school with no intent of further education. But he will probably have a good work ethic and, perhaps, a Leo career with some emphasis on creativity. Neither parent is going to push him toward a military career. Whatever he does, his personality and Uranus in the first house should be an indicator. Scorpio rising will be a detective or researcher. Pluto in the twelfth may indicate a prison career. Don't laugh as he lives in a town famous for its penitentiary.

61. Jackpot, 8-1-4
Saturn: 0N18, Jupiter: 0N01, Mercury: 0S57
Data: April 9, 1981, 9:37 p.m. EST,
Plattsburgh, New York, 44N30, 73W27

This and the next chart are the charts of the two teenagers who went on a rampage on the April 20, 1999 at the Columbine School in Littleton, Colorado, and shot themselves at the end of their spree. I decided to call this Jackpot because Jupiter and Mercury are also with Saturn at zero declination although Mercury is at South declination while the other two are at North. So now also note that Mercury is in a northern sign, while the other two are in a southern sign. The data for both is reputed to be birth certificate data, published by the NCGR Boston Chapter and forwarded to me by Edward Dearborn. Frances McEvoy, Boston astrologer actually saw the birth certificate of this youth. What the release did not say was that an astrologer, with a detective in tow, saw the Colorado birth certificate of the second youth, although they could not according to law be given a copy of the latter.

Since the identity has been revealed in the media, this is the chart of Eric Harris. It gives us chart with Scorpio rising, Sun in Aries, and Moon in Cancer. Mars is also in Aries but it is Uranus on the Ascendant which first catches our eye, and it is retrograde. Scorpio rising with Mars in Aries is going to look more like and Aries, and Uranus so close will either make the person either quite attractive or rather homely. Described in the media as a nerd and personality misfit, such descriptions are merely psychological generalities. What we have here is a deep and secretive personality, rather unconventional, but with a large ego and aggressiveness, and would like to appear as nurturing. By the way, if this chart were done in Placidus it will have Capricorn and Cancer intercepted in the second and eighth houses. Campanus gives us a first to seventh interception in Sagittarius and Gemini, and a nocturnal birth gives us the Part of Fortune in the Virgo Midheaven. Note further that the horizon is fixed while the vertical is mutable.

This is a chart with many difficulties. Unlike many charts of negative people and criminals, there are no grand trines although there are individual trines. Interesting oppositions, Sun and Venus to Pluto, and Mercury to Jupiter and Saturn. See that the Mercury opposition to Jupiter and Saturn makes a T-square to the Cancer Moon. Mars and Moon are dignified in their own signs, and most of the chart is disposed of by Mars.

I favor and pay attention to the locations of three things in any birth chart, where the Aries point is, where the Ascendant is and where Saturn is. The Aries point is in the fourth house, a need for security. The Scorpio Ascendant gives a depth which the Sun does not have. And Saturn retrograde is the condition of those who see relationships as highly necessary. Of course few start life with the Ascendant and Saturn together, and here Saturn is in the tenth, obviously a child heralded at his coming and facing a future of difficulties with a father figure. He has his first Saturn return in infancy and only lived just past Saturn opposed to natal Saturn, a crucial time in the life of any youth. What a youth he must have spent, briefly checking out his status without any prior experience, checking out those around him for friends, and then being in a position to analyze a past just barely started before Saturn goes into his first and allows him to experience the forging of a personality image for himself. A Saturn transit through the twelfth can be so difficult to an adult, so how much more difficult to a boy just about to start school.

This example was born with five retrograde planets, second hand Jupiter, relative Saturn, underdog Pluto, creative Uranus and prideful Neptune. So many retrogrades are difficult to handle and set him apart from his peer age group. We must count these as points of difficulty and add to them the closeness of Mars and Venus scorched by his ego Sun. This trio in the fifth house, the area of speculation, is hardly going to work well for the youth of this chart. Then we have the Capricorn Moon, and many who have that meet with much opposition.

Monday morning quarterbacking is futile. We are too late. And so are the psychologists and all people around him. This child, more than most, obviously needed acceptance. Shutting out his parents and keeping them blind to his activities is no more than second nature to adolescents. Notice the only aspect the Ascendant makes is the conjunction to Uranus. Think of the only aspect to the Midheaven as the trine to Chiron. Astrologers can decide from this chart whether, as it is in Campanus, the Moon is not intercepted, is less difficult than having the chart in Placidus, which would have the Moon intercepted, and whether Neptune intercepted is better than having it unintercepted.

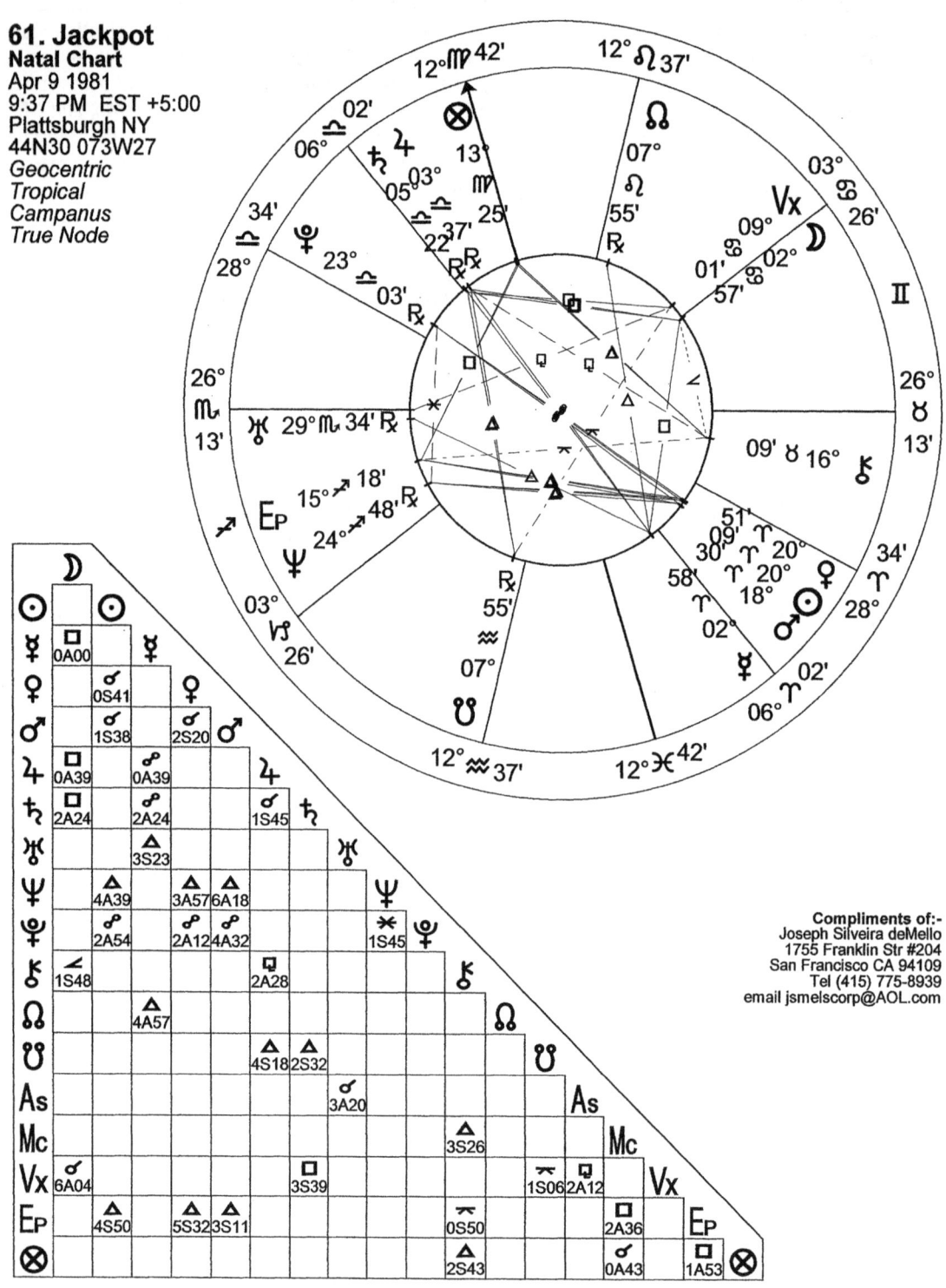

62. Jackpot #2, 7-6-11
Saturn: 1S02
Data: September 11, 1981, 9:11 a.m. MDT,
Denver, Colorado, 39N45, 104W59

This is the chart of David Klebold, the other young man involved in the Columbine High School massacre at Littleton, Colorado on April 20, 1999. He, too, ended the fracas by turning his gun upon himself. Two suicides, neither of which had the classical signature of Neptune in the twelfth house. And note the other boy had Neptune only trine to the trio in his Aries fifth house. Here we have Neptune square the Sun and sesquiquad Mars.

Some attention at the time was devoted to which of these two boys was the lead protagonist. My vote goes to this young man, who has a more complicated chart and what I think is the stronger of the two. And I am doing so despite the previous chart having been cardinal-fire, and here we have cardinal with air prominence. This chart puts great weight into twelfth and first houses, has a fence-sitting rising sign, a planning Sun and a knowing Moon. He would assume leadership. His Mars in the tenth is concerned with status, that in Leo Mars needs to be a leader and figurehead, and doubtless it was his idea to become a celebrity by playing with fire. With the majority of planets on the left side of his chart, he is more self-motivated, for good or evil, and he also has as many planets above as below. The previous chart was equal in distribution above and below and left and right.

Being entirely fair, Saturn in the twelfth of learning from previous experience and Jupiter in the twelfth as Guardian Angel placement are evidently negated in this chart. Pluto in the first house has as much prominence as Mars in this chart, and Venus in the first house is the only planet in the chart in its own sign. Pluto, sign of sabotage, occurs in his personality area. The Uranus of this chart is on the Ascendant of the previous chart. The Sun of this chart falls in the tenth house of the previous chart, while the Sun of the other chart falls into the seventh house of this chart. These also mark this young man as leader of the other. The other was his natural partner, while he himself would be instrumental in determining the status of the other young man. No study of these two charts is complete without checking progressions, solar returns and transits.

There were plenty of warning signs in this young man's behavior. He violated curfew, vented his frustration in throwing things or in physical attacks on his parents (in a society that now believes corporal punishment is child abuse and should be a reported offense), or physical attacks on the walls or doors of his room. No psychological authority will admit cases of such overt behavior to counseling for two reasons: 1) they are not a danger to themselves (even if he breaks his own hands) and, 2) they have not yet done anything for which they should be physically detained. And then we are told there are too many children and too few counselors.

Pause for Reflection

What a mixed bag we have in these 62 charts, so mixed that we are hard put to find one trait all of them have in common. Sixty-two is hardly a large enough chart sample for research, but already these samples divide themselves with Saturn retrograde or direct, those in Northern signs in Southern declinations and vice versa, and, of course, in a variety of signs and a variety of house placements. Meaning that merely being in zero declination is too wide a heading. We could have seen that Saturn has favorable, difficult or neutral aspects, and the work would expand to meet all the potential individual considerations exemplifying the very individual study that is astrology. These people are no more or no less Saturnian in their approach to life and living.

What this study has meant to do is to awaken the reader to the importance of any planet at zero declination. We have much to check in any chart, astrology being as wide as the human experience. But it is really important to consider declinations, not only in the birth chart, but how declinations manifest through progression and transits. No doubt the reader will have checked these things in his own chart and mull over meanings and directions life has taken, yea or nay, and pondered meanings. Tying in historical persons with known biographies will perhaps have been more help than those charts of modern and miscellaneous clients and friends from the author's files as impartial as I have attempted to be about all these charts. What the astrologer gets from study of his own chart is that he is right there to agree or disagree with all the checkpoints.

The hallmark of all these charts lies in the absolute seriousness of every person whose chart we have checked. We have to forget whether we like or dislike them, are at sympathy with them or critical of them. Every one of these samples lived or is living his life on his own terms and doing exactly what he wanted or wants to do. It is hoped that the Saturn qualities of these people shine through regardless of Sun, Moon or rising signs. The hallmark of Saturn is conservative, and all the other things Saturn may mean from years of all astrologers being Saturn watchers. But as many of them as might be seen to be conservative, there are also liberals in this group and eccentrics. I have commented on those who are homosexual to point up that these come in all varieties of occupations, habits and beliefs. To my amazement, the majority of the homosexuals in this group have been overt and unmistakingly so in their mannerisms. Only two of the homosexuals in this group easily pass as heterosexual, and both of them were bisexuals. This was a discovery for which I was not quite prepared even though Saturn is in every chart we look at. I would have expected anyone heavily saturnian, which is to say, Saturn importantly at zero degrees declination, if homosexual, to be concealed and closeted, but this was simply not generally true.

Charts with Saturn at Wider Orb

With these charts, we will explore how different or if different at all from the sorts of people who have Saturn in close orb to zero declination. This group will be treated in the same way we treated of the first sixty-two charts. Some of these charts will not be illustrated, but

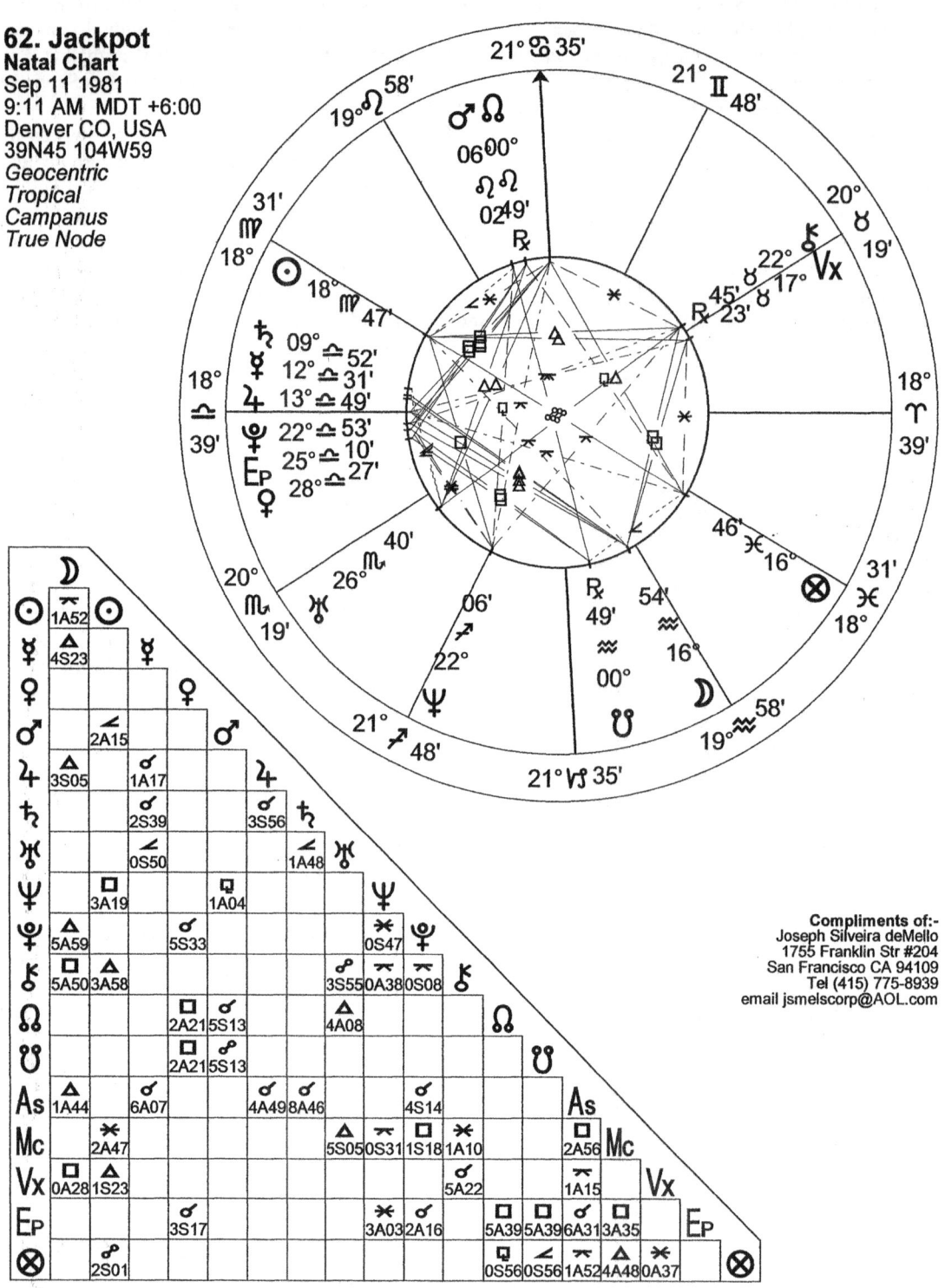

they will have the data and curtailed comments for readers who may wish to set up and look at these additional charts.

63. Eileen Garrett, 11-12-12
Wider orb Saturn: 1S39
Data: March 17, 1893, 5:25 a.m. UT, Drougheda, Ireland, 53N43, 6W15

Her advertisements in *Horoscope* magazine always carried a picture of this lady, and I had long made up my mind she must be an Aquarian, and sure enough, she turned out to be Aquarius rising. This chart was discussed at a lecture given by the late and wonderful astrologer Mary Vohryzek (nee Lynch) at one of the Saturday lectures in the rooms of the Theosophical Society in San Francisco. Everyone knew this lady as the first any only psychic to advertise in *Horoscope* magazine.

64. 20th Century Lady, 8-3-8
Wider orb Saturn: 1N26
Data: June 12, 1908, 4:00 p.m. EST,
Darien, Connecticut, 41N05, 73W28

I had a terrible time deciding on a descriptive tag which would fit this interesting lady. Truly born in the early 20th century, she lived in an era from the first automobile and so many inventions we take for granted in our daily living. Moreover, she learned how to cope with all of these. She remembers long train trips to the east and half a day to London by plane. Two world wars, and many other wars on the side, the Great Depression. Her father was a pioneer in the movie industry, and she married four times and had three children. She saw her children from ankle sox to residencies world wide.

Her father allowed her to do walk on bits, and it was a special privilege which let her appear on screen with some of the great figures of early cinema history. Her parents saw to it that she attended a proper well-known finishing school in the east. Although it was very glamorous, she was raised to decorum and the realities, but it was in the Hollywood setting that she came to the attention of an oil millionaire who all his life had an eye for young girls. He had known her in passing for several years and finally proposed marriage. It was her first marriage, but it was his third and destined not to be the last for either of them. From this marriage she had two sons, but her husband "traveled too much," was never at home, and she soon gave him the liberty to pursue other ladies. Divorce was becoming more popular in the 1920s, but in those days it was still a social stigmata. In this divorce, she never got alimony, and child support was a sometime thing. She married a New York stockbroker and had a daughter of that marriage which was also not successful. She then married a San Francisco attorney, having decided to return to California and not raise her family out here. This too ended in divorce. Finally, after many years, in London, her favorite city, she met the heir of a big pharmaceutical company who was also a neurosurgeon, trustee and professor of medicine at a prestigious eastern university. From then on, she basically lived in the university city, but she also had homes in Palm Beach, in Montego Bay and in the Napa Valley wine country, and annual stays in London.

She did not live a truly pampered life until her fourth and last husband. Forced quite often to raise her children as a single mother, she was determined that their growing up should be enjoyable. So she had done some wild and wacky things any bright young mother does to avoid making a chore of growing up. Once a figure skating champion, she was a lifelong national figure skating judge and loved to ski, hike and ride horses. In the 1950s she held a license as a California real estate broker. She loved opera and had a box at the San Francisco Opera and late in life had lavishly contributed to the staging of at least two operas. She seemed to do things with just the right flair. She was a bright optimist who enjoyed life right up to the day when her husband died. The life as a widow held no charms for her. She missed her husband so greatly that aloneness led to an over indulgence in alcoholic beverages. She seemed to go into the depths of despond. She spent more time traveling. She died of lung cancer 2:30 p.m. CST, 23 Jan 1988.

Her chart is Scorpio rising with the Moon in Scorpio in the first house. Everyone always knew exactly what she thought about any subject; she told them. Her Sun is in Gemini in the eighth house where she also has Pluto with her Sun and Vertex, and Mars, Mercury and Neptune in Cancer. The great majority of placements are in the third quadrant, objectively interested in other people. Jupiter in Leo in her ninth house would sometime in her life progress into her tenth house. It was always a pleasure to be in her company.

65. Nelson Aldrich Rockefeller, 7-4-8
Wider orb Saturn: 1N46
Data: July 8, 1908, 12:10 p.m. EST,
Bar Harbor, Maine, 44N20, 68W12

Grandson of John D. Rockefeller, Sr. of Standard Oil, this man served as governor of New York and as vice president under President Gerald Ford. Although a Republican, he was always a great admirer of Franklin D. Roosevelt, under whom he served as Coordinator for Inter-American Affairs and as an assistant secretary in the State Department. He also had a minor position in Eisenhower's Department of Health Education and Welfare. He played a prominent role in promoting the candidacy of Eisenhower, and it is said that without Nelson Rockefeller we never would have had a United Nations, NATO or the presence of a Republican ascendancy in the last half century.

But what he most wanted, the White House, eluded him, and that may be due to the criticisms made of him by Henry Kissinger who once worked for him, and by Eisenhower, not the brightest of intellects but still perceptive enough to doubt whether Rockefeller had the brains to be president. He was heir to the Standard Oil fortune, brought up frugally in a miserly Baptist household. He began life as a child with a thirty cent per week allowance (at a time when few children got any allow-

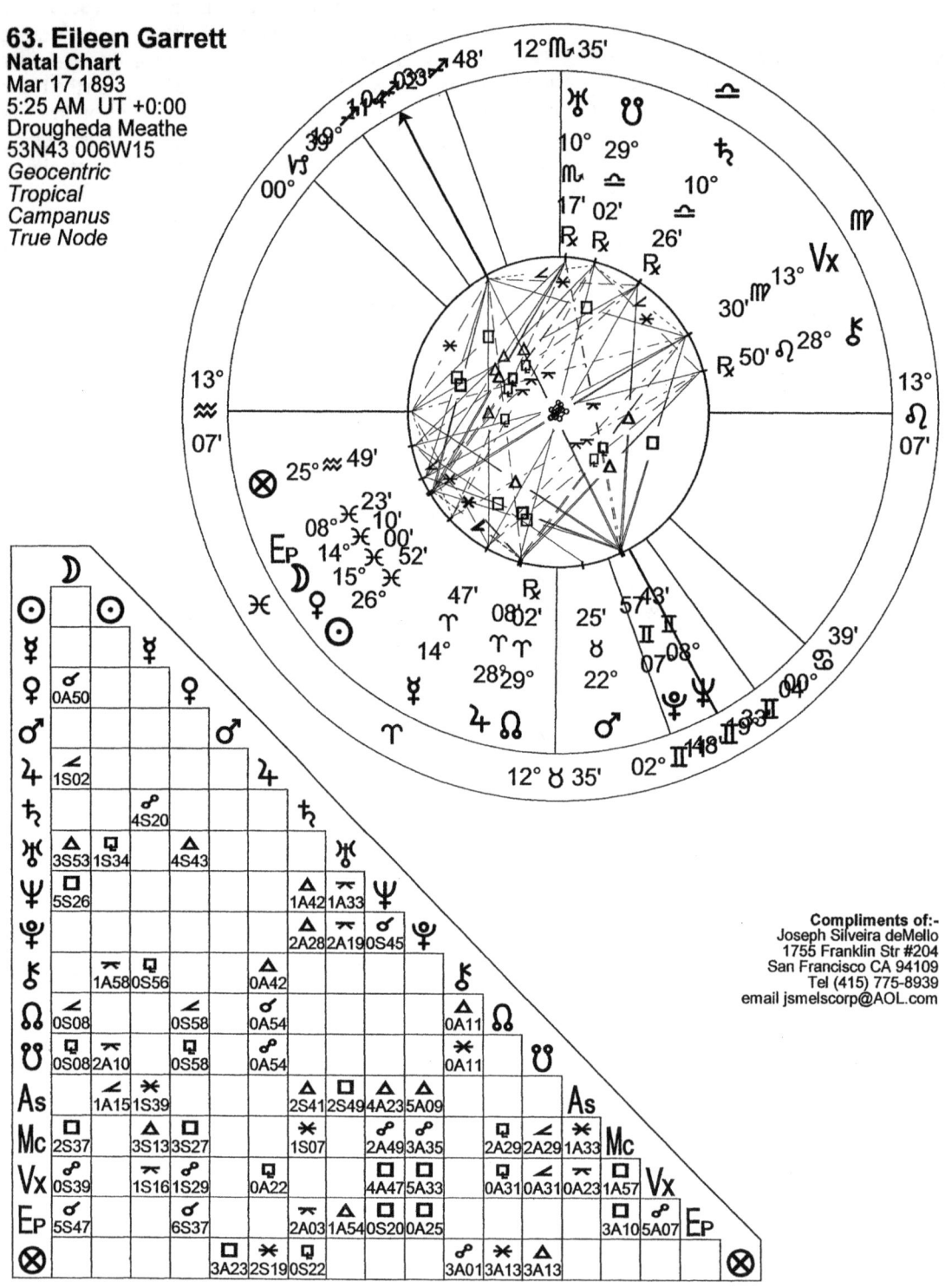

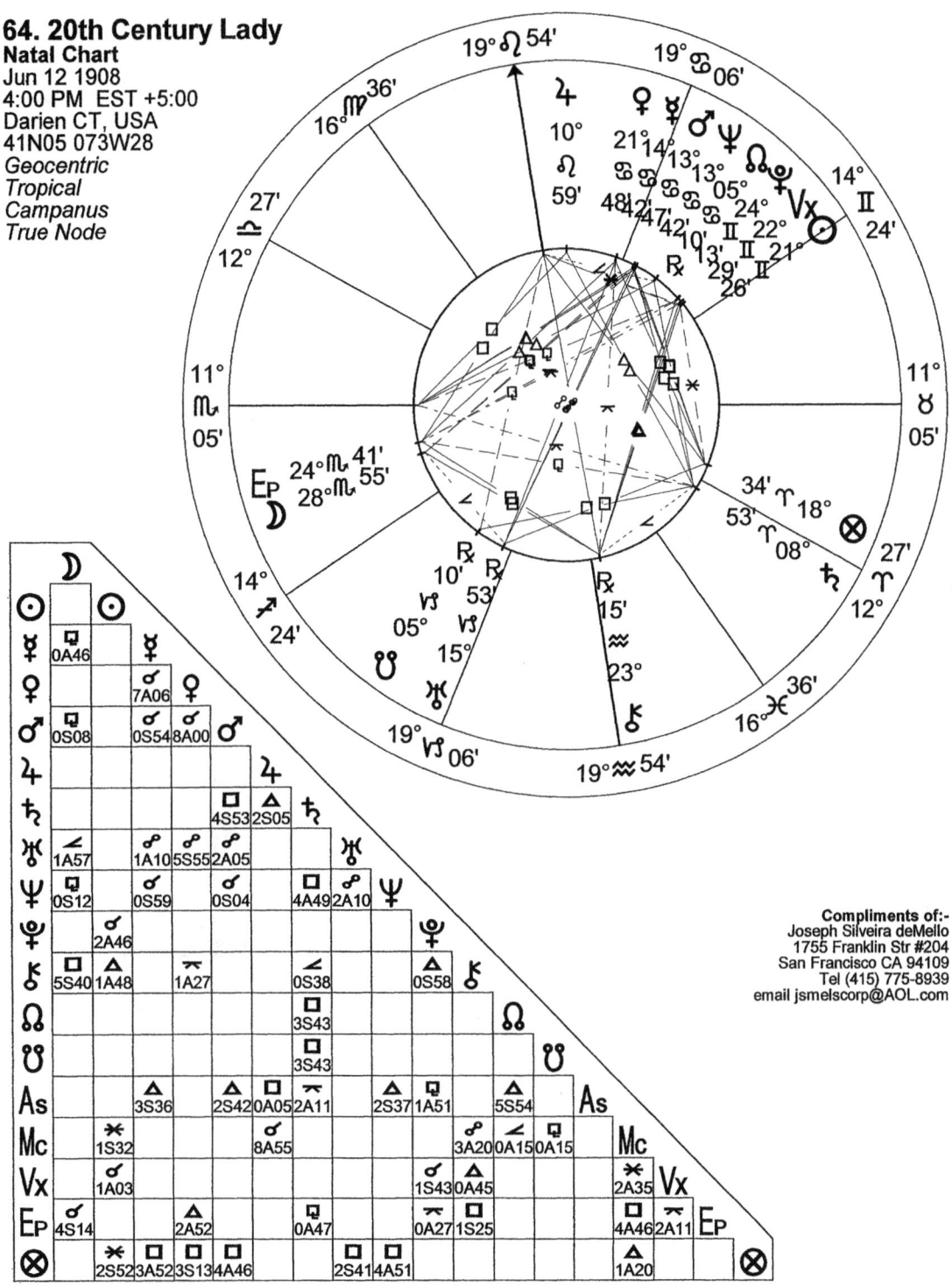

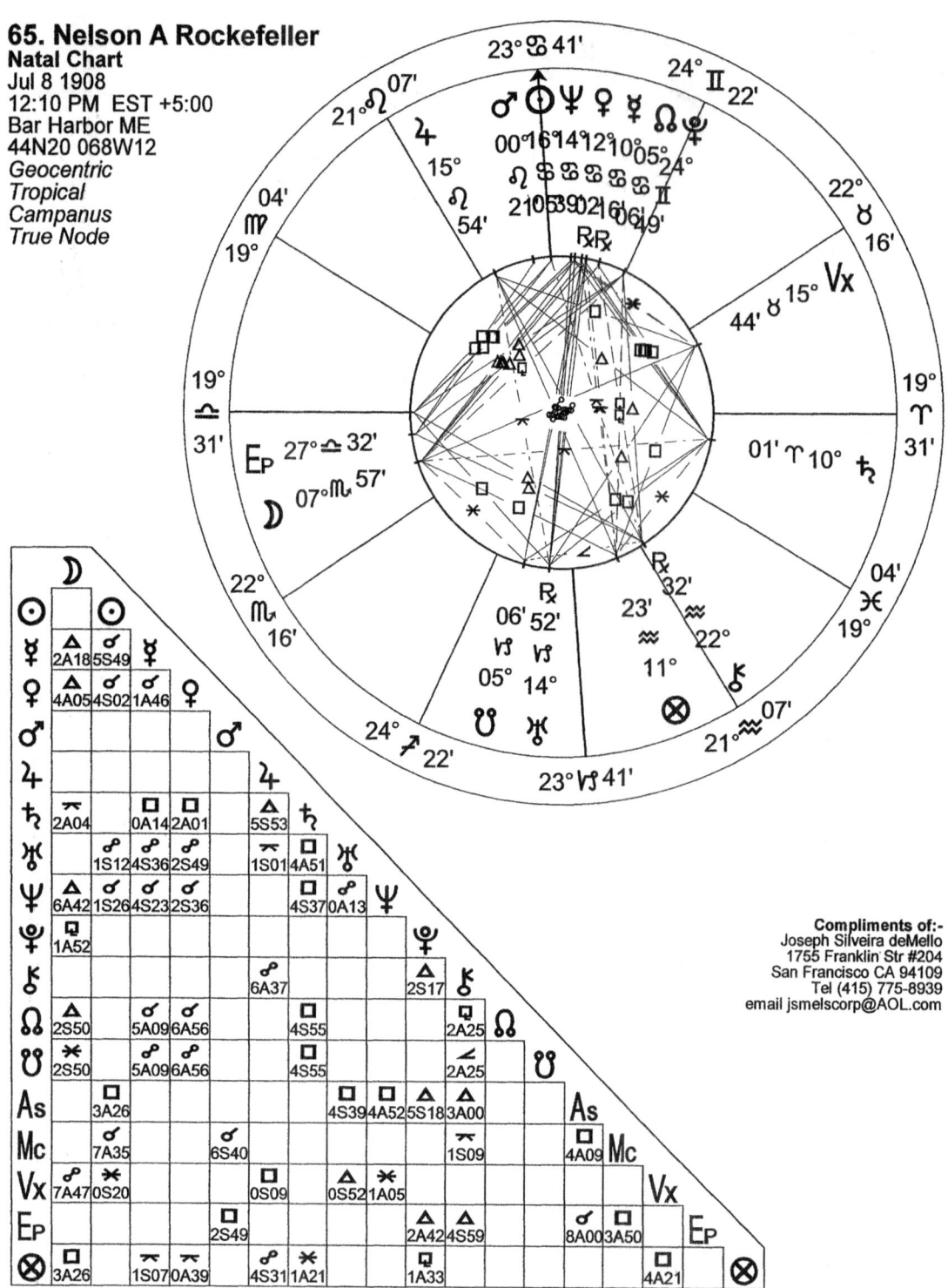

ance), one-third of which he was supposed to save, another third which he was supposed to give to charity (or the church) and, if he spent the remaining third frivolously, he was fined five cents. With all this modest lack of ostentation, the family was wealthy enough to support large estates and summer in Bar Harbor along with the Morgans and others who eschewed the Newport social scene or the north shore of Long Island.

He was to be active in all elements of business and philanthropy, but spending money was what he knew best and enjoyed most. He was a very balanced person, able to please his father and the political world. It is due to him that we have the term Liberal Republican. He much cared for the meaning of his social standing and place in society (Libra rising, Cancer Midheaven and Venus), and had a genius for knowing other people deeply and well. But as befits Mercury retrograde, he was dyslexic, which proved to be no handicap to him. And with Venus retrograde, he found some things funny that others found grim and found grim some things others thought hilarious. He died working at his desk, although there were rumors that it might have been the result of a romantic assignation.

If we think of Saturn as the epitome of conservative, it seems to have given him a bit of latitude. Aspirations to the presidency were to climax his life. Rockefeller was very loose with money. He defeated Averill Harriman to become governor of New York, and Alsop, the political columnist, used to refer to both of them as the "rich Siamese twins." As governor, Rockefeller became involved in a spending spree never seen previously or since in the history of New York State, one so serious that the state almost went broke. A great sponsor of modern art, he donated heavily to the New York Museum of Modern Art and passed out Picasso works almost as party favors to the ladies of his court. He was probably the best looking member of his family and society's darling. His Saturn is square the ninth house crowd of Sun, Mercury, Venus and Neptune, but Mars in the tenth is as ambitious as any ninth house placement. He spoke of himself as a man who had everything so that the only thing left to want was the highest office of his country.

With five planets in the ninth house, and Mars and Jupiter in the tenth, it cannot escape us that these were the important areas of the chart. Notice the order of these ninth house planets. Pluto is on the cusp of the house, making this an area of self-sabotage. The North Node is there—intake from philosophical attitudes, from ideas of why things are as they are—putting the South Node in the area, third, of release through the status quo. The crowd of planets around the Sun needs special attention. Usually planets combust the Sun are taken over by the person's ego needs. The Sun may scorch Venus, but Neptune would have survived and affected his ego. We may speak of the care and sensitivity of Cancer, but we won't get agreement from the people at Attica. Neptune would ensure that he see not too clearly. We should rather think in terms of the Sun besieged by Neptune and Mars. The "kicker" here is Uranus retrograde in the third house and opposite most ninth house placements. Retrograde Uranus is very creative, but basic Uranus is unconventional. Uranus rules his creative fifth house, where we cannot escape the presence of Chiron and wonder what he overlooked.

Note now that he was born with a Saturn that rules his fourth house but is in his sixth house and in fall in Aries. This tells us that he was born into responsibility inculcated or drummed into him from the start. For it is Saturn in the sixth that makes sixth house service karmic. Quite early in life Saturn went into his seventh, more knowledge of social responsibility. See Saturn as midpoint between Mercury and Uranus, or the focal point of a T-square.

But the executives of his party worried about the message Rockefeller would bring to national government. Perhaps it was his stance at Attica where he was, for a change, suddenly seen as more hard-nosed than liberal. His era was one of labor prosperity, an unusual situation in a Republican regime; he expanded public works, repairing potholed highways, mindless that he was financially burdening the state. Philosophy ninth ruled by Gemini is a challenge.

66. Lyndon B. Johnson, 5-6-6
Wider orb Saturn: 1N13
Data: August 27, 1908, 4:29 a.m. CST,
Stonewall, Texas, 30N15, 98W31

Johnson, a poor Texas farm boy, born some weeks after the previous sample, was radically different. He was born determined to attain status, and did so by very carefully calculated stages. His first sponsor was John Nance Gardner, a political power in South Texas, and later on his next mentor was Sam Rayburn, equally a driven Texan. He worked for both as an aide, and he could not have had better tutors for the power arena. The ultimate step was to move in timely fashion to get himself elected to the House of Representatives. With a solid marriage to a Virginia heiress, two daughters and a conservative family image, he had prime qualifications as a political hopeful. The crown of his career came when he was chosen by John F. Kennedy as running mate when JFK was going to need the Southern vote. Beside the suave charisma and Harvard image of JFK, Johnson sounded like any other backwoods Texan, a thick southern drawl with country figures of speech. When, at the death of Kennedy, he was sworn in as President of the USA, I cringed at his first speech when he drawled out the infamous date ending with a full scale elongation of "Nineteen hundred and Sixty-three." Regardless of how he sounded, here was a man well versed in the politics of consensus and coalition, famed for working both aisles of Congress. He was subsequently persuaded to smooth his voice by taking elocution lessons from Robert Montgomery who helped Johnson polish his voice and speech patterns. He completed the Kennedy term, and Congress let him have all the things they had refused to Kennedy, and got himself elected to a term of his own. Johnson is best summed up as political savvy and a power broker.

Raised absolutely in a work ethic that was thoroughly serious, when he became President, he was

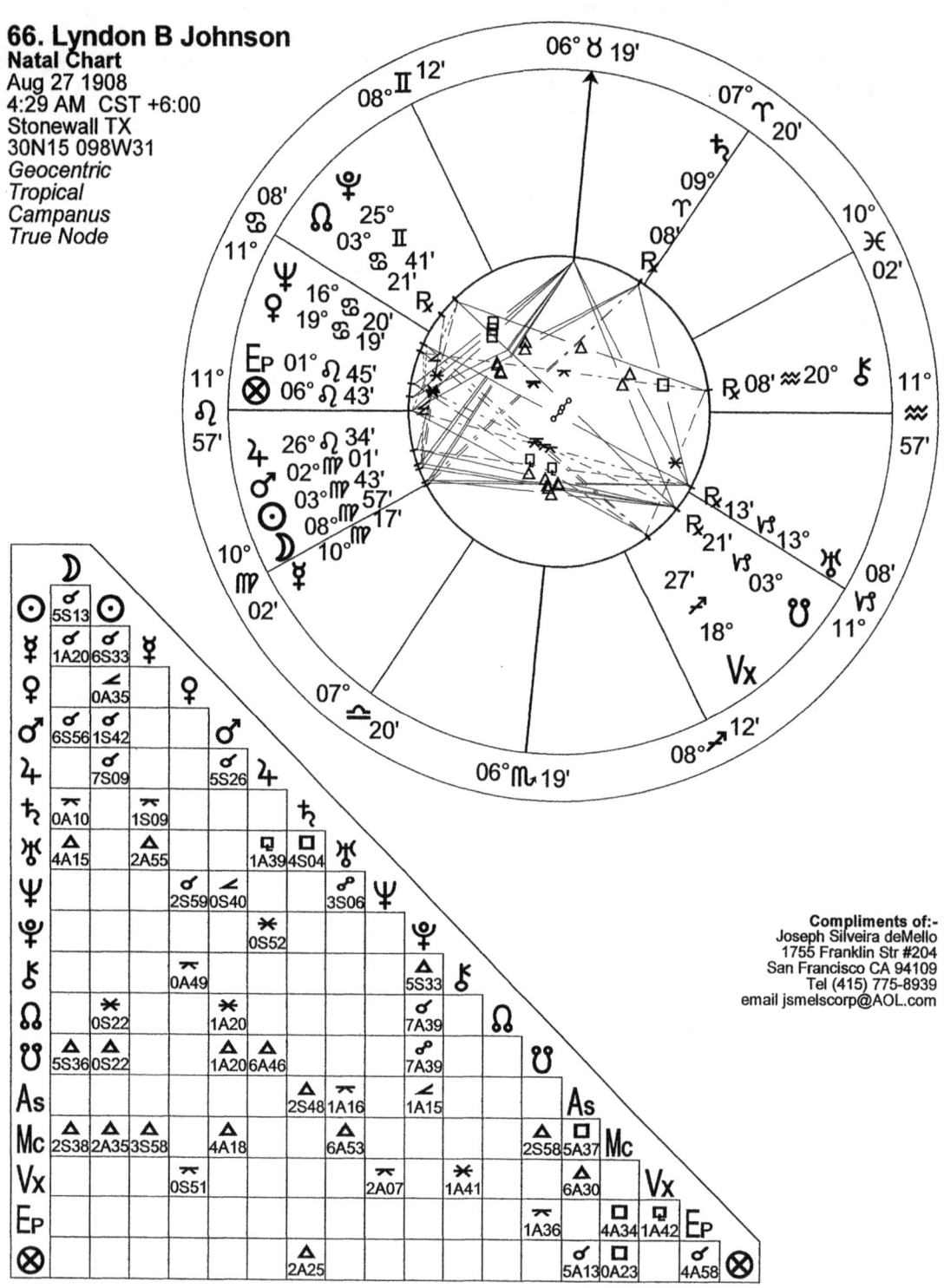

amazed by the number of people from the Secret Service who stood around watching him and doing absolutely nothing else. It drove him to distraction, and he would snap impatiently at them, "Don't just stand there, do something." Although a double Virgo, he was also Leo rising, so he had a proper estimate of his importance in the highest office when he got there. He was determined that everything which happened during his presidency be recorded for posterity. To this point he installed tape recorders throughout the White House. These were to remain there after he left office and ultimately performed a disservice and the undoing of Richard Nixon. Although he became more polished, he never lost the cajoling capacity for homey southern syrup.

It is most unfortunate that the astrologers of his time viewed Johnson and his chart in the light of rather misguided public feeling. Mark you, this was an age when Kennedy was highly popular and universally slandered. Even as he affected history, history was being revised under his feet. The public little remembered that Vietnam did not have its SEATO beginnings with his administration. Notice the closeness of Sun and Mars and see it as ego dominating military activity and rulership of the ninth house. He was determined we make as good a showing in Vietnam as possible and get it over with. This unfortunately was not to be. Vietnam was to dog his every waking moment. The biggest irony is that we were criticized by France, the very France who had been the first to fail in Vietnam, the France who obviously drove their former colony toward Communism, and the France whom we twice bailed out of European conflicts. Let no good deed go unpunished.

Now let us have some look at the chart. He has four planets in the first house, and these six houses of his chart. Ghandi only had three (Mercury, Venus and Mars) and most people think of Ghandi as a saint which he was not, he simply got his way). And note that only Jupiter is in the rising sign, so we cannot call him a war monger. As Vice-president, he stepped from leadership of the House to leadership of the Senate. His time there was not wasted. This was a man who knew personally every seat in Congress and had known them all for years. He also had an excellent memory and could cajole or flatter anyone to his needs. He expected to build a New Society, though how he was going to do so to a country more in tune to hedonism does make us look at his Neptune and find it cadent. Only by disastrous fate did he step in as our up front national leader, and neither Jupiter nor Sagittarius are at the top of his chart. Certainly Leo rising is a factor, but with Virgo Sun and Moon, oriented toward details, he could jolly well have freaked out. Notice that he was born after a New Moon, with the Moon in creasing in light, and if this is favorable in astrology charts it should also be favorable in his chart.

Johnson was as much a diamond in the rough as was Truman, both of them having been vice-presidents somehow left out of the loop of the real action until they discovered themselves waist deep in it. We have come to accept the greatness of Truman who said that the office of Vice-president was about just as important as warm spit; it should be about time we recognized the importance of Johnson. One must look at this chart without benefit of popular prejudice and revisionist history. Its one opposition from Venus-Neptune to Uranus does not have a mitigating kite formation, but Venus-Neptune is the focal point of a double quincunx to the Vertex and Chiron, and the quincunx is basically a nervous making aspect, one that astrology cookbooks will not interpret for us. It has sextiles and semi-squares. Moon-Mercury are trine Uranus, as well as trine Midheaven. The Midheaven is also trine Sun-Mars and Moon-Mercury, but Moon-Mercury also make double sesquiquads to Saturn and Uranus, with the latter two square each other. Thinking in terms of progressions, and without doing them, we realize that Leo and Virgo are slow as rising signs, but surely the Sun would have gone on to Scorpio by the time he became President and hit the bottom of his chart when he retired. Although he had all the career assistance any down-home politician could want, he would never have gone as far as he did without a great deal of determination and real work on his own behalf. He and Truman will always live in history as common men who rose to the heights of national prominence.

67. Entrepreneur, 9-12- 4
Wider orb Saturn: 1N31
Data: March 1, 1909, 12:02 a.m. CST,
Cottonwood Alabama, 31N06, 84W14

This man was born in rural Alabama east of Mobile and north of the Florida Panhandle. He made in his lifetime a great deal of money by investing in special business developments which always worked out well for him (retrograde Jupiter highest planet in his chart). Just before he died, he wanted to get into astrological software and gather together astrologers and computer people who would write a program to interpret any astrological chart by printing computer read-outs. This was in idea whose time was just around the corner. Another client brought him to me, and my first act was to make sure he understood what a monumental problem this might be. No interpretive program has ever been written to take into account how different positions and aspects mitigate each other, do not overlap, but necessarily have to change general interpretations. Unfortunately, all astrologers approached wanted to be the sole big cheese rather than part of a group of people working toward the same ends. This man had a genius for gathering around him people that he could mold into what he wanted them to be, and a record of having been successful with those people. But when he bumped into astrologers, they really dealt him a setback. and less than 20 years later, computer readouts were on the market.

The chart is Sagittarius rising with the Sun in Pisces and the Moon in Cancer. He was just as plain as an old shoe. Until he opened his mouth, you never would have suspected that he had business savvy and had money in the bank to attest to his success. I was impressed by him and wondered where he had seized the idea that astrology needed print-out computer readings. I knew that if he had this idea, so did someone else. It is in the grand

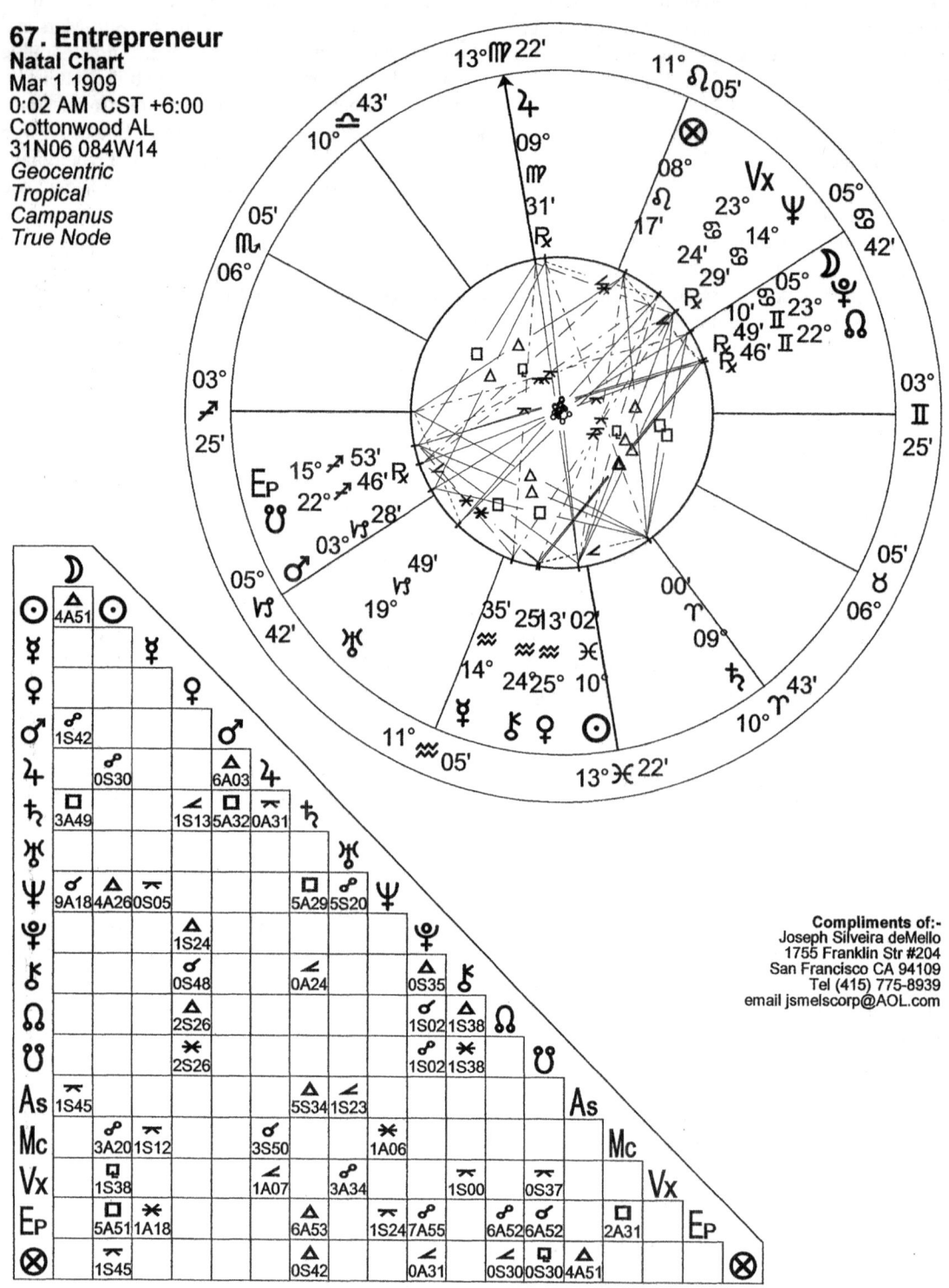

tradition of all inventiveness. It was going to be a case of who was going to bring forth this idea ahead of anyone else. The man had the wherewithal to make the investment and pay the salaries, but, interestingly enough, none of the astrologers I approached mentioned money or remuneration. As usual, this chart told of the man and told me of astrology, but more than anything else, it gave me a very jaundiced view of whatever it is that passes for the "astrological community." The client who brought him around, saw his idea as a way whereby all astrologers might benefit from his readiness to invest in the work. I explained to him that most real astrologers were not particularly partial to the idea of chart write ups being done mechanically. The problem was to find special programmers to create exceptions, weed out contradictions.

Later on, I had to tell him that every astrologer I'd approached and thought this could be done was not interested in a group undertaking but would be happy to take the job on all by him or herself. With such people the OED or the Encyclopedia Britannica could never have been written, the King James Bible never translated. I myself saw the only way to do it would be to give various segments of the monumental job divided up between the people wanting to do the work; no one person could ever accomplish it alone. This interesting chart has Mars in mutual reception to Saturn. Yet the basic motif of this man was Sagittarius rising with his chart significator almost on the Midheaven.

68. Retired WAAC, 5-12-6
Wider orb Saturn: 1N52
Data: March 6, 1909, 3:00 p.m. EST,
Belmont, Massachusetts, 42N24, 71W11

This is the chart of a very tall and handsome lady who began a career during the Second World War in the WAAC, stayed until retirement, and then studied astrology. She did this purely for her own interest. For years she attended all sessions of the astrology meetings at Theosophical Society. But going into her nineties, she has suffered a setback.

She has been in failing health since a small stroke (1996), and she cannot climb stairs or steep hillside streets. With Leo rising, she is as Leo as she can be with her upright carriage and bearing, and the Pisces Sun is far less visible than her Libra Moon which keeps her steering a moderate course. She has a mutual reception between Mars and Saturn which, in effect, gives her a Mars-Saturn conjunction, and we see here that Mars is out of bounds by declination. Connections between Mars and Saturn always seem to bring large quantities of frustration, impatience due to an inability to do everything one might wish to do. She very much enjoyed her career in the Army, and her life since then has been quiet, patrician, non-confrontational.

69. Ex-Nun and Teacher, 8-4-8
Wider orb Saturn: 1N31
Data: July 4, 1922, 4:00 p.m. EST,
Madawaska, Maine, 47N21, 68W21

I had studied astrology for six years, and I waited for Saturn to transit out of my twelfth house before I hung out my shingle as a professional astrologer. And in 1975, out of the blue, came a mature lady of some fifty years who wished to consult me on career guidance. In introducing herself, she told me she had been a teaching nun, having taken her final vows when she was twenty-seven, and that she remembered 1959 as her best year, but she had left the convent and teaching a few years ago and gone to work in a clerical job at a hospital. She felt, and had been feeling, she should make another change.

She was born in the most remote city at the very top of Maine. She had spent her life almost as far away as she could be from her place of birth, but it was no issue to her. I looked at her vacant ninth house with Neptune and Venus almost on the cusp of the ninth, and the cusp was Leo. One is creative in one's fifth house of speculations, in the area or of the things where the Sun is found (her eighth of gains from others and feedback), and in the area and of the things ruled by Leo (ninth of faraway places and philosophy). Mars the ruler of the fifth house is intercepted in the first house, giving privacy to Mars issues, and then noting that Mars is out of bounds, I concluded some weight was taken off Martian things. But Mars is also retrograde.

When considering career guidance, there are some practical non-astrological considerations. One must realize that a person over fifty is not going to easily find a job in private industry. One has to consider that her past experience must be of some value or a basic training bit for anything else she does. In leaving the convent and teaching, she had taken a job in a hospital run by nuns and gotten stuck with the paperwork mountain which can often happen to a Virgo Midheaven or sixth house. Is she meant to be in business, third house with Uranus there retrograde. Scorpio risings like jobs they can be left alone to do, and jobs which require some depth or research. Taurus on the sixth is not a very good sign for unpaid charity work and service, but not much of an issue since the sixth is unoccupied. The chart significator is Pluto, in mutual reception to the Moon, therefore giving courtesy placements of Pluto in the twelfth and Moon in the eighth, and Pluto close to the Sun in Cancer, gives Pluto greater strength. Both Pluto and the rising sign it rules have an abiding conviction that any change is always for the better. Then we find the Moon in Scorpio is also intercepted in the twelfth house but with a courtesy position in the house it rules, and gives greater outlet for the emotions. While she was more comfortable behind the scenes, interested privately in delving into the subconscious, the psychic and the intuitive, she had an outlet in feedback from others and handled that in a maternal manner. We can see here that the elements of the personality as equally Cancerian as they are Scorpionic. And Mars is retrograde, another element that puts the brakes on the usual operation of Mars.

In such questions we much look at personality, training, interest, job type, and the timing indicators for when the move should be made. All this may tell the astrologer is that the client may yet find her happy niche in public life and be rewarded. But it is never a happy thing to

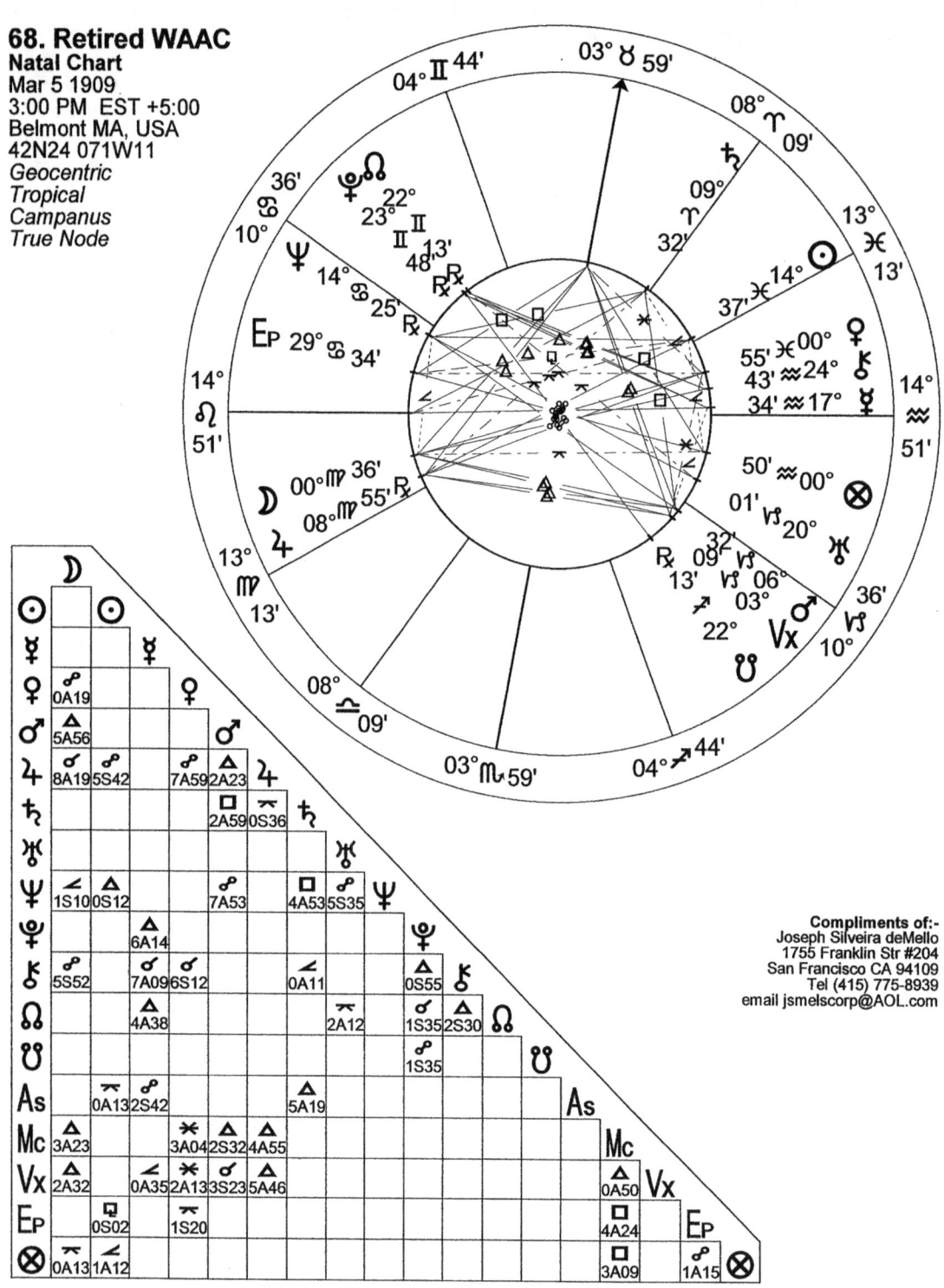

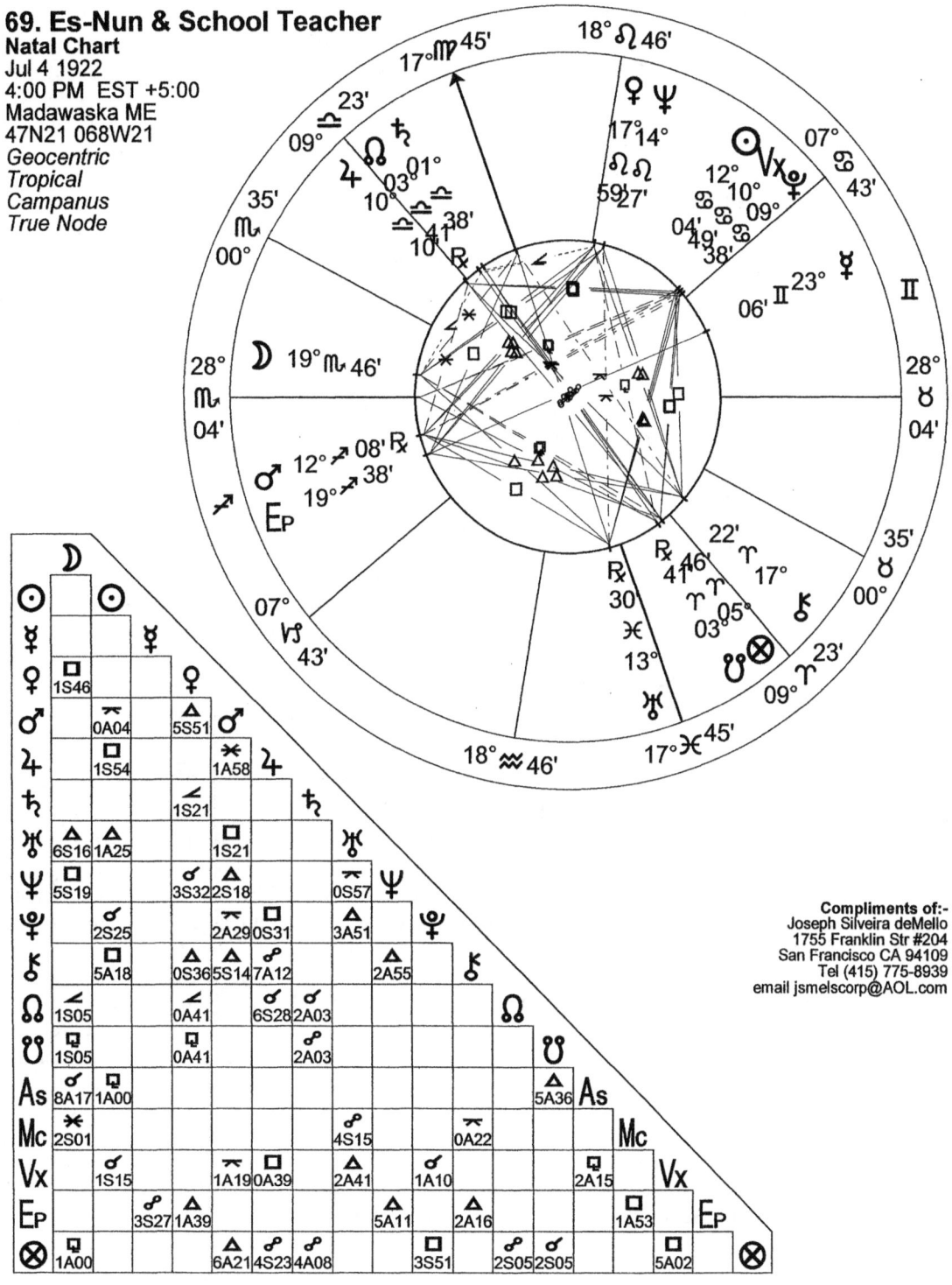

69. Es-Nun & School Teacher
Natal Chart
Jul 4 1922
4:00 PM EST +5:00
Madawaska ME
47N21 068W21
Geocentric
Tropical
Campanus
True Node

tell a client, who thinks change is overdue, that it may yet be some time before things are really right. And it does not specifically tell her where to send her resume.

I noticed Mercury not involved in the Moon-Pluto loop, intercepted in its own sign in the seventh house, and far behind the Sun: it must recently before her birth have been retrograde, and so it had been. Whatever may be said of Gemini, Mercury responds very intuitively to real emergencies. Note too that this Mercury is unaspected but for a wide opposition to the East Point, and an equally wide quincunx to the Ascendant. Such an unaspected Mercury becomes very strong, becomes the planet to watch, especially for times when it makes direct or retrograde stations or even when it changes signs, even if it is intercepted, and even in a chart where Mercury is not the chart significator. I felt every confidence that this client would make the right move on her own intuition.

70. Mark O. Hatfield, 7- 4-12
Wider arc Saturn: 1N19
Data: July 12, 1922, 11:30 a.m. PST,
Dallas, Oregon, 44N55, 123W20

This is the chart of the former governor and long-time senator from Oregon. From his youth he has retained amazing good looks. He was the only child of a railroad employee and a working mother who was a school teacher. When he was sixteen, first driver's license in hand, he drove down a street and hit and killed a girl who dashed out in front of his car. It was an unavoidable accident. He attended the small but well regarded Willamette University, interested in law, but changed to political science to get his masters from Stanford. He was a naval officer in the Second World War. With his masters degree there are but two possible options, teach or go into public life. Choosing the latter, he then single-mindedly took all the steps he felt necessary to make a success of his ambitions.

Having made his decision, he forthwith married and subsequently fathered four children and has lived a basically scandal-free life. All potential scandals have washed off him like water off a duck's back. This does not prevent his being the target of snide remarks about his aides being remarkably handsome males, but all attempts to trap him in political shenanigans have come to nothing. So great has been his popularity with voters that it is said that if his political opponents ran Jesus Christ in Oregon against Hatfield, Hatfield would win.

His chart has several indicators regarded as unfavorable by many astrologers. Immediately we see Pluto at the top of his chart, mercifully not close to the Sun, but Pluto is the highest planet in his chart, and we cannot fail to remember men in public life with Pluto there who have sabotaged their public status, Richard Nixon coming foremost to mind. Perhaps the Sun there, which is always most favorably regarded in astrology, saves the day. Saturn in the twelfth has a nice propensity for turning around potential contretemps in the career. Jupiter in first here does not give us a physically large person and note Jupiter is out of orb of a square to the Sun. Astrologers might be suspicious that this chart is not well timed, that perhaps he may have been born later. But this is birth certificate data. Then there is the Pisces Moon on the edge of a sixth house which also contains Uranus retrograde, both in Pisces and sensitive to the winds of chance. This is not the first time we will see a non-astrologer who seems to live as if he is entirely in tune with his own chart.

Libra rising is not unfamiliar to politicians, with Venus in Leo in eleventh does not consciously account for his retained good looks. Perhaps simply being Libra is enough for that for it is axiomatic in astrology that Librans wait until late in life to look their age. Then they are shocked to appear their real age in a short time period. Libra, the sign of the fence-sitter, also likes things to run smoothly. We see the Sun in Cancer, the sign of social reciprocity, adding to his acumen as a successful politician. The Ascendant at the midpoint of Saturn-Jupiter may well be a help, but we wonder about these square to Pluto. A few charts back we had an example of Jupiter conjunct Saturn which I described as karma together with its acceptance. This may give him both wariness and discipline.

We have already commented on how those who have Mars retrograde try to drive their cars without releasing the brakes. Perhaps that is just the check needed here. Note his Mars declination is well out of bounds, and he has Mars trine Neptune but square to Uranus, and the latter square is an astrological pointer to a murderer, say astrologers who so read it in the chart of O.J. Simpson, but not in the chart of Mark Spitz. This chart has no oppositions, no T-squares, no grand trines, which is to say, none of the big luck or disaster which those aspects usually signal to astrologers.

71. Saddam Hussein, 4-2-9
Wider orb Saturn: 1S45
Data: April 29, 1937, 8:55 a.m. BAT,
Tikrit, Iraq, 34N38, 43E42

Now we move years ahead to the chart of the military dictator of Iraq. When Saddam Hussein came to prominence, even his place of birth eluded the understanding of many of us. This data was published by Lois Rodden in *Today's Astrologer*, the AFA bulletin, of December 1990, but going back to check that issue, I do not find it, so undoubtedly my reference was poorly noted. This, as given, is his accepted data. We are faced with dealing with a man who culturally is a traditionalist settling all daily activity upon what is written in the Koran. However, human nature as the universal property of all men. They see the rest of the non-Arab world as infidels, and some of us think the same of them. Suffice it that he is very popular among his people. His people may parrot anti-American attitudes but lack no hesitancy in following American fashions and styles.

The chart has Cancer rising ruled by Moon in Sagittarius in the sixth house, and see the Moon give ambivalence toward things of that area. But we also have Mars there, the Mars position of an excellent work ethic. We can see Mars indicative of a military man, and the Moon

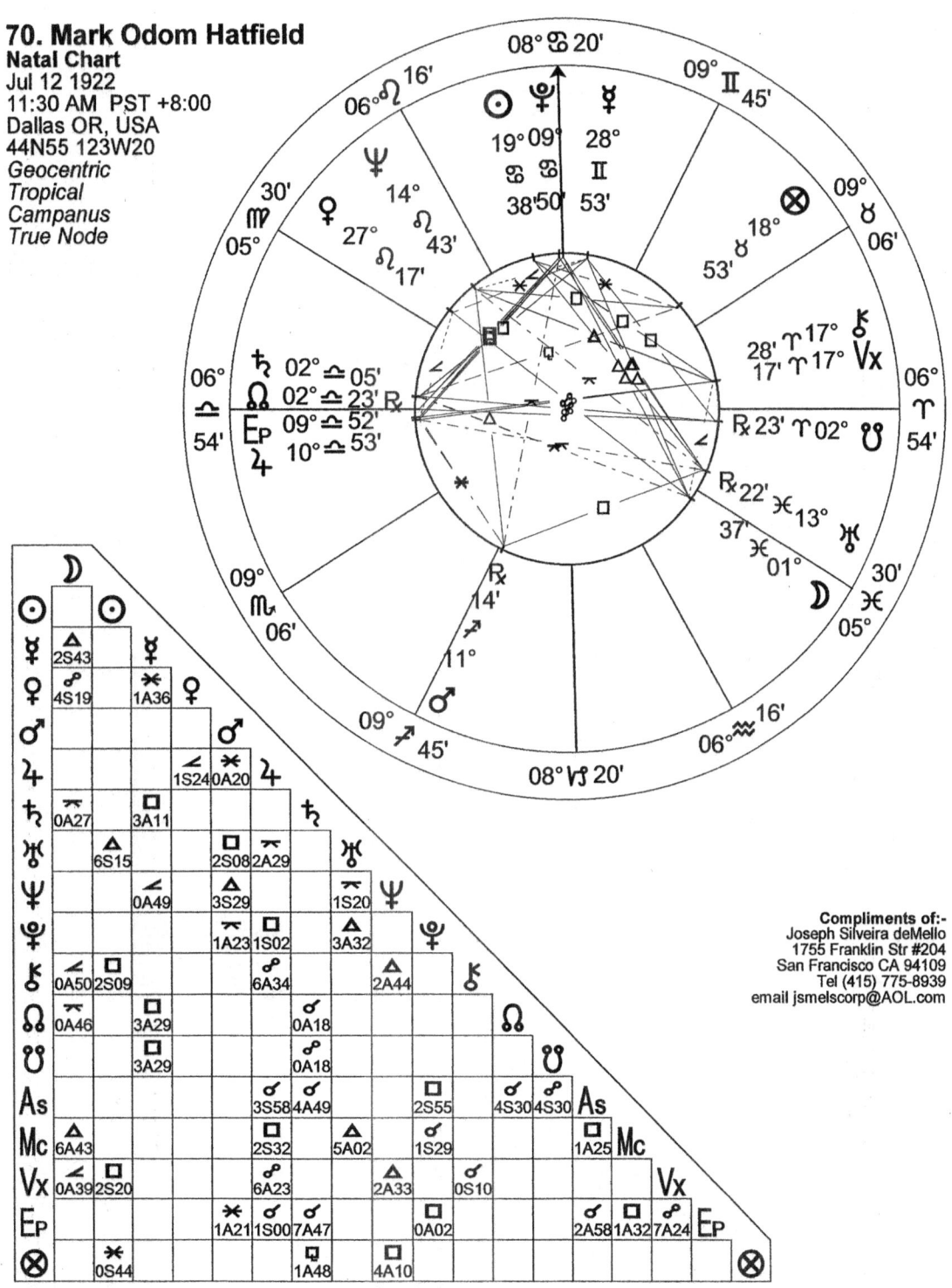

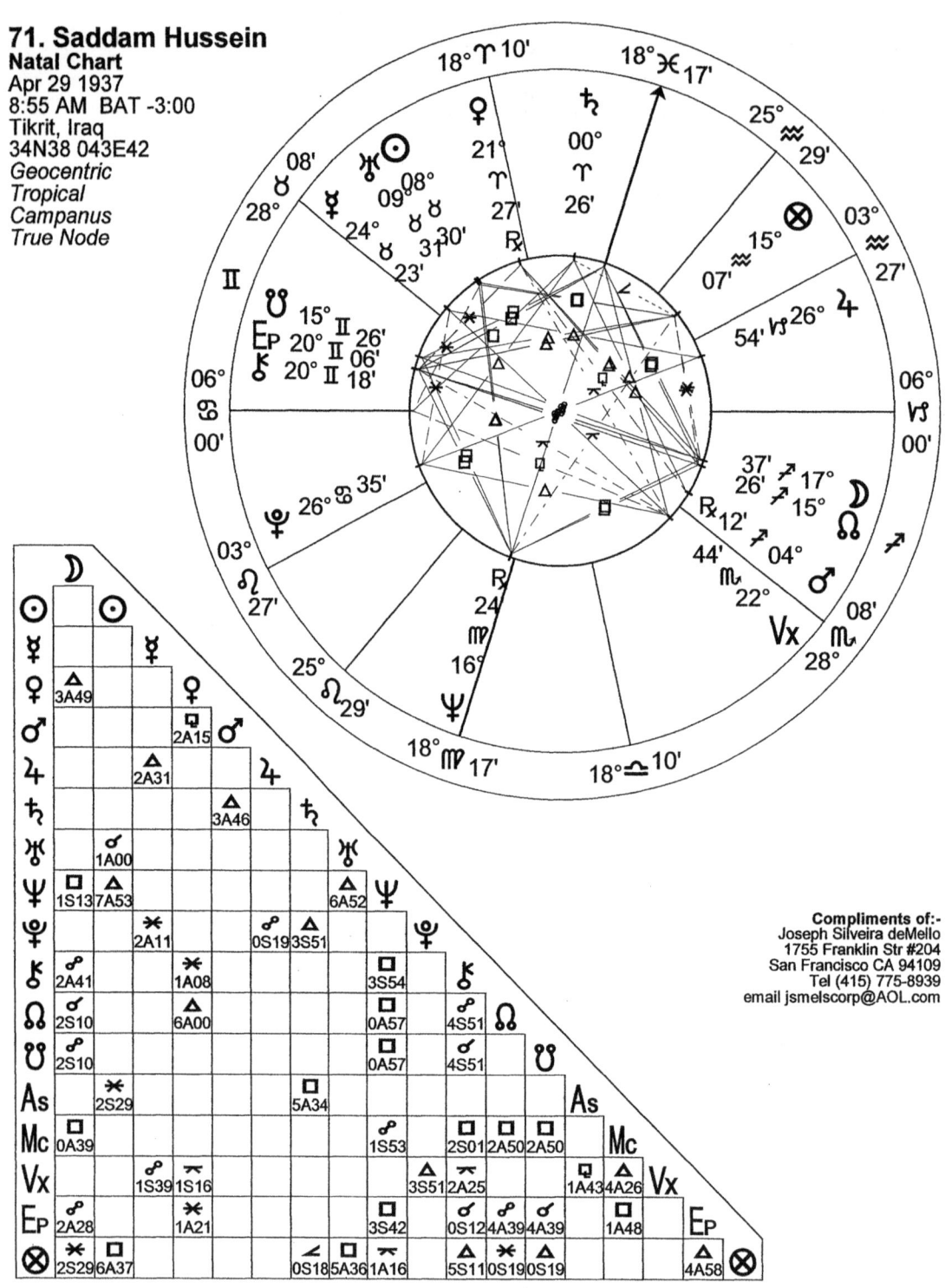

representing his emotional quotient of his pose, how he wishes to appear, so these ideas have to delineate that man. We also have to remember the downside of the Cancerian personality contains a large ability to acquire and store up resentments. Pluto in the first house tells of his ability to sabotage his own personality image. This has not destroyed his national popularity.

The Sun is in Taurus in the eleventh house, giving him a oneness with his community (which might have existed anyway due to shared ethnicity). The Sun in Taurus, if we are consistent, is mercenary and concerned with financial well being. The Sun is in one degree conjunction with eccentric and modern Uranus, and the closeness of Uranus to the Sun is not going to lessen the workability of Uranus. If we explore creativity, we see that he is creative in eleventh house of community, creative in the second and third houses, both ruled by Leo and, again being consistent, more expressive in the third house. The final creative area is the Libra fifth house, ruled by Venus in detriment in Aries and in the eleventh house. Note also that Venus is in retrograde denoting one who is amuse by the grim and grim about what others find amusing. The surprising thing to me is that this chart speaks to me of interest in the economy of his people, not just mercenary about his goods and self-esteem.

It is perhaps a good thing that the Moon has parted so far from the conjunction to Mars. Note that Mars is quincunx to Sun and Uranus and also quincunx to the Ascendant. Admittedly this is a large orb of aspect, but I have learned where there is a double quincunx an orb of five degrees is not excessive. We pause to say a word for the usual stubbornness of Taurus and wonder if the presence of Uranus alleviates it. While he may rely publicly on a traditional Koran based conduct, I think he could be a leader for more modern attitudes. But no Taurus is easily dislodged from his attitudes.

Looking for a chart dispositor to help us, we are left to wandering from Mars to Jupiter to Saturn and back to Mars. All else devolves to this circle. The fact that this chart has a mutable square is a surprise, a contradiction to fixity; say a man retains his attitudes but also rolls with the punches. This square ties in the Midheaven to the nodal axis and the Moon, and Neptune at the bottom of his chart. This square might also involve the twelfth house Chiron. We also note that Saturn is not part of this square and is in fall in Aries, while Neptune is in detriment and retrograde (hardly concealed pride) in Virgo. Saturn has to be important as highest planet, and the same must be said for Neptune on the fourth. Also Neptune is in the 165 degree aspect to Saturn. Does this aspect lead us toward thoughts of paranoia. Saturn is doubly important for being on the Aries point, and it is part of a grand trine to Pluto and Mars. This man has flirted with being judged terrorist and war criminal, taking us back to that ring of dispositors and suddenly seeing that his Jupiter is in fall.

It is rather interesting that this man waited until his Sun should progress down into his first house to make a world nuisance of himself. When he invaded Kuwait, he cannot have had any astrological advice. Few astrologer would have counseled this on his Saturn return, although astrologers also say that at Saturn return we feel free to do anything we want to do. When Cancer or Taurus is ready to do something, no further discussion is needed. What is natally in Cancer will progress slowly through Leo. Mars would long remain retrograde, would not get up to his seventh house where world leaders feel obliged to go to war, but on the road to Kuwait, his Mars was coming to a stationary direct at 19 Scorpio, the lovely degree of snakebite and almost quincunx natal Chiron and the East Point. The East Point is always in charge of the special events of life.

Now if we agree that Neptune on the IC will cloud his home and security, we will of course have seen natal Mercury on the not so fine degree in Taurus where Caput Algol easily causes the mentality to go off beam. But Mercury is trine Jupiter and sextile Pluto which mitigate the Jupiter opposite Pluto. In line with the 165 degree aspect of Neptune to Saturn, we should watch transits to two degrees Pisces and Aries to see what happens.

72. Wealthy Heir, 9-2-5
Wider orb Saturn: 1S04
Data: May 16, 1937, 8:01 p.m. MST,
Denver, Colorado, 39N44, 104W59

This financially well off scion of a family of three generations in an established local business habitually spends half a year living in Greece. He has had astrologers all his life, beginning with the services of the late Gavin Arthur who was grandson of President Chester A. Arthur. Gavin Arthur told this man that he would experience a very difficult year at age sixty-four, that at age sixty-five, were he still with us, he would lose all his money, and that at age sixty-six there would be a severe illness. He took all this information very seriously, has taken excellent care of himself and watches his investments. Gavin Arthur could only have been looking at his progressed Moon through Scorpio and Sagittarius, the progressed Sun coming to the natal Vertex and Pluto.

He is a typical jetsetter, well tanned leathery facial skin, looking gaunter as the years succeed, due perhaps to regular ministrations of cosmetic surgery. He is very careful where he goes and how he acts. He drinks moderately and drives a vintage big-name sports car, very James Bond in sense of style, powerful motor under custom chassis, and he is quite censorious of those who have had the bad luck to be caught with drugs in countries which have long term punishments in rather inferior jail facilities.

He has never held a job although he has Sun, Mercury and Uranus in the sixth house and could perhaps make a good CIA operative with Mars in the Scorpio twelfth house, but it is a retrograde Mars. He also has Mercury, Jupiter and Neptune retrograde. He ceased being a client of mine when another local astrologer became the most famous astrologer in the land. But he is serious about astrology, and he can afford the best. He was always guarded when around me. I have noticed how Sagittarians are wary of Scorpios but get along just fine with Capricorns, and his Sun and my Sun fall in each other's twelfth houses indicative of past life karmic situations.

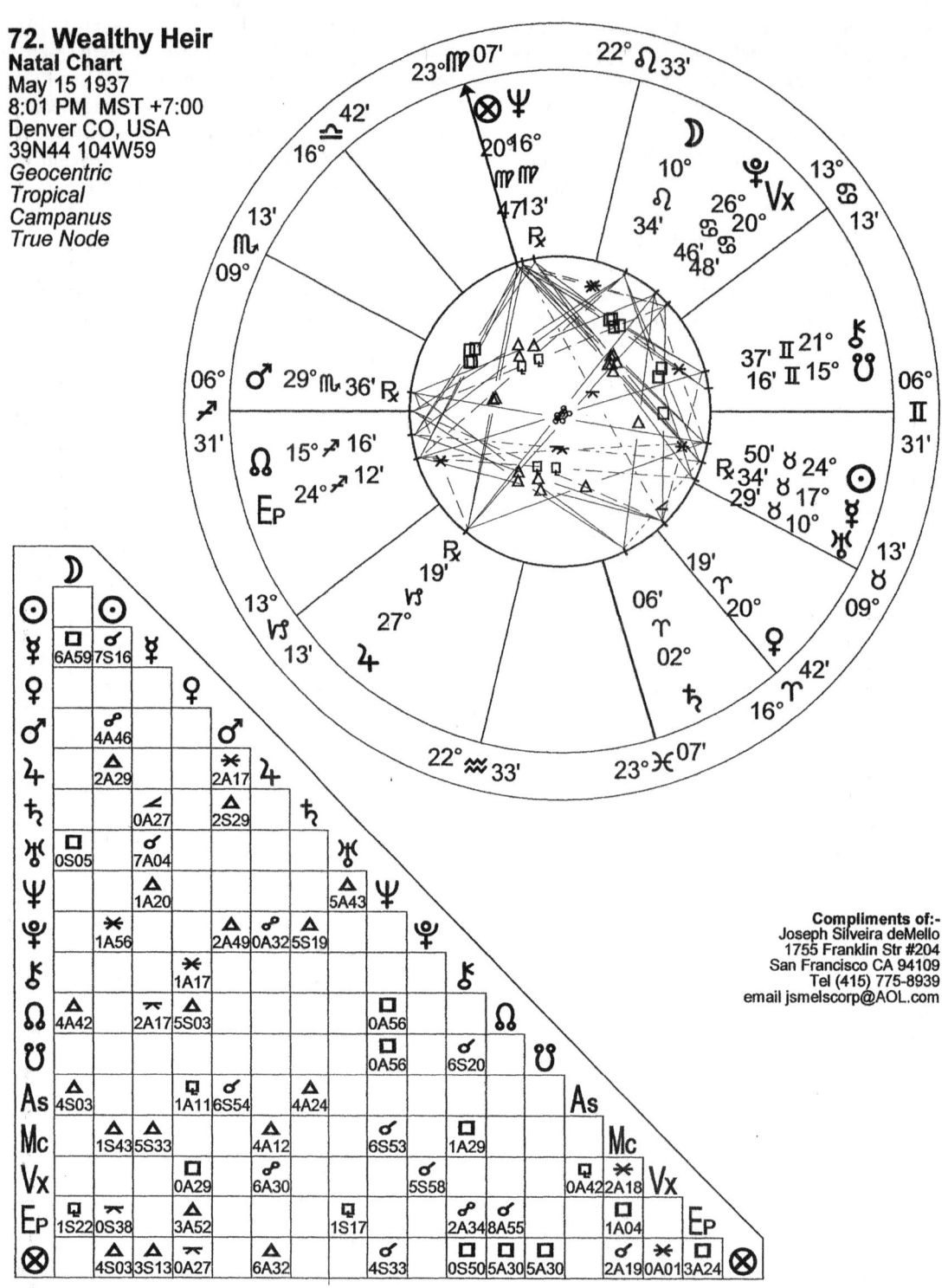

Sun in Taurus is interested in his money, but it is in a difficult degree. For most of his life he has been the most attractive man to grace any poolside. He has a lovely apartment, and, if he has any other thoughts in his head than personal gratification, it would be a nice surprise. I do not dislike this person. He is very amusing, and we have had many interesting conversations. Unfortunately we rarely see each other nowadays.

73. Retired Waiter, 7-6-2
Wider orb Saturn: 1S39
Data: September 23, 1937, 7:30 a.m. PST,
Auburn, California, 38N52, 121W05

This is the chart of a very good former waiter with Pisces ruling his sixth house and Neptune is on the cusp of his twelfth house. This is where we find the Neptune of people who at one time or another consider suicide, but there is no such history. Pluto on the tenth dismayed me for a short time. Then the place where he worked changed locations (was eventually to go out of business entirely), he became quieter, got into a relationship, and he and his partner bought an old wayside inn and converted it into a single residence in the late Seventies. He was entirely reliable, worked steadily while employed, and at the end of any evening sat himself at the bar to take copious doses of Vitamin V (for vodka). Unlike most of his co-workers, he took good care of his physical self. And all of this happened prior to the onset of AIDS which since that time has decimated many of his former co-workers.

74. Cafe Pianist, 4-11-2
Wider orb Saturn: 1S13

Data: February 6, 1938, 3:39 p.m. PST,
Las Vegas, Nevada, 36N10, 115W09

When I first saw the man of this chart, his red hair still golden, going into severe pattern baldness, blue eyed, pointed chin, I felt sure he must be an Aries. As it turns out, he has but Mars and Saturn in Aries in a Pisces-ruled ninth house. He was a fine piano player for sing along piano bars, was homosexual, played mostly engagements in gay bars.

Venus, too close to the Sun, is in mutual reception to Uranus. So, how to account for looking like Aries, unless Mars, the only planet in its own sign is not quite dispositor of the chart. His personality was entirely convivial and pleasant. The other task here is to account for his fine musicianship. Venus quincunx Neptune? He died in 1995, age fifty-seven, cause unknown, but note that Saturn and Moon were natally in 165 degree orb of cesquin or quindecile to his natal IC.

75. Richard Ideman, 7-11-3
Wider orb Saturn: 1S07
Data: February 8, 1938, 9:37 p.m. EST,
Akron, Ohio, 41N05, 81W31

Born two days after the previous example, we have now the chart of a man who made astrology fun and easy to learn. His lively lectures were widely popular, and since he had a swashbuckling image, he was especially popular with his women students. He was a big man, large and tall, and he had a wide infectious smile and facial dimples. He oozed sex appeal but never made an overt sexual advance toward any student. He augmented his income from astrology by going out with the local fishing fleet, work which requires a great deal of physical stamina. Everyone but I knew he was homosexual. It seems that he contracted HIV and then opportune infections of active AIDS situations, and, after a convalescence of five months, on the evening of February 22, 1987 at home in San Anselmo, California, he shot himself by putting a gun in his mouth. One assumes that he had no desire to face long periods of intense and debilitating medications. Note he had Neptune in the twelfth, a classical suicide placement. He deliberately prepared for his death making all his arrangements, and he carefully disposed of his astrological papers.

76. Medical Technologist, 1-11-3
Wider orb Saturn: 1S06
Data: February 9, 1938. 8:52 a.m. PST,
Los Angeles, California, 34N03,. 118W04

The data here is from the files of Don Borkowski who knew the subject. Although this man is a medical technician, he is also an astrologer. In his younger days, he was described as "kind of creepy" for his predilection to dressing entirely in whatever color he chose for any particular day. The only reason for including this chart is that it is a sort of upside down mirror image of the previous chart. Mars and Saturn rising are usually indications for surgeons. Perhaps having Aries rising with it's short attention span did not allow him toward deeper study. Saturn is not blessed in Aries. Mars and Saturn are semi-square to the Sun and Venus. We still have the mutual reception of Venus-Uranus. Also notice that Mars rising in the rising sign here really underlines the Aries personality.

77. Service Garage Employee, 3-1-12
Wider orb Saturn: 1N14
Data: March 30, 1938, 8:37 a.m. PST,
Portland, Oregon, 45N31, 122W41

From the files of Don Borkowski, this is the chart of a cousin. With this twelfth house and my own Ascendant, I was curious about solar and lunar returns for myself the year he was born and I was thirteen. The subject's mother married for a third time, and the subject, child of a former marriage, added the surname of his new step-father. Even though her third marriage ended in divorce, he retained the name. Originally Don had set this chart for 8:00 a.m. because the subject was born by c-section. I rectified the chart to fit with the date of his mother's death (November 16, 1996) and for the death of his step-father (died of Alzheimer's March 29, 1989). Don is not close to his cousin who lives at a distance from him. This man served two hitches in the Navy and

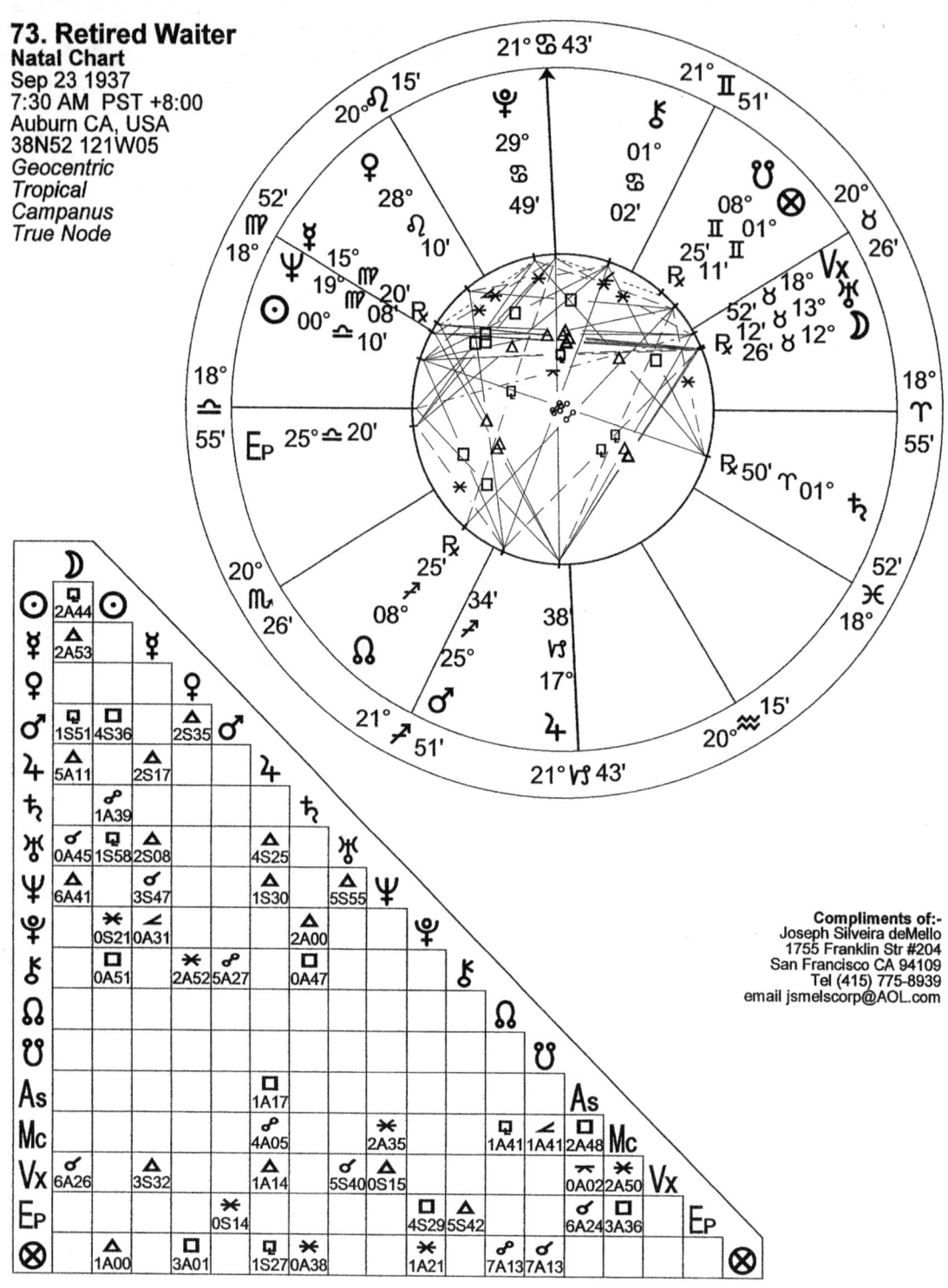

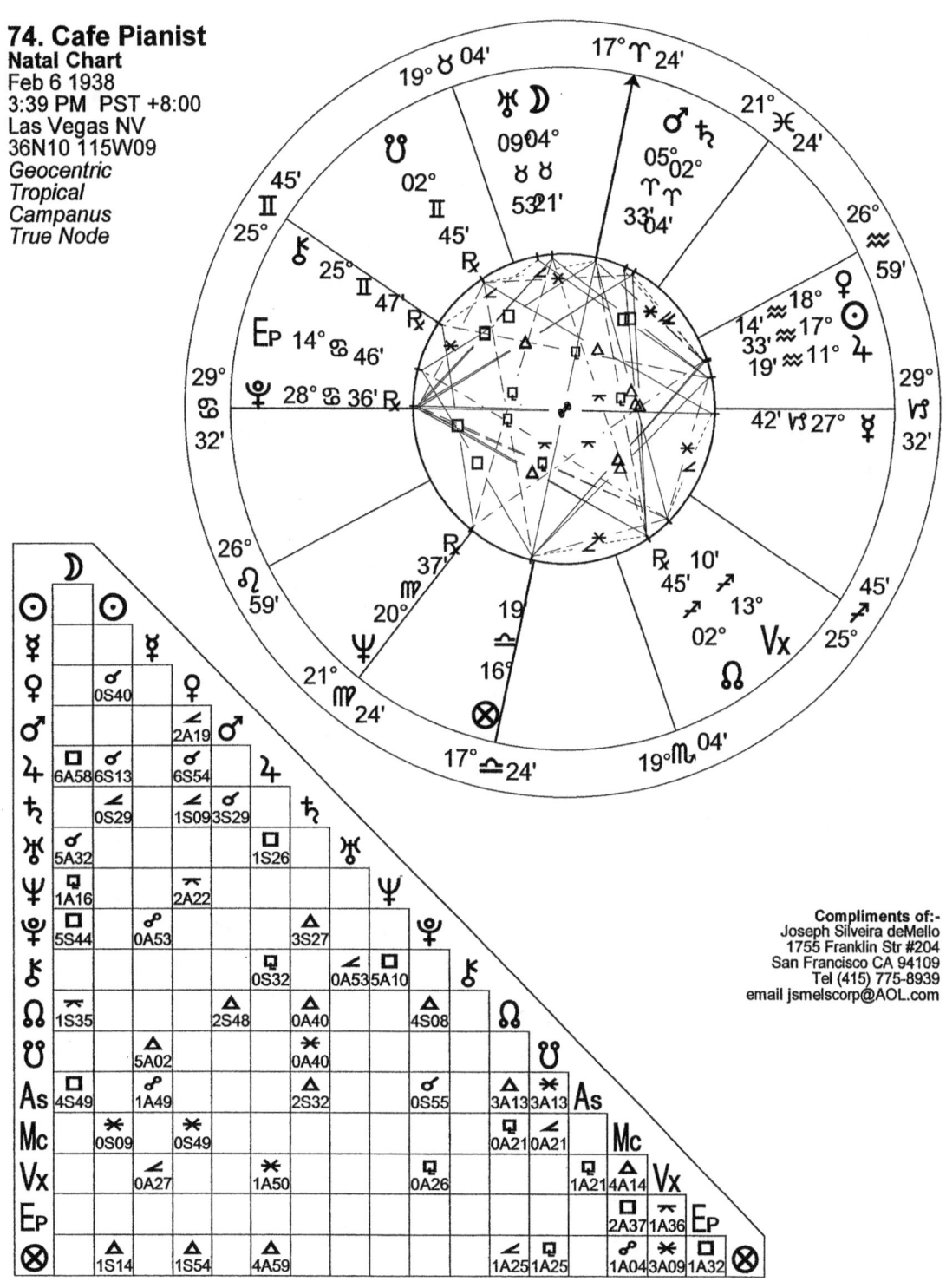

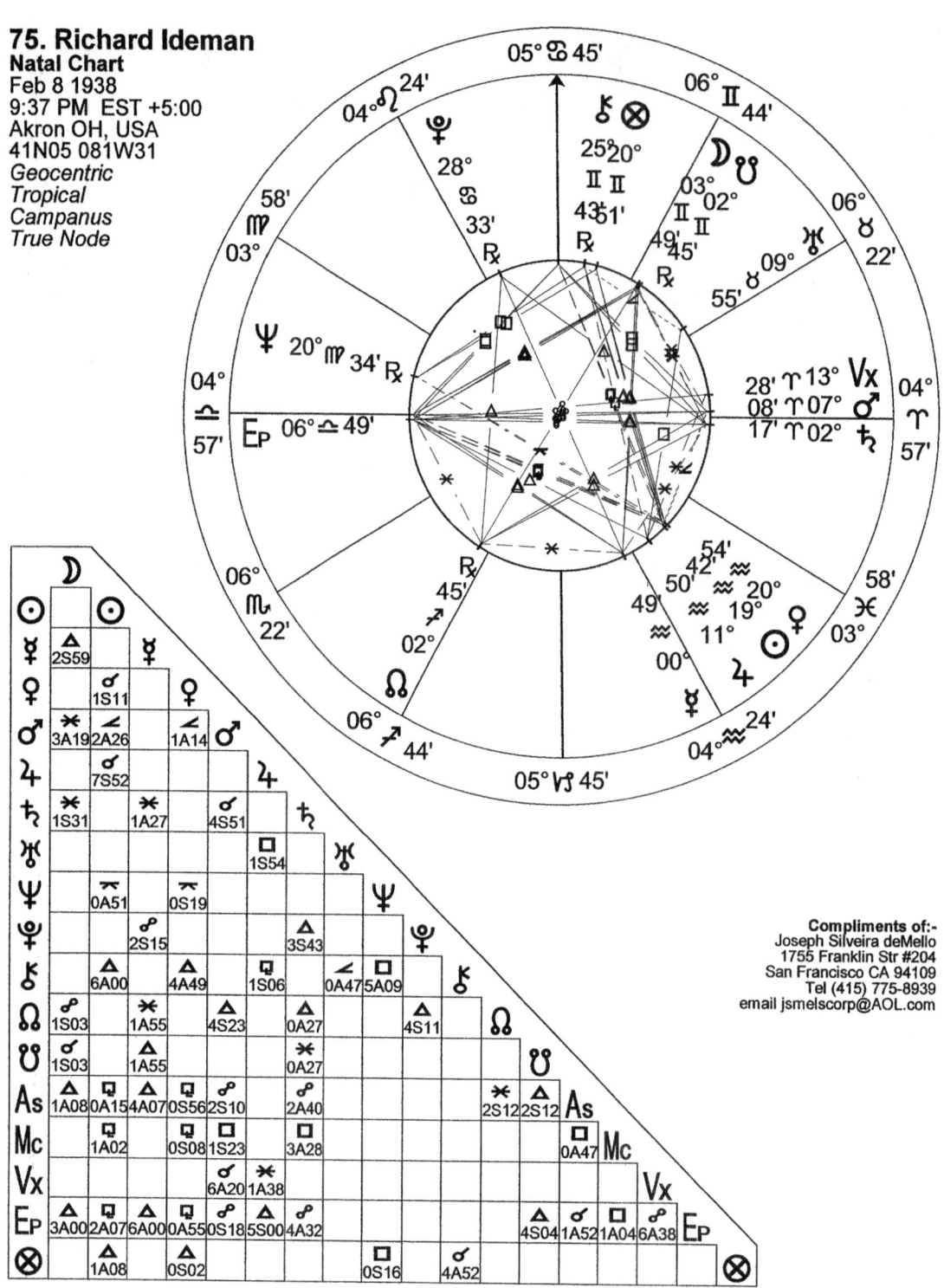

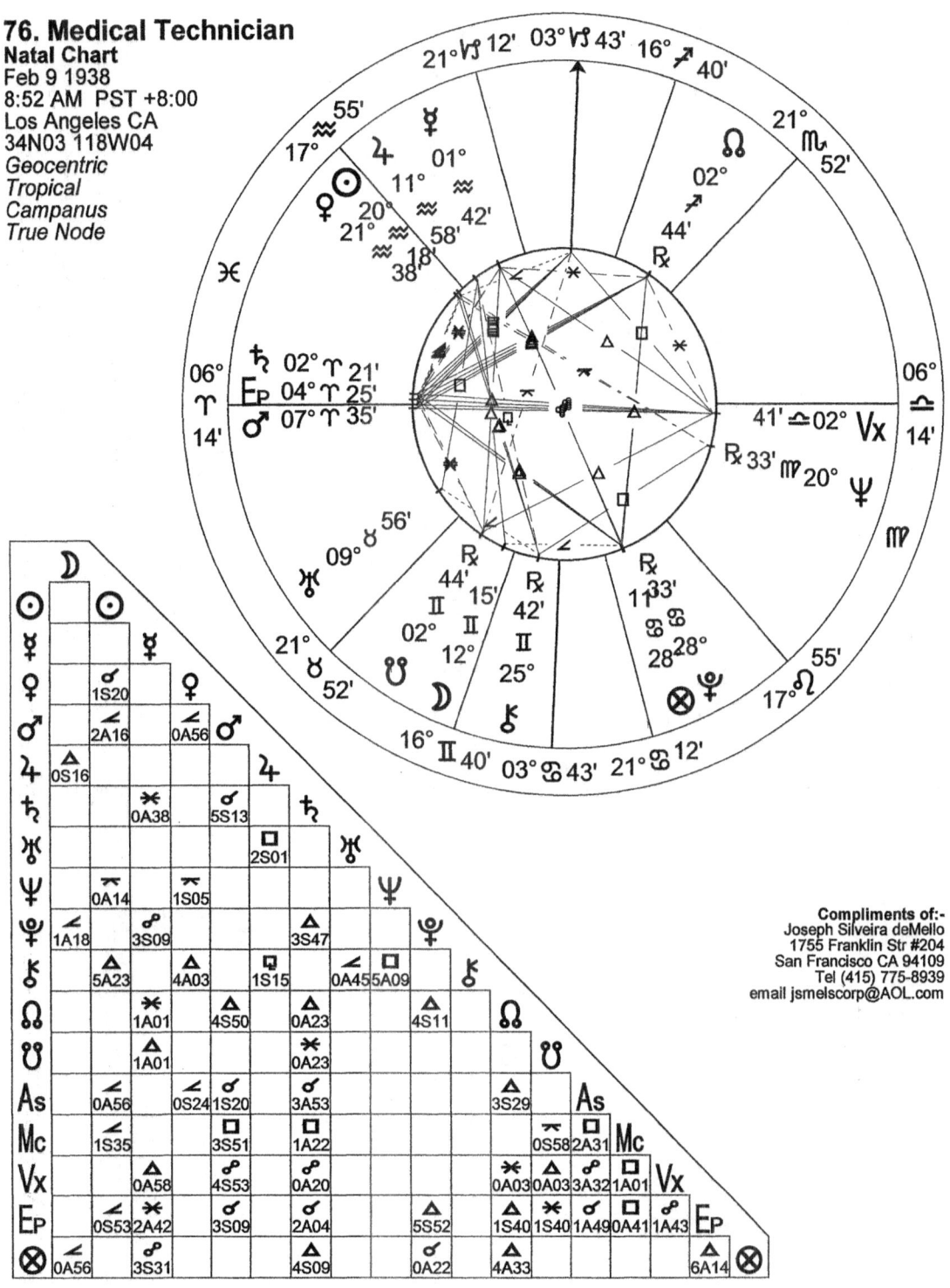

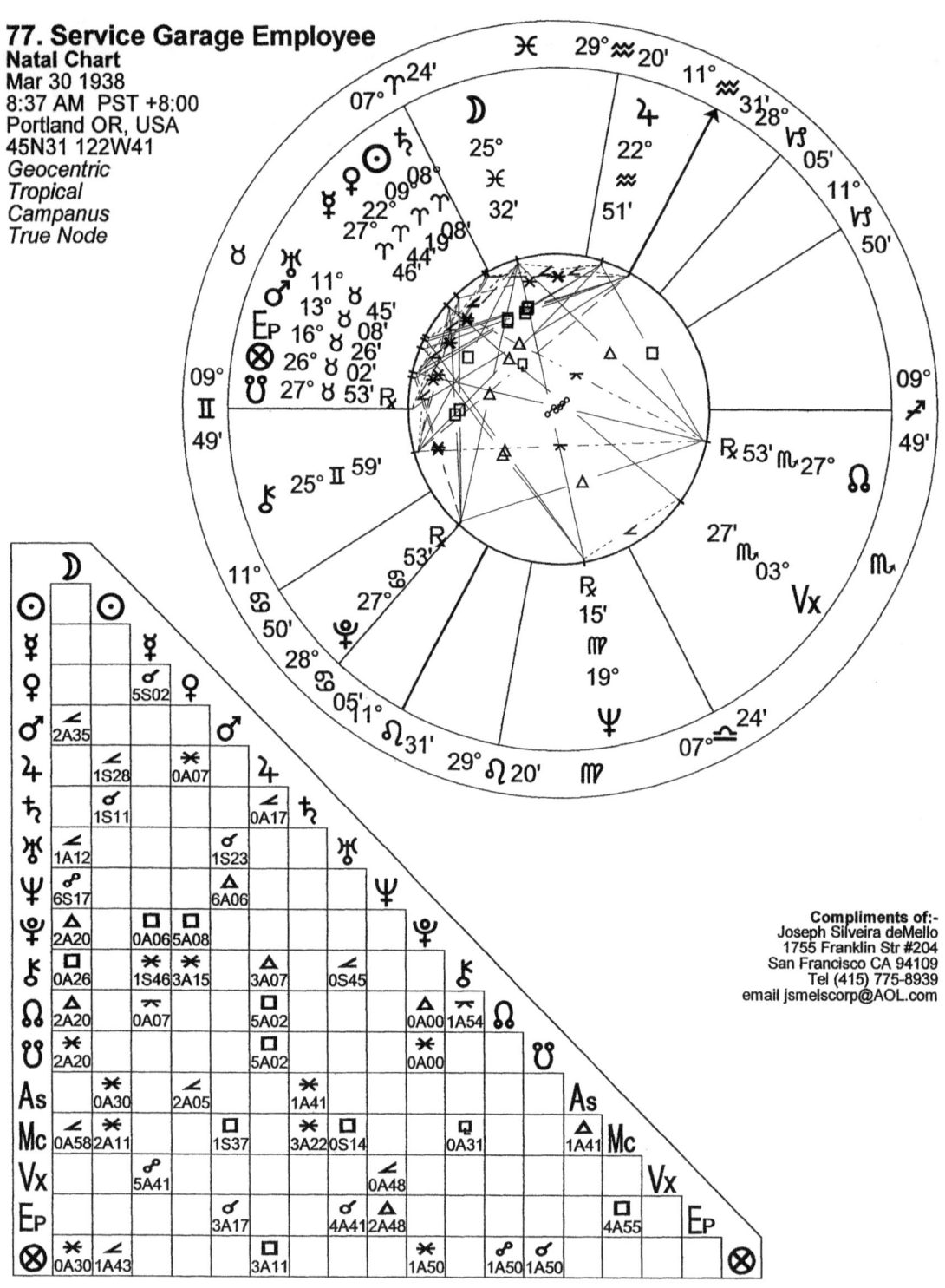

one in the Marines, in all of which he worked as a yeoman or secretary-typist. His service with the Marines was cut short by a nervous breakdown, and Don's comment is that with such a twelfth house as this chart has, it was an accomplishment he had only one such breakdown.

78. John Valle, 8-1-1
Wider orb Saturn: 1N16
Data: March 30, 1938, 7:50 p.m. PST,
Colton, California, 34N04, 117W20

This is the chart of a male homosexual cross dresser who was elected Empress Jonnie VII of San Francisco in 1972. Being an Empress is a position of gay community leadership, the quasi local Miss America (and there is also an Emperor. but it is the Empress which counts: she gets to wear all the finery, and this elective office lasts for a year). The chart has Scorpio rising, Sun and Moon in Aries, and much of the chart in the sixth and seventh houses where Venus and Mars are in mutual reception, courtesy positions put Mars too close to Sun and Saturn and that this mutual reception loop disposes of the entire chart. The subject died a number of years ago, but unfortunately my files show no note made of the passage.

79. Publisher's Representative, 9-1-3
Wider orb Saturn: 1N33
Data: April 5, 1938, 10:30 p.m. EST,
Burlington, Vermont, 44N28, 73W13

When I was book buyer for a nine-branch department store chain, he was a trade book publisher's representative who called on me. The chart is a prime example of Sagittarius, a man reticent to make social and personal contacts too quickly. It amazed me this man stretched the limits of his third house by having Jupiter in the area of short distance travel that covering eleven western states, a territory devised in New York.

He was an impressive publisher's representative. He appeared to have read every book on his seasonal lists. He personally had more information than revealed in the publicity material furnished by his publisher. He also understood the difference of approach in the way I bought books, not on literary content so much as to catch the impulse buyer who wandered through the book department on the way to luggage or kitchen wares, credit card at the ready. When he gave me his data, I guessed Sagittarius rising and told him he had to go to nature periodically to recharge his energies. He was amazed I knew that about him. He disliked the competitive push to ever increase sales figures. When I did the chart, I wondered when he would fulfill his fifth house Aries and if he was far enough from home to operate his ninth house. He seemed too well grounded to be bothered by Neptune at the top of his chart. This is another case of my doing a chart where my Sun fell in his twelfth, and his in my twelfth, which I think of as a very obvious past life connection. Our Moons were both in Gemini, and he is an example of where we matched very well in work. Sagittarius is as much a talker as any Gemini while still reflecting that Aries, as private as Scorpio, both having great ability to avoid topics they do not wish to share. I always looked forward to appointments with him.

80. Jerry Brown, 5-1-4
Wider orb Saturn: 1N3
Data: April 7, 1938, 12:43 p.m. PST,
San Francisco, California, 37N45, 122W26

Son of former California Governor Edmund "Pat" Brown, this man followed his father into politics and succeeded him in office. After this office, he attended to his law practice in Los Angeles and San Francisco until 1998, when he emerged and was elected mayor of Oakland, California, the city across the Bay east of San Francisco. Coming from an Irish-Catholic background with strongly stressed family ties, he has never married. He has at various times dated entertainment celebrities. A Democrat, staunchly liberal, he also took the Republican stance that the people could not have all kinds of give-away programs if they would not finance them. From the first, he went his own way, and refused to live in the Governor's Mansion. He said it was too big for his simple needs (a big Victorian which Nancy Reagan, when her husband was governor, called a fire trap), and instead maintained rooms at the Senator Hotel near the State Capitol. He refused to use the official limo which went with his office, and chose to drive himself in a shoddy Plymouth gas guzzler. He had an interest in Zen that earned him the media nickname of Governor Moonbeam.

I have never seen an astrologer read this chart without getting involved in the media hype around this man and the astrologers' own political bias. Jerry Brown was seen as liberal but not liberal enough for other liberals. Plus the fact that California politics are strange. All the metropolitan areas vote Democrat, but there is a larger part of the State which always votes Republican, and a Democrat Governor is usually rare. After he finished his term as Governor, entitled to be addressed as Governor for the rest of his life just as are Presidents or Senators, the logical political next step was to run for President or for a Senate seat. Due to the general weirdness of Californian politics, Senatorial seats are now filled by Feinstein and Boxer, and a goodly number of people waiting in the wings to succeed them should term limits force either one of them out.

No matter what is said of him, there is no way a Leo rising, Sun in Aries, or Moon in Cancer walks other than his own road, or takes a safe seat away from the torpedoes. He is a very ambitious man who really is concerned with public service, as traditional in his family as in the Kennedy's. He is not the least fazed that newspaper people took issue with his having studied Zen in Japan or mock his seriousness and integrity. The entire chart is disposed of by Venus and Moon, both of which are in their own signs.

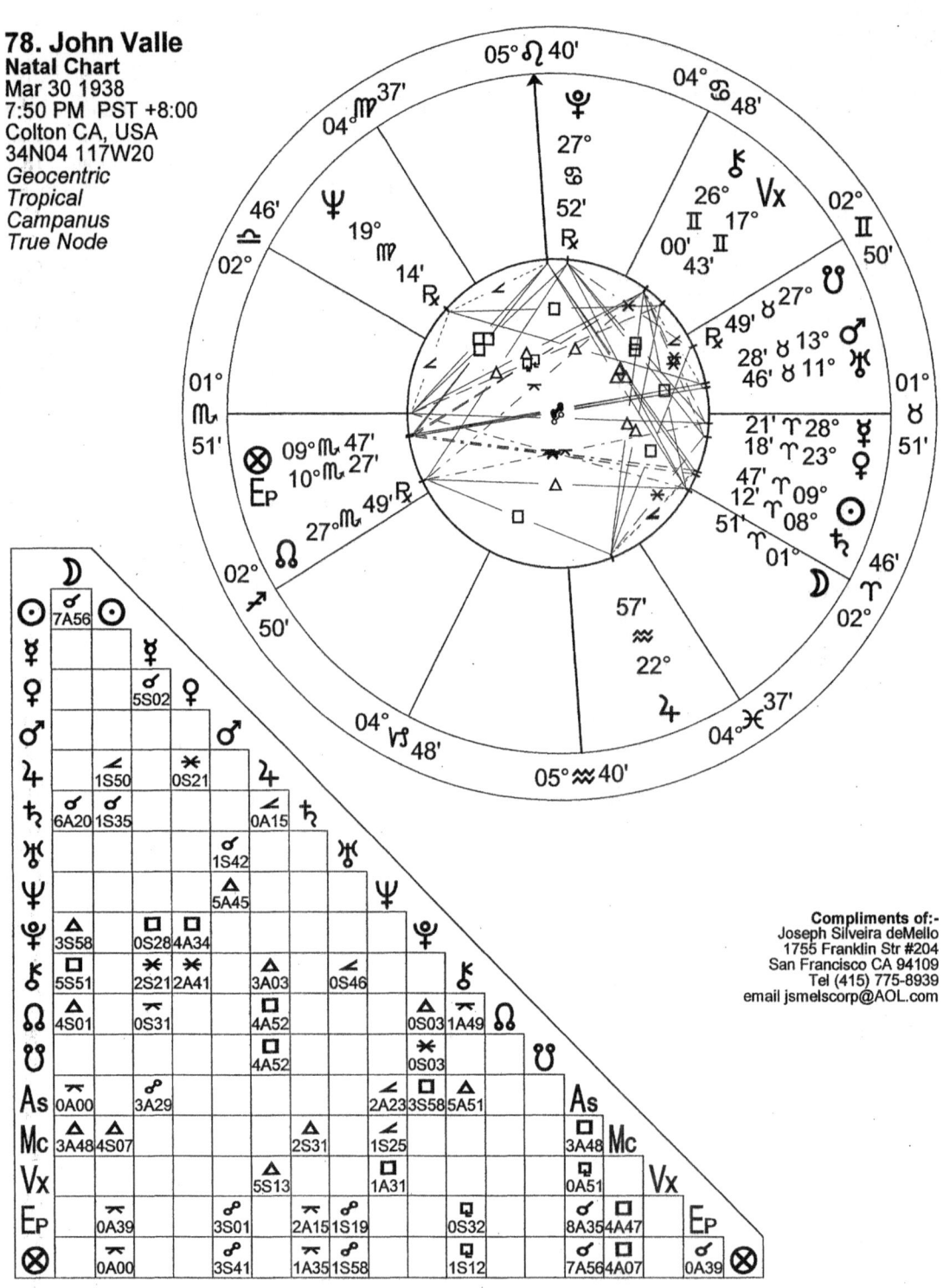

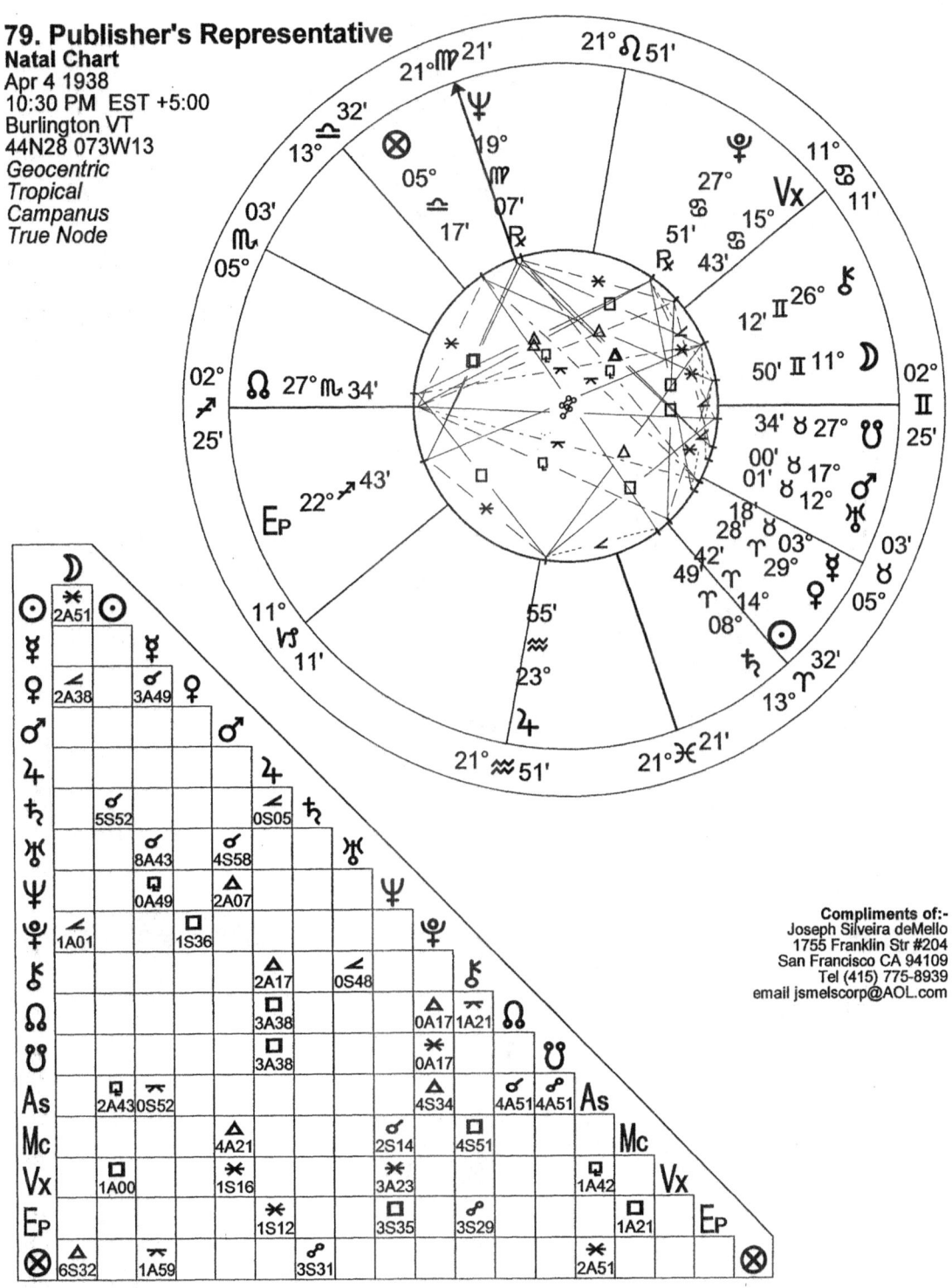

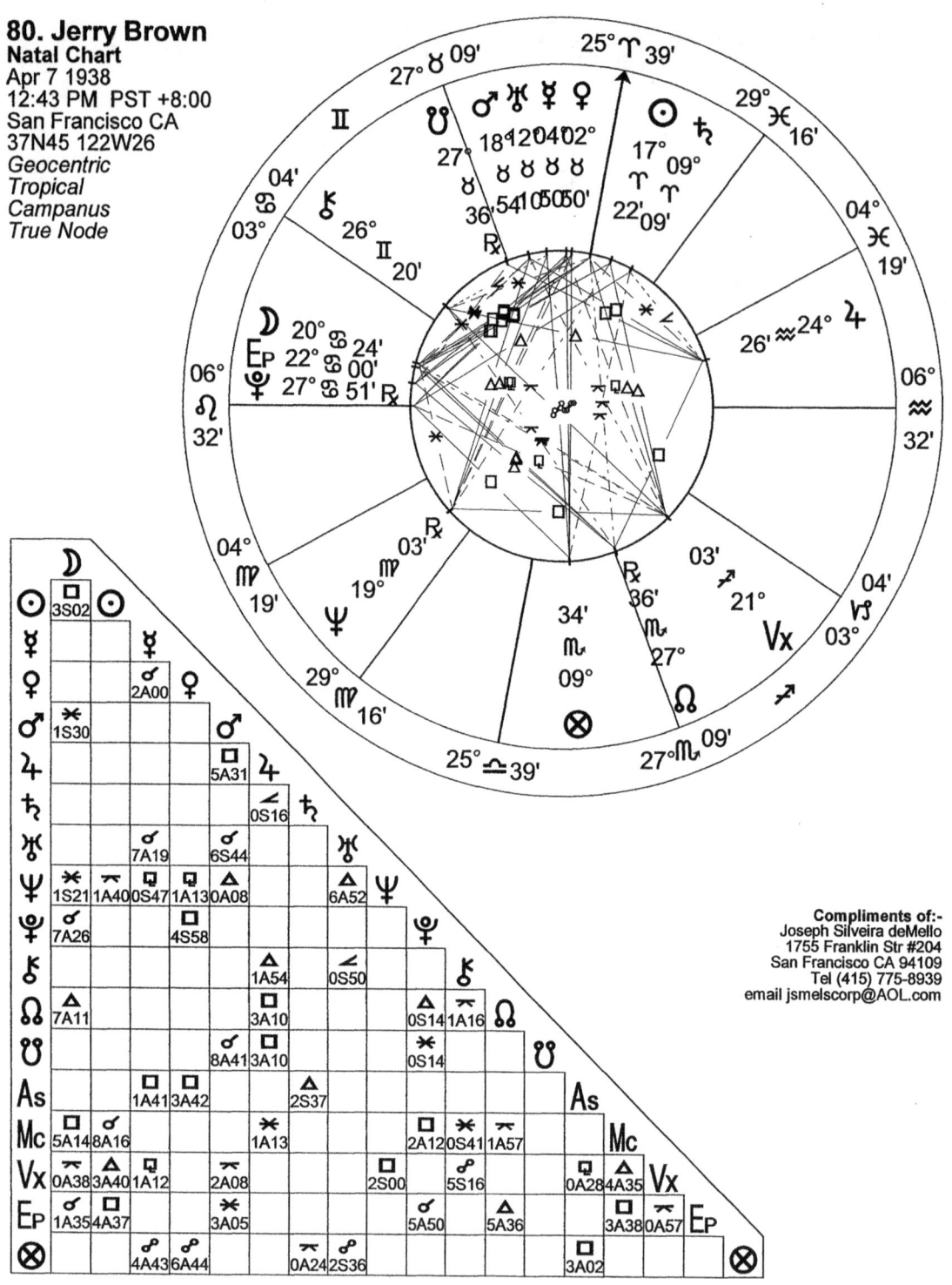

81. Architect/Restaurateur, 4-1-5
Wider orb Saturn: 1N43
Data: April 9, 1938, 9:35 a.m. EST,
Putnam, Connecticut, 41N55, 71W23

Born in rural Connecticut, he studied architecture and left home to find fame and fortune in Hawaii. He was a popular and successful architect and went from designing homes to the acme of building a skyscraper, designing a resort, and designing a state park, at which point he felt he had done it all. He felt it was time to walk away from his drawing board. So, in October 1977, he moved to San Francisco, just ahead of mid-life crisis. This in a man's chart happens when transiting Saturn is opposite natal Saturn (for which he was early) and transiting Uranus is opposing natal Uranus (on time).

But there were other problems. A lifelong bachelor and a homosexual, he had to find a way out of a life of failure in personal relationships. Looking around for something to do, he drank a great deal, and took a job as a bartender. Eventually he met a man who was partner in a restaurant and having problems with his partners to such an extent that he wanted out of it. They went on a motor vacation trip into the Sierras and gold country. There they found a big empty building and liked it so much that they purchased it that afternoon. They then remodeled it and opened a restaurant where one was very much needed. The place is a gem. He and his partner are diverse personalities, each needing his own private space, so that the partner lives over the restaurant and this subject lives in a condo mountain development above the town and straddles the mountains to give him a view for hundreds of miles east and west, a very dramatic venue. This change was eased by a nice inheritance when his father died.

His projects as a Leo Moon (such people are not easy to live with) clearly show in the dramatic design development of his restaurant and in the dramatic presentation of his menu items. This may even have to do with living in so dramatic a condo. As a Cancer rising, he really relaxes while cooking and no dish receives less attention than any other. But there is one very strange thing about the restaurant kitchen, for although it has toaster ovens, hot plates and microwaves, there is no stove in it. He does the cooking, while his partner does the seating and helps serve the clientele.

82. Groupie, 9-9-9
Wider orb Saturn: 1N26
Data: December 9, 1950, 7:14 a.m. EST,
Kalamazoo, Michigan, 42N17, 85W35

This man is one of a diverse group which regularly met to chat with an occult guru who spread out tarot cards but did not read them. The cards were used for subjects to have something to look at while the guru worked as a psychic. This chart has a crowded first house and is a triple Sagittarius, the personality broken only by Mars in Capricorn in his second house. Occasionally some pot was toked (marijuana is not a smoke). The subject and his girlfriend were the token heterosexuals. Everyone was excessively accepting of everyone else, and he attended only to keep up with his wife's interest in the occult.

83. Artist and Chef, 10-9-1
Wider orb Saturn: 1N18
Data: December 17, 1950, 8:35 a.m. PST,
San Francisco, California, 37N45, 122W26

Years ago there was a fine restaurant which originally also functioned as a plant nursery. The restaurant had a house psychic, and for a time I became its house astrologer. Later the nursery side of the business was abandoned although the dinning room still looked like a garden gazebo. While I was being the house astrologer, this man applied for the job as chef and was hired. He was of medium height, a bit round and overweight as chefs often are, even when they snack off bits and pieces and are never seem to sit down to a complete dinner. He had a ruddy complexion and ordinary features, none of which was in any way special or remarkable, just pleasant. He was so adept that he stepped right into the job, knew the recipes of the menu and always presented beautiful dishes. In his spare time he painted. He brought some of his pictures for exhibit, but he had no gallery connection. His stuff was more decorative (big floral canvasses) than great or fine art. But he was basically slack and easy going, unhurried, and a homosexual, also easy going, but definitely very interested in himself and his world. He preferred to work alone and, if he sold a picture, would quit working to do more paintings. But he was very secretive about himself. More than anything, he was always in control of every situation around him, without exerting control but taking casual pains to show no one controlled him, that he was always his own man.

84. Tennis Pro, 7-9-2
Beyond orb Saturn: 1N16
Data: December 21, 1950, 12:36 a.m. PST,
San Francisco California, 37N45, 122W26

I never met this man and knew of him only through his mother. He was an only son, and she regarded him as a satisfactory son who was married and had a life of his own in the suburbs. Uranus at the top of his chart is intriguing and it would seem he should do more with his life than be a tennis pro. Saturn in the twelfth is an indicator that he learns from his own experiences as well as a testament to the lack of a father who early disappeared from his life.

85. Waiter, 8-9-2
Wider orb Saturn: 1N15
Data: December 21, 1950, 5:32 a.m. MST,
Liberal Kansas, 37N01, 100W56

This man was a waiter in the restaurant in a multiplex entertainment complex where I was house astrologer. I was having dinner with a client whose chart we were discussing. Over desert and coffee, the waiter volunteered his chart data, and I subsequently did his chart and gave him a copy of it. But we never sat down and

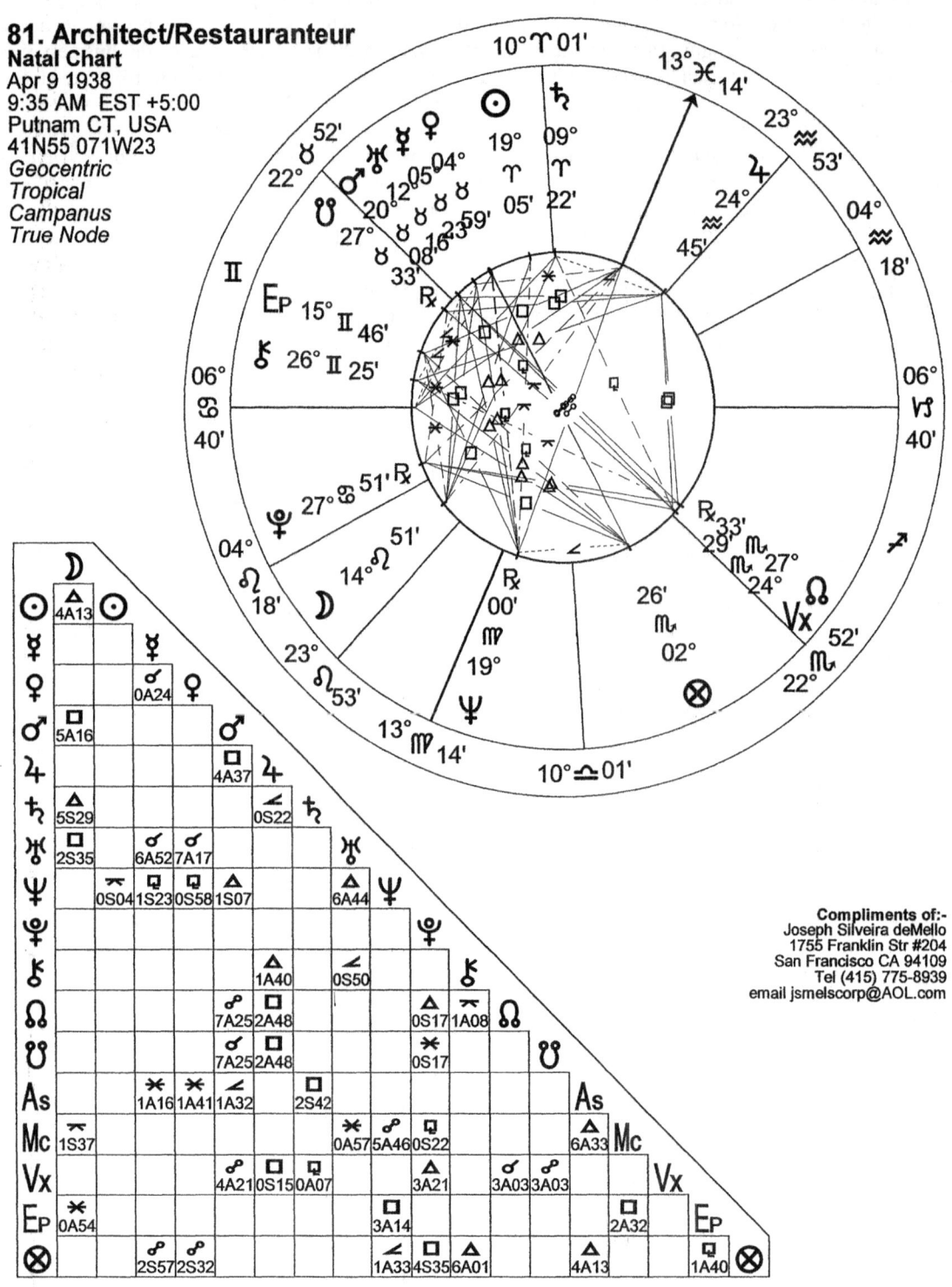

81. Architect/Restauranteur
Natal Chart
Apr 9 1938
9:35 AM EST +5:00
Putnam CT, USA
41N55 071W23
Geocentric
Tropical
Campanus
True Node

Compliments of:-
Joseph Silveira deMello
1755 Franklin Str #204
San Francisco CA 94109
Tel (415) 775-8939
email jsmelscorp@AOL.com

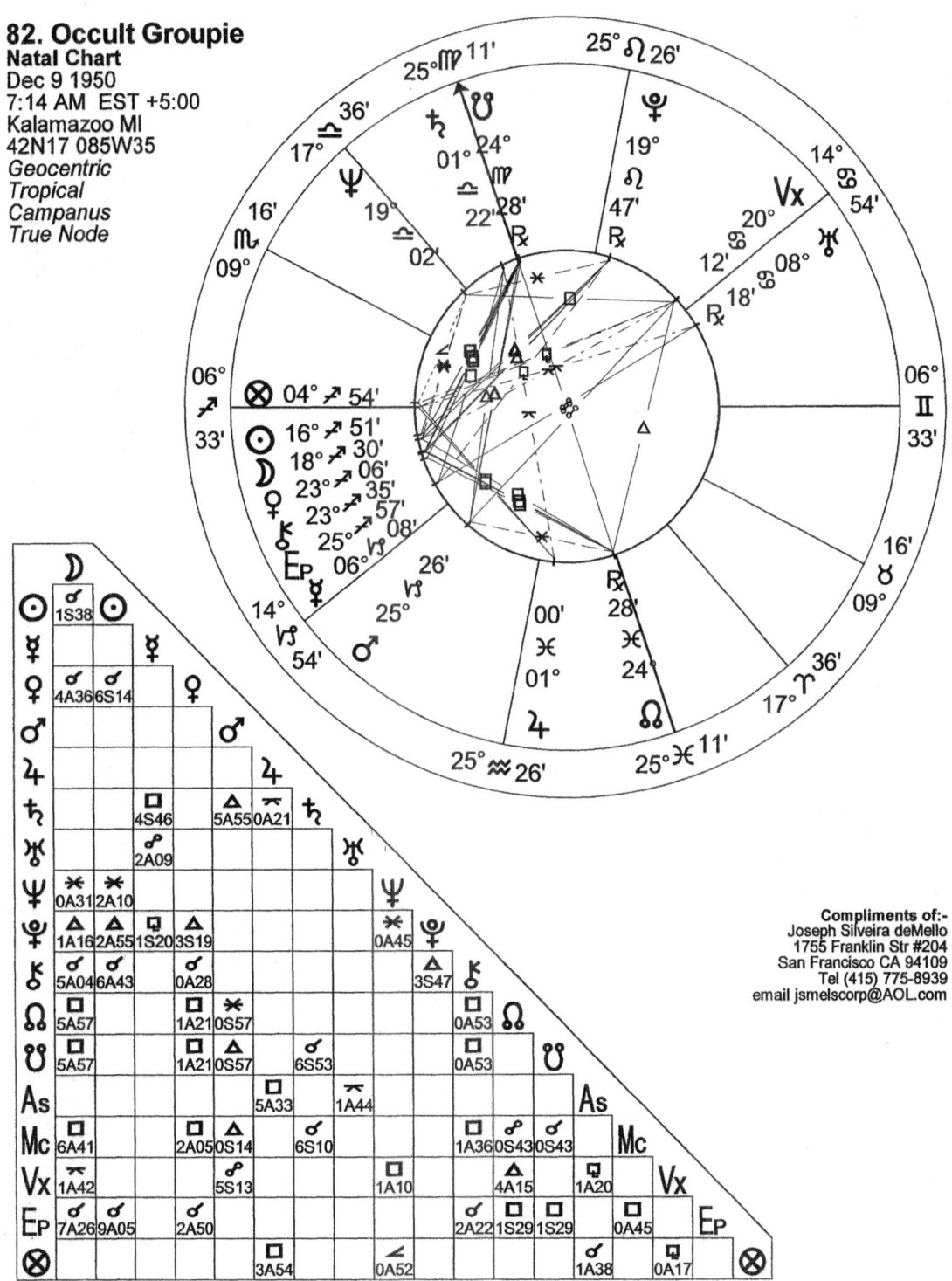

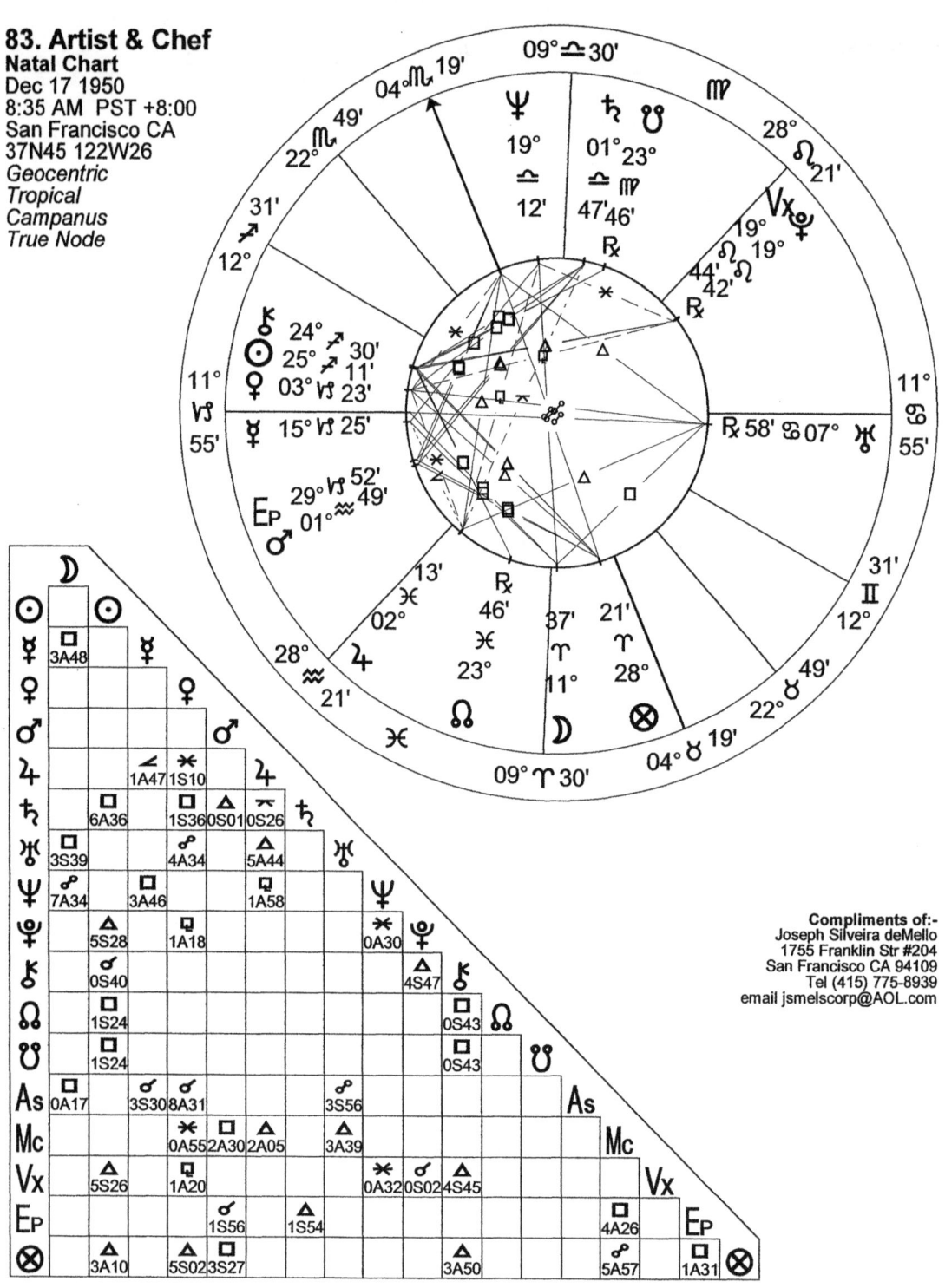

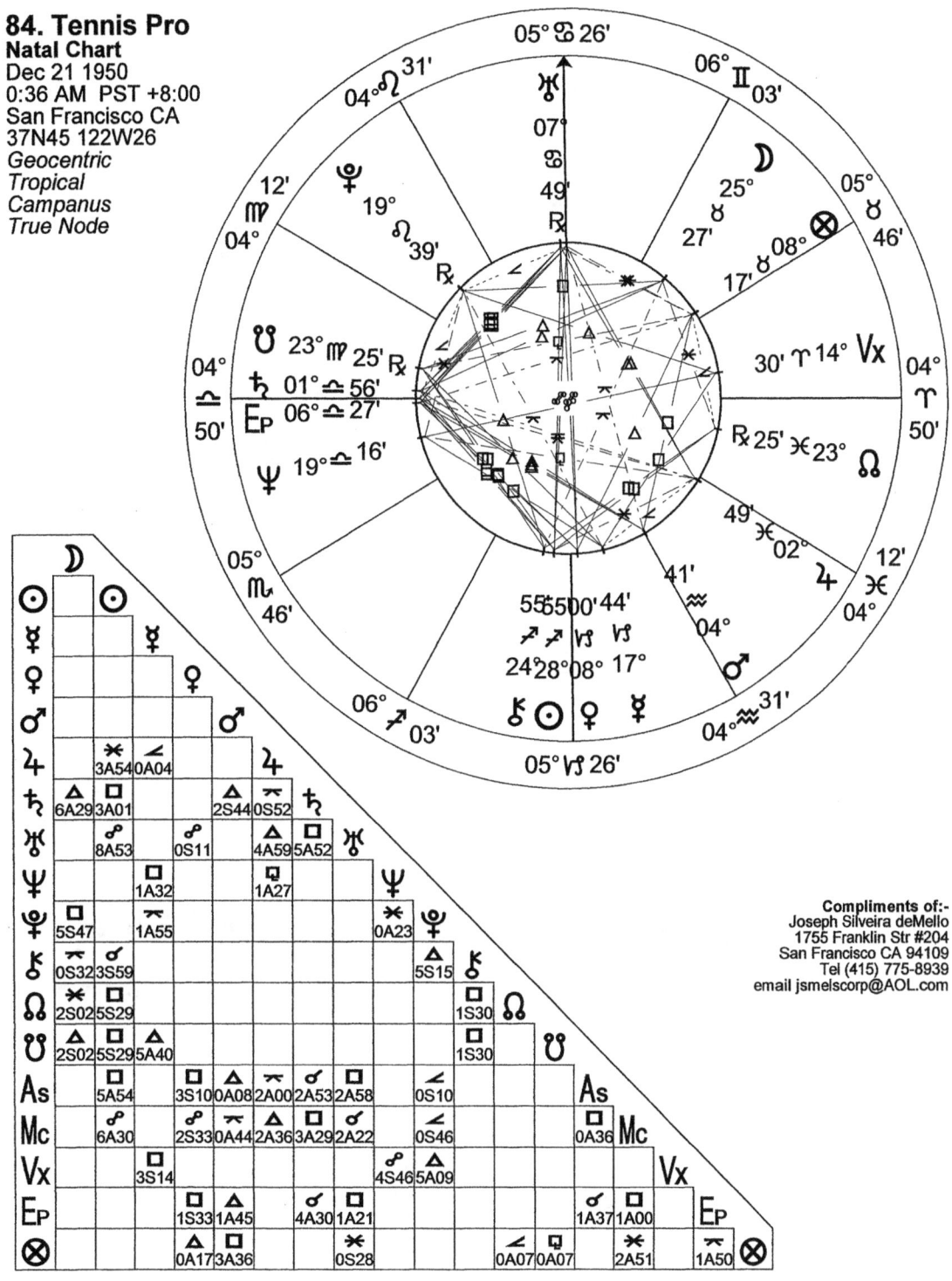

84. Tennis Pro
Natal Chart
Dec 21 1950
0:36 AM PST +8:00
San Francisco CA
37N45 122W26
Geocentric
Tropical
Campanus
True Node

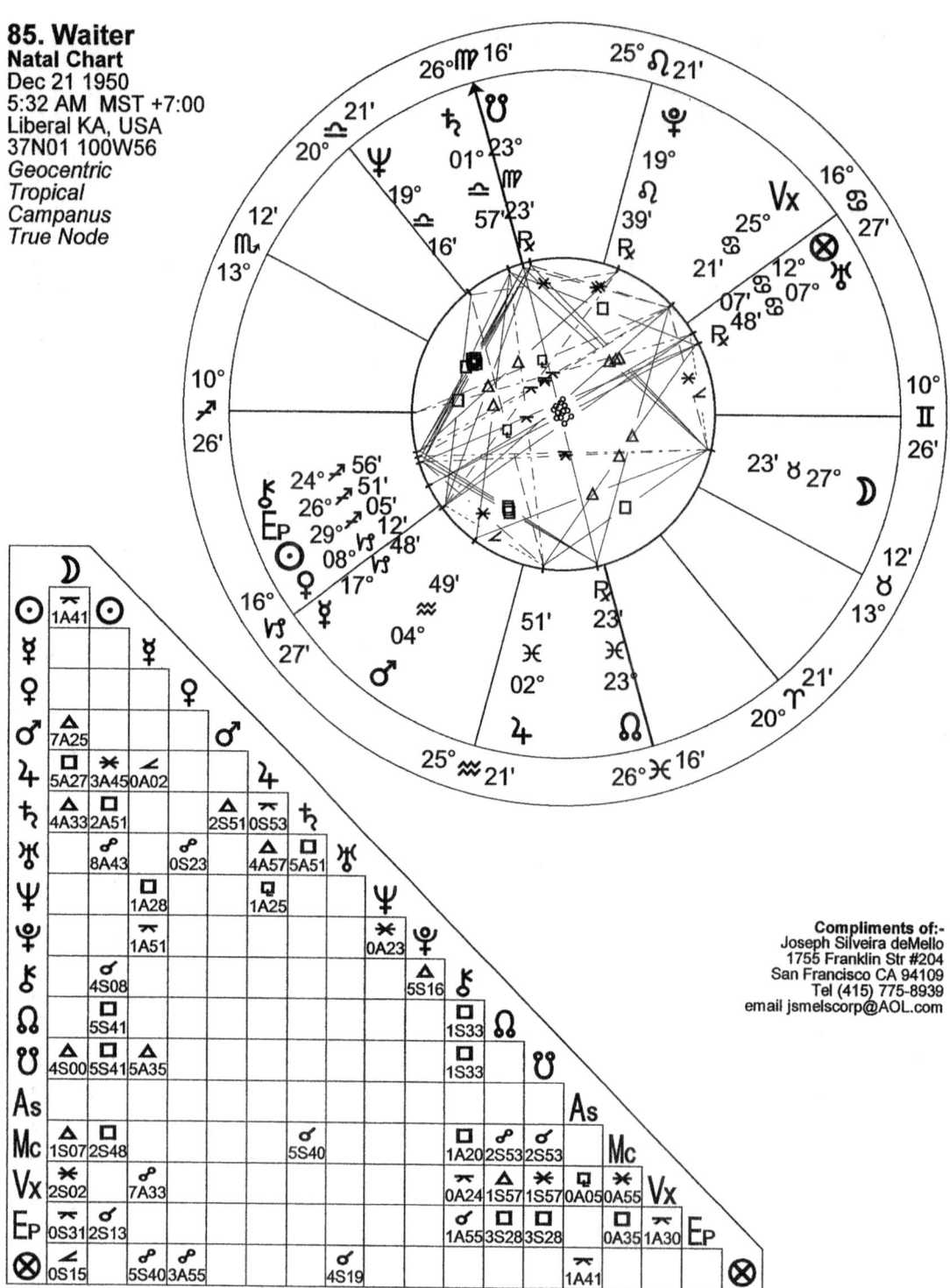

85. Waiter
Natal Chart
Dec 21 1950
5:32 AM MST +7:00
Liberal KA, USA
37N01 100W56
Geocentric
Tropical
Campanus
True Node

talked about it. He served pleasantly and efficiently, was homosexual, interested in doing his own thing, had no one really close to himself for very long. His recreation seemed to be in socializing with his coworkers.

86. Robert Schmidt, 5-10-3
Wider orb Saturn: 1N14
Data: December 22, 1950, 8:22 p.m. CST,
Rock Island Illinois, 41N30, 90W34

Everyone in astrology knows this tall, dark, erudite Illinois astrologer who with his wife, Ellen Black, are both always a pleasure to meet at any astrological conference. They and Robert Hand organized and worked with Project Hindsight, devoted to translating the works of ancient astrologers for today's astrologers. He was in charge of doing the Greek translations. He was a serious astrologer but is also well regarded for business ability.

The chart with Leo rising is no surprise to anyone who has every met him and seen how tall he stands and walks. The fact he has dark and plentiful hair may be due to Pluto on the Ascendant. His Sun is in Capricorn, testifying to executive and managerial work, and his Moon is in Gemini, a testament to humor and wide interests. Note that the Sun is at its Southern limit of declination due to his birthday, while the Moon is very out of bounds beyond the northern limit, and Venus and Uranus are both also out of bounds. There is a Venus-Saturn mutual reception which puts the courtesy position of Saturn rather too close to his Sun. Sun ruling the first house is an excellent position for any salesman or actor, giving a facility for changing personality to suit the requirements of any moment and very good for creative and speculative endeavors, Sun in a managerial creativity, while Saturn rules his sixth house of work and the Mars there shows where all his energies go, while his tenth of career is ruled by Venus back in his fifth.

87. Mother with Problems, 9-10-6
Wider orb Saturn: 1N12
Data: December 29, 1950, 4:35 a.m. MST,
Denver, Colorado, 39N45, 104W59

There are times when an astrologer finds himself among the world of the truly dysfunctional and the client for whom you can do absolutely nothing that is going to have any meaning. This client came to me because she had a son, born with minimal brain damage. The child tended to use his hands as if they were paws and had trouble separating his fingers from each other or coordinating with his hands. This the mother attributed to overly physical exertion in her first trimester, at which time she moved a great deal of heavy furniture. At least I knew better than disabuse her of her theories. But the reader can, no doubt, see how this reading went. And just as I suspected, although her reason for consulting me was her child's problems, she actually was far more interested in getting a reading on her own chart, and discussion of her child's chart was quickly relegated to the background. I did, however, get the child's data: August 27, 1971, 3:47 a.m. PDT, San Jose, California, 37N20, 121W53.

In the course of the reading, it was revealed that she had been born with speech problems which she has overcome. The phrase "born with a speech impediment" grated on me. It must have been quite some time before this came to light. She would not discuss how this "impediment" manifested nor what had been done to work out of it. Her third house had Jupiter, chart significator, nicely in Pisces, its own sign, but with Mars in Aquarius almost on its house cusp. Mars is in no aspect to the eighth house Uranus in Cancer, but her Sun is opposite Uranus and both square Saturn and Fortune. The mutual reception of Venus-Saturn disposes of the chart but for Jupiter.

During this reading, I had plenty of time to wonder which of us was doing the reading. I figured she wanted someone to whom she could talk, and it was not going to matter what I said. I resigned myself to being directed by her plentiful remarks. I noted with amusement that the Moon was opposite Jupiter, one of the meanings of which is "laziness." Although Jupiter is sesquiquad Neptune and quincunx Saturn, rather thorny aspects, Jupiter is also trine Uranus.

88. Divorcee, 6-10-7
Wider orb Saturn: 1N11
Data: December 31, 1950, 11:00 p.m. EST,
Johnson City, New York, 42N07, 75W58

This is a chart of a vivacious redheaded lady briefly part of our neighborhood club many years ago. She knew everyone and was well-liked by one and all. She had got married to an old friend of hers on November 3, 1974, but she separated from her husband two weeks after the wedding, said it was a mistake she should not have made. Additionally, her father died in January 1975. I remember that she had an exceptionally lush figure and a very outgoing personality. There was none of the shyness, inhibition or conservatism one might expect from Saturn in the first house, and this may have been due to Saturn not being in the rising sign, at zero declination, or in mutual reception to Venus. She had the wonderful ability to make the person to whom she was talking feel he was the only person in the whole room.

Even that early in my career as astrologer, I was aware of the differences between Virgo rising males and females. Virgo men are project coordinators who bring together people to work on any project with more personal friendliness than do Capricorn men.

Virgo women, Sun or rising sign, bring together socially people who want to know each other. But Virgo women have problems with personal and intellectual fads, a thing they routinely deny just before demonstrating how they do it. What may be "in" for them for any not too long period is supplanted by the next fad, and one never again hears of the previous favorite thing. In any case, this very nubile lady left San Francisco, returned to Los Angeles where she had previously lived.

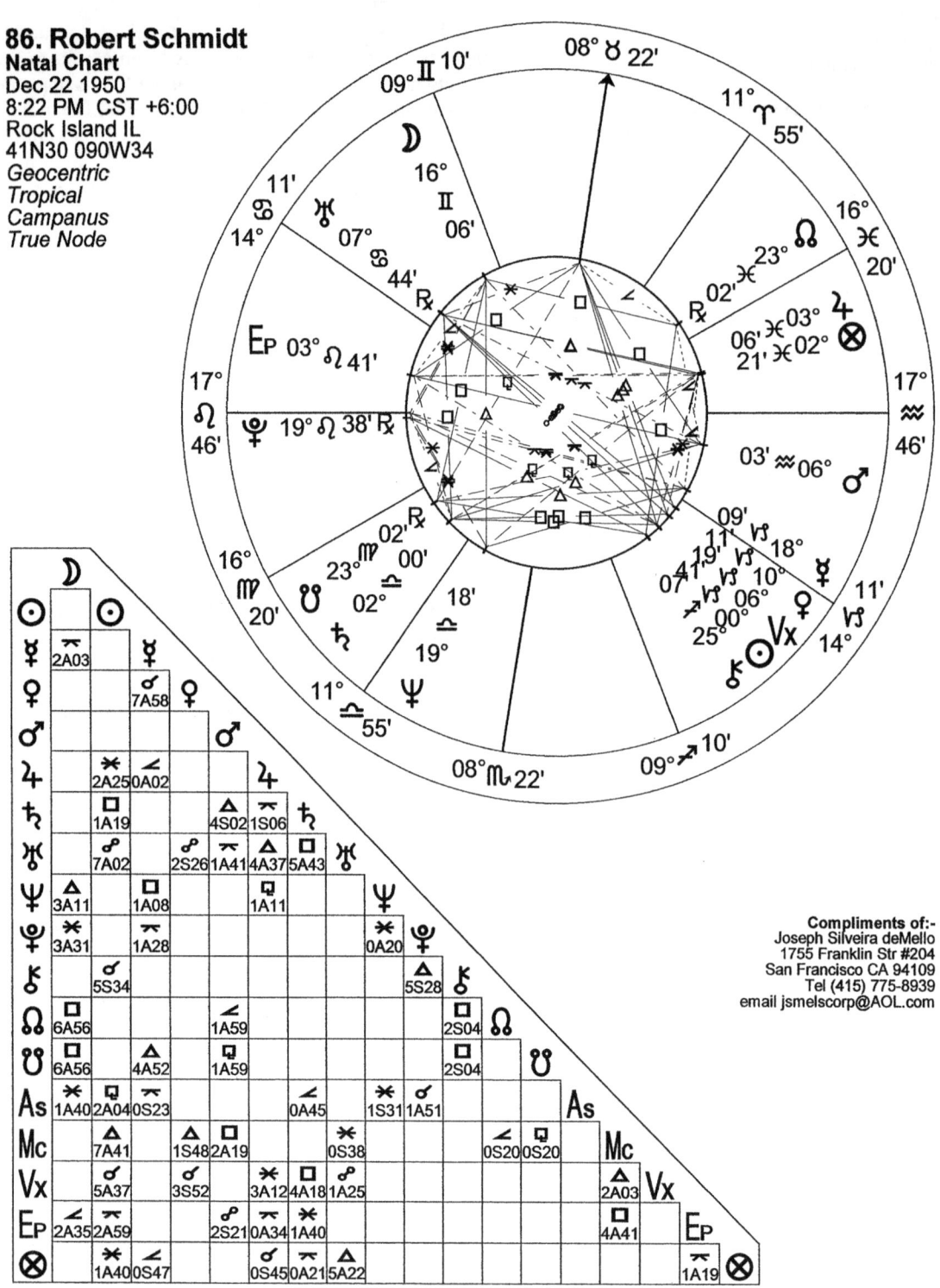

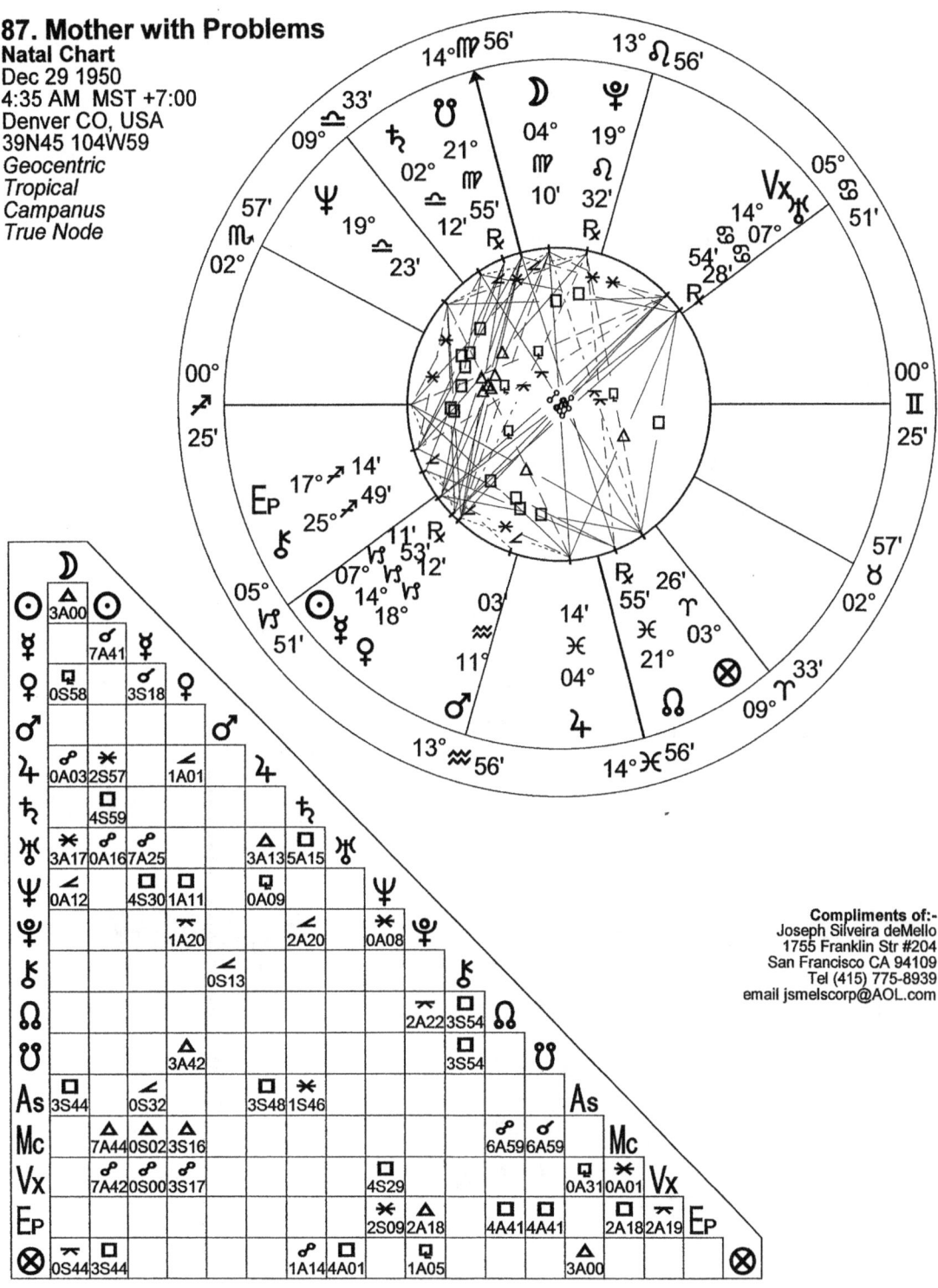

87. Mother with Problems
Natal Chart
Dec 29 1950
4:35 AM MST +7:00
Denver CO, USA
39N45 104W59
Geocentric
Tropical
Campanus
True Node

Compliments of:-
Joseph Silveira deMello
1755 Franklin Str #204
San Francisco CA 94109
Tel (415) 775-8939
email jsmelscorp@AOL.com

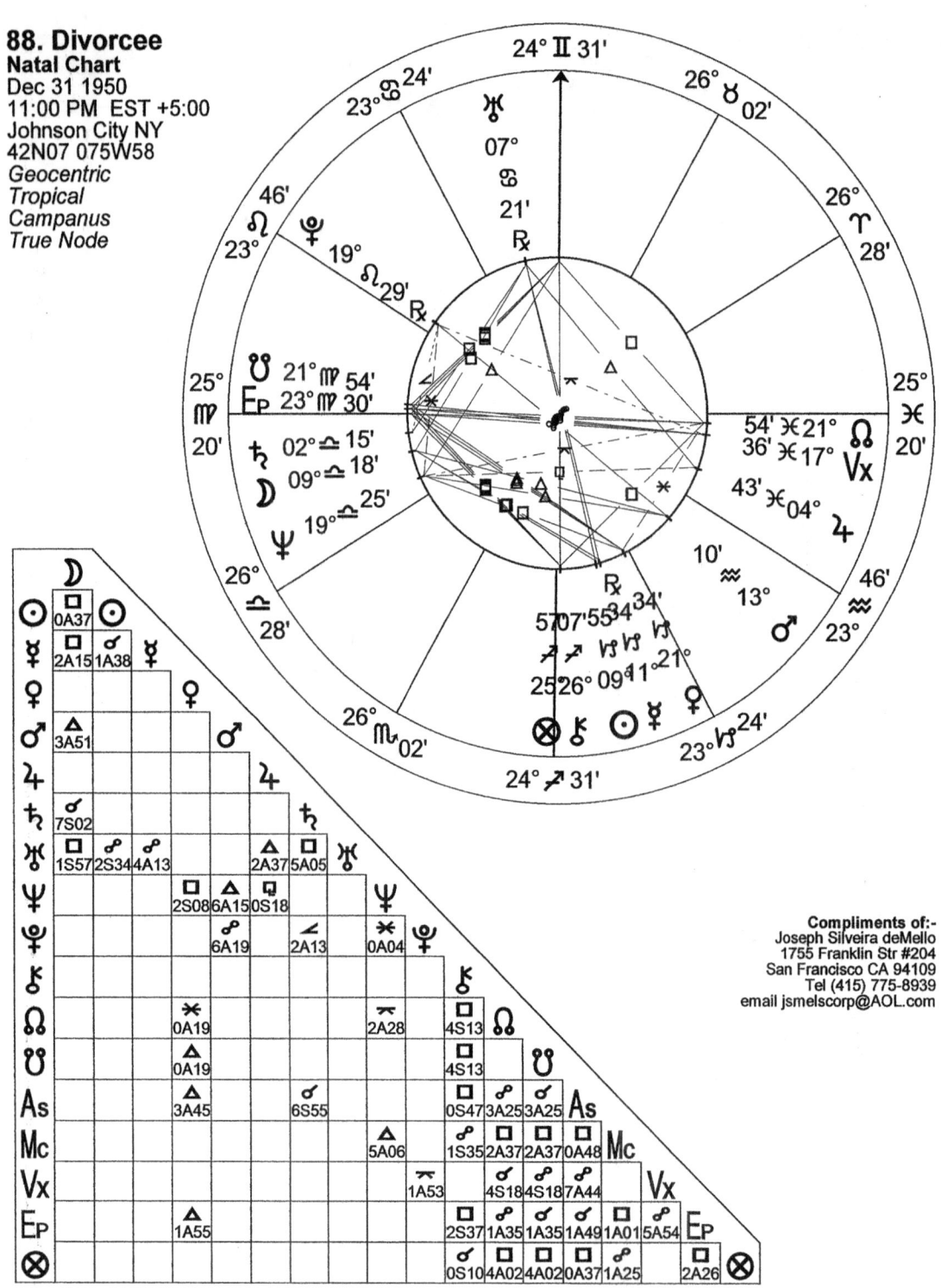

88. Divorcee
Natal Chart
Dec 31 1950
11:00 PM EST +5:00
Johnson City NY
42N07 075W58
Geocentric
Tropical
Campanus
True Node

Compliments of:-
Joseph Silveira deMello
1755 Franklin Str #204
San Francisco CA 94109
Tel (415) 775-8939
email jsmelscorp@AOL.com

89. Barman, 3-10-11
Wider orb Saturn: 1N11
Data: January 9, 1951, 3:15 p.m. PST,
San Francisco, California, 37N45, 122W26

This bartender worked briefly at a place which did not stay in business very long. He was slender, blue eyed, had red hair, and was homosexual. I knew him in 1978-79 at a time when he was planning to move to the Los Angeles area. He was rather sensitive and talented, very interested in everything around him. His chart has a dizzying number of aspects of every variety.

90. Rush Limbaugh, 11-10-12
Wider orb Saturn: 1N11
Data: January 12, 1951, 7:50 a.m. CST,
Cape Girardeau, Missouri, 37N19, 89W32

The astrologer has to be prepared for the unusual. The time originally given for Rush Limbaugh was 6:50 a.m., but his mother has nicely improved it by saying, in a radio interview, that it actually should be for an hour later. By adding an hour, he becomes an Aquarius rising, but we still have the Capricorn Sun, to which we then have the dread Pisces Moon in the second house. Sun and Uranus are intercepted, and two degrees apart by declination; Uranus is out of bounds, and Pluto is way up there, too. This is a daytime chart with modern rulerships although Jupiter must be enhanced in Pisces. Aquarians know what is best for everyone else (but seldom for themselves). The solutions or suggestions proposed by an Aquarian are usually poorly conceived and totally untenable to those for whom they are meant.

This chart gives us an interesting picture of the man, a right-wing radio commentator, further to right of God than God, somewhat lacking in humor, but sure his every stance is infallibly correct. The new astrology student first learns that humanitarianism and tactfulness are the basic qualities of Aquarius, but then the astrologer starts to find charts where both those qualities are not only absent but superimposed by redefining contradictions. So the conviction of Aquarius blends with controlling Capricorn, and a Moon sign that wishes to appear compassionate but will miss the mark. If we have a twelfth house and private Sun, we then have a Mars-Aries overtone, a definitive exception to the Mars rising, and a Moon allowing for a Christian consciousness that steps on too many toes for total effectiveness. The first house Venus supposedly improves his appearance and Jupiter does here attest to the full figured man. For it is the belligerence of Mars which is most visible. Uranus is chart significator. See Midheaven square Mars and both sesquiquad Uranus. Uranus is in the sixth house which is ruled by the twelfth house Mercury retrograde, and Mercury is square Saturn which is also retrograde, and as I write this, Saturn is coming to sesquiquad by transit to both of those. The Mars opposition to Pluto tends to be obsessive to a point where actions impact poorly on many people. The Moon in Pisces is more emotional than spiritual, and how a person projects may not be what others see.

With Limbaugh just past age fifty, check the Sun's progressed movement in this chart. It stayed in the twelfth for his first nine years, and went into his first house for a long stay of fifty-two years. The Sun left Capricorn for Aquarius and then Pisces. What a path for someone interested in Christianity. None of the planets on the right side of the chart are going to move much by progression. But the transits are a different story. What did the transit of Pluto do in its passage over his Midheaven, and next watch ahead for the movement of Saturn over his IC. There is much for future interest in this chart. But then take it a bit more deeply. His natal helio Mercury is 9 Virgo, helio Venus is 25 Virgo 29, and helio Mars is 13 Pisces 24.

91. Female Bank Clerk, 6-10-2
Wider orb Saturn: 1N13
Data: January 16, 1951, 8:00 p.m. PST,
Portland, Oregon, 45N31, 122W41

Chart of a bank clerk from the files of Don Borkowski. She was a beautiful bank teller married to a medical student. Don had been curious to see what sort of a chart she had. She had very large eyes, perhaps Neptune on the Ascendant, he thought, but she did not have that.

Virgo rising people attending to all the details is good for a teller, but what of Capricorn ruling the sixth, and Venus and Mars widely apart in Aquarius are intercepted. The career Midheaven is Taurus, and we know bank tellers are not highly paid. Mercury the chart significator is in Capricorn, well ahead of her Sun position. Mercury is opposite Uranus, and both make a T-square to her Saturn. Venus, on the other hand, makes only a semi-square to Fortune, so I would watch Venus as through it were unaspected. Planets which have no aspects are usually very strong, and they must be watched when they make retrograde/direct stations. Venus and Saturn are in mutual reception.

92. One Time Female Client, 11-10-2
Wider orb Saturn: 1N13
Data: January 17, 1951, 6:37 a.m. AHST,
Honolulu, Hawaii, 21N19, 157W52

Data from the subject was altered for correct time zone which changed in 1947 to AHST or CAT adding half an hour to previous HST. She was visiting San Francisco briefly and did not keep her appointment before returning to Hawaii. Data is from her and given since it is for the day following the previous example. Oddly, my Jupiter is on her Ascendant. Having the correct natal angles is of utmost importance if one is going to look at progressions. My best test of chart involves watching the transits of always timely Saturn. Any astrologer, asking the client the right questions, soon arrives at a sense that the chart matches events in the client's life. I worked on her chart in 1982. Moon and Uranus are out of bounds and parallel. Venus and Saturn are still in mutual reception. She was in a management

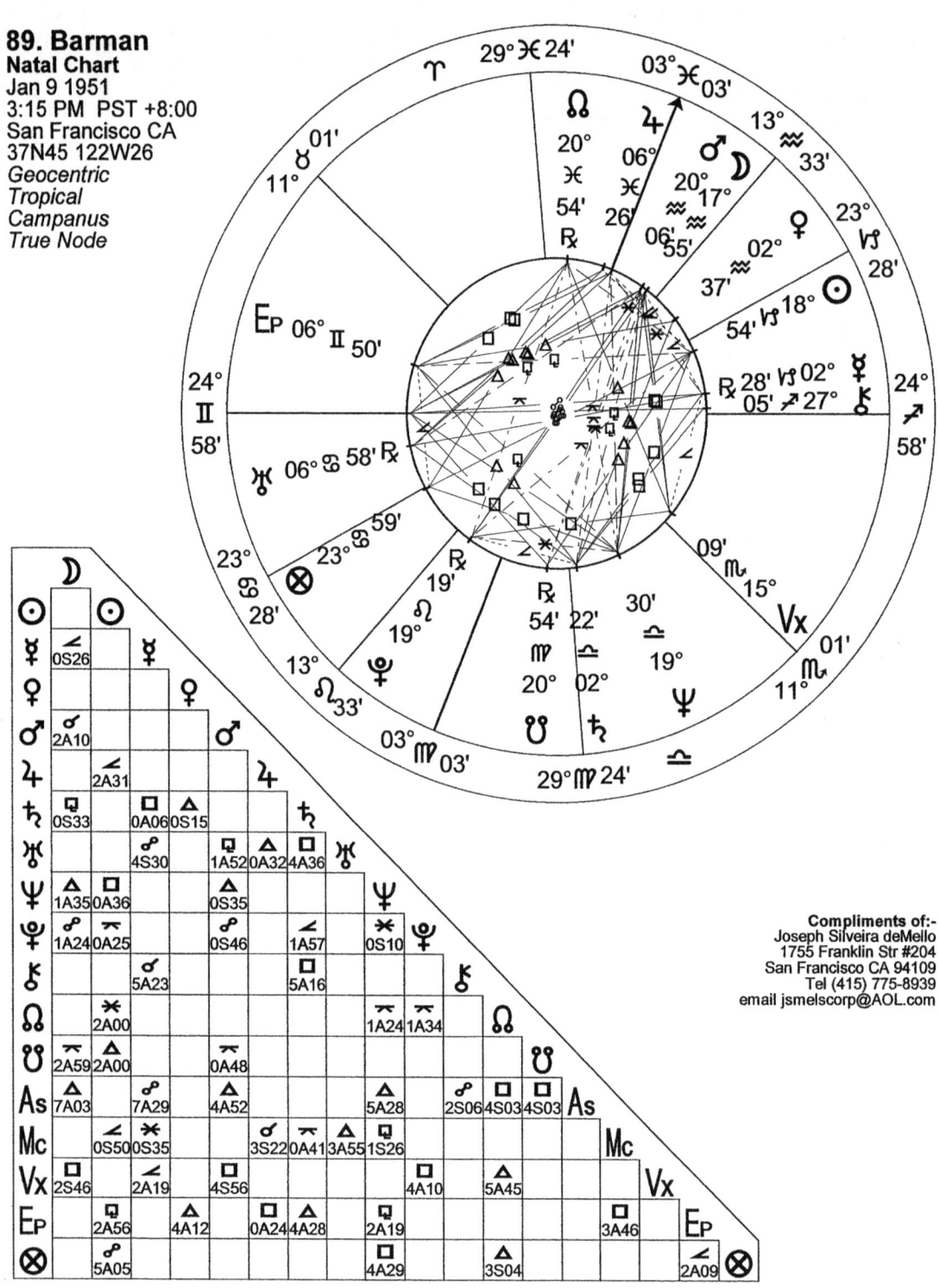

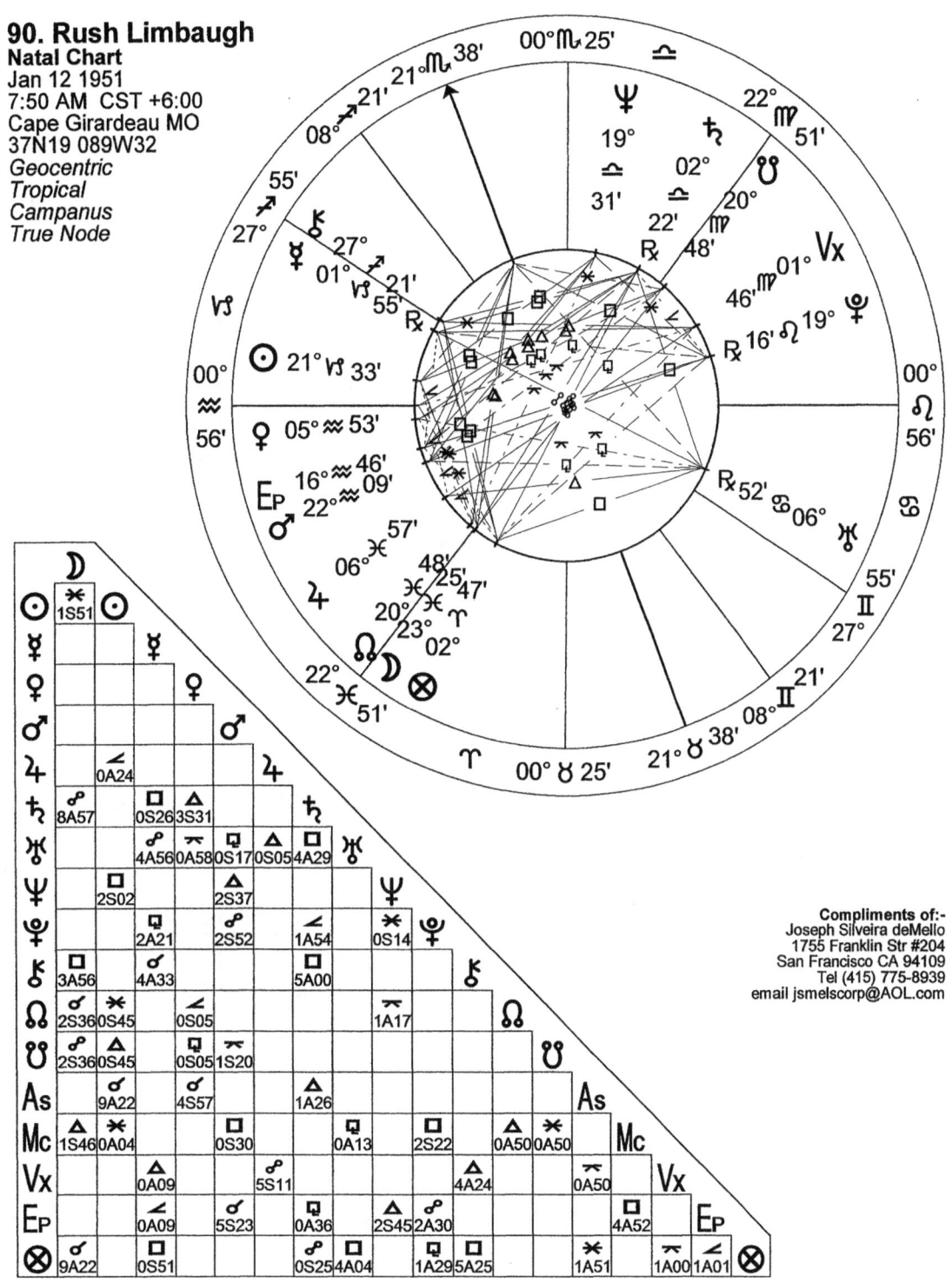

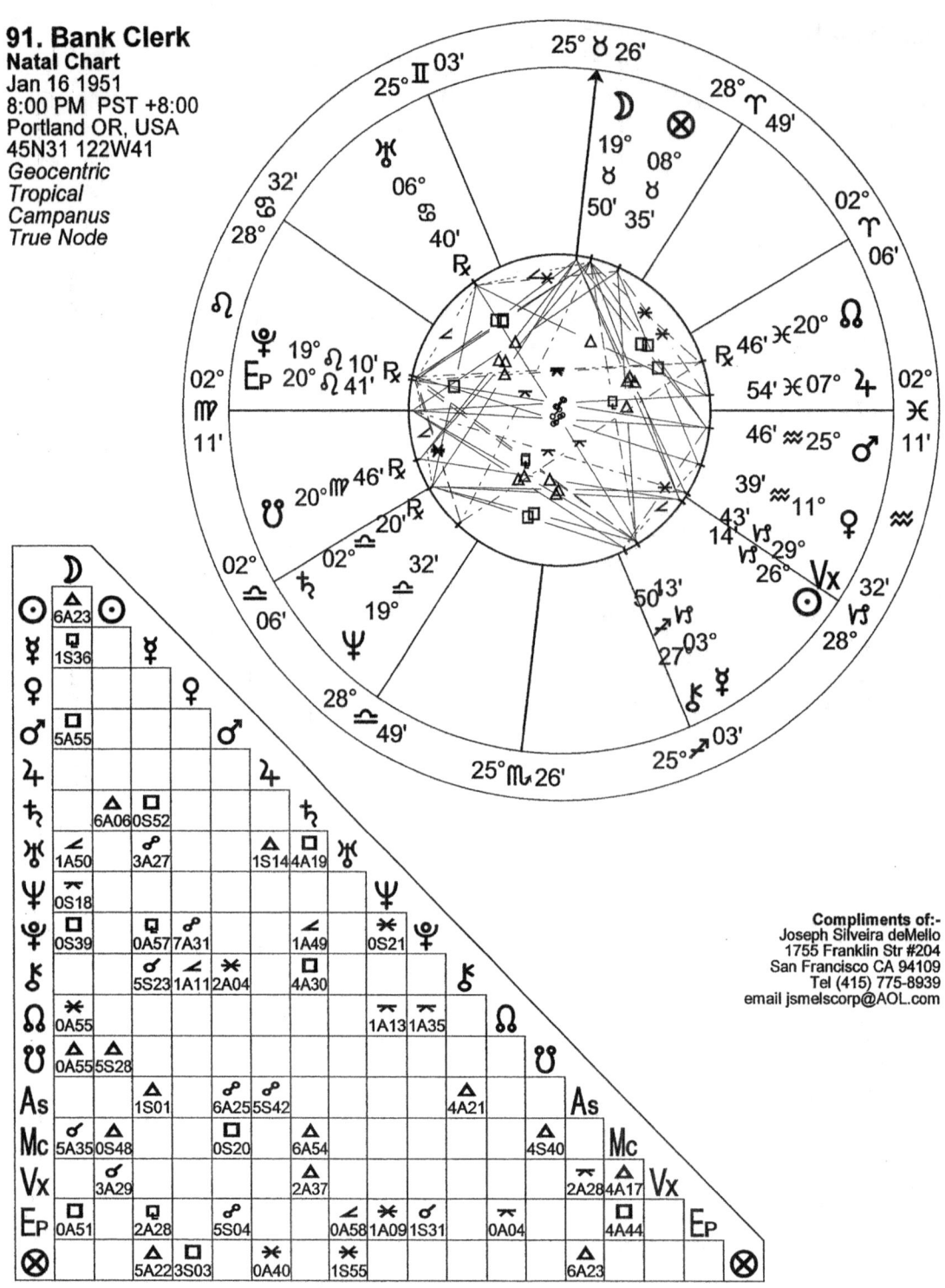

91. Bank Clerk
Natal Chart
Jan 16 1951
8:00 PM PST +8:00
Portland OR, USA
45N31 122W41
Geocentric
Tropical
Campanus
True Node

Compliments of:-
Joseph Silveira deMello
1755 Franklin Str #204
San Francisco CA 94109
Tel (415) 775-8939
email jsmelscorp@AOL.com

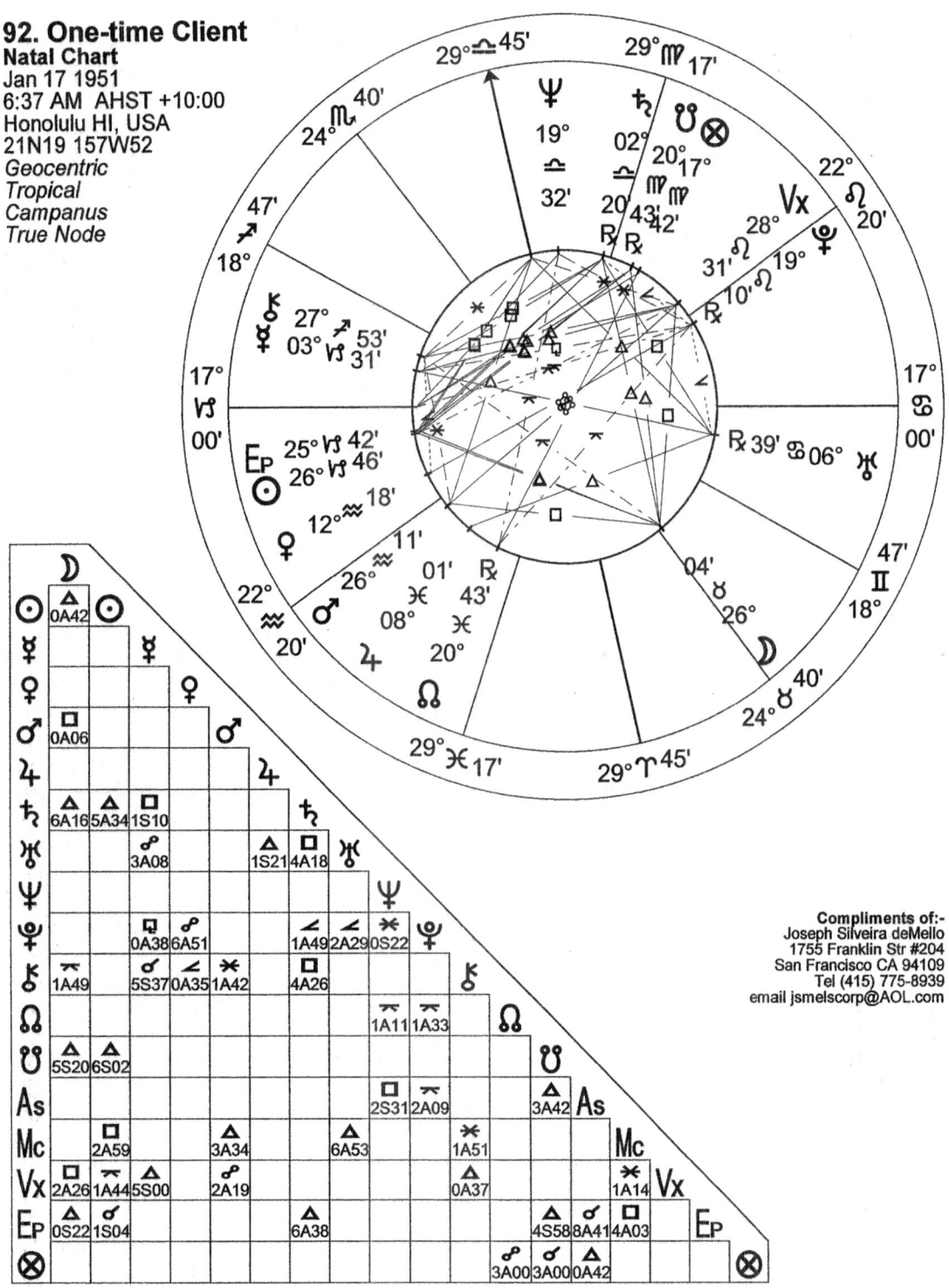

position, well employed and well-salaried, and money meant a great deal to her. She was much more focused in Hawaii.

93. Male Office Manager, 7-10-3
Wider orb Saturn: 1N14
Data: January 18, 1951, 10:44 p.m. EST,
Westerly, Rhode Island, 41N25, 71W50

This chart for one day later than the above. On his first visit to a social club in the early summer of 1978, I was immediately introduced to this man who was born near where I was born. I was supposed to make him feel welcome. He was of medium height and somewhat plump, pleasant, quiet, and he was employed as an office manager, a job with which he was unhappy. He thought he would like to get into banking, and thus he became a client, wanting to know about career and health, but he also asked about romance, of which my homosexual clients of either sex rarely ask. He was not involved in a relationship, but he did not expound on that. In March of 1978, he had been managing a retail shop that burned to the ground. He had taken his present job out of need of a steady paycheck. The progressed Moon then had been about to conjunct his natal Moon. Saturn at that time was in late Leo in retrograde, past his natal Pluto and opposite his natal Mars which Saturn did not natally aspect. Saturn would go into his twelfth in the fall.

I am still surprised in the timely way people consult me. Not only was Saturn going into his twelfth, but it would come to a Saturn return in another year. In the eleventh house transit he was deciding on what friends to have around him, what community he needed. In the twelfth house, the previous twenty-eight years are examined for what went right or wrong—an analysis rather than to lay the blame. The sojourn there was to take advantage of planning for the future and not a time to begin something new. His natal Saturn is in the twelfth and retrograde, and relating is important to him. A serious young man, it was time to take his life in hand.

The chart is Libra rising with Neptune in the first house. Such a person can always ask "who is the real me." Libra rising is always happiest in a relationship, but their people should be those of a high moral caliber. The Sun is in late Capricorn in the fourth house is both practical and creative in home and future planning (his eleventh ruled by Leo is also a creative area for him), and the Moon in Gemini (and well out of bounds as are Uranus and Pluto). In this nocturnal chart Venus and Saturn are in mutual reception, but Mercury is opposite Uranus with Saturn at the T-square midpoint in his twelfth house. He demonstrated psychic gifts or capabilities but was of no mind to put these to any sort of use, certainly not professionally, nor to use these as conversational ploys. He was shy and diffident of these abilities and preferred to suppress them.

Our client-astrologer relationship did not last beyond the series of meetings that led up to the reading. He wanted to be told that right then was a time to change, that in the near future he would find a serious lifetime partner. I saw that his Ascendant was trine my own and that his Moon was in Gemini, as is mine. I also saw that his Venus was on my Midheaven, my Sun fell on his second house cusp and his Sun fell close to my South Node. I am sure he did not view favorably that I counseled no immediate change and carefully quizzed him about what he might expect of a banking career. He was also disinclined to spend time being friendly with someone like me who was not a potential partner. The chart represents many contradictions. Libra may need a strong partner, but Capricorn is a control sign, and Aries or Cancer might be viable but are also too strong for his liking. Note Uranus as the highest planet in his chart, and the aspects made by Saturn and Uranus. I was also aware that it would take some time and a couple of trials for him to find a final career niche and success.

94. Band Vocalist, 8-6-4
Wider orb Saturn: 1N19
Data: August 28, 1951, 12:30 p.m. EDT,
Brooklyn, New York, 40N38, 73W58

This young lady is a long time close friend of a colleague who furnished me with her data. One of the most persistent dreams of young people is to become a star and rise to celebrity in the entertainment world. Quite often any astrologer is faced with such clients. A sensible astrologer knows that, in any one period, though many are called, only a very few get to the top forty. Perhaps that is why so many are told not to give up their day jobs. But this young woman stayed with her dream. She sings with a moderate sized band and performs at private parties and night clubs.

This chart has Scorpio rising. The Sun is in Virgo in the tenth house which has a Leo Midheaven, an excellent placement. Mercury is five degrees from the Sun, and so has the potential of being overtaken by the ego Sun, and here they are applying by progression since Mercury is retrograde. Of course it is necessary for someone looking for success in the world of entertainment to be possessed of an untrammeled ego. Too many dreamers seeking celebrity lack ego, in which case we can only recommend that they have top agents and managers to handle their careers. This chart has a problem in that my own Saturn falls on her Ascendant degree, and I perhaps should not seek to advise her.

In our look at declinations, the Moon is out of bounds, and she has Moon in Cancer, a bit beyond a trine aspect to the Ascendant, and we note that the Moon has but one aspect, a square to Neptune which should aid her as a vocal stylist. We also see that Mercury and Jupiter are parallel, but Venus and Saturn are contra-parallel. Mercury and Moon are chart dispositors. Most of the placements in this cart are above the horizon, another good thing for public image. A small side issue is that this young lady sings under a stage name, one she finds more romantic than her given name. Do not fail to notice that Mercury is on the South Node. Only the tenth is an active angular house.

If one checks progressions, the progressed Sun has now gone into her twelfth house which may put her career in the shade as she goes through her late forties,

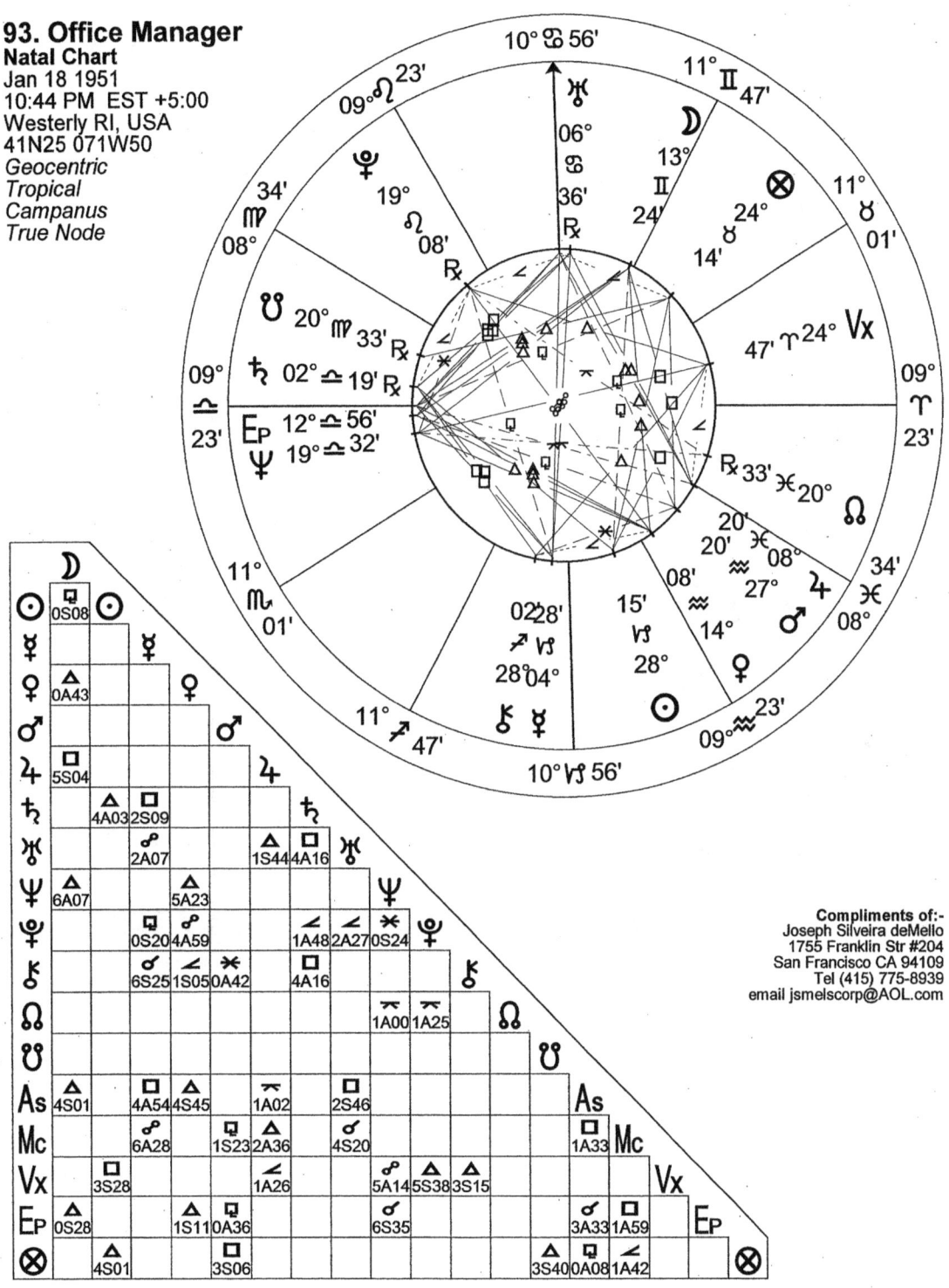

93. Office Manager
Natal Chart
Jan 18 1951
10:44 PM EST +5:00
Westerly RI, USA
41N25 071W50
Geocentric
Tropical
Campanus
True Node

Compliments of:-
Joseph Silveira deMello
1755 Franklin Str #204
San Francisco CA 94109
Tel (415) 775-8939
email jsmelscorp@AOL.com

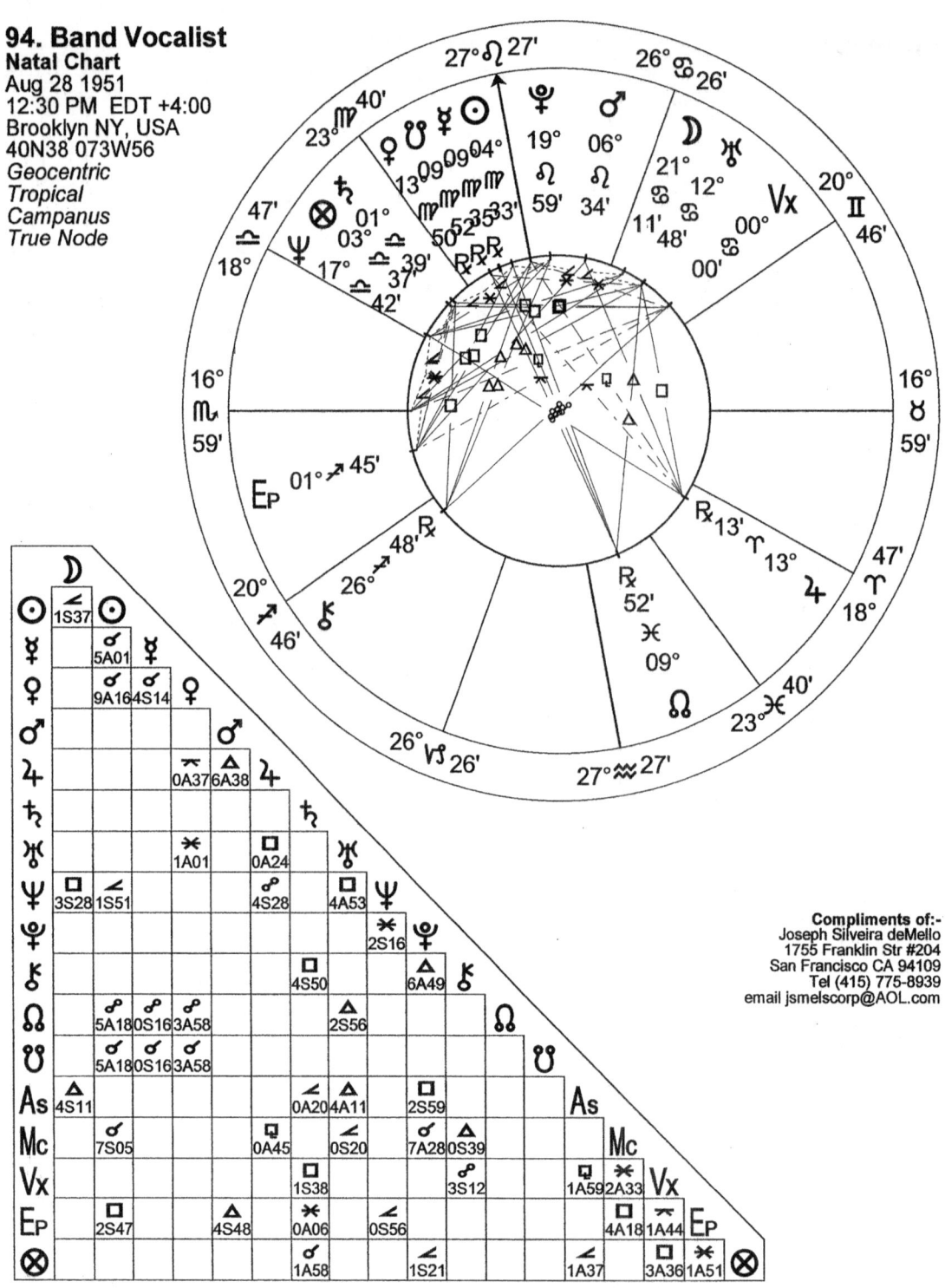

bearing in mind that if few find celebrity in youth, even fewer are still singing in or beyond middle age.

She has always kept very busy maintaining contacts and bookings. There is much on the face of this chart that is strong, many squares, but two T-squares, desire on the Ascendant, determination on the tenth, artistic ability, public image, and ambition.

95. Canadian Female Astrologer, 6-6-6
Wider orb Saturn: 1N07, Venus: 0S34
Data: September 2, 1951, 5:15 a.m. GMT,
Cambridge, England, 52N12, 0E11

This is a chart of a Canadian astrologer who lectured on depression at the 1985 FCA Convention in Vancouver. Data was given by her to Don Borkowski. She is a triple Virgo with nodal axis on the horizon, from seventh to first, or Sun conjunct South Node. and all but two planets in the twelfth and first houses. I maintain that having rising sign, Sun and Moon all in the same sign offers the person very little mitigation from being too much all of a kind. We see the Ascendant ruled by Mercury which also rules the Midheaven, but Mercury is on the twelfth house side of Virgo rising. There can be no doubt that she pays attention to all the details, is very practical. Mercury, the interest in the matter, is in the twelfth and retrograde, and this makes her an abstract thinker, which might give her a deeper more interesting mentality, less run of the mill.

While Saturn is out of orb to make it into our prime zero Saturn group, we see that she was born with Venus at zero declination. This should turn our thoughts further afield. It is not the Venus out of bounds which loves too well but not too wisely. For here we have a Venus which is much too close to the Sun (and Mercury is also close enough to give way to the ego Sun influence). Note that these planets are only in aspect to each other and the Ascendant. Mercury certainly bears watching when its transits change station. I would say this chart has to be self-centered. The doings of six houses of this chart are channeled through the first house, and of four houses of the chart channeled through the subconscious twelfth. The final personality indicator is Mars, and here we find Mars in dramatic Leo starting the twelfth house chain. At the end of this chain, we have Saturn in Libra exalted.

96. Female Astrologer, 6-7-2
Wider orb Saturn: 1S01
Data: October 16, 1951, 2:31 a.m. EST,
Hartford, Connecticut, 41N45, 72W40

This is another chart from the files of Don Borkowski, who collects charts of astrologers and Virgo females. She practices astrology in Oregon and is well known there. We do not now have the great twelfth and first house concentration, but we still have Saturn on the cusp of the second house. Also notice that Jupiter retrograde is on the cusp of her eighth and the Taurus Moon is on the cusp of her ninth house. And we still have the nodal axis on the horizontal axis. This lady has a genius and a history for stirring up trouble between everybody around her. This is, of course, a Libra hallmark, for Librans enjoy starting small wars with the option of later on making peace and getting to be known as peacemakers. Of her own telling, she claims to have very high standards of spirituality. I find such statements instantly suspect, and my first thought is that these are probably standards for other people to toe the mark and grace notes for her own ego. Virgo women are always in tune with the latest fads, or things have a habit of becoming fads with them. Going with her self-description, we start seeing anomalies to spirituality. I always look to Neptune for that, and while here the Sun (ego) scorches Mercury (mentality), Neptune can withstand the heat of the Sun, and she can say what she wishes of herself, regardless of what others may see in her chart. With four planets influencing the second, and Jupiter on the cusp of the eighth, not to mention Moon in Taurus, materialism has to loom rather largely somewhere there. If Neptune were angular, I would say things about the manner in which she might process reality, but that is not the case. Her creative houses are the twelfth (the dramatic subconscious ruled by Leo), the second house (where the Sun is aiding moneymaking) and the fifth, ruled by Saturn. Saturn also rules the sixth and influences the second. Since this is a nocturnal chart, Jupiter is the best ruler for the seventh and nicely placed on the eighth. Quickly note that Mercury and Venus are in mutual reception. This lady has probably processed out of her life many which should have stayed to be a real part of her life. One wonders at the effect of Mars on her South Node has been. So how does she think? Mercury is intuitive about her status but practical about her personality, while being a bit debilitated in the second house. The status quo third has Scorpio on the cusp, ruled by Mars in the twelfth, while the area of why things are as they are is ruled by Venus on her Ascendant. With the Moon on the cusp of the ninth, philosophy is probably going through constant shifts and revisions.

97. Policewoman, 1-2-2
Wider orb Saturn: 1S25
Data: April 25, 1952, 4:10 a.m. PST,
San Francisco, California, 37N45, 122W26

This interesting lady went from working in a welfare office to a job as a sheriff and finally applied for and went to the police academy and became one of the first policewomen at a time when political correctness took women from desk jobs and let them become street cops. Her family was reputed to have very close ties to the Mafia, easily said of anyone with an Italian family name, and it was gleefully purported that she married simply to change her name.

Unfortunately she and a male partner were responding to a complaint that a teenager on a hillside had a gun. When they arrived, the boy on the hillside pointed a sub-machine gun at her, and she shot him. Then the gun turned out to be a toy, and the boy turned out to be mentally deficient. Since both cops were white, and the victim was of mixed race, there was an inordinate hue and

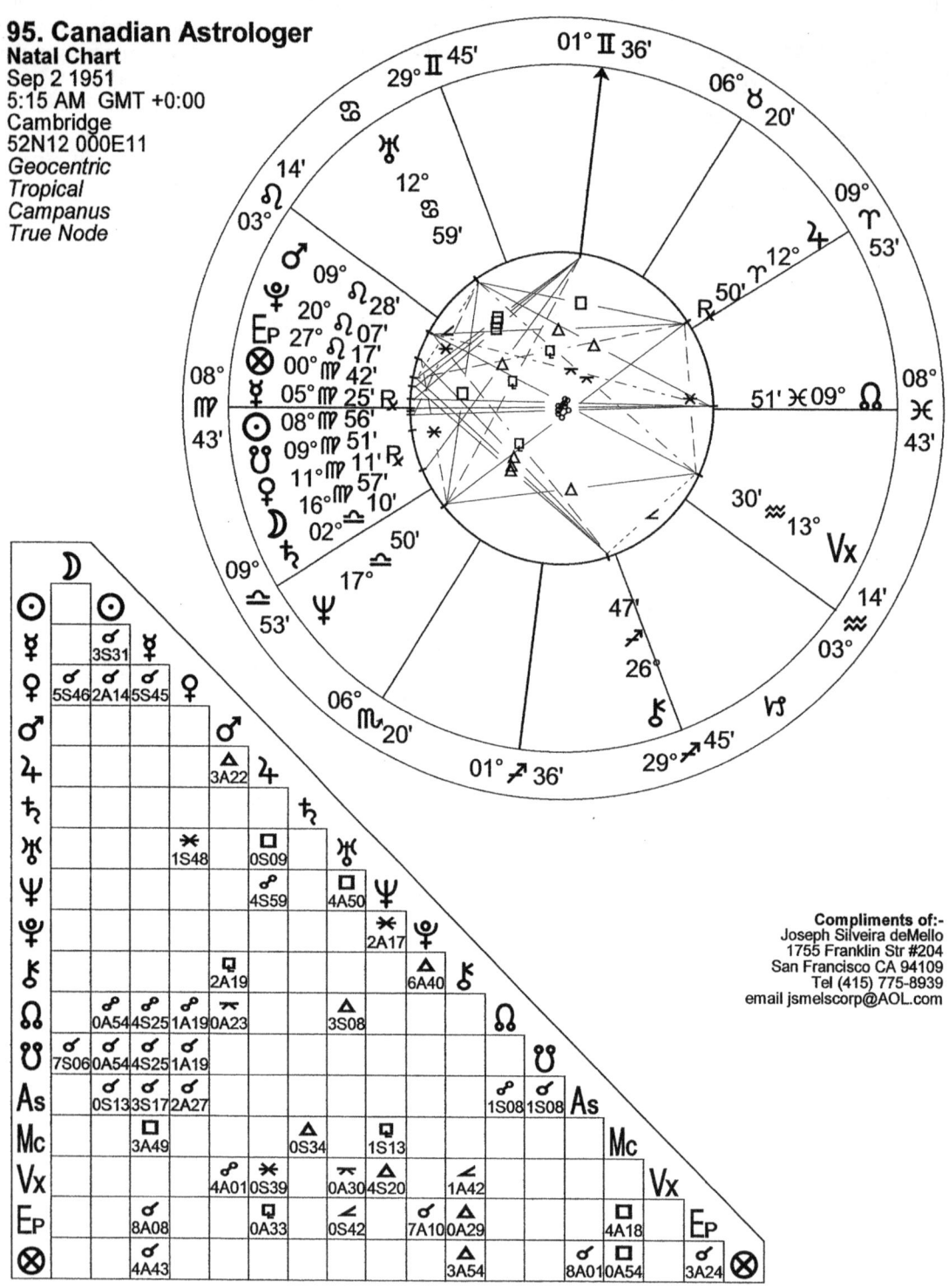

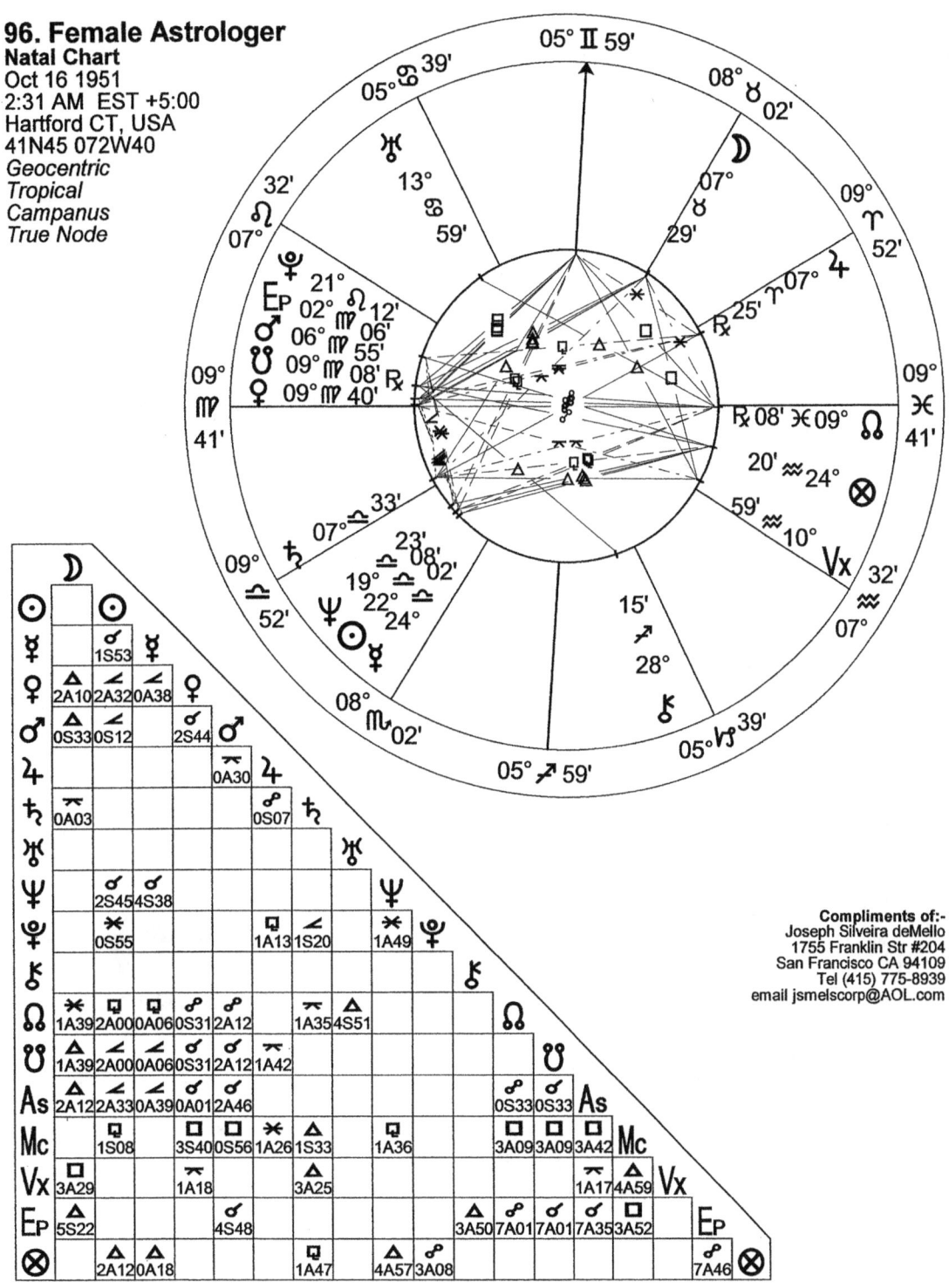

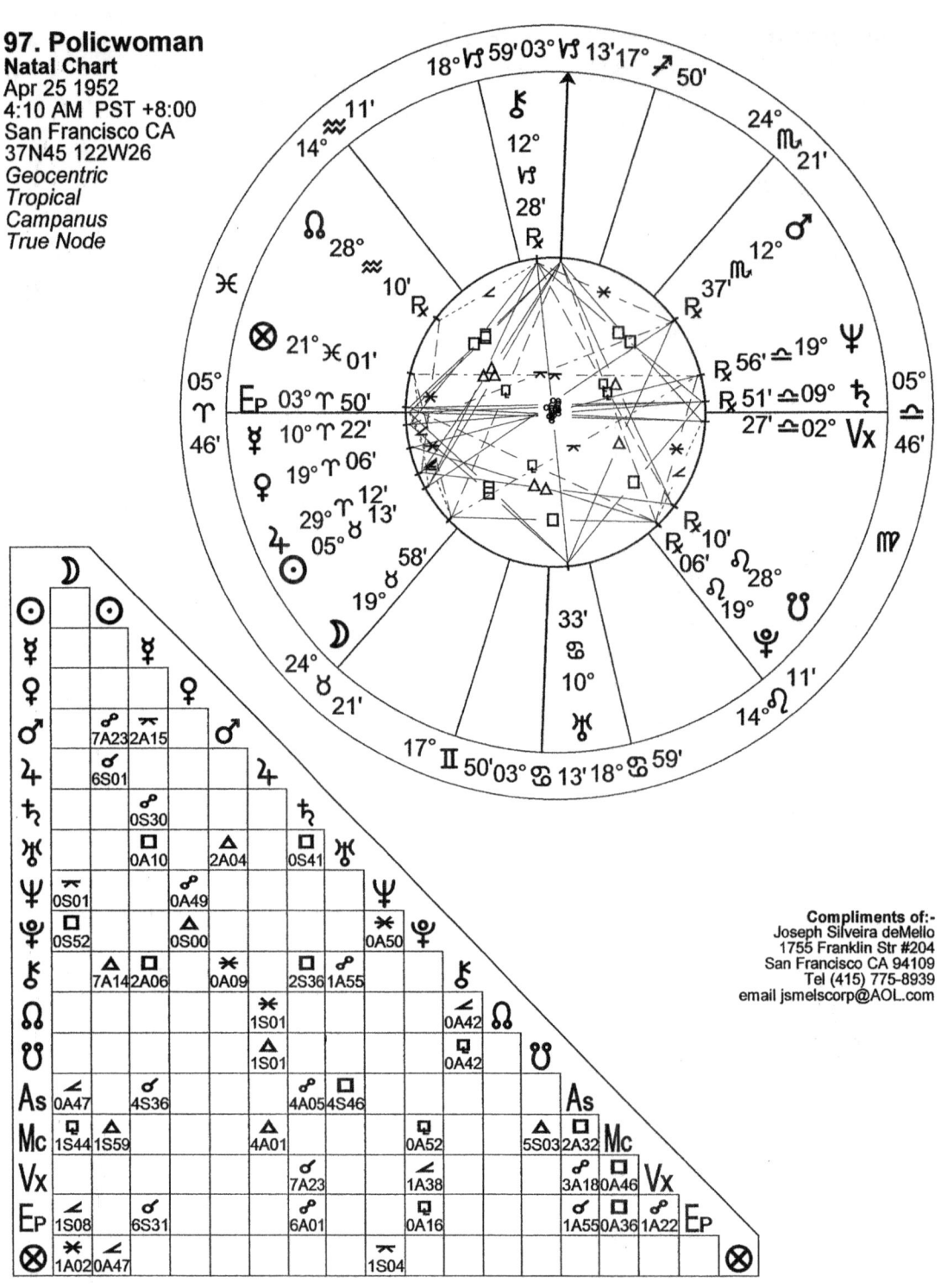

cry. The people who usually seek television exposure at whatever chance raised the ruckus shouting loudly about "white cop behavior." There was no way at a distance to determine that the remarkable weapon was, in fact, a toy, and no way to have a clue to the mentality of the boy on the hillside. Our policewoman was exonerated. But this incident very much shook her up and brought on questions of her own that made it imperative that she take a long disability leave. All of this happened in 1985. She is now a suburban housewife who raises dogs.

This is a vivid looking, attractive and strong featured woman with Aries rising where less of Aries shows than do her Taurus Sun and Moon, not to mention the chart significator Mars in Scorpio which disposes of the chart. She has a heavily tenanted first house, but Mars is in Scorpio in the seventh house, as are Saturn and Neptune which are in Libra. Although she has Aries qualities, she is quite Scorpio. This chart gives the lie to marriages of people with natal Saturn in the seventh house. Her husband is neither a father figure, nor older, nor more mature than herself. However, since she was married with transiting Saturn in the seventh, the marriage has been lasting. Pluto is in her sixth, is a position of people who sabotage themselves on the job. See the oppositions and the cardinal square. I can tell you that this Mercury in the first house was never at a loss for words.

98. Maitre'd, 5-2-4
Wider orb Saturn: 1S19
Data: April 29, 1952, 11:35 a.m. PST,
Corvallis, Oregon, 44N33, 123W15

I knew this man as a greeter and seater at a restaurant, and it was only an interim job while waiting for a more important job. I met this young man when he was twenty-three years of age through two clients while I was being house astrologer at a neighborhood garden restaurant. Among his friends he was known to have huge amounts of talent in many fields; hardly anything to which he could not turn a creative hand. In the realm of dubious claims to fame, he was also born with only one testicle without the possibility or potential to find a hidden or undropped second testicle. It was claimed that he was one of thirteen such cases in medical history. Elspeth Ebertin says such problems are indicated in Scorpio where we find his natal Mars retrograde in the fourth house. He was homosexual.

This chart has many things astrologers delight in finding, a tenth house Sun and Jupiter on the Midheaven, Mercury and Venus in Aries in the ninth house, while not the best for Venus as a sign, we are also caused to see Venus opposite Neptune, and there are also some debilitating aspects of laziness. The Moon out of bounds with Uranus almost out of bounds, and both in the twelfth can be very psychic. While his Saturn karma may be in communications, his energies go to Mars in the fourth and in Scorpio to achieve home and security, and the success of this will depend on how well he works with Sun opposite Mars. Most of our discussion revolved around the development of a time table for further planning and action.

99. Psychologist, 10-2-7
Beyond orb Saturn: 1S10
Data: May 7, 1952, 12:01 a.m. EDT,
New York City, New York, 40N40, 73W58

This is the chart of a very good looking and dapper young doctor who is also a psychologist. He was very quiet and self-contained, and very professional. He came to me at a time when I was doing some work with psychologists who were sending me some of their patients. The seriousness of this chart is seen from the very start of Capricorn rising with Saturn in Libra on the cusp of the ninth house, yet this placement, which should be ambitious, is rather daunted by the Libra Moon and Neptune in the ninth house, Moon indicating discontent, and Neptune bothering the reality of upper mind functions. In the normal Saturnian influence, and things of Saturn and Capricorn coming to the life rather later than earlier, the astrologer has to look closely at the movement of this chart to check future timing. He has the Sun in Taurus in the fourth with Jupiter and Venus also in Taurus on the IC, and these are opposite to Mars in Scorpio, highest planet in the chart testifying to the importance of career and status. He is a male homosexual with Uranus on the seventh opposite the Ascendant and Chiron, and these square Moon and Saturn. No question relevant to sexuality were explored for this client.

Career questions were what brought him to me as a client. He had a private clientele and did community counseling in a clinic, but he was looking for a position which might offer him more status and security. He was then seeking a managerial position in a large Welfare Department but realized he would have difficulties overriding affirmative action, where job preference was given to women even over minorities. He was Hispanic. There was no question of changing profession, and it was my job to find favorable times and dates for job interviews. Capricorns are good team managers who prefer to work alone or be in charge of projects.

100. Dorian Bagwell, 1-2-9
Wider orb Saturn: 1S06
Data: May 11, 1952, 3:12 a.m. EST,
Harrisonburg, Virginia, 38N27, 78W52

Every astrologer is familiar with recurrent periods when we get to run into people of all the same signs or configurations. This was the second of four men with the Sun in Taurus and Aries rising. One of these was a client whom I was following closely, and the others were friends of his, and I was meeting them every two or three days. An even larger surprise was they all seemed to get along well together, and although all were homosexual, they had no intimate relations with each other, and a very good thing, too, since this subject was an early AIDS patient. One does not expect a lot of Aries to hang out together, but these gathered almost on schedule. If two were there, a third or fourth would eventually show up, each professed to not quite understand why the

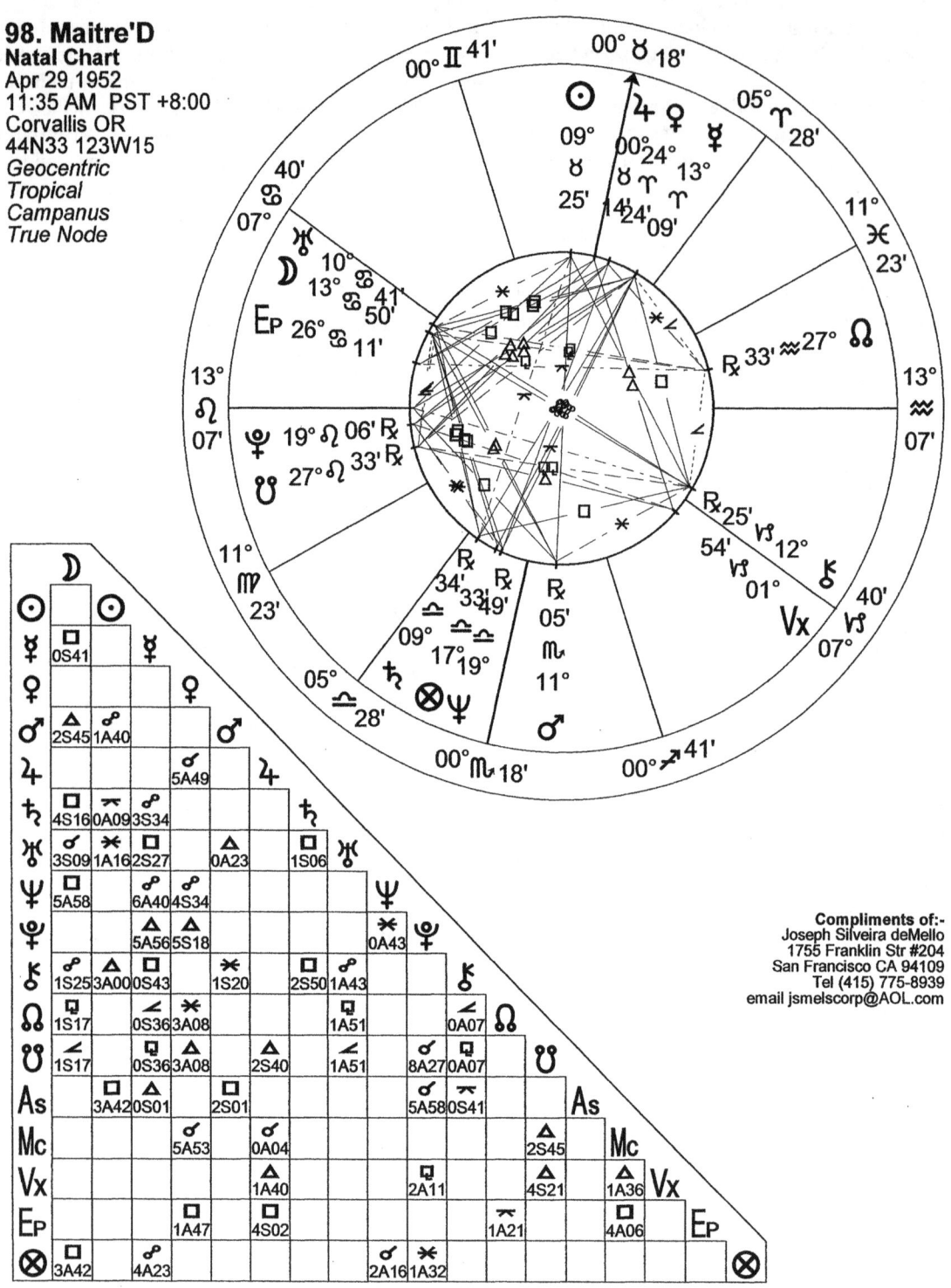

99. Psychologist

Natal Chart
May 7 1952
0:01 AM EDT +4:00
New City NY, USA
40N40 073W58
Geocentric
Tropical
Campanus
True Node

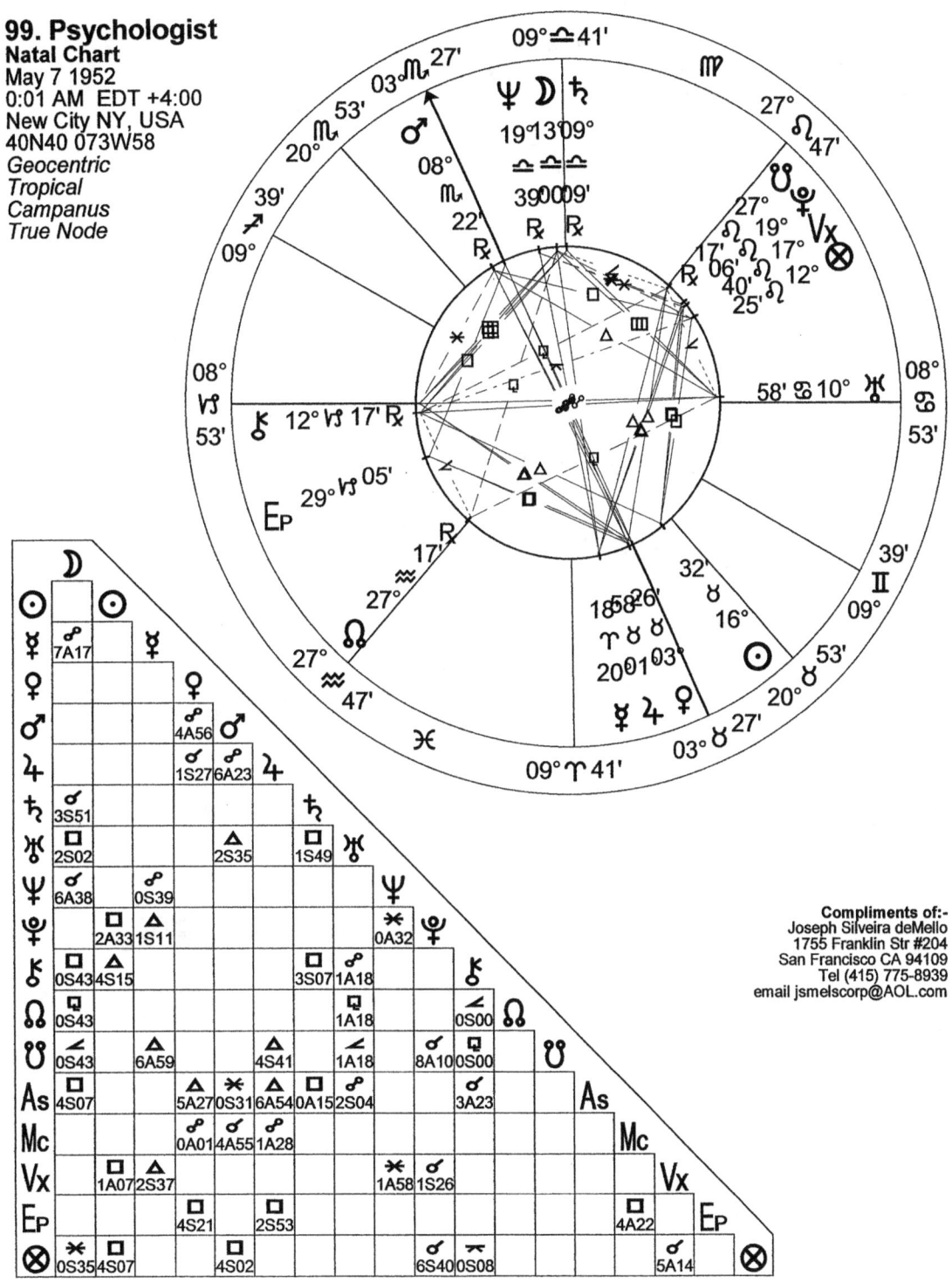

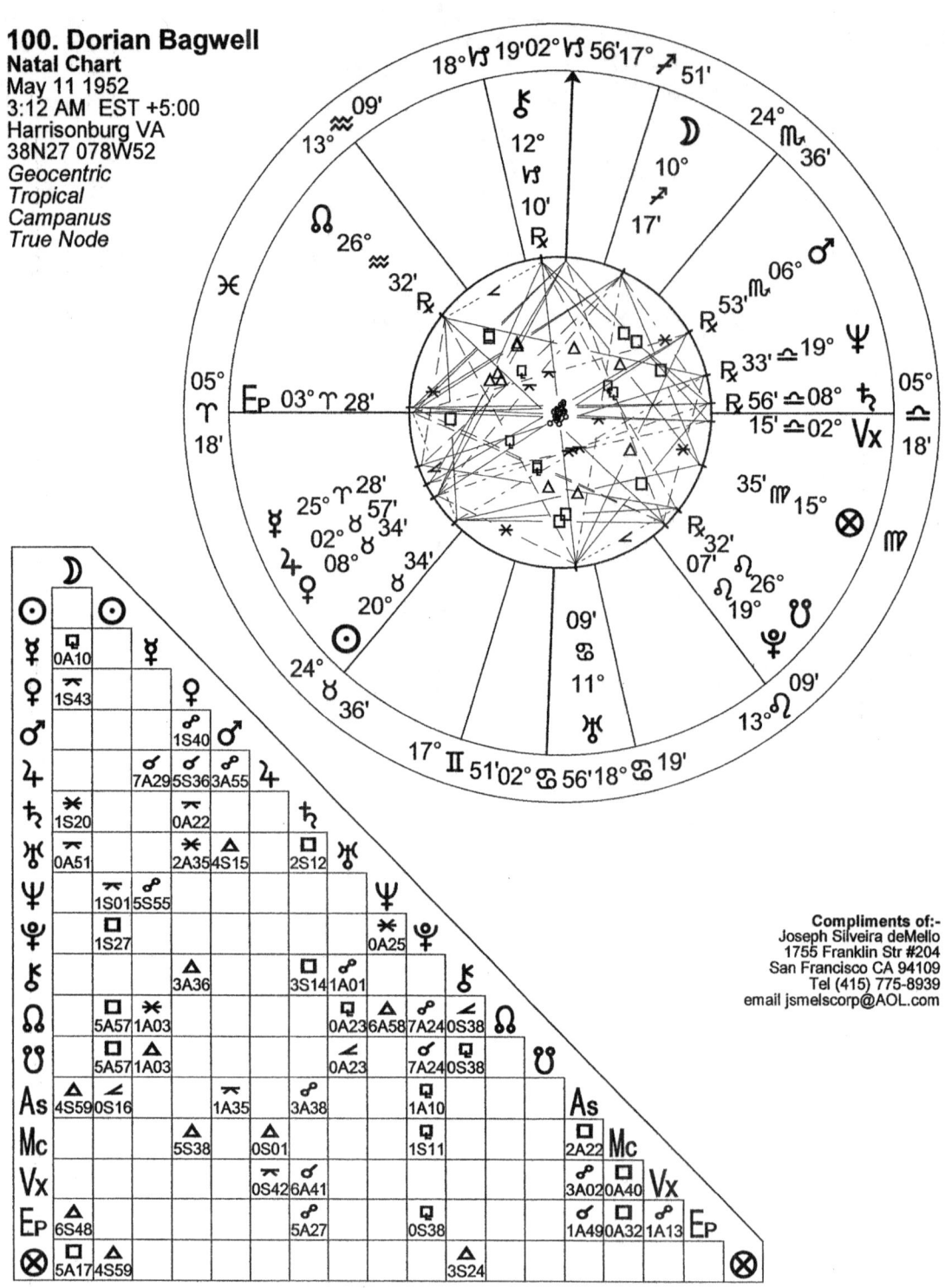

100. Dorian Bagwell
Natal Chart
May 11 1952
3:12 AM EST +5:00
Harrisonburg VA
38N27 078W52
Geocentric
Tropical
Campanus
True Node

Compliments of:-
Joseph Silveira deMello
1755 Franklin Str #204
San Francisco CA 94109
Tel (415) 775-8939
email jsmelscorp@AOL.com

others acted as they did. There were, of course, similarities between them (which none was ready to admit), and they did not always put aside competition. Conversations were always lively. All suffered pattern baldness which was emphasized by their insistence on dressing like hippies and wearing long hair which they refused to realize emphasized their hair loss. Dorian went one step further; he had a huge handlebar mustache and a thin and scraggly beard.

Dorian had begun his career as an accountant, switched with the times to doing his job on the computer, and later became a computer analyst, and he was very good at both occupations. Unfortunately when he became HIV positive, this was a real death sentence as the cases that went into remission in those early days were rare, the not unexpected psychological thing happened. Or not so strange. With Dorian, it was as if nothing any longer mattered except himself. He went into disability retirement. His perspective seemed to focus on the tip of his nose. If, in a gathering, he was not getting what he thought of as sufficient attention, he would simply disappear. He was also the sort of person who made gifts to others, but ritually refusing to accept gifts from others.

Dorian died of AIDS at home and in his sleep prior to 6:00 a.m., December 19, 1993, San Francisco, California. As the natal chart of a person with AIDS, his chart does not fulfill the criteria of having planets in aspect from the IC to fifteen degrees either side of his Midheaven. This I can accept, for no sooner do you formulate a thesis than along comes a chart that does not fulfill it. However, astrologers remember when Uranus and Neptune and Saturn were going through Capricorn. The day he was born, the Moon would have gone past 16-17 Sagittarius which would have fulfilled one cesquin (165 degree aspect) to the IC. AIDS has a huge incubation period, so it is difficult to tell exactly when he may have been exposed. Patients usually have no idea when or from whom they might have found contagion. All of these men acknowledged they had been regulars of a bar which had a ninety-five percent AIDS death rate among its customers.

Declinations show he had Moon and Pluto out of bounds, and an interesting array of parallels and contraparallels. The T-square with Saturn includes the opposition of Uranus-Chiron we saw in previous examples. He died with transiting Moon opposite Chiron, making a T-square to natal Moon and a double quincunx from Vertex to east point and the conjunction of Uranus-Neptune with transiting Venus at the opposition to the Vertex. Jupiter was on natal Mars with the diurnal Ascendant the day he died. Though he had been years in this wasting away illness, his death was both sudden and unexpected since he was suffering only a mild indisposition. This diurnal chart may be found in the diurnal section of this book.

101. Archaeologist, 8-4-4
Wider orb Saturn: 1S01
Data: June 23, 1952, 2:27 p.m. CST,
Lake Charles, Louisiana, 30N14, 93W13

This sandy haired young man of medium height has been a client since 1976. He was trained as an archeologist and has worked on dig sites around the world, with breaks to investigate Findhorn. When least expected, he always gets back to me. He has been married at least twice and early had a vasectomy so that he would not father children. This has been a problem since most of his girlfriends definitely wanted to become mothers. Defiantly a child of his times, no reference has ever been made to his childhood, obviously well put behind him, and much time has been spent with occult philosophies and religious systems as attested by an overly populated ninth house and Scorpio rising.

He has an early Scorpio rising with Mars on his Ascendant, and Mars here does not make him more Scorpionic. Not only does he behave more like an Aries, he even looks like an Aries right down to early pattern baldness. Mars in its own sign is the only planet not disposed of by the Moon in its own sign which also disposes of the Sun. This is most curious as the Cancerian side of him does not show with any prominence. The only generality one can make astrologically is that with Jupiter in the seventh house, he never lacked for close and intimate friends. There was a time when I did charts for all of his ladies. Instead, all that any astrologer might say about Aries applies to this man.

Being born on the Summer solstice, he has Sun on the boundary of declination, Moon, Mercury and Venus are out of bounds, and Uranus and Pluto minutes away from doing so. Note how all of these are North and parallel, underlining a conjunctive quality to the chart. He is heterosexual exclusively. He has a preference for not marrying. Pluto in his tenth contributes largely to his ability to sabotage his status, and any efforts I have made to discuss this with him have hit a hard wall of ninth house attitudes. This man is an idealist, yet there seems to be a lost quality about him. With a twelfth house Neptune, he has never thought of suicide.

102. Princess, 11- 4-8
Beyond orb Saturn: 1S09
Data: July 2, 1952, 9:43 p.m. CST,
Chicago, Illinois, 41N30, 87W38

This is the chart of a young mother, the divorced daughter of a movie distribution and theater mogul whose business was kept very quiet since the films and theaters in which he specialized were pornographic. Her chart was done at the request of her mother, but nothing I said was taken seriously since at that time I could not predict her finding Prince Charming then or in her immediate future.

Venus is out of bounds here, taken to indicate those who love too well but not too wisely. She seemed a pleasant normal sort of pleasant Jewish-American princess with no special talents. Venus with Uranus are both too close to the Cancer Sun, which may slant the meaning of Venus, but my bet is that Uranus wins out. Very much an Aquarius rising, pretty enough to make the competition, she has all the answers but cannot apply them to her own situation. She keeps very quiet about herself and what she wants out of life so that it is a ques-

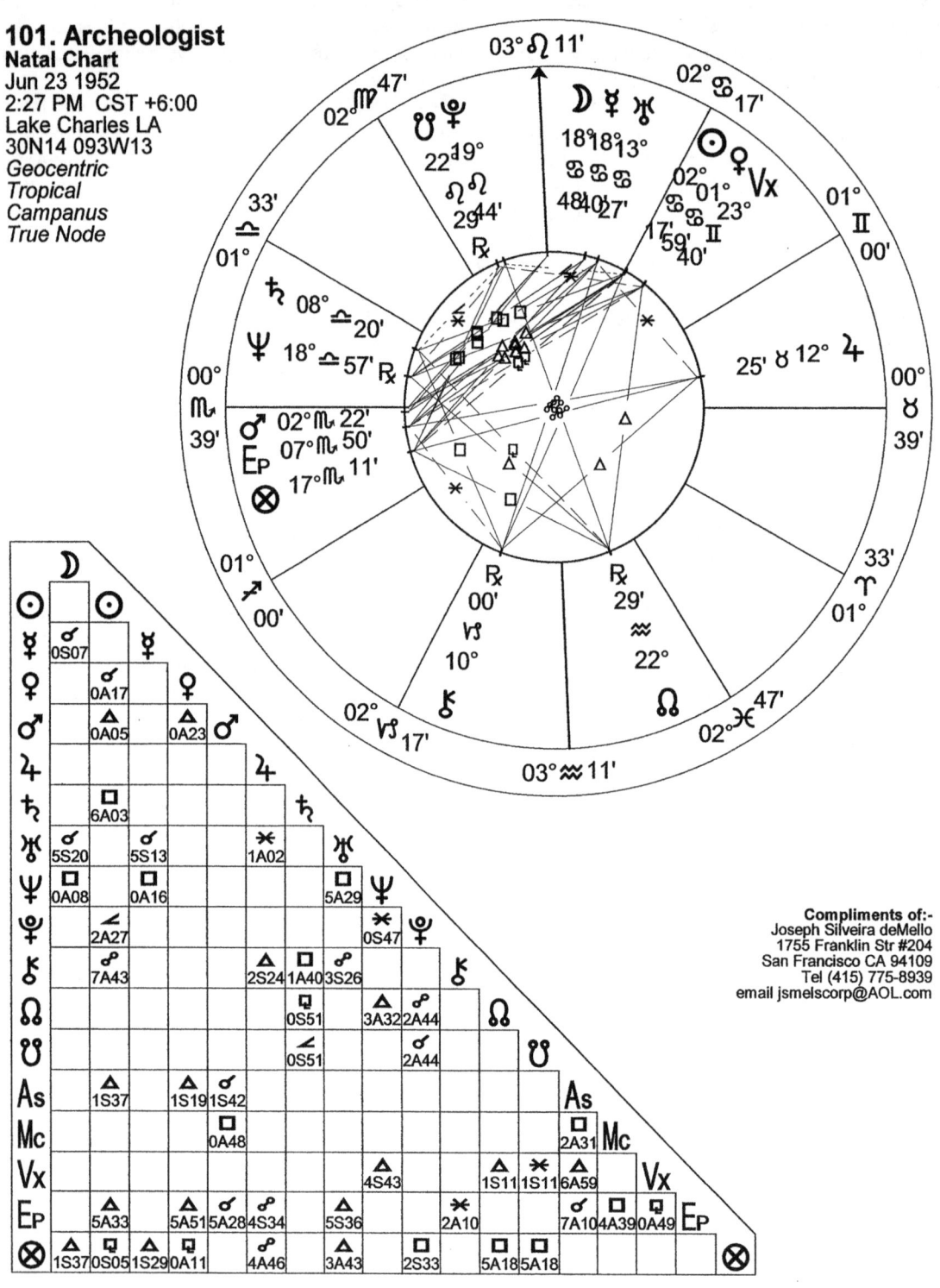

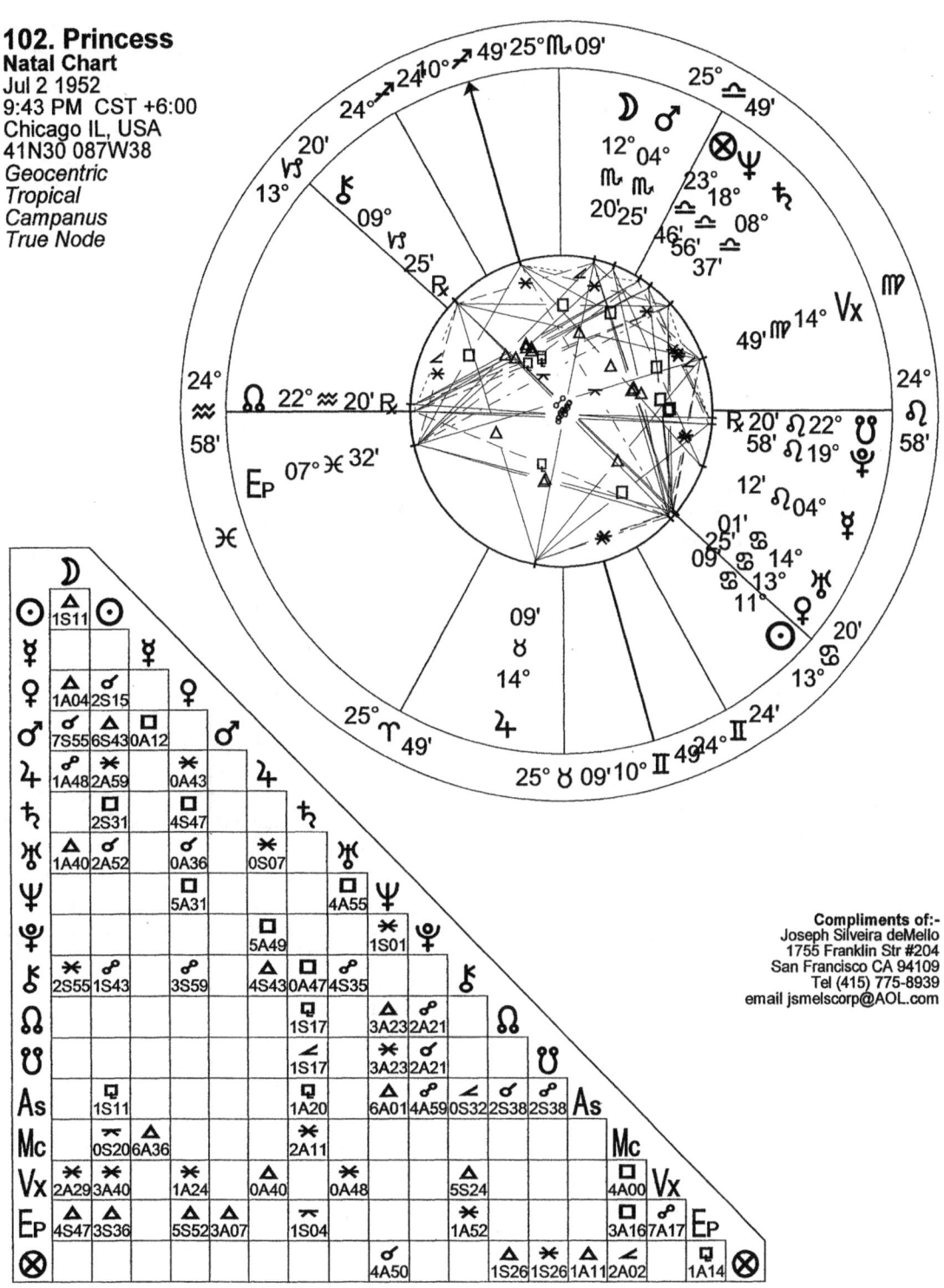

tion of whether she is maintaining privacy or really has no aims at all. With five planets to be interpreted in his sixth house, it is obvious she should be doing something in the line of work and service. In line with this sixth house, her work should be also Mercury and Pluto in style, and might even include Sun, Venus and Uranus. Her tenth house is Sagittarius which usually leads to being some sort of consultant. Saturn in the seventh has me hoping she would find a mature and serious partner rather than, which seems more likely, a father figure. Here we have a case where Moon and Mars are in Scorpio. And in the eighth house, she wishes to gain from others but keeps changing her mind about what she wished to gain. After her divorce, from a man who thought her father would make him rich, she returned to live with her parents and showed no inclination to find any other living arrangement.

***

This is the end of charts with Saturn in declination a bit more than the one degree orb or application. I have tired to make comments to show a difference between the people of these two groups and tried to allow the reader latitude to find differences.

Zero Jupiter People

Halfway through my study of Saturn at zero declination, I thought a proper foil for that collection would be charts of Jupiter at zero. In our studies we have found that Saturn is not always detrimental and obstructing and often brings rewards. Now we have Jupiter which our early teachers all assured us is basically benefic to the point that we never were prepared for Jupiter neutral or Jupiter idling. The karma of any chart is Saturn as planet of lessons to be learned. I see Jupiter in a chart as indicative of our acceptance of our karma. Saturn is always on time. You can set your watch by the movement of Saturn as it goes around any chart. I am reluctant to trust Jupiter as a timing planet. But you see, if Jupiter brings beneficence, we sail through those moments often without taking any notice of them. We snap to and sit up when we respond to difficult aspects. It was quite a day when we realized that Jupiter could bring such over-abundance that it sated and cloyed. When I had an evil aspect to Jupiter it most often manifested in writing checks when my funds were insufficient. I finally cured that by having a savings account from which funds may be deducted to cover bad checks. Haven't written a bad check in twenty years. In the achievement of Jupiter sanity, even of general astrological sanity, I have to thank Howard Hammitt, Jr, one time AFA recording secretary, for his local lectures. Howard was a genius of chart rectification. We wanted to rectify the chart of a reclusive millionaire, and everyone wanted to try Jupiter in the second house. I was for Pluto in the second house or even Neptune and our final solution did indeed put Pluto there.

The reader may well laugh, of course, as I have Pluto in my own second house, but I also have Pluto opposite to Jupiter in Capricorn in the eighth house, and I am no millionaire. My personal monitory gains from Jupiter are rare, meager and late, as befits Capricorn, and since Jupiter and Saturn in my natal chart are closely sextile, those gains come have come when Jupiter was in any aspect to Saturn. Having had to evaluate my Jupiter, I do think anyone can re-evaluate anything in their charts to get away from standard, general interpretations. Where Jupiter unfailingly stands me in good stead is that it brings me feedback which is invariably beneficial.

Jupiter is counselor and optimist. Jupiter people, especially if they are Sagittarians by rising or Sun sign, like others to bring them their problems for solution. They promise much they may fail to deliver. If they fail to follow through, they can be very offhand, knowing as they do that in three or four weeks anyone's problems are sure to change and their help will no longer be needed anyway. So for contrast to Saturn, let us look at some charts with Jupiter within a one degree orb of zero declination.

103. John Sutter, 10-11-8
Jupiter: 0S23
Data: February 15, 1803, 5:00 a.m. LMT, Kandem, Switzerland, 46N45, 7E40

The data for this chart comes from *Sabian Symbols*, not the most reliable source, so I can only say that it is what is generally most accepted. John Sutter was a Swiss emigre who set up a grist mill on the Sacramento River at a place he originally called New Helvitica. This in itself is strange since most people of other countries, usually seek to settle where others of their same culture settle, and most Swiss have settled in Wisconsin.

Instead, he came all the way West. It was here on his land that one of his employees discovered gold. News spread rapidly, sparking the Gold Rush of 1849, when he was 46, and prospectors came by the hundreds to overwhelm his original claim in the area. It was as if every six feet of the river had a different claimant. So great was the swarm of squatter claims that there was no way the tide could be stemmed. Sutter was the product of a very tidy and orderly old world culture. The onslaught he experienced was devastating. Though he owned the land, any adventurer could stake out mineral rights on that same land. Sutter himself could not start a war against the invasion, and no legal apparatus was in place to aid him. He knew he was in the right, and felt that his rights were being abrogated, but he had no recourse. He never made a cent from this great discovery, and he died a pauper.

This chart with Capricorn (the man who prefers to be self-employed or run his own business) and Venus rising (not easily seen in pictures of a man with a wild white beard), has the Sun in Aquarius (intercepted, but always sure he is in the right so he has no need to do anything to prove it or otherwise to protect himself), and Moon in the last degrees of Scorpio in the eleventh (ambivalent community feelings) not enhanced by the nearby presence of Neptune. His chart significator Saturn is in his eighth house and retrograde, disposed of by Mercury also retrograde, does not bode well for gains from other people. Nor does the nodal axis from his first to his seventh house, things flowed from him into other

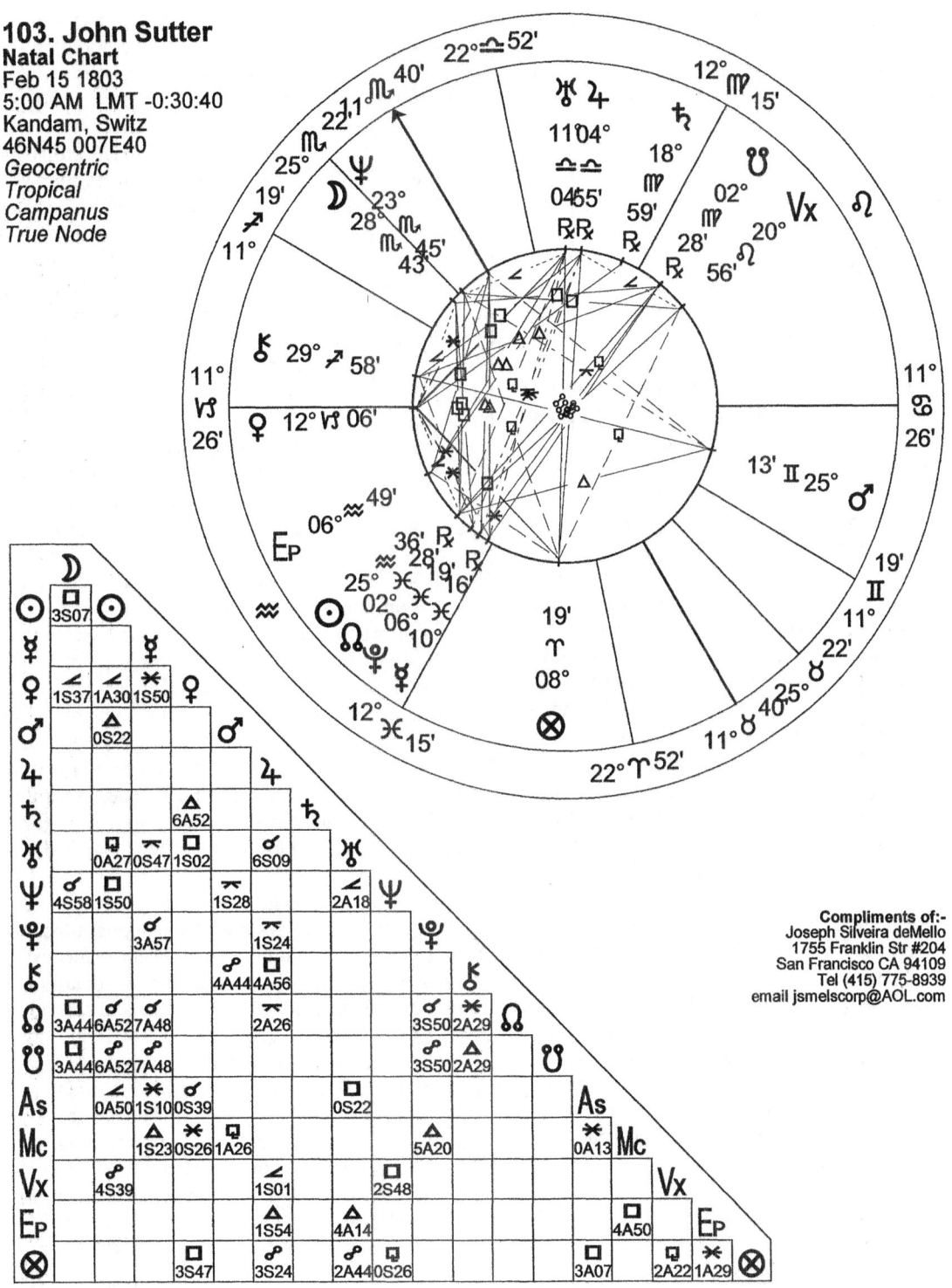

persons. The presence of Jupiter and Uranus, also in the eighth house and retrograde, is not helpful. Indeed, his four retrogrades only attest to his difference from the average man. Mercury is the abstract thinker, Jupiter which does best with second hand things or things abandoned by others, a Saturn which strives to make people relate well to each other and the world around them, and a creative Uranus. Notice the aspects these retrogrades make. Mercury is quincunx Uranus. The Moon and Mars in this chart are considerably out of bounds, while Jupiter is at zero declination. Note that he has Neptune and Pluto in mutual reception. Squares are more telling here, and he does not have the luxury of oppositions.

104. Sir Richard Burton, 8-12-7
Jupiter: 0N48, Moon: 0S24
Data: March 19, 1821, 9:30 p.m. LMT,
Hereford, England, 52N50, 2W44

This data is from *Sabian Symbols,* giving place of birth as Barham House, Herts, England. But his family eventually settled in Ireland, and in 1842 he joined the Indian army, about which he published a book in 1851. During service in the Sind, he became familiar with Hindustani and Persian and spoke Arabic like a native. Indeed he had an excellent facility for languages. He explored Arabia in disguise as an Afghani pilgrim, effectively exploring Medina and Mecca (1853) where non-Arabs were forbidden to go. His book on that experience was published in 1855. He then explored Somaliland and discovered Lake Tanganyika, even explored North America. In 1861, he married Isabel Arundell and occupied several posts as consul, and devoted much time to writing. He mastered thirty-five languages and was knighted in 1886. He combined a thirst for travel with studies as an anthropologist. What seems best remembered is that he and his wife traveled together, an oddly liberated couple who traveled in grand style as he investigated subjects rather taboo in Victorian England (homosexuality among other cultures), recording his explorations in more than thirty narratives.

Some will nod at the sight of this Scorpio rising chart with the Sun in Pisces and a Libra Moon. A nocturnal chart makes Mars in Pisces as chart significator. See the mutual reception between Jupiter and Mars. The Pisces and Aries stelliums in the fifth and sixth houses are impressive, and the Moon on twelfth is the only planet above the chart horizon. The Moon is also at zero declination but contraparallel to his zero Jupiter. At least we have Jupiter in North declination and in a Northern sign, while the Moon is in Southern declination and a southern sign. There are several interesting placements, North Node between Venus and Mars, Pluto conjunct the Sun in the fifth house, Uranus and Neptune, both retrograde, in second house Capricorn.

105. Woodrow Wilson, 7-10-11
Jupiter: 0S40
Data: December 29, 1856, 12:45 a.m. LMT,
Staunton, Virginia, 38N09, 79W05

President of the United States and educator (data recorded in the family Bible), he first ran for office in 1912, and four years later, he ran again as an isolationist bent on sparing the country from European conflict. "He Kept Us Out of War" was the trumpeted slogan for his second term election. But inevitably we became involved in the First World War, in the popular effort to make this the war to end all wars. In the peace settlement, his Fourteen Points won him European opposition in the face of mostly French needs for punitive reparations and revenge. Disabled by a stroke, there are rumors that the end of his Presidency was directed by his second wife, Edith Bolling Galt Wilson, but he did recover from the serious illness to resume the active reins of office.

Most marvel at the scholarly leader of Princeton University turned politician. But he had begun as a lawyer, advanced to studies in political science in which he had a doctorate, various teaching positions, became President of Princeton University at age 46, and Governor of New Jersey in 1910. Two years later he was the Democrat nominee for the presidency. In this election he was aided by the split between Teddy Roosevelt and the incumbent William Howard Taft. When he tried for a second term, he won over a much closer contender, Charles Evans Hughes.

We see a tremendously active chart with cardinal angles. We have already found Libra rising frequent among politicians. The Sun is executive in Capricorn, and the Moon is in Aquarius, the man who wants to appear as if he is all-knowing. Sun is opposite Saturn (contraparallel). Moon and Mercury parallel and out of bounds, with Jupiter at zero declination. Moon and Saturn are in mutual reception, Jupiter with sextiles to Moon and Chiron, all testifying to unsettling difficulty in the propagation of his programs. But let us not slide too quickly past Saturn, a great timer in this chart. We all know the one bonus of a Saturn return, no matter how bad it is, that after a Saturn return one feels free to do whatever he wishes. Saturn was retrograde, so a Saturn return in infancy, another around age thirty, and right after his next Saturn return, he married his second wife while in the White House.

This is one of the charts of famous people which should be famous for its squares and oppositions. The Wilson Presidency was not one of the most successful in the annals of American leadership, especially as it culminated in opposition both at home and abroad. At home, the country was glad of the end of a war with so many fatalities, so many men in the front lines gassed, and the final influenza epidemic which is said to have killed more men than died in the war. As aware of foreign involvements as we were at the founding of the country and again during Wilson's first term, the country was ready to go back into isolationism after the First World War. Part of that kept us out of the League of Nations to which Congress was not at all favorable. He was tall and lean, learned-looking and sternly serious. If we see politics as rancorous in our time, Teddy Roosevelt assessed Wilson as always having been "a thoroughly selfish and cold-blooded politician."

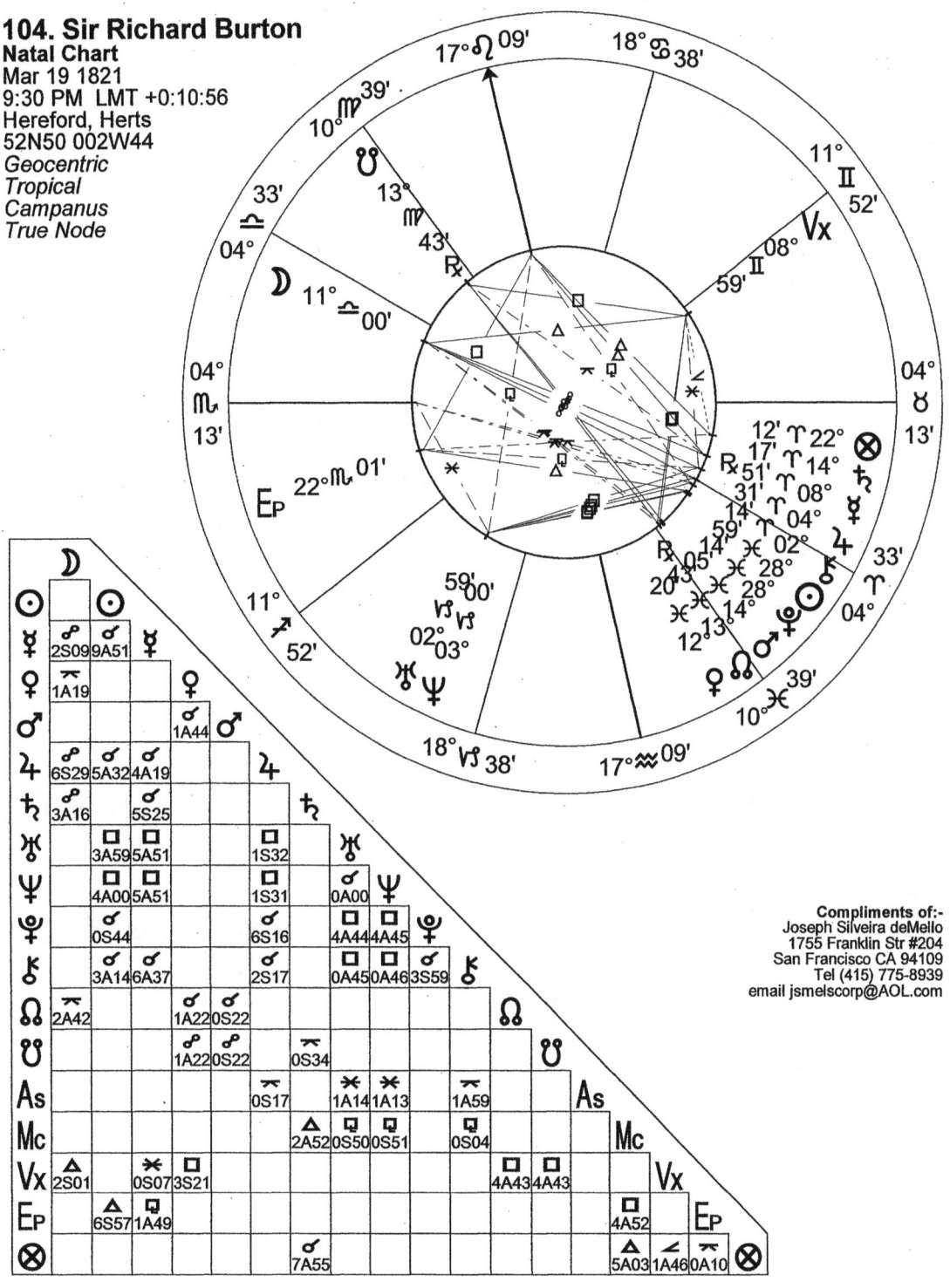

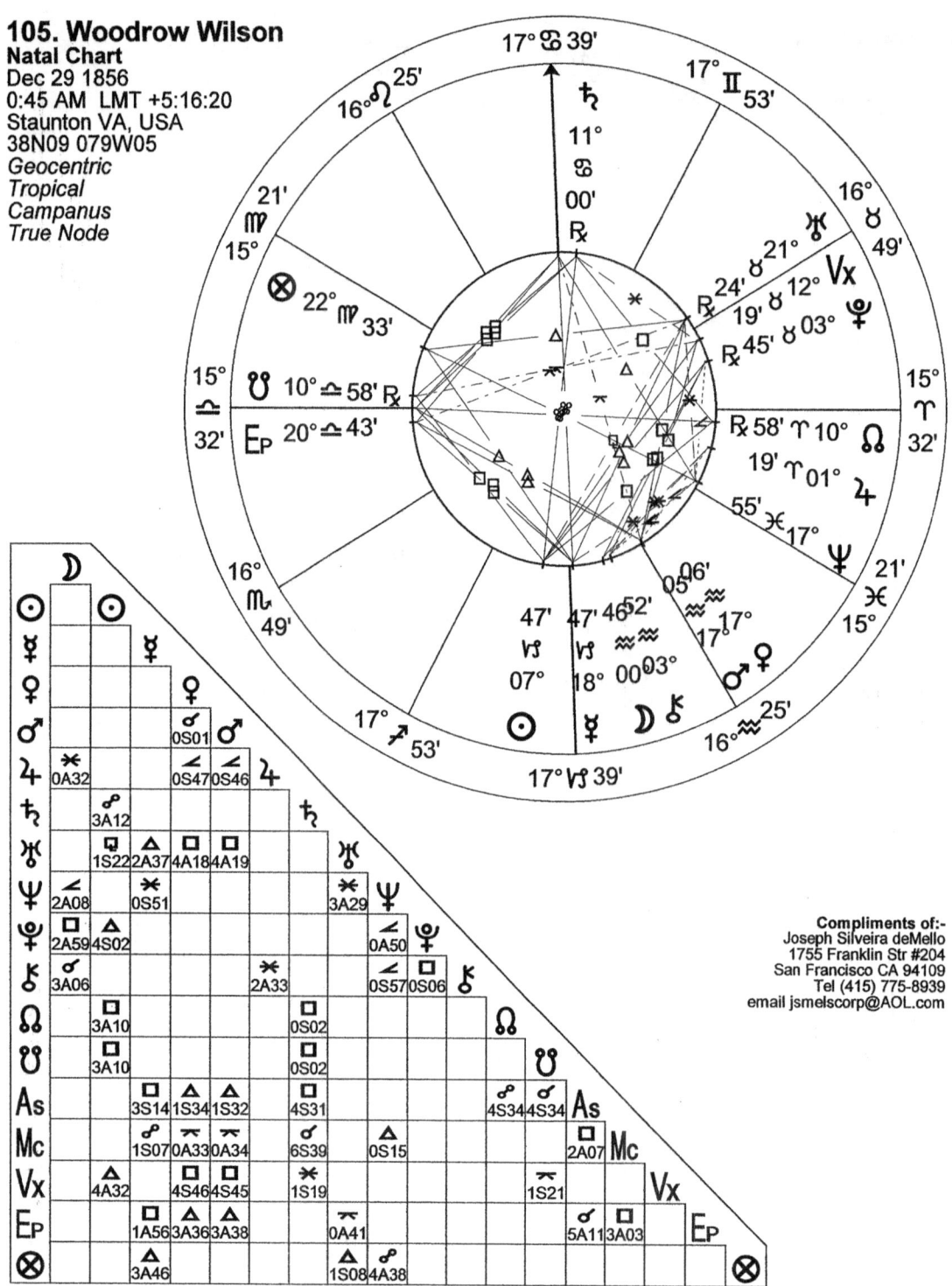

106. Gertrude Stein, 12-11-6
Jupiter: 0N50
Data: February 3, 1874, 8:00 a.m. LMT,
Pittsburgh, Pennsylvania, 40N27, 80W01

Data from the biography by Brinnin, Stein was born in the township of Allegheny, today part of incorporated Pittsburgh. In 1877, Pittsburgh adopted EST, so charts for prior to that time should be done in Local Mean Time. She trained in medicine at Johns Hopkins but never practiced, choosing instead to become an expatriate in Paris where her brother and his wife had become early art patrons and got her started in knowing and supporting up-and-coming artists working in Paris. There she met and began a lifetime liaison with Alice Toklas who took a secondary role in their household. Together the ladies operated an ambulance in the First World War and later held a salon of the best people in the art world of Paris, and where Gertrude insisted on first place as literary lioness. No one was welcome at her soirees who did not acknowledge her the greatest writer. Her unique method of writing, expressed in alliteration by which she repetitively developed her characters as in a flow of consciousness style which gave her much avant guard popularity but did not gain her commercial book publishing contracts. Where she was rich enough to self-publish, her attitude would not permit her this vanity role, and she remained relatively unpublished during her lifetime, while supporting the work of other writers whose styles were more traditionally narrative, far from her own methods of character and story development. Reading and critiquing a Hemingway piece, it was she who told him that "comments are not literature."

For a Pisces rising, Stein is remembered as a very strong character and a rather overbearing personality, and we might note that Neptune is in Aries. But, going on from that, Neptune is disposed of by Mars in the rising sign and in the first house, graphically underlining my insistence that the best thing which could happen to a Pisces would be to have Mars in the rising sign and in its location. Then we have the knowing Aquarius Sun in the twelfth and intercepted, disposed of by and in mutual reception with Uranus intercepted in Leo in the sixth house. With all this, almost reading too quickly, we have to emphasize that she was definitely not open to criticism from other people, just never heard any of it. What others said did not matter at all to her. For a Pisces rising, Stein had the thickest skin in the world. Her first nature was belligerence, no shrinking violet she, and Mercury with Venus get scorched by that Aquarian Sun. Ah but here Mercury here is two minutes from Sun, definitely cazimi, and so a very powerful Mercury, more powerful than the Sun. A case of mind over ego. She was sure of herself. We cannot attribute to Gertrude Stein the usual things we say of Pisces. She asked no quarter and gave none. No doubt the Moon in Virgo had much to do with her detailed stream of consciousness style. She takes character development beyond the method of Henry James. But, astrologically, we have to admit working creatively behind the scene (twelfth house Sun) and creative in writing (Gemini fifth house), creative privately in a modern manner (Uranus in the intercepted portion of the sixth), and then the important Sagittarius Midheaven. One gets far more out of reading Stein aloud, possibly with a southern drawl, as she meanders through her expositions. Note the Gemini IC and see she delighted in being interested in many things, and with Sagittarius on the Midheaven was judged for her willingness to help and play consultant to all who came near her. The opposition makes a fixed square to her nodal axis. There are no sextile-trine mitigations to this T-square. At her deathbed, she sat up from unconsciousness to ask "What is the answer?" Those in attendance were so surprised that none had a ready response, and, receiving no reply from those present, she asked, "In that case, what is the question?" at which she subsided back into her pillows and died.

107. Herbert Hoover, 2-5-5
Jupiter: 0N45, Venus: 0N34
Data: August 10, 1874, 11:15 p.m. LMT,
West Branch, Iowa, 41N39, 91W22

This data was given by Hoover for himself, although it was rectified by Doris Chase Doane to 11:29 p.m. and given by her in *Horoscopes of the US Presidents,* which hardly changes the angles of the chart. I have seen this chart done with Placidus and Koch house systems, and the reader should take pains to check this special chart in other than the Campanus system I prefer to use. The Campanus system puts Venus and Jupiter closer to the cusp of the sixth house so that they must be interpreted there. Note that in this Campanus chart, although there are wide sixth and twelfth houses, there are no interceptions.

Herbert Hoover was a Stanford University graduate in mining engineering, who married a Stanford coed who had his same interest in minerals. He and his wife were staunch Quakers, high ethical and moral standards as well as a sense of dignity of their positions. He had traveled extensively and developed business oriented philosophy. He subsequently built up an international business empire and a great personal fortune. He was a Cabinet member under Harding and Coolidge as secretary of commerce where he fostered the coming radio and airline industries. Becoming thirty-first President by a remarkable plurality, he followed Silent Cal Coolidge toward the end of the hedonistic Roaring Twenties and right into the great stock market crash eight months after he took office. This devastated the country's economy and had worldwide repercussions, especially in a Europe not yet quite recovered from the First World War. Few realize that Hoover inherited the administrative policies of his predecessor. While Coolidge remains a mythic figure of prosperity, Hoover, despite his career prior to and after leaving the presidency, remains damned in the public assessment of history.

Contrary to the roundness seen in portraits, he was 5'11" and broad shouldered and was so serious he is not known for showing any sense of humor. With such a late Taurus rising, one might expect him to be more of a Gemini, or as one astrologer puts it, to demonstrate the

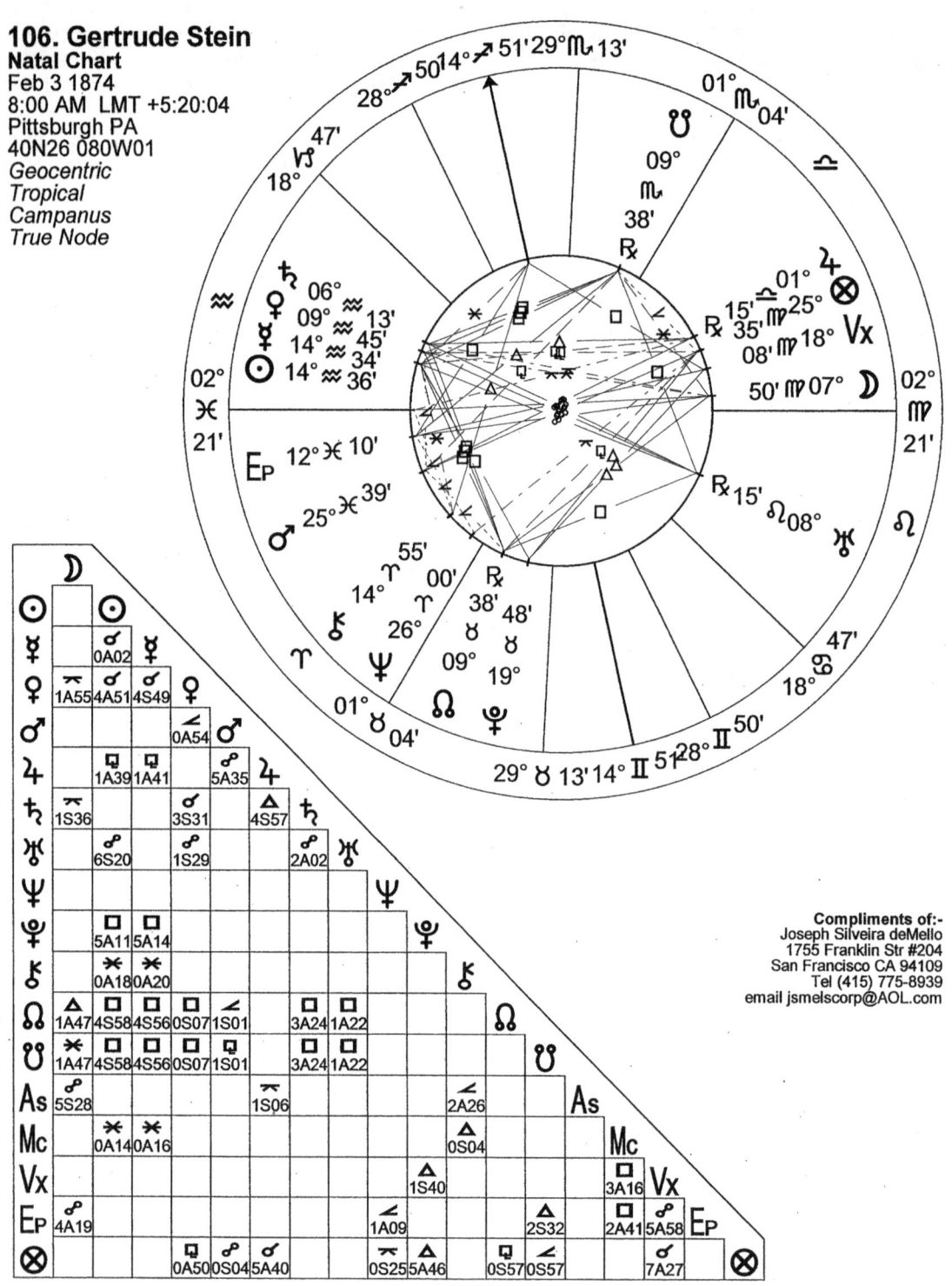

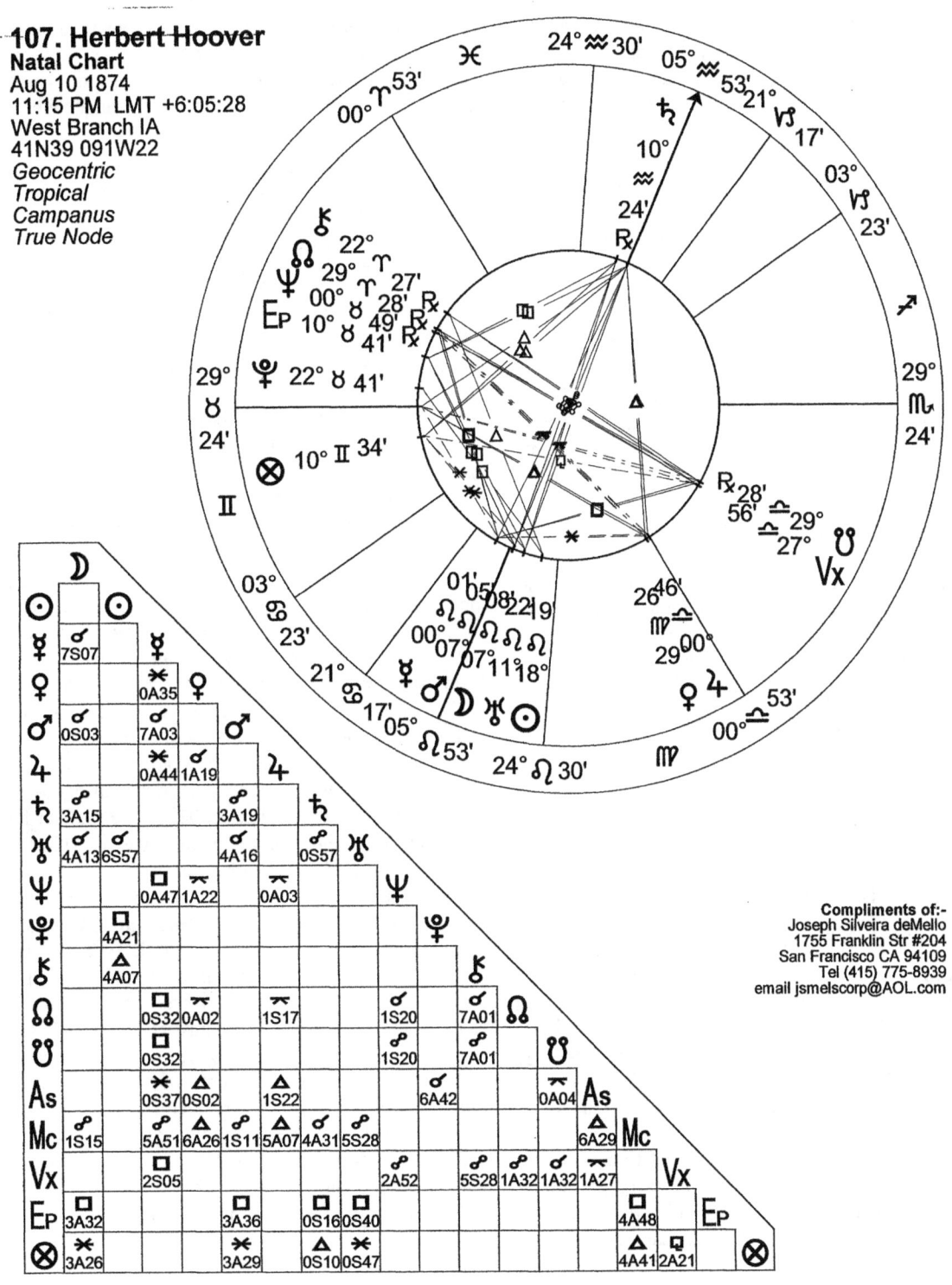

worst qualities of the next sign. Yet Hoover specifically has all the visible and generally attributed appearance of Taurus, with a slight nod to Venus in Virgo, again at the final degree of that sign. The Sun is the entire dispositor of this chart. There is much of his career that is Leo, but then again, it is less the Leo the figurehead for he was also a hands-on leadership man. His power as President seems to have been canceled by Congress, that branch of government which prevents the Executive from finding a way out of chaos. Voters never blame Congress, a fact well known to Truman of "The Buck Stops Here" fame. So Hoover lives in the memory of Shanty-towns which were "Hoover-villes," "Hoover Blankets" which were newspapers wrapped around the body for warmth, and "Hoover Wagons" which were broken down automobiles pulled by mules, while "Hoover Flaps" were empty pockets turned inside out. When he ran for a second term, his opponent was Franklin Delano Roosevelt who came along with charismatic bonhomie to lift the spirits of the electorate.

And thereby hangs a tale of astrological prediction gone wrong. At the time of this election, all astrologers said his chart was strongly for reelection. They must all have been Republicans. With transiting Saturn approaching Hoover's Midheaven and a soon to come Saturn return, which might have meant retirement, with an Ascendant on the Pleiades and the Nodes in zero Taurus, and natal Venus and Jupiter closely trine (although at that dreadful degree again) to the Ascendant. One by one, Herndon had to take fellow astrologers up to the chart of Roosevelt and insist the challenger's chart was the stronger of the two for election. He had been very successful in his programs for economic recovery of Europe after the First World War. But he lacked the common touch.

108. Josef Goebbels, 5-8-10
Jupiter: 0N50
Data: October 29, 1897, 10:30 p.m. CET,
Rheydt, Germany, 51N10, 6E27

Here we have the chart of the Nazi Propaganda Minister of Hitler's regime. This man was a cripple of wizen appearance. A club foot successfully kept him out of military service in the First World War. He began life as a rather unsuccessful novelist in Heidelberg. His public life began when he became Berlin editor of the Nazi newspaper. This led to his final position in the Nazi hierarchy which he held from 1929, as Hitler rose to power, Goebbels was in exactly the right place to rise when Hitler took over in 1933. He took his own life in April 1945, as Russian forces were invading Berlin.

The chart presents an amazing testament to a need for power with Leo rising by a man with his chart significator Sun in Scorpio, which gave him a thoroughly Scorpionic appearance, and then combined the Moon in Capricorn to give us a person with vivid control issues. The strong tenancy of the second quadrant, subjective knowledge of others, is a surprise, not so much his interest in others but for it being Leo-like in paternal subjectivity. Indeed this chart presents us with an overwhelming number of interesting minor aspects and mid-points. His varied inventiveness in the propaganda field, which led to his control of all German cultural life, is due to a strongly tenanted fifth house and Jupiter in Libra in his third house. We must be impressed by the number of untenanted houses in this chart and the nodal axis from seventh Descendant to his rising degree, and then we see Jupiter, Mercury, Saturn and Moon are in a zero and one degree positions in their respective signs, an interesting and not exactly benign run of semi-sextiles which develop into sextiles and trines. All these natal planets were activated by transits which would aspect the natal placements sensitively.

109. Golda Meir, 7-2-7
Jupiter: 0N56, Mars: 0N22
Data: May 3, 1898, 5:43 p.m. LMT,
Kiev, Ukraine, 50N27, 30E30

This data was arrived at by rectification done by Howard Hammitt Jr who was the astrologer who conducted Saturday astrological studies at the Theosophical Society in San Francisco. It is a time which works well with all events in her lifetime. Although born in Kiev (New Style), Golda Mabovich emigrated from Russia to Milwaukee, where her father had for three years previously started paving the way for his family to join him, which they did when she was eight years old. Her father worked as a carpenter when he could find work, and her mother set herself up in a small grocery where, as a girl, Golda kept shop and hated it. She had to run the store every morning while her mother was at market buying the day's supplies and stock. At age eleven, she organized her first public meeting and gave her first speech to raise money for school books. Her mother tried to get her to give up the idea of high school, wanted her to work in the grocery and marry a much older man. So at age fourteen, Golda ran away and went to live with her sister in Denver. There she met her future husband, a sign painter named Morris Myerson who had also immigrated from Russia.

Her father wrote her that she must return home to help her mother, which she did. But immediately she plunged into socialism, teaching, public speaking and Zionism. When there were attacks on Jews in Poland or in the Ukraine, she organized protest marches in Milwaukee. She pressed her future husband to go to Palestine, and when he agreed, in 1917, they were married, and in 1921 set off on an adventurous trip. They lived briefly in Tel Aviv and in Jerusalem, and in the latter place she gave birth to a son and daughter.

But her marriage ended in 1933, apparently by mutual agreement, and he died in 1951.

In the meantime, everything she did, every move she made was furthering the history of Israel. On May 14, 1948, she was one of the signers of the Israeli Declaration of Independence. By next day, the new State was under armed onslaught from Egypt, Syria, Lebanon, Transjordan and Iraq. Carrying the first passport issued by Israel, Golda Meir came to the United States to raise

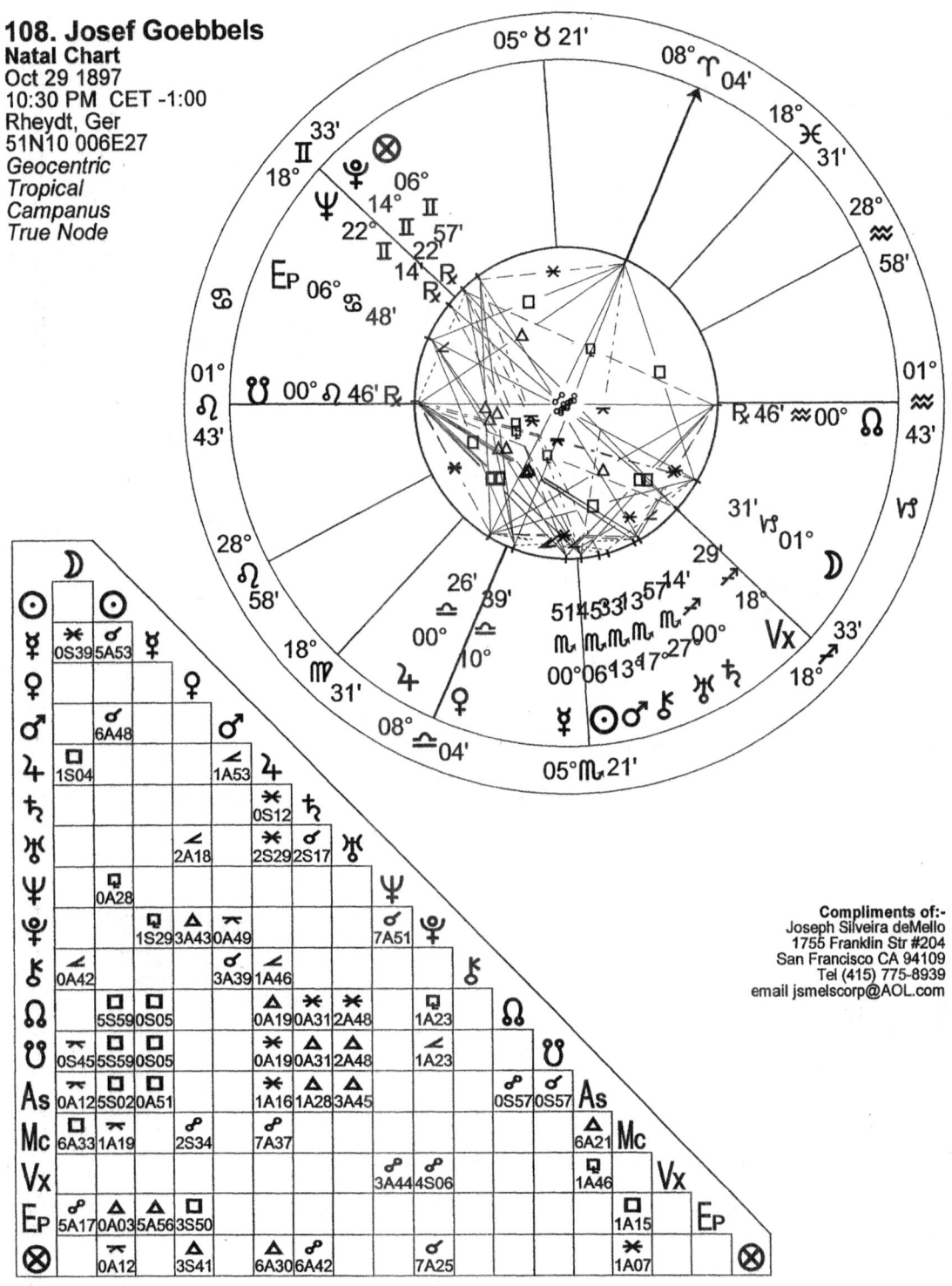

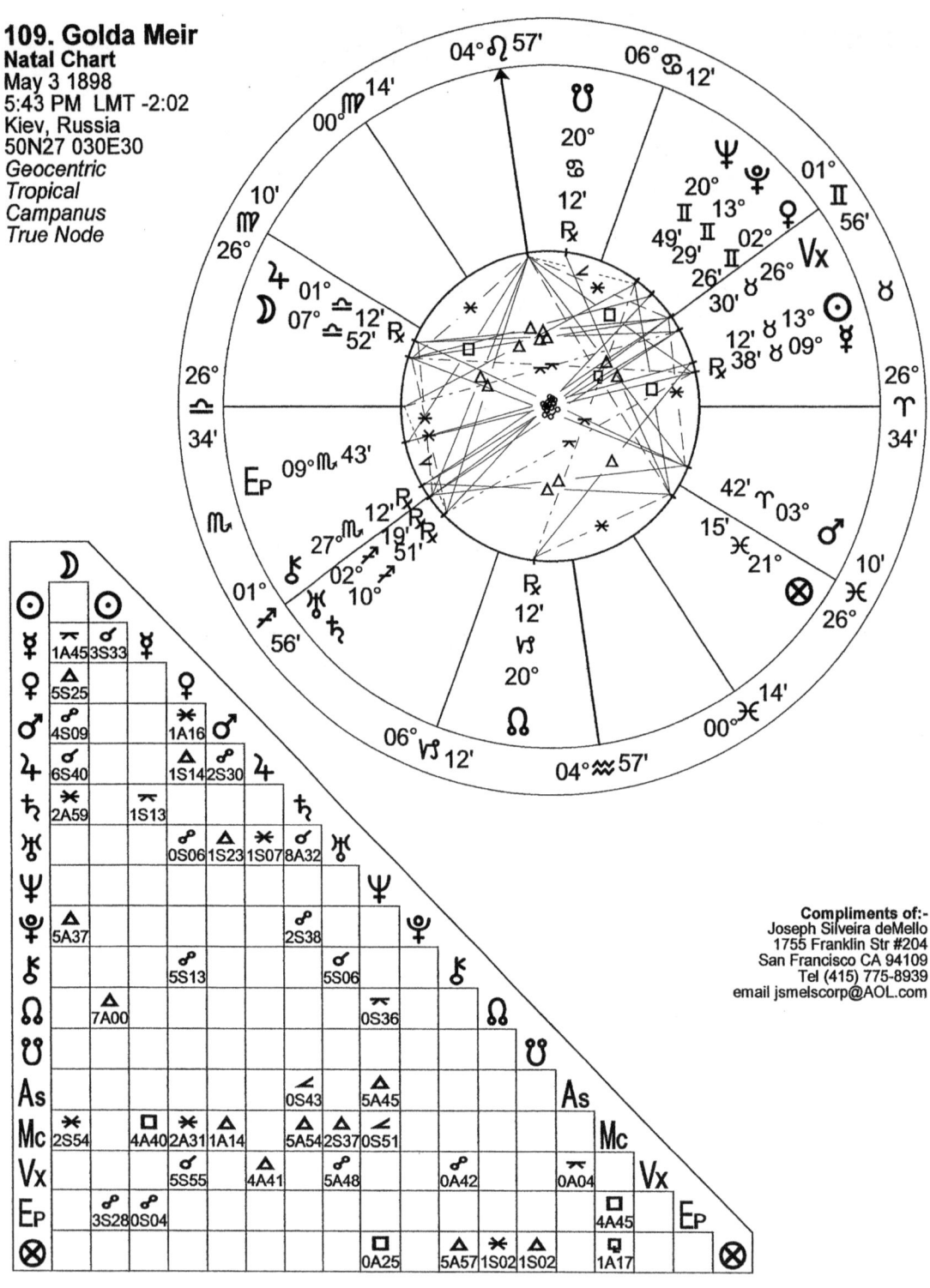

money. And back home, Israel confounded all expectations of its Arab neighbors and enemies by repelling all attacks and establishing its authority. Later that year she was made her country's first ambassador to Russia, but she returned the following year, 1949, to enter the Israeli Knesset (parliament) where she served until 1974. From 1949 to 1956, years of severe economic difficulty, she was minister of labor. In 1956, she became foreign minister serving under Prime Minister David Ben Gurion. He called her the only man in his cabinet and persuaded her to change her name from Myerson to Meir, although people had long known her simply as Golda.

In 1956, she, Moshe Dayan and Shimon Peres flew secretly to France to lay plans for an Anglo-French-Israeli attack on Egypt which had nationalized the Suez Canal and denied Israel access to the Red Sea. When the war came, Israel captured Gaza Peninsula in less than 100 hours. France and Britain having landed to the north, marched southward under the pretext of keeping the Egyptian and Israeli forces apart, but this was halted by pressure from the USA and Russia, so the Anglo-French withdrew.

Golda Meir had always put in long days of hard work at whatever post she held. In 1965, after much illness she resigned from the cabinet, but she was soon persuaded to become secretary-general of her party. Although she longed to retire, on the death of Prime Minister Eshkol in February 1969, she was persuaded to become prime minister. She was then seventy years old. She left this office finally on June 4, 1974 at age seventy-six.

In everything written about her, including her obituary notices, great stress is given to her public career, her struggle through socially conscientious issues, her place in history. Little attention is given to a private life which she kept separate from her public career. But she was the quintessential Jewish mother, her family playing a behind the scenes but very real part of her life. Her illnesses were kept out of the news, and her hospitalizations went generally unnoted in world news.

It is almost an astrological corollary that prominent people do not have easy charts. In the charts of many noted personages, we find oppositions and squares, and here we find one which also has a grand trine from Midheaven to Uranus and Mars. Although there are many oppositions, only one of them from the East Point axis to Sun-Mercury makes a T-square to the Midheaven. We look for angular planets and find only Sun-Mercury in the seventh house, on the other side of her chart. We look for cardinal and find but three such placements. Then we see she started out with a cardinal Ascendant-Descendant, but then graduated to a fixed Midheaven-IC axis. This is as if one begins life sure with great enterprise and that subsequent experience developed her along decidedly fixed ideas. More attention should be paid to the quality of the chart axes for we do not often find the horizon and vertical axes always in the same mode. Pause a moment to check your own charts in this regard.

Libra rising may be cardinal, but it is also an air sign, ruled by Venus in another air sign, Gemini, and on the cusp of her eighth house. Skipping astrological chauvinism, we should think more along the lines where we see Libra as the most suitable foil to Aries. Here we can also forget that Libra people operate best when married, definitely not the case in this instance. Marriage was hardly a life focus; she was more married to Zionism.

Note that Venus is in mutual reception with Mercury, so she winds up looking more Taurean, but only in her older years. In youth, she was thin and lithesome and quite pretty. Note that Mercury is retrograde but still too close to the Sun. Does the twelfth house Moon in Libra tell us she suppressed her emotions? At the same time we note the Guardian Angel placement of Jupiter in the twelfth.

This very political person actually was a leader, and not by virtue of Leo on the Midheaven, for we have to remember Leo likes to be seen to occupy the chair of leadership without doing much of the actual work involved. She was mindful of all gains she made, but it was natural for her to lead, so natural she could play it modestly.

We almost have complained of all the political charts with Libra rising; here is another. The chart of the prime minister can be the chart of the nation. And then we find the final quotient, Mars, strong in its own sign and definitely underlining her strong work ethic. This is a very strong Mars even if it is in the house behind that which it rules. Since we are studying zero Jupiter, we cannot fail to note that Mars is also at zero declination, and although both are opposite in the chart, they are both parallel by declination. Mars is further the only planet not disposed of by the Mercury-Venus mutual reception. We know that she was very well aware of the devastation of war and did all she could to avoid conflicts. But she was not one to be walked over, never flinched from war when war became inevitable, and then her resolve was always to fight and get it over with as quickly as possible. She let the military fight and win the war, and she even let the military make the peace. Her role was to get on with administration and national progress.

She died at 4:28 p.m., December 8, 1978, according to the Associated Press report. Family members attended her last hours. In the months leading to her death, she had been in and out of hospital. Her illnesses had always been held behind a screen of secrecy, privacy. Back problems, jaundice and viral infections were rumored. A hospital spokeswoman said cancer was the cause of death, and that it had originally been detected ten or twelve years prior to her death. She had at various times been treated with radiation and chemo therapies. Golda Meir insisted that as a private person the hospital was not to issue public statements on the course of her health. At her death, she had Sun and Jupiter and Venus and Pluto in mutual reception.

110. Robert W. Cooper, 3-12-9
Jupiter: 0N21
Data: February 27, 1916, 10:34 a.m. EST, Philadelphia, Pennsylvania, 39N57, 75W10

Now we come to a chart that surprised me at first look. This is the chart of the executive secretary of the

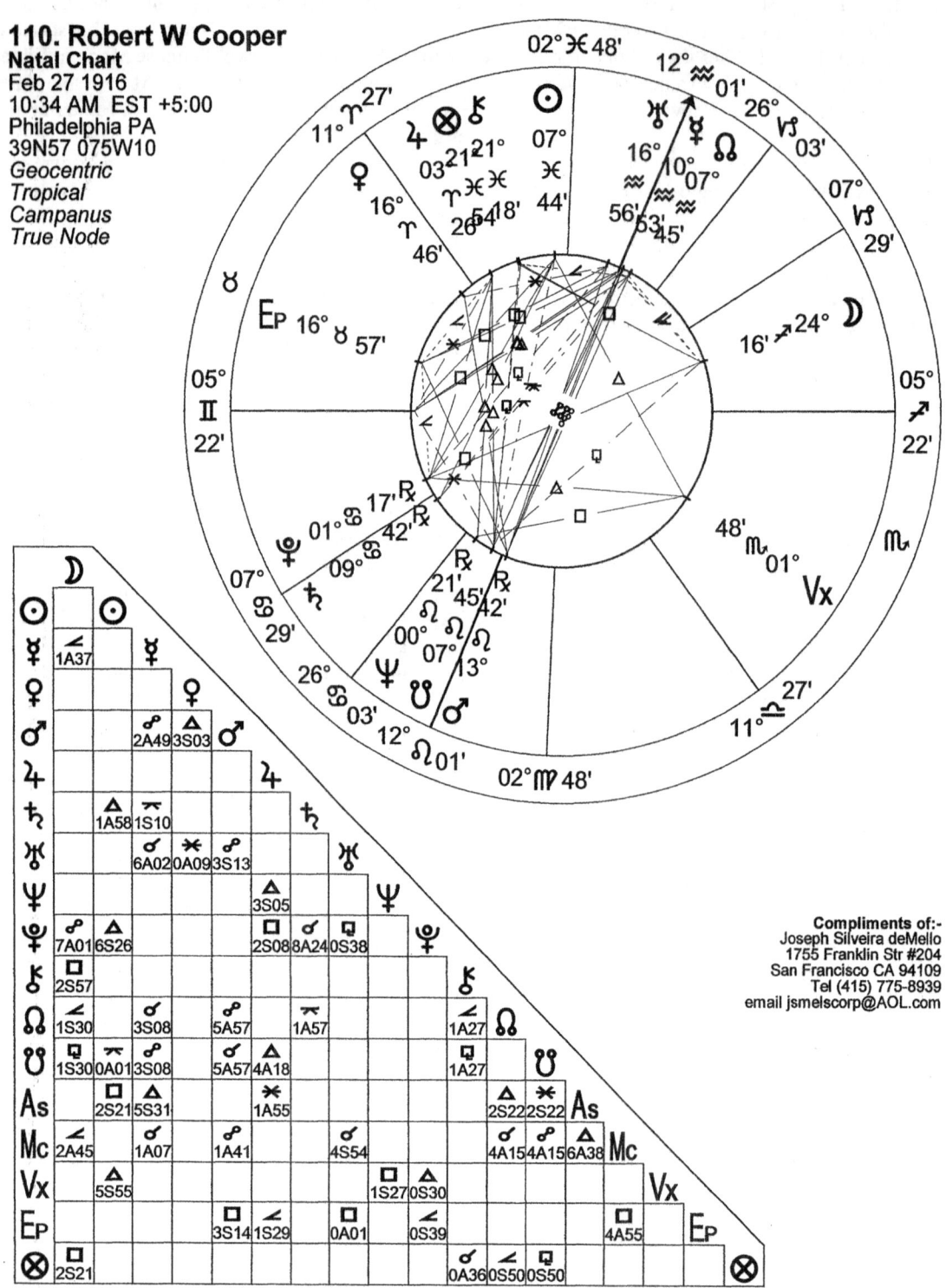

American Federation of Astrologers, Inc. Data is from birth certificate. With an Aquarius Midheaven, tenth house Aquarius Uranus and an Aquarius Mercury in the ninth, this is the chart of an astrologer. His occupation puts him in charge of the everyday operations of the leading professional astrological association, a group which is also a publisher and distributor of astrological books and supplies. In the community eleventh house is his Sun in Pisces, and there also are Chiron, Fortune in Pisces and Jupiter in Aries.

The Gemini Ascendant person always has many interests, and his activities encompass greater duties than he mentions or than the membership is willing to see. The chart significator Mercury is nicely placed as highest planet in the chart. Remember that the Sun represents the heart of the matter (community), while Mercury represents the interest in its status. Even with these obvious indicators of his chart suited to his position, it is puzzling that he has voluble astrological critics all demanding individual care and feeding without any consideration of other member astrologers. Practically all of this chart is on the left side, hallmark of the person who is a self-starter. Rather than be a procrastinating Pisces, he has personal impetus toward organization and schedules.

Then we see the Moon is in Sagittarius in the seventh house. Although this gives an optimistic turn of mind, the Moon in the seventh house is most indicative of changing ideas of what he wants and expects of the people closely around him. And despite the fact that this is a daytime chart, it is Jupiter which is so aptly placed. In any contact with him, the optimist is always evident. Note that the North Node is in the ninth house, hence South Node in the third, a natural teaching dichotomy from the knowledge of why things are to the understanding of how they really are. Neptune is in the third but rules the eleventh, so the affairs of the eleventh house are channeled through the third house of business and communications. Now see that Mars is in the fourth house, focusing his energies to the solvency and future planning toward security. Mars in Leo is very power conscious, calculated to hold and control power. Astrologers might like this better in their own charts than in the chart of someone of whom they prefer to be critical. Mars opposes the Midheaven positions, but oppositions give one the ability to seesaw between both ends of the opposition.

Obviously things are not as bad for eleventh house matters as some might say. Sun and Neptune are in mutual reception. The twelfth house position of Venus is of mundane interest. Venus rules the intercepted part of the twelfth and the sixth house of work and service, which we then say operates behind the scenes, and remind ourselves that he keeps quiet about the amount and variety of work he does. Even astrologers have to learn to adapt to their own charts as well as the charts of their clients and their betters. Saturn in the second house of his immediate future and ruling the eighth implies delays in money, both his own and that of others, but also says the last of life is better than earlier life. We note that, along with Jupiter at zero declination, the Moon is out of bounds by declination. Bear in mind that while the Moon is in the least of the fire signs, it is also in a sign which tries to be all things to all people. Do not fail to see the four retrogrades.

111. Lady Doctor, 8-4-8
Jupiter: 0N03, Uranus: 0N40
Data: July 10, 1927, 2:00 p.m. CET,
Sarajevo, Yugoslavia, 43N50, 18E26

This chart is from birth certificate data furnished by the subject, a tall upstanding lady whom I met socially at the house of a client while she was in California adding to her medical training and knowledge. My very first intuition was that she was a Scorpio. But when I asked her data, I was surprised that she had Sun in Cancer until I counted from a ninth house Cancer to Scorpio rising. She had style, dash and verve. She was serious and practical, and was armed with an elegant silver handled stick with which she was perfectly prepared to do battle. Although the idea was to see what the year would bring her, this was then years away from the fracture of her country into autonomous nations. With Scorpio rising, she has the Moon in Scorpio which is very outspoken in the first house (and Moon is conjunct Saturn there), and she has the Sun in Cancer with Pluto on the edge of her ninth house. Sun and Pluto are widely trine Moon and Saturn, in turn also trine to Jupiter and Uranus in her fifth house. Moon and Saturn are square to Mars, Neptune and Venus in her tenth house.

Although Jupiter is at zero declination, note that Uranus is also at zero, both parallel and trine. Mars, as the highest planet and the dispositor of the chart, is a driving force. Status and power are important to her, and she does not back down from confrontation. Mars and Saturn rising in a chart are fine and statistically prevalent indicators for medicine and especially surgery.

At the time, I was aware of a sizable community in San Francisco of rather contentious Croatian waiters as well as a fair historical knowledge of her birthplace. Bismarck said that if Europe was to have trouble it would most likely arise from the seething cauldron in the Balkans. I live down the street from the former Yugoslavian Consulate. One night in the late 1970s, a drum of oil was set on the front porch of that house and torched, searing the front of the consulate and the house next door. It was rumored this had been done by Croatian separatists.

This may look like an easy chart with a grand trine and no T-squares, but it is also a chart with striking energy fields and subtle minor aspects, as well as a Moon-Pluto mutual reception. After her sabbatical, she returned to Yugoslavia.

112. Architect, 7-4-9
Jupiter: 0N03, Uranus: 0N40
Data: July 10, 1927, 1:10 p.m. PST,
Oakland, California, 37N48, 122W16

Birth certificate data, only hours later than the previous example, this is the chart of the long time live in boyfriend of a lady who was an astrology student. As "astral" twin of the preceding chart, this man was tall and low key. The thing about having two charts close together is that, using progressions, the later born's Moon

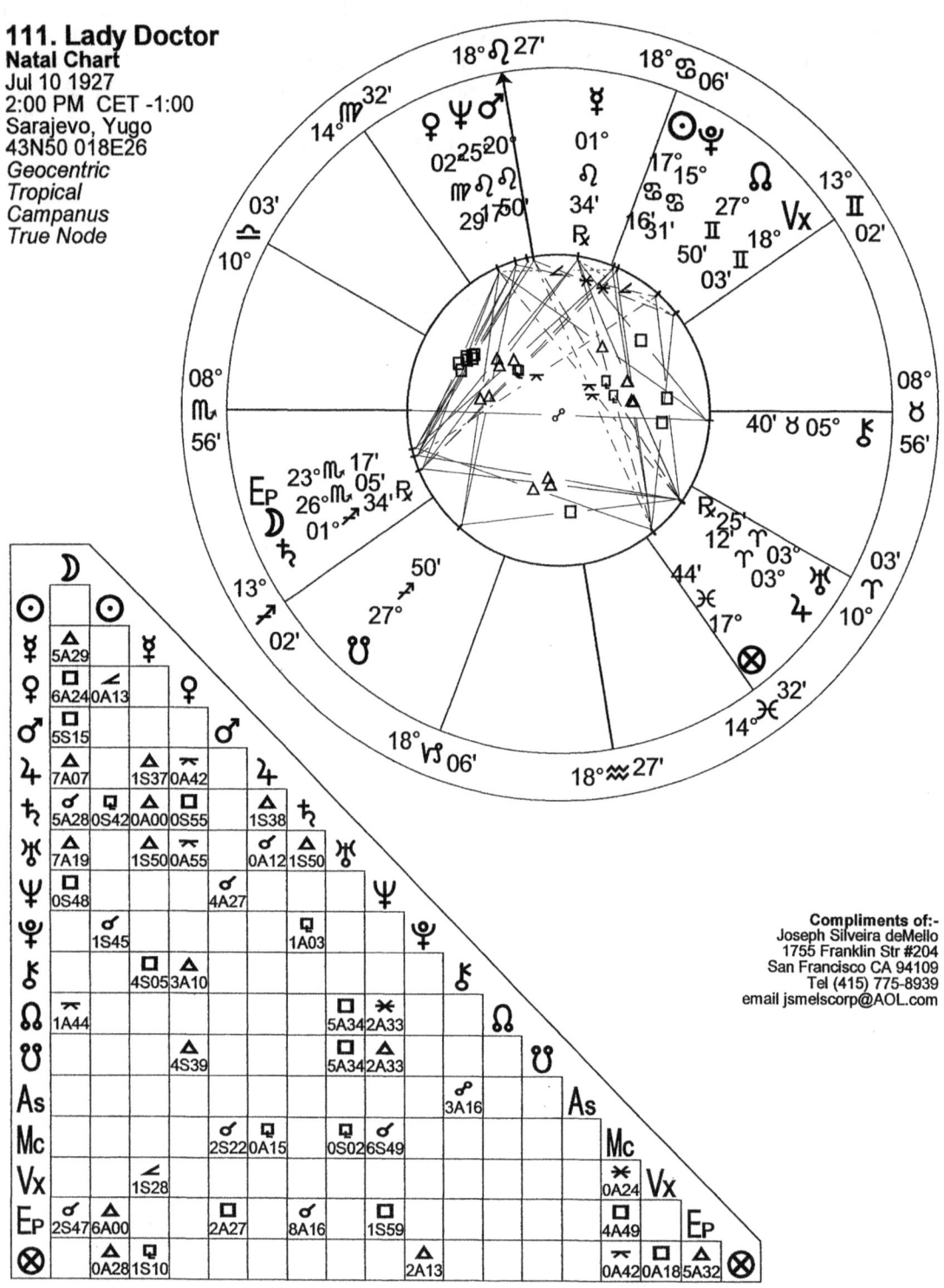

111. Lady Doctor
Natal Chart
Jul 10 1927
2:00 PM CET -1:00
Sarajevo, Yugo
43N50 018E26
Geocentric
Tropical
Campanus
True Node

Compliments of:-
Joseph Silveira deMello
1755 Franklin Str #204
San Francisco CA 94109
Tel (415) 775-8939
email jsmelscorp@AOL.com

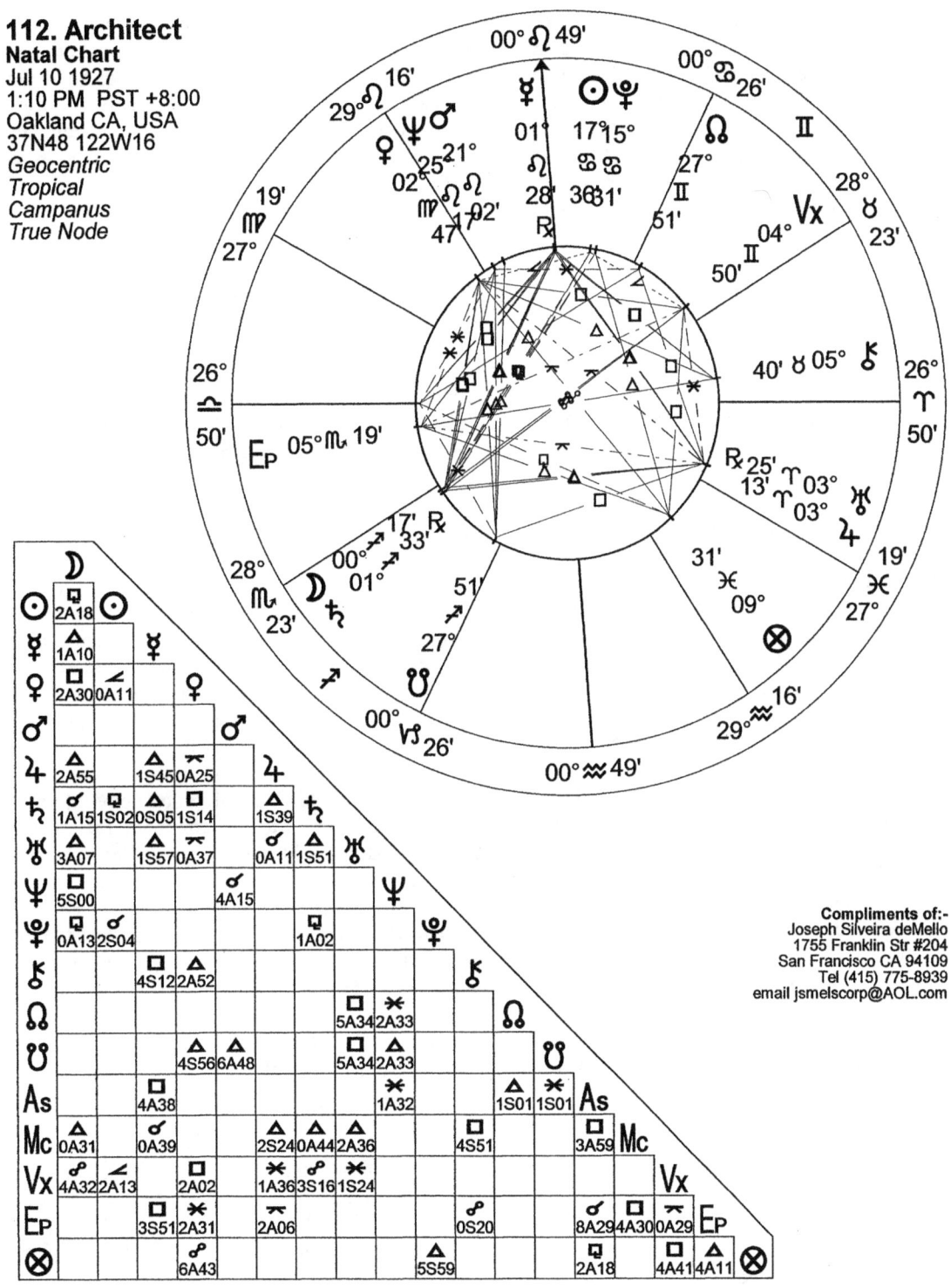

makes its aspects ahead of the earlier born. Venus in Virgo in the eleventh is his chart significator. His Sun in the ninth is overpowered too near Pluto, and the Moon in early Sagittarius with Saturn are sesquiquad to Sun-Pluto. Another close pair, Jupiter is conjunct the retrograde Uranus in the sixth house, ruled by Pisces. He is a successful architect with a quiet sense of humor and never discussed any of his projects.

Mercury retrograde of abstract thought as his topmost placement and part of the fire grand trine to Moon-Saturn and to Jupiter-Uranus. While this man is highly philosophical, he was undismayed by change, he has remained located in his birth locale with never an idea of distant relocation. Note that Jupiter-Uranus is underlined by both of them in zero parallel declination. Note that Libra rising is happiest in a durable relationship, this man is unmarried despite a better than twenty year liaison with the same lady.

113. Man with Broken Elbow, 5-4-12
Jupiter: 0N07, Uranus: 0N39
Data: July 18, 1927, 5:42 a.m. CST,
Decatur, Georgia, 33N47, 84W17

This is the chart of a highly successful real estate man. I met him in late March of 1976, and he immediately told of falling off the back of a truck while he was helping a friend move on March 5. As a result, he broke his right elbow and emerged with a right arm he would never be able to straighten out. It was a freak accident which he approached with grim self-deprecation in line with Chiron at the top of his chart. Here we have a Leo rising with a Cancerian Sun in the twelfth and a Pisces Moon in the eighth. He is sensitive to the needs of friends, and allows them to demand his attention. There is no question of his getting involved in confrontations though his Mars is with Neptune in Leo. There is little here of the expected Aries dominance other examples here get from Mars in the first house and in the rising sign. This man was divorced when he was forty-one, and unhappy to find himself unattached. He drifted into a homosexual lifestyle which he kept pretty much under wraps. He discovered young men in search of a father figure were attracted to him, probably the product of paternal Leo with maternal Cancer. This is a bit strange considering Saturn retrograde in the fifth house which is not good for parent-child relationships. This position of Saturn is one where his father had too high expectations of him and he has the same expectations of his own children. Notice that Saturn is part of the grand trine to Jupiter-Uranus and Ascendant. This man is living far from his natal place which he left for greater freedom. Check the Midheaven trine to Neptune-Mars. He lived more comfortably with his Jupiter-Uranus conjunction than he did with his Mars-Neptune combination.

114. Prison Guard, 4-5-7
Jupiter: 0S01, Uranus: 0N33
Data: August 4, 1927, 3:47 a.m. PST,
Sacramento, California, 38N35. 121W30

First quickly notice that we now have the Jupiter-Uranus conjunction contraparallel both still retrograde but higher in the ninth house. The wife of this man was in a carpool with suburban friends of mine, so I got data from her for herself, her husband and their four sons. Now retired, the husband was once a minor bureaucrat in his native city. At a critical time, middle age, he found himself shuffled out of his job and took the very next thing he could find, a job as a guard at a huge penitentiary. The family moved to a community closer to his place of work. His wife found a job as a civil servant in San Francisco, and they proceeded to raise their four boys. Our subject is very much a family man, paternally caring and highly practical. He puts all of his time into family and community. Home and family define his place in the world. Although he spends much time in his off hours watching television, but he has long had an interest in photography and was always taking pictures of high school athletic events, in some of which, his four sons participated. Although Cancer rising, he is very much a Leo, and the first house Sun is the hallmark of the salesman who easily assumes whatever mood and role he needs in any situation. But then his Libra Moon in the fourth and trine his Ascendant, home care and improvements are of active interest. There is, however, an element of frustration seen in Mars square Saturn, and anybody who has ever raised four sons is going to sympathize with Saturn in the fifth house. Doubtless his father expected more of him, and certainly he expects more of his sons, all of whom were just as normal as boys can be, never too far from getting into scrapes. Only one of his four sons has done exceptionally well, went from high school to work for a franchise food operation and rose to be in charge of his own area and is said to be a millionaire (but, married to an equally workaholic wife, both career oriented, he has not produced grandchildren). That is how any fifth house Saturn looks at children; there is always a fly in the ointment. I expected him to turn his photographic hobby into more than a minor business after his retirement. I felt that the fifth house Saturn could work in terms of late found creatively and that he might turn it into a maker of occasional pin money. But that also has to be revised due to Neptune also in his second house making the situations in that house a bit unreal. But he is happy enough merely puttzing in his retirement.

115. Marrying Man, 3-5-3
Jupiter: 0S32, Uranus: 0N22
Data: August 22, 1927, 12:00 a.m. EST,
Cincinnati, Ohio, 39N08, 84W30

This man has a sister who is an astrologer, but he came to me with a most unusual tale of woe (one which he could not willingly share with his sister). One afternoon I just popped into an almost deserted neighborhood bar where the bartender was a client. The bartender made a reference to my involvement with astrology, and this man, sitting one barstool away got into conversation. Well primed by his sister, he immediately gave me his birth data. As his story unfolded, he was entirely het-

113. Man with Broken Elbow
Natal Chart
Jul 18 1927
5:42 AM CST +6:00
Decatur GA, USA
33N47 084W17
Geocentric
Tropical
Campanus
True Node

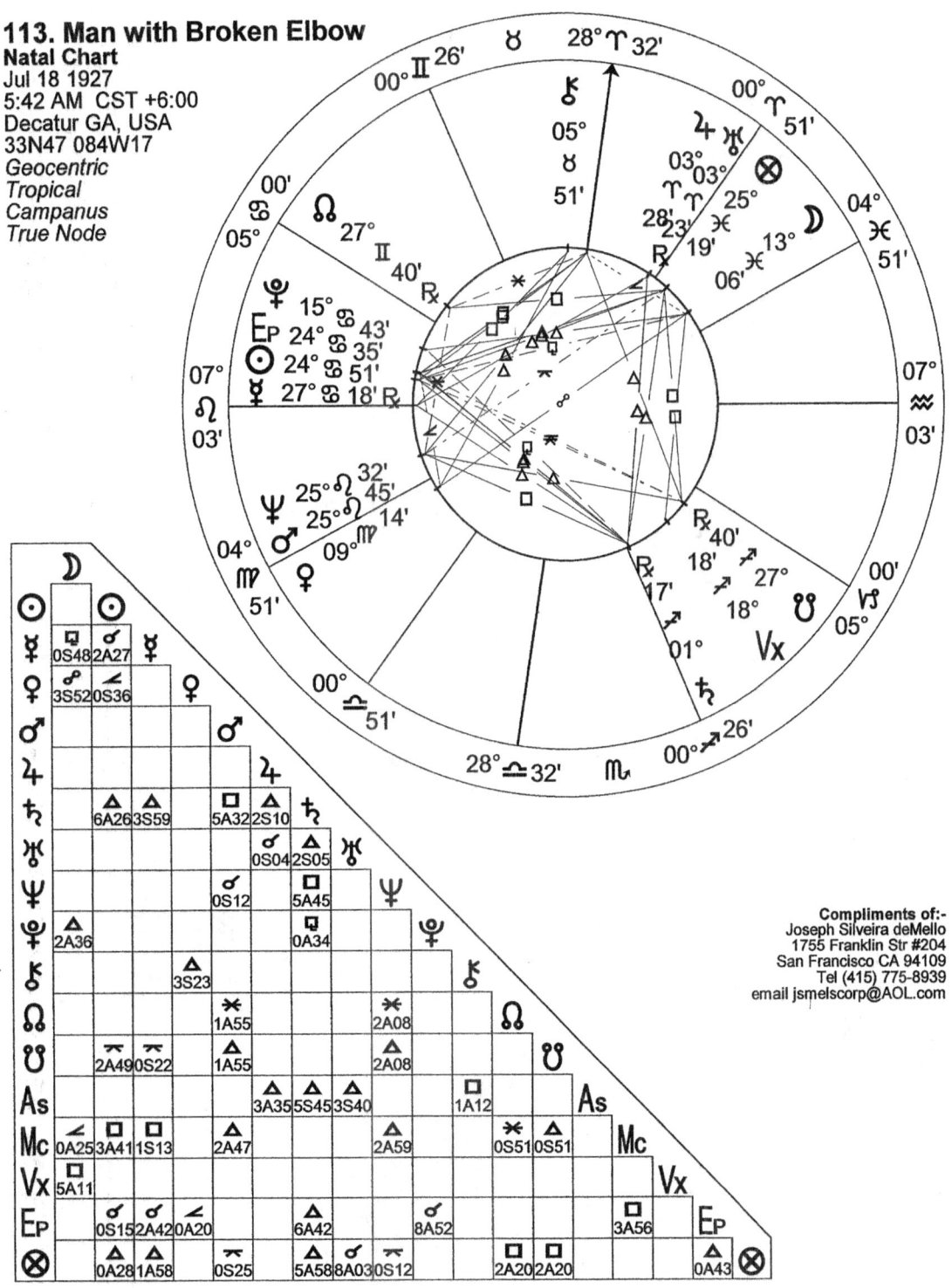

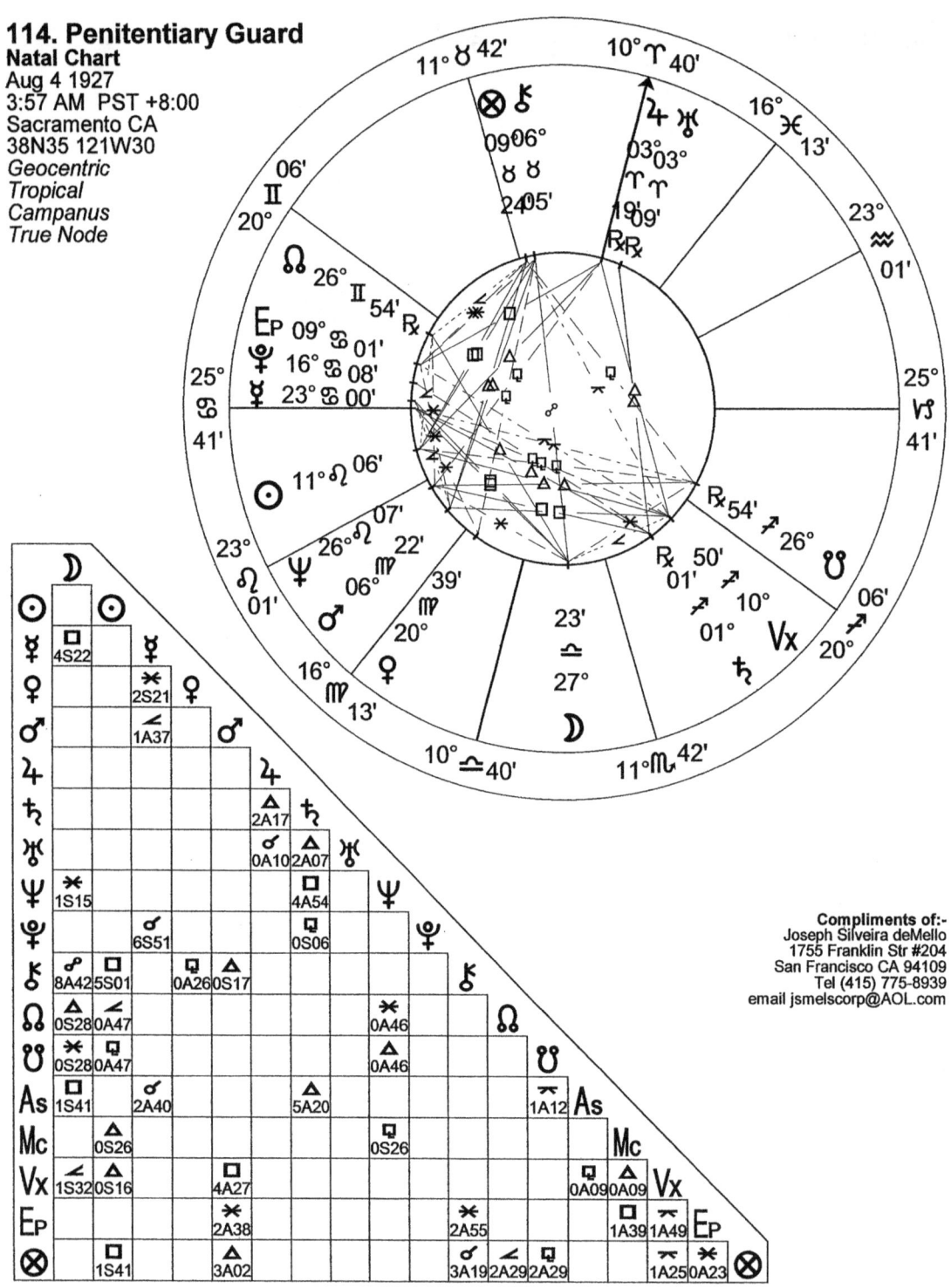

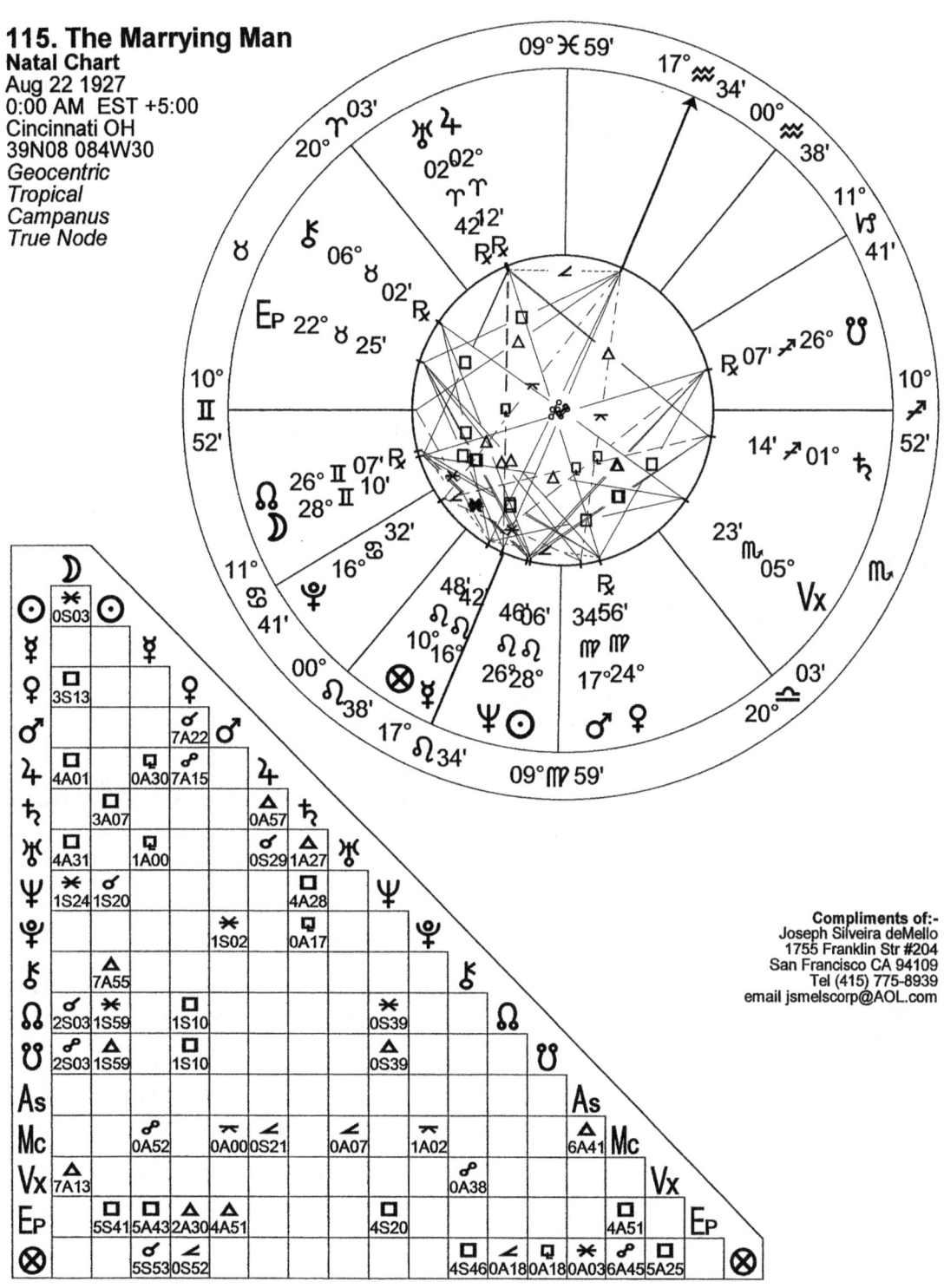

erosexual, in fact preferred to be married, and that all his troubles stemmed from a recent effort to remarry.

His first wife died in 1968, and he subsequently remarried only to get divorced in August 1976. He then quickly took up with a girl and they set up a date to marry on September 4, 1977, but three weeks before that date, she admitted to him that she had been stealing from her employer to invest it in his art gallery and make herself his business partner. So he took her to his attorney, and research revealed she had stolen in excess of $100,000. His attorney got him disentangled from the partnership and marital plans. He got his gallery building free and clear of her on October 4, 1977. His girlfriend had always been busy pulling deals, improving her credit lines, and she would go from one excellent temporary job to another with large companies all over town. All of a sudden she cleared out, became an office manager in the West Indies, and moved into the apartment of the man who interviewed and hired her for a magazine job. All of this left my casual saloon companion back in the singles limbo.

In this Gemini rising chart, the angles closely similar to my own, and the Moon is also in the same sign in the first house as is mine. No wonder he so easily went from casual stranger to the revelation of personal details of his life. The chart significator Mercury is on the IC in Leo. The Sun is also in Leo in the fourth, too close to Neptune, so that it is Neptune which exerts its influence to cloud the Sun operation with a sense of unreality about home and security, particularly important to him. The Moon is out of bounds, while Jupiter and Uranus are both at zero declination but contra-parallel. Mercury is not well-aspected and at the midpoint of Mars-Pluto (via semisextiles). Moon is square to the Jupiter-Uranus conjunction. As I recall the original meeting and subsequent reading session, the subject was frank and detailed on his circumstances which made for an easy and productive reading.

116. Psychic's First Husband, 3-6-6
Jupiter: 0S47, Uranus: 0N17
Data: August 27, 1927, 11:50 p.m. CST,
Bartlesville, Oklahoma, 36N44, 95W58

Thirty years ago, when I was teaching astrology at the Metaphysical Center in San Francisco, a psychic lady was also giving classes to help others improve their own psychic senses. She had some while back divorced her first husband and had just met a man who was to become her future husband. She gave me birth data for herself, her former and future husbands, and their extended families. Life with her ex-husband was quite a saga. He was as close to a harum-scarum ne'er do well type as ever existed. He never stayed long enough with any one job to do well at it. Originally an oil-field worker, he quit this line because the work was too hard. By whatever quirks of fate, this man and his ex-wife are the in-law parents of #49 Oil Field Worker. In the course this man's marriage and career, his wife went into real estate and got part-time work as the manager of apartment complexes which kept them and their only daughter in living accommodations. In those situations, he sometimes got involved as resident handyman.

This was a very inventive rationalizer, never saw himself as a failure. All he wanted was universal approval and sympathy and the cheapest possible ticket for getting from day to day. His inventive fabrications were rich in convoluted detail and all highly dramatic. He pretended at Russian roulette but never managed to do any harm to himself while working the nerves of everyone around him. When his first wife was on the verge or remarriage, he called his former mother-in-law to inform her that he had glandular cancer and three months of life expectancy. He was sure this information would be passed on and lay a guilt trip on both ex-wife and daughter. Needless to say, he is still alive, still concocting wild scenarios with no notion he long ago lost all credibility.

Imagine my amazement when I first saw his chart, the Gemini rising and Aquarian Midheaven so close to my own. Even before going further, I remembered the old axiom that cautions against being critical of others because those same criticisms can apply to the critic. But all I have in common here is the similarity of angles. I have always been interested in the two faces of Mercury, Gemini and Virgo, in the same chart. Here we have Gemini rising with significator Mercury in Leo conjunct Neptune, and both too close to the Virgo Sun in the fourth house. Adjacent this group, and at the other end of the fourth house, we find Moon in Virgo conjunct Mars conjunct Venus, also in Virgo, but the latter two in the fifth house, and Venus retrograde. Compare this to the previous example born five days earlier and with the same angles. Give close attention to the planetary movement and placement at the bottom of both charts. For those astrologers who say that the IC is the indicator of how a person sees himself, Leo here, and the MC is the indication of how the world sees them, Aquarius, this chart and person are excellent examples that this particular insight is worthy of consideration.

For many years, he has lived with a girl friend in a trailer in southern Nevada. He has finally, in failing health and old beyond his years, left that situation (or got pushed out of it) and returned to the city where his ex-wife and his daughter and he once lived and to which now all three have returned. His infirmities are real but lack drama, testaments of old age and neglect of his own health. He returned with the notion that he could move in with either his ex-wife (now widowed by her second husband) or his daughter, but he was quickly disabused of that idea. His daughter found him a place to live but made it very plain that neither lady wished his company. The car in which he returned is so decrepit that it is not expected to be able to carry him many miles in their direction, but no one is letting their guard down. At this writing, his transiting Saturn is aptly going through his twelfth house. Times are not of the best for him. The sesquiquads from Jupiter-Uranus to Mercury and the Vertex do not bode well for health. His ex-wife has late Aries rising, a Gemini Sun and Sagittarius Moon.

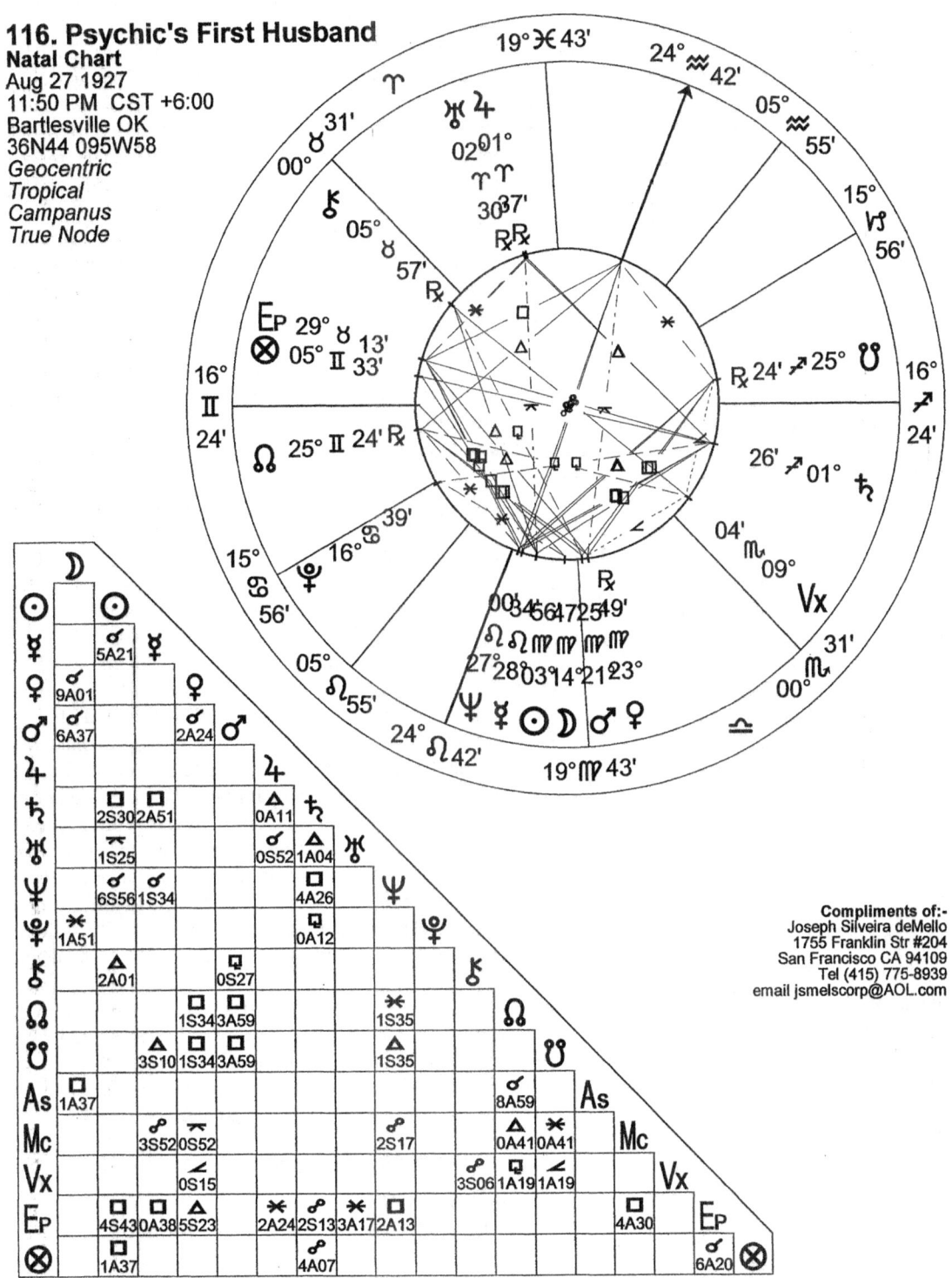

116. Psychic's First Husband
Natal Chart
Aug 27 1927
11:50 PM CST +6:00
Bartlesville OK
36N44 095W58
Geocentric
Tropical
Campanus
True Node

Compliments of:-
Joseph Silveira deMello
1755 Franklin Str #204
San Francisco CA 94109
Tel (415) 775-8939
email jsmelscorp@AOL.com

117. Man with Brittle Bones, 7-6-5
Jupiter: 0N23
Data: September 17, 1933, 7:04 a.m. CST,
Cammeron, Texas, 30N51, 96W59

Finally we have got away from Jupiter conjunct Uranus and the latter at zero declination. This is the chart of a very quiet and pleasant man I have known for thirty years. He is a court reporter and was once active in a local softball league. He is of medium height, a dark abundant head of hair, crinkly laughter lines around his eyes, and facial dimples as befits a Libra rising. He is very quietly homosexual and has lived with the same life partner almost the entire time I have known him. Unfortunately in 1979 and on May 11, 1980, he broke the same ankle playing softball. His doctor told him he had unusually brittle bones which prohibit him from taking part in sports activities and put the fear of God into him about the effects of any sudden movement. He seldom talks about himself, and the only time he came close to manifesting a Leo Moon was when he was active in sports.

He is a Libra rising with Sun, Mercury and Jupiter all in the twelfth house (Neptune is also there but not part of the stellium). Venus is in the first house but in Scorpio almost on the second house cusp, and Mars in Scorpio is in the second house. The preponderance of twelfth house placements may account for the sort of privacy to which Mars in Scorpio can contribute. Now, as I write, Saturn is transiting his seventh house as he heads toward retirement. Will he actually retire? We see Saturn will go over the Vertex which is so often a health indicator, and Uranus of the sudden and unexpected (often divorce) but may mean surprises in career status if he does not intend to retire. Jupiter just above the Ascendant is still by progression in zero declination. Saturn is the best chart timing device, now climbing up his chart toward the Midheaven. He is asking himself what he needs or does not need of people close to him, will ask what he wishes to gain from them, and finally will be studying what he is going to be doing when Saturn does go over his Midheaven.

118. The Bon Vivant, 5-7-9
Jupiter: 0S18, Sun: 0S35
Data: September 25, 1933, 1:10 a.m. PST,
Los Angeles, California, 34N03, 118W44

This is the chart of a man who is happiest partying and exchanging stories and jokes. He goes from one to a long series with great facility as if he knows each story and has found the most effective way of telling it. While he is also a writer and has a photographic hobby, his prime career has been in commercial real estate. In the early Nineties as he neared the age at which most people retire, he was living high on the hog and paying quite high rent for a fabulous apartment. All of his living and social expenses were being charged off as business expenses. His expense account attracted unfavorable notice, and his firm decided to dispense with his services. He has been rarely seen locally since 1995, returning here only to pursue a legal suit he has pending in local courts contending unjustified termination. He has moved to southern California. He is very active and not the sort of person who would retire. Over the years he did extended luncheons and often did not return to his office, merely calling in to check messages. Most of us see it with dismay that he is no longer in our social group.

He is unmistakably Leo rising, a good sign for a salesman, and his Libra Sun is in the third house rather close to Jupiter and with Mercury also there. Obviously he should be in the business world. He has the Moon in Sagittarius, intercepted and conjunct the Vertex, and the Moon is in his fifth house and well out of bounds. Note that his third house is ruled by Virgo, the house of sales, and Virgo rising probably richly contributed to his detailed expense reports. What is foremost is the creative personality and creativity in business activities and all communications, and then a fifth house ruled by Scorpio, the sign of research. He exudes an air of confidence, optimism and a great elan, due to Moon in Sagittarius. Remember that in sales, appearances are always a big asset.

Although basically bi-sexual, with a prior history as a serious family man, he has no compunction at revealing his current homosexual attractions when among others of that group. We may consider Mars in Scorpio as an additional clue to him, but cannot do so without seeing Venus debilitated in Scorpio nearby. The real clue to the chart and his fantasy lifestyle is the Uranus Midheaven. Note that Uranus is square Pluto in his twelfth house. Uranus is sesquiquad Neptune, but there are pattern sesquiquads from Pluto to the Moon and Vertex and to the North Node. He has Sun conjunct and parallel with his zero Jupiter declination. Have the combust Jupiter and Mercury helped or hindered his life? It is the usual tendency of astrologers to view well a Sun-Jupiter conjunction, a thing this chart and life contradicts. Since he made it easy for his firm to make him redundant, a look at Chiron is expected, and we find that Chiron is trine his Sun-Jupiter with the Ascendant sextile and at the midpoint of both ends of the trine.

We have one major event in his lifetime. On November 15, 1942, he was in the Navy serving around Guadalcanal when his ship was shot out of under him. A diurnal chart for that occasion, however, only has diurnal Jupiter on the diurnal Ascendant, where we need at least two angular placements for a really serious event. He always laughed at this misadventure, treating it very lightly, for he was hardly in any real danger, and he was rescued after several days in a lifeboat wandering in the South Pacific. I cannot remember whether he was alone or accompanied by other shipmates.

119. General's Aide, 4-7-11
Jupiter: 0S37
Data: September 28, 1933, 11:05 p.m. CST,
Ridgeville, Indiana, 40N17, 85W02

I first met this man as next door neighbor of an old friend. I was told that he set off for work every day by loading his golf bag into the trunk of his sports car, himself attired for a day on the golf links. A quiet man of me-

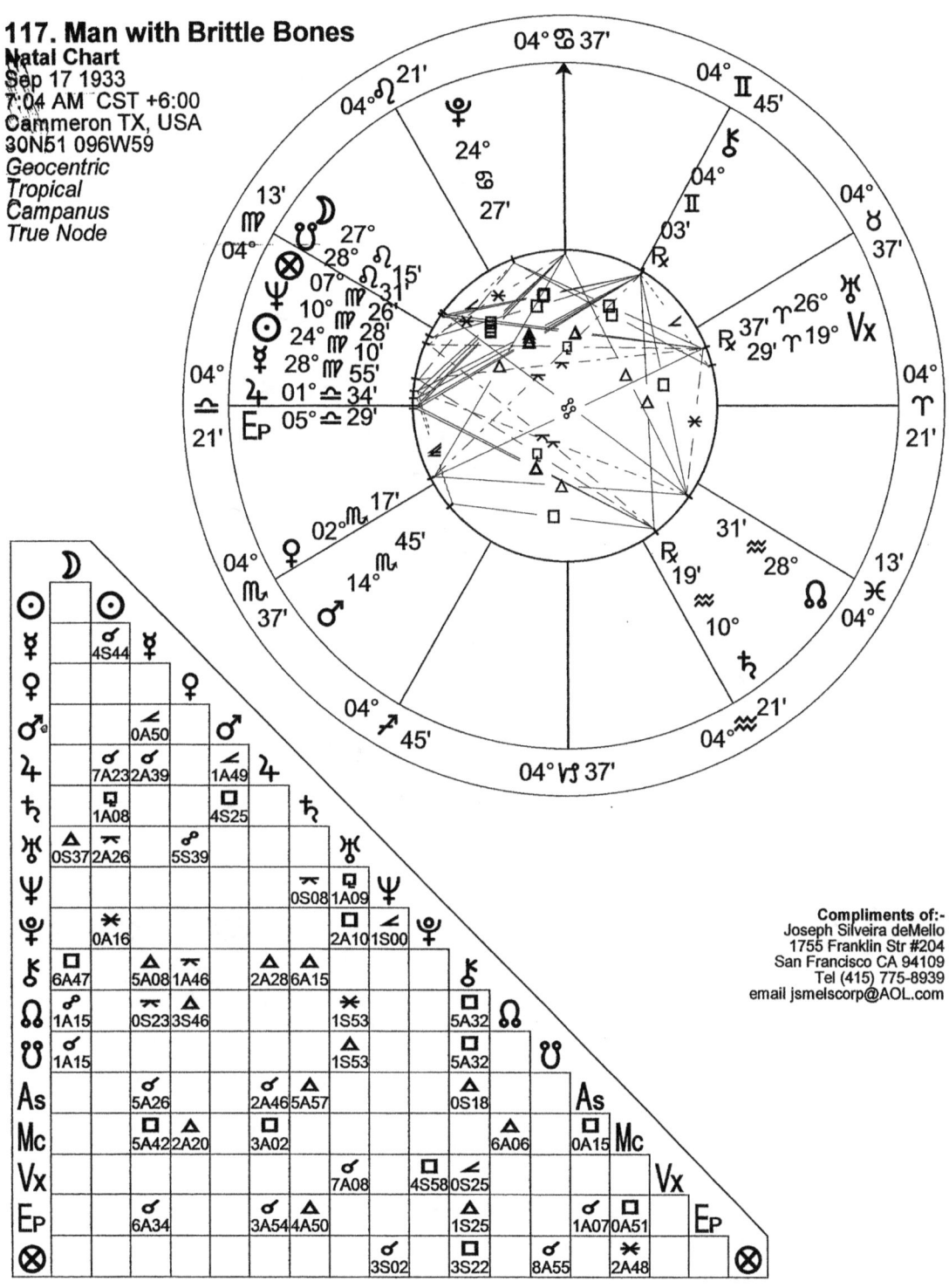

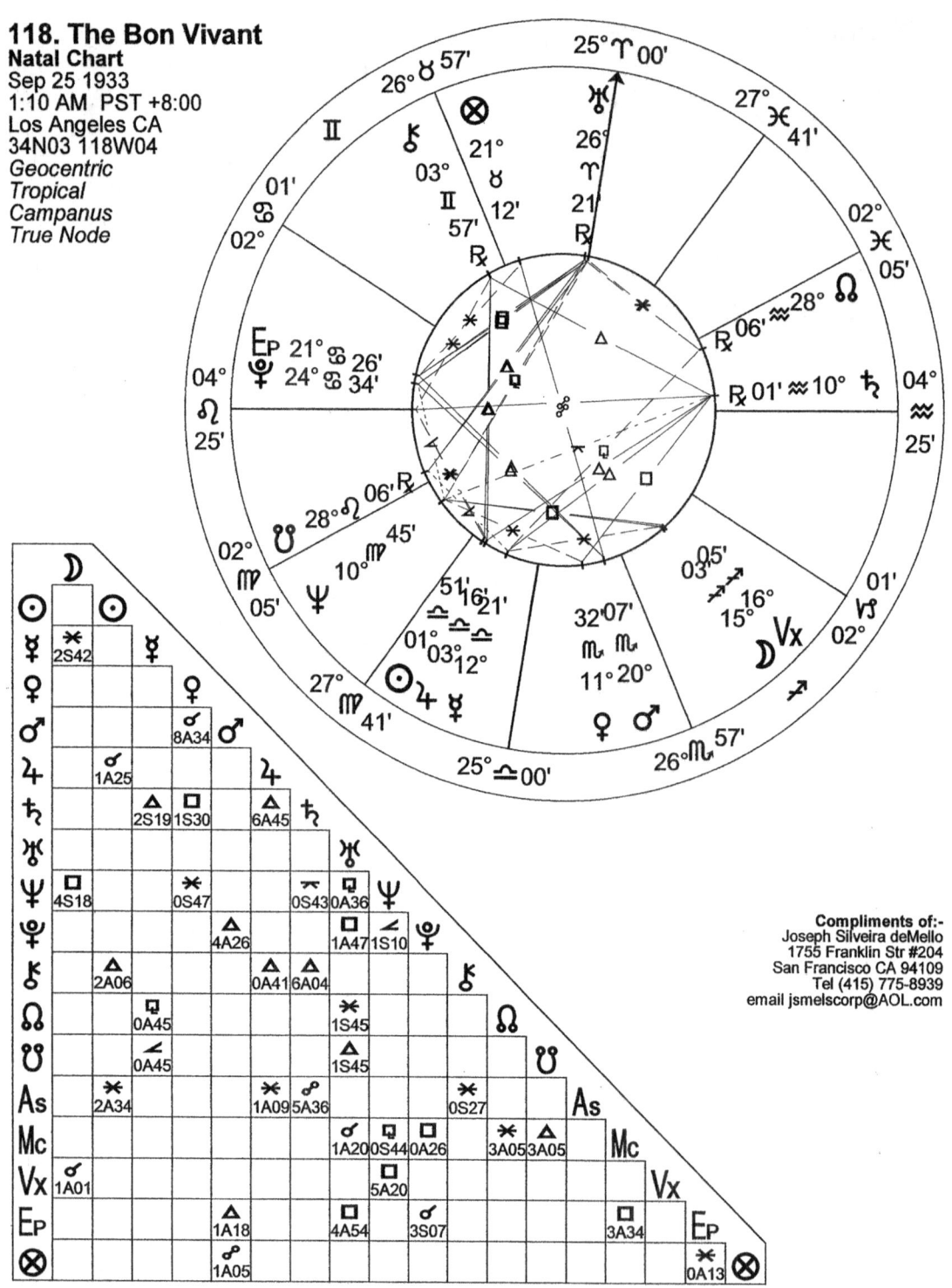

dium height and stature, he was a career Army officer who chose to live off base. He kept his uniforms at work, strictly for official occasions. He was approaching retirement and joked that his chief occupation was as golfing partner of his general. He is now retired and living just as quietly and privately in the same neighborhood. Birth data is from him.

The chart is only three days later than the previous example. Cancer rising with Pluto in the first house has certainly not lead him to self-destruct his personality image. The Sun is in Libra, still conjunct Jupiter, but more distant from Mercury, and the Moon is with Saturn in Aquarius at the end of a seventh house ruled by Capricorn. Here with Sun leaving a conjunction to Jupiter in the fourth house, these make a trine to Moon-Saturn which goes on to form a grand trine with Chiron. And although the Sun and Jupiter are opposite the mid- heaven, there are no T-squares or kite formations to mitigate one opposition (Sun-Jupiter to Midheaven), but the opposition of Chiron to Vertex, has Sun-Jupiter trine Chiron and sextile the Vertex.

120. The Irishman, 8-7-11
Jupiter: 0S45
Data: September 30, 1933, 11:05 a.m. EDT,
Jersey City, New Jersey, 40N43, 74W05

Two days after the previous example, this is the chart of a red-headed, blue eyed, man who is a professional Irishman, of a heavy and very solid build. Being Irish was the most important factor in his life, and his work and career were never revealed. His chart has two double bi-quintile with quintile formations which should attest to the presence of a talent which he should be teaching to others. The focus of one of these is the Moon, going out to Sun-Jupiter and to Pluto, while the other focuses on Uranus and goes out to ASC-Mars and to MC-Neptune. The trouble with this and the last two examples is that Jupiter is too close to the rays of the Sun. This is the chart of a homosexual, but he would have to tell you himself as casual acquaintance did not reveal any such activity. He was bluff and hearty, held very well his liquor, knew a lot of people but only casually.

The chart is Scorpio rising with Mars and Venus in Scorpio just above the Ascendant. The Sun is in Libra with Jupiter in the eleventh house, while the Moon is in the latter degrees of a third house Aquarius. The reader of course realizes that Scorpios have their secrets and half-truths. But it is Neptune on his Virgo Midheaven, and the highest planet of the chart that tells us that this man is a Neptunian, has a special way of processing information or living an image which is real only in his own imagination. Mars might tell that his job is in the twelfth and see Aries ruling his seventh house. I might guess at law enforcement, but that remains a guess.

121. Union Administrator, 1-2-2
Jupiter: 0S36
Data: May 17, 1939, 2:57 a.m. EST,
Detroit, Michigan, 42N20, 83W03

If Evangeline Adams deftly predicted a hotel fire and got out of legal troubles by successfully analyzing the chart of the judge's son, I, on the basis of delineating this chart was taken on to deliver a course of astrology lectures at a local community college. He was then a civil servant in executive position, a liberal Democrat, very interested in politics and union affairs. In recent years he has moved from this city leaving the education field for a position as a union administrator. He is single, lives very quietly and conservatively.

This chart is unusual in that he has Ascendant, east point and anti-Vertex (secondary Ascendants) and Jupiter in the same degree of Aries-Libra, the Aries zero point, which more astrologers should look upon as of high significance. And then the Midheaven is zero Capricorn. His chart gives him very wide twelfth and first houses (and their opposites) and only Pisces and Virgo are intercepted. The Aries rising was a surprise to me, since he is not a typical Aries personality, which may be because his Mars is in Capricorn and his looks and career are more along Capricorn lines. However, his size matches having Jupiter on his Ascendant, and every planet in the first house serves to bring too many additional factors into any assessment of looks or personality. It is a mind-bending stellium which begins with Fortune and goes through the second house Sun. Uranus is seven degrees away from the Sun and while I limit combust Sun degrees with a five degree orb, I am aware most astrologers give greater orbs in their readings. The crowd in the first house channels the affairs of most of the houses of the chart to what he personally wants of them. Needless to say, he is very focused, and any self-interest is well concealed. However, he is quite outspoken against situations with which he does not agree. His image and actions are as conservative as his appearance. Mars in mutual reception to Saturn must have special meaning in this chart.

122. Male Nurse, 5-2-2
Jupiter: 0S30
Data: May 18, 1939, 10:19 a.m. EST,
Glade Springs, Virginia, 36N48, 81W47

This chart moves the Aries-Taurus crowd of planets from first to tenth house and surprisingly makes this man a more vivid personality, as if Leo rising were not enough of an indicator. This chart places Saturn and Venus around the Midheaven. Data from birth certificate. This man was a tall, burly, upstanding Leo rising, heavily bearded (going gray to pure white), a man who kept his body in good shape, was a motorcyclist often clad in the almost formal and total biker leather gear. It was a surprise to see him and his shorter friend on huge BMW bikes. One day his smaller friend sedately drove up to a stop at a traffic light, forgot to put out his feet, and his huge machine tipped over. The bike well out-weighed his friend and was very difficult to get upright. The other side of our example is that he and his friend enjoyed classical music and were never far from opera house or symphony hall. He was an intensely serious ombudsman ready to serve in any labor dispute re-

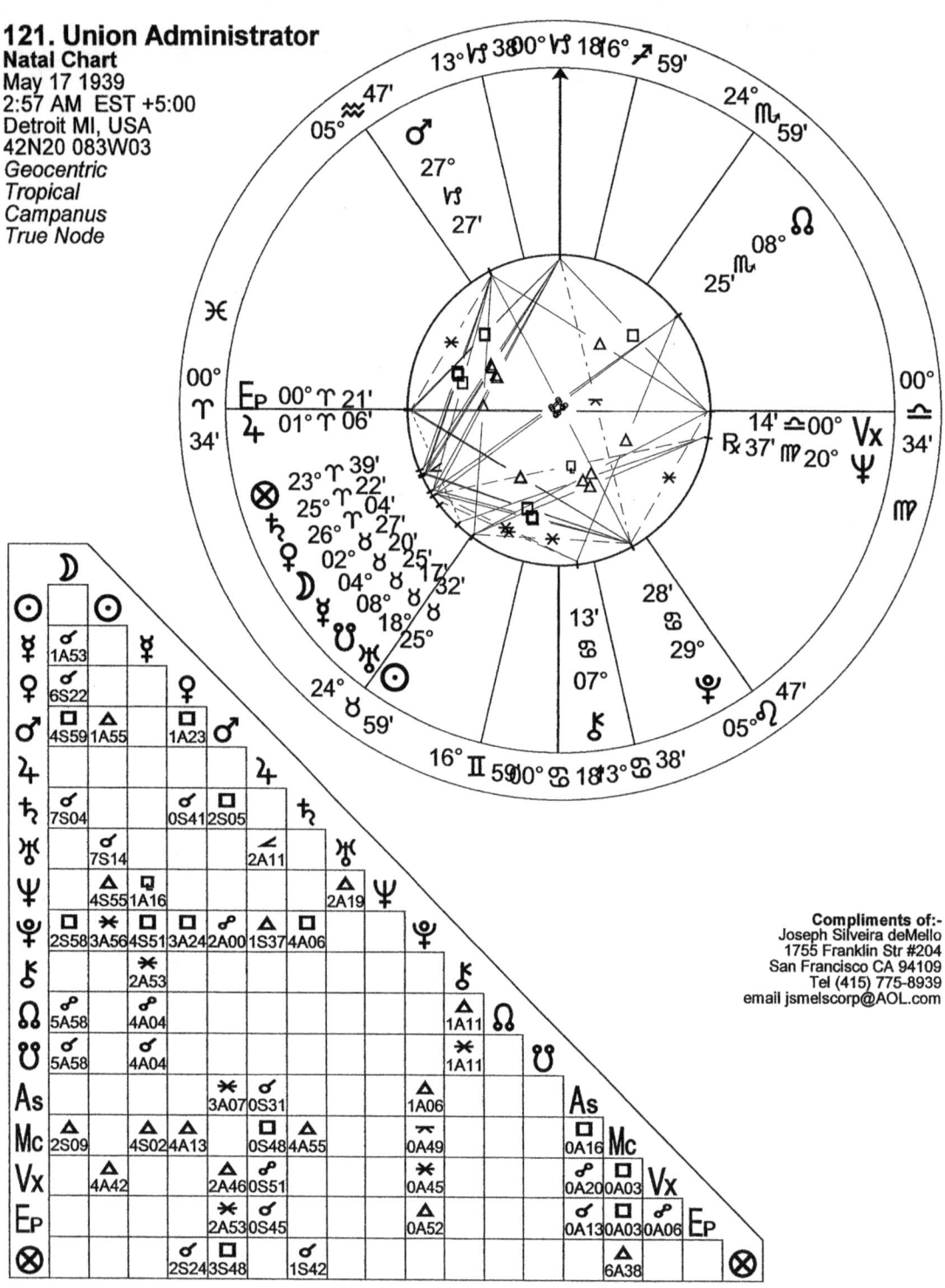

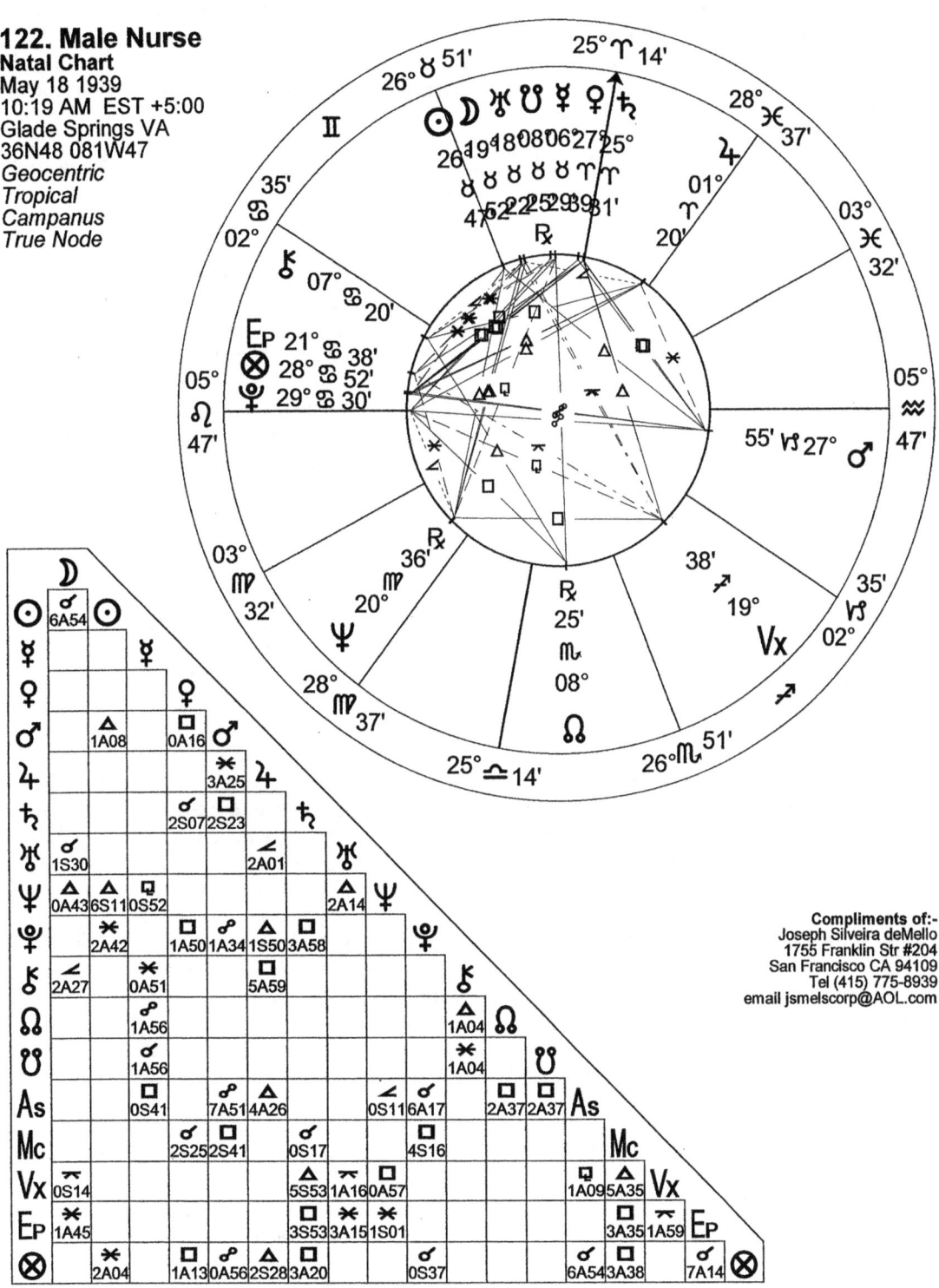

gardless of its merits so long as the basic principle was right. By the time I came to know him, he had worked at almost every hospital in the city as a nurse, and in his final hospital caring for geriatrics. He was such a thorn in the side of every hospital administrator, bucking even the County health system, and at the point where he became unemployable, decided to work out of various nursing registries, accepting assignments as he chose. To my amusement, his friend was a retired executive who was Jesuitical and had unremittingly rode roughshod and hard-nosed as if a little martinet keeping his employees in line without almost being politically incorrect. It appeared the meaning of life was outlined by how big a thorn both of them could be among the softer thinkers around them. But Leo and Taurus best describe him.

Venus-Saturn straddling the Midheaven is amusing since it is general astrological myth that such people are very cold. He and his friend were so intense in what they believed and so serious that it was difficult to see them as the liberals they were. It amused me they got along so well together, even thought as one, ruled by logic and reason. Note that Mars in late Capricorn is in the sixth house. In this chart Pluto is out of bounds, that it is opposite his Mars, and this opposition forms a T-square to Venus-Saturn on the Midheaven. He died in the spring of 1992, after a brief bout with AIDS. I was out of town then, and have never learned his exact date of death.

123. Male Astrologer, 5-3-10
Jupiter: 0S39
Data: June 5, 1939, 10:28 a.m. PST,
Orange, California, 33N47, 117W51

This is the chart of a serious astrologer and lecturer who also has a musical career. He has been thrice married, and was highly interested in astrological relationship studies and lectured on chart comparisons. At a lecture he once gave, I was surprised at his use of examples from his only family problems and a bit embarrassed that he had no idea how much he revealed of himself, yet managed to remain completely unaware of himself as the problem. But then, he was a Leo rising, which makes such obtuseness no more than normal. The surprise is that neither the Gemini Sun nor the Capricorn Moon, not to mention the Aquarius Mars, gave him more perspective. All but the Sun were involved in control factors. With a Midheaven combining with Caput Algol, I suppose permission was granted him to lose his head. There is the idea that those with positions in the final degrees of a sign often partake of the worse elements of the following sign. Certainly at his lecture he was swamped with the Virgo details of the charts he presented. And what we have here is another example of Mercury too close to the heat of the Sun. If his work was presented in great detail, the Leo still shone through as super paternalistic and the concept that no Leo could ever possibly be in any way at fault. I puzzled that Neptune in the first was not in the rising sign which should have me describing him as Neptunian. Had the Neptune been in Leo, I would have no reservation.

124. Robert Nicholas Denham, 3-3-12
Jupiter: 0N55, Moon: 0N00
Data: June 10, 1939, 5:00 a.m. EST,
New Baltimore, Michigan, 42N37, 82W46

This is the chart, birth certificate data, of a real estate management mogul who met his death at 5:00 a.m. PST, May 9, 1978, Palm Springs, California, the victim of murder. He was a big man, well over six feet tall with a corresponding weight of well over two hundred pounds. He was inclined to heaviness and said he worked at keeping his weight down, but not to the point of cutting down on booze. His face was well rounded but basically square featured with a prominent nose and rather noticeably pock marked. He was quite an active real estate operator and investor. All his life he had operated with other people's money. In San Francisco, he owned a string of hotels advertised as catering to young men but meaning homosexual clients. He owned motels and other income property both in San Francisco and in Palm Springs.

A very alert businessman, usually private and quite reserved, he loosened up considerably when he was with his intimate group. Anyone who watched him would always be aware of some reserve (watchfulness) and reticence. Always pleasant to get along with, affable, socially oriented in small groups, he said he avoided large social gatherings. He always traveled with a large entourage of hangers-on, and he did not see dinner for ten or twelve as a large group. He drank rather heavily but had a good tolerance of alcoholic beverages, but he could not hide the bloating effects of such heavy indulgence.

One of his investors was a lady over sixty years of age who had invested her life savings of $12,000 in his enterprises, and there was talk Bob had gone through that money for his personal expenses. She had gone on a brief trip but had returned to Palm Springs to live with Bob and his lover Gregg. Two days before his death, Bob had suggested that his lady investor not stay at the main house but to move to a motel he owned three blocks away so he could have the guest room free. She did as he suggested without demure and was back next evening to attend a dinner party on the evening of May 8, which was also attended by Bob's attorney. The party was entirely agreeable, pleasant and successful. When it broke up, the lady had left the party for her room at the motel.

Police said she must have stayed up all night and begun to get increasingly agitated that she was being eased out of the group since she had no further money to invest with him. Going on to five o'clock the next morning, she had walked back to the main house, let herself into the house with her key, took off her shoes in the entry, tiptoed upstairs, entered the bedroom where Bob was sleeping with Gregg, held a gun with both hands to Bob's head and shot him twice, missing the first shot. She then tried to shoot Gregg, but he was instantly wide awake and wrestled the gun away from her.

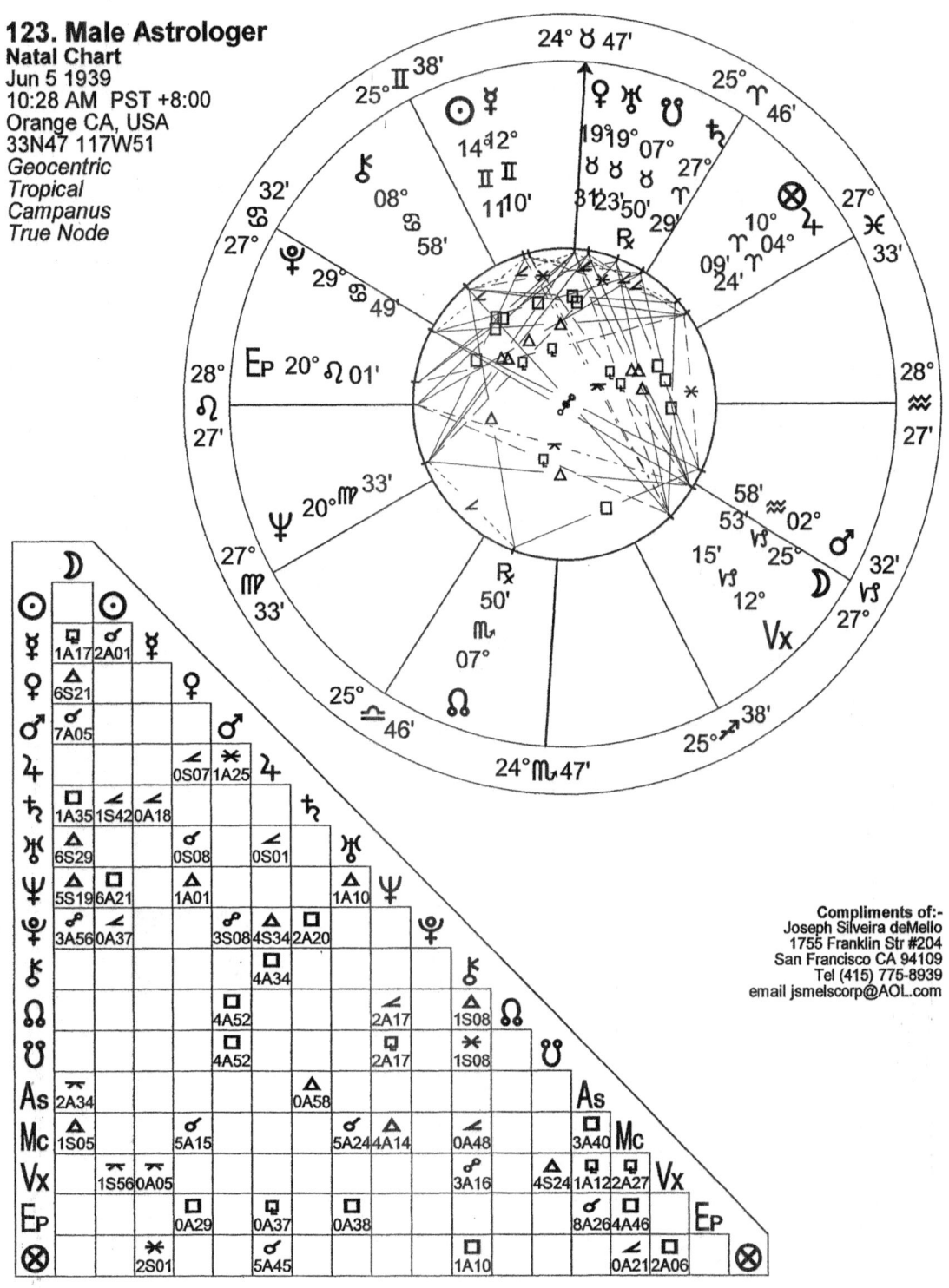

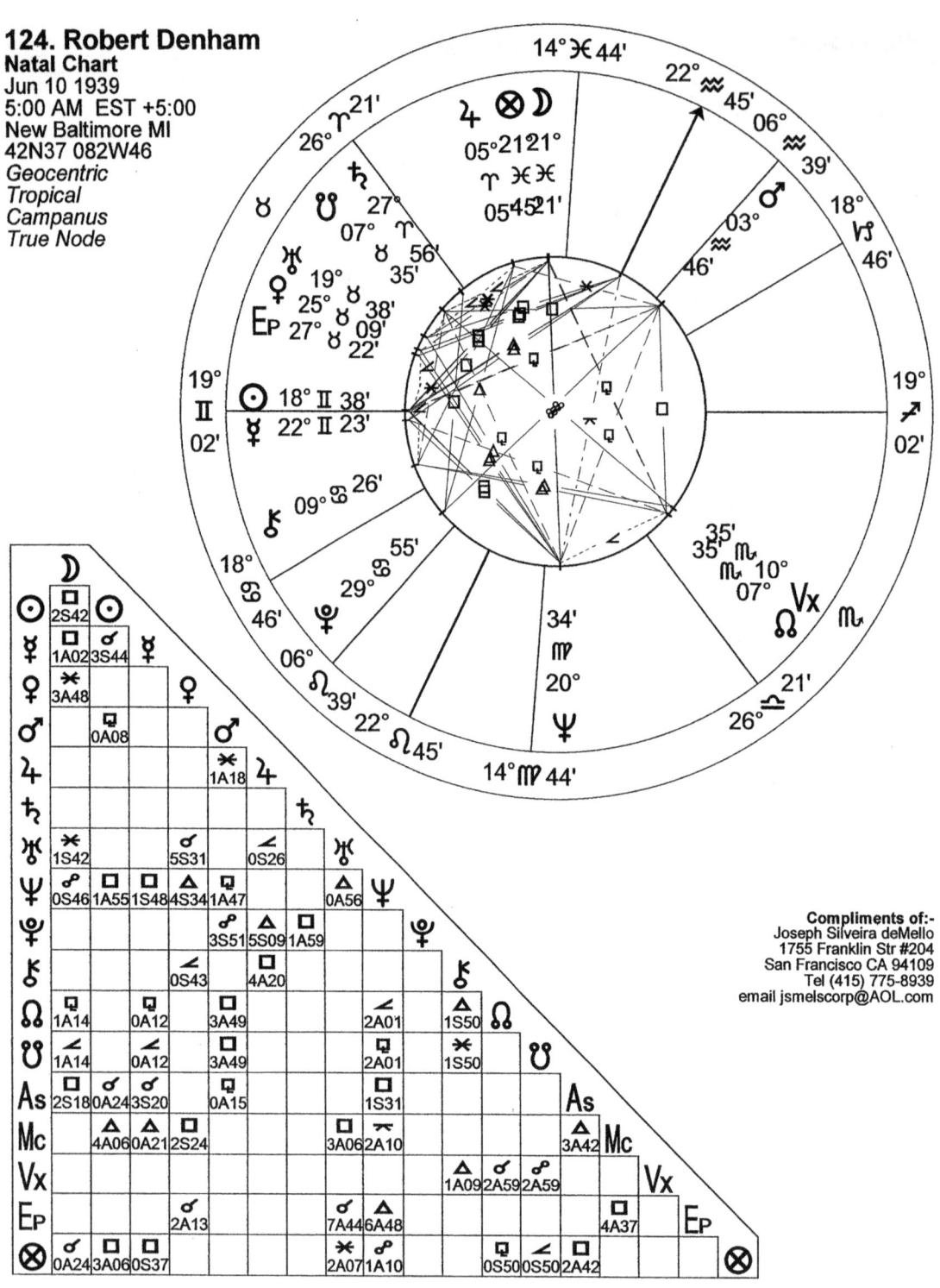

Since someone is bound to notice, we once again have similar angles to my own. Moreover his Sun on my Moon did not give him ascendancy over me as any astrologer might expect. The chart is double Gemini with the Sun on the Ascendant and Mercury in Gemini in the first house a bit too close to the Sun. He had created his own personality and continued to do so, but note that the Sun rules both third and fourth houses, perhaps the latter more strongly. Saturn begins the twelfth house in which position it often shows people to make and loose a couple of fortunes before they finally make it on the third try. It usually also allows people to learn from their own experiences, but I suppose this is provided they live long enough to do so. Venus and Uranus are in separating conjunction and intercepted there. We see that matters of the sixth, eighth, ninth and tenth houses are channeled through the twelfth house and provide a key to his *modus operandi*.

He was such an operator that one wondered how much his closest intimates really knew of what was going on in his entire structure of living. Not that his intimate crowd much cared. They seemed to be sitting around waiting for some sort of main chance. Climbers by association. Notice this double Gemini which should have been quite a bit intuitive also had his Moon in Pisces, which I do not regard as a helpful influence. This uncertain Moon is in the eleventh and Jupiter testifies to many friends but also to his ambivalence in their regard. At the time of his death, Saturn had progressed to zero Taurus, Pluto to zero Leo, and Moon to zero Virgo, so a square and a trine, but these three things into zero of new signs shows probable change worth noticing and should be correlated by aspect to the Aries point. Older astrologers were much in dread of when too many things in a chart changed into zero of a new sign. And not the least of it, progressed Mars was retrograde at zero Aquarius and so opposite to Pluto.

The Ascendant for the moment of murder was zero Taurus, the Sun at 18 Taurus was on his natal Uranus. The Moon and Venus were transiting his twelfth house at 14 Gemini quincunx transiting Uranus at 14 Scorpio. Moon and Venus were trine transiting Pluto at 14 Libra, in a permissive trine. In retrospect there is much to see by doing a series of charts for sensitive moments. Any astrologer would have frowned to see so much about to happen. I might have been reassured by transiting Saturn going over his natal IC, and this is the first chart where I have seen this transit behave drastically there. One has to remember with Saturn that what one gets is what one deserves and remember that Saturn can be a stern master. If ill results from Saturn going over an angle, it can always be said to be a result of wrongdoing in the immediate past (while Saturn was transiting the previous cadent house). So, although in a rather negative sense, this was just the sort of astrological lesson I needed. Just as soon as you are certain of something, you get put right back in your place as a mere mortal.

I also want to make clear that my original readings for this client were done in 1976 and in 1977, and that it was after this second year that he was spending more time in Palm Springs and his trips to San Francisco grew briefer. I did not go as far ahead as 1978, I was a bit uneasy about the lot of zero progressions, though I did not foresee either death or murder. But, after all, astrological climate changed before I began to study astrology in 1963. By the 1960s, it became incorrect to predict death astrologically. This can only be as foolish as to believe that if a thing is not talked about, it will go away. Death and taxes are inevitable. And here we had a preponderance. As a final note for this study we see the natal chart with Jupiter at zero declination parallel to Moon also at zero declination. We see Mercury out of bounds as well as Pluto and note that Mars will spend some years out of bounds by progression.

125. Career Manager, 9-6-4
Jupiter: 0N57
Data: September 9, 1939, 12:29 p.m. CST,
Dayton, Ohio, 39N46, 84W12

Frequently when I would do the chart of one young man in San Francisco, his significant other of the same sex would also come for a reading. This and the next are such a couple who wanted me to do a comparison series in the late 1970s with some attention to the chart of this man as agent-manager for his friend, ten years younger, who was an aspiring singer-dancer. The results of this survey revealed strong karmic ties and many conjunctions and permissive trines between them as well as one of the largest number of semi-sextile aspects as I have ever seen between any two people (these indicate all of the things that each will defer to any demands of the other). This would be a fine relationship and might even work into a professional association. The problem was going to be whether the individual charts were right for the roles they wanted to play. It was also meant that such career concerns involved a move either to Los Angeles or New York.

This chart has Sagittarius rising with Jupiter in Aries toward the end of his fourth house. Here we are faced with Jupiter retrograde to be interpreted in the fifth house, creative with things or people abandoned by others. Right away we see that Saturn, also retrograde, will be interpreted in the sixth house which contains Uranus retrograde. Of course the Sun is at the top of the chart, is too close to Venus, and followed by the presence of Neptune which is very strong for being angular and not giving a clear look at reality. This man might combine optimism with attention to details, but reality is questionable. The Moon is in Cancer in the eighth house, indicative of discontent, with Chiron of overlooking the obvious, and then Pluto in Leo bringing big changes or sabotage to the area. Mars is in Capricorn in the Saturn ruled second house and is out of bounds. This chart is strong, replete with oppositions, squares, trine and sextile pairs to mitigate the oppositions, and a grand trine from Neptune to Mars to Uranus. Saturn is the focal point of a T-square between the Moon-Mars opposition.

In the late 1970s, transiting Saturn was going over the top of this chart. The passage of Saturn through the

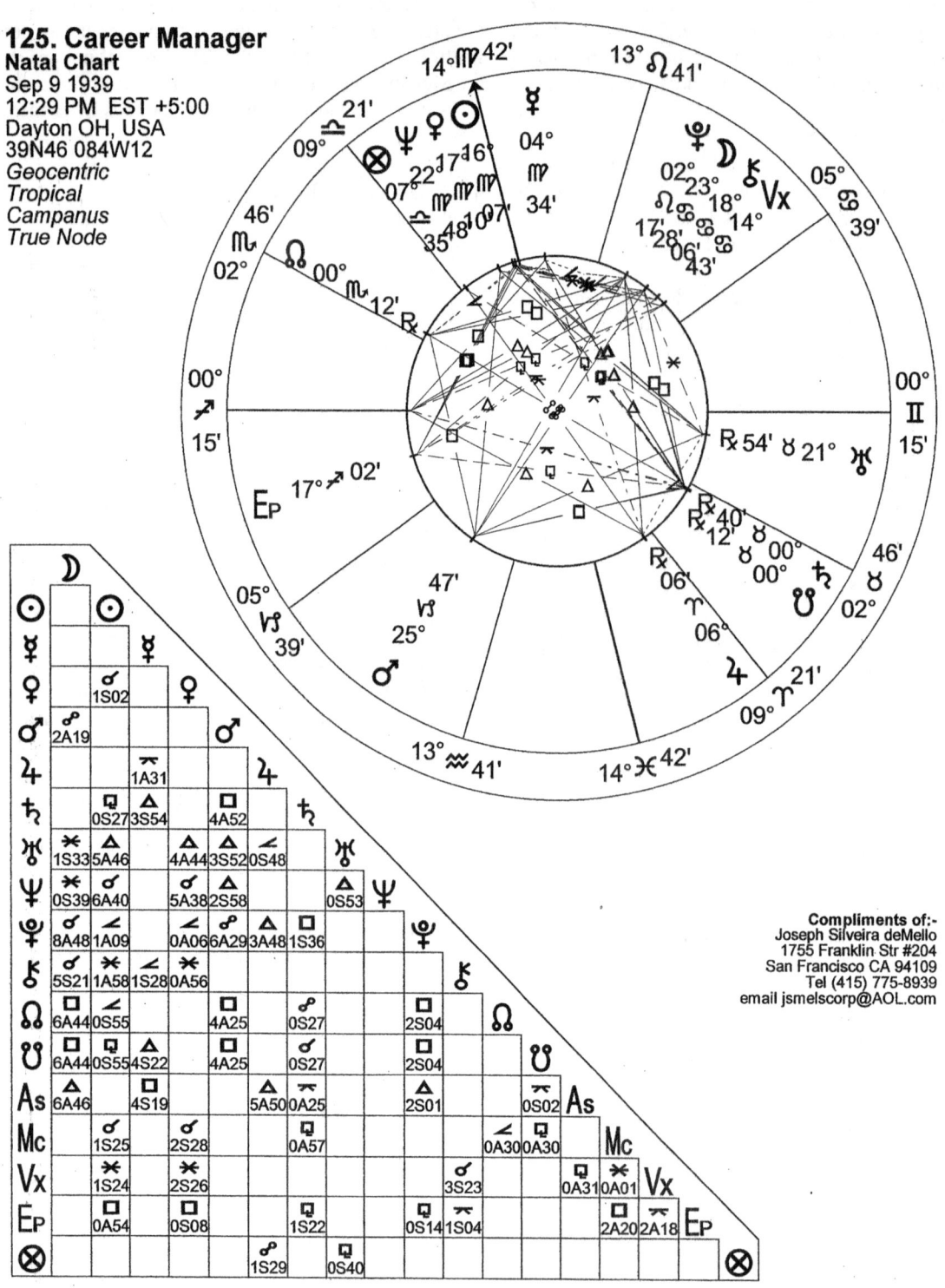

125. Career Manager
Natal Chart
Sep 9 1939
12:29 PM EST +5:00
Dayton OH, USA
39N46 084W12
Geocentric
Tropical
Campanus
True Node

ninth house was a time for study of the problems of career. I do not remember what this would be manager's business career was at that time, but it was in San Francisco and not connected to the entertainment world. Did he think he could make the upheaval into a career where he had no background and no connections.

How could he go to, say, Los Angeles and hang out his shingle as a manager-agent and be able to support himself in this new and untried field? It had to be established how aware this client might be of the pitfalls and whether he could roll with the exigencies he would meet breaking into a field from which monitory gain might be more slender than demanded of his second house Mars.

126. Singer-Dancer, 7-5-4
Venus: 0N44
Data: August 20, 1949, 9:28 a.m. EST,
Cincinnati, Ohio, 39N08, 84W30

This chart does not have Jupiter at zero, but it has Venus at zero declination. It is included here only as a tie in to the preceding chart. This young man embarking on a career as singer-dancer to be managed by his friend. He is ten years younger, but already thirty, rather late for an aspirant. Although he has cardinal angles, he has only three placements angular. Mars and Jupiter angular are fine, but a Neptune in the first house impinges on reality. The presence of Moon-Uranus on the Midheaven is of dubious help. Both had problem Neptunes, akin to the blind leading the blind.

First of all, it is not the astrologer's role to tell people they cannot have what they most wish for. But the astrologer has to look at ego, ambition, charisma and talent. Not to mention how these ambitions would fit into the real world. The era of the big musical and the style of entertainment has changed. This young man had a repertory of fine songs, but they were the ones of his early years, mostly romantic ballads. Singing and dancing disappeared long ago. I did not think the young man very disciplined. Nor did I feel they understood the need for coaches, trainers, arrangers, all the people who stand behind any entertainment career. Clearly these young men had to understand the pitfalls they would meet in pursuit of a career where the competition is extreme.

Both Mars and Jupiter are in fall, but a tenth house Mars is going to put energy into status. The Moon at the top of his chart in conjunction with Uranus increases or speaks of emotional tension and the presence of less conventional ways of doing things. Remember that the Moon mostly tends to ambivalence and lack of assurance. The Sun is in the eleventh in Leo besieged between Pluto and Saturn. The Sun progressed at age eleven into the twelfth house where it would spend thirty-five years behind the scenes, years of work but not of prominence or public notice. He would be forty-six before the progressed Sun would get into his first house. Even before he is off the ground into the career he wants, there are too many years of preparation before real achievement and public notice. At the time of this reading, he had just had a Saturn return, and Saturn was then transiting his twelfth house, not a location for new beginnings. There was no question I should thwart him in any way, nor would suggestions of any other career sit well with this man. I could only recommend that he get involved in the local musical scene and suggest that he was in a time of planning and working up to a career and make it understood that people do not usually break into a career from the top. I hardly hoped that he would take a gig with any local groups whether he stayed in this town or moved to Los Angeles. And perhaps I also had a real sense through the problems a nephew was having though better equipped than this man.

127. Porn Star, 5-6-5
Jupiter: 0N52
Data: September 11, 1939, 3:00 a.m. EST,
Circleville, Ohio, 39N35, 83W00

At about the same time that I did the two previous charts, I was talking to this man in a local bar, and there were two other astrologers present. He was quite happy to give to give us his data. He grew up in rural Ohio, the above city being the closest to his place of birth. He then made his home in Los Angeles, was in San Francisco only on a brief visit. He had hit Los Angeles years ago and been so intent on getting into the movies that he finally fell into the porn industry where he made a good living as a star in male porn films. What were his personal sexual preferences never came up. He was not dismayed to learn that none of us had ever seen him in films. One of the other astrologers present was the sort of astrologer who carries an ephemeris around in his head and with the aid of pen and cocktail napkins we got an idea of his chart even before I actually did the chart.

This man was almost forty, tall, thin, dark, with abundant hair, and very long sideburns, early swashbuckler style. He was glib, seemingly open, and fit Leo rising and Moon in Leo in the first house. I was put off by his name, an obviously contrived film alias. I let one of the other astrologers do most of the talking. Privately I thought about his aging and how long he could expect to remain a star, ready to suggest that he should be thinking of directing rather than continuing to act. He had no illusions of ever making it in the standard movie industry.

I was surprised to find Saturn at the top of his chart and Uranus in his tenth. Nor was I particularly happy to see the South Node on the Midheaven. With Leo rising, a natural good opinion of himself and a facility of matching his personality to whatever the demand of any situation. Mercury, Sun, Venus and Neptune, all in Virgo, are second house. It was of prime importance was to keep on making good money. Mars in Capricorn in his sixth is out of bounds applying to a square to Saturn, leads us to Venus as dispositor or the chart, and Venus as well as Neptune are too close to the Sun. I wondered into what career he would wander later on in life. The key might well be found in Jupiter retrograde in his tenth and trine the Ascendant.

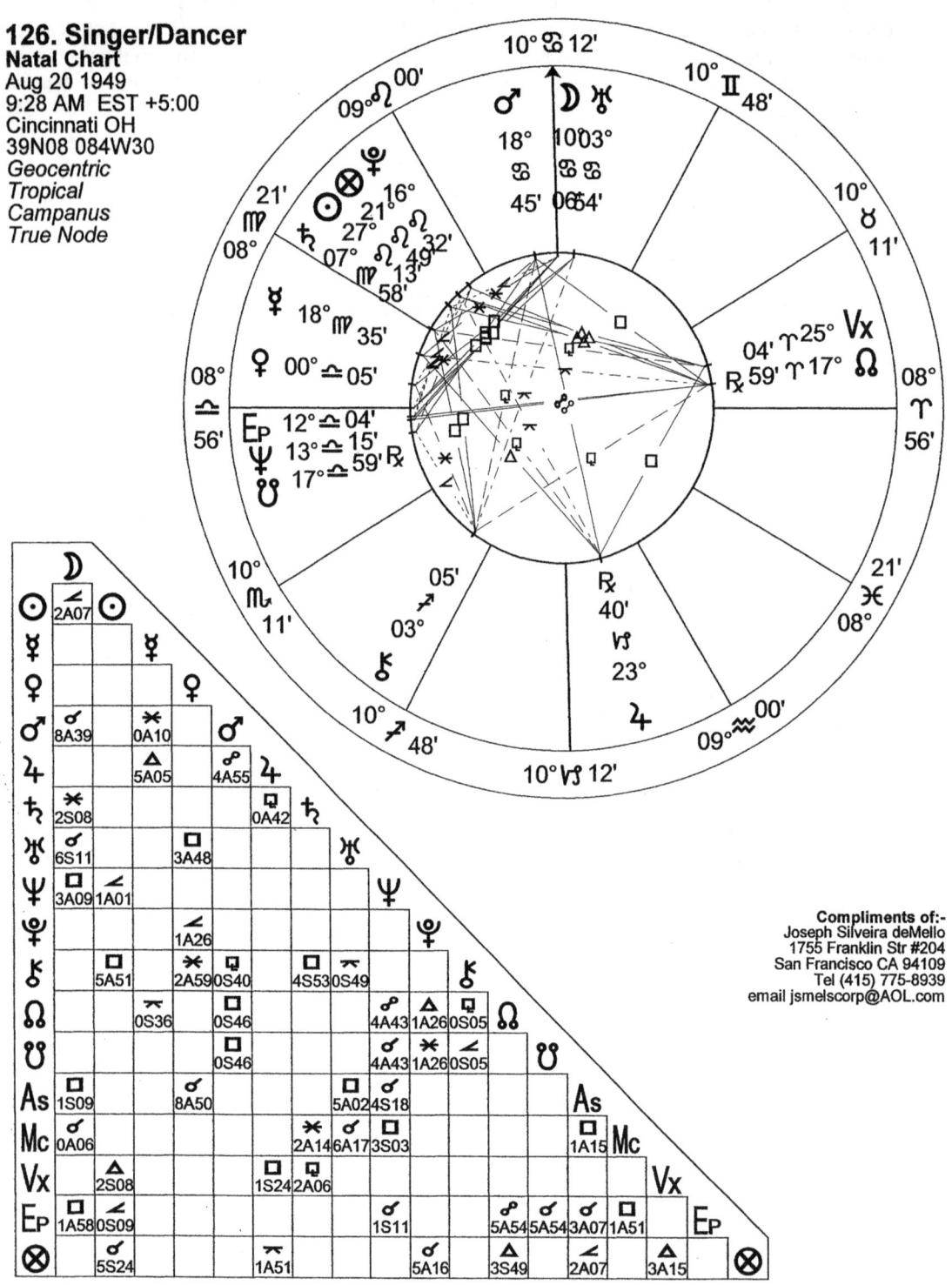

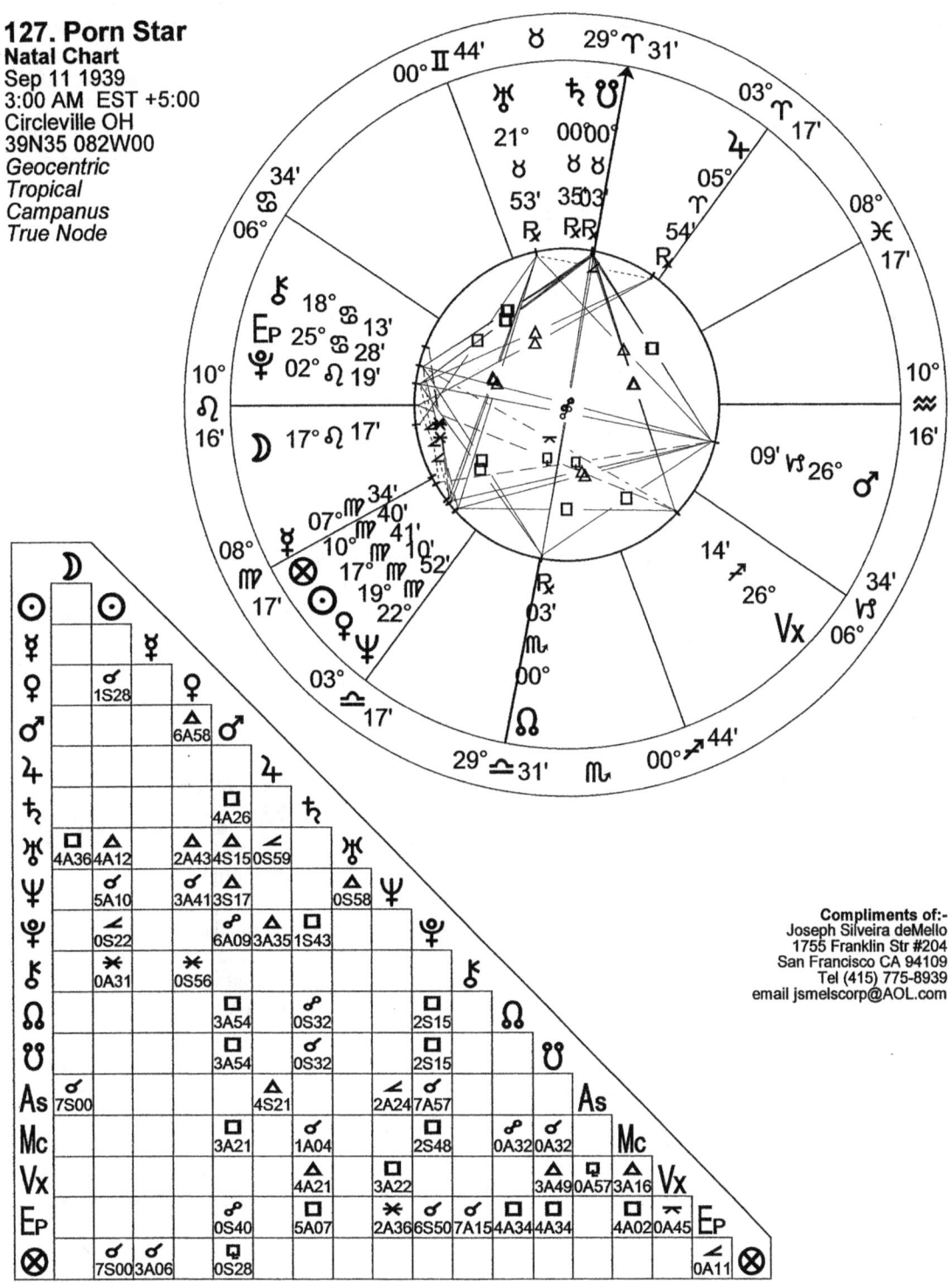

127. Porn Star
Natal Chart
Sep 11 1939
3:00 AM EST +5:00
Circleville OH
39N35 082W00
Geocentric
Tropical
Campanus
True Node

128. Legal Lady, 9-6-6
Jupiter: 0N44, Moon: 0S48
Data: September 13, 1939, 2:00 p.m. CST,
Mankato, Minnesota, 44N10, 94W00

This is the chart of a woman who was client of a psychic I have known for many years. She was a legal secretary on her way to being a paralegal but could not get along with co-workers. She had mastered the specialized vocabulary and was a crack typist, and with the advent of computers, she became one of the earliest home workers. Somehow, perhaps the ninth house stellium in Virgo, gave her the idea her fortune would be made if she sued someone to win a huge court settlement which would keep her the rest of her life in indolent comfort. As she went from job to job, each less important, less well suited, less gainful, she also (circa 1990) contacted muscular dystrophy. She allowed her disability status to make herself a dependent personality. She refuses all advice, even the most basic, as roads she could never consider taking. She is chronically unemployable. Any potential employer can spot her as arriving trouble. She has been trained as a medical transcriptionist and as a court reporter, both dead end jobs, and has never worked at either. A third try at special training involving a special computer program, she was constantly on the telephone to technical support complaining that the program did not work. She gave them such unremitting grief that they asked her to send it back to them and they would most happily grant her a total refund.

She has made a thorough study about her personal status as physically challenged. There is no way she will go back to her original career, for she does not want to work that hard. It would be very nice if she could be supported by others without turning a hand. Personally, she is the most inconsiderate, overbearing, demanding, selfish person who has ever graced the earth. It never strikes her that her rudeness is a very real reason why others are rude to her.

Several years ago, she moved into an apartment complex where she had heard that Jewish tenants were not wanted. Immediately on moving in, she announced she was Jewish to all her neighbors and proceeded to document offenses. Of course she opening herself to a life of misery without quite being able to catalogue the misery into a genuine legal action. As with other ill-conceived scams, her legal process was thrown out of court, and she did not even manage a negligible settlement. She simply had to move.

My original reading for her was rather plain-spoken. She did not protest it did not fit her, but she tried to get me to tone it down. Nor was I open to myriad telephone consultations where I had to drop everything to give her immediate answers. To this day she regards her psychic as a personal friend and calls several times daily, interrupting the psychic's other work and has yet to pay for the impromptu readings she demands.

In late 1998, she almost got what she wished for. She was in an automobile accident. A car on her left suddenly decided to make a right turn and drove into the side of her car. Her car was totaled, and the other driver told her she had no right being where she was. On the following day, she woke for find her face contorted and her mouth twisted out of shape. She went to the emergency room to be diagnosed with palsy due to trauma, and with a definite-maybe prognosis for improvement. Her next stop was at an attorney's office. However, her potential case suffered a setback when the palsy decided to disappear a few weeks later.

Note that she not only has zero Jupiter, but she also has zero Moon, with Mars pretty far out of bounds (which Mars does about once a year) and Pluto close to doing so. When she was first a client, she asked about romance. She was and is a rather large, squarely built, indeed, stocky lady, not especially attractive and taking no care of her appearance. I looked at her chart and noted that, although Mercury is ahead of her Sun and out of combust, Venus, Neptune and Moon are all combust the Sun. Weighing double Virgo against non-competitive Sagittarius rising, I told her I did not think she would ever find a man clean enough that she would not bore before they got to first base. Mars is intercepted in her first house and is square to its ruler Saturn in her fourth house. She is decidedly heterosexual but no longer asks questions about love and romance.

Despite the fact that she has so much Virgo, she refuses all dietary advice whether from her doctor or from her psychic. She really does have health problems, but she will not deprive herself of what she wants to eat when she wants it. Her sixth is ruled by combust Venus. Any suggestion that Venus and Neptune together might engender poetry and music has never been applicable here. On June 19, 2000, she was found dead sitting up against her bed. Cause was a heart attack and advanced arteriosclerosis.

129. Potential Suicide, 9-6-7
Jupiter: 0N39
Data: September 15, 1939, 12:32 p.m. EDT,
Freeport, New York, 40N39, 73W35

There was always much talk of death and suicide with this male client. There was also a great deal of paranoia. I met him through a longtime friend and client, and he would not reveal his surname though he did consult his birth certificate to give me his chart data. He was cagey about having his whereabouts revealed, as if police were after him or the Internal Revenue, and wanted to know if he should move to Mexico. Much later I was given more information about him. Child of Russian-Jewish emigree parents, he was doomed from infancy by being named for a ponderous but acclaimed Anglo-American author, and he had no literary bent. But there is the warning Saturn in the fifth house, hallmark of the child whose parents expect more of him than he wants to give them, and had he children, he would do the same to his own offspring.

He was vacationing in San Francisco when I met him. He did not know which way to turn. His passport was coming up for renewal, and he felt if he renewed it, authorities would apprehend him. In which case the only way out was to commit suicide. In doing this chart, I saw that he did not have Neptune in the twelfth house

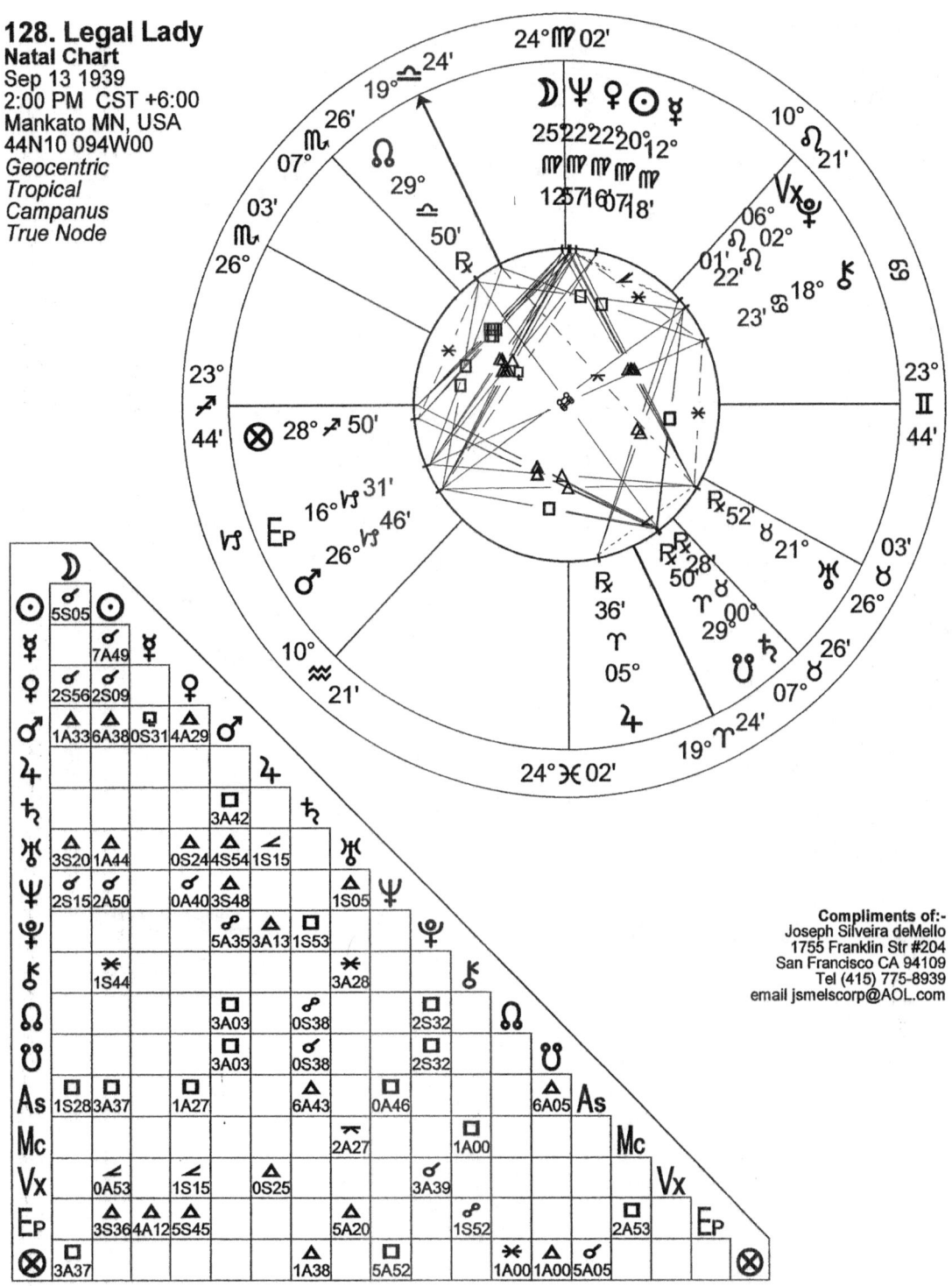

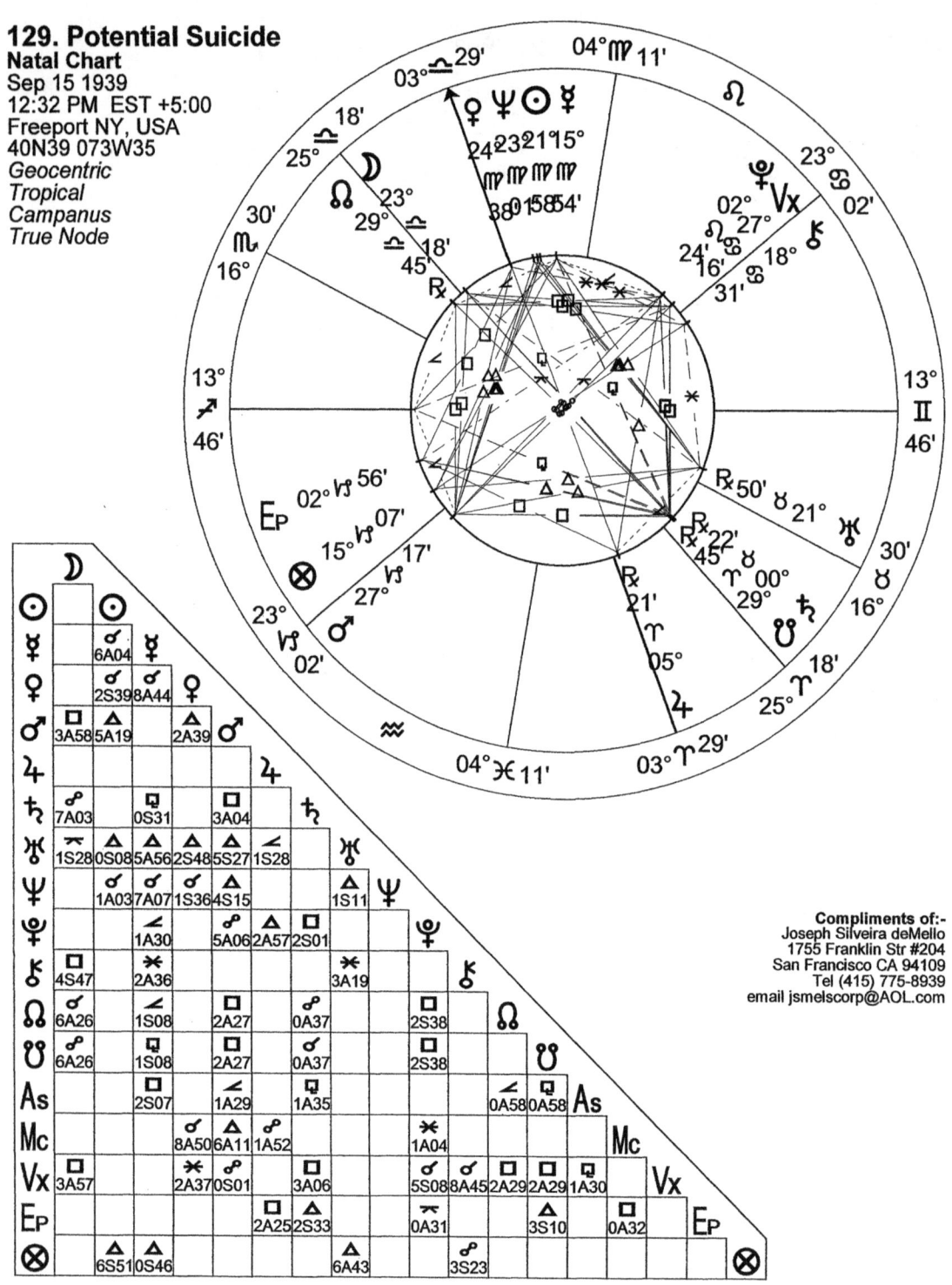

129. Potential Suicide
Natal Chart
Sep 15 1939
12:32 PM EST +5:00
Freeport NY, USA
40N39 073W35
Geocentric
Tropical
Campanus
True Node

Compliments of:-
Joseph Silveira deMello
1755 Franklin Str #204
San Francisco CA 94109
Tel (415) 775-8939
email jsmelscorp@AOL.com

(people with this position of Neptune do not always kill themselves, but they do seriously think about it). I checked his Arabic Parts of Death and Suicide. Death fell on the cusp of his ninth house, and the Part of Suicide at 29 Scorpio just above his Sagittarius Ascendant. I looked at his ninth house collection of placements and decided that suicide was the sort of play acting that Virgos do when they want to dramatize themselves.

Mars is still out of bounds with Pluto nearly so. Although he had a very good, active and successful 1976 and busily went into 1977, his chart became somewhat less active after the spring of 1978, and, of course, it did not sit with very well with him to be told that he would have to wait a few months to regain the swing of life. If he wanted to lie low, this was a good time for it, but with Saturn transiting his ninth, he really should be studying something seriously with regard to his future career. I hoped he knew better than to run drugs across the border, and he allowed he did know better, and I felt that if he were to renew his passport, he might as well quietly do so from a San Francisco address. He seemed to be well-heeled financially, but his grasp of reality really bothered me. Notice the likeness of this chart to #121 Singer Dancer. He has the same angles and house cusps and the same arrangement of Jupiter-Saturn-Uranus in the second quadrant of his chart.

130. Hawaiian Male, 6-6-8
Jupiter: 0N33
Data: September 17, 1939, 5:37 a.m. HST,
Honolulu, Hawaii, 21N18, 157W50

This chart is of a Hawaiian-born man who was vacationing in San Francisco and intended to go on to Los Angeles. Chart data is from his birth certificate. Two days after the previous example, the chart orientation is different, although he was also lost and on a quest with notions of living on the mainland. The Virgo stellium now shows up on the Ascendant. Sun is too close to Venus, but Neptune takes over on both, although his Venus did improve his physical appearance. He was attractive, outgoing, personable, charming and would always have a weight problem common to his heritage. Two things bothered him. He had never had a job which was of real interest to him, and his "love life" was a disaster area. He was homosexual.

When an astrologer looks at any chart, the difficulties loom rather large, but the eternal question is how to help this man to improve his life with the chart he has. Virgo pays attention to detail, needs a project to run and some command of people to assist so that he does not get bogged down in the details. Aquarius on the sixth would indicate that the job should not be humdrum or, rather, should be a very today sort of job, such as with computers. Gemini at the top of the chart indicates communications, but the third house Scorpio Moon wants to think deeper, do some sort of research work. But I had to consider that he was already close to forty, perhaps too late for any career involving more training, but approaching mid-life crisis, a time of Saturn opposite natal Saturn and Uranus square natal Uranus.

While the Sun in the first house allows people to suit their personality to the needs of any moment and often indicates success at sales, in this chart such an idea is doomed by the Moon on the edge of the third house, for the Moon cannot make up its mind on what it wants from business or communications. But, the Gemini Midheaven can spin off into lots of socializing, even though he has Mars in the fifth of speculations as a creative area, creative personality and creativity in the twelfth behind the scenes. At the time I knew him, Saturn was into a transit of his second house, and if he was going to make a serious residential change, I felt sure he would make his most serious residential change when Saturn transited his IC or shortly thereafter.

Regarding his love live, he has Jupiter in the seventh in Aries, a precipitous sign, but Jupiter still means many people close around him, and Jupiter retrograde is the person who does well with people discarded by other people. But by his count, he had never found anyone to interest him or stay with him long. I had to remember that earth signs are difficult to please. Taureans are money minded, Virgos are hygienically minded and Capricorns wish to control. All three signs are wary of anyone who initiates friendship. They are unready to deal with overtures and suspicious of them. But when it is their own idea, they can be quite overwhelming. When someone tells of homosexual interests, I am not going to talk in terms of women partners. Even the Moon opposite Uranus would not permit that. It seemed to me that what he wanted from others was of a Martian sort, someone both forceful and creative, dominant in fact, perhaps even a father image. And with Saturn in the eighth house, and himself close to forty, he might find what he wanted of others later in life, which would probably be true of his creativity.

His trip to San Francisco and Los Angeles was not merely a vacation. He wanted to check what these cities might have for him. I questioned him closely about how he would adapt to our climate versus the Hawaiian climate, and what sort of prejudice he might encounter there less acceptable than his life in Hawaii. It was impossible to discus creativity with him. He did not expect to be creative on a job. I pointed out the nature of creativity as I saw it and the problem was Neptune in his personality area not assisting reality in his ideas about himself. Mars in the fifth house I regarded as indicative of sex life, recreation and other speculations. Virgo made him super-critical and Pisces expected those close to him to be total ideals. It is not that he would have to settle for second best or that his intimates were the cast-offs of others (Jupiter retrograde seventh) with which he would always have success. The problem is that he himself was no god, so he should not expect others to be gods.

Mars is opposite Pluto in the eleventh, and both make a T-square focusing on Saturn. The nodal axis and Saturn are part of a fixed square. I despaired he could be keyed to changes in any of his basic attitudes. Only the Moon opposite Uranus is mitigated by a kite formation to Chiron, but I did not find that reassuring. Almost any

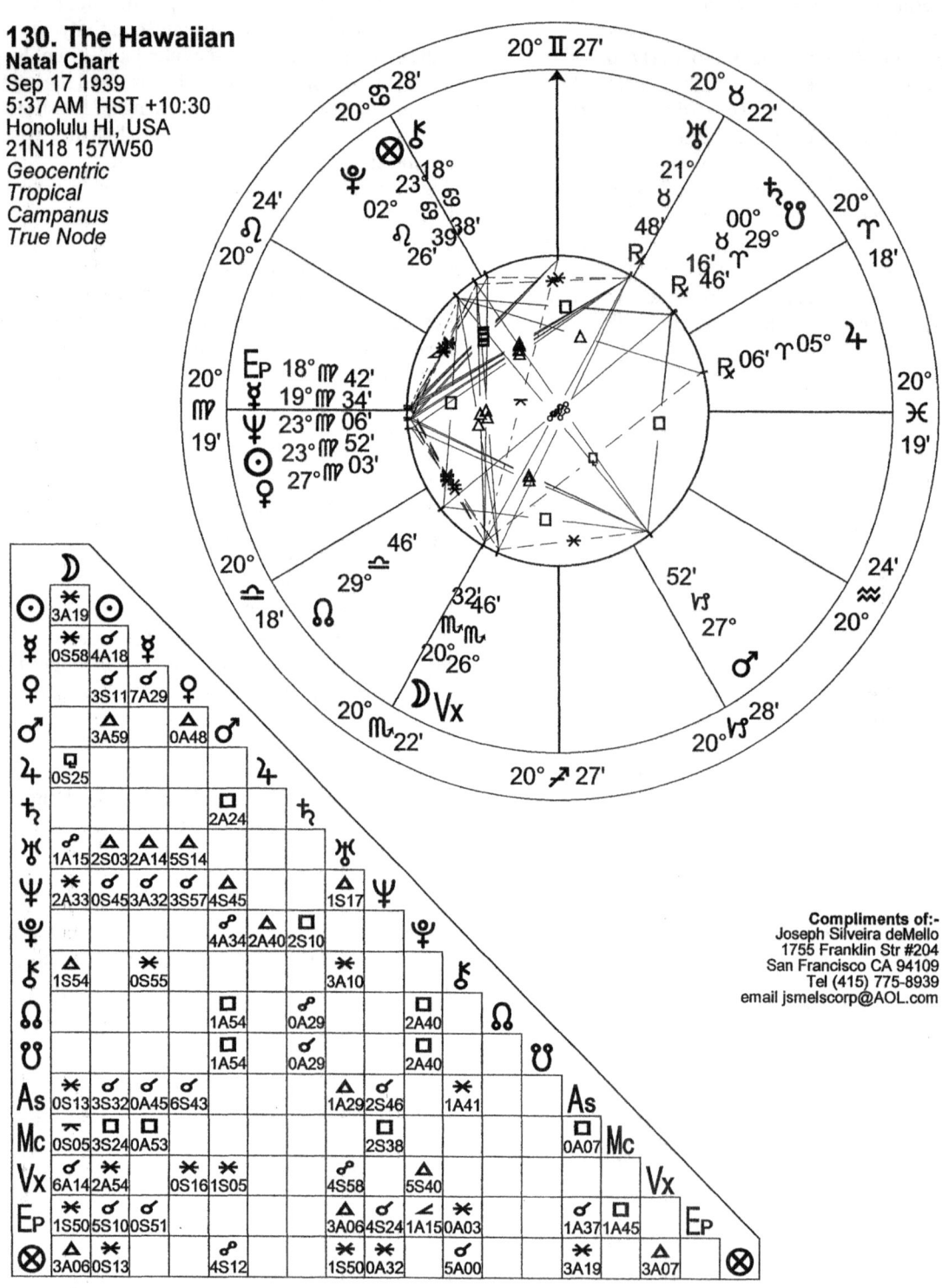

130. The Hawaiian
Natal Chart
Sep 17 1939
5:37 AM HST +10:30
Honolulu HI, USA
21N18 157W50
Geocentric
Tropical
Campanus
True Node

suggestion I could make would be greeted as impossible and untenable. Everything in the chart is disposed of by Mercury and for once I wished this man had been born with Mercury retrograde, with some capacity for objective and abstract thinking. I struggled mightily giving him as good a reading as I could. But I do not feel much was achieved and had little hope he would keep in touch. If you criticize a Virgo, you never hear from them again.

131. Hip Replacement, 12-7-4
Jupiter: 0N28
Data: October 8, 1939, 4:01 p.m. EST,
Rye, New York, 40N59, 73W41

This man worked as a chef at a neighborhood restaurant. He was of middle height, quiet, and rather private sort of person. Although well regarded and well-liked by his coworkers, he did not socialize much with them. He was having deteriorating hip problems when I first met him, and I was amazed how he could function so well in a busy kitchen and do so on aluminum crutches. The hip replacements were done six months apart at the end of 1975 and again in May 1976. But for hospital stays around the times of the operations and short convalescences, he returned to work as early as possible. Just as soon as he was mended from the second operation, the restaurant went belly-up, and he and a friend opened a delicatessen business in another part of town which they still operate rather successfully.

I caught as a fragment of overheard conversation that he was in a "committed homosexual relationship." Notice that his Mars is intercepted in Aquarius in his twelfth house. It is past an opposition to Pluto which is intercepted in his sixth house. His personal privacy may also be remarked by Sun, Mercury and Venus in Libra intercepted, and Jupiter and Saturn intercepted. People with these interceptions have little problem living with them, but they make the things of those planets unreachable to other people and much more of a problem to others who are denied interference. He is Pisces rising with Sun in Libra and the Moon in Cancer. Thus the Moon hangs alone, with all else in the chart disposed of by Venus. He was a good chef and enjoyed his work never complained when he was rushed. He was not much dismayed when his job ended. It simply provided the time for moving on into establishing his own place of business.

132. Lesbian Lady, 11-7-6
Jupiter: 0S3
Data: October 9, 1939, 3:00 p.m. PST,
San Francisco, California, 37N47, 122W26

This is the chart of a lesbian, known as such only because she told me so herself, and data is from her birth certificate. Notice its similarities to the previous chart. Her chart has interesting aspect patterns to either side of the nodal axis with Saturn on the South Node. On the left side of the chart, she has Jupiter trine mid-heaven with Mars in the twelfth making a sextile to both but not exactly on midpoint. Midheaven and Jupiter are part of a fire grand trine to Pluto. We primarily see Aquarius rising with an Aquarius Mars in the twelfth house, Sun in Libra and an intercepted Moon in Virgo where we also find Neptune.

She was a creative woman in business as a graphics designer, and with Sagittarius at the top of her chart, might eventually lead to being a consultant. I could only wish that her Mars was elsewhere than in the twelfth of behind the scenes energies. At the time I knew her, much of her work was done on computer and personal publishing was the coming thing. Sun in eighth attests to interest in gain from others. She confessed to poor luck with male friends while she knew herself popular with and gaining gifts from female friends, but she also accepted that she changed her mind a lot about the people she wished close around her. She was a very attractive career woman.

133. Businesswoman, 7-7-8
Jupiter: 0S51
Data: October 14, 1939, 7:00 a.m. PST,
Oakland, California, 37N48, 122W16

I was amused that this serious businesswoman had a show-girl name. She and another woman owned a diet center, and she wished me to do a comparison survey of their charts. She was, however, planning to sell out her interest in the diet center in order to go into business as a real estate financing consultant. She had recently ended a romance of some long standing, and she and the man involved were suing each other to come to a settlement of mutual properties. Like most of my real clients she did not ask about the status of her romantic affairs but rather wanted to know more about career and business matters, when to close one and open another. She took care of her own romances and although things were not settled yet with her former partner, she had already moved in with another man. She did not ask me to do his chart and, in fact, had no birth data for her past or present men.

Remembering Richard Nixon, we see again Pluto at the top of the chart, and here it has Mars leaving an opposite in the fourth house (and home and security were her serious goals), and both of these are square to the East Point and Mercury. Another interesting thing is late Libra rising, and she did indeed have Scorpio qualities underlined by Moon in Scorpio. The Sun is in Libra in the twelfth, and while not egotistical, she certainly took a back seat to no one. Her first house is excessively tenanted with North Node, Venus, Mercury and Moon, not to forget Fortune also there. The final part of the personality equation is Mars in the fourth house in Aquarius, and financial planning for the future was very important to her. To assuage the Pluto Midheaven, she always kept meticulous records and competent legal counsel. With this chart, I would say she relied on herself and her abilities to get ahead with her life. My files reveal that she was involved in an accident where she cut her left heel on August 2, 1986, and that she opened her new business on January 7, 1987.

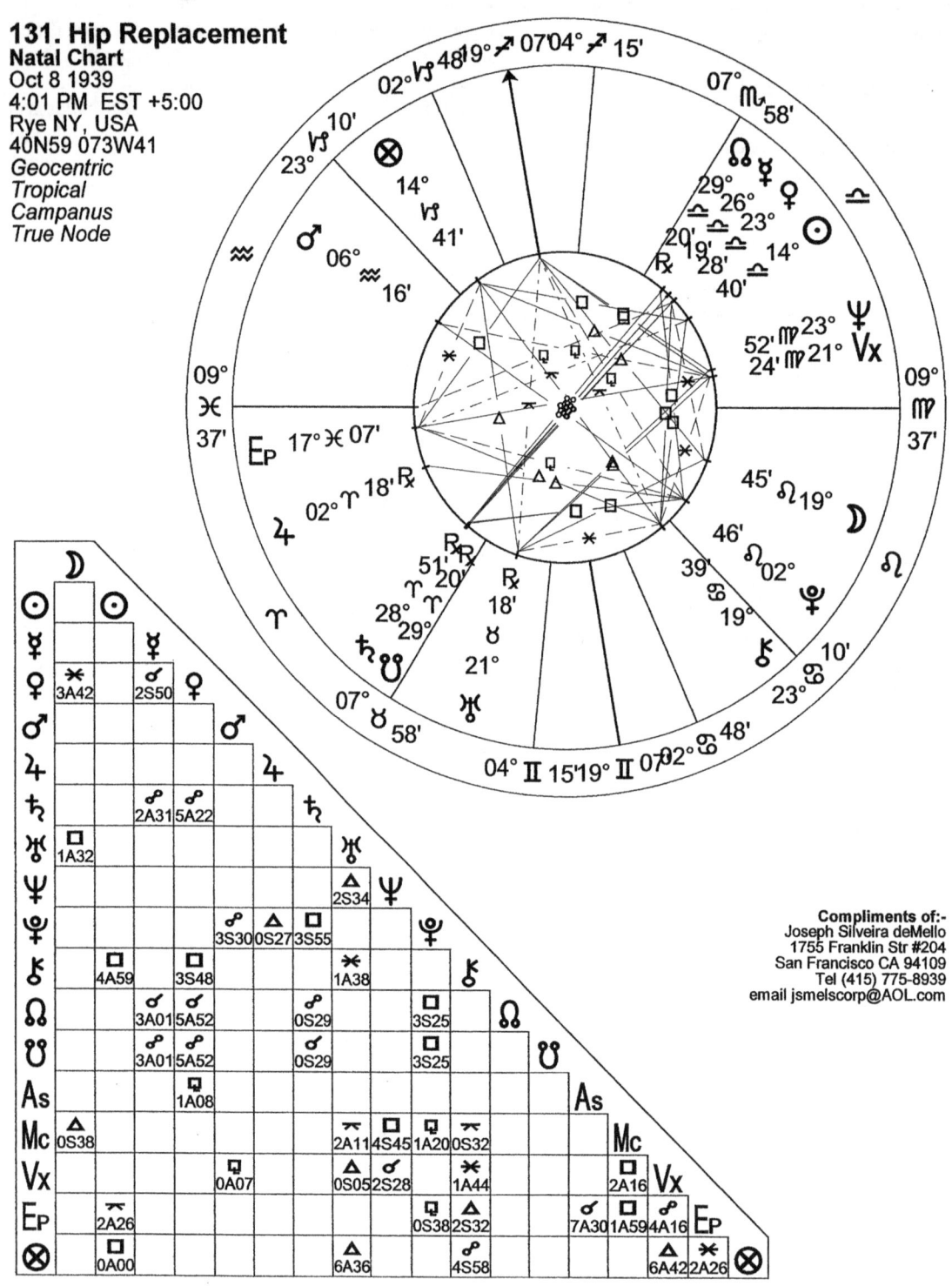

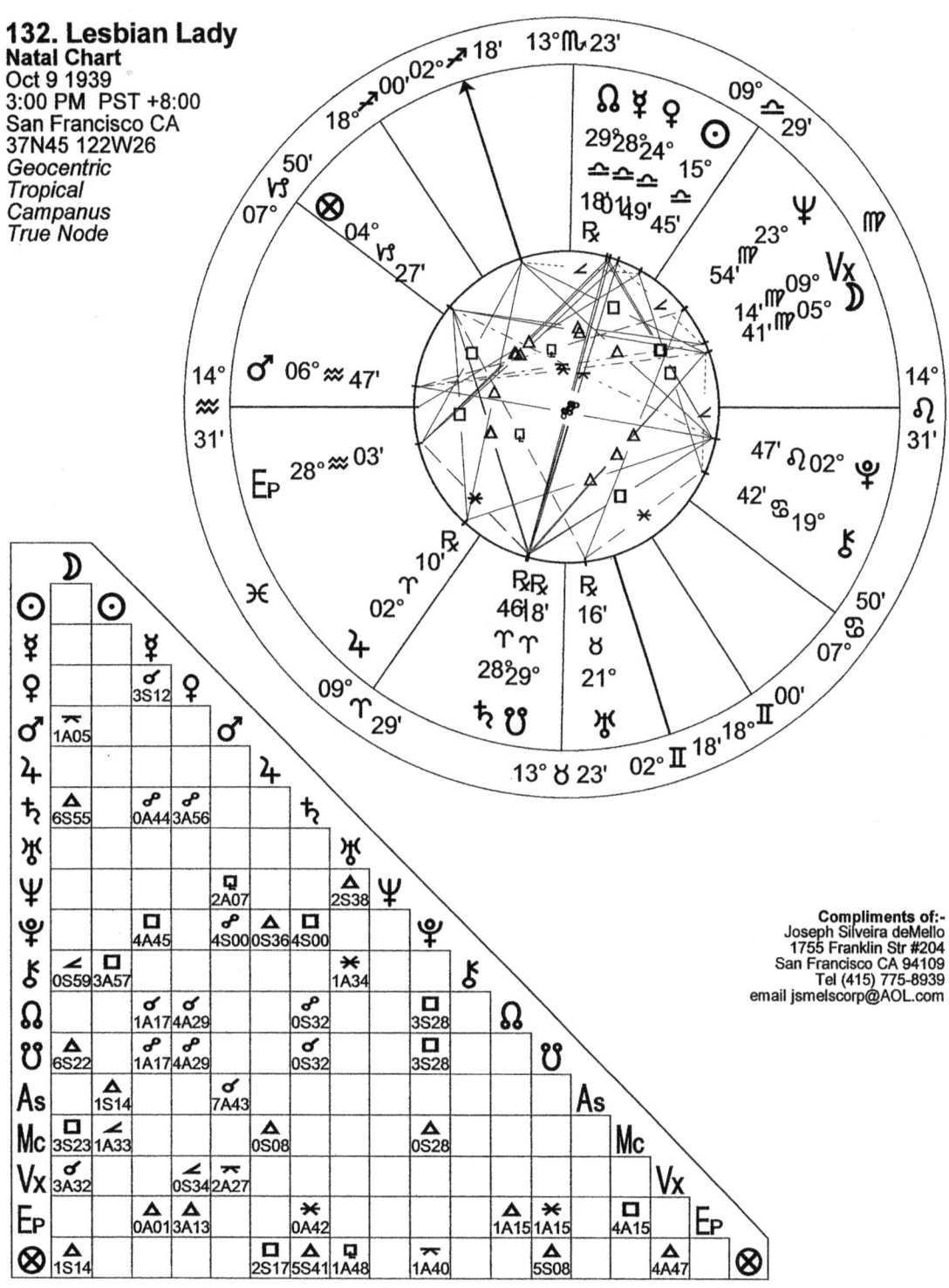

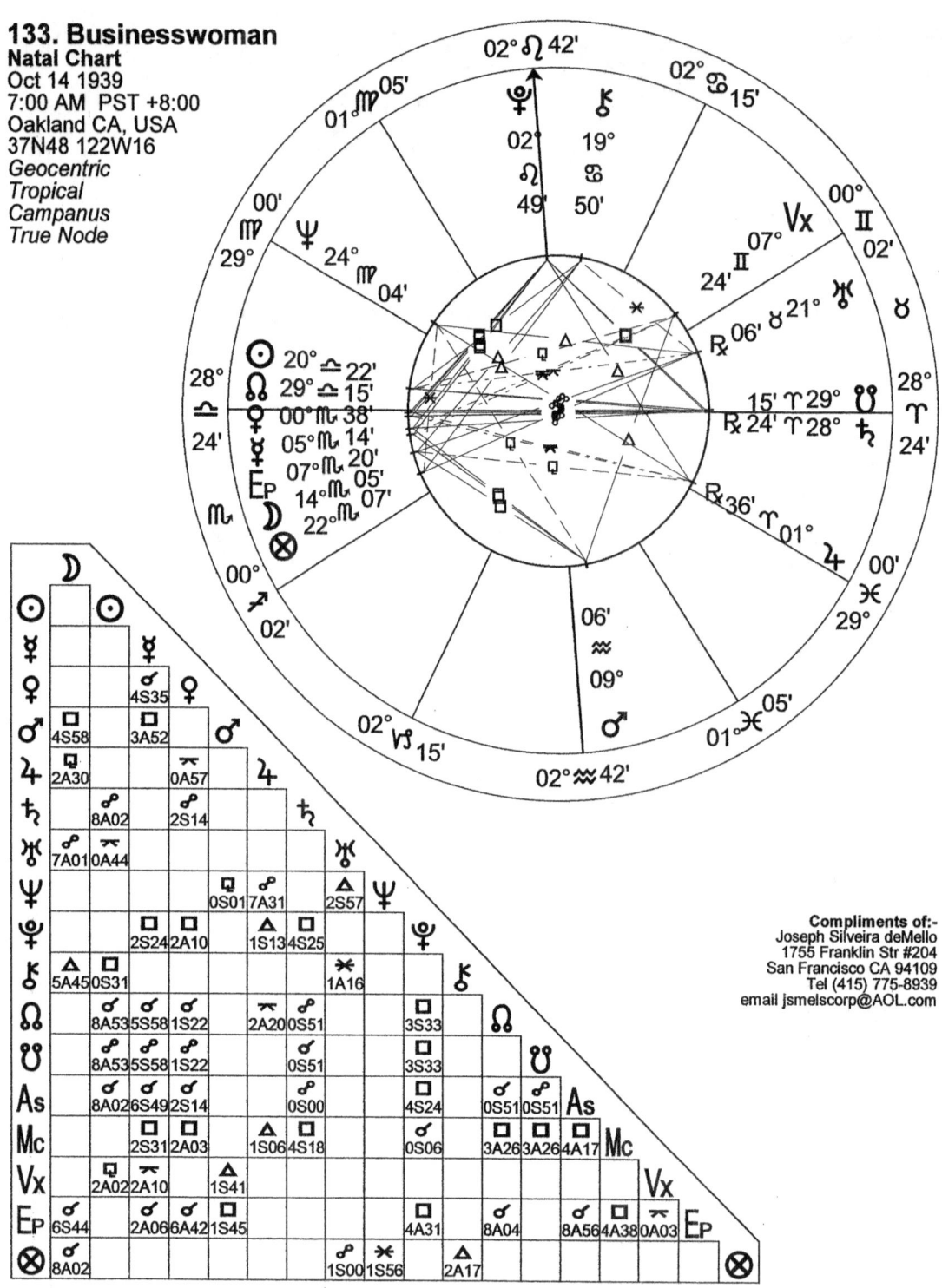

134. Unknown Lady, 11-7-9
Jupiter: 0S54
Data: October 15, 1939, 2:00 p.m. PST,
Maywood, California, 33N59, 118W11

This is the chart of a prospective client who did not keep her appointment and did not reschedule. She was a small, rosy-cheeked lady, who was sitting next to me at a bar and sailed into immediate serious conversation. She talked and talked. Almost as if she were a maniac depressive, and, of course, she was in psychotherapy. One supposes that since she knew all the answers (as an Aquarius rising), she probably decided that she really had no need of outside sources. But it is so typical of Mars on the Ascendant to be all gung ho initially and then make real efforts to disappear. All she really wanted to know about was her situation with a particular man for whom she had no data whatsoever, and I later discovered she hardly knew the man and that he had no idea of her interest in him.

135. Lee Harvey Oswald, 4-7-10
Beyond orb Jupiter: 1S03
Data: October 18, 1939, 9:55 p.m.,
New Orleans, Louisiana, 29N57, 90W04

In the course of choosing sample zero Jupiter declination charts, I ran into this chart and noted that it was three minutes out of orb with zero position Jupiter. I could not resist presenting it here, even though much has already been written about this chart. The data comes from his mother, given originally to astrologer T. Pat Davis. Perhaps at a distance of thirty-five years, making this ancient history, this Cancer rising, Libra Sun and Moon in Capricorn will be new to some readers.

None of the positive ways we may speak of Cancer rising seem to apply here. If he was a caring person, it was strangely expressed, but no more strangely than Cancer's nature of giving 100 percent of what is not really wanted. As for keeping his family together, he was having a bad time of it close to the end. He was living in a rented room far from his wife and family staying with a sympathetic Quaker lady in the suburb of Irving. The job he had paid no more than a minimum wage for unskilled labor. Cancer will not let go and will not be shaken off. And then his whole history is banked by resentments over the fact that no one was particularly sympathetic to him. With this we have the Libra Sun on the edge of the fifth house with the ruler of the house (Venus in Scorpio) therein. And of course the Scorpio planets are intercepted as is Uranus in Taurus. Libra is a need of everything nice and pleasant, but here we might expect creativity where we obviously got speculation. His other creative house is the second ruled by Leo and there we find Pluto on the cusp of it. Now add to this the Capricorn Moon, famous for attracting opposition and wanting to come off as being in charge, and we see it unhappily in the seventh as surely an unsteadiness toward those closest to him. We can say his personality and his emotions are in conflict, or his sense of being in charge is at variance with the personality. Above it in the eighth house we see Mars in Aquarius ruled by Saturn and in mutual reception, an avidity for gains from others, and his whole history says he got shorted.

We see in this chart an abundance of squares and oppositions. But nowhere is there a complete square or grand trines. In fact the only T-squares involve Sun opposite Saturn with Pluto at the focus, and Jupiter opposite Neptune which focuses on the East Point. If nothing else, this latter T-square might say he was indeed the assassin. But the main point is what aspects are lacking. Everything has one or two aspects, and there are areas of total lack of connection. These sextiles do not connect to trines. There are no kite formations to aid the oppositions. Mars squares Mercury and Venus and is semi-square the Midheaven, but that is it for Mars. Jupiter opposes Neptune but trines Pluto. Too often what is not there is as significant as what we do find. Jupiter gloriously at the top of his chart is retrograde and not in the sign on the Midheaven, but in Aries, and the Midheaven tells us he was sensitive, perhaps. Anyone would be sensitive if whenever he sat down to play he was consistently dealt a hand of poor cards.

And then think of the era in which he grew up. The big war was his infancy. He missed Korea and did not live long enough for Vietnam. He grew up in the South between New Orleans and Dallas, and with Uranus in the eleventh, though intercepted, he could have found community in military service but seems also to have found outre non-conservative friends. Surely civil rights legislation and its changes hardly impacted many people among whom he lived for it is difficult to legislate old prejudices which mostly remained intact in so many people. Think of a strange climate: school children of tender age applauded the death of JFK.

To many of us all over the country, the assassination of John F Kennedy was such a historical landmark that I seldom meet anyone of my age who does not remember precisely what he was doing in those fateful days. Fifteen minutes before the shooting of Kennedy, I was among the bystanders as his motorcade drove toward downtown Dallas, and I took a snapshot which surprised me by coming out pretty well. We returned to our office where everyone told slanging and slaying anecdotes about the Kennedys, the Johnsons and the Connallys. The situation was entirely sacrilegious. Our office sound system turned into a local radio station was drowned out when the first announcement came and I interrupted their joking by relaying the message. I was not believed, but sure enough a second announcement followed and was heard. Everyone's attitude changed, and blame was assigned to Communist Cuba. Transistor radios, a big fad then suddenly were brought out. I went down to my car where I tried one radio station after another. A wanted description of Oswald as suspect was aired about twenty minutes after the first shooting newscast. Not much work got done that afternoon in our office as we sorted conflicting reports.

Sunday morning, November 24, 1963, I saw on television the shooting of Oswald as he emerged from Dallas City Hall jail, saw on his face absolute recognition as

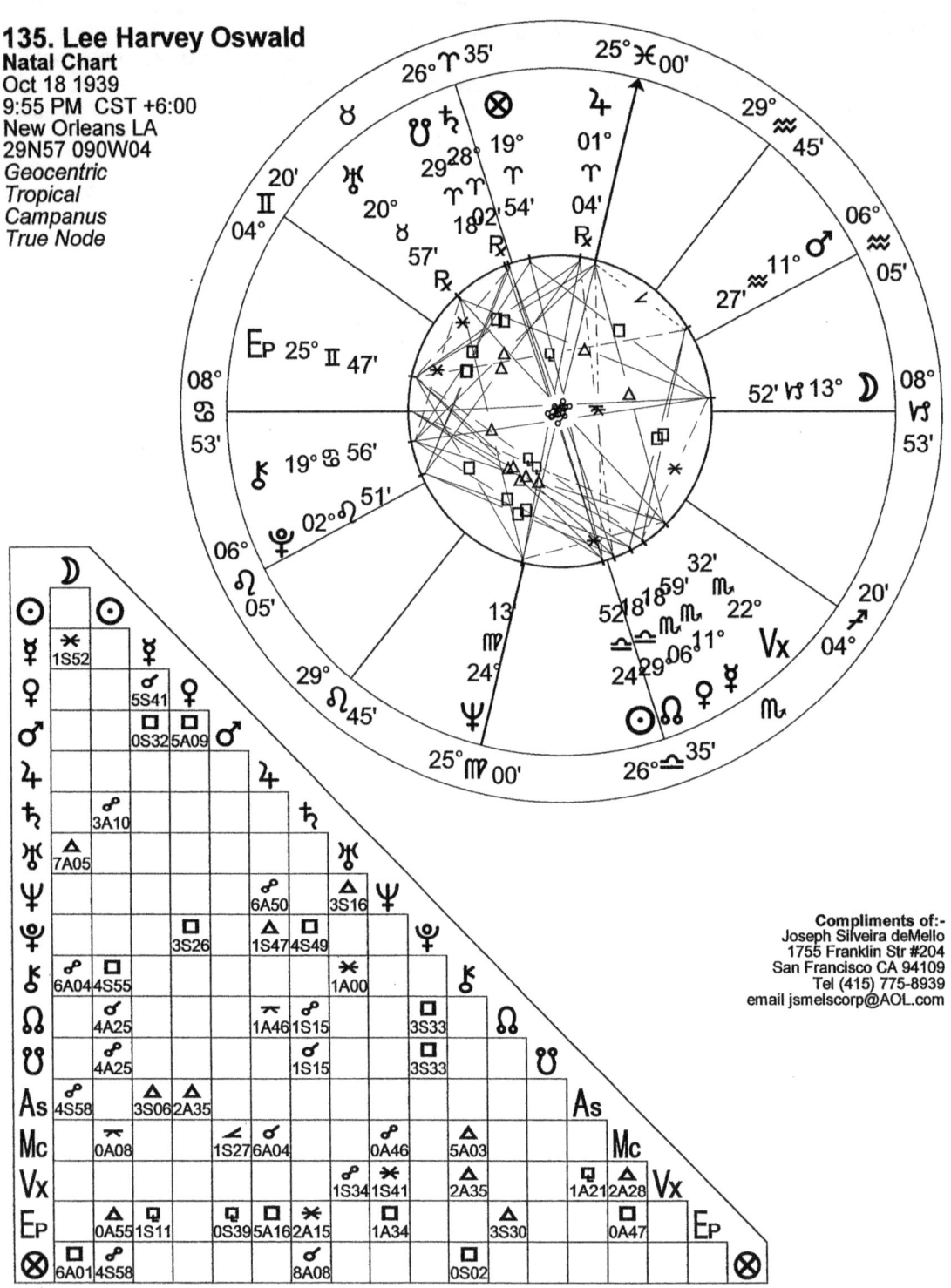

Jack Ruby walked right up to him. All of this was televised live. Every policeman mugging for the cameras. But only the first two showings of this film contained those frames of blatant initial recognition. Every subsequent showing of this scene deleted the recognition frames.

It is hard to believe there was no basis for conspiracy theories. Oswald was shot at 11:21 a.m. CST, November 24, 1963, Dallas, Texas, and was declared dead at Parkland Hospital at 1:07 p.m. CST, quite close to where Kennedy had been declared dead, at 1:00 p.m. CST two days previously. Such are the facts (given in EST) recorded in Manchester's *Death of a President*.

The history of Oswald who had certainly shot the police officer in the movie theater came out in full blown stories. The product of a broken home, and an environment where he was pretty much left to his own devices as his mother went out to work. He got through only enough school to join the Marines where he did get a badge for sharpshooting. But he was dishonorably discharged and had a beef with Governor John Connolly who had been Secretary of the Navy. Some claimed that Connally was his actual target. He conceived of the brilliant idea of defecting to Russia who found he had little to give them and shunted him to a job in Minsk he met and married his wife and had a daughter. He is quoting as wishing he had a son who might someday be president. Even in those days there was no idea that a girl child could get to be president, but he also did not seem to know that a president had to be born in the United States.

Evidently no notice was taken that Oswald was working in a building alongside the Kennedy motorcade route. Although Kennedy had been warned by astrologers and others to not go to Dallas, he said it was a risk that came with his job and went anyway.

The months that followed the Kennedy assassination made it difficult to live in Dallas. The police who badly handled the Oswald transfer went into overdrive. All men driving anywhere alone were stopped and subjected to a complete car and personal search.

Cars containing females were not stopped. Even the Chief Engineer of the Ford Motor Company plant was stopped and searched as he headed to work at 4:30 a.m., much to the delight of his employees who used the same route to get to work. In the following weeks, strange people appeared all over town, mostly in bars. All of them were men just passing through, picking up a friend with whom they would travel on to a job in some other city. I have never met so many people using the same cover scenario. If I went out to walk my dog I was fine, but if I went to the corner mailbox alone, I was stopped by police. Conspiracy theories flourished and could hardly be easily discounted since many had a basis in fact. It is indeed strange that a disproportionate number of witnesses who testified for the Warren Commission subsequently died under strange circumstances in the three years following their testimony. On the other hand, District Attorney Jim Morrison of New Orleans, striving for publicity, never quite realized that any motorcade going down Main Street in Dallas had to dog leg to access the ramp to the Harry Hines Freeway, for jersey walls prevented access to the highway ramp if the motorcade had kept to Main Street under the viaduct.

There are people still alive who will testify that the Kennedy frontal head wound was an entry wound, the bullet exiting the back of his head with a much larger wound, so that the bullet would have had to come from the top of the grassy knoll ahead of the motorcade. Oswald shot from above and behind. Then there was the report that Oswald was with Ruby at Ruby's downtown second floor topless night club usually more frequented by commercial travelers than by locals. The rifle Oswald "used" was tested and no expert could fire it as rapidly as Oswald had fired three shots from a supposedly inferior piece of equipment.

Oswald was twenty-four when he died. With Saturn retrograde, he had a Saturn return in infancy but had Saturn had not yet made a complete circuit of his chart.

136. The Mathematician, 6-7-10
Beyond orb Jupiter: 1S03
Data: October 19, 1939, 3:45 a.m. EST,
Rochester, New York, 43N15, 77W35

As long as we saw the previous chart, I cannot leave out another beyond the orb of one degree of Jupiter delineation, a man born almost six hours later than Oswald. This man is a huge contrast. Now we see Virgo rising, Sun in Libra and the Moon in Capricorn. If the Moon in Capricorn is the property of so many people who meet with much opposition, it has not proven that way in this man's life. By contrast, this man was brought up in an excellent home, educated at the best schools, and has a chart which shows attentiveness to detail, a balanced ego and a desire to be in charge. He is very tall, married to a most successful and stylish lady who has always been in great demand throughout the Middle East as a classical belly dancer. He is a bit unhappy about his wife's international fame, despite the high fees she commands and a nice collection of Cartier's pieces with which she has been tipped. At this writing he teaches mathematics in the United Arab Emirates where he as his family and two daughters reside.

The Sun here is in the second house, and Moon is on the cusp of the fifth. We see Neptune is with the Ascendant. There is something a bit unreal in his tidy manners, but one wonders if Neptune can equate with chauvinism. His chart has no interception, and Mars is in his fifth house. He is entirely devoted to wife and family. And with Jupiter in the seventh and retrograde has not picked up close associates discarded by others. Virgo rising must blend with Mercury in Scorpio and is not a wide open personality. As a teacher of mathematics, he does not have his nodal axis from third to ninth or vice versa. His sixth house cusp is Aquarius which does not indicate teaching, and his Gemini Midheaven might say business and communication and a vacant third ruled by Scorpio. With his earth grand trine and tendency toward detail and critical acumen, he is seen to be very meticulously attentive, intellectually clear-headed. He has a good opinion of himself and the Libra Sun falls on a critical degree. Mars in Aquarius is in his house of specula-

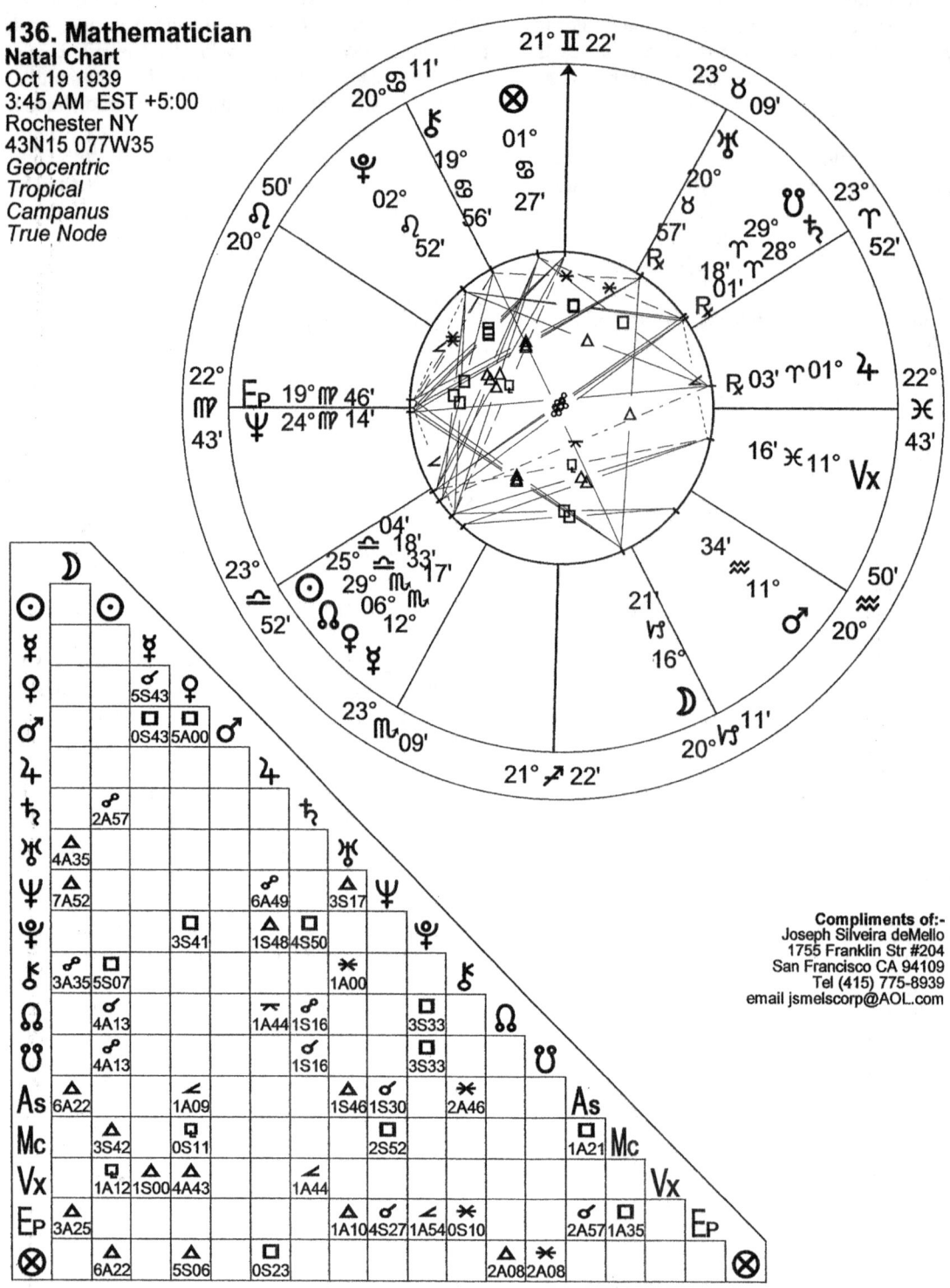

tive affairs is still square Venus and in mutual reception to Saturn. Mars is square Mercury and Venus, and once again note here what is seen as well as what is missing. It is easy to say this chart is more favorable than the Oswald chart, but we should rather say that this chart has its own issues which just happen to be very different than those in the Oswald chart. This may be simply seen that both charts are nocturnal charts, Jupiter rules Oswald's sixth and tenth, but in this chart Jupiter rules the fourth and seventh houses.

137. Psychic Healer, 6-10-9
Jupiter: 0S24, Mars: 0N40, both in northern Aries, but Jupiter S declination
Data: January 6, 1940, 9:00 p.m. PST,
Oregon City, Oregon, 45N21, 122W37

As with the former example, this chart is nocturnal, has similar angles, Virgo rising, and Jupiter rules the fourth and seventh. This is a chart of a man who, when I first knew him in 1976, had been a student at the Berkeley Psychic Institute for two years. He believed he had psychic sensitivities and was interested in developing them to the point where he might use his talents for healing. I am never quite sure this means that the psychic does all the work and the person being healed need make no effort. This man never explained how his psychic gifts manifested, and not then need healing, I did not pursue this. Virgo is the ultimate sign for a service oriented career, but we want to see how a spiritual psychic combines with the practical nature of this chart. Or, come to some notion of how these elements combine with the Capricorn Sun. The Moon in Sagittarius, how he wishes to perform, combines well with Virgo. Chart significator Mercury is more important and is trine to the Ascendant and Saturn.

Notice that he has both Mars and Jupiter at zero declination and Mercury out of bounds, with Pluto on the verge of going out of bounds. This is a chart more particularly worth studying to those who do midpoint analysis for there is more here than meets the eye. Mars and Jupiter are the focal point of a semi-squares to both Venus and Uranus, and the semi-square indicates friction. This would seem to have more to do with an erotic love nature than healing. Venus and Uranus are also in mutual reception. In our conversations, sex or romance were never topics. Mars is the dispositor of the chart. Neptune in the first house may indicate the healer, but far too often it indicates one who has an unreal perception of the self, if not faulty judgment. The conjunction of Mars and Jupiter gives an ability to concentrate and stick to one's goals. Note also that Mars is behind the house it rules, while Jupiter rules its house but is in Aries rather than in Pisces. Also put some emphasis of the fact that not only are these energies combining by conjuncting, the parallel here is off by having Jupiter in a northern sign and a southern declination. This will not work as well as it should if both were north declinations to go with the northern sign. If you look at the ephemeris, both were South prior to his birth and that progressed to eight years old, both are again in North declination although by then Mars has sped away from zero declination.

Of course, Aquarius ruling the sixth house might be suitable to either psychiatrist or healer, but it also presupposes that the person knows all there is to know about sickness and health and service. The Sun in the fifth house may speak of creativity, and Leo ruling the twelfth creates behind the scenes (but note Pluto on the twelfth cusp). The Midheaven is at the midpoint of Mars-Jupiter and Pluto, and Mercury is at the midpoint of Midheaven and Pluto. At the time when he was still studying, the progressed Saturn was going through his twelfth house, and he had the same situation as I when I was first studying astrology. It should be assumed that when Saturn progressed into his first house, he would hang out his own shingle as a professional practitioner.

138. Barman, 10-11-3
Jupiter: 0N35
Data: January 22, 1940, 6:30 a.m. EST,
Milford, Connecticut, 41N41, 73W04

This hefty built bartender was remarkable for his equanimity, great sense of humor and sociability. He was always in complete control of his saloon, and he tended to practice psychology from his runway. But he was not sure what sort of work he ought to do, which is not surprising with an end of Gemini Moon in his sixth house. Being a bartender is a sort of dead-end job, its only outlet being to become proprietor of one's own establishment. This is easier to wish on than to actualize for it involves much special planning, not to mention quantities of money.

His chart with Capricorn rising, at the outset, suggests one who would rather be self-employed, so far achieved only by being in complete charge of his workplace during his shift. Saturn in his third house attests well for his being in business, and with Saturn in Aries (in fall) he is seen not to be the least reticent in communications. With the Sun in Aquarius, although intercepted, there is still a distinct psychological theme, and we can only say of the Moon in Gemini that it lightens up his personality image. Note that he has Mars in Aries, and at some time he went through a seven year period of having Mars progress over his natal and progressed Saturn, never an easy and often a frustrating period which probably happened at the end of his teens and into is early twenties. He was already going on age forty when I first did his chart.

Patterns made, especially by minor aspects, are strong because we use close orbs for them, and the closer any aspect is, the stronger it is. Sun and Mars are quintile, and so are Mercury and Midheaven, while the Midheaven is 165 degrees to Mars. He left San Francisco and returned to New England.

139. Quiet Young Man, 3-11-5
Jupiter: 0N49
Data: January 25, 1940, 3:40 p.m. CWT,
Houston, Texas, 29N45, 95W23

I met this man through a client who had polio when he was two years old and was subsequently to die of

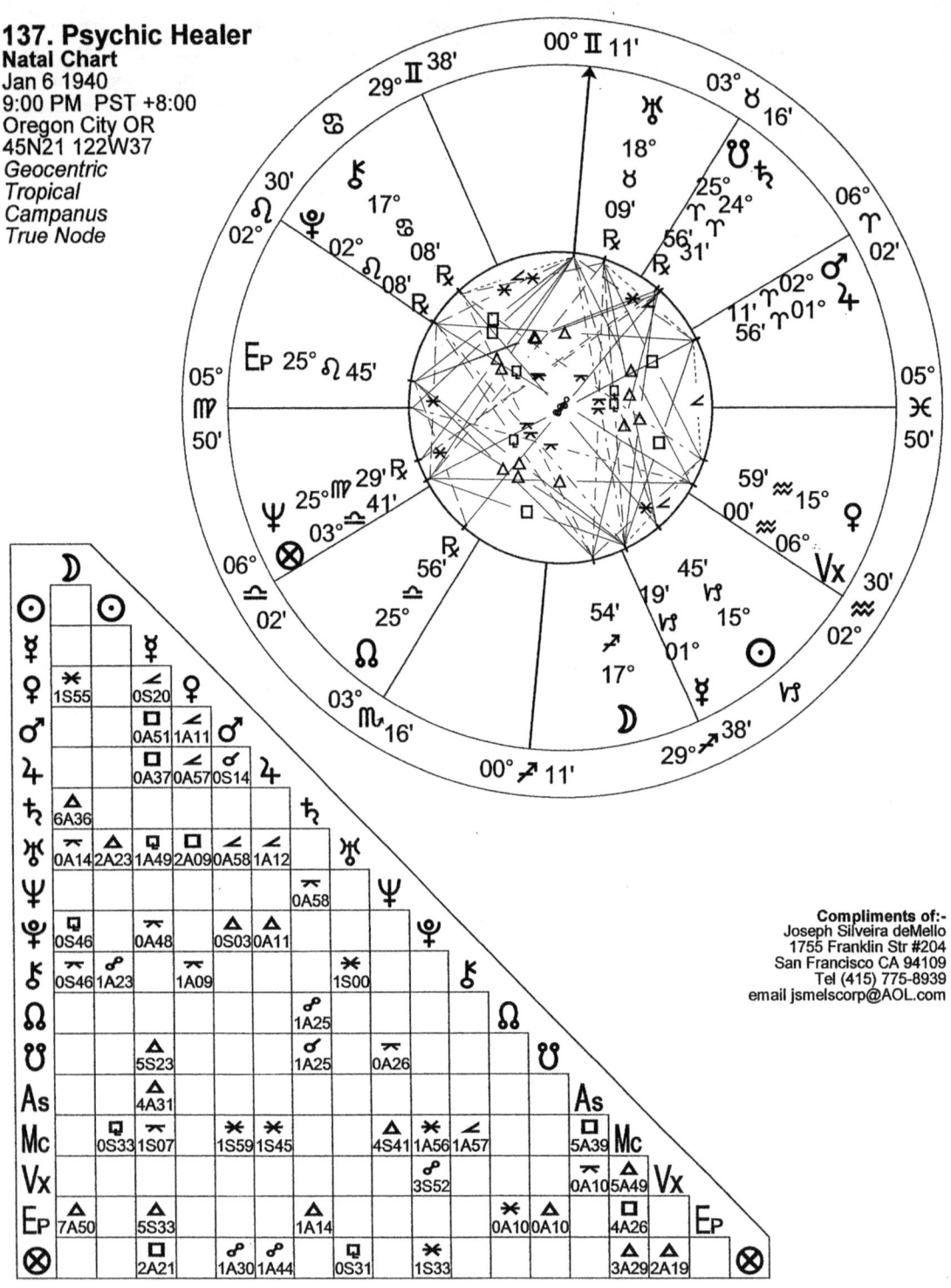

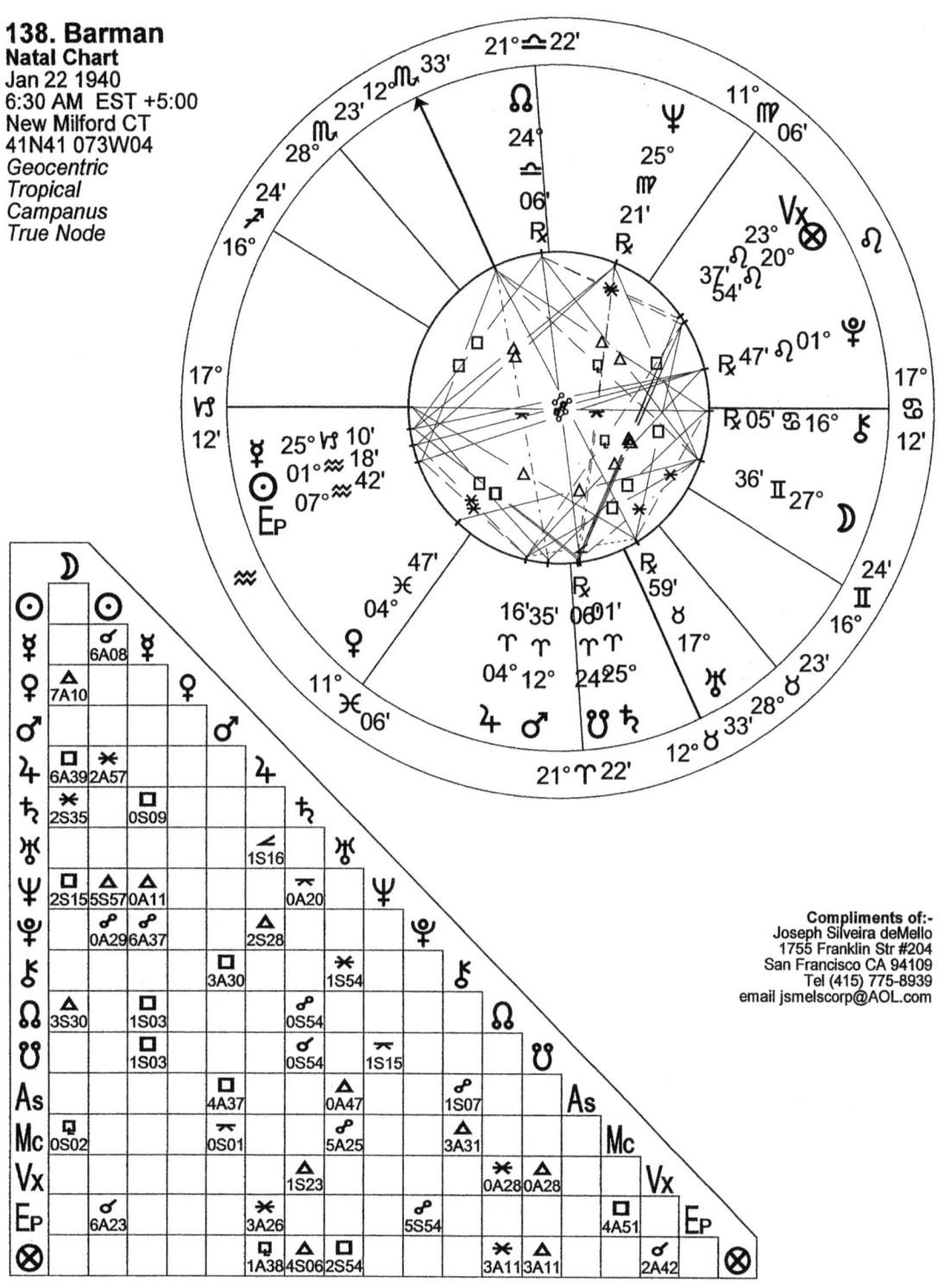

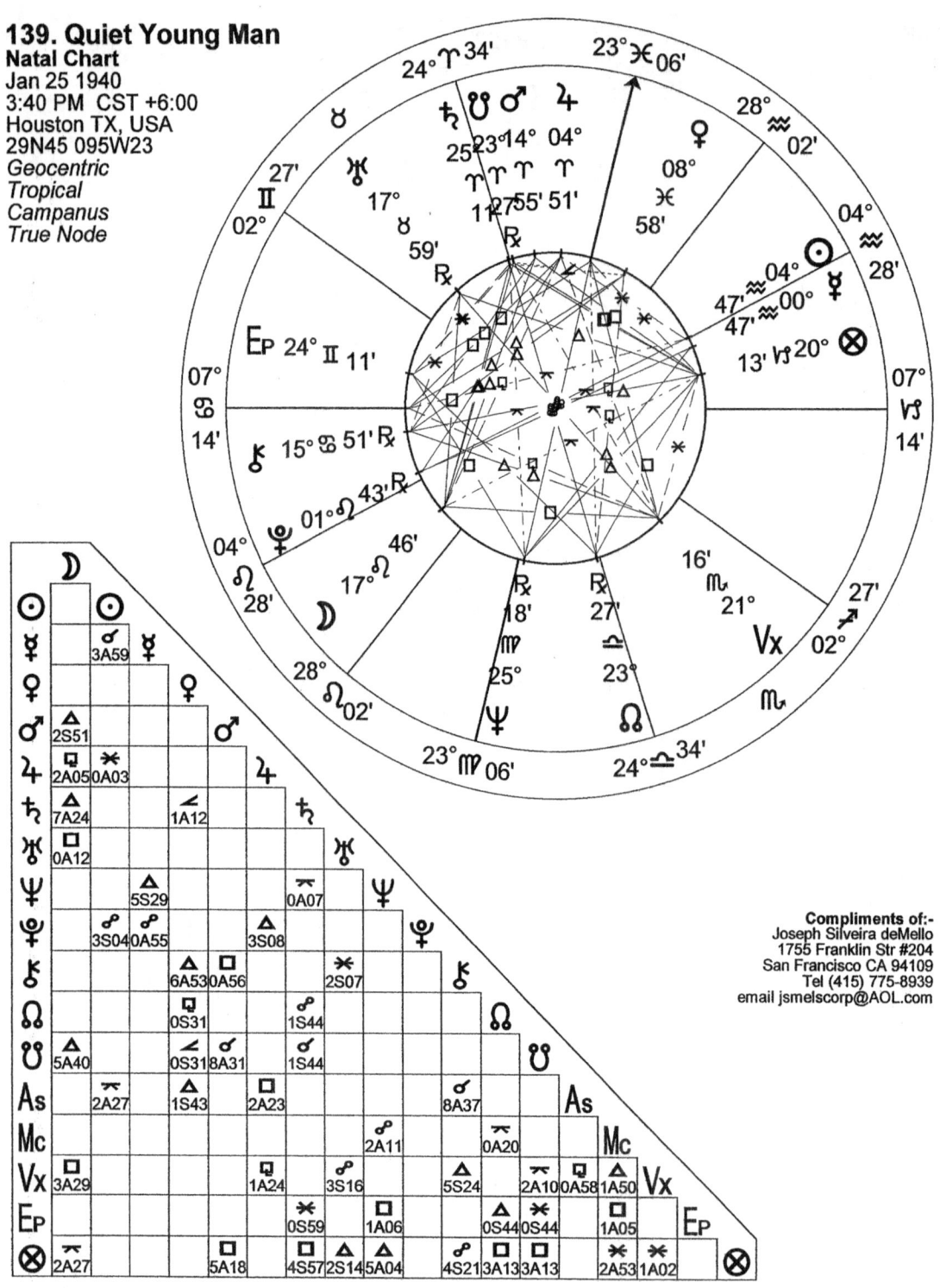

139. Quiet Young Man
Natal Chart
Jan 25 1940
3:40 PM CST +6:00
Houston TX, USA
29N45 095W23
Geocentric
Tropical
Campanus
True Node

AIDS. This is the chart (birth certificate data) of his significant other, who at first meeting hung back and let his more vivacious companion do all the talking. They were totally opposite types, and this man was steadily and gainfully employed. Where his close friend was quite obviously homosexual, this man was not.

Once I had done his chart, he became more voluble. In those days the diagnosis of AIDS as a modern plague was some years ahead, also before we learned that people who have once recovered from polio may suffer a relapse in later years. Although I have lost touch with this man, I cannot assume that he, too, may have succumbed as did his friend. I now looked for the AIDS "signature" of placements quindecile from the IC, Venus ninth, while Jupiter may progress to 8 Aries.

The Sun in Aquarius is usually a quiet Sun sign, with the Sun in detriment, and his chart significator Mercury is also in Aquarius and too close to the Sun. Most Aquarians can refrain from opinions until actually asked for them. With a Leo Moon, always wanting to be dramatic, there was no indication that this man had such a need. Mars in its own sign, but Venus is on the Midheaven making a quintile to Uranus and a quincunx to Pluto. Pluto is out of bounds in the second house and opposite to Sun and Mercury. But it is Pluto from where the kite formation starts with a trine to Jupiter, and Jupiter sextile Sun-Mercury. Saturn is on the South Node in the eleventh house where we also find Mars trine the third house Moon. Neptune retrograde in the fourth house, difficulty with prescription dosages and, sometimes, with alcoholic beverage intake did not seem a problem here.

140. Man with Alias, 5-6-1
Jupiter: 0N51, Neptune: 0S41 (both in southern signs)
Data: August 27, 1945, 5:40 a.m. CWT,
Sioux City, Iowa, 42N30, 96W24

This man hated, as people often do, the name given him by his parents. He is not the first such case in this group. There was nothing wrong with his name except that it was rather ordinary, and he longed for something more "today." The problem was that the name he chose was one being given to every baby boomer born while this man was growing up, and its overuse was already a cliché of the times. He lived but briefly in San Francisco around the spring of 1974, very much a transient, always meaning to find his fortune in Los Angeles.

This Leo rising aspired to find fame in the entertainment world. His Mercury is in Leo on the Ascendant, general indicator of a constant talker, It is also retrograde but well before the Sun in Virgo in the first house and in mutual reception with Mercury, chart dispositor. Oddly, courtesy placements of these two in their own signs would give a courtesy Sun in the twelfth and courtesy Mercury in the second house. This chart has a great deal of personal drive and much self-interest. Moon in Aries (but square Venus in Cancer and sextile Mars in Gemini) shows a desire to come off as a real go-getter. Mars is in Gemini, leaving a conjunction to Uranus in the eleventh house, indicating that he might get sidetracked down any path of least resistance. Saturn, Venus and Pluto are all in the twelfth house. The question is whether I could find an alternate occupation where potential exists and the thought he was starting too late in life on his desired role. Good sense has to prevail. There are interesting vocations open to him.

141. The High Roller, 7-6-2
Jupiter: 0N40, Neptune: 0S43
Data: August 29, 1945, 8:30 a.m. PWT,
San Diego, California, 32N43, 117W10

This man was vacationing in San Francisco, staying with a client of mine. My client told me his friend probably had a very interesting chart I should like to see, and that the man was in a dilemma and needed the sort of advice I could give. I was not fooled for a minute. What my client seemed to imply was that his friend was not listening to the advice my client was giving him and he hoped that I would give the man the very same advice from his horoscope. In getting his data, his friend refused to give me more than his first name. He had been keeping a low profile in Mexico living under an assumed name and he felt that this trip to San Francisco was a bit risky. He looked far from the drug-toting hippie, so crossing the border should have been easy. He said he was thinking of moving from Mexico to Jamaica, but his current passport was running out and would soon have to be renewed and that might set official inquiries in motion. He felt that his passport should always be indisputably legal. I was told that he was hiding out from possible prosecution by the authorities. Not another one of those, I thought. (See #129)

Every question I asked got a careful and hesitant answered. His credibility was fast eroding. Money, he said, was no problem. Talking about himself evidently was. In his extensive business background, he had put together some really big real estate deals and it was hinted some may have been dubious, but he had been inactive for some time.

My friend later told me that this man was a borderline paranoid schizophrenic. He had in the past witnessed episodes of this man's uncontrolled temper and learned to make himself scarce when he saw his friend going toward the edge. I concentrated on the Libra rising chart and seeing within a little more than a trine. His Sun in Virgo might stabilize and so might his Moon in Taurus. Mars getting away from a conjunction to Uranus in the ninth house and in Gemini was a bit of a puzzle. Alas Neptune in the first house was a real problem Venus as chart significator is in the tenth house at the end of Cancer and leaving a conjunction with Saturn. Venus is sextile Moon and Jupiter. Venus in mutual reception with Moon disposes of the chart except for the mutual reception of Sun and Mercury.

With such a clumped together chart some astrologers might say such people should be specialists in whatever field they put themselves. I had set up his progressed chart for 1977 and noted that the progressed Sun had five years previously moved into his first house Libra

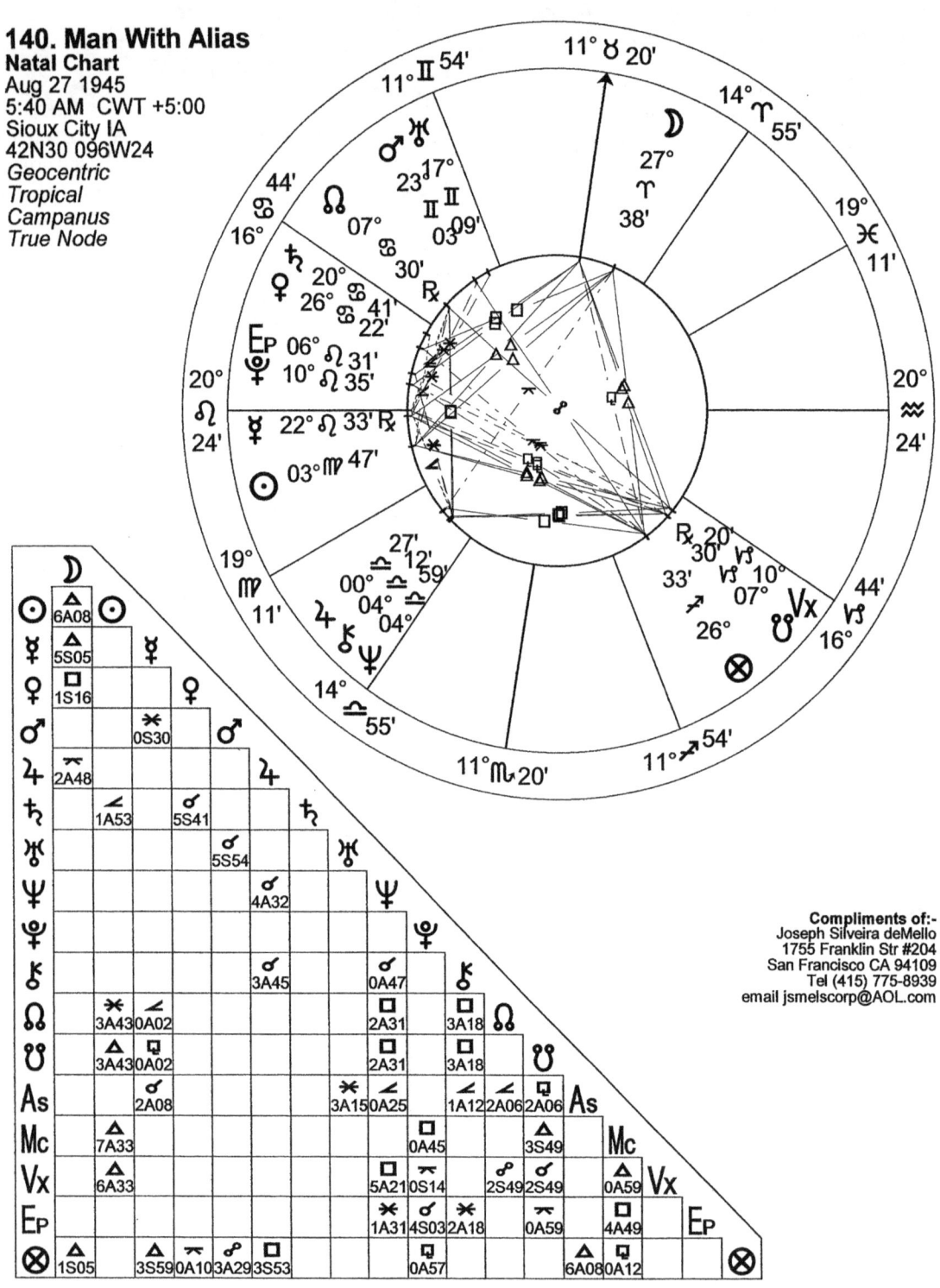

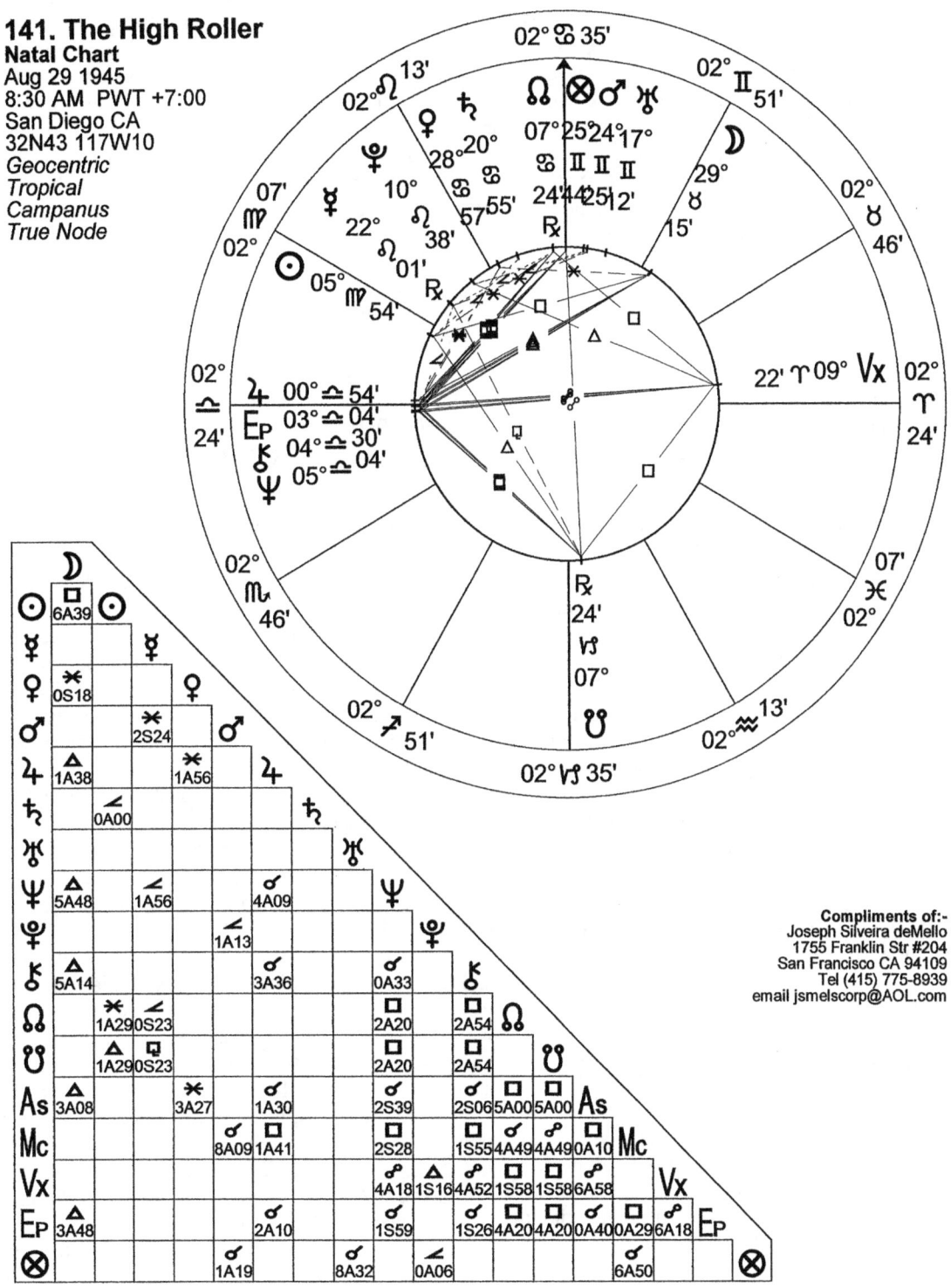

141. The High Roller
Natal Chart
Aug 29 1945
8:30 AM PWT +7:00
San Diego CA
32N43 117W10
Geocentric
Tropical
Campanus
True Node

and contacted his natal Neptune two years prior to my reading for him.

Also at the same time, progressed Venus had gone over his natal Sun. His progressed Mars was chasing his Saturn but had still years to go before they made contact. His progressed Ascendant was about to move into Scorpio, always a significant indicator of coming changes, and I believe progressed Ascendant over the second house cusp usually indicates the year of biggest change in a life. His progressed Mercury and Neptune were still close to natal Neptune, and the progressed Sun and Jupiter were together. In the meantime he had no strong progressed aspects that I thought were favorable to change, and I suggested he put off making any changes for more than a year. When I had related the movement of progressed Venus, he then mentioned that he had been twice married and divorced but gave no dates. He said that he had come to terms with himself as actually bi-sexual, finding people of both sexes attractive to himself. Well, hooray for him.

142. Cemetery Dweller, 4-6-4
Jupiter: 0N41, Neptune: 0S43
Data: August 29, 1945, 2:41 a.m. PWT,
San Francisco, California, 37N45, 122W26

Almost six hours later than the preceding example, Cancer is now rising. Now the planets rule other houses and activities. The amusing thing when I met this man was that he lived in Colma, a small town south of San Francisco where the majority of its residents are dead and buried in the many cemeteries which crown its hills. Economic considerations had made moving there attractive, and his sense of humor was not the least impaired. The chart runs from Moon in Taurus in the eleventh to the trio of Jupiter, Chiron and Neptune in early Libra in his fourth house. Jupiter and Neptune rule his sixth and ninth houses. Cancer is rising with Saturn in the first house and is not indicative of any personality impairment. The Sun is in Virgo on the edge of his third house is in mutual reception with Mercury, and Moon the same with Venus. I did his chart in 1975, merely for my own study, and I made no notes of any social or business connections. I met him but once and had an interesting and extended conversation with him but never saw him again.

143. Female Attorney, 6-6-4
Jupiter: 0N20, Neptune: 0S46
Data: September 2, 1945, 7:30 a.m. PWT, Redwood City, California, 37N29, 122W13

Now, a few days later, we see the trine chart layout from the tenth to the first house and now Neptune in first is no longer in the rising sign. When I first met this lady, she was celebrating in December 1975 with a group of neighborhood friends for she had just passed her Bar examination. She joined the family firm in the San Francisco financial district with which she is still affiliated.

The chart, besides having Jupiter and Neptune in contra-parallel and at zero declination, conjunct Chiron in the first house. The problem is to see this as the chart of an attorney. Virgo of details highlights the Ascendant. Mercury is chart significator in Leo, but it and the Sun are both in the twelfth house, creativity behind the scenes. The family law firm is not such that its clients litigate in courtrooms. Sun and Mercury are also still in mutual reception. The Moon has sped into Cancer, separating from a conjunction with Saturn, and Venus has moved on into Leo. But Uranus is now the most prominent at the very top of her chart, from which Mars is separating. Tall, she is thin and stylish. She did not become a client.

In these tight charts, everything in less than a trine and many squares. Every year in Summertime, transits are moving over this tight collection of planets, while in Winter, they are in opposition. You can see that she possibly passed the Bar with Sun opposite Uranus and then Mars and then North Node. Her future career activities were to be conducted quietly and efficiently behind the scenes. Uranus high in the chart should find novel ways to proceed, and Mars in the tenth should testify to a very energetic career.

144. Carpenter, 9-6-4
Jupiter: 0N19, Neptune: 0S47
Data: September 2, 1945, 2:37 p.m. PWT,
Hermosa Beach, California, 33N51, 118W24

Seven hours later, we have another location of the trine pattern. Nothing could be so different as the people of previous examples. Sometimes I wonder where some of my clients find the men on whom they get romantically fixated. No sooner had I been introduced to this man and been persuaded to do his chart, in 1983, than he was stopped by a traffic patrolman and arrested when his record showed how many unpaid traffic and parking tickets he had. Although he has the surname of a prominent family, he is a drop out from the establishment and preferred to make his living at carpentry. Yet the amusing thing was that my client and this man had so many conjunctions to placements in each other's charts that karmic ties would have drawn them together. They would probably have fallen all over each other in the dark.

Again we see the tightness of placements in this chart and the sort of generational indicators. This man was, when I met him, basically a loner, typical of his times, with all the liberal attitudes and conspiracy theories. His placements are in the third quadrant of a need to understand others objectively. But with everything on the right side of his chart, we have to see that he achieves through the good will of other people, but is not aided by the Moon on the edge of his eighth house of gain from others and ambivalence about what, from time to time, he really wants that gain to be. Those who work with comparison surveys had better pay attention to more than planetary contacts. In this case, his Sun falls in her seventh, while her Sun falls in his eighth; he might have married her, but she was not quite sure he was what she wanted. Her Saturn fell in his eighth, while his fell in her sixth, showing the areas where they might hinder each

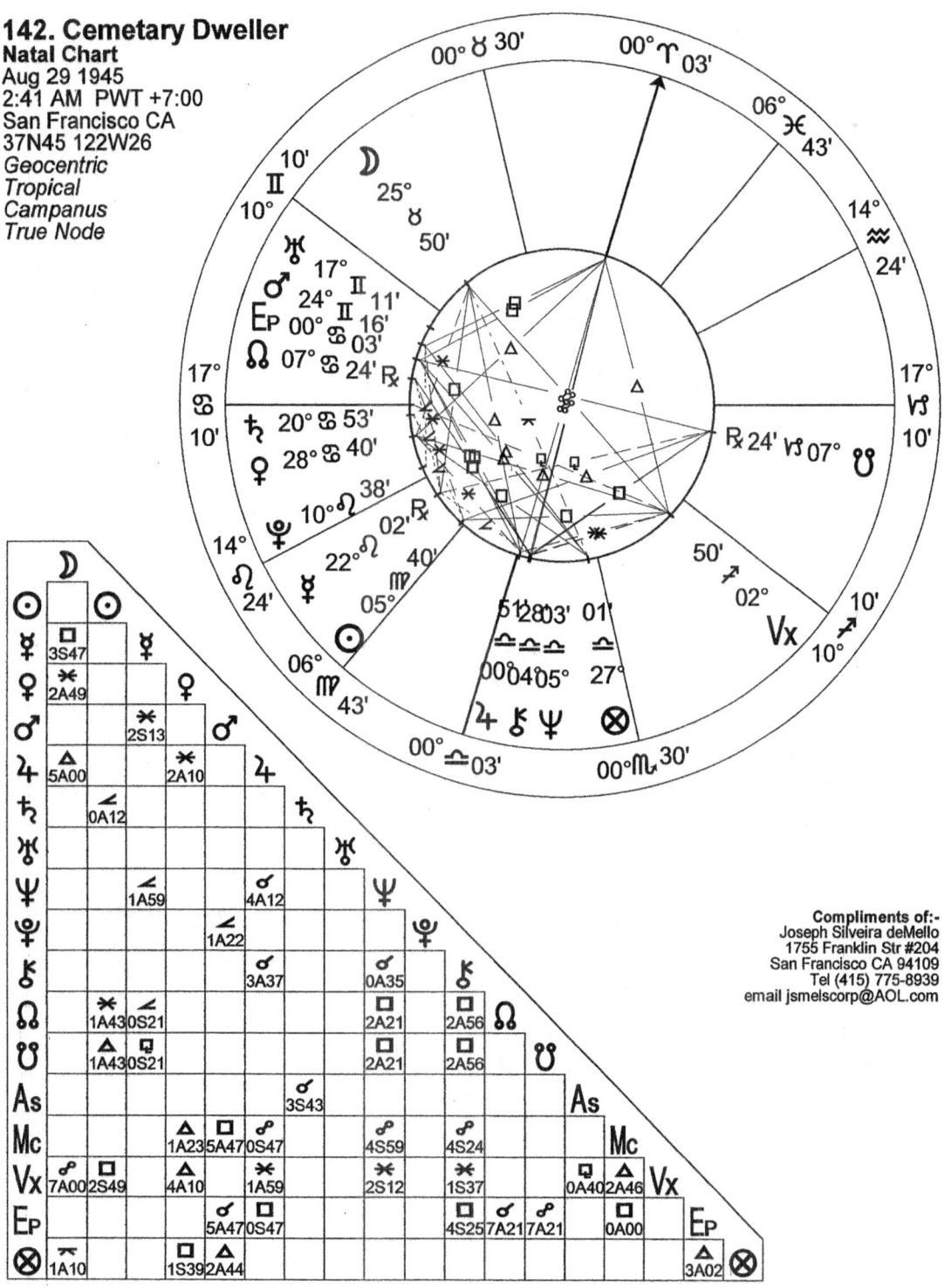

142. Cemetary Dweller
Natal Chart
Aug 29 1945
2:41 AM PWT +7:00
San Francisco CA
37N45 122W26
Geocentric
Tropical
Campanus
True Node

Compliments of:-
Joseph Silveira deMello
1755 Franklin Str #204
San Francisco CA 94109
Tel (415) 775-8939
email jsmelscorp@AOL.com

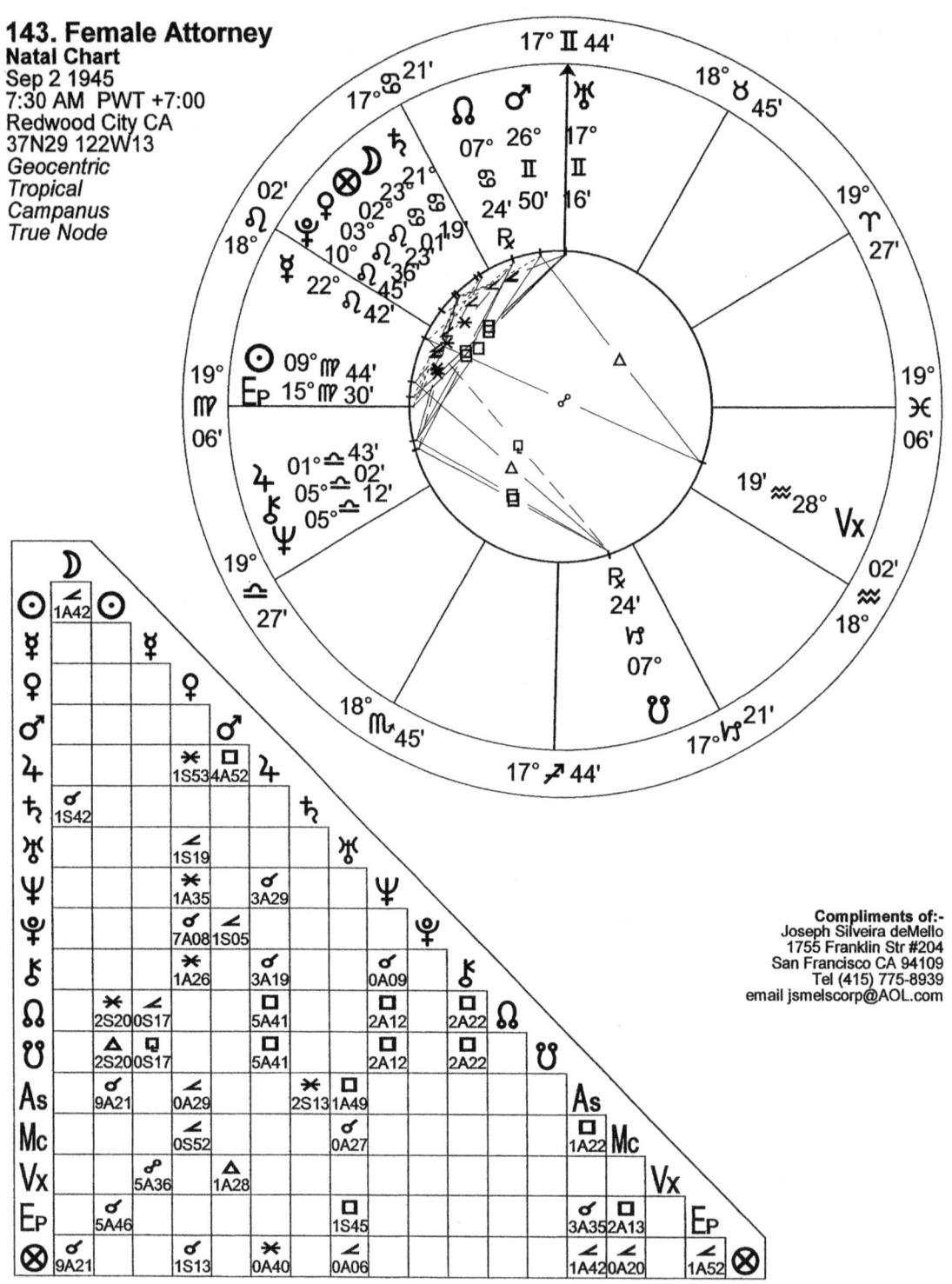

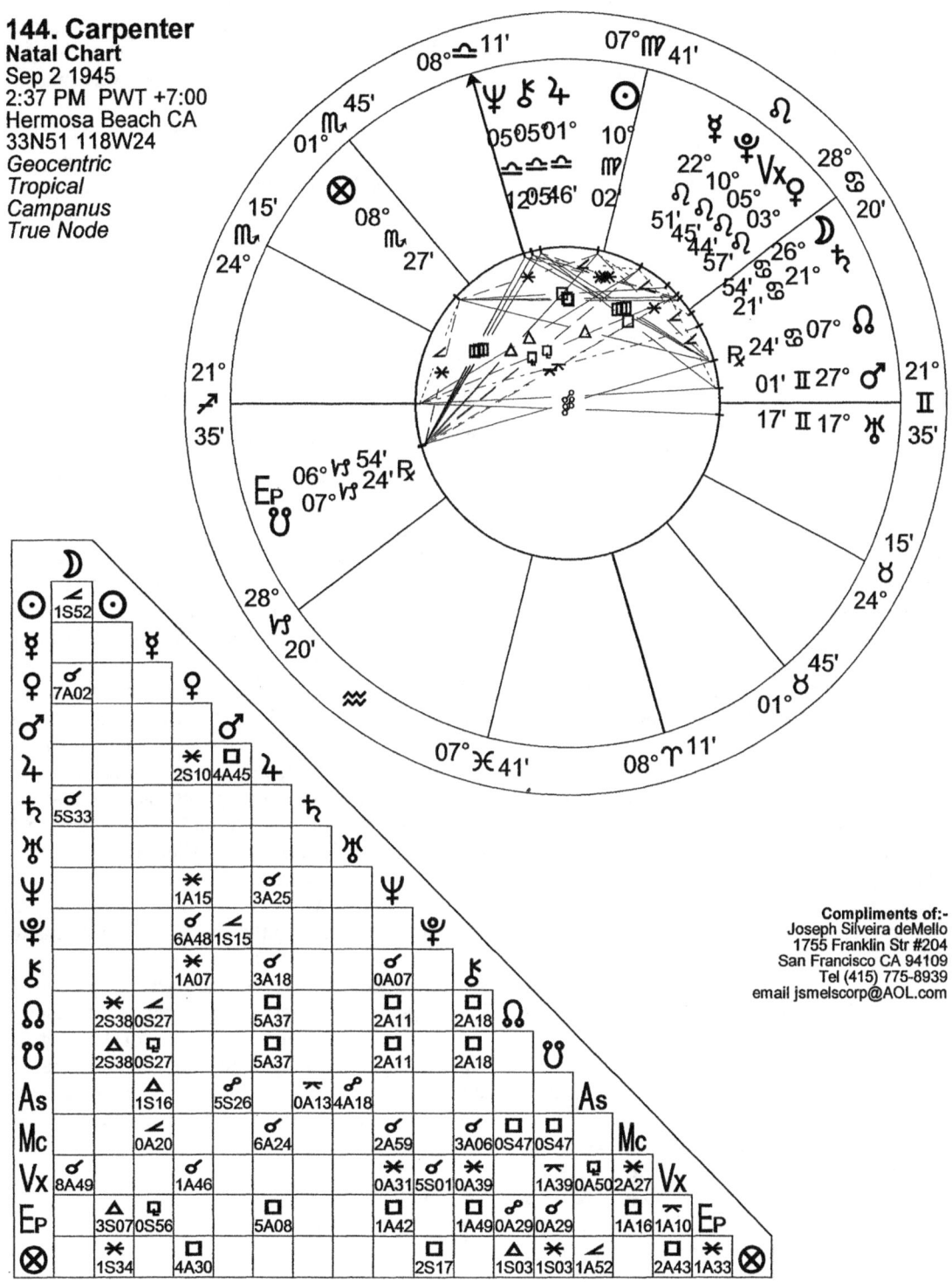

144. Carpenter
Natal Chart
Sep 2 1945
2:37 PM PWT +7:00
Hermosa Beach CA
33N51 118W24
Geocentric
Tropical
Campanus
True Node

other. She was Capricorn rising Leo. The touches of their charts might have been karmic, but he should thank his lucky stars he got away from all her control and direction.

Due to the historical time at which these people were born, at the end of the Second World War, the first of the crop of baby boomers, growing up too young to be hippies, their hippie involvement reminds us that those who never have their own ideas are not so badly off as those who accept and spout the poorly founded ideas of others, (so said Cicero in ancient Rome). Too young for the Korean War, more the Vietnam generation. He was quite content to be an itinerant workman with his own pickup. Although this young man was heterosexual, he moved unbothered in a mixed social group where people gave each other space without judgmental moral prejudices or censures.

145. Astrologer and Author, 7-6-5
Jupiter: 0N16, Neptune: 0S47
Data: September 3, 1945, 9:04 a.m. EDT,
Waterbury, Connecticut, 41N33, 73W03

This is the chart of an astrologer who is also the author of an excellent book on horary astrology, but who also has a professional career as a psychiatrist. I first met him at a small luncheon when he had finished writing his book. Unfortunately another guest at luncheon was one of those women who prefer to talk mostly about themselves, and we got little chance to talk astrology. He prefers to keep his two major interests very seriously separate, and authored his book under a *nom de plume*, yet did publish his own chart, I will stay with the game of preserving his anonymity.

Besides the fact that he has Jupiter and Neptune at zero declination and Mars and Pluto within orb of almost out of bounds and parallel, this chart is distinguished by being entirely within the ninth to twelfth houses, like some previous examples, everything is within the trine from Uranus to East Point. Astrologers will easily see that the major annual events of his daily life are going to be signaled by the Sun passing over this tenanted area, and monthly by the passage of the Moon passing over from Uranus to Neptune-Chiron, Ascendant and east point. By the way, from student days, we were told that our lives were in low when the Sun transited the bottoms of our charts, and in high when it transited the top of the chart. Try that on your own charts to see if you agree. In this case, life was best for him in June and July, worse in December-January.

Looking at the zero declination planets in this chart, Jupiter and Neptune in the twelfth house, Jupiter rules the third house and Neptune rules the sixth; compare to the chart of our High Roller #163 and see the dissimilarities. The nodal axis runs from ninth to third houses, great for a teacher who is also a psychiatrist. I was pleased to see that astrology does not get spoken of in psychiatric terms. The Sun is on the twelfth and all the placements of this chart are above the horizon. He has Libra rising with the Sun in Virgo, but here the Moon is in Leo, rather too close to Venus and Pluto. I dare say if Mars were not in Gemini and in ninth house, and setting, this man might have been a neurosurgeon, but in his ninth house with Uranus more of his time is spent on intellectual concepts in both his fields. Saturn in Cancer (in detriment) is important as the highest planet in the chart. This opens great interest when we follow Saturn transits around the chart. Following the Saturn cycles is productive in any chart, for after his Saturn return, Saturn conjuncts the Sun and later the Ascendant, and then is square its natal position, squares natal Sun, then is conjunct the IC, square Ascendant, and opposite its natal self. These cyclical contacts give us all very different rhythms of life and insist that astrology is very much an art.

The subject is creative in the community and behind the scenes and in fifth house speculations. Uranus in the ninth ruling the fifth will probably keep astrology as a creative avocation. He is quite conservative, married, a family man. His book on horary astrology examines both old and new horary techniques. It is a basic book and is entertaining.

146. Lady Psychiatric Patient, 3-6-10
Jupiter: 0S48, Neptune: 0S58
Data: September 15, 1945, 11:00 p.m. EWT,
Buffalo, New York, 42N53, 78W52

From time to time, psychiatrists have sent me their patients. I believe this was an attempt to expand the patients' sense of themselves and to show them what a stranger would think of their potentials. This client was a people person but had real difficulties in relating easily to people. I found her to have remarkably varied interests and quite a creative potential. She was probably seriously hurt growing up.

Now notice that the Jupiter-Neptune zero declinations have become parallel, and bear in mind that this posed no problem in the previous charts above. This client was very attractive, and she had perhaps too much energy, wanted to move too quickly. Note that Mars is with her North Node opposite the Moon, and both make a T-square to Jupiter-Neptune-Chiron. Our consultation was very interesting and productive. I am not the sort of astrologer who gets psychological with my clients, and since this client was in therapy, such matters were best left to her therapist who had referred her. What we discussed were how I saw her basic personality and her potentials. I therefore gave her a fairly standard reading, focusing on the tenanted areas of her chart, personality, self-esteem, communication, home, creativity and people who came close to her. As in the previous chart, there are no retrograde planets, nor are there intercepted planets.

147. Neighbor Lady, 10-6-11
Jupiter: 0S57, Neptune: 0S59
Data: September 17, 1945, 4:30 p.m. EWT,
Buffalo NY 42N53, 78W52

One day I went out to my mailbox and found a very pretty next door neighbor with her infant daughter close to my gateway. She was a single mother living with her

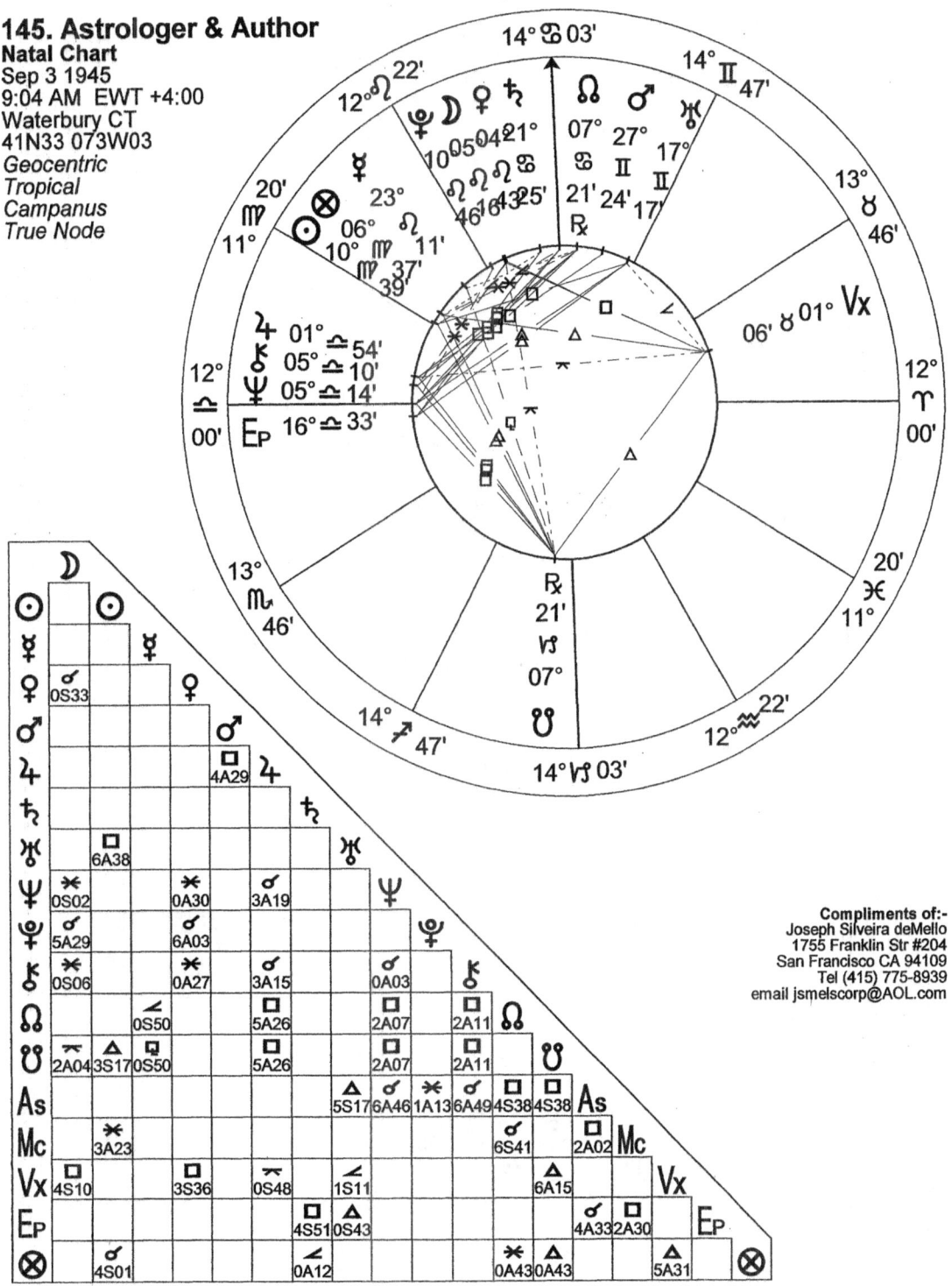

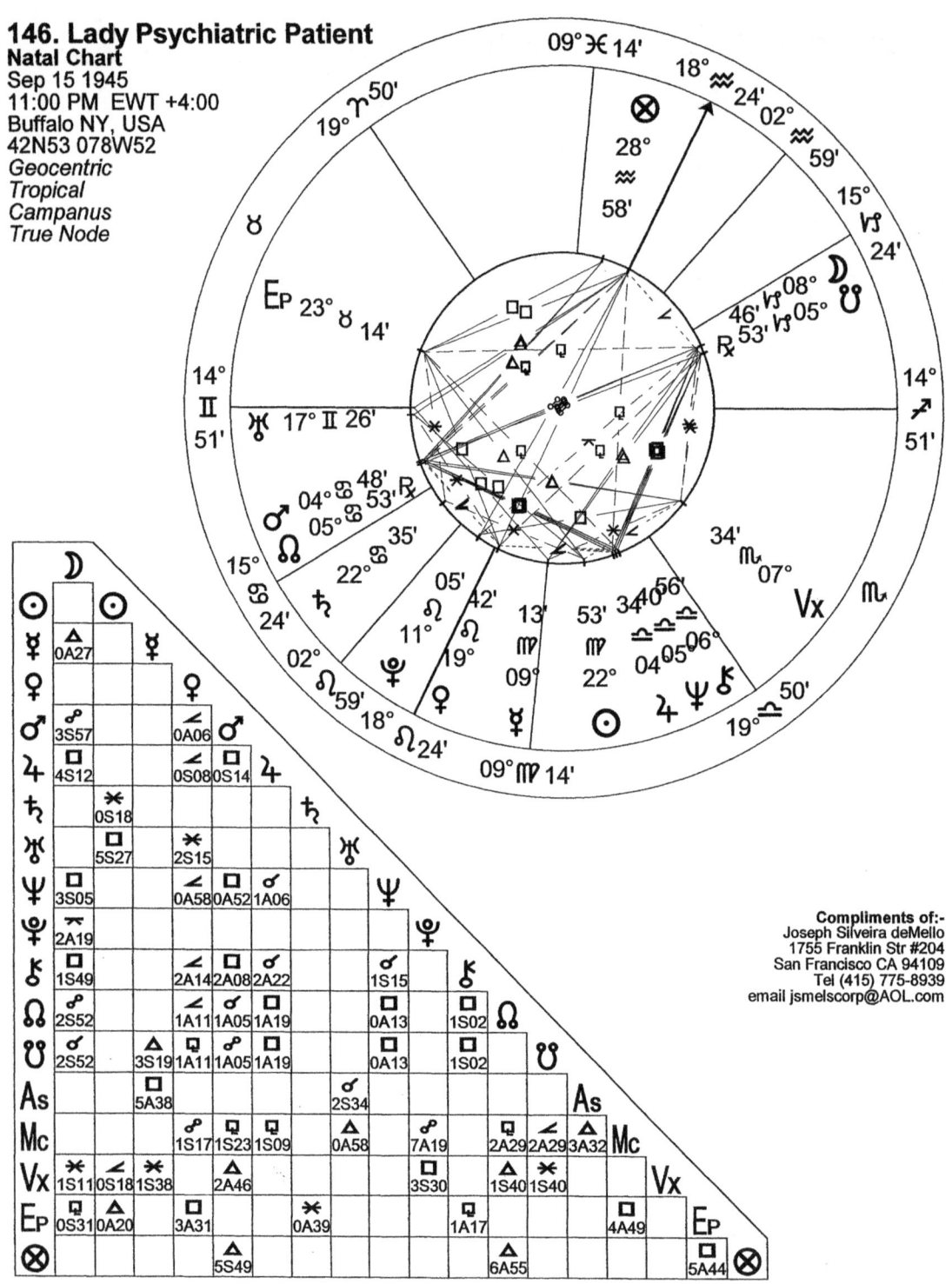

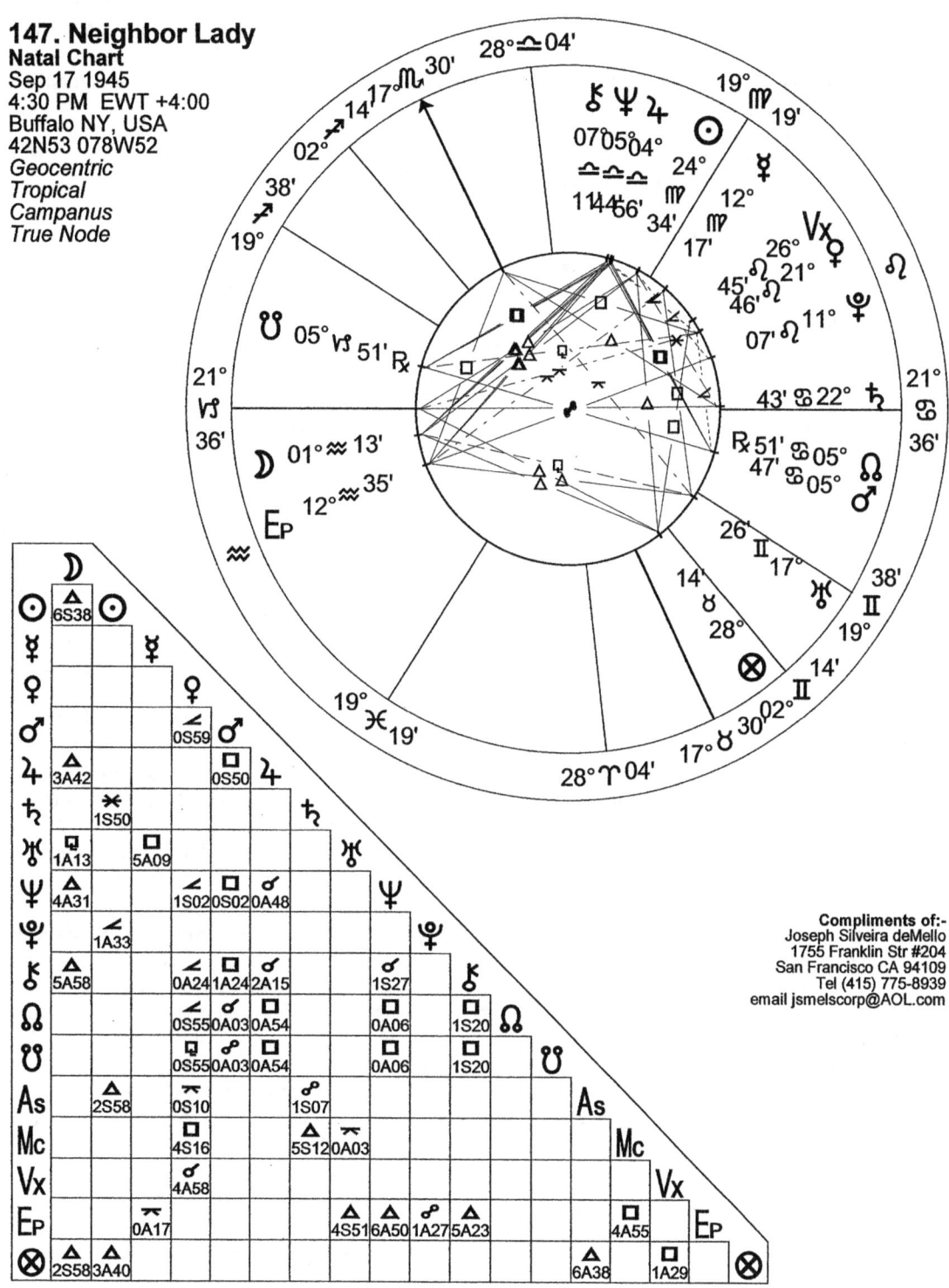

mother. She was pleasant, totally open, and, because I had pulled some astrology mail from my box, we began to talk about astrology, and she gave me her data. When I did the chart, I noticed that it was close to the previous chart which I had done three years earlier and that both had been born in the same city. Of the same age, this lady did not know the previous client. Soft and a little plump, she was neither nervous nor hyperactive.

Here we have the classical panhandle chart with the Moon in Aquarius in a first house ruled by Capricorn, but already in Aquarius. Saturn we then see is opposite the Ascendant in the seventh house. Mercury disposes of everything in the chart but for Moon and Saturn in mutual reception. Jupiter and Neptune at zero declination and parallel, in the eighth house Libra with Virgo Sun also there. There were contradictions. She was not controlling, nor was she dour or shy. Virgo manifested better than Capricorn, and the Moon in Aquarius was also quiescent. What had happened to her regarding the father of her child was looked upon practically, and she was not seeking future romances or partners, though she may have wished for a father figure in her life. The Moon is intercepted, and so are Pluto and Venus. Tenanted houses contain the important problems. She was resolved at that time to be the best mother she could be to her child and she had the complete sympathy and backing of her own mother.

148. Chef, 11-2-12
Jupiter: 0S09
Data: May 1, 1951, 1:58 a.m. CST,
Little Rock, Arkansas, 34N42, 92W16

This is the chart of a young man who had been living in Texas before moving to San Francisco. He took a job as chef at a garden restaurant where I was resident astrologer. It was only natural that I immediately got his data, and he also gave me the data for his sister to whom he was very close. This restaurant was owned by a gay man who habitually preferred to hire young gay men, and both employer and employee have long since succumbed to AIDS, and though I have no data of when this man died, I do know that his employer became infected with AIDS long after this man worked for him.

Although this new chef was a good and able worker, there was little favorable or easy between his chart and that of his employer who was prominently a Leo and had Aquarius rising, and two know-it-alls do not meld harmoniously. The employer had Sun in Leo and a Libra Moon, and we see here Sun in Taurus, Moon in Pisces. Once again two fixed signs do not adjust easily. In his brief tenure as chef, and chefs easily come and go, employee and employer tiptoed around each other. The chef was not overwhelmingly grateful that he had been hired, maintained his independence and his own friends, and preferred to do his work with his boss out of his hair, not the sort of thing easily asked of a Leo. One day he walked off and was gone as suddenly has he had come on the scene.

Of course today we have more knowledge of AIDS thanks to the research of French astrologer Guy dePenguern who found a preponderance of AIDS victims had placements at 165 degrees from the IC. But not in this chart, nor did anything progress to fifteen degrees either side of the Midheaven. However, transits in the early 1980s had Venus in Scorpio and Neptune in Sagittarius, and the monthly Moon could any time have filled the gap. Although the chart shows no predisposition to a weak immune system, giving a glance to the permissive grand trine between Neptune, Ascendant and Venus, see sixth house ruled by the Moon and with Pluto in the sixth, plus the connection of Moon and North Node in opposition to the Vertex, hindsight provides room for speculation.

149. Male Referral, 7-2-1
Jupiter: 0S01
Data: May 2, 1951 4:42 p.m. EDT,
Boston, Massachusetts, 42N22, 71W04

This client came through a chain of referrals. A woman sent me her printer, and I did several charts for him and his employees and for this homosexual young man who stayed with him for a while. The comparison between boss and employee had a large number of contacts. This young man had a mutual reception of Mercury and Venus. Between them, there were eight conjunctions (karmic contacts), nine sextiles, ten trines, ten squares, five oppositions, thirteen semi-sextiles (things where they would defer to each other), and eleven quincunxes (adjustments they would loath to make). It is not often you see comparisons with sixty-six contacts between the two. The quincunx aspects between both can send any relationship up a tree. The employer was Capricorn rising with Taurus Sun and Aries Moon, not a very easy person as either boss or personal friend.

This chart has a cardinal grand cross with Uranus as the highest planet in the chart. Uranus is out of bounds and rules the fifth house of speculations and love affairs. Saturn in the twelfth is good for learning from his own experiences, plus the fact that Saturn is retrograde and thus given to being motivated to make everything around him relate.

Mercury retrograde allows for abstract thinking, and Neptune retrograde indicates a detrimental pride and defensiveness. There is an old adage that when people of fixed signs get together, the only solution is for each of them to come to terms and assign each other specific areas of responsibility. Since both this young man and his employer had Sun in Taurus, this might be a paramount suggestion except that the employer had the very controlling Capricorn rising and a need for total control in his own hands all the time.

The Sun here is applying in five degrees to Mars, so the ego takes over on the energy, setting up an internal war with himself. The Moon is in Aries, so there is a desire to appear more aggressive, and here the Moon is close enough to be interpreted in the seventh house, indicative of constantly changing ideas regarding the people he drew close to himself. This young man was thoroughly ambivalent about the sort of people who came close to him. This, of course, is not out of line with

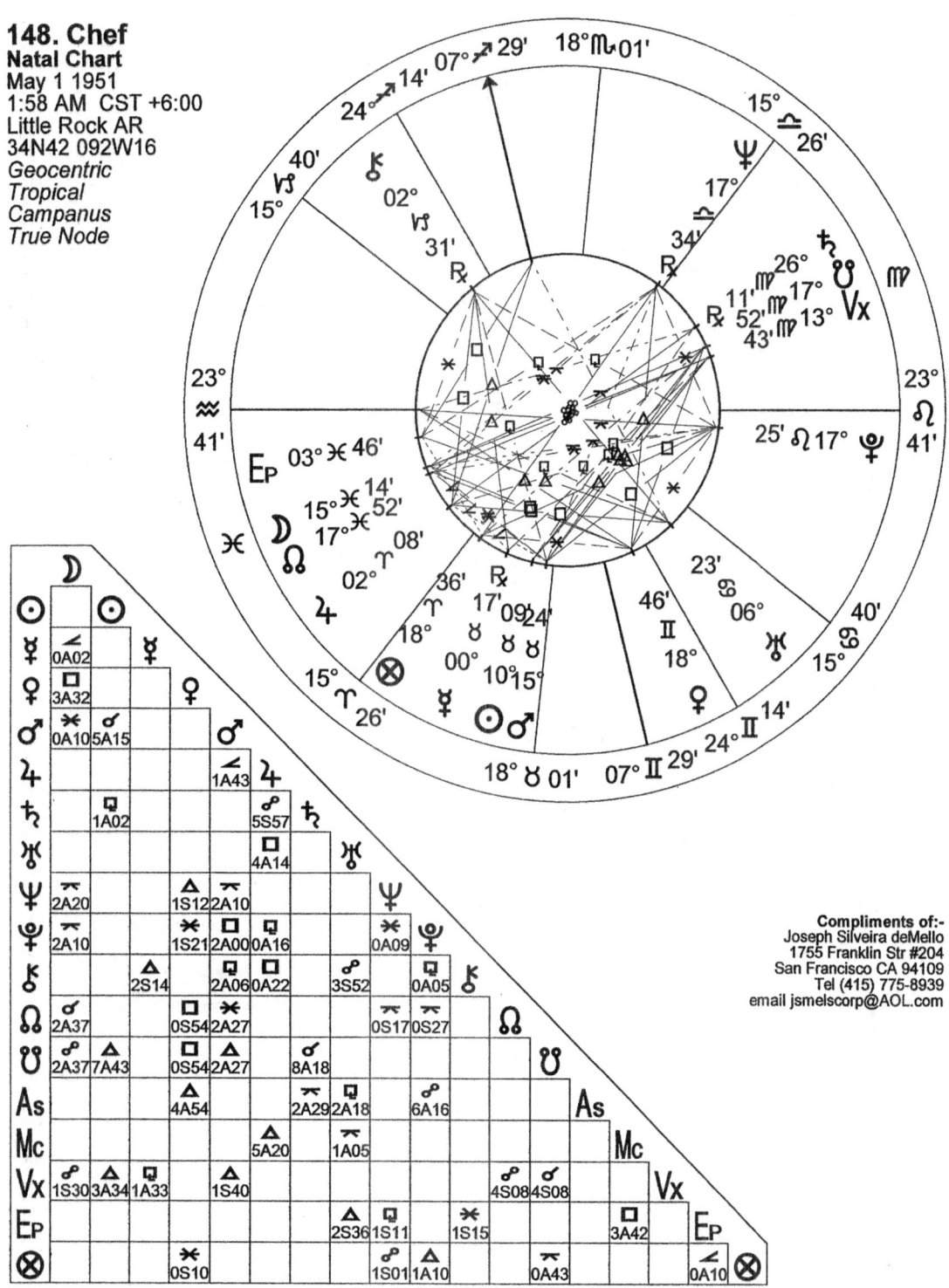

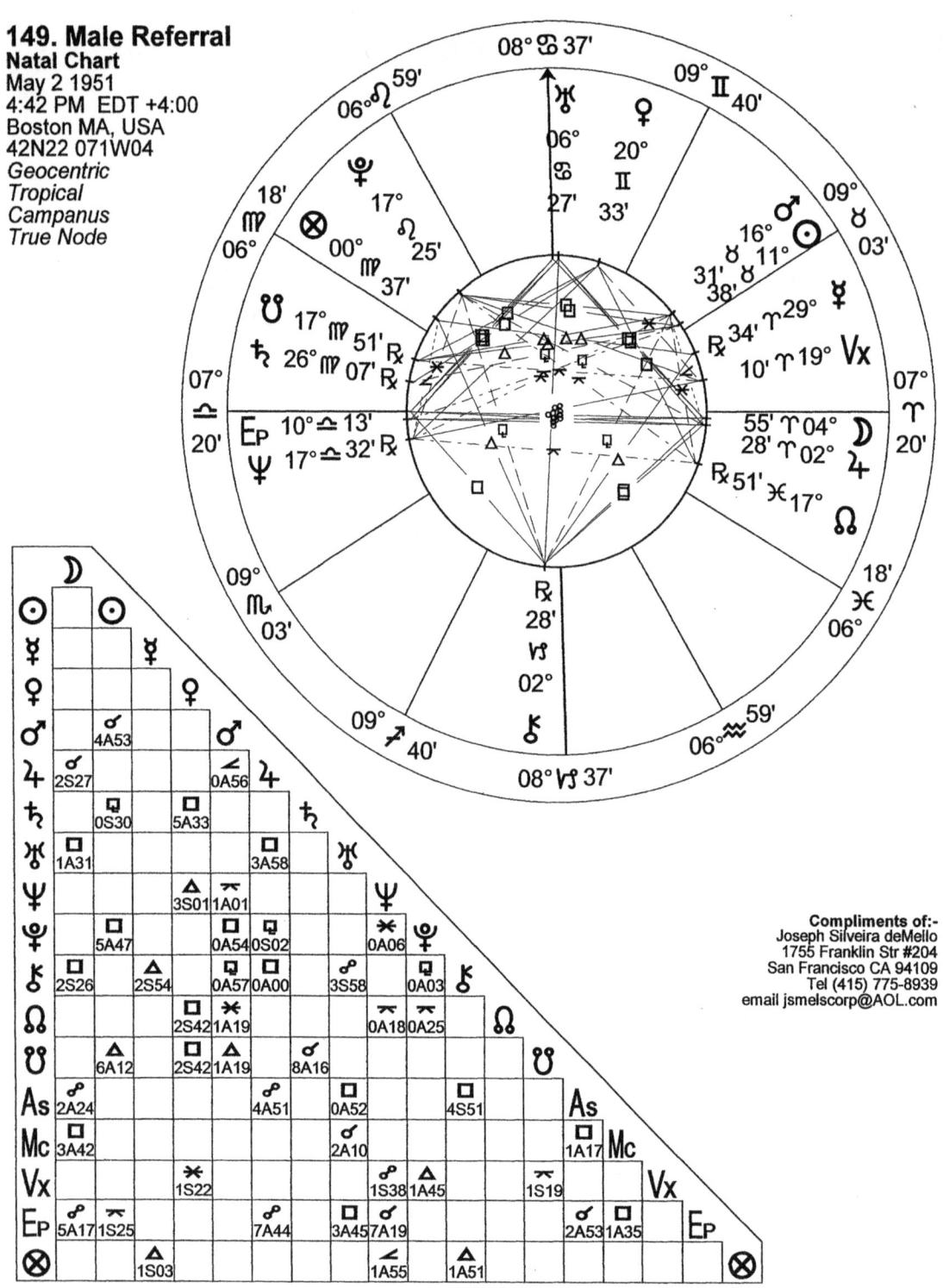

Libra rising, the sign which needs people but those people should be of good moral character. Jupiter is in zero declination, again close to the seventh, so there was no lack of people around and close to him. Venus, chart significator, is in Gemini in the ninth house separating to a trine from Neptune in the first house, a grace aspect denoting talent, but Neptune in first brings unreality of judgment. This is not aided by Moon ruling the tenth, Uranus on the cusp of tenth which does not guarantee great stability. The closeness of Mars to the Sun is not helpful.

150. Female Student, 10-2-2
Jupiter: 0N10
Data: May 5, 1951, 12:25 a.m. EST,
Indianapolis, Indiana, 39N46, 86W10

This was a female student who attended a series of classes I gave in elementary astrology. I always did charts on all my students. Here there was a big question about her time data, even from birth certificate, which plagues all charts for people born in Indiana. Businesses observed EST all year in 1951, but in summer they opened an hour earlier, which is probably to say they did not close an hour earlier. Clocks were not changed. It was finally resolved that EST was in use that year, and the student lost interest, since her only reason for attending class was to arrive at a viable chart built and interpreted (less expensive than becoming a client) when she saw that every lesson was not going to be exclusively devoted to the interpretation of her chart. I remember one corollary from my student days: When you have Cancer on the seventh, double check your work for error. Once I determined her time zone, and I double-checked my arithmetic. When I got into computers for astrology, I was again amazed at how closely my hand done chart came to what the computer generated, seldom more than two minutes difference between them.

Capricorn rising is ruled by Saturn retrograde in Virgo in the eighth house which seems to have only one aspect, a square to Venus. Mars, the great innovator and energizer is in Taurus (detriment) close to the Sun and possibly overcome by the Sun in the fourth house of home and security. The waning Moon is exalted in Taurus in the third but still gives vacillations to matters of communication and security. Venus and Uranus are here out of bounds and both of them in the sixth house of work. So here we have an executive who might get bogged down in the widely dispersed job requirements. Yet this seems a chart well keyed to prosperity, a karma of how she handles what she gains from others and good success in a research career.

151. Scorpio Lady, 8-2-6
Beyond orb Jupiter: 1N01
Data: May 15, 1951, 7:00 p.m.,
San Francisco, California, 37N45, 122W26

This chart is already a minute beyond the one degree orb we have allowed our- selves in the study of zero Jupiters and is included only because it has interesting aspect patterns and midpoint structures. A chain of noviles running from Sun-Mars to Venus-Uranus to Midheaven-Pluto and on to Saturn. Sun-Mars at the start of this chain makes a bi-quintile to Neptune, while Saturn at the end of the novile chain makes a biquintile back to Mercury. And Venus-Uranus is part of a grand trine to Ascendant and Fortuna. The data is from birth certificate.

The immediately visible placement is Pluto, the chart significator, on the Midheaven, and we note that Venus, Uranus and Pluto are all out of bounds. Further, Pluto is sesquiquad to Chiron, square to East Point, and the usual sextile from Neptune which is common to the generation of baby boomers. The Sun is not in a pleasing degree of Taurus (the one where you have to watch you don't lose your head). The Moon in Virgo surprises us by being on the South Node. The lady was obviously more Scorpio with Leo overtones determining a strong status need which might lead to status sabotage. She is a member of an important local Italian family.

She was interested in romantic relationships, was interested in marrying, and available to doing so (which most people seeking romance are not). Here Sun and Mars are closer than in previous charts, Sun ruling status, Mars ruling work, both conjunct in the seventh house. This should indicate a real need for prospering in association with a close partner. Or, Sun close to Mars, her personal ego burning up her energy and in the seventh house of other people. Mars rules the sixth, is not well placed by sign or closeness to the Sun, but is in the house after the one it rules. Any reading for this person would involve many cautions and warnings, and this chart is quite an exercise for any astrologer. Even if the Sun and Mars are not exactly opposite the Ascendant, they are opposite the East Point, a secondary Ascendant very evident as an event determiner. This opposition is, however, mitigated by a trine to Saturn sextile the East Point. There was no discovered interest in suicide with Neptune twelfth, and an alternative interpretation might be that she should pay attention to her own dreams as a help in finding answers to her own problems.

152. Lady Librarian, 1-2-6
Beyond orb Jupiter: 1N03
Data: May 16, 1951, 3:33 a.m. EDT,
Brooklyn, New York, 40N38, 73W56

Although this chart is three minutes out of orb of our zero Jupiter declinations, I cannot resist including it. Not only is it close to the previous example, but it is personally important to events in my life. I was clerk in charge of the film library of the radiology department of a large county hospital. In my tenure, I had almost completed a total remake of the film library, acquired new shelving to modernize the stacks, done the first complete purge of old files, and collating all files into our specially coded indexing. Two months before the job was completed, we acquired a new non-medical administrator, the same described in chart #19. This administrator courting me to find exactly what I did and then acted as if I had lost all knowledge by having told it to

150. Female Student
Natal Chart
May 5 1951
0:24 AM EST +5:00
Indianapolis IN
39N46 086W10
Geocentric
Tropical
Campanus
True Node

Compliments of:-
Joseph Silveira deMello
1755 Franklin Str #204
San Francisco CA 94109
Tel (415) 775-8939
email jsmgemscorp@juno.com

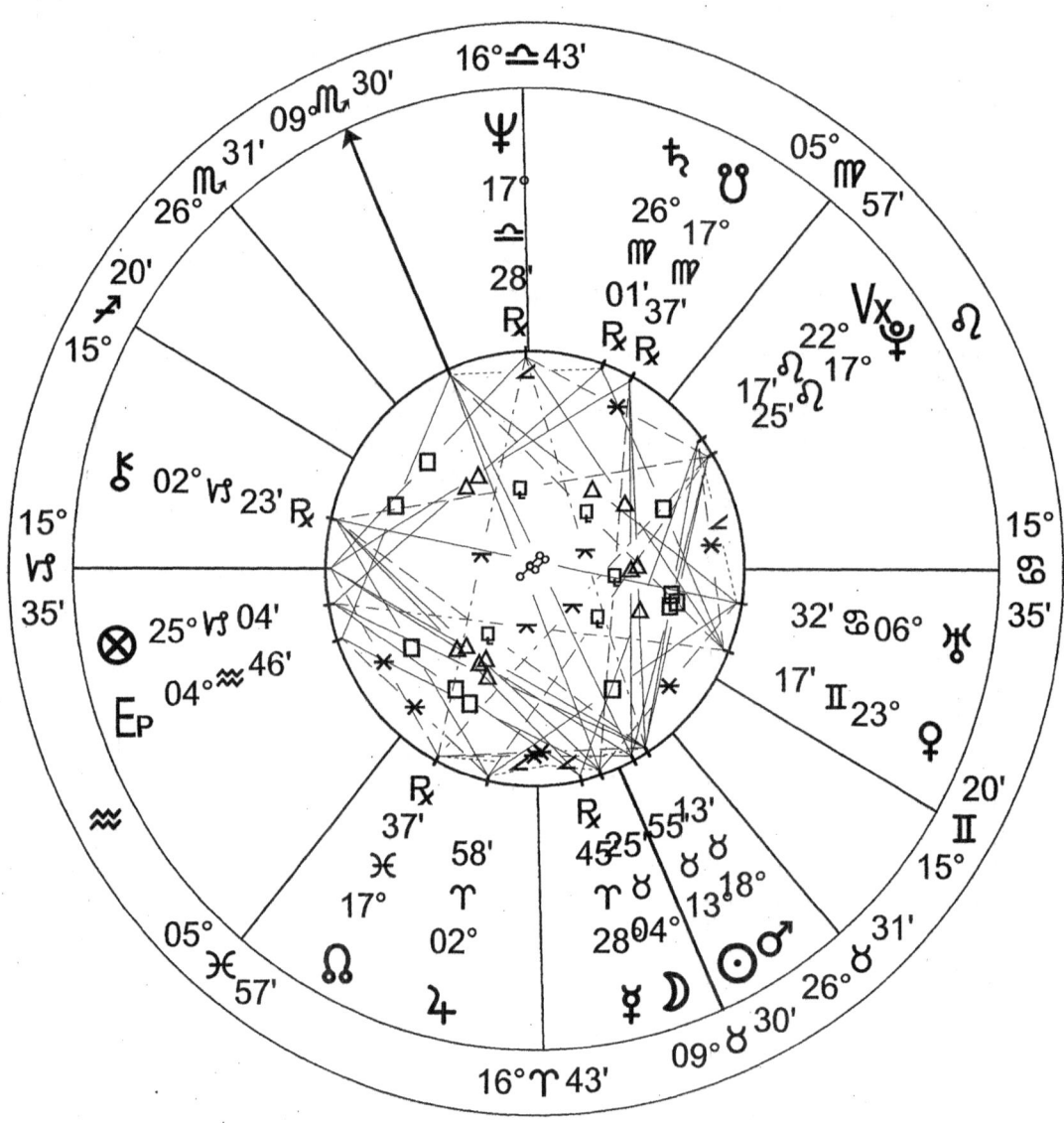

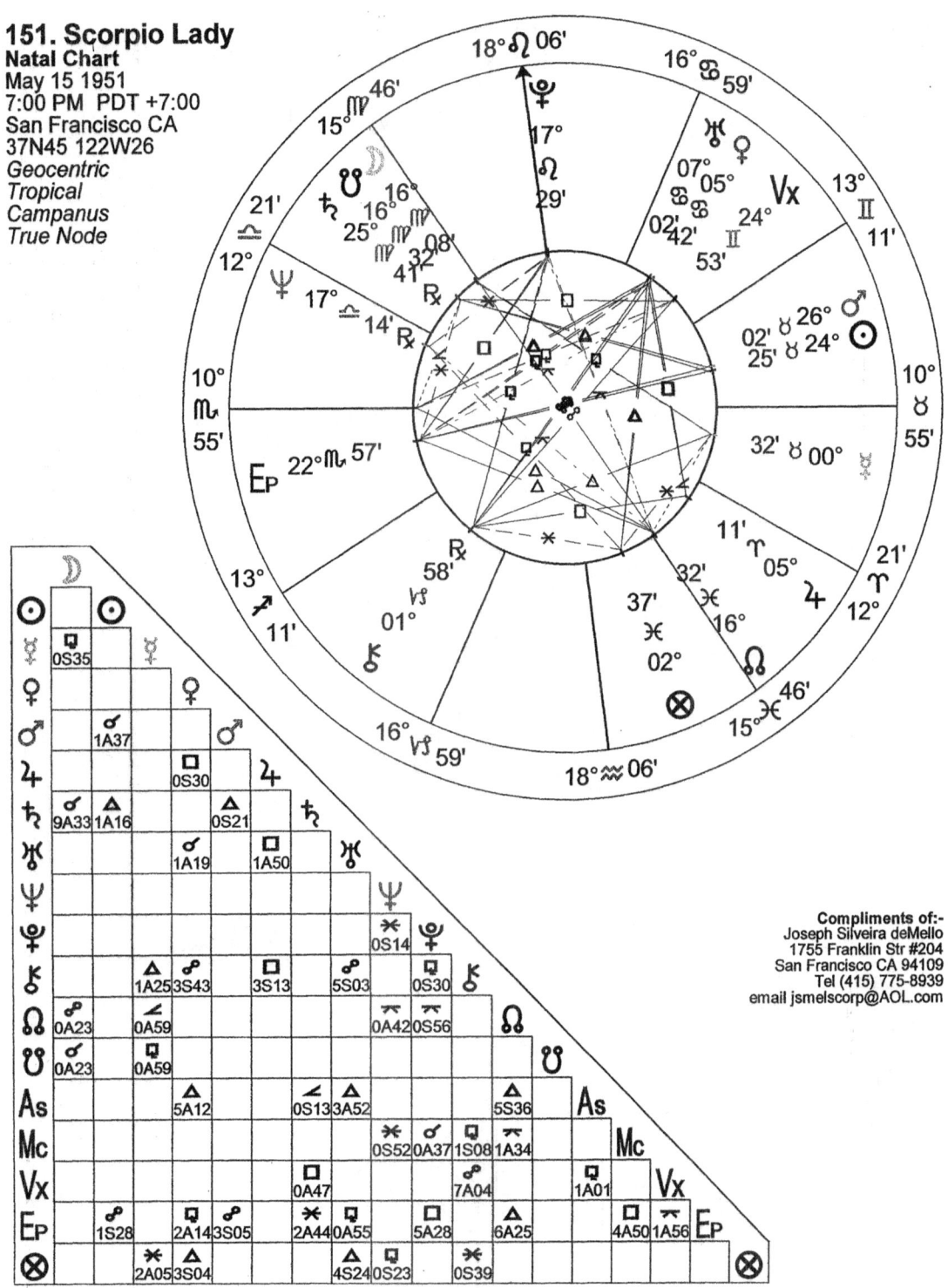

151. Scorpio Lady
Natal Chart
May 15 1951
7:00 PM PDT +7:00
San Francisco CA
37N45 122W26
Geocentric
Tropical
Campanus
True Node

Compliments of:-
Joseph Silveira deMello
1755 Franklin Str #204
San Francisco CA 94109
Tel (415) 775-8939
email jsmelscorp@AOL.com

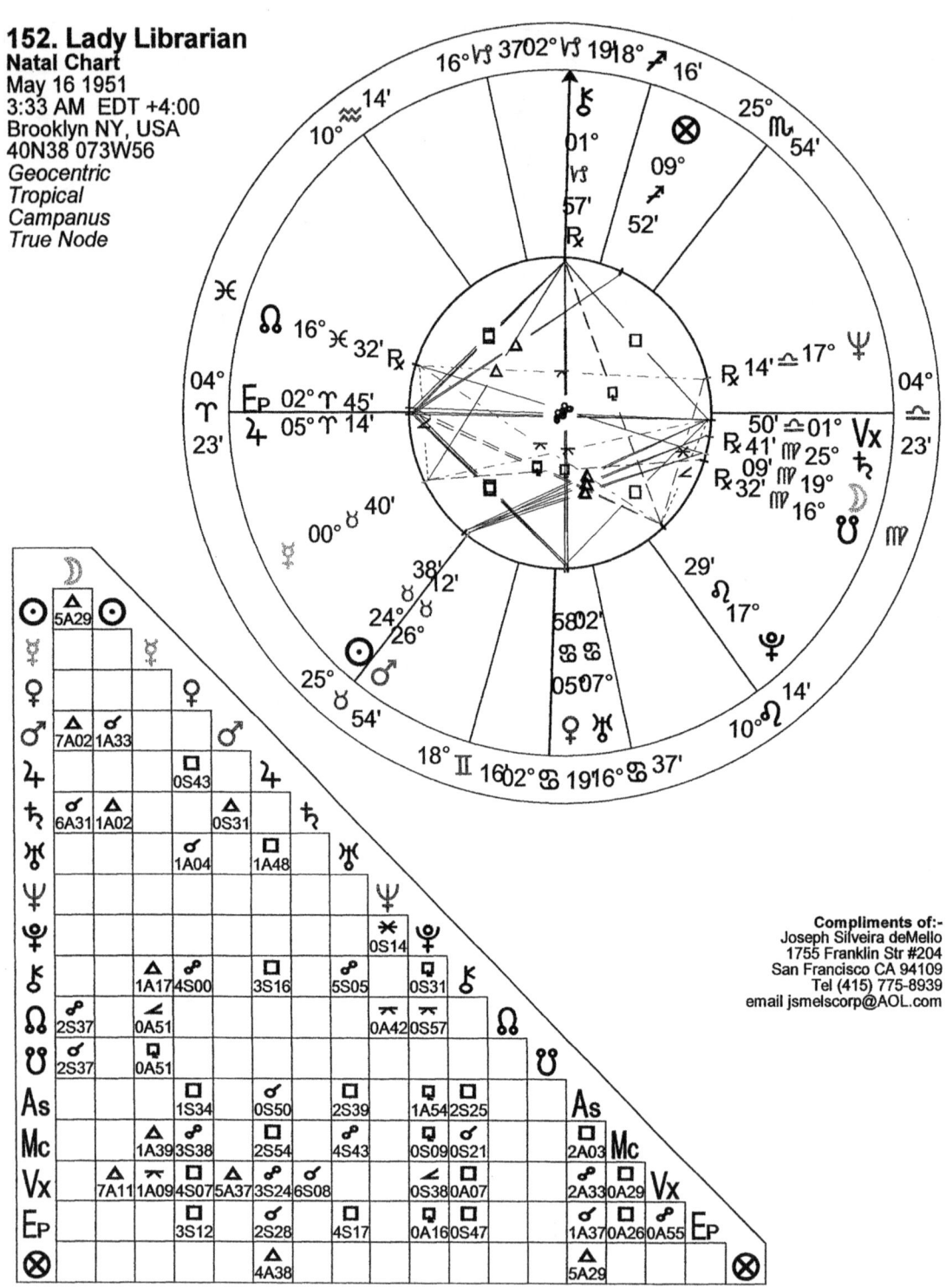

152. Lady Librarian
Natal Chart
May 16 1951
3:33 AM EDT +4:00
Brooklyn NY, USA
40N38 073W56
Geocentric
Tropical
Campanus
True Node

her, and she was now my grand instructor and director. I like nothing so much as to be left alone to do my job, and I proved, one by one, that her ideas for greater efficiency were poorly conceived, did not work, and were, in the matter of file purging using a computer program not keyed to our legal guidelines, an idea whose time had not come. She retaliated by deciding to upgrade my job. To wit, the film library should be headed by someone with library training, especially ridiculous since our code was not the Dewey decimal system. In effect, I was made redundant by a rewritten job description. I had been in charge only by virtue of being one grade higher than the employees whom I supervised. So one day, a lovely young lady arrived to take over my job. I introduced her to her staff, and found I had to teach her the unique code system by which film envelopes were filed.

Of course I had job security, and was assigned to other duties. I took a great liking to my successor and determined I would be of as much help to her as possible. In as many ways as they could, her workforce tested her to see with how much they could get away. The staff was the sort which knew exactly what their duties were not, and gave minimal attention to what their duties actually were. The taking of mandated breaks and lunch times had far greater priority than whether or not the area was covered at all times.

As new head of section, the new librarian found it hard to believe she would have to take a hard line with her workforce. They drove her to distraction, frustration and tears. In addition, after a week, I was told to stay out of anything to do with the library. The medical staff had relied upon me to find lost films in emergency situations. They should now be directed to the new librarian. But my services were still retained for the setting up of films for the AIDS ward and the ICU. This was considered a ten minute job three times daily. In fact this duty took all told two hours daily. All film library staff had proven untrainable for this duty. It was considered too low grade a chore for the status of the new film librarian. The last months I was on this job also coincided with a severe knee injury I exacerbated on the job, so that I had to take time off for therapy which did not aid relations with our civil administrator.

As a sidelight, the Virgo administrator learned that I did astrology and challenged me to be able to tell her anything about herself. Of course she gave me her data with the wrong year of birth, and I immediately found that the chart did not fit her. Several months later, our personnel department had a crisis to prove that all hospital staff came within the guidelines of affirmative action. I was loaned to personnel for this project, and one of the files I had to check happened to be the file of the administrator, and I discovered she had made herself one year older than she actually was.

I originally did my successor's chart in 1983, and I was surprised that what, at the outset seemed a strong chart was in fact flawed. The lovely and willowy lady had Aries rising with Jupiter on the Ascendant; she was quite tall, but also quite thin. She exhibited no Aries qualities whatsoever. Even if this is birth certificate data, she was much more of a Pisces rising with the rulership of Jupiter. Yet this chart went well (and on time) with progressions and transits. She had the Sun with Mars unfortunately in Taurus and both on the second cusp which might have done better in her third house. Moreover, her Moon was in Virgo, the Sun sign of her administrator. The librarian had a cardinal square, one of its points was Chiron on the Midheaven, and the other was the Vertex. She had a Venus-Uranus conjunction in the fourth house opposite Chiron, and perhaps most damaging for her, she had Neptune in the seventh house. Our librarian was surprised to learn that her new job involved doing disciplinary write-ups on the most minor infractions of her staff; this sat no better with the librarian than it had with me. She found her new job neither decorous nor civil. I wondered how long she would last. Of course I did progressions and a solar return, and I readily saw that a change in job and a possible marriage were both in the offing. She married October 29, 1983. I also predicted and prepared her for a job change. Her future husband was supportive, and I found good dates for her to seek other employment. She quickly found a new job and left for greener and calmer pastures. Her Taurus Sun fell in my twelfth indicating past life karmic ties. There is little coincidence in the people who come our way whether as relatives, friends or clients. Although my Sun fell in her seventh house, her Ascendant ruler is in an opposite sign to my Ascendant ruler, her Descendant ruler and mine are also opposite. In comparison charts this is important and shows that there is easy exchange between the two people involved attesting to a cross of responsibility between them.

153. Cystic Fibrosis Victim, 8-8-8
Jupiter: 0N51
Data: October 30, 1951, 7:08 a.m. CST,
Des Moines, Iowa, 41N35, 93W37

One of the great tragedies in the life of a former editor was that he had a step-brother and step-sister, children of a subsequent marriage of his mother, who were the victims of cystic fibrosis. This is the birth certificate data for the step-brother. The data for the younger sister, who died in the fall of 1961, is January 18, 1954, 7:21 a.m. CST, Cedar Rapids, Iowa. The young man of this chart died at noon on his thirteenth birthday, poisoned by a new experimental drug he was testing. A medical dictionary will tell us that cystic fibrosis occurs in the pancreas, a hereditary situation, usually causing death prior to adulthood. It manifests as a widespread dysfunction of the endocrine glands, characterized by signs of chronic pulmonary disease, pancreatic deficiency, abnormally high levels of electrolytes in the perspiration, and occasionally by biliary cirrhosis. "The degree of involvement of organs and glandular systems may vary greatly, with consequent variations in the clinical picture," says *Dorlan's Medical Dictionary*. All that tells us is that this is a complicated situation without much in the way of a favorable prognosis. Cornell, which needs modernizing, notes under "fibrosis" that this is a Saturn ailment.

I have no charts of the fathers, either of my friend or his siblings. The mother married twice more but had no

153. Cystic Firbrosis Victim
Natal Chart
Oct 30 1951
7:08 AM CST +6:00
Des Moines IA
41N35 093W37
Geocentric
Tropical
Campanus
True Node

Compliments of:-
Joseph Silveira deMello
1755 Franklin Str #204
San Francisco CA 94109
Tel (415) 775-8939
email jsmgemscorp@juno.com

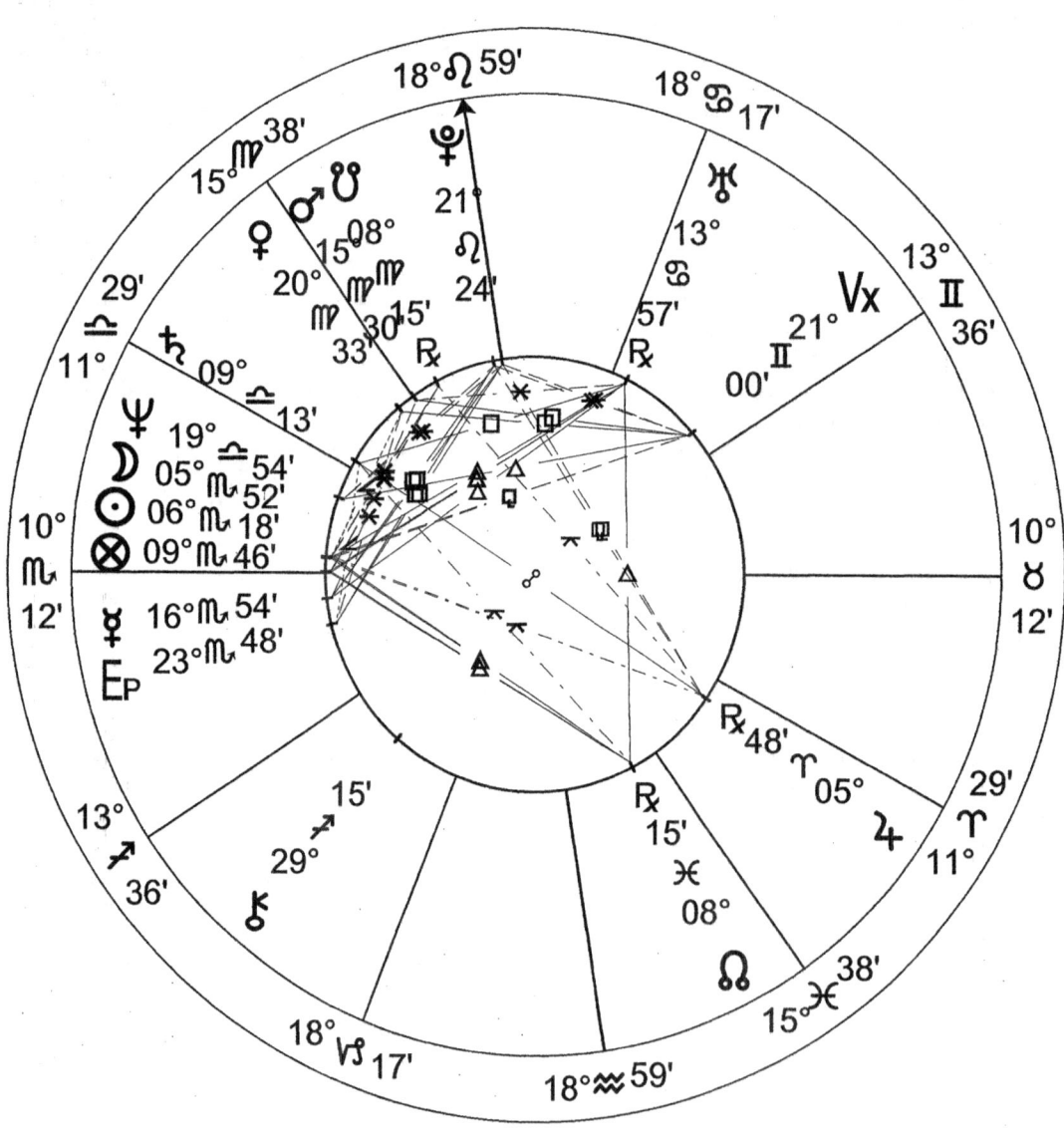

other children. From this chart of a New Moon baby born with a Scorpio Sun-Moon in the twelfth quincunx the Vertex, this chart was indicative of a serious medical situation. Jupiter is quindecile (165°) Venus and Neptune, and Jupiter is opposite Saturn. It is interesting that Pluto highest in the chart indicative of self-sabotage of status is in a chart where the victim elected to be in the drug testing program which proved fatal to him. All of this was forty years ago, far from the genetic research being done today. The problem was that the parents may have been screened for social diseases to get a wedding license, but no notice was given to incompatible blood types.

The large occupation of the twelfth house with Saturn on the cusp sets this up as a karmic situation. What also got to me was data revealed by his progressed chart of the slow movement of Sun and progressed Ascendant and 19 and 20 of Scorpio square natal and progressed Pluto. These progressed Scorpio positions are conjunct the fixed star Serpentis, and I remember several difficult years in the life of my friend, his older brother, when his Ascendant progressed to these Scorpio degrees. I seem to be the only astrologer who takes Serpentis as more serious than mere superstition.

It was bad enough that the girl had gone before she was seven years old, but far worse when the boy lived to his thirteenth birthday and then died that day at noon. The decision to join the test program was okayed by his mother and his doctors. Pluto at the midpoint of Vertex and Neptune is meaningful. The Sun and Moon together is not good. Being a triple of any sign offers no mitigation. The longer you look at this chart, the more dismaying it gets, for it is hard to see with natal and progressions anything rosy to say about it.

In doing the normal chart series, I came to the solar return for his thirteenth birthday, the solar return is the day before the birthday, and the Midheaven of the solar return is Sagittarius, indicator that this is going to be a serious year. Who is to dream that the serious day is the very next day? Three days maybe, at least get the Sun over on the natal Ascendant and Fortune which in the natal is in Scorpio and then called misfortune. In a solar return one of the best indicators is a solar return planet on a natal planet, and here we have Pluto in Virgo on natal Mars and practically a Mercury return in the eighth house and Mercury rules the natal eighth as well as fourth and seventh of the Solar Return. The solar return also has Mars and Moon opposite Saturn. Now the Mercury return also involves Solar Return Neptune and what else could indicate the involvement of a medication in the death. Perhaps under diurnals we can contrast the diurnal chart with one that simply shows the diurnals as transits around the natal chart. His progressed Venus was at 0S19 when he died.

154. The Girlfriend, 4-8-2
Jupiter: 0N29, Venus: 0S20
Data: November 12, 1951, 8:26 p.m. EST,
Quonset, Rhode Island, 41N40, 71W23

This is the chart of an early girl friend of a nephew. This girl always sounded like a heroine or author of bosom ripper romances. Over the years, she has had two children and two failed marriages. She has become something of an Earth Mother and makes costumes for fairs and a scant living selling her own country crafts at such fairs.

The chart has Cancer rising with the Taurus Moon in the eleventh house, and Sun in Scorpio (and Serpentis) in the fifth house. She not only has Jupiter at zero declination, but she has Venus also at zero and contraparallel. This underlines both planets in natal opposition. Then, too, Mercury is out of bounds and Uranus close to that boundary. Venus and Mars are part of a cardinal cross which includes a cardinal cross which includes East Point and Chiron with Venus and Jupiter. She has been very enterprising and is also very creative. My nephew's interest in her was a poetic schoolboy crush and an instance where she matured earlier than he, she being more possessed of depths than he, an Aries person. There are many and various aspects in this chart but no grand trine and kite mitigation exists with the opposition of Fortune and Uranus, the latter being trine-sextile Moon. I should like to recommend that she try her hand at writing since I have found that many people with Mercury out of bounds write with great facility, but I have reservations since she has Virgo ruling her third house. Note Jupiter on her Midheaven.

155. Man About Town, 4-8-6
Jupiter: 0N22
Data: November 21, 1951, 6:52 p.m. EST,
Englewood, New Jersey, 40N53, 73W58

In his recent book the subject says that all the tag lines which might be used to describe him are merely fine ways to call him a d-r-u-n-k, which, of course, he is not. It is well known perhaps worldwide that anyone can drink more in San Francisco than anywhere else. I met this man when he was briefly chef at the garden restaurant where I was the house astrologer. As Cancer rising he was a natural chef. He was also one of the rare non-homosexual employees of this restaurant which was owned by Robbie Campbell and a gathering place for any show business people passing through town. Robbie himself was celebrated as the very handsome black man who in 1950s Paris was the warm up act for Josephine Baker's cabaret show. Our subject was about to work his way through music school. Newly arrived, his first expense was for formal clothes he would need as a concert soloist or man about town.

Eventually his studies were financed by a benefactress who gave him a scholarship, and he was able to leave his chef's job and find part time work in various trendy bars, as bartender, and perhaps not in exact order, he has sung in opera, worked in news radio, and written newspaper columns. Initially he became a regular contributor to the column of the late and great San Francisco columnist Herb Caen. He was affable and interested in everyone he met. He made friends easily. People told him things, and any Cancerian can retell a story better than he originally heard it. Any Scorpio gets told more than he wants to know. Seeing his Mercury far beyond the Sun, I checked the ephemeris to see that Mercury

154. The Girl Friend
Natal Chart
Nov 12 1951
8:26 PM EST +5:00
Quonset RI, USA
41N40 071W23
Geocentric
Tropical
Campanus
True Node

Compliments of:-
Joseph Silveira deMello
1755 Franklin Str #204
San Francisco CA 94109
Tel (415) 775-8939
email jsmgemscorp@juno.com

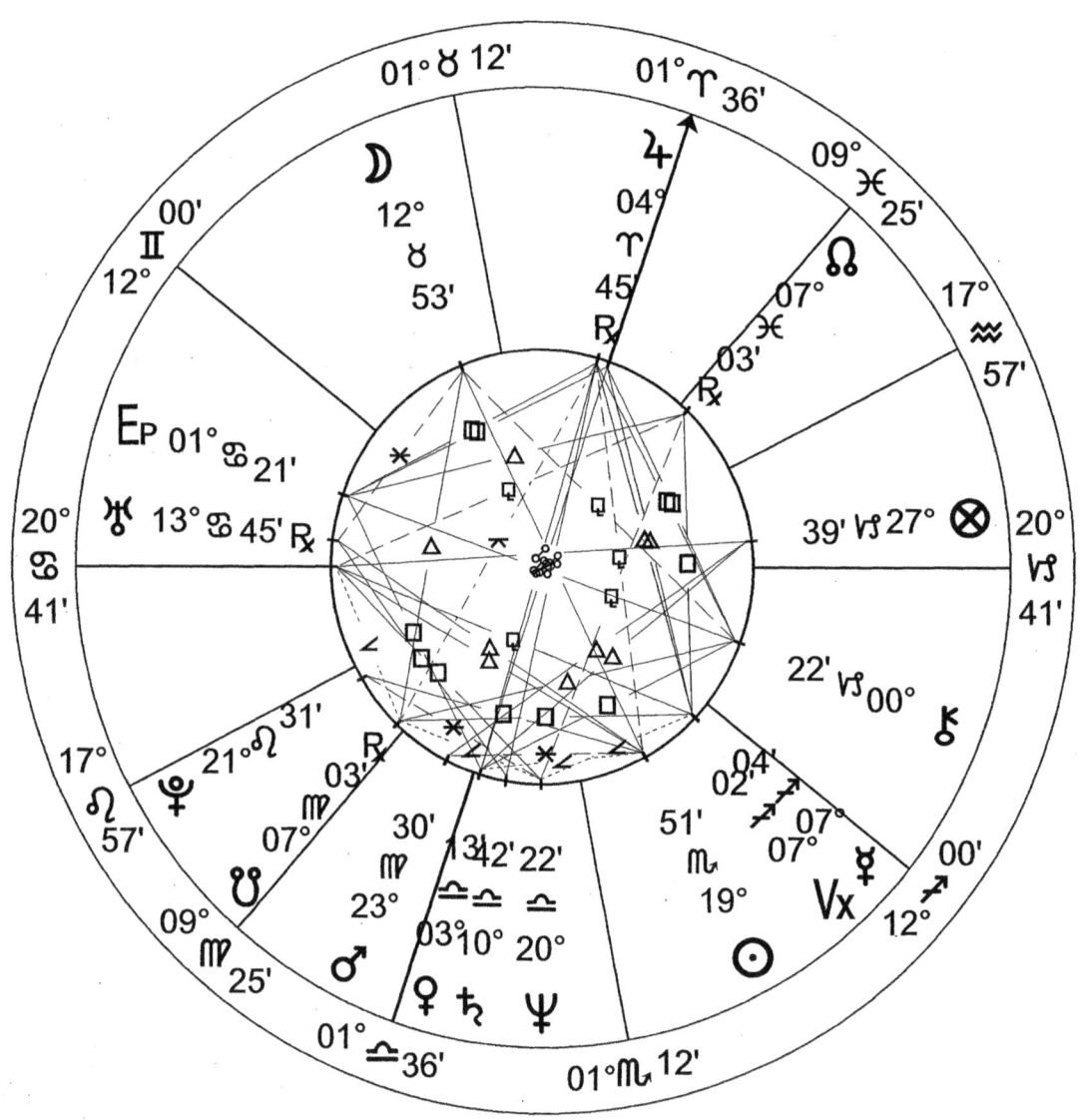

155. Man About Town
Natal Chart
Nov 21 1951
6:52 PM EST +5:00
Englewood NJ
40N53 073W58
Geocentric
Tropical
Campanus
True Node

Compliments of:-
Joseph Silveira deMello
1755 Franklin Str #204
San Francisco CA 94109
Tel (415) 775-8939
email jsmgemscorp@juno.com

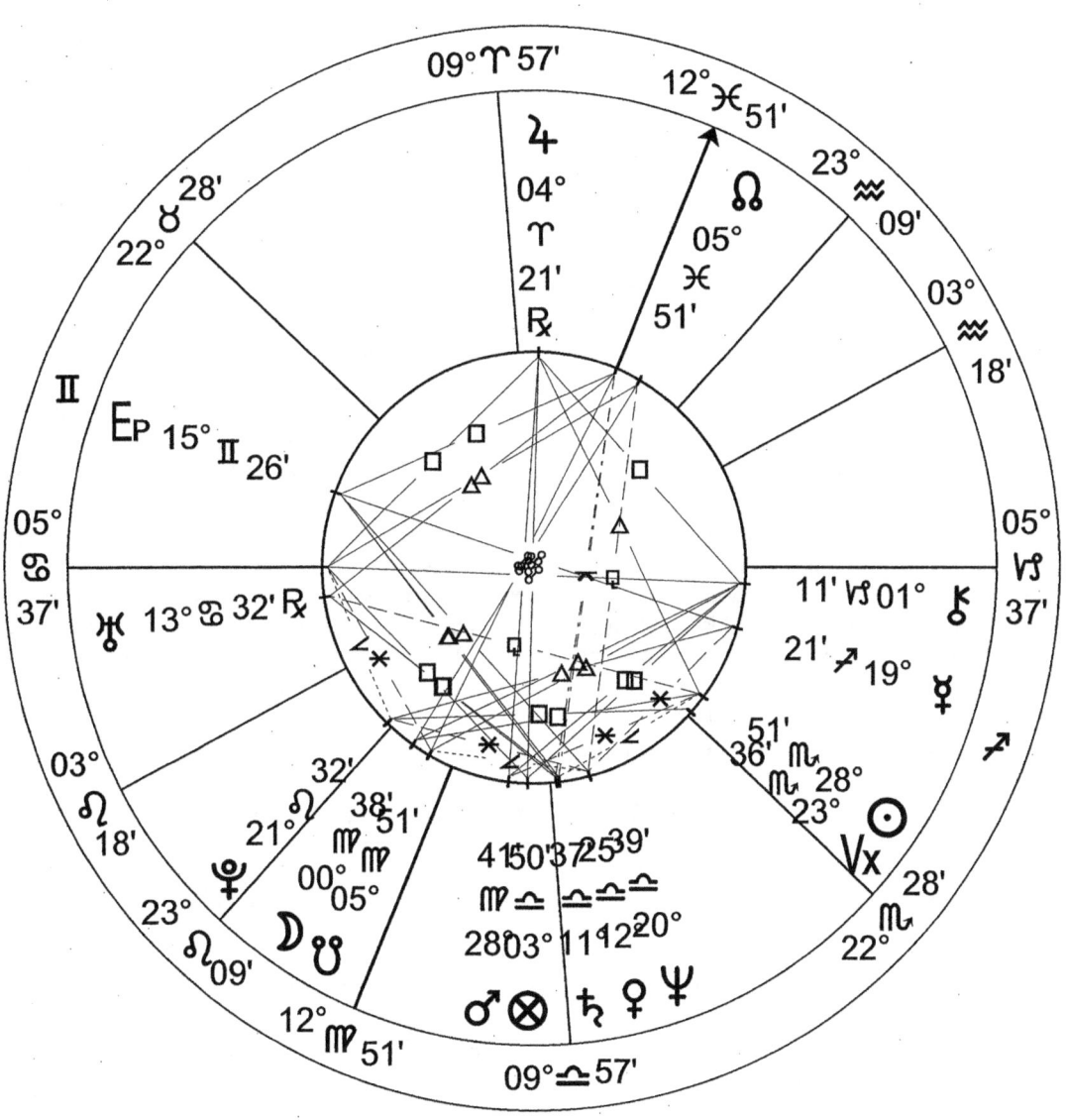

would progress retrograde from ages seventeen to thirty-eight. But this is not so important since Mercury does not rule his angles. Indeed, this chart is a perfect example of what astrology should weed out as less important than what deserves our first attention.

Cancer rising, this Scorpio Sun is ruled by Moon in Virgo in his third house. Uranus on the Ascendant is a creative contributor to his personality, the more so retrograde, and his Mercury is out of bounds, good for a writer. Creativity in this chart is where Leo rules and where the Sun is located as well as the Libra fifth house where he has Saturn, Venus and Neptune. With Uranus first, he is neither exceeding handsome nor plain. He has a round head and face, a medium full beard which is red. The chart does not have a grand trine. Mars in Virgo in the fourth is opposite Jupiter retrograde in the tenth. Mars is also an out of element part of a cardinal grand cross.

156. Career Woman, 8-9-7
Jupiter: 0N21
Data: November 24, 1951, 5:12 a.m.,
Cincinnati, Ohio, 39N06, 84W31

This is the chart of an insurance actuary with whom I had several great conversations backing up everything I have ever known about research probabilities and insurance company attitudes. Insurance companies are made of more sleaze per linear inch than almost any other business. Comparatively, shilling for a medicine show is more honest and more entertaining. My experience as an insurance investigator taught me a great deal but left me with a very jaundiced attitude toward the industry.

Of course, being myself a Scorpio Sun, I was destined to enjoy talking to this Scorpio rising. My Sun falls in her first house which introduces an element of competition between us, while her Sun would fall in my sixth house, describing our relationship entirely with her being a ship which, for me, passed in the night. Our contact was of the moment and may have filled some karmic need between us. I like looking at charts where the rising sign and the Sun sign are adjacent signs, for then the person exhibits personality traits which match well with ego expression. By progression, the Ascendant will become Sagittarian, and the Sun will go on to be Capricorn. Later in life when the Ascendant gets to Capricorn, the Sun will go into Aquarius. She was a really laid back Scorpio. The Moon introduces a spirit of greater balance. Note that Moon and Mars are rather close together, energizing the emotions but often indicative of rather thin skinned responses.

Those are the elements of personality. But it was the career that most interested me. Leo on the Midheaven shows a need for dramatic status, though I blink at the presence of Pluto there. Jupiter on the sixth cusp and opposite to the Moon and Mars, indicates a lot of work and a work ethic. Actuarial insurance work is very Scorpionic, while it also is a non-competitive Sagittarian endeavor, while Moon and Mars in Libra and almost behind the scenes aims for a balanced and almost non-committal air to statistical evaluation. No doubt Mercury out of bounds contributes nicely to this chart and life. In short, the same weighing of all factors which her work requires are the very same sort of things every astrologer meets with every chart.

157. Male Client, 6-9-7
Jupiter: 0N21
Data: November 25, 1951, 1:30 a.m. EST,
DeLand, Florida, 29N02, 81W19

This interesting Libra stellium runs from the first to second house, Mars to Netpune. He was happily working as a bartender-philosopher. However, the astrologer who uses Placidus houses would automatically read Saturn and everything after it in second house. Note that at some time, by progression, this man is going to have a five year period when Mars progresses over his natal and progressed Saturn, not usually a jolly time. Also at some time we must check to see if he will have Mercury going retrograde by progression. The sixth house has Aquarius on the cusp, and even though the pictograph shows pouring water, that does not usually denote tending bar. But he was happy as a clam doing so. He paid attention to his customers, never slighting one to spend more time with another. Happier still was he when he directed all his customers into the same conversation. Virgo at best is critical and discerning and seemed to work that way for him. The chart ruler, Mercury, is in the fourth, opposite the Midheaven and out of bounds, but there was then no known intent to write. This is a chart of power with all those first house planets. The affairs of seven houses are channeled through that area. To properly assess this chart and the personality, all these planets and the aspects they make must be taken into consideration. The Sun, the heart of the matter, communications and business, and Mercury are what is important, home and security. The weight is lessened that they are not in the rising sign. At least in this chart Neptune is already in the second house. Combinations of Venus and Neptune usually give some move toward artistic endeavor. Note that his North Node of intake is in work and service, release through the South Node in twelfth house.

158. Upscale Man, 3-9-9
Jupiter: 0N21, Mars: 0N10 (but Mars in southern sign Libra
Data: November 29, 1951, 6:11 p.m. PST,
San Francisco, California, 37N45, 122W26

Although born the same day as the previous client, these men never met. The previous man was Caucasian, and this man is Black. This man had a sister and mother also very ambitious, and the family had decided as a whole in what upscale manner they would rise. He was a student majoring in political science, and he and his family were active in social causes and very polished. They divided their time between San Francisco and New York, but always preferred to return west. This chart has Gemini rising in a late degree, but he had too many interests to dwell on negativities. He was born

156. Career Woman
Natal Chart
Nov 24 1951
5:12 AM EST +5:00
Cincinnati OH
39N06 084W31
Geocentric
Tropical
Campanus
True Node

Compliments of:-
Joseph Silveira deMello
1755 Franklin Str #204
San Francisco CA 94109
Tel (415) 775-8939
email jsmgemscorp@juno.com

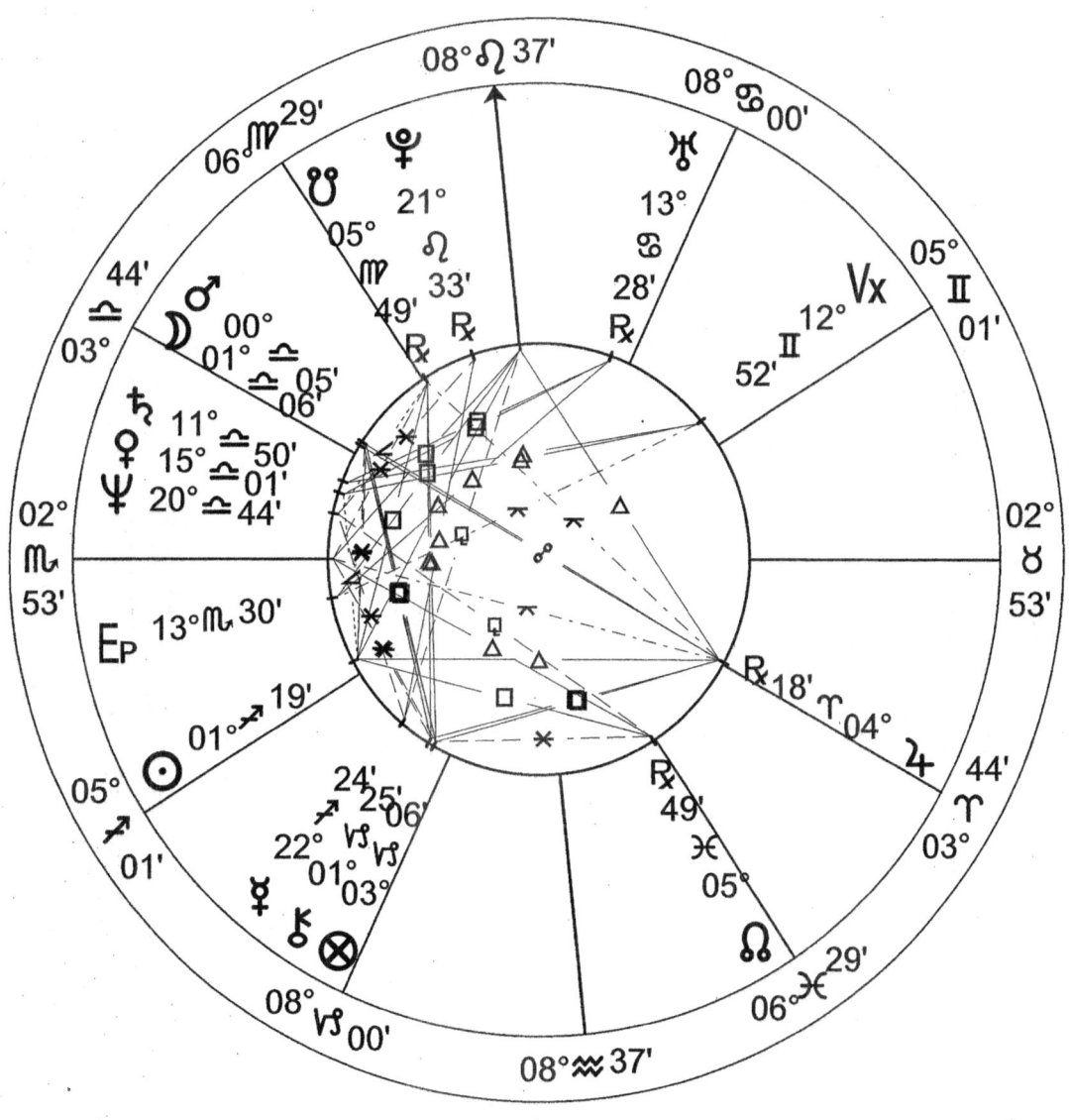

157. Male Client
Natal Chart
Nov 25 1951
1:30 AM EST +5:00
De Land FL, USA
29N02 081W19
Geocentric
Tropical
Campanus
True Node

Compliments of:-
Joseph Silveira deMello
1755 Franklin Str #204
San Francisco CA 94109
Tel (415) 775-8939
email jsmgemscorp@juno.com

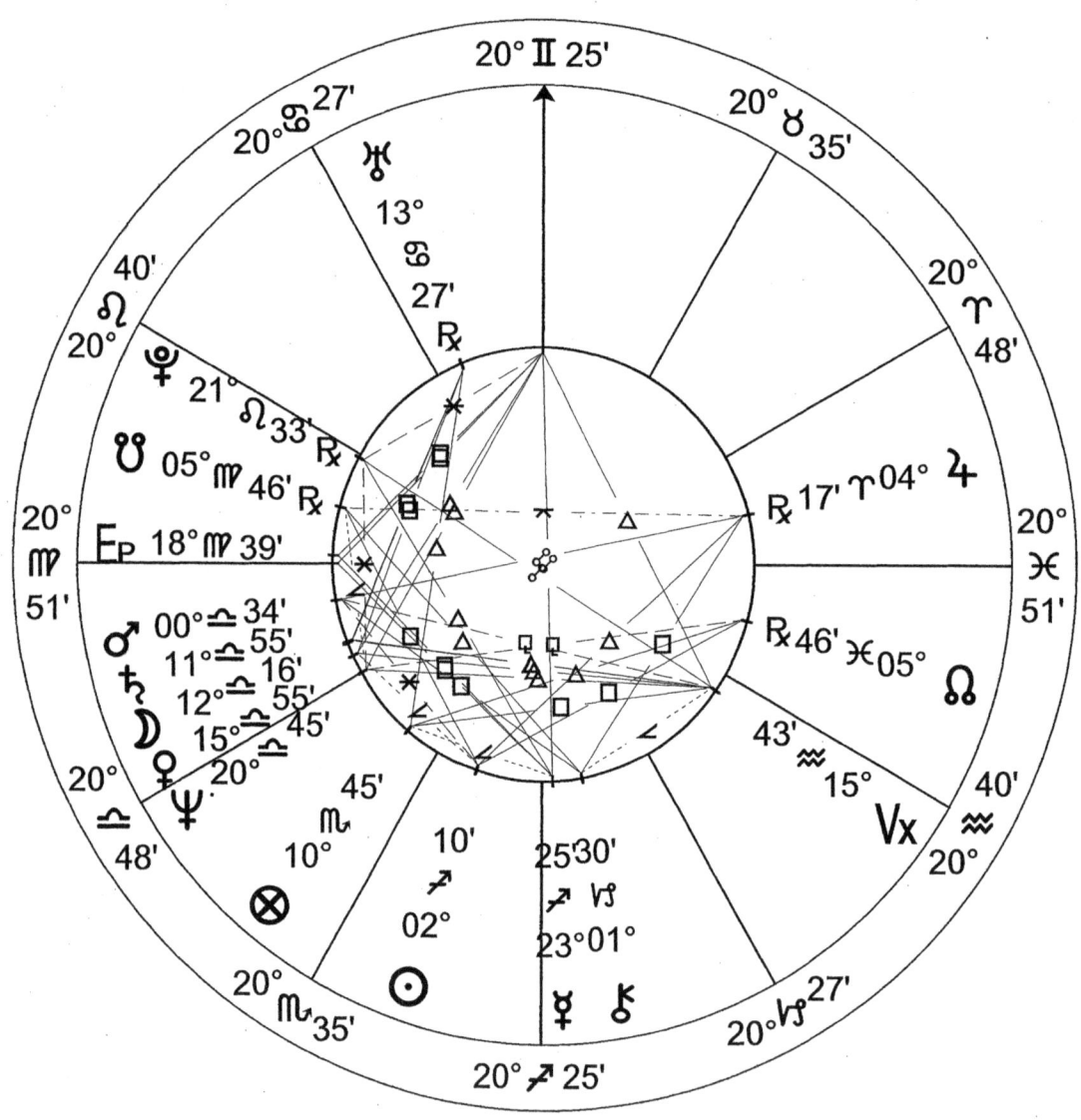

158. Upscale Male
Natal Chart
Nov 25 1951
6:11 PM PST +8:00
San Francisco CA
37N45 122W26
Geocentric
Tropical
Campanus
True Node

Compliments of:-
Joseph Silveira deMello
1755 Franklin Str #204
San Francisco CA 94109
Tel (415) 775-8939
email jsmgemscorp@juno.com

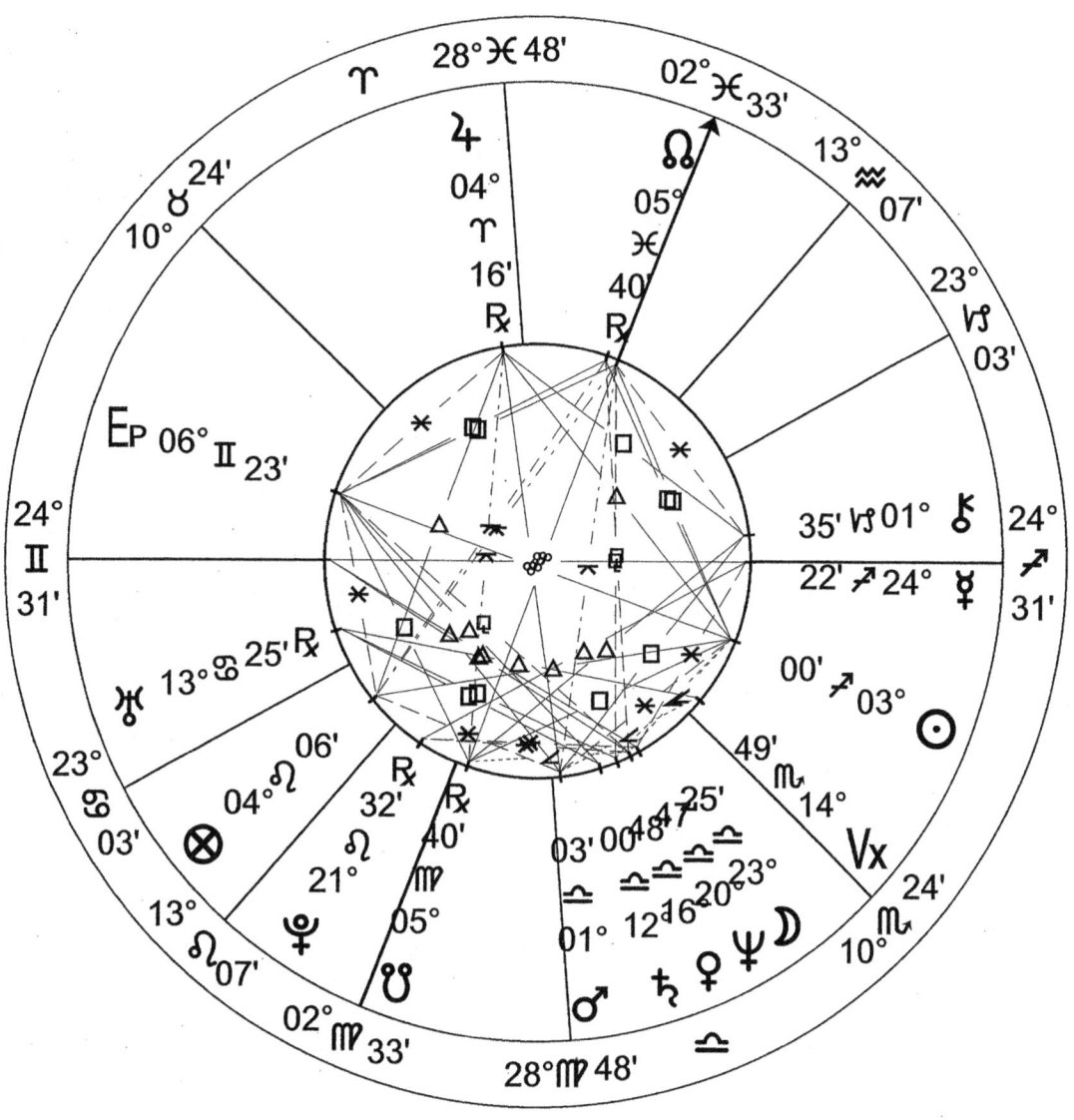

with both Sun and Moon in Sagittarius to balance Gemini rising, and his chart significator, Mercury in Sagittarius, opposite his Ascendant. It was thought he might go into politics, a family desire, but he did not. The last time I touched base with his family, I was told he is married and has two children, but nothing was said of his career. Not only is Jupiter at zero declination, but so is Mars (Mars is North, but in a southern sign). Mercury and Moon are out of bounds. Of all the careers astrology might pick for him, we finally have to take notice of Saturn in the fifth house, where perhaps more was expected of him than he wished to give.

159. Career Concerns, 10-9-9
Jupiter: 0N21, Mars: 0N17 (but Mars in Libra,
a southern sign)
Data: November 29, 1951, 9:15 a.m. EST,
Jenkentown, Pennsylvania, 40N05, 75W08

This young man came to me when he and his new partner were in a dilemma. They had just recently started to share their lives in a new apartment. They had found a very nice place, moved in, made essential purchases, and done a bit of decorating. So what should be more timely to surface but a career situation. He was offered a promotion too good to pass up. And off course the promotion involved a transfer to another location. There was no question of turning down the promotion. But both were also in an economic crunch. They had just put down big money on first and last month's rent and a hefty security deposit. They had spent every cent they had to spare on their new home. This man had a real power job in the financial community, while his friend, six years older, was bartender in a fashionable watering hole. Should they go where his career would take them or defer to their preference for staying in San Francisco?

First of all, it was obvious that the bartender could easily move and get another similar job anywhere in the world. The problem was that the bartender had Leo rising, Sun in Taurus, and the Moon, alas, in Pisces. So it wasn't that obvious, not without a lot of talk of all the sacrifices they would have to make. The other man does not have Jupiter at zero declination, but this man has both Mars and Jupiter at zero declination and parallel in the sense that Mars is in a southern sign but is zero North. Sun is highest planet in his partner's chart, and it was obvious both from personal observation of the men involved and their charts that the bartender was the father figure of this younger businessman who was being promoted. The charts of both men loom large with drama of one and control for this one, but this is the cardinal and mutable chart. They really needed someone to talk as a sounding board, and the odd thing is that neither chart by progressions or transits had any indication of moving.

This is a Capricorn rising chart with birth just after a New Moon in Sagittarius and in the twelfth house. Although this is a strong twelfth house, with a very ambitious stellium in the ninth house consisting of Mars, Saturn, Venus and Neptune and Mars is directly opposite Jupiter retrograde in the third house. This young man had quite an important job for his youthfulness, and his job was very important to him. It was obvious they would have to move. Neither of them could afford the new apartment by himself, nor with their newly found relationship were they willing to be parted. The final upshot was that they did indeed move away from San Francisco and would probably try to angle a future promotion that would let them return here.

160. Female Client, 3-9-1
Jupiter: 0N26
Data: December 7, 1951, 3:45 p.m. CST,
Princeton, Minnesota, 45N34, 93W36

This client and her mother came to me for readings and brought birth certificate records. The mother was a career employee of a credit union in the suburban area, this, the daughter, round, a bit overweight, was employed editing and publishing in the legal field. I told of potential big changes coming upon her three years hence, stressing the importance of being ready for these, going on a diet, readying to direct her attention to the people close around her. Although one change involved transiting Saturn close to going into her seventh house, she was not interested in relationships or romance. It is not often that one finds a Gemini rising wary of social intercourse, but the Sun is in Sagittarius seems to have been more powerful with this lady than Gemini rising. Like most Sagittarians, she was wary of people and held back on any new encounters not wishing them to come too close too quickly. It seemed obvious to me that she would be more creative if she had a partner. She was content to live with her mother. Her fifth house ruled by Leo only underlined a need of creativity, but with Pluto on its cusp did not ready her for big changes before she felt herself ready to proceed. Note that Mercury the chart significator is at the end of the seventh house with Chiron in early Capricorn, but Mercury is out of bounds by declination.

Work was what mattered to her, and she had a very wide sixth house with four planets in it, including Mars, all of them in Libra. Note that sixth and twelfth contain two intercepted signs. Now we see the stellium of Mars, Saturn and Neptune has been robbed of Saturn at the midpoint of Mars and Neptune, and Venus has gone further onward so that what we have here is Neptune at the midpoint of Saturn-Venus. Check also how Mars and Moon-Jupiter have moved in regard to their opposition to Mars and Saturn. When I see Mars before Saturn, I always check for when Mars will progress across natal and progressed Saturn usually involving about five years of difficult frustrations. Further note that Jupiter is no longer retrograde as in the immediately preceding examples. This chart has a grand trine from Midheaven to Ascendant to Saturn. But instead of having a cardinal square, she has two quite separate T-squares. The first is an opposition of Moon to Saturn with Uranus at the midpoint, the second, Jupiter-Fortune with Mercury-Chiron at the midpoint. She was a most interesting person to read for and I remember the session as quite successful, a thing one cannot often say and at first rather doubtful.

159. Male Career Concerns
Natal Chart
Nov 29 1951
9:15 AM EST +5:00
Jenkentown PA
40N05 075W08
Geocentric
Tropical
Campanus
True Node

Compliments of:-
Joseph Silveira deMello
1755 Franklin Str #204
San Francisco CA 94109
Tel (415) 775-8939
email jsmgemscorp@juno.com

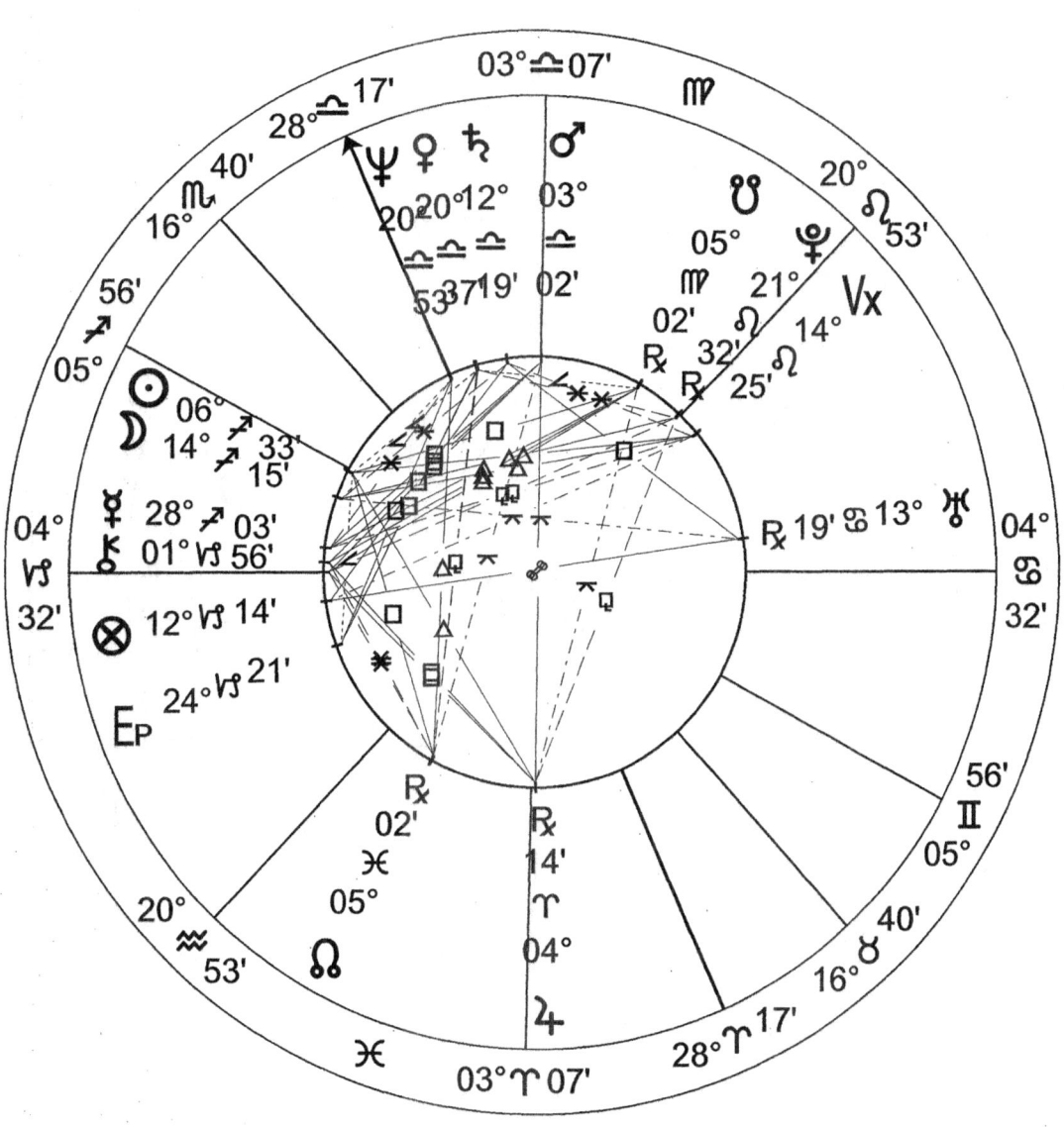

160. Female Client
Natal Chart
Dec 7 1951
3:45 PM CST +6:00
Princeton MN
45N34 093W36
Geocentric
Tropical
Campanus
True Node

Compliments of:-
Joseph Silveira deMello
1755 Franklin Str #204
San Francisco CA 94109
Tel (415) 775-8939
email jsmgemscorp@juno.com

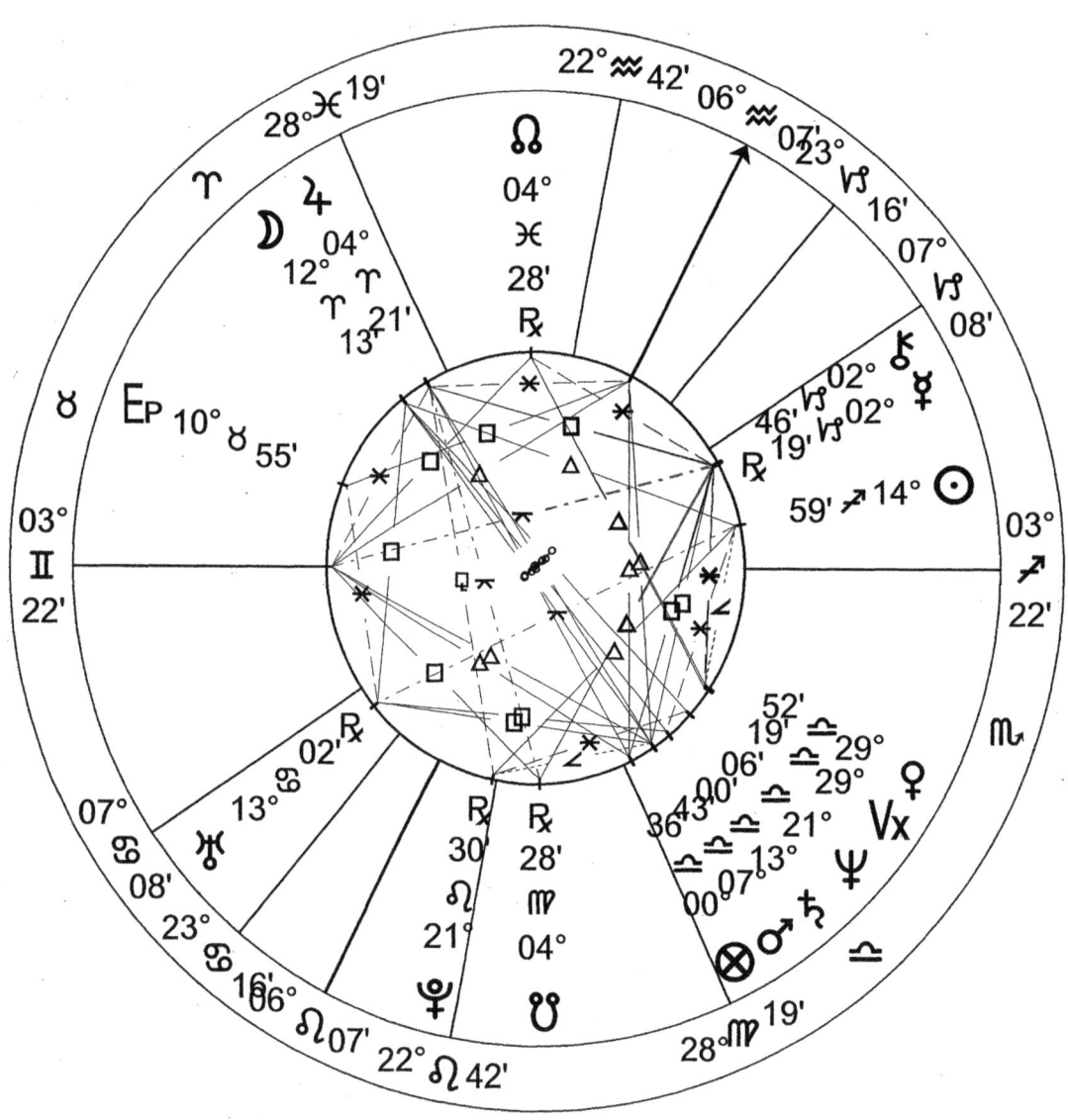

161. Troubled Brother, 4-10-7
Jupiter, 0N50
Data: December 23, 1951, 5:02 p.m. CST,
Springfield, Illinois, 39N49, 89W39

This chart is that of the uncle of #55, Child of Gender Problem. I knew him as brother of the father of #55, but it would later turn out that he was that indeed, but that the father of #55 was actually #55's birth mother who had decided to change to the male gender. The origins of the family were Mexican and Roman Catholic, but both siblings had been born and raised in Illinois. Later the family moved to the San Francisco area.

This chart has Cancer rising, and it is the Cancers of this world who keep families together. He was also godfather of the two children. The Capricorn Sun is in the late sixth house applying to an opposition to the Ascendant, and its ruler Saturn is in the fifth house with Mars separating from a conjunction. With this Saturn, much was expected of this young man by his parents, and it did seem he was a stabilizing influence in this group of people. Combined with Mars, we see much frustration, and the chart is not aided by the further closeness of Neptune, or from a Moon about to go into Scorpio.

162. Spiritual Lady, 10-10-8
Jupiter: 0N52
Data: December 24, 1971, 7:30 a.m. PST,
San Francisco, California, 37N45. 122W26

This is the chart of a well to do Descendant of a banking family who had cut off her heritage to live a permissive lifestyle and adopted a spiritual Hindu name. She was living with a long time client who had been a hooker, a dope dealer, and who had even served a jail term. My original client was very interesting. I was very curious and predisposed to do as she asked, which was that I make a house call to give her new friend a reading. This new client hated having to get dressed and to leave her home.

The subject of this chart was very beautiful, and since she was being a Hindu lady at home, she insisted on not wearing clothing to conceal her upper body. But, of course, I should not be uncomfortable. That is rather easier to say than to do. I took refuge in professionalism, like a doctor examining harem girls, divided my attention between eye contact and studying the chart as I spoke. Of course I had studied the chart as I had set it up, a double Capricorn clued me to a person of a rather controlling disposition, the Sun but a few minutes above the Ascendant, personality in charge of ego, and Chiron of obvious agendas also on the Ascendant. If Chiron rules Libra, here Libra was the Midheaven of the chart with Neptune right up there, and as highest planet in the chart, I was inclined to see her as a Neptunian, processing information wildly to suit herself. She had a need to run things despite the fact that her girlfriend, my original client, really was the one in total control. In any case, though she touted herself as spiritual, she was as hard as nails as insistent spiritual people so often are.

I might add that both ladies had a fondness for drugs which at that time had gone beyond marijuana to nose candy. What really made me more uncomfortable was the presence of drug paraphernalia on every end table and coffee table, a full array of oval mirrors, razor blades, little plastic rulers, and tiny plastic straws. I kept wanting to ask my friend what would happen if the police were ever to arrive unexpectedly with all that stuff laid out all over the place. I had read for my old client of specific dates when she should be wary of being involved in drug activity. It was in that period that a friend of hers had invited her to accompany him on a ride to the airport where he was to pick up a package. She had declined. He went alone, his package contained drugs, and he was arrested.

At every turn, the subject of this chart insisted on her very high evolvement as a spiritual persona. I did not challenge her. Not my business to be rude. Now I had chart and person together to match one with the other. Five planets to the east, five to the west, but nine above the horizon, and what you see is what you get. Mercury retrograde in the twelfth rules her ninth house which is further dubiously occupied by Mars separating from Saturn and applying to Neptune, and what would surely be some interesting progressions. The sixth house is just as unoccupied as it might be by a rich girl who had never worked and ruled by Gemini which is not exactly a service sign. Spiritual she might be, but she was also permissively self-indulgent, the only trine being from Mercury to Pluto in the eighth. There are just too many contradictory indicators in the chart that required real attention.

This young lady had found a cozy nest with an equally well-to-do partner and preferred to live a lesbian lifestyle as well. Actually money, sex and drugs were her main interests. Status also meant a great deal to her even if she kept changing her mind about it, denying her innate social status, going with the Scorpio Moon, she would have liked to appear deeper, but Scorpio, though deeper, is also more sexy than spiritual. I emphasized her ninth house collection of three planets. Saturn might be exalted, but Mars was in detriment, and Neptune hardly penetrates philosophy with reality. Viewing her Virgo ninth and its tenants, one can only wonder what philosophy she might go to as she grows older.

I honestly did not think that I might have been the right person to give this young lady a reading as my Sun is exactly on her Moon. The assorted aspects in this chart are troublesome, such as Venus square Pluto and both sesquiquad Jupiter. And I wondered how the energy of a cardinal chart with all those squares went with an indolent life. I was kept busy a bit over an hour and I was relieved when this reading finally came to an end. My original client hoped for a word with me about her own chart, but this was not to be, as her friend was not interested in her partner's chart and insisted my time there was to be hers exclusively. My original client had no need that I do a comparison chart between them as she was confident she could handle any thing that came up in their relationship.

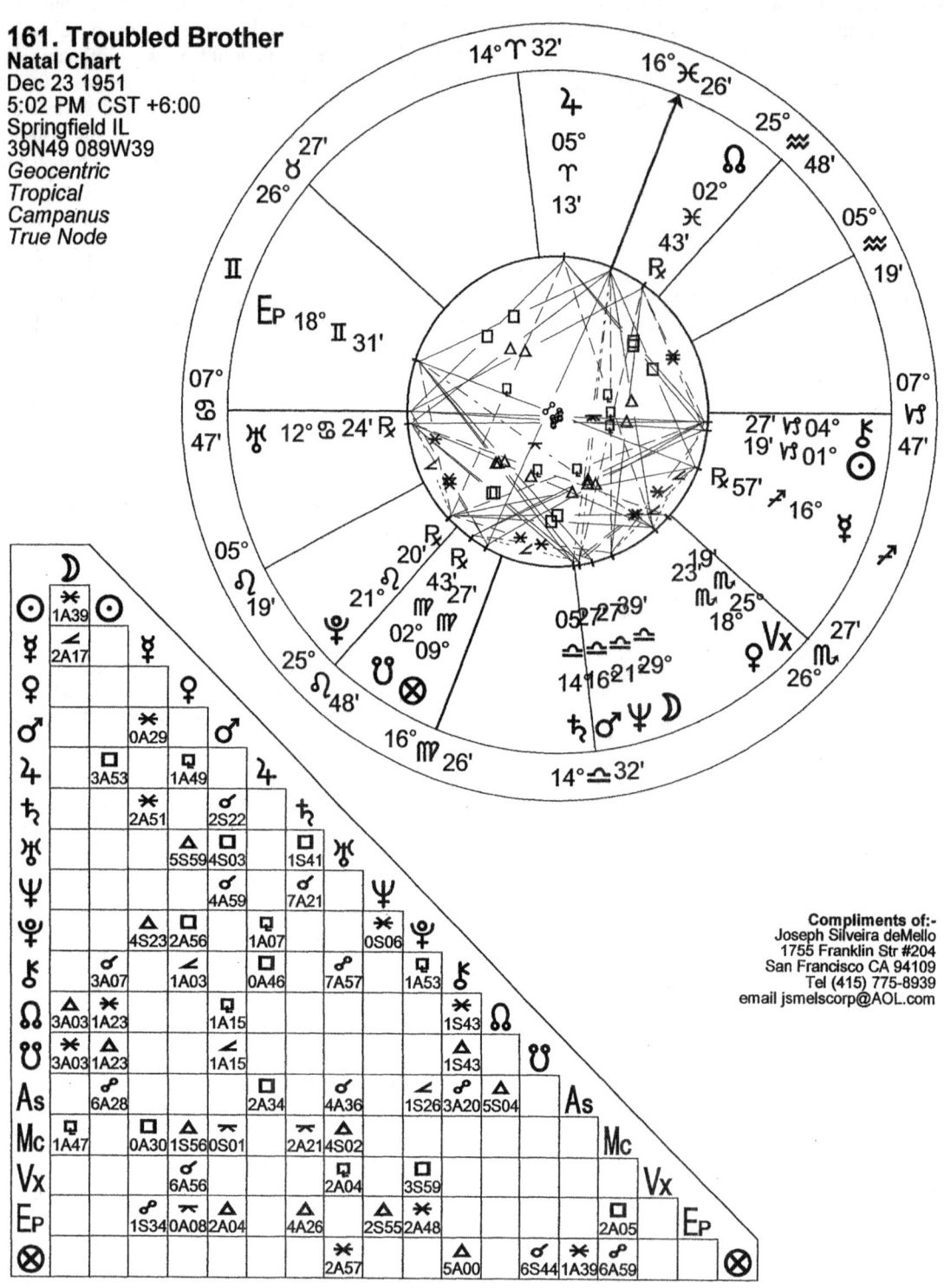

161. Troubled Brother
Natal Chart
Dec 23 1951
5:02 PM CST +6:00
Springfield IL
39N49 089W39
Geocentric
Tropical
Campanus
True Node

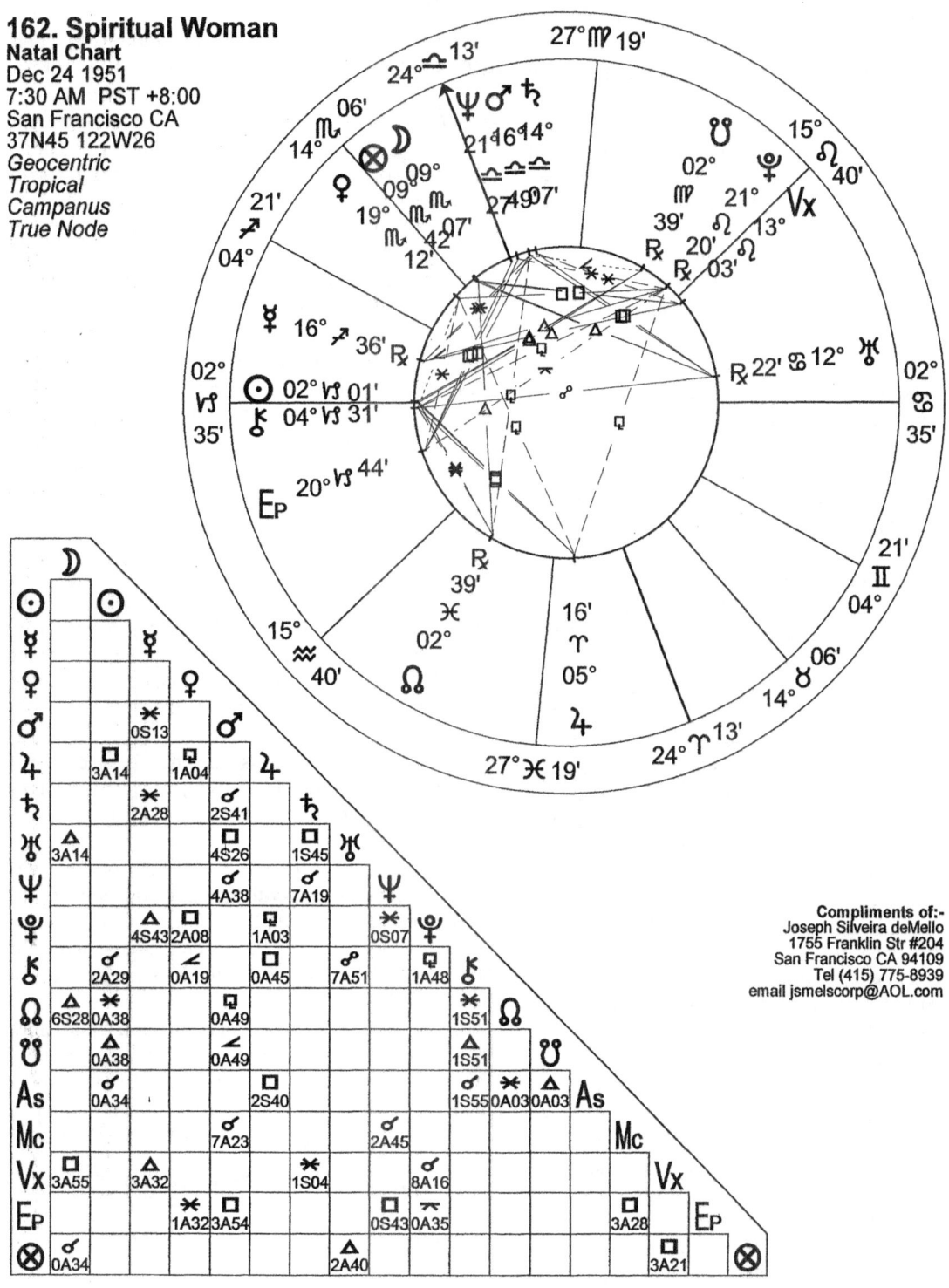

163. Blond Young Man, 11-11-2
Jupiter: 0N58
Data: February 8, 1957, 7:26 a.m. CET,
Hamburg, Germany, 53N33, 10E00

This is the chart of an army brat, son of a father who was a career man in the US Army of Occupation in Germany. Whatever may be said of the offspring of such families, the usual difficulty is serving a dominant father who's structured career is carried over into child rearing in the home. Of course, due to his early European education, this young man grew up fluently able to make himself understood in three languages. He was small-boned and blond and just the sort of young man to attract the attention of the owner of the garden restaurant previously mentioned. This young man had walked into this situation as if he had found a bird's nest on the ground. Psychologists notwithstanding, he knew exactly what the situation was. Any father image was preferable to the father he already had, and his basic criteria was to find a totally approving and non-critical parental figure. Luckily this young man was on the scene and away (gone just as suddenly as had been his arrival) long before his employer acquired immune deficiency syndrome.

Although he had just turned twenty-one years of age when I met him, he was so boyish that one might have said he was a high school freshman. He had run away from home, could have turned into a street urchin, but he quickly found a job, and had papers to prove his age since the restaurant served alcoholic beverages. He was as bright as a new penny. He was very proper and deferentially polite and well mannered. Aquarius rising, he could have been in motion pictures, a career choice not the least interesting to him.

When I did the chart, I was surprised to see Venus just above the Ascendant and wondered what I had missed when I looked at him. When Venus is in the twelfth house, there is usually some clearly visible facial blemish. There was none. He was Aquarius rising with the Sun in the first house but also Chiron. His employer, by the way, was a Leo with Aquarius rising. So we have a double Aquarian teamed up with a double of Moon and Mars in Taurus, the latter duo in his second house. He indeed wanted to make money, and he would rather it be given him than he work for it. Fortune and Neptune on the cusp of his eighth and both are opposite Mars. But his chart significator is Saturn in Sagittarius in his tenth house. The chart is complicated by too many aspects, grand trines and fixed squares.

In any house system this chart would have widely skewed houses due to his birth location. But it certainly tells the astrologer what matters of his chart are more important to him. The young man was in very mild revolt, unlike his American counterparts, was a fine conversationalist on a wide variety of topics. His Mercury is in Capricorn, intercepted in the twelfth house, but rules the fourth, fifth, and sixth houses, as well as an intercepted portion of his eighth house. If he had a plan for tomorrow, he may have been living it right then, but no one was privy to it. His intercepted Jupiter in the seventh house is at the midpoint of his mid-heaven and Uranus and is in a grand trine with Mercury and Moon and South Node. Saturn is in the tenth house not only bring his father into career concerns but indicate late career development. Note that Sun-Uranus are in mutual reception.

164. Pretty Girl, 8-5-12
Jupiter: 0N43
Data: August 11, 1957, 12:30 p.m. PDT,
San Jose, California, 37N20, 121W53

I have a client of many years for whom I have done many charts and many comparison surveys with the girls of his dreams. This client, once married and the father of a grown daughter, has been divorced, due to his philandering, and he has no contact with his past family. He is the sort of man who has aged but whose girl friends seem to get ever younger. He also has the dubious habit of courting the mothers of the girls who attract his interest in the hope the girls will notice him or wish to vie with their mothers for his affections. So far as I know, he has never been very successful.

The major interest here was to do a comparison survey between his chart and that of this young lady. There were scant touches between the two charts. Furthermore, the comparison survey rather plainly revealed that the tables would turn against him, and it would be she who would eventually cheat on him. This survey joined all the other such surveys I did for this man in never getting to first base with the mothers or the daughters.

Although we are looking at this chart because of her zero Jupiter declination, here we note Jupiter on the edge of the twelfth house in early Libra, in a north declination and in a southern sign, and Neptune barely into Scorpio is above the Scorpio Ascendant. We cannot escape her tenth house, Leo on Midheaven and Sun in tenth, but Uranus out-ranks the Sun by being the highest planet in the chart. Notice also that the Sun is "besieged" between Uranus and Pluto, the Sun, though in Leo, is debilitated between two malefics. And then we have to deal with Mars and Pluto conjunct in different signs also in the tenth. Pluto is chart significator. I find this a very interesting chart in line with the opposition aspects. Sun and Uranus are opposite Chiron; Pluto and Mars are opposite the Moon in early Pieces on the edge of the fifth house; the East Point and North Node are opposite the South Node and Fortune. The Sun is focal at the T-square midpoint of this latter opposition while Chiron is at the T-square opposition of the same opposition, thus forming a fixed square. This chart is far stronger than the chart of her would be swain, and he may be lucky this potential romance was never realized.

165. Thomas, Earl of Craven, 2-6-5
Jupiter: 0S18
Data: August 24, 1957, 9:30 p.m. GMT,
London, England, 51N31, 0W06

Some will be familiar with this chart of a client of the late English astrologer Judith Gee which she shared with readers of Mercury Hour many years ago. We were

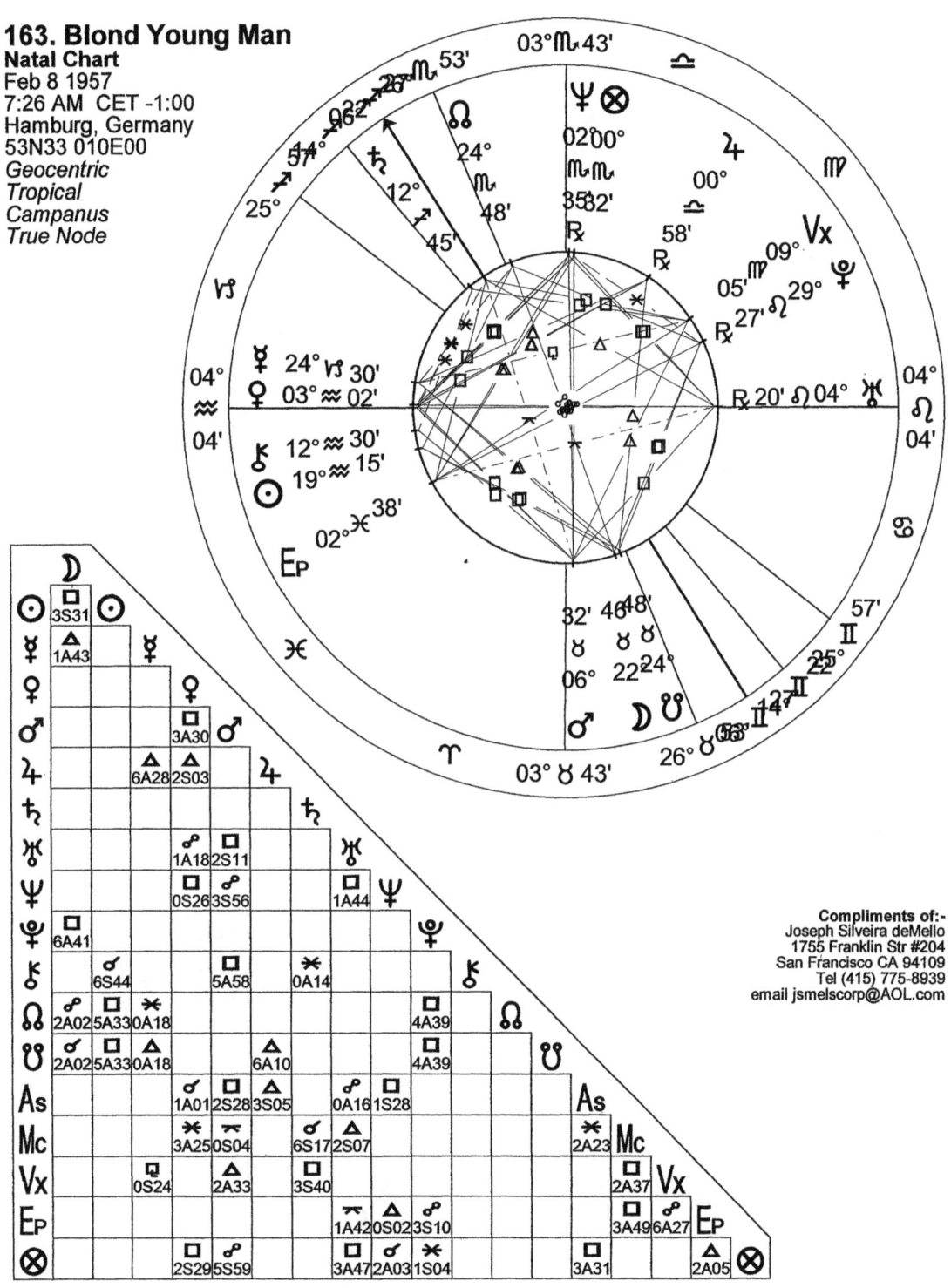

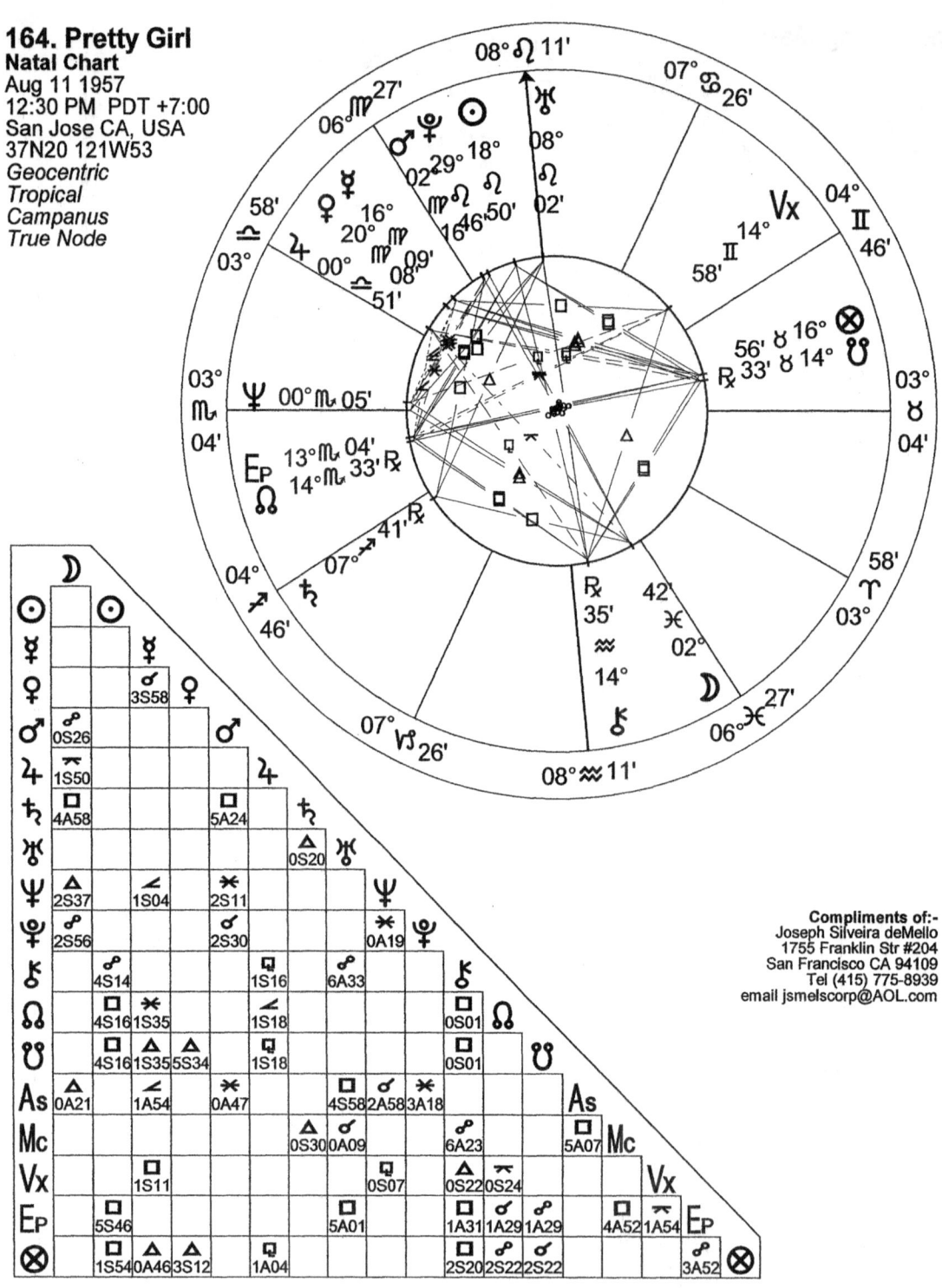

164. Pretty Girl
Natal Chart
Aug 11 1957
12:30 PM PDT +7:00
San Jose CA, USA
37N20 121W53
Geocentric
Tropical
Campanus
True Node

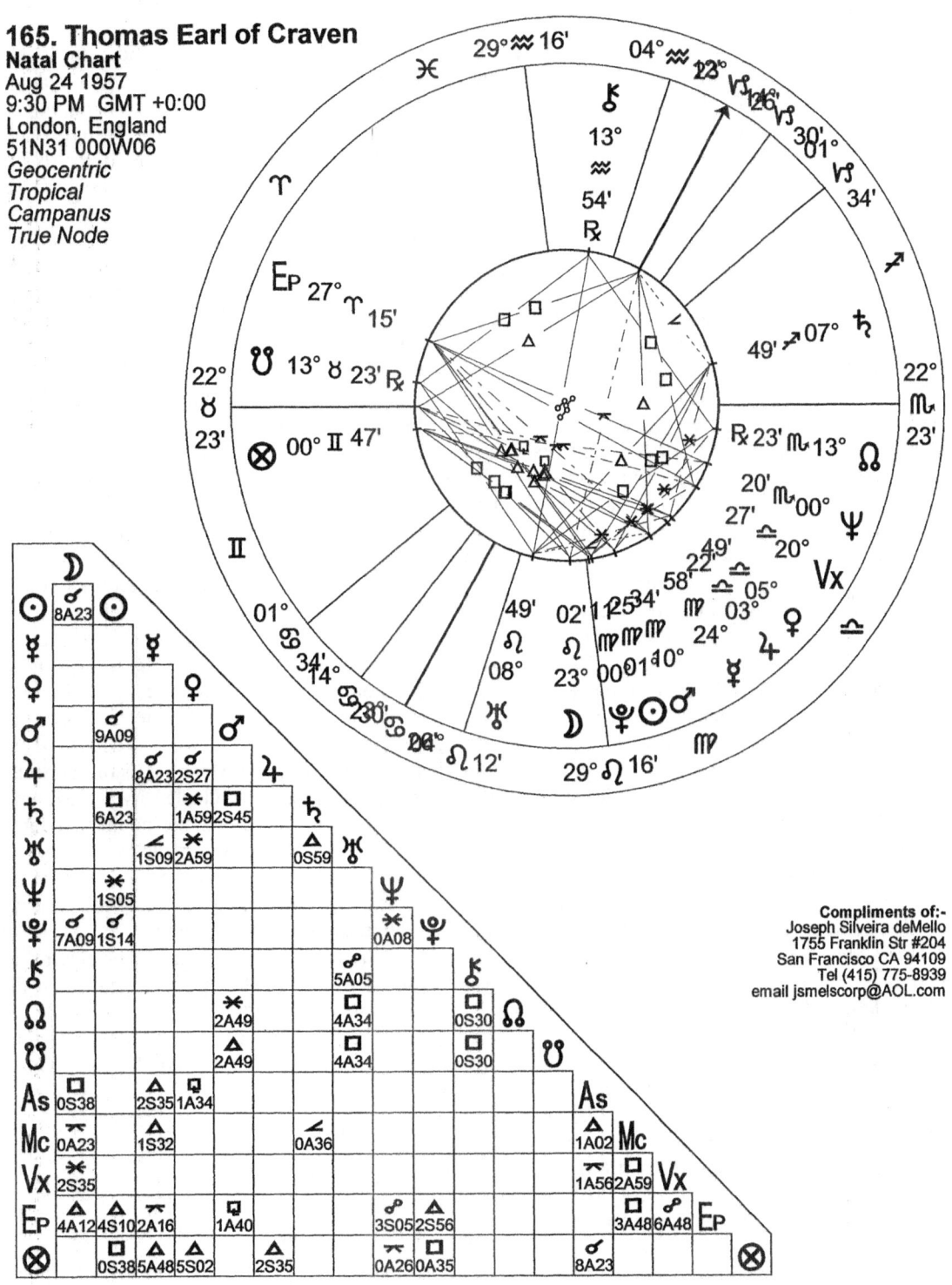

told that all the males in this family always have died early as if due to a family curse. There have twice been earls of this name, the most noted being Sir William who was Lord Mayor of London in 1610, the only known ancestor who lived a long life from 1606 to 1697 and supported Charles I and Charles II but spent his career in the Palatinate and Bohemia.

The present title was created in 1801, during the reign of King George III, the older title having died out in the 17th century. The earl who is the person of this chart is the seventh earl in the more recent line. That means seven earls in 183 years, which gives us a new one every twenty-six years. These are indeed brief lives. He inherited the peerage when he was eight years old in 1965. He committed suicide by shooting himself on October 22, 1983 at his home in Sussex. The earl was not married but had an illegitimate son by a woman who was married to another man. This lady was also a client of Judith Gee.

Although doomed by the "family curse" to an early death, he was a weak child who growing up missing out on a lot of normal childhood activities. And while very wealthy, he was beset by agents in control of his estate who were of suspected probity. Again we have the situation of very wide and very narrow houses, the widest being sixth and twelfth, while first and seventh are just a bit wider than average. Almost everything in this chart is within the space of a trine, and most of that in the second quadrant of subjective understanding of other people. And then the preponderance of planets is in the area of works and services, and we have no indication he was devoted to either. Judith Gee felt that this narrowness of aspect indicated a person with a very limited vision and experience of life. She thought he should have found it difficult to understand other people, and I must disagree on that point. For those wishing to read the comments of his astrologer, they are in the forty-first edition of *Mercury Hour*, April 1984. The suicide raised inheritance questions. The Earl had a younger brother, but medical tests were admitted in court in an attempt by the child's mother to have the Earl's illegitimate son declared the proper heir. Normally this legal ploy would be doomed to inadmissibility.

Taurus is rising with the Sun in early Virgo, and the Moon in late Leo, so that he was born on a waning Moon cycle. Here the sixth house opens with Sun conjunct Pluto, and we have concluded that in the case of the outer planets, Pluto would be stronger than the Sun, an outer or heavy planet.

We are informed that birth data is approximate for the British would have only recorded time of birth had the Earl been born a twin, so this time of birth comes from family records. For the aggressively superstitious, the earl was born and died on Saturdays, days ruled by Saturn, transiting at 6 Scorpio when he died. Progressed Venus was at 6 Scorpio and transiting Moon was at 5 Taurus. The progressed Ascendant was 25 Gemini the year of death with its ruler Mercury at 11 Virgo stationary direct on his natal Mars, to which transiting Jupiter was square. Transiting Mars was 13 Virgo the day he died having just made a Mars return. We are given no motive for suicide except that the Earl was living in a state of constant despair. Of course he was born with Mars square Saturn and Saturn trine Uranus. The part of Fortune changes from twelfth house Taurus to zero Gemini in his first house. In the twelfth (had he been born in day time, Fortune would have been on his natal South Node

The true role of the astrologer is to delineate a chart so that the interpretation helps the client understands himself. The client should be shown what ever may be seen as a more helpful role in life for the client. Every astrologer looking at this chart must ask what he or she would recommend to this client. It would seem to me that ego expression is in the hands of Pluto in this chart, change for the sake of change, not always an easy way to go. Still, the client should have been in tune with change, all he needed to learn was how to master his situation. The chart shows obvious difficulties in doing this.

The zero Jupiter declination in this chart is contra-parallel to Mercury and Venus, and Venus is conjunct Jupiter with Mercury applying widely to the same conjunction. The karma of this chart is relationships with persons close to him, but the absolute crux of this chart is work and service. He should have found a specialty and stuck with it. His sixth house is the end of Leo. Note that the only planet in the sixth not in interception is Neptune. If he was in such grand despair, it must have been because he could not get a handle on how to work, how to serve. Everything in interceptions is kept private, and then we turn around and see that Neptune rules an intercepted portion of the twelfth house. It is as if there is no way out. The nodal axis speaks of intake through work and service, and release into the subconscious. And then, looking at the fifth house, we have another puzzle to find that it has Leo on the cusp. But Leo is on two cusps, more important on the second of the two, which weakens by putting fifth into a twelfth house position to the sixth. And in the fifth we have Uranus of unexpected methods, and Moon which vacillates. Sun with Pluto intercepted (private) in mutable Virgo here is not a stabilizing influence. The conjunction might have fared well in Leo, but here it is in Virgo. On the whole, this chart is more mutable than it is fixed, waiting to see if he will continue to roll with the punches until the fatal day when action must be taken. Despite the grand trine of Midheaven to Ascendant to Sun-Pluto, none of it makes a kite formation to mitigate an opposition. Even the T-squares ties to no opposition but the nodal axis. Even Saturn, in interception, and the tenth it rules, if promising of good action later in life, cease to have any meaning for someone who hardly went the distance

166. Jennifer Collegio, 2-9-3
Jupiter: 0S02, Uranus: 0S42
Data: December 4, 1968, 2:32 p.m. EST,
Brooklyn, New York, 40N38, 73W56

The parents of this young lady were buying a house from a real estate woman who is also an astrologer in Oregon. Jennifer, then 12 years old, told the real estate woman that she wanted to be a doctor, so the real estate lady took down the chart data from the young lady and her mother and passed it to Don Borkowski who, when he had set up the chart, said that he thought she might, but said she wouldn't be just any ordinary doctor. Now a dozen years later, Jennifer was in the newspapers, and her real estate lady cut all the news clippings she could find and went through her files. She found the chart and the original write up and sent them back to Borkowski, who, mildly chagrined, still sent the whole thing on to me because the Jupiter in her chart is at 0S02. I saw that Uranus in her natal chart was also at 0S42 declination.

What put Jennifer in the news was that she was an Army Captain and the pilot of a twin-rotor Ch-47 Delta Chinook transport helicopter on a test flight after routine maintenance. Flying out of Ft. Hood, Texas with a crew of five other soldiers, they were about forty miles north of Austin TX (or fourteen miles south of Killeen, the town closest to Ft. Hood), when the helicopter disintegrated in midair. Everyone perished at 11:15 a.m. CST on the April 25, 1995. A witness said there was just a sort of pop as the aircraft broke in half.

Jennifer had attended the University of Oregon where she majored in physical education and in the ROTC program. Flying had become an absorbing interest, and, out of school, she joined the Army and received flight training at Ft. Ruger, Alabama. Transferred to Ft. Hood, Texas, on December 30, 1994, she had married Army Capt. Dean Varney, who survives her.

What on earth would lead her to join the Army, except as a natural outgrowth of the university ROTC program, for a career as a pilot. She is a Taurus rising, not a sign conducive to work and service. The Sun is in Sagittarius and Moon in Gemini. She has a hugely occupied sixth house with Virgo on the cusp, and Virgo is tuned to services, and all those planets are intercepted in Libra. Note that Fortune is out of the interception and in Scorpio. Saturn is rising in the twelfth, but it is opposite Mars. Capricorn on the Midheaven as a career indicator hardly points to flying. We cannot fail to note that Venus, chart significator, is the highest planet in the chart, disposed of by Saturn, in turn disposed of by Mars in Libra, disposed of by Venus, making a full circle.

A check of *The Rulership Book* by Rex E. Bills gives pilots of airplanes as Uranus, Aquarius and Neptune with Sagittarius on the ninth as secondary. Uranus in this chart is in the sixth, Aquarius rules the eleventh, Neptune is in the Scorpio in the seventh, and here Sagittarius here rules the eighth house. Mars is, of course, a prime indicator of an army career, as is the sign Aries, here intercepted in the twelfth house. Would an Army test pilot have Virgo on the sixth house? We must conclude that Venus as significator and at the top of the chart had to be the guiding influence in her career choice.

We have here a pretty young lady compatible with Taurus rising chart but not with Venus in Capricorn and disposed by Saturn to which it is in square. She was warm and outgoing, so we can discard the "coldness" interpretation for Venus in Capricorn. We do remember that Capricorn prefers to be in control, to run things. She was a total team player, but she liked tennis as much as she enjoyed playing softball. One thing to note here is that, while Jupiter and Uranus are parallel at zero South declination, Venus is out of bounds, and the Moon is also considerably out of bounds. Moon out of bounds, an indicator of death by drowning is also wrong here. She was born with the Moon increasing in light. The Moon in the first house is not in the rising sign.

Four planets are in the sixth house, and three in the seventh house so that these houses are the most complicated in the chart. (The Placidus system puts Mercury and Sun in the eighth house.) The sixth house is ruled by Mercury, Virgo on the cusp, and starts off with Pluto in Virgo, and Pluto is the planet of sabotage. Other charts in this sample with sixth house Pluto are charts of people who have difficult on-the-job situations. Then we have Jupiter, Uranus, South Node, and Mars intercepted in Libra, and we might say that she has a lot of involvement in work, that the work is unusual or modern, that she releases through her work, and that she has a positive work ethic. We can notice that the Vertex in Libra is opposite to Saturn and should have given us health qualms.

In the seventh we find Neptune in Scorpio. In this chart we might wonder at a lack of realism about those closest to her. Mercury is too close to the Sun in Sagittarius and less powerful for not being cazimi. Note that while the ruler of the sixth house is in the house ahead of that which it rules, Mars and Pluto which rule the seventh house are in the house behind that which they rule. In actuality this chart is well balanced, equally above as below the horizon, though mostly on the right side of the chart, more dependent on the people in her life. The chart is as strongly cardinal as it is mutable, and stronger on earth practicality, than with air and fire, and a lack of water placements. Her aspects are strongest but positive in oppositions, and, but for conjunctions, are intensely of negative weights in all other aspects.

Saturn is retrograde at birth, and this is a very good thing. Such Saturns are avidly interested in trying to make all around them relate to others and the world around them. And a twelfth house Saturn always learns through personal experience. It should also be pointed out that so much is intercepted, fenced off from the importunities of others, a nice balance to find in a chart otherwise given to much influence from others.

Another puzzle is to find what in this chart would indicate death so spectacularly. I did secondary progressions, solar return, diurnals for the day of her death, and an event chart for the disastrous moment of death. In secondary progressions, the progressed Ascendant was a tiny bit more than one degree from natal Moon. Progressed Mars had just entered Scorpio. Progressed Vertex was on natal Fortune, and progressed Mercury was on natal Venus. In amused passing, her progressed angles are almost exactly my own natal angles, the cause of my great interest in this chart.

In the diurnal chart for her day of death, transiting Jupiter is on the IC of the chart also occupied by natal Mercury and Sun, while natal Moon is on the diurnal MC. A further check around the diurnal shows diurnal North Node on natal Fortune. The diurnal or transiting Sun is

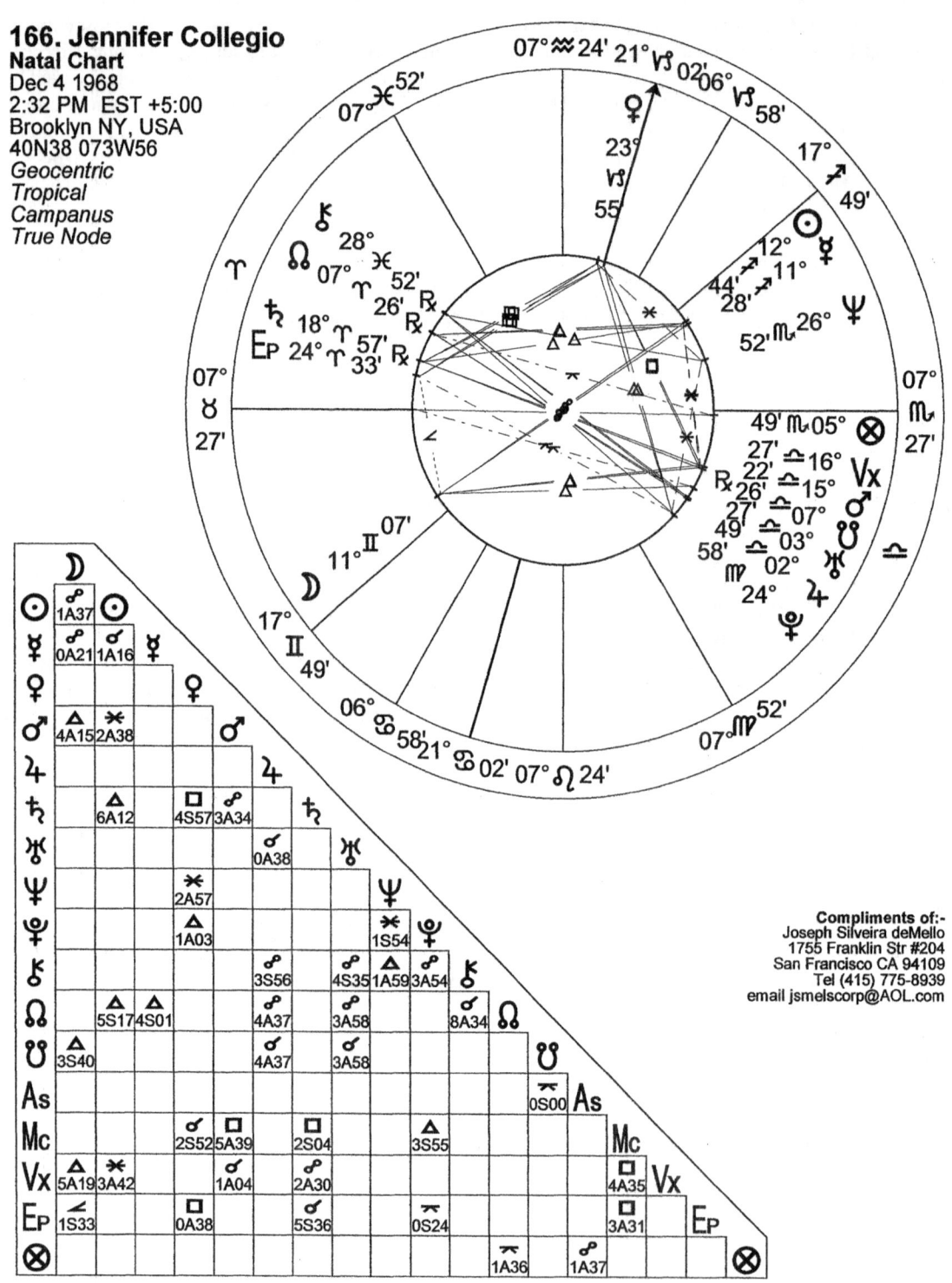

opposite North Node and Fortune, so, South Node with Sun, not a pleasant indicator. This is a surprise diurnal in that there are angular and other touches in the chart of the subject, things not generally found in the diurnal technique where most usually, as you will see in the diurnal portion of this book, death usually shows best in the chart of the mourners even in charts for a disastrous death.

A chart was done for the time of the disaster, 11:15 a.m. CDT, April 24, 1995. Ft. Hood, Texas, 31N26, 97W44, although the actual disaster occurred south of Ft. Hood and closer to Fort Hood than the forty miles north of Austin, Texas. This chart has Cancer rising, falling in her natal third house of brief trips. Late Pisces is on the event Midheaven, in the same degree as her natal Chiron, so that something fateful was overlooked. As in her natal chart, Venus is on the event Midheaven but in the sign Aries. Moon, which rules the event chart, was in Pisces about to enter her natal twelfth house, let's say four hours early of doing so. The chart has Neptune in Capricorn and Uranus at zero Aquarius, both in the event seventh house. The event Vertex at 25 Scorpio was on her natal Neptune, but, more telling, the event North Node was on her natal Fortune.

So much did this chart interest me that I shared it with astrologer T. Patrick Davis, knowing she would be equally interested. Pat Davis used heliocentric astrology which is very in tune with public events and disasters. I suppose I could have done that work myself, but I regard her as an authority, willing to take a back seat to what she might find. She did a three-ring chart which she sent me. On it were natal, progressed and death transits in both geocentric and heliocentric positions. The very first thing that hit my eyes was natal Venus, surmounted by progressed Mercury, and that surmounted by helio Neptune, all at 23 Capricorn. Starting around the chart from the Midheaven, we next encounter transiting helio Venus on progressed Midheaven and quincunx natal helio Mars as well as trine natal geo Mars. Then comes transiting Midheaven on geo natal Chiron. Pat Davis then noted that the subject's natal Saturn retrograde has progressed stationary direct when she was 17 years of age (the career change had its seeds then). Progressed geo Venus was just two degrees past her natal Ascendant, quincunx Jennifer's natal helio Mercury. Transit geo Mercury was exactly quincunx her natal geo Mars, and progressed Moon was exactly quincunx progressed Mars. Pat found progressed Ascendant less than one degree from Jennifer's natal Moon, exactly opposite natal geo Mercury. Another very interesting finding was that progressed geo Pluto had been stationary retrograde at Jennifer's twenty-third birthday. The stationary status was still in effect at the time of her death. Pat Davis states that she finds air disaster charts among the most difficult to read even after all the facts are known.

Here is a case where six people met their deaths all at the same time. It reminds me of the in-depth research done after the second NASA disaster where all the charts except that of school teacher McAuliff, held exactly similar positions to each other, and the chart of the school teacher which did not fit was, for that day, so bad she should not even have been on roller skates. Pat Davis states rather factually that Don Borkowski should not lash at himself for not having foreseen a military career for a twelve year old girl. Such a career was not yet all that frequent for women and even less frequent is a flying career. Not all boys who want to be firemen in their pre-teens follow up on careers as fire fighters. For those who like conspiracy theories, there is much grist in this chart to favor unknown causes for the disaster and the potential that faulty maintenance was done to the aircraft prior to its test flight. This could not be proven by the aircraft remnants, twisted junk.

167. Kidney Patient, 9-1-8
Jupiter: 0N08
Data: March 30, 1975, 12:15 a.m. EST,
Newport, Rhode Island, 41N29, 71W19

One final sad tale. This is the chart of a grand-nephew who was unfortunately born with the family hereditary tendency toward kidney ailments. His maternal grandmother and one of her sisters, and three of her four brothers have all died of kidney problems. Others in our family show this same tendency, but none are so afflicted as is this young man. He had his second kidney transplant at the age of sixteen and rejected it in 1994. In October of 1995, he had two cardiac arrest episodes brought on by not going regularly for dialysis. It is supposed he was feeling suicidal at that time. Currently he has to have dialysis once a week.

Things have gone poorly for him since birth. His mother had four children when she divorced his father. Since the father did not contribute to child support, and soon died, this young man's mother had to apply for help from social services. She immediately ran up against the strange ways of bureaucracy. They would contribute to support of the other children but not for this boy's medical expenses if he remained with his family, mother and siblings. To them it was obvious that, with the other children, this boy and his ailment would prove to be too much for the mother to handle, and they insisted that a foster home be found for him. Of course, he wanted nothing but to remain with his mother, but this cut no ice with social services. Anyone but a social psychologist would have seen the error of such a decision. Luckily a fine foster home was found for him which regularly permitted maternal visits and contact with his siblings.

Unable to live with his natural mother, he found mean ways to express negative feelings toward his fine foster parents. Nothing done for him has ever suited him, and he has never thanked anyone for anything done for him. At school, his nun teachers lost no opportunity to criticize in class his divorced mother as morally reprehensible, and all the more so as she had to resort to welfare aid. He is a prime example that suffering does not ennoble. When he got to high school, he met another boy who was also a kidney patient. They became fast friends. This other boy shared with our subject the idea that his foster parents were very well off from the money they were being paid by social services to keep him.

167. Kidney Problem
Natal Chart
Mar 30 1975
0:16 AM EST +5:00
Newport RI, USA
41N29 071W19
Geocentric
Tropical
Campanus
True Node

Compliments of:-
Joseph Silveira deMello
1755 Franklin Str #204
San Francisco CA 94109
Tel (415) 775-8939
email jsmgemscorp@juno.com

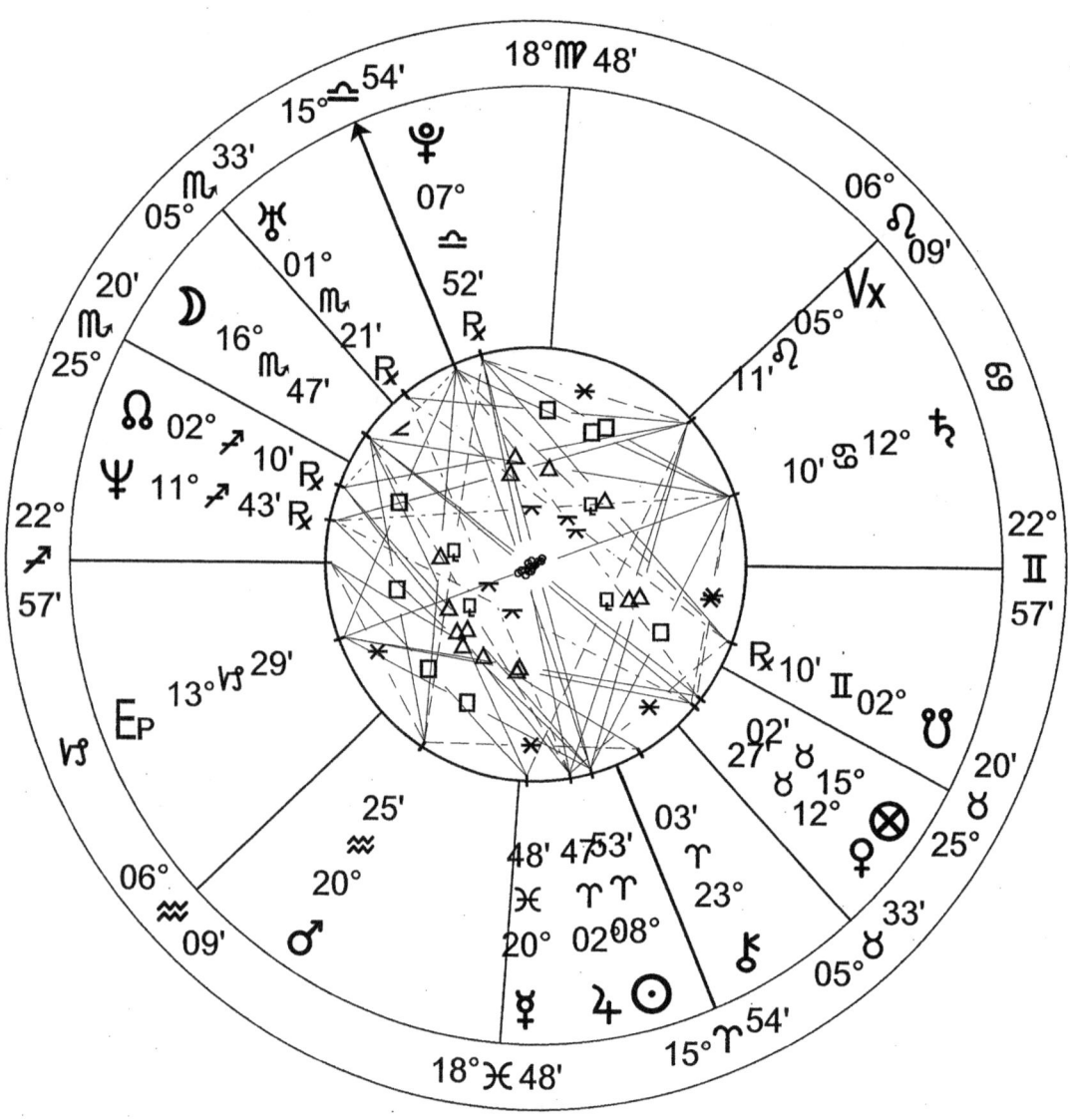

Our young man went home and demanded that his foster parents give him the money they were being paid. It was pointed out to his chagrin that Social Services would not give any money directly to him until he was of age and out of foster care. From then onward, he became abusive toward his foster parents and made their lives difficult to the point where the foster father got so stressed he had to seek hospital treatment. As soon as he turned eighteen, Social Services switched him to SSI and told him he could now assume responsibility for himself.

He set up housekeeping in his own apartment. At regular intervals a man from social services checks that he is regularly going to dialysis and managing to care for himself. He is not a happy person, is stocky and under-developed due to the lifelong kidney situation. His mother has remarried and moved at a distance from him, but he still wants to go live with her. Authorities, for some unknown reason, tell him that he cannot move away from the state where he has lived. His mother visits him regularly but is not permitted to adopt him back into her home. He has no contact with his siblings since he has treated them with nothing but jealousy and acrimony. He has no known interests or hobbies, is not known to have any friends. When visited, he retreats into silence, rarely has any conversation, rather like his grandfather who was a very silent man.

He was born with Sagittarius rising, Sun in Aries, and Moon in Scorpio. He has frequently thought of suicide but only by neglecting treatment, and he does have natal Neptune in the twelfth house quincunx his Saturn. He has Moon square Mars, so an attitude that the whole world is against him is not unfounded. The Sun is trine Neptune, not doing much for reality perception since conspiracy theories easily proliferate, and there is a grand trine from Jupiter to North Node to Vertex which may be quite connected to his kidney ailment. The degrees of Pluto and his Midheaven directly refer to kidney disorders and ailments (Elspeth Ebertin).

He has never had any training to fit him for any occupation. The general attitude is that he will never be well enough to hold a job. Throughout his life, the prevalent opinion has revolved around an early expectancy of death. He has come close to death on at least half a dozen occasions. Sagittarius rising has a natural reticence to step into friendships, but Aries Sun which should have made him enterprising, seems to have failed him even though it is part of a cardinal square. Jupiter in the third is his chart significator. Mercury in Pisces could indicate a lack of realism in his mental processes. Regardless of what an astrologer might say of a third house with three planets in it, the real third house significator is that Pisces is on the house cusp. Because this is a nocturnal chart, we should say that the third is ruled by Jupiter rather than by Neptune, and here Jupiter is in Aries. Jealous of his siblings, he does not have much interest in his personal environment since it has always been a second class choice, and it has certainly not led to writing or any interest in business. He writes no letters and is not known to use a telephone. He does not contact any family members; they contact him. From other examples of Aries people here, we might judge that Aries usually evinces bad behavior when not receiving sufficient attention to his personal wishes.

Astrologers should have a field day with this chart. Note first all the oppositions and note they are all mitigated by kite trine-sextile patterns. True he is a Sagittarius rising which is a sign not noted for competitiveness, but also note that he has never been much in the way of being an optimist. The world has taught him otherwise. One just does not turn away an Aries with any good results. The Moon in Scorpio is another bit of the personality quotient; he wishes to be thought much deeper, and to this point melds keeping silent in both the Aries and Scorpio manners, taking refuge in silence and refusing to talk about himself. After all, the world can never know how stupid you are if you keep your mouth shut. The Sun is in such exact opposition to Pluto in the ninth which has to aid strange notions. Uranus in the tenth indicates an unpredictable life style. Moon in the eleventh is not conducive to stable expectations from friends or community. Mars, the final personality quotient is in Aquarius in his second house. He has never earned a penny in his life, living always on a limited income.

Everything in this chart, but Venus in Taurus, is disposed of by the mutual reception between Mars and Uranus which are not in aspect to each other. Venus in the fifth would suppose some creativity, but none is known. Nor is anything known about his sex life. His only two consuming preoccupations are his mother and his money. He is not a pleasant person and evinces no responsibility toward anyone else, hardly any toward himself. Medical science has done all that it can in his case, much of it with scant cooperation from him. You can see that he became emancipated when his Ascendant progressed to his East Point. Saturn intercepted or fenced off in the seventh has indeed manifested strangely for him. His karma is involves the people close to him, and those are certainly few. The seventh house is also the area of open enemies, and that may indeed be how he sees other people. Blaming others for his vicissitudes is given total precedence.

The Road to Conclusions

You have now seen 167 charts. This collection is meager for a bona fide research project, especially since the 167 charts can be further subdivided into those with Jupiter and Saturn in interception, Jupiter and Saturn direct and retrograde, both planets in all sorts of locations in the chart, in all sorts of aspects, and then the times when these planets are in North declination in Southern signs and vice versa. All of these variations dilute the basic choice which only took into account that these were at zero declinations. It might be said I have done a research project using only one chart.

It is expected that readers will be able to add to this collection with charts in their own files. The reader will also, as I did, find charts of persons with other planets at zero declination and other planets out of bounds. This variety complicates assessment. The aim was to find special meaning to placements at zero declination. In the course of this work I have further noted that while natal charts have planets at zero declination, these and other planets will be either secondary progressions and by transits continue to move during each individual life. While the natal chart is a spot picture of the heavens that remains with each person of the chart for a lifetime, these two planets may not move much by progression but have greater movement as transits throughout any lifetime.

I chose Saturn because Saturn is the great teacher, the planet which is always exactly on time in any event with which it is involved. Basically Saturn is conservative and Jupiter is the bringer of hopeful optimism. But Saturn may be rewarding while Jupiter's manifestations are often curtailed in some signs and locations in any chart. I believe that whatever you get from Saturn is exactly what you give, and give you must before you can receive. How your Saturn works for you at any given time depends upon whether you have worked well with and in accordance to the Saturn needs as its passage dictates. If you make the right moves, Saturn approves and rewards. Saturn gives nor permits any alibis. If Saturn punishes, you have strayed from your personal meaning of Saturn.

I chose to check out Jupiter at zero because Jupiter might be the suitable foil to Saturn. Jupiter's power is second only to the Sun power in any chart. Astrologers know that the planets are more individual than their basic cookbook meanings, astrology stresses the individuality of all people and their charts. This study here is the distinct product of how Jupiter acts in my chart. So many contributed charts to the study. Just as Saturn may prove rewarding, Jupiter can bring us more than we can handle. I have always thought of Jupiter as a window on our ability to accept and work with our Saturn karma.

If there is one thing I did not do in this study was to take into account Ptolemy's Table of Essential Dignities. These tables are well known to practitioners of horary astrology. This table takes in triplicities, terms and faces of the planets although prior to the discovery of Uranus, Neptune and Pluto. This table is often reproduced in the best horary books. When this table is checked we find that beyond the basic dignity and exaltation of planets, there is frequently a larger presence of planets not basically suggested by a particular planet being chart significator or dispositor (things on which I seem to have placed the greatest significance).

The study was to find special meanings for Saturn and Jupiter at zero declination. Though the sample is small, still a variety of people are presented and no chart is quite really like any other. Since the periods of zero declination in both planets come in batches, many charts are close to each other in date but change to move all the planets into other areas of the chart. The task of finding a common denominator only became more difficult. In the first place, this is in danger of becoming derogatory as well as negative. Most of us would rather work on a positive level, regardless of the fact that it is the negative which always shows up most easily. These are not all saints, not all sinners.

At zero declination, I first thought these zero declinations worked as an engine idling in neutral. I soon had to scratch that idea. Saturn is never neutral. I tried to see if those planets responded better for being at zero. This, too, had to be scuttled. I was not overwhelmed by a cohesive and significant picture of marvelous synthesis. The historical figures in this sample had widely known biographies. I tried to assess them in their own time rather than from the skewered revisions of modern enlightenment. I surprised myself at finding I had great personal bias against some of these people. They knew only their own time and lived with the sins of their fathers, never thinking that the future would more drastically write differing epitaphs. With contemporary unfamous clients and friends, I had to take into account my personal acceptance of the foibles of human nature. In all cases, I found I had a great interest in these people as individuals. Some of them surprised me by being people who have acted independently, people who have paid little or no attention to opposition, people who are essentially untouched by the machinations of others. For example, George Washington got well around opposition. Who knows how well he coped with a stony-faced mother so incapable of being pleased. Lyndon Johnson, on the other hand, viewed the opposition of others as a game he knew he could win.

Many kept their dignity intact regardless of the world around them, through both success and failure. I prefer a study of human nature to a study of psychological types and why the latter should be any less various than astrological meanings. Human nature should not surprise us. Men created in the image of God have turned out not to be gods, and that should not be news to any astrologer. Too many people slide down the paths of least resistance. And then there were the rare few who were so in tune with their charts and not know it. To find such people is always a glorious bonus to any practicing astrologer. I would have liked to find my zero Saturn people on a quest for perfection. From those I asked about this. I got resounding negation of this notion. One of them realized a quest for perfection as a source of problems and difficulties. Only one was the example of a lady who deviled herself for her failure at perfection. The idea of perfection seekers had to be dropped. And then as many were serious as were frivolous, others fairly out of touch with any larger meanings of life.

So, although we have 167 charts, what a mix they are. And astrological truth is as varied as the charts and the people themselves. This gets to be as if the family of man has almost only the most basic similarity, two arms, two legs, hearts which beat and lungs which fill with hardly any personal effort. Indeed, if any of us had to devote conscious effort to keep ourselves breathing, or to attend to our own heartbeat, all other daily activities would go wanting or disappear from our major consciousness. The inventor of man gave him capacity to think and in some naive slight of hand let man forget his motor operations.

With few of these examples some were either out of control or had no clue to the ways they might fulfill themselves. Since man has the capacity to think and decide, man is responsible for all his acts but negates this in a constant need for alibis to all his acts. Regardless of what his planets show, if one believes in reincarnation, man is responsible for the karma which he chose to work out in his lifetime and, in selecting it, saw that such a karma could be worked out in the lifetime. Some came to life with genetic problems. Their grand design must have involved doing the best they could to transcend heavy problems. Some were lucky enough to find other paths than blame and rancor.

Now comes the question of control. This is a difficult concept, especially as we have here many charts of control personalities. This does not mean, of course, that they control themselves. Control oriented people only wish to control others, seldom themselves. Perhaps those with Saturn or Jupiter at zero declination do as they wish and are not have subject to the control of others. Those with intercepted houses show us their freedom from interference, free-wheeling, untrammeled, and working their way around the slings and arrows of public opinion.

Several things in this study have surprised me, and you will perhaps have become aware of them as you studied these charts. Knowing Saturn as conservative, it was a surprise to find that those with Saturn at zero declination were not that all conservative. Expecting to find Jupiter more ebullient and sanguine, those with Jupiter at zero declination tended to be far more conservative than the Saturns. This, amounting to almost a reversal of roles, should be something to watch for.

In this study I have made special point of telling you whether the person of the chart, regardless of gender, is or is not homosexual. Quite a number of charts in my files are the charts of homosexuals (a tribute to my Uranus in the eleventh house and allowing that Uranus may refer to astrologers and their role in a community and Uranus as ruler of non-conformists). For the homosexuals with Saturn and Jupiter at zero declination, I found that zero manifests oddly indeed. Those homosexuals with Saturn at zero declination are easily identifiable by anyone on the street, they seen to be obviously effete or effeminate as men, and quite "mannish" if women. Few cases of zero Saturns were not obvious homosexuals, and those were the charts of male bisexuals. I would say in passing that cases where homosexuals discover their sexuality after marriage are about equal in both genders. We must bear in mind that it is a suspicious theory that female homosexuals are more prone than males to return to straight relationships after participation in another lifestyle. Those homosexuals with Jupiter at zero declination are closeted or easily pass as straight. This collection also contains two zero Jupiter bisexuals. The zero Jupiter people had to tell me of their sexual preferences or I would never have divined it. I must also say that the variety of homosexuals in my files runs the full gamut of every imaginable role or type of homosexual activity as well as their various political or religious persuasions.

Another surprise to me was to find quite a few charts of homosexuals with out-of- bounds Moon placements. Equating the out-of-bounds Moon with homosexuality was not going to be something to carve on stone as I began to find heterosexuals with Moon out of bounds. I have not made a specific study of the astrology of sexual preferences or of astrological indicators of homosexuality. Very few of my homosexual clients ever ask me about sex or romance. The last planets I should have picked as sexual significance would have been Jupiter and Saturn. But I feel confident enough to say that an afflicted Moon is but the tip of the iceberg, as are the conditions of Venus, Mars and Uranus in the horoscope. I do not find that retrogrades influence sexuality. We do have to remember that anything we see in any chart should be backed up by three indicators. Experience has taught me that, unless sexual preference is mentioned by the client, no astrologer should lift the lid of Pandora's box. Many people live all their lives without any hint, suspicion or question regarding their sexuality. I have seen charts, as I have pointed out, where I saw or felt homosexuality in the chart and there really is no way that I would suggest that the client check out any other lifestyle than the one being lived. And it is not all a matter of preferences but also of the ways these preferences manifest. Believe me, these are as various as all the reasons why a person becomes an alcoholic, especially in the case where a couple of avowed alcoholics never drank anything but beer.

One final word on the tendency of Saturn zeros to seek perfection. It was Maritha Pottenger, astrological author and editor, who informed me that she was unaware of any undue search for perfection despite the detailed work involved in her own books. In the face of this astrologer's opinion, I was not about to argue with her, and not devastated to abandon that concept. Having checked 167 charts and finding only so very few concerned about perfection, so abandoning the notion was easy. The search for perfection did not even surface in the charts of those with Jupiter at zero though there were some of these who were surprised at the lack of perfection among people around them. This goes hand in hand with the search for spirituality.

Another strange discovery or, perhaps, call it a revision of standard meanings which deviate from basic astrological thought, relates to the effect of Mars in the first house but in the same sign as the rising sign. Such a person is much more an Aries than he is his own rising sign. A first house position of Pisces Mars for a Pisces rising person born either at day or night, is probably the best thing that ever happened to the basic Pisces personality. On the other hand, in Scorpio rising charts with a Scorpio Mars in the first house did not produce a more Scorpionic type. Mars in any rising sign produces only an Aries type. A first house Mars in other than the rising sign does not do this.

Edward L. Dearborn is the astrologer who motivated and founded Declination SIG, a special group under the NCGR family, devoted to the study of declinations. As I came to the end of this section, he wrote me about an additional bit of research which I might care to undertake. When two planets are in contra-parallel, because the orb of aspect is so narrow, we frequently find one planet North, the other South, and then we find that the one North is in a southern sign, or the one South is in a northern sign. They do of course stand the chance of having exact zero as the midpoint between them.

He then pointed out to me that people with two planets, one at ten or, say, fifteen north and another at the same degree south, the midpoint between those two parallels would be zero degrees declination. In any case, whoever undertakes this research will have much work to do. It will mean going through many files. First, the search for files poses a meticulous search and assembly of data. One far more difficult that my own search for two planets at merely zero declination. It will be your task to made decisions on each chart, judge which of the two planets is most favored, and then judge what meaning this has to the condition of life of the person of the chart and whether you can justify reading these contraparallels with midpoint significance. There will be no problem of coming to quick conclusions, bearing in mind that conclusions are often what we make when we are too tired to keep on thinking of the task in front of us.

www.ingramcontent.com/pod-product-compliance
Lightning Source LLC
Chambersburg PA
CBHW060311240426
43661CB00059B/2729